$SAGE edge™

SAGE edge offers a robust online environment you can access anytime, anywhere, and features an impressive array of free tools and resources to keep you on the cutting edge of your learning experience.

▶ edge.sagepub.com/bryant

SAGE EDGE FOR STUDENTS provides a personalized approach to help you accomplish your coursework goals in an easy-to-use learning environment.

- **Original video cases** feature in-class footage, teacher interviews, and accompanying reflection questions

- Mobile-friendly **eFlashcards** strengthen your understanding of key terms and concepts

- Mobile-friendly practice **quizzes** allow you to independently assess your mastery of course material

- A complete online **action plan** includes tips and feedback on your progress and allows you to enhance your learning experience

- **Chapter summaries** with **learning objectives** reinforce the most important material

- **Multimedia resources** and meaningful web links make it easy to mine internet resources, further explore topics, and answer critical thinking questions

- EXCLUSIVE! Access to full-text **SAGE journal articles** that have been carefully chosen to support and expand on the concepts presented in each chapter

SAGE EDGE FOR INSTRUCTORS supports your teaching by making it easy to integrate quality content and create a rich learning environment for students.

- **Test banks** provide a diverse range of pre-written options as well as the opportunity to edit any question and/or insert your own personalized questions to effectively assess students' progress and understanding

- **Sample course syllabi** for semester and quarter courses provide suggested models for structuring your courses

- Editable, chapter-specific **PowerPoint® slides** offer complete flexibility for creating a multimedia presentation for your course.

- EXCLUSIVE! Access to full-text **SAGE journal articles** that have been carefully chosen to support and expand on the concepts presented in each chapter

- **Multimedia content** includes original SAGE videos that appeal to students with different learning styles

- **Lecture notes** summarize key concepts by chapter to help you prepare for lectures and class discussions

- Chapter-specific **discussion questions** and **class activities** help launch classroom interaction by prompting students to engage with the material and by reinforcing important content.

- **Course cartridge** for easy LMS integration

D0073783

To our special mothers and special brothers.

And to our children, who make our lives so very special.

TEACHING STUDENTS WITH SPECIAL NEEDS IN INCLUSIVE CLASSROOMS

Diane P. Bryant
The University of Texas at Austin

Brian R. Bryant
The University of Texas at Austin

Deborah D. Smith
Claremont Graduate University

Los Angeles | London | New Delhi
Singapore | Washington DC

Los Angeles | London | New Delhi
Singapore | Washington DC

FOR INFORMATION:

SAGE Publications, Inc.
2455 Teller Road
Thousand Oaks, California 91320
E-mail: order@sagepub.com

SAGE Publications Ltd.
1 Oliver's Yard
55 City Road
London EC1Y 1SP
United Kingdom

SAGE Publications India Pvt. Ltd.
B 1/I 1 Mohan Cooperative Industrial Area
Mathura Road, New Delhi 110 044
India

SAGE Publications Asia-Pacific Pte. Ltd.
3 Church Street
#10-04 Samsung Hub
Singapore 049483

Printed in Canada.

ISBN 978-1-4833-1925-4

Acquisitions Editor: Theresa Accomazzo
Associate Editor: Jessica Miller
Editorial Assistant: Georgia McLaughlin
eLearning Editors: Lucy Berbeo and
                               Robert Higgins
Production Editor: Olivia Weber-Stenis
Copy Editor: Tina Hardy
Typesetter: C&M Digitals (P) Ltd.
Proofreader: Scott Oney
Indexer: Molly Hall
Cover and Interior Designer: Scott Van Atta
Marketing Manager: Ashlee Blunk

This book is printed on acid-free paper.

16 17 18 19 10 9 8 7 6 5 4 3 2 1

BRIEF CONTENTS

DETAILED CONTENTS

PREFACE

TO OUR READERS

We came together to write this text with one main purpose: to help teachers complete their special education/inclusion course *inspired* to teach students with disabilities in inclusive settings and *equipped* to do so effectively.

With the increased reliance on accountability systems and high-stakes testing, the number of students who struggle and who are at risk for school failure has become increasingly apparent to educators. Today, the vast majority of students with disabilities spend more than 80% of their school day learning in general education classrooms. Unfortunately, many classroom teachers working in inclusive settings believe they are unprepared to meet the challenges these individual students bring to the learning environment. So we wrote this text to fulfill what we see as our two critical responsibilities to our readers:

- **To increase knowledge of *proven* practices.** A wealth of information exists about instructional practices that are evidence-based and effective for students with special needs who are learning in inclusive settings. We have worked to make this information accessible to you by analyzing the body of research that exists, selecting those practices that have proved to be most effective (and that will be of most help in the teaching situations you will encounter most often), and presenting that information in the context of real classrooms. To that end, our text discussion and supporting features focus on *what works.*

- **To improve instructional decision making.** The ADAPT framework that we have integrated throughout this text will help you determine *how, when,* and *with whom* to use the proven academic and behavioral interventions in your repertoire to obtain the best outcomes. The ADAPT framework will help you develop the "habits of mind" needed to respond thoughtfully and flexibly to the challenges you will meet in your classroom long after your coursework is over.

We hope that by the time you have completed your reading of this text, we will have met these responsibilities and you will have confidence in your ability to meet the needs of *all* students in your classroom. We are confident that with the appropriate knowledge and tools, all teachers can make a positive difference in the educational lives of students with special needs.

ORGANIZATION OF THIS TEXT

The content of this text is organized in three parts. Chapters 1 through 4 comprise Part I: Foundations of Inclusive Education. Chapters 5 through 8 are the focus of Part II: Planning for Exceptional Learners. Chapters 9 through 12 cover Part III: Adaptations to Meet Individual Learner Needs.

PART I: FOUNDATIONS OF INCLUSIVE EDUCATION

The first four chapters of this text provide an overview of inclusive education and the nature and characteristics of students with disabilities and special learning needs. Chapter 1 examines the meaning of the term *disability*, what is meant by *inclusive education*, and the key legislation that has affected the development of inclusive classrooms: the Individuals with Disabilities Education Act of 2004 (IDEA), the No Child Left Behind Act of 2001 (NCLB), and the Assistive Technology Act of 2004 (ATA or the Tech Act). Chapter 2 presents information about high-incidence disabilities—those that teachers are most likely to encounter in classrooms—such as learning disabilities, attention deficit/hyperactivity disorder (ADHD), speech or language impairments, mental retardation or intellectual and developmental disabilities, and emotional or behavioral disorders. Chapter 3 discusses low-incidence disabilities: deafness and hard of hearing, physical disabilities, low vision and blindness, autism spectrum disorders, developmental delay, and other conditions. Chapter 4 offers information about student learners whose needs are not specifically covered by IDEA '04 legislation, including students who are English language learners, students who come from challenging living situations, and students who are gifted and talented.

PART II: PLANNING FOR EXCEPTIONAL LEARNERS

Chapter 5 focuses on the importance of collaborative relationships with professionals, paraprofessionals, and families. In Chapter 6, we discuss individualized education programs (IEPs) and other special services that help teachers meet the needs of their students. Chapter 7 addresses differentiating instruction to promote access to the general education curriculum. This chapter focuses on the steps of the ADAPT framework and the four categories of adaptations and the universal design for learning (UDL), which are then integrated into Chapters 9 through 12. Chapter 8 discusses the evaluation of students' learning and how to modify and adapt assessments for students with special needs.

PART III: ADAPTATIONS TO MEET INDIVIDUAL LEARNER NEEDS

Chapter 9 discusses the importance of creating a positive classroom environment by communicating effectively with students, arranging your classroom, teaching social skills, and addressing problem behaviors. In Chapters 10 through 12, we focus on specific content areas: reading, writing, mathematics, and content-area reading and study skills. In these chapters, we present practical, evidence-based strategies for adapting instruction to meet the needs of all students.

SPECIAL FEATURES

- An **Opening Challenge** case study begins each chapter. It describes in some detail a specific teaching challenge at the elementary and secondary level (middle school and high school), which is then revisited throughout the chapter. Students are asked to reflect on their knowledge of the subject matter before reading the chapter and are encouraged to record their responses to **Reflection Questions** in a journal.

- **ADAPT in Action** sections are integrated directly within the text discussion in Chapters 5 through 12. This illustrative section applies the ADAPT framework, a research-validated problem-solving approach, to the student and teacher introduced in the **Opening Challenge** scenarios. In these features, the teacher "thinks out loud" using the ADAPT framework, thus allowing the reader to go through the problem-solving steps with him or her.

- The **ADAPT framework** charts summarize the ADAPT model and apply it to practical, oft-encountered teaching and learning topics.

- The UDL approach to instruction is integrated in several chapters, through the **UDL in Action** feature, with specific lesson activities as examples of how the principles of UDL can be accounted for as part of instructional design.

- **Working Together** features offer practical advice on how an idea or concept can be taught using a collaborative approach that involves other school professionals and/or family members. Questions are posed for deliberation of how professionals tackle issues together.

- **Instructional Strategies** feature key research-to-practice, classroom-based activities that are relevant to topics in the chapter. Sample lessons for teaching the skills that students need to succeed in each area include the instructional objective, instructional content, instructional materials, a means to deliver the instruction, and methods to monitor student progress.

- **Considering Diversity** features examine various issues from a cultural or linguistic perspective; they illustrate how the diversity of our school populations is related to academic instruction and management.

- **Tech Notes** features provide readers with information about assistive and instructional technologies that can be employed with students who have learning or behavior problems. Examples from classrooms are used to show practical applications.

- The Response to Intervention (RTI) model is described in Chapter 6. RTI is a model for delivering scientifically based schoolwide, multitiered systems of support (MTSS), which is designed to promote improved academic performance for all students and minimize behavior problems.

- Each chapter closes with a **Summary** section, followed by **Review the Learning Objectives** with answers to help readers review material and assess their understanding of key topics. **Revisit the Opening Challenge** questions return readers to the scenarios presented in the **Opening Challenge** and monitor their learning of key concepts in relation to the development of the teacher and student scenarios. Examples of professional standards also are included at the end of each chapter.

- All chapters include **Video Cases**, with actual classroom footage to help illustrate how the strategies are implemented, and follow-up questions.

ONLINE RESOURCES

PREMIUM VIDEO AND SAGE JOURNAL ARTICLES

Each chapter is accompanied by original Video Cases featuring in-class footage and teacher interviews, with follow-up reflection questions to promote student engagement with course content. Students also have access to a robust assortment of supplementary video clips, bonus instructional strategies, and exclusive full-text SAGE journal articles that have been carefully chosen to promote mastery of learning objectives. These resources are available at the open-access SAGE edge website, **edge.sagepub.com/bryant**, described in more detail below.

The text can also be paired with an Interactive eBook that contains carefully placed links to each of these study tools for a seamless learning experience. Look for the following icons accompanied by labels in the margins of the print book that signal when you can visit the SAGE edge website or Interactive eBook to access these online resources:

 Watch an original Video Case to see teaching strategies in action.

 Watch a supplementary clip for further context and enrichment.

Read a SAGE journal article to sharpen your comprehension skills.

 Access a bonus instructional strategy for additional practice.

SAGE EDGE FOR INSTRUCTORS

SAGE edge is a robust online environment featuring an impressive array of free tools and resources. Instructors using this book can access customizable PowerPoint slides and an extensive test bank built on Bloom's taxonomy that features multiple-choice, true/false, essay, and short answer questions for each chapter. Lecture notes, discussion questions, and class activities are provided along with sample syllabi for semester and quarter courses.

SAGE EDGE FOR STUDENTS

At **edge.sagepub.com/bryant** students can access a complete online action plan that includes tips and feedback on progress through the course and materials that allow students to enhance their learning experience. Chapter summaries with learning objectives reinforce the most important material, while multimedia resources help further classroom-based explorations of key topics.

Students can also practice with mobile-friendly **eFlashcards** and take the **Web Quiz** at SAGE edge to find out what they've mastered.

ACKNOWLEDGMENTS

Thanks to our colleagues who contributed their writing and expertise to Chapter 4, "Other Students With Special Learning Needs": the late Janette K. Klingner, University of Colorado at Boulder, for her sections on culturally and linguistically diverse students, multicultural education, bilingual education, and culturally and linguistically diverse students and special education; and Margarita Bianco, University of Colorado at Denver and Health Sciences Center, Denver, Colorado, for her section on students who are gifted and talented.

Our gratitude goes out to the many reviewers, focus group attendees, and advisory council members who have greatly enhanced this project over the years of its writing. Your thoughtfulness and commitment to the project have made this a better book.

For the current edition:

Dona C. Bauman, University of Scranton

Nancy Beach, Ferrum College

Judy Bentley, State University of NY Cortland

Pamela Brillante, William Patterson University of New Jersey

Kimberly Boyd, Virginia Commonwealth University

Melinda Burchard, Messiah College

Nancy G. Burton, Concord University

EunMi Cho, California State University, Sacramento

Su-Je Cho, Fordham University

Hollie C. Cost, University of Montevallo

Susan Courey, San Francisco State University

Aaron R. Deris, Minnesota State University, Mankato

Jason Fruth, Wright State University

Heather Garrison, East Stroudsburg University of Pennsylvania

Terri M. Griffin, Westfield State University

Vicki Jean Hartley, Delta State University

René Hauser, St. Bonaventure University

Jude Matyo-Cepero, University of Nebraska Kearney

Virginia McLoughlin, St. John's University

Carol Moore, Troy University

Wendy Pharr, Northeastern State University

Jazmine Ramirez, Miami Dade College

Bruce Saddler, University at Albany

Thomas Simmons, University of Louisville

Linda Smetana, California State University, East Bay

Shanon Taylor, University of Nevada Reno

Harriet L. Thompson, Western Governors University

Colleen A. Wilkinson, Medaille College

Jie Zhang, The College at Brockport State University of New York

For the previous edition:

Judith Ableser, University of Michigan, Flint

Lynn Bagli, Old Dominion University

Mary Banbury, University of New Orleans

Heather Barker, University of New Hampshire

Dona Bauman, University of Scranton

Kimberly Bright, Shippensburg University

James Burton II, Marshall University

Debbie Case, Southwestern Oklahoma State University

Walter J. Cegel, St. Thomas University

Marlaine K. Chase, University of Southern Indiana

Vivian I. Correa, Clemson University

Kevin Costley, Arkansas Tech University

Christina Curran, Central Washington University

Helen T. Dainty, Tennessee Technological University

Sarah De Haas, Juniata College

Audrey T. Edwards, Eastern Illinois University

Joseph Feinberg, University of North Carolina at Wilmington

Dan Fennerty, Central Washington University

Marion Fesmire, Florida State University

Connie Flood, State University of New York at New Paltz

Regina Foley, Southern Illinois University, Carbondale

Barb M. Fulk, University of Illinois

Raymond J. Gallagher, California State University, Dominguez Hills

Laurel M. Garrick Duhaney, State University of New York at New Paltz

Gordon S. Gibb, Brigham Young University

Gary Goodman, University of Houston

Paul C. Gorski, Hamline University

Char Gottschalk, State University of New York at New Paltz

Elizabeth L. Hardman, East Carolina University

Genevieve Howe Hay, College of Charleston

Susan Hupp, University of Minnesota

Kimberlye Joyce, University of Richmond

Kim Kelly, Southwestern Oklahoma State University

Timothy Lackaye, Hunter College

Phil Lanasa, Cameron University

Michelle LaRocque, Florida Atlantic University

DeAnn Lechtenberger, Texas Tech University

Robert B. Lee, Fort Valley State University

Gary Louis, Wilmington College

K. Alisa Lowrey, University of South Carolina

David J. Majsterek, Central Washington University

Linda Mechling, University of North Carolina, Wilmington

Heeral Mehta, Columbia University Teacher's College

Susan P. Miller, University of Nevada, Las Vegas

Susan O'Rourke, Carlow University

Theresa Pedersen, Northern Illinois University

John Platt, University of West Florida

Wayne Pyle, Lipscomb University

Melisa Reed, Marshall University

Laura Reissner, Northern Michigan University

Patricia Renick, Wright State University

Joy L. Russell, Eastern Illinois University

Edward J. Sabornie, North Carolina State University

Bruce Saddler, State University of New York at Albany

Mary Schreiner, Alvernia College

Amy Staples, University of Northern Iowa

Qaisar Sultana, Eastern Kentucky University

Donna E. Wadsworth, University of Louisiana at Lafayette

We are deeply grateful for the expertise, support, and commitment of the SAGE team to see this project to fruition. Their belief in us and in this project exceeded all reasonable expectations. Many people comprised the team who worked on this book. Although we do not know all of them by name, their expertise with their craft is truly evident; to this team we express our gratitude. We thank Terri Accomazzo—editor—for her support, advice, and wisdom as this writing journey unfolded. Terri inspired us to begin this project and remained steadfast with her encouragement and support throughout challenging times. We could not have finished this work without her continuing encouragement. To Jessica Miller, our associate editor, we extend our thanks for keeping us on track and enduring the evolution of this book. Jessica's ideas and wisdom are found throughout the book; her partnership was evident as the project evolved in scope and content. Elisa Adams, our developmental editor, helped us through the numerous reviewers' comments by providing advice about important changes to ensure the high standards and excellence readers expect. We would like to thank Olivia Weber-Stenis, our production editor, whose high standards and expectations helped us throughout production; to her we are truly grateful. We greatly appreciate Erica DeLuca and Amy Lammers's work as marketing managers. Erica and Amy helped us focus on ideas to make important personal connections with our colleagues. We thoroughly enjoyed working with them! We would also like to thank Nick Pachelli and Lucy Berbeo, eLearning editors, for expertly coordinating the book's supplemental resources, and to Georgia McLaughlin, editorial assistant, for her continued help throughout the process.

We would also like to thank Tina Hardy, copyeditor, who did an excellent and thorough job in making this book clear to read. Bringing closure to this project could not have occurred without the hard work and attention to detail she demonstrated. Her keen eye, efficiency, and professionalism were greatly appreciated to ensure a high quality product for our readers. Tina was a joy to work with through the endless number of details that required careful scrutiny. It is because of Tina that this text is easy to read. Thanks also to Jessica Miller for her fine work in researching the photos that appear in the book. And, finally, we greatly appreciate the work of Scott Van Atta, who created the beautiful cover and interior design.

We would like to thank Dr. Kavita Rao, University of Hawaii, for helping us to create a format for the UDL lessons. Her contributions (e.g., suggesting that we provide information on UDL checkpoints rather than principles; editing our early work) have been invaluable, and we appreciate her taking the time to provide excellent guidance.

We would also like to extend a special thanks to the teachers and administrators who graciously allowed us to film their schools and classrooms: Principal Lou Lichtl and instructors Jason Brown, Jeff McCann, Brinden Wohlstattar, and Melissa Wood-Glusac at Thousand Oaks High School in Thousand Oaks, California; and instructors Jan Evans, Tema Khieu, Lisa Sigafoos, and Mia Tannous at the University of Texas Elementary School in Austin, Texas.

You have a textbook that we hope will inspire you as educators to reach out to all students. You will hear the voices of many as you read and learn numerous, practical ways to work with all students across the grades. We wish you the best!

D.P.B.

B.R.B.

D.D.S.

ABOUT THE AUTHORS

Diane Pedrotty Bryant is a professor in the Department of Special Education, College of Education, The University of Texas at Austin. She is the graduate adviser for the Department of Special Education. She holds the Mollie Villeret Davis Professorship in Learning Disabilities (LD). She is a member of the board of directors for The Meadows Center for Preventing Educational Risk, the project director for the Mathematics Institute for Learning Disabilities and Difficulties, and the co-coordinator of the Assistive and Instructional Technology Lab in the College of Education. Dr. Bryant is principal investigator on a U.S. Department of Education, Institute of Education Sciences grant on algebra-readiness interventions for middle school students with mathematics difficulties. Her line of research focuses on the development and validation of intensive interventions, which can be utilized by mathematics interventionists to teach students with mathematics learning disabilities and mathematics difficulties. She has published numerous articles on technology and academic instructional strategies and is the coauthor of textbooks on methods for teaching struggling students. She is the co-editor-in-chief with Dr. Brian R. Bryant of the *Learning Disability Quarterly*.

Brian R. Bryant lives and works in Austin, Texas. He served as director of research for PRO-ED, Inc., for 10 years and has since served as director of the Office for Students with Disabilities at Florida Atlantic University (where he also served as instructor in the Department of Special Education), as project director of the Texas Assistive Technology Partnership (Tech Act project), and as a private consultant. Brian held an adjunct faculty lecturer appointment in the Department of Special Education at The University of Texas at Austin for many years. For several years, he also had an appointment as a research fellow and research professor with The Meadows Center for Preventing Educational Risk at The University of Texas at Austin. In addition to his book, *Assistive Technology for People With Disabilities* (Pearson, 2011) with Diane Bryant, Brian is the author or coauthor of more than 100 psycho-educational tests, articles, books, book chapters, professional development materials, and other products dealing with remedial education, learning disabilities, intellectual disability, assessment, and assistive technology. His primary research interests are assessment and intervention in learning disabilities and intellectual disability and the exploration of assistive technology applications across the life span. He is currently serving as president of Psycho-Educational Services, an Austin-based publishing and consulting company.

Deborah Deutsch Smith is a professor of special education at the School of Educational Studies at Claremont Graduate University. She currently is coproject director of the IRIS Center (http://iris.peabody.vanderbilt.edu or http://www.iriscenter.com), which is funded by the U.S. Department of Education's Office of Special Education Programs. The national center is charged with developing modules and other resources about students with disabilities. These enhancements are designed for use in coursework by university faculty and in professional development activities for education professionals working in inclusive school settings. She also directs IRIS@CGU, where the national training and dissemination component for the IRIS Center is based. She is the author of *Introduction to Contemporary Special Education: New Horizons* (Pearson Publishing, 2014), was the recipient of the 2015 TED/Pearson Excellence in Teacher Education Award, and was the lead researcher for the Special Education Faculty Shortage Study.

PART I

FOUNDATIONS OF INCLUSIVE EDUCATION

1

INCLUSIVE TEACHING AS RESPONSIVE EDUCATION

LEARNING OBJECTIVES

After studying this chapter, you will be able to answer the following questions:

- What is the ADAPT framework and how do I use it?

- What is a disability?

- What are some reasons for disabilities?

- What are the characteristics of students with disabilities?

- What are the origins of special education?

- What laws and court decisions protect students with disabilities?

- What is special education?

- What is inclusive education?

ELEMENTARY GRADES It is the week before the first day of school. Ms. Smith, a first-year teacher, sits in her empty fourth-grade classroom thinking about what it will be like to finally have her own students to teach, her own classroom to organize, and a real paycheck! She remembers spending years in hard study, taking many late-night classes, traveling across town to observe classroom after classroom, doing week after week of student teaching, staying up late revising lesson plans one more time, and being so excited when she saw the great scores she and her friends received on the state's competency test for teachers. She feels well prepared to assume the responsibility of educating a class of general education students. Ms. Smith has waited so long for this day to arrive; she has wanted to be a teacher since she was in elementary school. She begins to prepare for the school year with great excitement and anticipation.

But as she looks at her class list of 18 students, matching their names with their student files, she is worried. *"The range of their academic skills is so wide; their achievement test scores are all over the map. One of my students has been identified for gifted education, two come to me with individualized education programs, and three of my students are English language learners. Plus, I see a couple of the boys are due to continue receiving speech therapy in a group session from the speech/language pathologist twice a week. I haven't heard from any other teachers or resource professionals about special schedules for any of my students. I wish I could go back and take that inclusion course again!"*

SECONDARY GRADES Mr. Salazar is getting ready for the first day of school where he will be teaching ninth-grade English I as a new teacher. His department has five English teachers, most of whom have had many years of experience, and some have offered advice about how to prepare for the first week. He is nervous but knows that his preparation in the subject matter is strong and his education classes provided lots of information regarding pedagogy and management. Student teaching gave him experiences working with students from diverse backgrounds, including students with learning disabilities (LDs). He learned about adapting instruction but didn't have many experiences with people who provided support services to students. Now, he is reviewing the student folders. *"I am glad for the student teaching experiences because now I have five students with LD. I have one student who uses an assistive technology device for accessing print; who is going to help me with this? I took an introduction to special education course but I am still concerned. I have 250 students each day; how am I going to meet the needs of all students?"*

Ms. Smith and Mr. Salazar share similar concerns. They are first-year teachers and although their preparation was strong, they must now apply what they have learned with diverse groups of students. Are they ready for the challenge?

REFLECTION QUESTIONS In your journal, write down your answers to the following questions. After completing the chapter, check your answers and revise them on the basis of what you have learned.

1. Do you think Ms. Smith and Mr. Salazar are overly concerned about their students' varied needs? Do you think they are just having first-year-teacher jitters? Why or why not?

2. What advice would you give them about planning for their students with disabilities and for those with other special learning needs?

3. How can they learn more about the special education services their students should be receiving this year?

4. In what ways can Ms. Smith and Mr. Salazar be responsive to all their students' special needs?

SETTING THE STAGE

Paul is 62 and lives in alternative housing responsive to his special needs. There are grab bars in the bathroom, an alarm system in case he needs help, and a contact person to answer questions. He has cerebral palsy, which affects his muscles. Writing and completing tasks that require using his fingers (such as buttoning his shirt and tying his shoes) are difficult for him. He walks with crutches, has good communication skills, and manages his daily living needs. He takes special transportation to attend work and physical therapy and to go shopping and visit the bank.

As a young child, Paul attended a state-funded school for children with physical and cognitive disabilities. It was isolated from the public schools and Paul took a special bus to get there. After school, he spent afternoons sitting at home or participating in physical therapy at the Children's Hospital. Paul's mother believed the school system could do better. She believed Paul was perfectly capable of attending public school with neighborhood children. She also thought he should be able to graduate from high school like other children. Paul's mother spent years making her case to the local school board, city officials, and state legislators. After her determined advocacy for her son's right to a public education, Paul started attending public school classes in the mid-1960s, when he was 10.

At that time, specialized instruction and services for students with special needs were not available. In elementary school, Paul was carried up the stairs to class because there were no elevators and he could not manage stairs with his leg braces. He learned basic school skills and went on to graduate from high school with a special diploma and later from a two-year vocational training school. He held various part-time jobs and to this day works at a special workshop for individuals with disabilities. In essence, his work environment is a segregated setting. His social world is restricted to telecommunications such as the Internet and cell phone. But even so, Paul is determined to live independently.

We have come a long way since Paul started school in terms of society's perspective on disability, and we have dismantled many of the barriers to individuals' living independent, productive lives. We have laws to protect individuals in most aspects of life, and we have public school systems that must include all students with special needs. We know a great deal about appropriate instruction and services for students with special needs. Yet there is still work to be done to ensure an appropriate education for all students with special needs and to help them make successful transitions to the independent adulthood with employment, social relationships, and living arrangements that all of us strive to achieve.

You might wonder how teaching can be responsive to the needs of students with special learning needs such as Paul's. The simple answer is that education becomes responsive when an array of *individualized* educational interventions, which are monitored for the student's progress, are implemented to improve the outcomes of infants, toddlers, children, and youth with disabilities (U.S. Department of Education, 2006). Education is responsive and, we believe, responsible, when teams of educators work together to address the unique challenges each student brings to school.

You have the opportunity to be part of this work to ensure that all individuals with special needs receive a quality education. However, if you find this opportunity a bit daunting, you are not alone.

Have you had much personal interaction so far with persons with disabilities in your home, school, or community life? If not, you are probably much like many of your colleagues preparing to become classroom teachers. Do you begin this course about teaching students with disabilities with some anxiety about your ability to meet the needs of these students? If so, again, you are not alone. Although almost two-thirds of students with disabilities spend more than 80% of their school day in general education classrooms, most recently graduated general education teachers report they do not feel adequately prepared to teach them. Their principals agree: New teachers are not doing as well as they should in managing behavior or instructing "difficult-to-teach" students (Futernick, 2006; Gaetano, 2006). But rather than being daunted by these reports, we hope you'll recognize in them the great opportunity they present as you prepare to enter the teacher ranks. You can make a tremendous difference in the lives of these students. And the mission of the course (and the text) you are now beginning is to give you the tools to do just that.

Throughout this text, we describe proven practices that will equip you to teach students with special needs in your classes. We focus on *instructional strategies* and provide *video exemplars* so that you can readily incorporate these practices into your teaching with confidence. We provide the ADAPT framework to help you develop the habits of mind to respond thoughtfully and flexibly to the varied challenges you will face in your classroom long after your brief university and in-service coursework is over. The ADAPT framework we have integrated throughout this text will help you *learn, remember,* and *know when to apply* proven practices in your classroom.

Our goal is for you to develop the confidence you need to teach all students in your classes. Our many years working with preservice and K–12 teachers convince us that teachers want to help their struggling students become successful learners but simply feel ill-equipped to do so. In this text, we focus on those practices that have been proven to work and show you *how, when,* and *with whom* to use each to the best effect. Nothing builds confidence better than good preparation.

We write this text out of the mission we share with your course instructor: By the conclusion of this course, you will leave wanting to teach students with disabilities and other special learning needs in your classroom and feeling equipped to do so effectively. You will find (and those of you who have been teaching have already discovered) that every student in your classroom comes to you with his or her own areas of strength and struggle, parts of the school day that she or he absolutely enjoys or does not exactly relish, and personality traits that make you laugh, make you cry, or leave you scratching your head.

In this respect, the students in your classroom with identified disabilities are no different from the rest of their peers: They're just kids. But the nature and extent of their particular struggles often require certain specialized teaching approaches to help them succeed.

The good news is that we know what those effective approaches are, research has proved they work, and they can be done with a reasonable amount of preclass preparation and in a reasonable amount of class time. (And, as a bonus, they usually benefit all the students in your class, with and without disabilities.) You will learn that even students with the most difficult challenges can overcome, compensate, and achieve remarkable outcomes when your instruction is responsive to their learning needs. You will come to understand across your teacher education program that as a teacher, you can make a real difference in the lives of your students. To begin, we situate the content of this text in the importance of understanding and appreciating the diversity of our society. The Considering Diversity feature provides recommendations for your reflection. We then introduce the ADAPT framework.

CONSIDERING *diversity*

CONSIDER HUMAN DIVERSITY

Diversity in our society is evident in terms of disabilities; social, cultural, and linguistic differences; economic backgrounds; gender differences; family structures; race and ethnicities; and religious beliefs. The students who attend our schools and their families represent these many diverse differences in our society that we embrace. Educators bring to schools their experiences with and understanding of human diversity and its influence on families, cultures, schools, and the delivery of educational services. All children bring a social, academic, economic, and cultural background to class with them, and these backgrounds are part of the environment in which learning takes place. The cultural heritage of all students is an important factor to consider when designing educational programs to meet the needs of exceptional students. Good teaching practices will benefit all students, whatever their background.

WHAT IS THE ADAPT FRAMEWORK AND HOW DO I USE IT?

The ADAPT framework we have devised is a tool for instruction and assessment of struggling learners that reflects proven best practice in the field. It will help you develop a mind-set for the selection of effective interventions and teaching practices. The framework, discussed in detail in Chapter 7, reflects and underscores the mind-set we want you to take away from your course. You can use its five steps to help you make informed decisions about adapting your instruction based on individual students' needs and the tasks all students must complete in school. For now, here's just a quick look in Table 1.1 at what the ADAPT framework looks like. Along with this framework, we provide ADAPT in Action, which is a scenario that describes an instructional situation. Then, the ADAPT framework, as shown in Table 1.1, provides a quick reference for how to frame the ADAPT in Action scenario. We suggest practicing the acronym by naming each letter and what it represents until you can talk about the parts without visual reminders.

With the ADAPT framework in mind, let's begin by first considering disabilities and the special challenges they create.

WHAT IS A DISABILITY?

Some of you might have answered the question "What is a disability?" by expressing the notion that **disabilities** are absolutes—something an individual simply does or doesn't have. You might have said the concept of disability is complex and that there are many different perspectives on what it is and what it means to each individual, family, and culture. You might have included in your answer that the intensity of a disability is the result of different conditions or experiences and that the response to it—the intensity of instruction, types of services, and community supports—depends on an

| TABLE 1.1 | INTRODUCING THE ADAPT FRAMEWORK |

A	D	A	P	T
ASK "What am I requiring the student to do?"	DETERMINE the prerequisite skills of the task.	ANALYZE the student's strengths and struggles.	PROPOSE and implement adaptations from among the four categories: • Instructional activity • Instructional content • Instructional delivery • Instructional material	TEST to see whether the adaptations helped the student accomplish the task.

Intellectual and Learning Disabilities

individual's unique needs. These answers reflect the idea that individualized accommodations and assistance can reduce the impact of the challenge presented by a disability.

Why did we ask how disability is conceptualized? First, the concept of disability is not as simple as it initially appears. Second, the way people, groups, and cultures think about what it means to have a disability affects the way they interact with people with disabilities, and those interactions in turn become events that influence individuals' outcomes (Branson & Miller, 2002; Winzer, 2007). For example, some responses—such as low or unreasonably high expectations—can have long-term negative results (Harry, 2007). So let's think together about various ways to conceptualize "disability" and also about how attitudes toward disability can influence students' lives.

Different disciplines, cultures, and individuals disagree about what disabilities are or how to explain them (Lynch & Hanson, 2004; Utley & Obiakor, 2001). For example, many psychologists, education professionals, and medical professionals describe children and youth in terms of various characteristics, such as intelligence, visual acuity, academic achievement, or behavior. In its manual, *Diagnostic and Statistical Manual of Mental Disorders* (DSM-5), the American Psychiatric Association (APA) describes many characteristics that help to describe or define a condition or a disability because they set the individual apart from "normal," "typical," or "average" (APA, 2013). In this common approach, human characteristics or traits are described as a continuum; at one end very little of the target behavior is observed, and at the other end an unusual amount of the trait is expressed. Here's an example. In the DSM-5, the APA (2013) describes hyperactivity and impulsivity as including the following behaviors:

a. often fidgets with hands or feet or squirms in seat.

b. often leaves seat in classroom or in other situations in which remaining seated is expected.

c. often runs about or climbs excessively in situations in which it is inappropriate (in adolescents or adults, may be limited to subjective feelings of restlessness).

d. often has difficulty playing or engaging in leisure activities quietly.

e. is often "on the go" or often acts as if "driven by a motor."

f. often talks excessively. (p. 60)

Note that all the behaviors described in the DSM-5 account of hyperactivity are expected in children to some extent. What identifies hyperactivity is that an individual exhibits "too many" of these behaviors. Now let's look at the reverse situation, when displaying "not enough" or "too few" of the behaviors of concern leads to the identification of a disability.

Other perspectives can also provide a framework for understanding disabilities and special needs. Let's turn to four different ways of thinking about disabilities:

- Deficit perspective
- Cultural perspective
- Sociological perspective
- People with disabilities as members of a minority group

THE DEFICIT PERSPECTIVE ON DISABILITIES

The *deficit perspective* reflects the idea that behavior and characteristics people share are distributed

Some students exhibit problem behaviors and need exemplary teachers. How do federal laws distinguish between students who exhibit problem behaviors and students with attention issues or learning disabilities?

along a continuum, with most people falling in the middle of the distribution, where they make up the average. For example, some people are short and some tall, but most people's height falls somewhere in the middle; the average of everyone's height is at the center of the distribution. The scores from most human characteristics create such patterns, forming what we call a **normal curve**, like the one shown in Figure 1.1. Because of the way the distribution tends to fall, with the highest number of scores in the middle and proportionally fewer as the distance from the average score increases, the distribution is also referred to as the **bell-shaped curve**.

Suppose we plotted the number of students obtaining each academic achievement score on the graph. Few students would obtain low scores, and their scores would be plotted at the left-hand side of the graph. The number of students receiving higher scores increases as we move to the right until we reach the average or mean score. Somewhere in the middle of the distribution are **typical learners**, whose behaviors and characteristics represent the average or majority of students. The progressively fewer students who obtain higher and higher scores on the test complete the right-hand side of the distribution or curve. The number of characteristics we can count in this way is infinite, and each individual student probably falls at a different point on each dimension measured. Thus the unusually tall student might have slightly below-average visual acuity and an average score on the distance he or she can kick a ball. Clearly the hypothetical average student, or typical learner, does not actually exist—or exists very rarely—because the possible combinations of human characteristics are endless.

Regardless, in mainstream U.S. society, the most common way we describe individuals is by quantifying their performance. Unfortunately, this way of

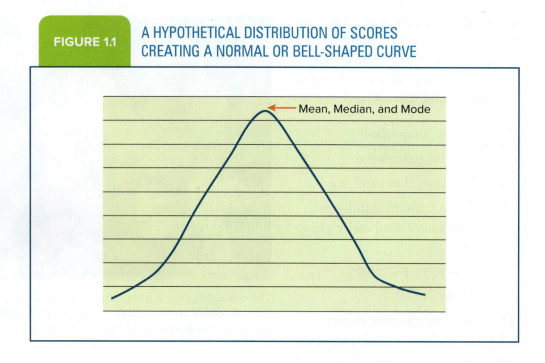

FIGURE 1.1 A HYPOTHETICAL DISTRIBUTION OF SCORES CREATING A NORMAL OR BELL-SHAPED CURVE

thinking forces us to consider everyone in terms of how different they are from the average, and half the members of any group will be below average. The approach also contributes to the tendency to think about students with disabilities as deficient or somehow less than their peers without disabilities.

THE CULTURAL PERSPECTIVE ON DISABILITIES

A second way to think about disabilities and the people who might be affected does not use a quantitative approach; rather, it reveals a *cultural perspective* that reflects the diversity of our nation. Alfredo Artiles of Arizona State University aptly pointed out that the United States today includes many different cultures, some of which embrace concepts and values that differ greatly from mainstream ideas. Nonmajority cultures often hold different views of disabilities, and many do not think about disabilities in terms of deficits or quantitative judgments of individuals (Artiles, 2003). The beliefs of teachers and other professionals who work with students are important to understand because different perspectives result in different responses to a disability.

First, education professionals and the families with whom they work might not share the same understanding of disability. Second, they might not have a common belief about what causes disabilities. Knowing this helps us understand why different families approach education professionals differently when told their child has a disability. Because disability does not have a single orientation or fixed definition, it is not thought about uniformly or universally (Harry, 2007; Lynch & Hanson, 2004). The same individual might be considered "different," or as having a disability, in one culture but not in another (Utley & Obiakor, 2001). Or the degree of difference might not be considered uniformly across cultures.

THE SOCIOLOGICAL PERSPECTIVE ON DISABILITIES

Instead of focusing on people's strengths or deficits, the *sociological perspective* views differences across people's skills and traits as socially constructed (Longmore, 2003; Riddell, 2007). The way a society treats individuals, not a condition or set of traits the individual exhibits, is what makes people different from each other. If people's attitudes and the way society treats groups of individuals change, the impact of being a member of a group changes as well. In other words, according to this perspective, what makes a disability is the way we treat individuals we think of as different.

Some scholars and advocates hold a radical view, suggesting that disabilities are a necessity of U.S. society, structure, and values. Some scholars, such as Herb Grossman, believe that when societies are stratified, variables such as disability, race, and ethnicity become economic and political imperatives (Grossman, 2002). They are needed to maintain class structure. Classifications result in restricted opportunities that force some groups of people to fall to the bottom (Erevelles, 1996; Grossman, 2002). Clearly, this rationale or explanation for disabilities is controversial, but let's see how the sociological perspective might apply to at least one disability. Using this perspective, intellectual disabilities (referred to as mental retardation in the Individuals with Disabilities Education Act, 2004; see Rosa's Law in Table 1.4) exist because society and people treat these individuals poorly. If supporting services were available to help every individual when problems occur, then people with intellectual disabilities would not be negatively treated and would be successful. In other words, if individuals with significant differences are treated like everyone else, problems associated with intellectual disabilities will disappear.

Serious issues have been raised about sociological perspectives on disabilities. Jim Kauffman and Dan Hallahan, scholars at the University of Virginia, maintain that disabilities are real, not just sociologically constructed, and significantly affect the people who have them no matter how they are treated (Hallahan, Kauffman, & Pullen, 2011). To these critics, sociological perspectives arise from a need for "sameness," in which everyone is truly alike. They contend that this position is dangerous because it (a) minimizes people's disabilities, (b) suggests that individuals with disabilities do not need special services, and (c) implies that needed services can be discontinued or reduced. All three scenarios leave individuals with disabilities vulnerable to diminished outcomes. Whether or not you believe the sociological perspective can be used to explain disabilities, it does explain why people with disabilities feel they experience bias and discrimination, just like members of other minority groups. Let's turn our attention to these issues now.

PEOPLE WITH DISABILITIES AS MEMBERS OF A MINORITY GROUP

Paul Longmore—a founder of the disabilities studies movement, director of the Disability Studies Department at San Francisco State, and also a person with disabilities—maintains that like other minority groups, individuals with disabilities receive negative treatment because of discrimination (Longmore, 2003). The ways in which people are treated by society and by other individuals erect real barriers that influence their outcomes. Many individuals with disabilities believe their disabilities then **handicap** them by presenting challenges and barriers. This belief leads many people to think of people with disabilities as belonging to a minority group, much as the concepts of race and ethnicity have resulted in African Americans, Hispanics, Native Americans, and Asian/Pacific Islanders[1] being considered part of historically underrepresented groups. Difficult situations occur not because of a condition or disability but, rather, because people with disabilities are denied full participation in society as a consequence of their minority status (Winzer, 2007). In fact, the law that guarantees children with disabilities a right to a public education, the **Individuals with Disabilities Education Act (IDEA, 2004),** is often referred to as a civil rights law. This places IDEA in the same category as the Voting Rights Act of 1965, which put an end to discriminatory practices that denied some citizens their right to vote in state and national elections. Next, we discuss reasons for disabilities.

WHAT ARE SOME REASONS FOR DISABILITIES?

We have just discussed four very different perspectives on disabilities. Let's return to more traditional views of disabilities and the conditions that cause them. (We discuss other special learning needs that schools and society do not consider disabilities, including those prompted by giftedness, social and economic inequities, and cultural and linguistic differences, in Chapter 4.)

One way to organize the causes of disabilities is to divide them into three groups by time of onset, whether before birth, during the birth process, or after birth. **Prenatal** or **congenital** causes occur before birth and are often genetic or inherited. Heredity is responsible for Down syndrome and congenital deafness. Diseases and infections in expectant mothers, such as HIV/AIDS, can devastate an unborn baby, and such events are also considered prenatal. **Perinatal** causes occur during the birthing process. They include low birth weight and injuries due to oxygen deprivation, umbilical cord accidents, obstetrical trauma, and head trauma. One common perinatal cause of disabilities is cerebral palsy (CP). **Postnatal** causes occur after birth, and here the

---

[1]Although regional and personal preferences about specific terms used to identify ethnic and racial groups vary, these terms are the ones used by the federal government. Throughout this text, we use a variety of terms in an attempt to achieve balance.

environment is a major factor. A few examples of postnatal causes are child abuse and neglect, environmental toxins, and accidents.

Another way to consider why disabilities and special needs arise is to classify the reasons in terms of biological causes, environmental causes, and other risk factors. Many of these occur during all three periods of onset. Let's briefly consider them.

BIOLOGICAL CAUSES OF DISABILITY

Heredity is a biological cause of disabilities, as are diseases and health conditions. Thus a virus that results in a severe hearing loss is considered a biological cause. Seizure disorders such as epilepsy are biological reasons for special health care needs, as are diseases such as juvenile arthritis and polio. In Chapters 2 and 3, where we present information about specific disabilities, we will have more to say about some types of conditions students bring to school.

ENVIRONMENTAL CAUSES OF DISABILITY

In addition to biological factors, other situations can cause challenges that result in educational difficulties. Some of these are environmentally based. Many are preventable, but many others cannot be avoided.

Toxins abound in our environment. All kinds of hazardous wastes are hidden in neighborhoods and communities. For example, one toxin that causes intellectual disabilities is lead. We can pinpoint (and, you would think, eliminate) two major sources of lead poisoning in the United States today: lead-based paint and leaded gasoline. Neither product is sold today, but unfortunately lead has remained in the dirt children play in and on the walls of older apartments and houses where they breathe it directly from the air and household dust, eat paint chips, or put their fingers in their mouths after touching walls or window sills. The Children's Defense Fund (CDF) reports that some 16% of low-income children in the United States have lead poisoning, compared with 4% of all U.S. children (CDF, 2004). Lead is not the only source of environmental toxins government officials worry about; other concerns include pesticides, industrial pollution from chemical waste, and mercury found in fish (Keysor, 2006).

Other environmental issues can trigger problems for children as well. Asthma, a health condition covered in our discussion of Section 504 later, is the leading cause of school absenteeism. Teachers and schools can reduce problems with asthma through the use of simple interventions. For example, asthma is often triggered by exposure to specific allergens. For some students, the chance of an asthma attack is reduced when the classroom is free of chalk dust, plants that generate pollen or mold, cold and dry air, smoke, paint fumes, and chemical smells. For others, the fur of classroom pets can cause an episode. Clearly, exposures to toxins are preventable, and the effect of a condition can be reduced. Let's learn now about students with disabilities.

Students With Disabilities

WHAT ARE THE CHARACTERISTICS OF STUDENTS WITH DISABILITIES?

Nationally, some 6.4 million children and youth ages 3 to 21, or about 13 percent of students in public schools, are identified as having disabilities and are receiving special education services from prekindergarten through 12th grade (U.S. Department of Education, Office of Special Education Programs [OSEP], 2013). The federal government describes 14 disability-specific categories that can be used to qualify infants, toddlers, preschoolers, and young students eligible to receive special education services. Within these categories are many conditions. For example, stuttering is included as a speech impairment, attention-deficit/hyperactivity disorder (ADHD) is included in the category of other health impairments, and Tourette's syndrome is included in the emotional disturbances category.

People think about these **special education categories**, or disabilities requiring specialized educational responses, in different ways. First, the names for these categories differ slightly from state to state, and parent and professional groups do not necessarily prefer the terms. Second, some categories—such as deafness and hard of hearing—are often combined. And they are often ordered and divided by **prevalence**, or the size of the category: **high-incidence disabilities** occur in greater numbers and **low-incidence disabilities** occur less often. Some people mistakenly think incidence or prevalence relates to the severity of the disability. Remember, however, that all disabilities are serious, and mild to severe cases occur within each range of incidence.

Table 1.2 shows an overview of the disabilities and the different ways they are referred to in school settings. The Individuals with Disabilities Education Act (IDEA) of 2004 requires states to use these disability areas to qualify children and youth for special education services. Note they are listed by whether the federal government considers them high or low incidence. Check carefully to see how your state views these determinations about prevalence. In Chapters 2 and 3, we discuss each of the disability categories, including their prevalence rates. In the next section, we discuss the origins of special education.

WHAT ARE THE ORIGINS OF SPECIAL EDUCATION?

Although many people believe U.S. special education began in 1975 with the passage of the national law we now call IDEA, it actually began more than 200 years ago. The legend of special education's beginnings is not only famous; it's true. In 1799, farmers in southern France found a young boy living in the woods, and they brought this "wild child" to a doctor in Paris. Jean-Marc-Gaspard Itard, the doctor who now is recognized as the "father of special

TABLE 1.2	SPECIAL EDUCATION CATEGORIES	
Federal Term	**Other Terms**	**Comments**
High-Incidence Disabilities		
Specific learning disability	Learning disabilities (LDs)	Includes reading, language, writing, and mathematics disabilities
Speech or language impairments	Speech disorders or language disorders; communication disorders	Includes articulation, fluency, and voice problems
Intellectual disability	Cognitive disabilities; intellectual disabilities	Ranges from mild to severe but often overlaps with low-incidence disabilities
Emotional disturbance	Emotional/behavioral disorders (EBDs)	Includes schizophrenia; does not include children who are socially maladjusted unless it is determined they have an emotional disturbance
Low-Incidence Disabilities		
Multiple disabilities	Multiple-severe disabilities; developmental disabilities	Does not include all students with more than one disability; criteria vary by state
Hearing impairment [includes deafness]	Hard of hearing and deaf	Includes full range of hearing losses; the term *deaf* is used to signify those who consider themselves part of the deaf community
Deafness	Severe hearing impairment	Signifies impaired ability to process linguistic information because of the severity of the hearing impairment with or without amplification
Orthopedic impairments	Physical impairments (PI); physical disabilities	Is often combined with health impairments because there are many overlapping conditions
Other health impairments	Health impairments; special health care needs	Under IDEA '04, includes attention-deficit/hyperactivity disorder (ADHD)
Visual impairments [includes blindness]	Visual disabilities; low vision and blind	Includes full range of vision loss
Autism	Autism spectrum disorders (ASD)	ASD is more inclusive; autism is considered one of five ASD conditions; actual national prevalence numbers place this group of learners in the low-incidence category, although many consider it more frequent
Deaf-blindness	Deafblind	Causes severe communication and other developmental and educational needs
Traumatic brain injury (TBI)		Must be acquired after birth
*Developmental delay		Allows for noncategorical identification from age 3 to the 9th birthday.

* States and school districts may use the term *developmental delays* for children with delays in cognitive, social, communication, physical, and/or adaptive development. Children may be identified if they have a diagnosed condition (physical or intellectual) that will likely result in a developmental delay. Children under the age of 3 may also be identified if they are at risk for developmental delays without intervention services.

education," used many of the principles and procedures of explicit instruction still implemented today to teach this boy, who was named Victor and who probably had intellectual disabilities.

In the early 1800s, Edouard Seguin, one of Itard's students, came to the United States and began efforts to educate students with disabilities. In fact, these early efforts were taking root across Europe as well. For example, in Italy, Maria Montessori worked first with children with cognitive disabilities and showed they could learn at young ages through concrete experiences offered in environments rich in manipulative materials. Meanwhile, Thomas Hopkins Gallaudet began to develop deaf education, and Samuel Gridley Howe founded the New England Asylum for the Blind (later the Perkins Institute). Elizabeth Farrell initiated public school classes for students with disabilities in 1898. Although special education and the idea of educating students with disabilities are not new, they were not uniformly accepted. In the United States, it was another 75 years before education became a right, something all students with disabilities were entitled to receive. You may be surprised to learn, in the next section, that the guarantees in place today were adopted rather recently.

INCONSISTENT OPPORTUNITIES

Although positive attitudes about the benefits of educating students with disabilities emerged centuries ago, the delivery of programs remained inconsistent for almost 200 years. In 1948 only 12% of all children with disabilities received special education (Ballard, Ramirez, & Weintraub, 1982). As late as 1962, only 16 states had laws that included students with mild intellectual disabilities under mandatory school attendance requirements (Roos, 1970). In most states, these children were not allowed to attend school, and those with more severe disabilities were routinely excluded.

In the early 1970s, Congress studied the problem, and here's what it found (20 U.S.C. section 1400 [b]):

- One million of the children with disabilities in the United States were excluded entirely from the public school system.

- More than half of the eight million children with disabilities were not receiving appropriate educational services.

- The special educational needs of these children were not being fully met because they were not receiving necessary related services.

- Services within the public school system were inadequate and forced families to go outside the public school system, often traveling great distances from their residence and at their own expense.

- If given appropriate funding, state and local educational agencies could provide effective special education and related services to meet the needs of children with disabilities.

Congress realized that special education, with proper financial assistance and educational support, was necessary to make a positive difference in the lives of these children and their families.

COURT CASES: A BACKDROP FOR NATIONAL LEGISLATION

The end of World War II ushered in a time of increased opportunities for all, eventually leading to the civil rights movement of the 1960s and to advocacy for people with disabilities during the 1970s. Before then, concerns about unfair treatment of children with disabilities and their limited access to education were being brought to the courts and legislatures state by state. Table 1.3 summarizes landmark state and local court cases that prepared the way for national special education to be consistently offered to all children with disabilities. After years of exclusion, segregation, and denial of basic educational opportunities, consensus was growing that a national civil rights law, guaranteeing students with disabilities access to the education system, was imperative. Next, we discuss laws and court decisions regarding special education.

WHAT LAWS AND COURT DECISIONS PROTECT STUDENTS WITH DISABILITIES?

The nation's policymakers reacted to injustices revealed in court case after court case by passing federal laws to protect the civil rights of individuals with disabilities (Florian, 2007). Table 1.4 lists some of the important laws passed by Congress that affect individuals with disabilities. As you study these, notice how one law set the stage for the next.

TABLE 1.3 LANDMARK COURT CASES LEADING TO THE ORIGINAL PASSAGE OF IDEA

Case	Date	Issue	Finding
Brown v. Board of Education	1954	Overturn of "separate but equal doctrine"; integration of Kansas public schools	The case was the basis for future rulings that children with disabilities cannot be excluded from school.
Pennsylvania Association for Retarded Children (PARC) v. Commonwealth of Pennsylvania	1972	Access to public education for students with intellectual disabilities	In the state of Pennsylvania, no child with intellectual disabilities can be denied a public education.
Mills v. Board of Education of the District of Columbia	1972	Access to special education for all students with disabilities	All students with disabilities have a right to a free public education.

TABLE 1.4 LANDMARK LAWS GUARANTEEING RIGHTS TO INDIVIDUALS WITH DISABILITIES

Date	Law or Section	Name and Key Provisions
1973	Section 504	Section 504 of the Rehabilitation Act • Set the stage for IDEA and ADA • Guaranteed basic civil rights to people with disabilities • Required accommodations in schools and in society
1975	PL 94-142	Education for All Handicapped Children Act (EHA) • Guaranteed a free appropriate education in the least restrictive environment
1986	PL 99-457	EHA (reauthorized) • Added infants and toddlers • Provided the Individualized Family Service Plan (IFSP)
1990	PL 101-476	Individuals with Disabilities Education Act (IDEA) • Changed the name of PL 94-142 to IDEA • Added transition plans (ITP) • Added autism as a special education category • Added traumatic brain injury as a category
1990	PL 101-336	Americans with Disabilities Act (ADA) • Barred discrimination in employment, transportation, public accommodations, and telecommunications • Implemented the concept of normalization across U.S. life • Required phased-in accessibility in schools
1997	PL 105-17	IDEA '97 (reauthorized) • Added ADHD to the category of other health impairments • Added functional behavioral assessments and behavioral intervention plans • Changed ITP to a component of the Individualized Education Program (IEP)
2001	PL 107-110	Elementary and Secondary Education (No Child Left Behind) Act of 2001 (ESEA) • Required that all schoolchildren participate in state and district testing • Called for 100% proficiency of all students in reading and math by 2012
2004	PL 108-364	Assistive Technology Act of 2004 (ATA) (reauthorized) • Provided support for school-to-work transition projects • Continued a national website on assistive technology (AT) • Assisted states in creating and supporting device loan programs, financial loans to individuals with disabilities to purchase AT devices, and equipment demonstrations
2004	PL 108-446	IDEA '04 (reauthorized) • Required special education teachers to be highly qualified • Mandated that all students with disabilities participate annually either in state and district testing with accommodations or in alternative assessments • Eliminated IEP short-term objectives and benchmarks, except for those who use alternative assessments

Date	Law or Section	Name and Key Provisions
		• Changed identification procedures for LDs
		• Allowed any student to be placed in an interim alternative educational setting for involvement in weapons, drugs, or violence
2008	PL 110-325	Americans with Disabilities Amendments Act (ADAAA) (reauthorized)
		• Restored workplace protection diminished by previous court decisions
		• Redefined "major life activities" to enable individuals with disabilities to be protected against discrimination in the workplace
2010	PL 111-256	Rosa's Law
		• Changed the terms *mental retardation* and *mentally retarded* to *intellectual disabilities* and *intellectually disabled* in federal laws
2010	PL 111-148	The Affordable Care Act
		• Prohibited exclusion for preexisting conditions
		• Eliminated caps on benefits
		• Prohibited discrimination based on disability and health status

SECTION 504

In 1973 Congress passed **Section 504 of the Vocational Rehabilitation Act**, intended to prevent discrimination against individuals with disabilities in programs that receive federal funds. Section 504 required public buildings to provide **accommodations**, such as wheelchair ramps, to allow or facilitate access by people with disabilities. This means public schools must provide accommodations to students whose disabilities or health conditions require some special attention in order to allow them to participate fully in school activities. This law set the stage for both IDEA and the Americans with Disabilities Act, because it included some protection of the rights of students with disabilities to public education and many provisions for adults with disabilities and their participation in society and the workplace. Let's direct our attention now to the law that specifically targets schoolchildren and their families.

AMERICANS WITH DISABILITIES ACT (ADA)

Congress first considered the civil rights of people with disabilities when it passed Section 504 of the Rehabilitation Act of 1973. However, after almost 20 years, Congress became convinced by advocates, many of whom were themselves adults with disabilities, that Section 504 was not sufficient and did not end discrimination for adults with disabilities. It took stronger measures by passing yet another law. On July 26, 1990, President George H. W. Bush signed the **Americans with Disabilities Act (ADA)**, which bars discrimination in employment, transportation, public accommodations, and telecommunications. Bush said, "Let the shameful walls of exclusion finally come tumbling down."

Senator Tom Harkin (D-IA), the chief sponsor of the act, spoke of this law as the "emancipation proclamation" for people with disabilities (West, 1994).

ADA guarantees people with disabilities access to all aspects of life—not just those supported by federal funding—and implements the concept of normalization across all aspects of U.S. life. Both Section 504 and ADA are considered civil rights and antidiscrimination laws (deBettencourt, 2002). ADA supports and extends Section 504 and ensures adults with disabilities greater access to employment and participation in everyday activities that adults without disabilities enjoy. It requires employers not to discriminate against qualified applicants or employees with disabilities and mandates new public transportation (buses, trains, subways) and new or remodeled public accommodations (hotels, stores, restaurants, banks, theaters) to be accessible to persons with disabilities.

ADA has had a substantial impact on the daily lives of people with disabilities. For example, it requires telephone companies to provide relay services so deaf individuals and people with speech impairments can use ordinary telephones. It is thanks to ADA that curb cuts for wheelchairs also make it easier for everyone to use carts, strollers, and even roller skates when crossing streets. For students making the transition from school to adult life, improvements in access and nondiscrimination should allow genuine participation in their communities.

Section 504 and ADA also affect the education system, but there are some important differences between them and IDEA. Section 504 and ADA incorporate a broader definition of disabilities than does IDEA, because they guarantee the right to accommodations even to those who do not need special education services and to those beyond school age. For example, it is under the authority of ADA that college students with special needs are entitled to special testing situations (untimed tests, Braille versions, someone to read the questions to them) and that schoolchildren with ADHD who do not qualify for special education receive special accommodations.

Like IDEA, the ADA law has sparked controversy. On the one hand, some members of the disability community are disappointed because they still cannot find jobs suited to their interests, training, or skills. On the other hand, many small-business owners claim that ADA requires them to make accommodations that are expensive and rarely used.

INDIVIDUALS WITH DISABILITIES EDUCATION ACT (IDEA)

We've seen that Congress found widespread patterns of exclusion, denial of services, and discrimination (Knitzer, Steinberg, & Fleisch, 1990). Therefore, it decided that a universal, national law guaranteeing the rights of students with disabilities to a free appropriate public education was necessary. The first

IDEA

version of the special education law was passed in 1975 and was called **Public Law (PL) 94-142, Education for All Handicapped Children Act (EHA)**. (The first set of numbers refers to the session of Congress in which the law was passed, the second set to the number of the law. Thus EHA was the 142nd law passed in the 94th session of Congress.) Congress gave the states two years to get ready to implement this new special education law, so it was actually initiated in 1977. It was to be in effect for 10 years, and for it to continue, a reauthorization process was required. After the first 10-year period, the law was to be reauthorized every 3 years.

Federal legislation broadly defines disabilities and impairments that significantly limit one or more major life activities, including walking, seeing, hearing, and learning.

EHA was reauthorized the first time in 1986. (Congress gives itself a couple of extra years to reauthorize laws so they do not expire before the congressional committee can complete the job of rewriting them.) Congress added services to infants, toddlers, and their families in this version of the special education law. In its next reauthorization, Congress (retroactively) changed the name of the law to PL 101-476, the Individuals with Disabilities Education Act (IDEA), added autism and traumatic brain injury as special education categories, and strengthened transitional services for adolescents with disabilities. In the 1997 reauthorization of IDEA, issues such as access to the general education curriculum, participation in state and district-wide testing, and discipline assumed prominence. When the law was passed again in 2004, many changes were made in the way students with learning disabilities can be identified. This version of the law also encourages states and school districts to help all young students who are struggling to read, in hopes of preventing reading/learning disabilities and also getting help as early as possible to those who need it (U.S. Department of Education, 2006).

COURT DECISIONS DEFINING IDEA

It is the role of the courts to clarify laws passed by Congress and implemented by the administration (implementation of IDEA is the responsibility of the U.S. Department of Education). Although Congress thought it was clear in its intentions about the educational guarantees it believed necessary for children with disabilities and their families, no legal language is perfect. Since 1975, when PL 94-142 (IDEA) became law, a very small percentage of the children served have been engaged in formal disputes about the identification of students with disabilities, evaluations, educational placements, and the provision of a free appropriate public education. Most disputes are resolved in non-court proceedings or **due process hearings**. Some, however, must be settled in courts of law—a few even in the U.S. Supreme Court. Through such litigation, many different questions about special education have been addressed and clarified. Table 1.5 highlights a few important U.S. Supreme Court decisions.

The issues and complaints the courts deal with are significant, and the ramifications of those decisions can be momentous. For example, a student named Garret F. was paralyzed as the result of a motorcycle accident at the age of 4. Thereafter, he required an electric ventilator (or someone manually pumping an air bag) to continue breathing and to stay alive. When Garret was in middle school, his mother requested that the school pick up the expenses of his physical care while he was in school. The district refused the request. Most school district administrators believed providing "complex health services" to students was not a related service (and hence not the district's responsibility), but rather a medical service (excluded under the IDEA regulations). In other words, across the country, districts had interpreted the IDEA law and its regulations to mean that schools were not responsible for the cost of health services.

The Supreme Court, however, disagreed and interpreted IDEA differently. The justices decided that if a doctor is not necessary to provide the health service, and the service is necessary to keep a student in an educational program, then it is the school's obligation to provide the "related service." The implications of this decision are enormous (Katsiyannis & Yell, 2000). Not only are the services of additional staff expensive—between $20,000 and $40,000 per school year—but to them must be added increased liability for schools, additional considerations for individualized education program (IEP) teams, administrative costs, and the complications of having yet another adult in a classroom.

Now let's turn our attention to a law that addresses the education of all students, with and without disabilities.

NO CHILD LEFT BEHIND ACT (NCLB)

In the last reauthorization of the Elementary and Secondary Education Act, known as the **No Child Left Behind Act of 2001 (NCLB)**, students with disabilities were included in many ways. This law requires that 95% of all schoolchildren be full participants in state and district testing. One major goal of NCLB is to raise academic achievement for all students while closing the achievement gap between poor, inner-city schools and schools in middle-class suburban areas. Here are a few of the main features of NCLB related to students with disabilities (Browder & Cooper-Duffy, 2003):

- Use of scientifically based programs and interventions
- Access to the general education curriculum
- Insistence on highly qualified teachers
- Evaluation of students' performance with appropriate accommodations

Special
Education Law

TABLE 1.5 LANDMARK U.S. SUPREME COURT CASES DEFINING IDEA

Case	Year	Issue	Finding/Importance
Rowley v. Hendrick Hudson School District	1982	Free Appropriate Public Education (FAPE)	School districts must provide those services that permit a student with disabilities to benefit from instruction.
Irving Independent School District v. Tatro	1984	Defining related services	Clean intermittent catheterization (CIC) is a related service when necessary to allow a student to stay in school.
Smith v. Robinson	1984	Attorney's fees	Parents are reimbursed legal fees when they win a case resulting from special education litigation.
Burlington School Committee v. Department of Education	1985	Private school placement	In some cases, public schools may be required to pay for private school placements when the district does not provide an appropriate education.
Honig v. Doe	1988	Exclusion from school	Students whose misbehavior is related to their disability cannot be denied education.
Timothy W. v. Rochester, New Hampshire, School District	1989	FAPE	Regardless of the existence or severity of a student's disability, a public education is the right of every child.
Zobrest v. Catalina Foothills School District	1993	Paid interpreter at parochial high school	Paying for a sign language interpreter at a parochial school does not violate the constitutional separation of church and state.
Carter v. Florence County School District 4	1993	Reimbursement for private school	A court may order reimbursement to parents who withdraw their children from a public school that provides inappropriate education, even though the private placement does not meet all IDEA requirements.
Doe v. Withers	1993	FAPE	Teachers are responsible for the implementation of accommodations specified in individual students' IEPs.
Cedar Rapids School District v. Garret F.	1999	Related services	Health attendants are a related service and a district's expense if the service is necessary to maintain students in educational programs.
Arlington Central School District Board of Education v. Murphy	2006	Fees	Parents are not entitled to recover fees for expert witnesses in special education due process hearings.
Forest Grove School District v. T.A.	2009	Private school tuition reimbursement	Parents are entitled to tuition reimbursement for private school special education services regardless of whether the child had received special education services in a public school setting and the public school had not provided a free appropriate public education.

ASSISTIVE TECHNOLOGY ACT OF 2004 (ATA)

On October 25, 2004, President George W. Bush signed the reauthorization of the **Assistive Technology Act** (ATA; PL 108-364), or the Tech Act as it is more commonly known, into law. People with disabilities find this law of growing relevance because they are confident that increased accessibility in the future depends, in part, on technology. The following Tech Notes provide information from the Tech Act about assistive technology (AT).

TECH *notes*

ASSISTIVE TECHNOLOGY LEGISLATION

The term **assistive technology** device was first defined in the Technology-Related Assistance for Individuals with Disabilities Act of 1988 (PL 100-407). In this legislation, AT devices were defined as "any item, piece of equipment, or product system, whether acquired commercially off-the-shelf, modified, or customized, that is used to increase, maintain or improve the functional capabilities of individuals with disabilities" (Sec. 3). Individuals with disabilities can use technology, whether disability-specific (e.g., Braille printers, speech synthesizers), specialized (e.g., devices such as "good grip" utensils, ergonomic seating), or general (e.g., organizing tools), to help them become more independent citizens (Carey, Friedman, & Bryan, 2005). The Tech Act applies to the education system and the federal legislation, IDEA (2004), mandates that IEP teams must consider whether the student needs AT to receive a free appropriate public education (FAPE). School districts have become increasingly aware that IEP team members need knowledge and skills to make informed AT decisions.

AT is critical to the participation of people with disabilities in the workplace, in the community, and in school; it removes barriers that restrict their lives. For example, AT allows people with hearing problems to go to their neighborhood theaters and hear the movie's dialog through listening devices or read it via captions. It allows people with physical disabilities to join friends at a local coffeehouse by using a variety of mobility options. It provides text-to-audio translations to those who cannot access printed passages because they cannot see and provides immediate audio-to-text translations to those who cannot hear lectures (Hitchcock & Stahl, 2003). The potential is limited only by our creativity and innovation.

However, AT is expensive and far beyond many people's budgets, particularly those who are underemployed or unemployed. For both students and adults, the Tech Act offers (through the states' loan programs) training activities, demonstrations of new devices, and other direct services. This law allows students to test equipment and other AT devices both at school and at home before actually purchasing them.

Access to information technology is important and unfettering to all of us, and restricted access to it results in barriers with considerable consequences. Here's how the National Council on Disability (NCD) advised the president of the United States about this issue:

For America's 54 million people with disabilities, however, access to such information and technology developments is a double-edged sword that can release opportunities or sever essential connections. On the one hand, such developments can be revolutionary in their ability to empower people with seeing, hearing, manual, or cognitive impairments through alternative means of input to and interaction with the World Wide Web, information transaction machines, and kiosks. On the other hand, electronic information and technological developments can present serious and sometimes insurmountable obstacles when, for example, basic principles of accessibility or universal design are not practiced in their deployment. (NCD, 2001 p. 1)

Influential court cases, landmark legislation, and laws related to education and to the greater society have paved the way for special education services as we know them today. We now turn our attention to a discussion about what makes special education "special."

WHAT IS SPECIAL EDUCATION?

Special education is designed to meet the unique learning needs of each infant, toddler, preschooler, and elementary through high school student with disabilities, and individuals up to the age of 21. This instruction might be delivered in many different types of settings, such as hospitals, separate facilities, and homes, but it is most commonly provided at the student's local school in the general education class with neighborhood friends. Special education reflects a variety of instructional targets: Braille for students who are blind, manual communication systems for students who are deaf, social skills training for students with emotional or behavioral disorders, and so on.

General education and special education differ along some very important dimensions. First and foremost, they are designed for students with different learning, behavioral, social, communication, and basic functional needs (such as the need to learn daily living skills). Second, some differences are based in law—what is stated in IDEA and its regulations—and result in key components of special education. Third, general education tends to focus on groups of learners, whereas the special education approach focuses on individuals.

One way to gain a better understanding of special education is to study some of its key distinguishing features. Although we cannot put forth a single description because these services must be designed for each individual to meet his or her unique learning needs, some fundamental tenets provide the foundation:

- Free appropriate public education
- Least restrictive environment

- Systematic identification procedures
- Individualized education programs
- Family involvement
- Related services
- Access to the general education curriculum
- Evidence-based practices
- Frequent monitoring of progress

Let's examine each of these features that form the foundation of special education.

FREE APPROPRIATE PUBLIC EDUCATION (FAPE)

From the very beginning of IDEA, Congress stipulated that educational services for students with disabilities are to be available to parents at no additional cost to them. These students, despite the complexity of their educational needs, the accommodations or additional services they require, and the cost to a school district, are entitled to a **free appropriate public education (FAPE)**. Note that Congress included the word *appropriate* in its language. FAPE must be individually determined, because what is appropriate for one student with a disability might not be appropriate for another.

LEAST RESTRICTIVE ENVIRONMENT (LRE)

The second key feature of special education is that students with disabilities must receive their education in the **least restrictive environment (LRE)**. In other words, special education services are not automatically delivered in any particular place. Today, LRE is often misinterpreted as meaning placement in general education classes. IDEA does not mandate that students with disabilities receive all their education in the general education setting. The U.S. Department of Education, in its 2006 regulations implementing IDEA '04 (the most recent law), explains LRE in this way:

> To the maximum extent appropriate, children with disabilities, including children in public or private institutions or other care facilities, are educated with children who are nondisabled; and that special classes, separate schooling or other removal of children with disabilities from regular educational environment occurs only if the nature or severity of the disability is such that education in regular classes with the use of supplementary aids and services cannot be achieved satisfactorily. (U.S. Department of Education, 2006, pp. 46764–46765)

The federal government identifies an array of placements, in addition to the general education classroom, that are appropriate for some students with disabilities. These placements include resource rooms, special classes, special schools, home instruction settings, and hospitals. For some students, exclusive exposure to the general education curriculum is not appropriate. For example, a secondary student with significant cognitive disabilities might need to master **functional** or **life skills** essential for independent living as an adult. That student might also need to receive concentrated instruction on skills associated with holding a job successfully. To acquire and become proficient in skills necessary to live in the community and be employed often require instruction outside the general education curriculum, outside the general education classroom, and beyond the actual school site. This instruction is often best conducted in the community, on actual job sites, and in real situations. In fact, **community-based instruction** is a well-researched, effective special education approach (Dymond & Orelove, 2001). Thus there is no single or uniform interpretation of LRE. A balance must be achieved between inclusive instruction and a curriculum that is appropriate and is delivered in the most effective setting.

SYSTEMATIC IDENTIFICATION PROCEDURES

To decide which students qualify for special education—those who actually have disabilities—and of what that education should consist requires systematic identification procedures. Because current methods tend to overidentify culturally and linguistically diverse students as having disabilities and to underidentify them as being gifted and talented, many professionals conclude that the special education identification process is flawed and needs a major overhaul (MacMillan & Siperstein, 2002). Educators must be careful not to identify students without disabilities. New procedures are being developed to identify students with disabilities and to qualify them for special education. We discuss these procedures in greater detail later in the text, but know that the role of general education teachers in the identification process is evolving and growing. Teachers have primary responsibility for the **prereferral process**, which includes gathering the documentation necessary to begin the special education referral process (Fuchs & Vaughn, 2012).

The first task is to ensure that difficulties are not being caused by a lack of appropriate academic instruction. The next is to collect data about the target student's performance, showing that high-quality classroom procedures do not bring about improvements in academic or social behavior for this particular student. Then, for those students who do not make expected gains, further classroom evaluations are conducted. The ensuing classroom assessments include comparisons with peers who are achieving as expected, careful monitoring of the target student's progress (through curriculum-based measurements), and descriptions of interventions tried, accommodations implemented, types of errors made, and levels of performance achieved (Fuchs, Fuchs, & Compton, 2004; Fuchs & Vaughn, 2012). Students who continue not to profit from instruction in their general education class are referred for formal evaluation and probable provision of special education services.

INDIVIDUALIZED EDUCATION PROGRAMS (IEPS)

At the heart of individualized programs are **individualized education programs (IEPs)** for schoolchildren ages 3 to 21 and **individualized family service plans (IFSPs)** for infants and toddlers (birth through age 2) with disabilities and their families. Each of these students is entitled to an individually designed educational program complete with supportive (related) services. In some states, the guarantee of an individualized education is extended to gifted students as well, but because federal law does not protect gifted students' special education, this is not a requirement.

IEPs and IFSPs are the cornerstones that guarantee an appropriate education to each student with a disability. The IEP is the communication tool that spells out what each child's individualized education should comprise. Therefore, every teacher working with a special education student should have access to the student's IEP. They should all be very familiar with its contents because this document includes important information about the required accommodations, the necessary special services, and the unique educational needs of the student. We devote an entire chapter to IEPs (see Chapter 6).

FAMILY INVOLVEMENT

Expectations of parent and family involvement are greater for students with disabilities than for their peers without disabilities, and the strength of families and their engagement with the school can make a real difference in the lives of their children (Garcia, 2001). For example, parents are expected to participate in the development of their children's IEPs and become partners with teachers and schools. Families have the right to due process when they do not agree with schools about the education planned for or being delivered to their children. They are also entitled to services not usually offered to parents of typical learners. For example, parents of infants and toddlers with disabilities (birth to 2 years of age) receive intensive instruction through special education along with their children.

Recognizing the challenges parents often face in raising and educating their children with special needs, advocacy groups and professional organizations have formed over the years to support families and those who work with them. For example, the Learning Disabilities Association of America has a long history of advocacy on behalf of individuals with learning disabilities and the professionals and families who work with them. The ARC, formerly known as the Association for Retarded Citizens of the United States, is another advocacy group. Its focus includes ensuring that all students are provided appropriate public education services. CHADD (Children and Adults with Attention Deficit/Hyperactivity Disorder) is made up of hardworking volunteers who provide support and resources to parents and professionals. The Federation of Families for Children's Mental Health (FFCMH) exists to provide national-level advocacy for the rights of children with emotional, behavioral, and mental health challenges and their families. It works collaboratively with a national network of family-run organizations.

Leaders in these organizations, who often are parents, have succeeded in influencing funding at the state and national levels for appropriate educational services for students with disabilities. Parent advocacy groups are very powerful, as shown by their contribution to key court cases resulting in legislation that now protects students with disabilities in all aspects of the educational system.

Parents and family members of students with disabilities have important roles to play. Linking home and school communities is the responsibility of both families and teaching professionals.

RELATED SERVICES

Another important difference between general and special education is the array of services the latter offers to help students with disabilities profit from instruction. **Related services** are the multidisciplinary or transdisciplinary set of services many students with disabilities require if their education is to be truly appropriate. They are specified in the student's IEP and can include adaptive physical education (PE), assistive technology, audiology, diagnosis and evaluation, interpretation for the deaf, family therapy, occupational therapy (OT), orientation and mobility, the assistance of paraprofessionals (paraeducators and teacher aides), physical therapy (PT), psychological services, recreation and therapeutic-recreation therapy, rehabilitative counseling, school counseling, school nursing, school social work, speech/language pathology, special transportation, vocational education, and work study (U.S. Department of Education, 2006). For example, in some cases a **paraprofessional**, sometimes called a **paraeducator**, supports the special education program and works with a special education student in the general education classroom (Allen & Ashbaker, 2004). These professionals' services often make inclusion possible because they provide individualized assistance to students with disabilities for extended periods of the school day (Trautman, 2004). **Multidisciplinary teams** of related services professionals go into action to meet the individual needs of students with disabilities. The federal government considers the cost of these professionals—such as school nurses and school counselors—to be covered in part by funding from IDEA '04 (U.S. Department of Education, 2006). You will learn more about collaboration and how to work with students who exhibit special needs in Chapter 5, and more about related services in Chapter 6. The following Working Together feature provides an example of how professionals from different services work together to benefit students, educators, and families.

thinkstock/Jack Hollingsworth

WORKING *together*

COLLABORATION FOR SUPPORTING STUDENT LEARNING

A school's child study team, consisting of the classroom teacher, school counselor, assistant principal, and special education teacher, was concerned about the behavior of a 6-year-old, first-grade boy. Information from the classroom teacher indicated that the boy exhibited erratic, unpredictable behavior, throwing chairs in the classroom and having temper tantrums when things did not go his way. The classroom teacher was concerned about how to stop these behaviors, teach the student appropriate ways to behave, and keep all her students safe. The child study team worked collaboratively with the school psychologist, district behavior specialist, and parents to problem-solve the situation.

The team decided to collect further information to better understand the needs of the student and ways to help the classroom teacher. The school psychologist was going to conduct an assessment to better understand the emotional and social well-being of the student. The district behavior specialist was going to conduct classroom observations to determine events that led up to or followed challenging behaviors. The school counselor was going to interview the parents to hear their perspectives about the student and challenging behavior. The team's collective information would be used to determine a plan to help the student and classroom teacher. In the meantime, the district behavior specialist worked with the classroom teacher to address immediate behavior issues in the classroom.

QUESTIONS

1. What information from the parents could help school professionals better understand the needs of the student?

2. What information from the classroom teacher could help the child study team better understand the student's behavior in the classroom?

3. What questions might you ask the classroom teacher about the student's behavior?

Most related services specialists are **itinerant,** working at several schools during the same day and at many different schools across the week. Scheduling their time can be complicated, but it is vital to ensure no educational opportunity is missed. Multidisciplinary teams of experts not only deliver critical services to students with disabilities and their families but also serve as valuable resources to teachers as they strive to meet the needs of each student. Despite the remoteness of a school, the distance a specialist might have to travel, or the shortage of related services specialists, there is no excuse for not making these experts available to teachers or their students with disabilities.

ACCESS TO THE GENERAL EDUCATION CURRICULUM

Another key feature of special education is access to the general education curriculum. In response to the fact that only 54% of students with disabilities leave school with a standard diploma, parents, policymakers, and advocates insist such students participate in the general education curriculum and be assessed in the accountability measures (state and district-wide tests) that monitor all students' progress (OSEP, 2006). Advocates contend that students who receive their education in inclusive general education classrooms are more likely to have greater exposure to the standard curriculum and a better chance of graduating with a standard high school diploma than those students who receive their education in more restrictive environments, such as self-contained special education classrooms. Therefore, when IDEA was reauthorized in 1997, it required that all students with disabilities have access, to the fullest extent possible, to the general education curriculum and its accountability systems.

The 2001 NCLB law strengthened such requirements and expectations by including most students with disabilities in state and district-wide testing. IEPs must address students' access and participation in the general education curriculum and justify limitations (Wehmeyer, Lattin, Lapp-Rincker, & Agran, 2003). IDEA '04 requires that when a student is removed from the typical general education curriculum, the IEP must specifically explain why the student cannot participate at this particular point in time (U.S. Department of Education, 2006). One interpretation of this requirement is to define "least restrictive environment" as meaning access to a curriculum, rather than to a place or service.

Of course, access to the curriculum and to a specific place often go hand in hand, because the general education classroom is the place where students have the greatest opportunity to access the standard curriculum. The general education curriculum is not appropriate for all students with disabilities, however. Some require an alternative curriculum, intensive treatment, or supplemental instruction on topics not available or not suitable for instruction in the general education classroom. Examples include orientation and mobility training for students who are blind, job skills training in community placements, public transportation instruction, social skills training, physical therapy, speech therapy for a student who stutters, and phonics instruction for a third grader. Placement issues, LRE, access to the general education curriculum, and alternative curricular options are not mutually exclusive. Each can be in effect for part of the school day, school week, or school year.

EVIDENCE-BASED PRACTICES

Passage of NCLB in 2001 and IDEA in 2004 emphasized teachers' applying **evidence-based practices**, sometimes referred to as scientifically based practices. These tactics have been proven effective through systematic and rigorous research. In fact, according to IDEA '04, documentation that evidence-based practices were implemented must exist before a student believed to have a learning disability can be referred. The student's responses to these practices must also be documented as part of the process of identifying the disability. This new process, promoted and endorsed in IDEA '04, is known as **response to intervention (RTI)**.

We define special education, in part, by its practices, which are more intensive and supportive than those for students without learning problems. Many of these proven interventions share six common features (Coyne, Kame'enui, & Carnine, 2011; Swanson, Hoskyn, & Lee, 1999):

1. Validated (using practices proved effective through research)
2. Individually determined (matching teaching procedures to individuals)
3. Explicit (directly applying interventions to content and skills)
4. Strategic (helping students apply methods to guide their learning)
5. Sequential (building on previous mastery)
6. Monitored (evaluating progress frequently and systematically)

Most students with disabilities and most of those with special needs do not require this intensive instruction for all their education. But when their learning is not on a par with that of their general education peers, it is time for action.

FREQUENT MONITORING OF PROGRESS

Even when teachers carefully select validated practices, there is no guarantee the individual student will respond positively or sufficiently. For this reason, teachers use **progress monitoring**—a set of evaluation procedures that assess the effectiveness of instruction on skills while they are being taught. The four key features of this approach are that students' educational progress is measured (a) directly on skills of concern, (b) systematically, (c) consistently, and (d) frequently.

The most effective means of implementing progress monitoring is **curriculum-based measurement (CBM)**. In this approach, the areas of most concern are measured directly to check progress on the curricular tasks, skills, or behaviors to which interventions are being directed (Deno, 2003; Fuchs, Fuchs, & Powell, 2004). These assessments occur often (perhaps weekly) and provide educators with useful feedback, on the basis of which they can quickly modify their instructional approaches (McMasters, Fuchs, Fuchs, & Compton, 2000). Because it tailors the special education a student receives, by guiding the selection of practices and monitoring their effectiveness, CBM must not be omitted. You will learn more about monitoring student progress when specific curriculum targets (such as reading) are discussed in Chapter 8. We turn our attention now to discussing inclusive education.

WHAT IS INCLUSIVE EDUCATION?

The term **inclusive education** usually means that students with disabilities access the standard curriculum in the general education classroom. Miscommunication can easily occur when the term *inclusion* is used: Whereas one person might use the word to mean that a student attends a neighborhood school and receives most instruction in the general education classroom, to another it might mean all the student's instruction is delivered in the general education classroom. It is easy to assume everyone is truly communicating about where a student should be educated, but it is wiser to be sure everyone is using the same definition before having an in-depth discussion of students' education. To understand the concept of inclusive education better, let's review how it emerged and developed.

ORIGINS OF INCLUSION

The basic concepts of inclusion and integration of students with disabilities into the public education system have their roots in the original IDEA law passed in 1975. Remember that before 1975, many children with disabilities were denied access to public education. To those who were instrumental in developing the original IDEA law, inclusion probably meant that children with disabilities had the right to go to public school and receive a free education. Neither the type of school nor the location where the education was delivered was the focus of advocacy efforts.

When education became mandatory for all students with disabilities, the nation saw a rise in the number of separate schools built specifically for them. Real growth also occurred in the number of special classes—sometimes on the grounds of neighborhood schools but often in basements and portable buildings—for this newly included group of students. The first model for inclusive education reflected the idea that whenever possible students with disabilities should be included in the public education system and **mainstreamed**, or educated together with peers without disabilities, such as in art, music, and physical education.

Was the creation of segregated programs for these students contrary to the concept of inclusion? Most likely, at that time, the answer to this question would have been a resounding "no." Special schools and special classes offered highly specialized programs to students with disabilities and their families. Some special schools offered facilities and services that are feasible to deliver only when students with similar needs are congregated. For example, when all students with severe physical disabilities in one school district attend the same school, the building can include a special therapy pool and the full-time services of many related services professionals like physical therapists, occupational therapists, and speech/language pathologists. When these students attended their neighborhood schools, they were spread across many different buildings and large geographic areas, diluting the intensity of

VIDEO CASE 1.1

Inclusive Education

1. The teachers in the video discuss inclusive education in their schools and classrooms. What practices are used to support successful inclusion? What are the similarities and differences between the elementary and high school levels?

2. What are the advantages of inclusive education? How do these advantages support teachers' and students' success within the inclusive classroom?

Inclusive Education

services available to them. Many families believed the potentially negative aspects of segregation were outweighed by the highly specialized services it made possible.

As time passed, however, dissatisfaction with segregated programs grew. Parents began to question whether separating youngsters from their siblings and neighborhood friends was the best strategy for their education. Professionals and policymakers were concerned about the efficacy of special education programs and practices (Finn, Rotherham, & Hokanson, 2001; Gartner & Lipsky, 1987). Professionals and policymakers came to believe separate programs were ethically and morally wrong (Sailor, 1991; Snell & Brown, 2006). In particular, advocates for students with severe disabilities maintained that the benefits of having "typical" role models (illustrating how children without disabilities behave and interact with each other) outweighed intensive services that might be more readily available when groups of youngsters needing a particular program were clustered together (Turnbull, Turnbull, Wehmeyer, & Shogren, 2016). Across the years, thinking about special education and the students it serves evolved. To many, LRE—that is, access to the general education curriculum—has emerged as the more critical variable to be considered when decisions about special education placement are made.

Of course, participation in the general education curriculum does not automatically result just because students with disabilities are placed in typical classroom settings (Zigmond, 2003). Something special needs to happen. One approach, **universal design for learning (UDL)**, focuses on the curriculum so a broad range of students with very different learning preferences can approach it and learn without an intervention being made especially for them. A second approach focuses on helping students, via assistive technology, to compensate for challenges they bring to the instructional situation. The third and most commonly used approach focuses not on the curriculum but on making adaptations to the instructional situation that match specific students' needs (Fisher, Frey, & Thousand, 2003). In Chapter 7, you will learn about universal design for learning and assistive technology. You will also learn about specific adaptations to help students access the general education curriculum so they can learn alongside their peers without disabilities.

INCLUSIVE EDUCATION PRACTICES

As you have read, inclusive education has many different interpretations. The range of interpretations is the foundation for different inclusive education practices. For example, one interpretation of inclusive education is called **full inclusion** using **pull-in programming**, where students receive all educational services in the general education classroom. With this practice, speech/language pathologists come to the general education class to work with a student who needs speech therapy, rather than removing the student for individualized work. Another interpretation is called **coteaching**, wherein special

Inclusion

education teachers come to general education classrooms to work with students needing intervention or share instructional duties across academic content for all students in the class (Friend, 2000; Villa, Thousand, & Nevin, 2004). You will learn more about coteaching in Chapter 5.

The **array of services**, or what is often called the special education **continuum of services** (an older term is *cascade of services*), offers additional practices for serving students with disabilities when they are not receiving some or all of their education in the general education classroom. **Pullout programs** include resource rooms, partially self-contained special classes, self-contained special classes, and special education schools (center schools). For the vast majority of students who receive most of their education in general education classes, the resource room is the option for pullout special education services. Resource room instruction often consists of small-group instruction focused on areas most in need of intensive intervention. This instruction may occur for 30 to 60 minutes several days a week. However, the number of these classes is shrinking because many students who attend resource room settings now receive most if not all of their education in general education classrooms (inclusive settings), thus leaving a reduced number of options available for even short-term, intensive intervention (Moody, Vaughn, Hughes, & Fischer, 2000). For example, in the 2005 school year, 79% of all students with disabilities—those with mild to moderate disabilities as well as those with severe disabilities—received at least 60% of their education at local public schools in general education classes (OSEP, 2006). The participation rates for students with disabilities in general education classes have increased consistently over the past 15 years, and only 4% of those students attend separate schools or facilities today, down from 20% in 1993 (U.S. Department of Education, 1995). Clearly, these data demonstrate a trend toward more inclusive education practices.

THE INCLUSION DEBATE

At the heart of discussions about inclusive education, particularly full inclusion, is the dynamic tension between FAPE and LRE: the delivery of an appropriate education and participation in the least restrictive environment possible. Let's think about how some of these conversations might unfold.

For example, should full-time placement in a general education setting be a goal for every student with a disability, even if some elements of an educational program that an individual needs to achieve to his or her full potential have to be sacrificed? For a high school student with severe disabilities, parents and educators might have to decide which is more appropriate or more important: access to the standard high school curriculum leading to a diploma (including science and foreign language requirements) or community-based instruction where on-the-job training, independent transportation, and home management are taught in real-life settings.

VIDEO CASE 1.2

Challenges of Inclusive Education

1. What challenges do schools face when implementing inclusive education? How can these challenges be even more significant for small school districts? What solutions does Mia Tannous share?

2. Which challenges mentioned in the video are directly related to funding issues? How can educational funding impact the quality of inclusive education?

A dilemma for parents and educators of high school students with severe disabilities is which is more appropriate or more important: access to the standard high school curriculum leading to a diploma, or community-based instruction where on-the-job training, independent transportation, and home management are taught in real-life settings.

Some scholars argue that full inclusion, where students with disabilities receive all their education in a general education setting, is not sufficient to support those with more severe needs, whether academic, emotional, social, or physical. Other scholars believe all students have a right to fully inclusive educational practices where they can benefit from being integrated into a school setting with their peers and gain a sense of belonging and active participation in the mainstream. Thus the role of special education services is to support all students with special needs in general education classes by designing instruction and applying adaptations that accommodate individual learning needs. The inclusion debate more often includes perspectives and discussions that range along a continuum where professionals and parents embrace the strengths of different inclusive practices and make decisions based on individual student needs.

Some guidelines can help when challenging decisions are being made. First, special education placement decisions must be individually determined, because services should be tailored to the needs of each student with disabilities. Second, no single answer is possible for all students with disabilities. Third, students with disabilities need an array of services (and placements) available to them for the delivery of individualized education programs that range in intensity and duration (Deshler, 2001; Vaughn, Elbaum, & Boardman, 2001). Few professionals or parents advocate either for fully inclusive settings or for fully segregated settings. The guiding principle must be based not on placement alone but on how students can best access the general education curriculum, master academic targets, and develop life skills they need to succeed when they are adults.

SUMMARY

You have now embarked on what we believe is an exciting course of study. You have begun to learn about the challenges that exceptionalities and special needs present to the individuals involved and to their families, teachers, and friends. You have already learned that many of these challenges can be overcome when the educational system is responsive to the individual needs of these students. You also know that responses to such challenges must be rich with evidence-based practices that are supported by teams of professionals working together in collaborative partnerships. For students with disabilities, the education system should be inclusive but also flexible enough to strike an intelligent balance between FAPE and LRE—types of education, services, and placement—for each individual. As you are coming to learn, many provisions, requirements, and legal mandates guide your role as an inclusive educator. Sometimes, these principles can seem overwhelming and confusing, but when all of the hard work pays off, and students soar, the accomplishments are everyone's to share. As you read this text, the puzzle of inclusive education will come together as you reach an understanding about how to teach and accommodate every academic and social area where students with disabilities and special needs require intervention.

REVIEW THE LEARNING OBJECTIVES

Let's review the learning objectives for this chapter. If you are uncertain about and cannot talk through the answers provided for any of these questions, reread those sections of the text.

- **What is the ADAPT framework and how do I use it?**

  The ADAPT framework we have devised is a tool for instruction and assessment of struggling learners that reflects proven best practice in the field. It will help you develop a mind-set for the selection of effective interventions and teaching practices. The framework, discussed in detail in Chapter 7, reflects and underscores the mind-set we want you to take away from your course. You can use its five steps to help you make informed decisions about adapting your instruction based on individual students' needs and the tasks all students must complete in school.

- **What is a disability?**

  The concept of disability is complex, is not absolute, and is influenced by individuals' and groups' orientations (psychological, medical, sociological). The way groups think about what it means to have a disability affects the way they interact with people with disabilities.

- **What are some reasons for disabilities?**

  One way to think about the reasons for disabilities is to divide them into three groups by time of onset, whether before birth,

during the birth process, or after birth. Three other ways to consider the reasons include biological causes, environmental causes, and other risk factors.

- **Who are students with disabilities?**

  Nationally, some 6.4 million children and youth ages 3 to 21, or about 13% of students in public schools, are identified as having disabilities and are receiving special education services in prekindergarten through 12th grade. The federal government describes 14 disability-specific categories that can be used to qualify infants, toddlers, preschoolers, and young students eligible to receive special education services. These special education categories are often ordered and divided by prevalence or the size of the category: high-incidence disabilities occur in greater numbers and low-incidence disabilities occur less often.

- **What are the origins of special education?**

  Many people believe U.S. special education began in 1975 with the passage of the national law we now call IDEA, but it actually began more than 200 years ago. In 1799, farmers in southern France found a young boy living in the woods, and they brought this "wild child" to a doctor in Paris. Jean-Marc-Gaspard Itard, the doctor who now is recognized as the "father of special education," used many of the principles and procedures of explicit instruction still implemented today to teach this boy, who was named

Victor and who probably had intellectual disabilities. In the early 1800s, Edouard Seguin, one of Itard's students, came to the United States and began efforts to educate students with disabilities. In the United States, it was another 75 years before education became a right, something all students with disabilities were entitled to receive.

What laws and court decisions protect students with disabilities?

Section 504 requires public schools to provide accommodations to students whose disabilities or health conditions necessitate some special attention in order to allow them to participate fully in school activities. ADA bars discrimination in employment, transportation, public accommodations, and telecommunications. Public Law (PL) 94-142, the Education for All Handicapped Children Act (EHA), was the first version of a universal, national special education law passed in 1975 that guaranteed the rights of students with disabilities to a free appropriate public education. The most recent reauthorization of this law, the Individuals with Disabilities Education Act of 2004, mandates participation of students with disabilities in state and district-wide testing, offers more specific guidelines about discipline, and helps explain how students with learning disabilities can be identified. It encourages states and school districts to help all young students who are struggling to read, in hopes of preventing reading/learning disabilities. Finally, it includes the following key components: free appropriate public education, least restrictive environment, systematic identification procedures, individualized education programs, family involvement, related services, access to the general education curriculum, evidence-based practices, and frequent monitoring of progress. The No Child Left Behind Act of 2001 (NCLB) requires that 95% of all schoolchildren be full participants in state and district-wide testing. The Assistive Technology Act of 2004 applies to both the education system

and community access, recognizing that AT is critical to the participation of people with disabilities in the workplace, in the community, and at school; it removes barriers that restrict people's lives.

What is special education?

Special education is designed to meet the unique learning needs of each infant, toddler, preschooler, and elementary through high school student with disabilities and individuals up to the age of 21. This instruction might be delivered in many different types of settings, such as hospitals, separate facilities, and homes, but it is most commonly provided at the student's local school in the general education class with neighborhood friends. General education and special education differ along some very important dimensions. First and foremost, they are designed for students with different learning, behavioral, social, communication, and basic functional needs (such as the need to learn daily living skills). Second, some differences are based in law—what is stated in IDEA and its regulations—and result in key components of special education. Third, general education tends to focus on groups of learners, whereas the special education approach focuses on individuals.

What is inclusive education?

Inclusive education means integrating students with disabilities with peers who do not have disabilities by using neighborhood schools, general education classrooms, and age-appropriate peers to maximize LRE and increase students' access to the general education curriculum. Inclusive education practices include using universal design, differentiating (adapting) instruction, and providing assistive technology.

$SAGE edge™ **Test your understanding of chapter content. Take the practice quiz.** edge.sagepub.com/bryant

REVISIT THE OPENING CHALLENGE

Check your answers to the Reflection Questions from the Opening Challenge and revise them on the basis of what you have learned.

1. Do you think Ms. Smith and Mr. Salazar are overly concerned about their students' varied needs? Do you think they are just having first-year-teacher jitters? Why or why not?

2. What advice would you give them about planning for their students with disabilities and for those with other special learning needs?

3. How can they learn more about the special education services their students should be receiving this year?

4. In what ways can Ms. Smith and Mr. Salazar be responsive to all their students' special needs?

KEY TERMS

accommodations, 19

Americans with Disabilities Act (ADA), 19

array of services, 35

assistive technology, 24

Assistive Technology Act, 23

bell-shaped curve, 9

community-based instruction, 27

congenital, 12

continuum of services, 35

coteaching, 34

curriculum-based measurement (CBM), 32

disabilities, 7

due process hearings, 21

Education for All Handicapped Children Act (EHA), 21

evidence-based practices, 31

free appropriate public education (FAPE), 26

full inclusion, 34

functional, 27

handicap, 12

high-incidence disabilities, 14

inclusive education, 33

individualized education programs (IEPs), 28

individualized family service plans (IFSPs), 28

individuals with Disabilities Education Act (IDEA, 2004), 12

itinerant, 30

least restrictive environment (LRE), 26

life skills, 27

low-incidence disabilities, 14

mainstreamed, 33

multidisciplinary teams, 29

No Child Left Behind Act of 2001 (NCLB), 22

normal curve, 9

paraeducator, 29

paraprofessional, 29

perinatal, 12

postnatal, 12

prenatal, 12

prereferral process, 27

prevalence, 14

progress monitoring, 32

Public Law (PL) 94-142, 21

pull-in programming, 34

pullout programs, 35

related services, 29

response to intervention (RTI), 32

Section 504 of the Vocational Rehabilitation Act, 19

special education, 25

special education categories, 14

typical learners, 9

universal design for learning (UDL), 34

SAGE edge™ Review key terms with eFlashcards. edge.sagepub.com/bryant

PROFESSIONAL STANDARDS AND LICENSURE ········•

For a complete description of Professional Standards and Licensure, please see Appendix on page 569.

CEC Initial Preparation Standards

Standard 1: Learner Development and Individual Learning Differences

INTASC Core Principle

Standard 1: Learner Development

Standard 2: Learning Differences

Praxis II: Education of Exceptional Students: Core Content Knowledge

I. Understanding Exceptionalities: Basic concepts in special education

II. Legal and Societal Issues: Federal laws and legal issues

III. Delivery of Services to Students with Disabilities: Background knowledge

 ···························•

Review ➡ Practice ➡ Improve

Get the tools you need to sharpen your study skills. Access practice quizzes, eFlashcards, video, and multimedia: **edge.sagepub.com/bryant**

PRACTICE AND APPLY WHAT YOU'VE LEARNED

▶ edge.sagepub.com/bryant

CHECK YOUR COMPREHENSION ON THE STUDY SITE WITH

- Mobile-friendly practice quizzes on the open-access study site that give you opportunities for self-guided assessment and practice!

2

UNDERSTANDING LEARNERS WITH SPECIAL NEEDS

High-Incidence Disabilities or Conditions

LEARNING OBJECTIVES

After studying this chapter, you will be able to answer the following questions:

- What are the categories for students with disabilities?

- How are disabilities organized for special education?

- What are the attributes of students with learning disabilities?

- What are the attributes of students with speech or language impairments?

- What are the attributes of students with attention deficit/hyperactivity disorder (ADHD)?

- What are the attributes of students with intellectual and developmental disabilities?

- What are the attributes of students with emotional or behavioral disorders?

OPENING *challenge* ·······························

Working in Inclusive Classrooms

ELEMENTARY GRADES Ms. Clarkson is several months into her second year of teaching and is so glad that she was assigned to third grade both years. She loves working at Jackson Elementary School, and she has great kids. The more experienced teachers are always there for her. They answer questions and help her navigate the bureaucracy, figure out how to get paperwork through the system, and think through issues related to her students' programs and how to respond well to their learning challenges. The teachers and administrators all work together as a team. When Ms. Clarkson received a note from Central Office asking her to come to a meeting because the IEP team was considering a change of diagnosis for one of her students, she went to some of the senior teachers at her school.

The IEP team was concerned about her student Darren, who has received special education services since kindergarten. Ms. Clarkson knows Darren's history well and has met with his parents on several occasions. Darren didn't begin talking until he was about 3 years old. As a kindergartner, he was unable to rhyme words, couldn't identify sound-letter relationships as well as his peers, was behind in language development, and seemed to have difficulty keeping up with classmates. In kindergarten, Mr. Frank, Darren's teacher, referred him for speech and language services. Darren qualified for special education and was identified as having language impairments. Now, the speech and language therapist thinks it's important to reclassify Darren as having learning disabilities. Ms. Clarkson can't understand the concern. Darren is receiving special education help, and he is improving. She wonders, *"Why are we going to spend so much time on changing a special education label for Darren? Do all these different special education categories make a difference in the way we teach? Will all the professional time spent on reclassification actually benefit Darren?"*

SECONDARY GRADES Mr. Suarez is a 10th-grade history teacher at Jackson High School. He is getting ready for his third year of teaching and is reviewing student record folders to learn about his class and their individual needs. The special education teacher is meeting with him to review the IEPs of three students he will have in his classes. One student has a learning disability (LD), another has attention deficit/hyperactivity disorder (ADHD), and a third student has a mild emotional/behavioral disorder (EBD). The students will be in his third-period class, and the special education teacher will work with him in his class during that period. Reading is an issue for the student with the LD; the student with ADHD needs assistance with paying attention, and the student with EBD is on a behavior plan. Mr. Suarez starts to think about questions for the special education teacher. *What are the learning characteristics of these three students? How severe is their disability? How can the special education teacher help me?*

REFLECTION QUESTIONS In your journal, write down your answers to the following questions. After completing the chapter, check your answers and revise them on the basis of what you have learned.

1. Do you think identifying students by specific disability is useful?

2. Why do you think Darren's special education label is being reconsidered at this point in his schooling?

3. Is Darren's situation unusual? Why or why not?

4. Will a change in category influence the way Ms. Clarkson teaches Darren?

5. Will it change the services Darren receives?

6. What do you think are some learning characteristics of the three students in Mr. Suarez's class?

7. What help might he be looking for from the special education teacher for these three students?

About 6.4 million or 13% of U.S. public schoolchildren, ages 3 to 21, have a disability that affects their educational performance to such a degree that they require special education services (U.S. Department of Education, OSEP, 2013). Looking at the statistics by age-groups shows the need to provide children and youth with special education services. About 2.8% of the population of infants and toddlers, birth through age 2, were served under IDEA, Part C (Chapter 6 provides more information about this population), and for children ages 3 through 5, about 5.9% of the general population were served under IDEA, Part B. In 2011, approximately 68 million students ages 6 to 21 attended school in the 50 states and the District of Columbia. Of this group, about 8.4% were identified with disabilities and were eligible for services under IDEA, Part B (U.S. Department of Education, Office of Special Education and Rehabilitative Services, Office of Special Education Programs, 2014). Figure 2.1 illustrates the percentage of students ages 6 to 21 with disabilities across the special education categories identified in Chapter 1. Clearly, the learning disabilities category and the speech or language impairments category together account for more than half the percentage of students with disabilities.

The "other disabilities combined" category includes deaf-blindness (less than 0.03 percent), developmental delay (2.1 percent), hearing impairments (1.2 percent), multiple disabilities (2.2 percent), orthopedic impairments (0.9 percent), traumatic brain injury (0.4 percent), and visual impairments (0.4 percent).

Disabilities create very special needs for individuals, their families, and the education system. Teachers and other educators can help students achieve their potential by addressing their special needs, by providing them with many opportunities for learning and for success, and by ensuring they receive a high-quality educational experience in order to succeed at school. Teachers who are well-prepared, use proven practices and instructional procedures, and provide students with additional assistance or accommodations do make real differences in the educational lives of these students (Futernick, 2006). In this text, we provide you with tools that improve the results of all students. Before you learn about how to teach these students effectively, let's think more about students with disabilities and specifically about the special education categories considered to be high-incidence disabilities. More information about prevalence figures for students from diverse backgrounds is provided in the Considering Diversity feature.

FIGURE 2.1 PERCENTAGE DISTRIBUTION OF CHILDREN AGES 6 TO 21 SERVED UNDER IDEA, PART B, BY DISABILITY TYPE: FALL 2012

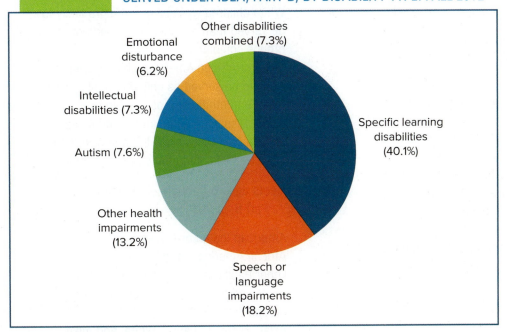

SOURCE: U.S. Department of Education, National Center for Education Statistics [NCES], Common Core of Data [CCD] (2012). These data are for the 50 states; Washington, DC; Bureau of Indian Education schools; Puerto Rico; the four outlying areas; and the three freely associated states. For actual data used, go to http://www.ed.gov/about/reports/annual/osep.

CONSIDERING *diversity*

OVERREPRESENTATION AND UNDERREPRESENTATION IDENTIFICATION ISSUES

As we discuss in other chapters, the overrepresentation of schoolchildren from some racial and ethnic groups has been an issue in the field of special education for many years (Yates & Ortiz, 2004). The underrepresentation of schoolchildren from other racial and ethnic groups, for example, those of Asian heritage, also has been an issue for different reasons. As you review the statistics that follow, think about why children and youth from various racial and ethnic groups are identified for special education services while others are identified to a lesser degree. The following statistics report information about special education service under IDEA by ethnic and racial group for

(Continued)

(Continued)

infants and toddlers birth through age 2, children ages 3 to 5, and children and youth ages 6 to 21.

- Infants and toddlers served under IDEA, Part C, in 2011:

  o White and Native Hawaiian or Other Pacific Islander children were somewhat more likely to be served than children of other racial and ethnic groups combined.
  o Black or African American children were as likely as children of all other racial and ethnic groups combined to be served.
  o American Indian or Alaska Native, Hispanic/Latino, Asian, and mixed races children were by group somewhat less likely to be served than all other racial/ethnic groups combined.

- Children ages 3 through 5 served under IDEA, Part B, in 2011:

  o American Indian or Alaska Native, Native Hawaiian or Other Pacific Islander, and

White children were by group more likely to be served than all other racial and ethnic groups combined.
  o Black or African American children were as likely to be served as children in all other racial and ethnic groups combined.
  o Asian, Hispanic/Latino, and mixed races children were less likely to be served than all other racial and ethnic groups combined.

- Students ages 6 through 21 served under IDEA, Part B, in 2011:

  o American Indian or Alaska Native, Black or African American, and Native Hawaiian or Other Pacific Islander were more likely to be served than all other racial and ethnic groups combined.
  o Asian, Hispanic/Latino, White, and mixed races children were less likely to be served than all other racial and ethnic groups combined.

SOURCE: U.S. Department of Education, Office of Special Education and Rehabilitative Services, Office of Special Education Programs (2014).

WHAT ARE THE CATEGORIES FOR STUDENTS WITH DISABILITIES?

Only students with disabilities are eligible for special education services, but not all of them actually require special education services to meet their special needs. For example, many students with physical disabilities do not require special education services. They excel as they learn the content of the general curriculum alongside their peers who do not experience physical challenges. These students may or may not need assistance or accommodations, such as special floor mats so their wheelchairs can glide easily into the school building or the classroom. These are students who have a disability and special needs, but they are not special education students because their disability does not negatively affect their educational performance.

Some physical disabilities do result in the need for special education services—possibly from a physical therapist and an assistive technologist—to reduce the impact of the disability on learning. Other students may have special needs and are entitled to accommodations as well as extra help, but they do not have a disability. For example, some students may require help managing their own behavior so they do not disrupt the learning environment and so they themselves profit maximally from instruction, but they do not have an emotional or behavioral disorder. And, as in the case of ADHD, some students with a specific condition qualify for special education services, but many do not. In this and the next two chapters, you will learn about students who have special needs because of the disabilities or special conditions they have. You will learn that some of them are eligible for special education services and supports, whereas others need accommodations or adaptations to overcome the learning challenges they face.

There are many types of disabilities, each requiring unique services, and they are not equally distributed; some occur more often than others. For example, many more students have learning disabilities than have vision or hearing problems that hinder their educational performance. According to the federal government, of students ages 6 to 21 who are served under IDEA, Part B, about 73% have a learning disability, a speech or language impairment, a mild to moderate intellectual disability, or an emotional or behavioral disorder. These frequently occurring disabilities are often referred to as **high-incidence disabilities** and make up about 8% of the school-age population (U.S. Department of Education, OSEP, 2013). The remaining disabilities recognized in IDEA '04 (the national special education law)—orthopedic and other health impairments, low vision and blindness, hard of hearing and deafness, traumatic brain injury, deaf-blindness, autism spectrum disorders, and multiple-severe disabilities—are sometimes grouped together and called **low-incidence disabilities** because together they affect a very small proportion of students with disabilities (U.S. Department of Education, OSEP, 2013). You will learn about these disabilities and the individuals affected in Chapter 3. In Chapter 4 you will learn about other groups of students who do not qualify for special education services and supports but still require accommodations or extra assistance to fulfill their potential. All these students have special needs that must be addressed for them to succeed in school.

Students with identified or documented disabilities are eligible for additional services and supports through special education. As you learned in Chapter 1, the vast majority of students with disabilities receive nearly all their education in inclusive general education settings alongside their classmates without disabilities. Although it is not common for students with high-incidence disabilities to be grouped together by their identified special education category (students with learning disabilities in one group and students with intellectual disabilities in another group), the federal government does require that all students older than age 8 be identified and counted in one of the 13 special education categories called out in IDEA '04 (see Chapter 1 for a review). As

VIDEO CASE 2.1

Meeting the Needs of Students With Disabilities

1. What supports does Nicole Santana provide to illustrate the concept of "fair is not always equal"? How do these supports assist the students with disabilities who are included in her classroom?

2. What advice does April Jacobsen offer to new teachers to help them meet the needs of students with disabilities who are included in their classrooms? How can teachers increase the acceptance of students with disabilities in their general education classrooms?

discussed in Chapter 1, children between the ages of 3 and 8 may fall under the developmental delays category.

HOW ARE DISABILITIES ORGANIZED FOR SPECIAL EDUCATION?

Three major schemes are used to group disabilities for the purposes of meeting educational needs. One classification system uses disability types or special education categories (learning disabilities, intellectual disabilities). Another groups students by the severity of the disability (mild, moderate, severe). And the third considers disabilities in terms of how often they occur (high incidence, low incidence). Let's look at each organizational system in turn.

SPECIAL EDUCATION CATEGORIES

IDEA '04 and many parent organizations (such as Learning Disabilities Association of America and Autism Society of America) encourage the use of disability labels, which translate into special education categories. When it comes to schoolchildren, the government has elected to define disabilities by using a categorical approach, and states are required each year to use these categories to report the numbers of students with disabilities being served (U.S. Department of Education, OSEP, 2013). Although many states use terms slightly different than those used by the federal government, the similarities are obvious (Müller & Markowitz, 2004). Within each of the 14 categories defined as disabilities in IDEA '04 and listed in Chapter 1 of this text, many conditions are included. For example, ADHD, asthma, sickle-cell anemia, and many other health conditions are part of the "other health impairments" category, not separate categories of their own. Notice that giftedness is not included in the prevalence figure because it is not part of IDEA. Its prevalence rate is estimated to be about 3% to 5% and includes students who can benefit from services to address their intellectual levels, talents, and creativity.

Possibly because it is so difficult to change federal and state laws, the names some government agencies use for disabilities might not always be what parents and professionals consider modern or up to date. In this text, we have tried to use terms preferred by individuals who have each specific disability, parents of children with each disability, and the respective professional organizations. Here are a few examples of how terms and thinking about specific disabilities vary. Ideas and research about autism have been developing rapidly. Today, this disability is considered a spectrum of at least five similar disorders, of which autism is one (DSM-5, APA, 2013). Thus, although IDEA '04 still uses the term *autism*, the more current conceptualization of this disability is much broader, as reflected by the name *autism spectrum disorders* or ASD.

Perspectives on Disability

As another example, IDEA '04 uses the term *specific learning disabilities,* but parents, professionals, and individuals with the condition use the term *learning disabilities.* And although IDEA '04 separates deafness from hearing impairments, it does not separate visual disabilities into two groups (blindness and low vision).

These categories developed because at one time, they related directly to how and where students with specific disabilities were educated and what they were taught. For example, years ago, the category called "mental retardation" signaled separate classrooms, separate schools,

Although not found in a separate disability category, asthma is a common chronic illness among children and is classified in the "other health impairments" category. ADHD is a more common condition and is also found in this category.

even separate living and schooling in institutions, and strict adherence to a curriculum of life and self-help skills and training for low-level jobs. Today, the public, professional organizations, educators, and policymakers embrace the term "intellectual disabilities" to replace an outdated view of this disability and believe alternate curricula should not be matched to specific disabilities; rather, the general education curriculum should be offered to all students. Different curricular options are then extended to individuals who have demonstrated that they cannot successfully access the standard curriculum offered in general education (McLaughlin & Nolet, 2004).

Also, instructional methods are not uniformly effective for all students labeled with a specific disability. Knowing a student has learning disabilities does not help a teacher figure out which reading method to use. Educational interventions must be matched to the individual learner's performance, not to a special education category (Fuchs, Fuchs, & Vaughn, in press). Many interventions effective with one student with disabilities are also powerful for classmates without disabilities who find learning a challenging situation. Thus, although special education categories have proved not to offer precision in guiding instructional decision making, they remain the primary way students are identified and labeled and qualify for special education services.

SEVERITY OF DISABILITY

As we have just noted, many educators believe that special education categories and the resulting labeling of individuals have little or no educational function (Fisher, Frey, & Thousand, 2003; Gargiulo, 2003). These

VIDEO CASE 2.2

Including Students With High-Incidence Disabilities

1. Students with a variety of disabilities are often included in general education classes. Students with which high-incidence disabilities may be included in Tema Khieu's class?

2. What strategies does Ms. Khieu use to support the students with disabilities who are included in her general education class? Which of these practices are you already familiar with?

professionals prefer a noncategorical approach that groups students by the severity of their problems, not by the type of disability they have. How does this system work?

Instead of thinking about the specific disability, educators consider how the condition influences an individual's performance. Typically, they use four groupings: mild, moderate, severe, and profound. This system reflects the types of supports the individual needs in life and at school (Luckasson & Schalock, 2013). Individuals with mild disabilities require some accommodations, and those with severe disabilities require intensive supports and assistance for a long time. We must be very cautious, however, when thinking about disabilities by level of severity. First, it is a mistake to assume that one disability, such as intellectual disability, is more severe than another, such as stuttering. All disabilities are serious, and the effects on the individuals and their families should never be minimized. Second, each disability grouping takes in a continuum of severity from mild to severe. It is incorrect, for instance, to think all learning disabilities are mild.

Today, both the categorical and noncategorical approaches are used in classrooms. Students are identified and reported to the federal government by disability, but fewer and fewer separate schools or classes are available for students with a specific disability (OSEP, 2006). Some professionals and advocacy organizations (such as TASH, an organization representing individuals with severe and profound disabilities) have advocated for the closure of all segregated programs for students with disabilities (TASH, 2004). Thus, although IDEA '04 requires that students qualify for special education by being identified as having a specific disability, schools typically serve these students according to their needs and educational performance. In both general education classes and special education classes, students with disabilities are classmates but do not always share the same disabilities.

Neither of these first two organizing systems—by category or by severity—is related to the number of individuals affected. Another way to organize our thinking about disabilities is thus to group them by how often they occur. For example, some disabilities (such as learning disabilities) occur more frequently than others; more students have mild disabilities than have severe disabilities. Let's consider organizing by prevalence.

PREVALENCE OF DISABILITY

Figure 2.2 illustrates that disabilities are not equally distributed across special education students. Almost half of all students with disabilities are identified as having learning disabilities, and most other disabilities are very rare. Some believe educators' response to high-incidence disabilities should be different from their response to low-incidence disabilities.

FIGURE 2.2 PREVALENCE OF HIGH- AND LOW-INCIDENCE DISABILITIES

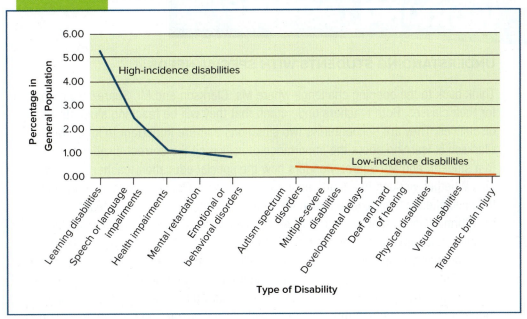

SOURCE: U.S. Department of Education, 2012.

The latter often require specialized services from a multidisciplinary team of professionals, such as an orientation and mobility specialist, assistive technology specialist, and vision teacher who knows Braille instruction. General education teachers work with many students with high-incidence disabilities every school year, but across their entire careers, they may never work with a student with a specific low-incidence disability such as blindness or deafness. In this chapter, we discuss ADHD and those disabilities considered high-incidence conditions. In Chapter 3, we discuss low-incidence disabilities.

We decided to organize our discussions about students with disabilities and special needs by prevalence. Although they are not comprehensive, several tables in this chapter provide commonly adopted definitions for each high-incidence condition. Compare these definitions and think about the different perspectives that contributed to each definition's development to gain a better understanding of the condition and the students affected. Let's start learning about high-incidence conditions by thinking about the one most common among schoolchildren: learning disabilities. Clearly, educators encounter students with this disability every school day in almost every classroom. Therefore, it is important that educators and specialists work together to ensure that all students are receiving an appropriate education. The Working Together feature illustrates how educators and specialists can collaborate for educational planning and instruction.

WORKING *together*

UNDERSTANDING STUDENTS WITH SPECIAL NEEDS

Think back to the opening challenge where Ms. Clarkson and Mr. Suarez are preparing for their classes. Both teachers understand that they will be teaching students with disabilities. They are encountering two situations that are important to know. Ms. Clarkson is learning about the importance of assigning the correct disability label to a student, and Mr. Suarez wonders how the special education teacher can help him. Whether working in a team, as in Ms. Clarkson's situation, or consulting with the special education teacher, as in Mr. Suarez's situation, classroom teachers must be informed about special education and collaborative practices to promote student success. It is important for Ms. Clarkson to understand why reclassifying a label (e.g., language impairment to learning disability) promotes appropriate services, such as providing more academic support, for the student with a disability. Mr. Suarez needs to work with the special education teacher to ensure that when they are teaching together, the needs of his three students with disabilities are addressed according to the IEP requirements. Both situations necessitate conveying of information to the classroom teachers to benefit their students with disabilities.

QUESTIONS

1. What questions might Ms. Clarkson ask at the IEP team meeting?

2. How can the speech and language therapist help Ms. Clarkson understand why the label is being changed?

3. What information should the special education teacher provide to Mr. Suarez?

4. How can the special education teacher work with the three students with disabilities in Mr. Suarez's class?

WHAT ARE THE ATTRIBUTES OF STUDENTS WITH LEARNING DISABILITIES?

Often incorrectly considered a mild condition, learning disability (LD) is a serious disability. It is a severe, pervasive, and chronic condition that requires intensive intervention (Bender, 2007; Pierangelo & Giuliani, 2006). Over the years, debate has focused on whether there is a difference between low achievers and students with learning disabilities. Some still question the validity of classifying learning disabilities as an actual disability (Fletcher et al., 2002). However, parents and researchers are confident that having learning disabilities is a complex and lifelong condition (Goldberg, Higgins, Raskind, & Herman, 2003; Lerner & Kline, 2006).

DEFINITION

Although definitions for learning disabilities differ across the states, the federal government's definition, the one included in IDEA '04, is the basis for them. The IDEA '04 definition, along with that of the National Institutes of Health (NIH) and the latest version by the American Psychiatric Association (APA, 2013), is found in Table 2.1. Like the NIH definition, many states' definitions reflect a more modern approach that has less of a medical orientation, acknowledge that *learning disabilities* is a general term referring to a heterogeneous group of disorders, allow for other conditions such as visual disabilities to coexist with learning disabilities, and recognize the problems many affected individuals have with social skills (Müller & Markowitz, 2004).

Look at Figure 2.2 again to see the disproportionate percentage of students included in this special education category. Clearly, parents, policymakers, and education professionals are most concerned about the number of students included in the learning disabilities category. Another concern stems from the way the identification process works. The traditional process requires that a student's achievement be two years behind the expected level. In other words, a third grader reading at the first-grade level is a prime candidate for referral to special education because of a reading/learning disability. However, this scenario also means the student has struggled for at least two years and has not received specialized attention in a timely fashion. Many maintain such students struggle without assistance unnecessarily. They can be identified as demonstrating academic difficulties as early as kindergarten, and for many, supplemental evidence-based reading and mathematics intervention prevents years of failure (Bryant et al., 2011; Fuchs & Vaughn, 2012; Vaughn & Linan-Thompson, 2004).

Therefore, IDEA '04 allows for a different way to intervene early and provides systematically more intensive instruction to all students struggling with reading and mathematics during their beginning school years. The law also allows for a new way to identify students as having learning disabilities; no longer must there be a significant discrepancy between their ability and their academic performance before they get the individualized instruction they need to succeed in school (U.S. Department of Education, 2006). This system, called response to intervention (RTI), incorporates multitiered systems of support before the devastating effects of school failure take their toll (Fuchs & Fuchs, 2006; Kukic, Tilly, & Michelson, 2005; The Consortium for Evidence-Based Early Intervention Practices, 2010). This method is also referred to as early intervention because it is applied as early as possible to every student who is struggling, particularly those having difficulty learning basic reading, writing, and mathematics skills. According to the RTI system, those who do not learn sufficiently with high-quality instruction, and those who do not learn reading, writing, and mathematics skills well enough after supplemental, intensive, evidence-based intervention, are referred for special

Learning Disability Definition

TABLE 2.1	DEFINITIONS OF LEARNING DISABILITIES
Source	**Definition**
IDEA '04[1]	*Specific learning disability* means a disorder in one or more of the basic psychological processes involved in understanding or in using language, spoken or written, that may manifest itself in an imperfect ability to listen, think, speak, read, write, spell, or do mathematical calculations, including such conditions as perceptual disabilities, brain injury, minimal brain dysfunction, dyslexia, and developmental aphasia. Specific learning disability does not include learning problems that are primarily the result of visual, hearing, or motor disabilities; mental retardation; emotional disturbance; or environmental, cultural, or economic disadvantage.
National Institutes of Health (NIH)[2]	Learning disabilities are disorders that affect the ability to understand or use spoken or written language, do mathematical calculations, coordinate movements, or direct attention. Although learning disabilities occur in very young children, the disorders are usually not recognized until the child reaches school age.
DSM-5[3]	Learning disabilities or *specific learning disorders* can be manifested in impairments in reading, writing, and mathematics. The types of impairments are clinically diagnosed with the level of supports (mild, moderate, severe) that are needed to support the individual. Academic learning symptoms must have persisted for a minimum of six months even though intervention support has been provided. Difficulties with academic skills are significant and affect the individual in various ways throughout life.

SOURCES: [1]U.S. Department of Education (2006); [2]National Institutes of Health, National Institute of Neurological Disorders and Stroke (2006); [3]American Psychiatric Association (APA, 2013).

education evaluation. The outcome of this evaluation may be the identification of learning disabilities (The IRIS Center, 2006). Once they are eligible for special education services, they receive intensive, *individualized* intervention.

TYPES

To better understand the diversity—the heterogeneity—of students with learning disabilities, let's examine these common profiles or types of learning disabilities:

- Overall underachievement
- Reading disabilities
- Mathematics disabilities
- Written expression disabilities

Despite having normal intelligence, students with learning disabilities do not achieve academically on a par with their classmates without disabilities. Some face challenges in almost every academic area. Most experts are certain that cognitive problems, poor motivation, and/or an insufficient instructional response to their learning disabilities can be at the root of some of these students' learning challenges (Compton, Fuchs, Fuchs, Lambert, & Hamlett, 2012). Some experts have long thought learning disabilities reflect deficits in the ability to process or remember information (Torgesen, 2002). What appears quite certain is that learning disabilities are **resistant to treatment** or "resistant to intervention" (Vaughn et al., 2011). Affected students do not learn at the same rate or in the same ways as their classmates (Fuchs & Fuchs, 2006; Vaughn, 2005). The instruction or intervention typically used in general education programs is not sufficient and does not help them improve; more intensive individualized intervention is necessary.

Reading difficulties—very low reading abilities—are the most common reasons for referrals to special education (Fuchs & Fuchs, 2001). Because reading and writing are related, most students with reading learning disabilities (sometimes called dyslexia) have written expression learning disabilities (Graham & Harris, 2011; Hammill, 2004). Reading and writing, obviously, are important skills; in school, students must be able to read information from a variety of texts (social studies, science, literature) and write in varying formats (essays, reports, creative writing, notes). As the complexity of academic tasks increases, students not proficient in reading and writing become unable to keep pace with academic expectations (Jenkins & O'Connor, 2002). As they progress through school, reading disabilities compound and make it almost impossible to perform well on other academic tasks, contributing to overall underachievement.

Problems associated with academic learning can be overcome with explicit instruction and intensive efforts. What benefits might this student receive from individualized instruction?

Although reading problems are the most common reason for referral, more than 50% of students with learning disabilities also have mathematics learning disabilities (Fuchs, Fuchs, & Compton, 2013). Some seem to have difficulties with mathematics alone, but for most, this difficulty is part of an overwhelming and pervasive underachievement (Bryant, Bryant, Porterfield, et al., 2014). Even so, as you will learn later in this text (in Chapters 10, 11, and 12), many of these problems associated with academic learning can be overcome with explicit instruction and intensive efforts.

CHARACTERISTICS

Unexpected underachievement is the defining characteristic of learning disabilities (Vaughn, Elbaum, & Boardman, 2001), meaning affected students perform significantly below their peers and below levels that teachers and parents would expect from children of their ability. Although some students have problems in only one academic area, most have pervasive problems that affect the entire range of academic and social domains (Bryant, Bryant, & Hammill, 2000; Gregg & Mather, 2002). Teachers often cite this group's heterogeneity as challenging because it seems that each student requires a unique response

(Fletcher et al., 2002). For example, some students might demonstrate difficulties with reading and writing, yet their mathematics abilities are in the average range. Other students could have difficulties in reading, writing, and mathematics plus exhibit problems with social interactions. The characteristics listed in Table 2.2 are usually evident to varying degrees.

Compounding these general characteristics are frustrations with the difficulties of learning academic tasks that classmates seem to easily understand and master. Students with learning disabilities cannot see the relationship between effort and accomplishment. When teachers and parents remind them that working hard, studying, and applying effective learning strategies to their schoolwork pays off, youngsters also learn that their efforts can lead to success.

Many of these students are said to be inattentive (Pierangelo & Giuliani, 2006). Either they do not focus on the task to be learned or they pay attention to the wrong features of the task. They are said to be distractible, disorganized, and unable to approach learning strategically (Bender, 2007). Most students with learning disabilities also have problems with generalization; that is, they have difficulty transferring their learning to different skills or situations (Vaughn & Bos, 2012). They might apply a newly learned study skill in history class but

TABLE 2.2	CHARACTERISTICS OF STUDENTS WITH LEARNING DISABILITIES	
Academic	**Social**	**Behavioral Style**
• Prone to unexpected underachievement	• Immature	• Inattentive
• Resistant to treatment	• Capable of socially unacceptable behavior	• Distractible
• Difficult to teach	• Prone to misinterpret social and nonverbal cues	• Hyperactive
• Unable to solve problems	• Poor decision-making skills	• Impulsive
• Demonstrate uneven academic abilities	• Victimized	• Poorly coordinated
• Weak in basic language skills	• Unable to follow social conventions (manners)	• Unmotivated
• Possess poor reading skills in word reading, fluency, and/or comprehension	• Rejected	• Dependent
• Possess poor written language skills in spelling, grammar, and written expression	• Naive	• Disorganized
• Possess poor mathematics skills in numbers sense, calculations, math reasoning, and problem solving	• Shy, withdrawn, insecure	
• Have difficulties with metacognitive and cognitive abilities	• Unable to predict social consequences	
• Have memory deficits		
• Unable to generalize		

not in English class. Teachers can encourage generalization by making clear connections between familiar problems and those that are new or novel (Fuchs et al., 2002). When teachers carefully broaden the categories—either the skill or the situation—and point out similar features, students extend their learning more readily. Thus, if a student knows how to solve subtraction problems that require regrouping without zeros in the minuend, for example, the teacher should carefully point out the similarities between problems that include zeros (500 − 354 = ?) and those that do not (467 − 189 = ?).

Another long-standing explanation for these students' learning problems is that they have trouble with information processing (Hallahan, Kauffman, & Pullen, 2015). A break occurs somewhere along the processing chain that leads from gaining the information, or input, to understanding the information, to finding an effective means of using new knowledge, or output. The break may be attributed to memory difficulties and the way students receive, organize, and store information to aid in recalling it. Many students with learning disabilities benefit from being taught strategies to help them identify, organize, understand, and remember important information in their textbook reading. For learning arithmetic facts, students can be taught strategies for retrieving answers quickly and correctly. Other students with learning disabilities may need to use alternative means or assistive technology to do their schoolwork. For example, a student with severely impaired writing abilities may find that the speech recognition system, a standard feature of personal computers, is helpful when writing term papers. Another student who cannot read well enough to keep up with classmates as they read their sixth-grade social studies textbook might profit from using the digital version of the text and the speech output option. This chapter's Tech Notes feature provides information about the use of computer tablets as an example of how technology can promote access to the curriculum and independence.

TECH *notes*

MOBILE DEVICES

The use of mobile devices rather than desktops or laptops has been gaining in popularity as a means for delivering instruction and helping students to access the curriculum. Mobile devices, such as small and handheld computing devices (e.g., smartphones, iPads), typically have a touch-screen display and allow for Internet access. These devices have the potential for being useful tools for students with disabilities due to the following reasons: (a) the availability of downloadable, inexpensive apps; (b) the touch-screen feature that allows students with disabilities to use the device without having to operate a mouse or a touchpad; (c) instant turn on/off ability; and (d) Internet access and built-in video, a camera, and audio hardware features. Instructional applications, commonly called apps, have gained in popularity for use with mobile technologies to help students acquire skills in various academic areas.

Finally, it is estimated that about three-fourths of individuals with learning disabilities have problems with social skills, and the results are negative self-concepts, an inability to make friends, ineffective approaches to schoolwork, and poor interactions with others (Bryan, Burstein, & Ergul, 2004; Vaughn & Bos, 2012). For example, many students with learning disabilities are naive and unable to judge other people's intentions accurately. They cannot understand nonverbal behaviors, such as facial expressions, and therefore they do not comprehend other people's emotional messages (Dimitrovsky, Spector, & Levy-Schiff, 2000). This inability puts them at a great disadvantage and results in low acceptance by their peers and teachers. Difficulty with social skills, coupled with low achievement and distracting classroom behavior, in turn influences the social status of children with learning disabilities. Peers consider them overly dependent, less cooperative, and less socially adept (Kuhne & Wiener, 2000). Consequently, they are less likely to become leaders—or even to be included in groups. Teachers can play an instrumental role in reducing peer rejection. One approach is to pair these students with classmates without disabilities in areas of mutual interest (Harris & Graham, 1999). For example, teachers might assign students with common interests like sports, music, or a hobby to work together on an academic task such as a science report.

PREVALENCE

Learning disabilities form the largest special education category (review Figure 2.2), including about 5% of the total public school enrollment and about 40% of all students identified as having a disability (U.S. Department of Education, OSEP, 2013). Although prevalence has declined slightly, the rates of learning disabilities remain the highest of all disability groups. Two-thirds of students identified with learning disabilities are male; gender is evenly split in public school enrollment. Parents, educators, and policymakers are concerned about this special education category for this and other reasons (Bradley, Danielson, & Hallahan, 2002).

1. Prevalence: About 40% all students identified as having a disability are identified as having learning disabilities.

2. Cost: Although variation exists across the nation and even between districts, every student with a disability costs more to educate than a classmate without disabilities, usually almost three times as much (Parrish & Esra, 2006).

3. Misidentification: Some experts have called the category of learning disabilities a "dumping ground" where any student unsuccessful in the general education curriculum can be placed (Reschly, 2002).

Not surprisingly, the field of learning disabilities has been in a state of transition. For example, because of the RTI focus, students no longer must fail for years before receiving specialized and intensive help. It is possible that the RTI multitiered systems of support have contributed to the recent decline in the number of students identified as having learning disabilities. These are exciting times, in particular for those concerned about students who struggle with reading, writing, and mathematics, because many have great confidence that ongoing changes will positively affect the lives of these students and their families (Bradley et al., 2002; Kukic et al., 2005). However, more research is needed on the long-term benefits of the RTI system as a valid model for early intervention and disability (Compton et al., 2012).

WHAT ARE THE ATTRIBUTES OF STUDENTS WITH SPEECH OR LANGUAGE IMPAIRMENTS?

Learning disabilities form the largest special education category, but the federal government allows students with disabilities to be reported in only one special education category. Thus, a fourth-grade student with reading/learning disabilities and also a speech problem might well be included in the learning disabilities category but also receive services from a speech/language pathologist (SLP) as a related service. Speech problems and language impairments go hand in hand with learning disabilities; in fact, their rate of co-occurrence is estimated to be 96% (Sunderland, 2004). Students with cognitive disabilities typically face challenges in the area of language development (Taylor, Richards, & Brady, 2005). Therefore, many students with disabilities receive services from *both* special education teachers and SLPs. Also, because of the relationship between having language problems as a preschooler and having later problems with reading and writing, as Figure 2.3 shows, during the early school years speech and language impairment is clearly the larger special education category. When we consider both primary and secondary disabilities, speech or language impairments are clearly the most common disability among schoolchildren. Speech and language are the foundations for many things we do as human beings. Let's briefly think about how problems in these areas affect learning.

Communication requires the receiver to use eyes, ears, and even tactile (touch) senses (as do those who use Braille) to take messages to the brain where they are understood and to interpret the sender's code so it has meaning. If either the sender or the receiver has a defective mechanism for sending or receiving the information, the communication process is ineffective. We distinguish among three related terms: *communication, language,* and *speech.*

- Communication: the process of exchanging knowledge, ideas, opinions, and feelings through the use of verbal or nonverbal language

- Language: the rule-based method of communication relying on the comprehension and use of the signs and symbols by which ideas are represented

- Speech: the vocal production of language

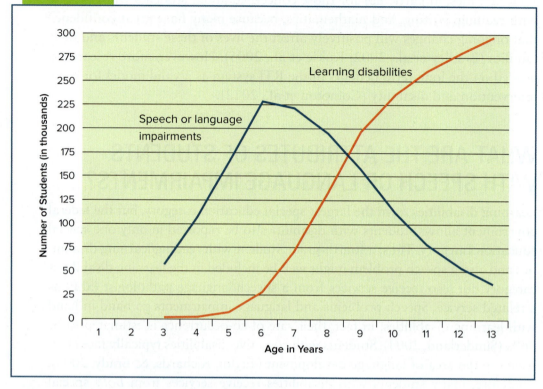

FIGURE 2.3 INDIVIDUALS WITH SPEECH OR LANGUAGE IMPAIRMENTS AND WITH LEARNING DISABILITIES SERVED THROUGH IDEA '04

SOURCE: U.S. Department of Education, National Center for Education Statistics [NCES], Common Core of Data [CCD] (2012). These data are for the 50 states; Washington, DC; Bureau of Indian Education schools; Puerto Rico; the four outlying areas; and the three freely associated states. For actual data used, go to http://www.ed.gov/about/reports/annual/osep.

Now let's turn our attention to problems that can interfere with communication by impeding either language or speech.

DEFINITION

Although they make up a single special education category, speech impairments and language impairments are really two separate but related disabilities. A speech impairment exists when a person's production of speech sounds is unintelligible, is unpleasant, or interferes with communication (Bernthal & Bankson, 2004; Hall, Oyer, & Haas, 2001). Speech impairments are distracting to the listener and can negatively affect the communication process. A language impairment disrupts communication and interferes with accurate understanding of messages, the intent of communications, and interactions among people. See Table 2.3 for the IDEA '04 definition, as well as the one adopted many years ago by the American Speech-Language-Hearing Association (ASHA), the nation's largest organization representing professionals in the areas of speech, language, and audiology.

TABLE 2.3	DEFINITIONS OF SPEECH OR LANGUAGE IMPAIRMENT
Source	**Definition**
IDEA '04[1]	*Speech or language impairment* means a communication disorder, such as stuttering, impaired articulation, a language impairment, or a voice impairment, that adversely affects a child's educational performance.
American Speech-Language-Hearing Association[2]	A speech and language disorder may be present when a person's speech or language is different from that of others of the same age, sex, or ethnic group; when a person's speech and/or language is hard to understand; when a person is overly concerned about his or her speech; or when a person often avoids communicating with others.
DSM-5[3,4]	Language Disorder: Persistent difficulties in the acquisition and use of spoken, written, or sign language. Language abilities are quantifiably below those expected for age with an onset of symptoms in the early developmental period. Speech Sound Disorder: Persistent difficulty with speech sound production that interferes with speech intelligibility or prevents verbal communication with an onset of symptoms in the early developmental period.

SOURCES: [1]U.S. Department of Education, 2006, p. 1265; [2]American Speech-Language-Hearing Association Ad Hoc Committee on Service Delivery in the Schools, 1993, pp. 40–41; [3,4]American Psychiatric Association (APA), 2013.

TYPES

Both types of communication disorders—speech impairments and language impairments—can be further subdivided. The three types of speech impairments follow:

1. Articulation problems: The process of producing speech sounds is flawed, and resulting speech sounds are incorrect. Table 2.4 describes each of the four articulation problems.

2. Fluency problems: Hesitations or repetitions interrupt the flow of speech. **Stuttering** is one type of fluency problem.

3. Voice problems: The voice is unusual in **pitch** or **loudness** given the age and gender of the individual.

Some young children between 3 and 5 years of age demonstrate misarticulations and dysfluencies (nonfluencies) in the course of normal speech development. These mistakes are not usually indicative of a problem in need of therapy (Conture, 2001; Ramig & Shames, 2006).

TABLE 2.4	TYPES OF ARTICULATION ERRORS	
Error Type	**Definition**	**Example**
Omission	A sound or group of sounds is left out of a word.	Intended: I want a banana. Omission: I wanna nana.
Substitution	One sound is used for another; a common misarticulation among small children.	Intended: I see the rabbit. Substitution: I tee the wabbit.
Distortion	A variation of the intended sound is produced in an unfamiliar manner.	Intended: Give the pencil to Sally. Distortion: Give the pencil to Sally. (the /p/ is nasalized).
Addition	An extra sound is inserted or added to one already correctly produced.	Intended: I miss her. Addition: I missid her.

Language impairments are not typically broken down into types, but we often discuss problems with language in terms of the aspect of language where the problem exists.

- **Syntax:** the rule system used for all language (oral, written, and sign)
- **Semantics:** the intent and meaning of spoken and written statements
- **Pragmatics:** the application of language based on the social content

Rules in each language govern the way vowels, consonants, their combinations, and words are used (Small, 2005). The relationship between development of an awareness of sounds in words (phonological awareness) during the preschool years and later ease of learning how to read is now clear (Bishop, 2006). To prevent reading failure later during the school years, teachers should refer preschoolers who have problems mastering phonology to specialists for early intervention.

CHARACTERISTICS

The ability to distinguish among these three language-related situations helps general education teachers make prompt and correct referrals and avoid misidentifying students:

1. Language impairments
2. Language delays
3. Language differences

A typical child at the age of 3 can use some fairly sophisticated language. At the same age, a child with language impairments might speak in only two-word combinations. We look not just at how quickly or slowly a child develops language but also at how the child's language development is different from that of typical peers.

Children with **language delays** generally acquire language in the same sequence as their peers but more slowly. Many do not have a disability and catch up with their peers. However, some children who acquire language in the correct sequence do so very slowly and never complete the acquisition of complex language structures. For example, most children with intellectual disabilities have language delays, and their language development is below the norm for their age (Wetherby, 2002).

What about children who are learning English as a second language? Many teachers have difficulty determining whether a child who is not a native speaker of English is merely **language different** or has a language impairment (Baca & Cervantes, 2004; Salend, 2005). Truly mastering a second language takes a long time. Many **English language learners (ELLs)**, now beginning to be referred to as **English learners (ELs)**, may appear to be fluent because they converse with their classmates on the playground and express their basic needs in the classroom, but even so, they may not yet have developed sufficient English fluency to participate fully in academic instruction. Speaking English as a second language does not result in a disability, but some ELs may be slow in mastering their second language, particularly because of the impact of poverty, and some do have language impairments.

Dialects of American English are not impairments either (Payne & Taylor, 2006). They result from historical, social, regional, and cultural influences on speech, but children who speak them are sometimes perceived by educators as inferior or misidentified as having language impairments. Teachers need to understand and be sensitive to the differences between dialects and language impairments, but when in doubt, they should seek the advice of specialists. SLPs who can distinguish between language differences and language impairments are proficient in the rules of the particular child's dialect and in the use of nondiscriminatory testing procedures. It is equally a mistake to assume students have disabilities simply because of their cultural or linguistic backgrounds and to fail to qualify students for services they need for fear of being discriminatory. We discuss linguistically diverse students again in Chapter 4.

PREVALENCE

As we saw in Figure 2.1, speech or language impairments accounted for 18.2% of students ages 6 to 21 with identified disabilities. In Figure 2.2, official reports show speech or language impairments as the second-largest special education category, behind learning disabilities. In 2013, nearly 1,373,000 school-age children were identified as having a speech or language impairment, representing 2.8% of the school-age population. And remember that when we consider both primary and secondary disabling conditions, speech or language impairment is clearly the largest special education category.

During the 2013 school year, speech or language impairment was the most common label used for children between the ages of 3 and 5.

Look again at Figure 2.3 to see how quickly the balance shifts: By third and fourth grade more students are included in the learning disabilities category, while the size of the speech or language impairment category declines. Clearly, the prevalence of speech or language impairment is associated with the age of the student and the demands of the curriculum (Bakken & Whedon, 2002). The data shown in Figure 2.3 also confirm what you learned earlier about students with learning disabilities. They tend not to be identified early, at the beginning of their school careers, when their struggle to succeed in the curriculum begins. These data contributed to justifications found in IDEA '04 for the application of early intervening procedures and new ways to identify students with learning disabilities.

WHAT ARE THE ATTRIBUTES OF STUDENTS WITH ATTENTION DEFICIT/ HYPERACTIVITY DISORDER (ADHD)?

The American Psychiatric Association places the percentage of children affected by ADHD at about 5% (APA, 2013); ADHD falls under the Other Health Impairments special education category (see Chapter 3). Here are some interesting facts about ADHD to help you better understand this condition:

1. ADHD is not a separate category called out in IDEA '04, so states do not report ADHD students separately to the federal government. Not all students with ADHD are eligible for special education services. If the condition does not adversely influence their academic performance, they are not reported to any agency and instead receive accommodations for their unique learning needs through Section 504 of the Rehabilitation Act (see Chapter 1).

2. Few additional students are identified as having a disability because of ADHD. Many were already being served in other categories, such as learning disabilities or emotional or behavior disorders, before the condition was called out within the "other health impairments" category.

3. Many ADHD symptoms overlap with those of other disabilities.

4. It is estimated that more than half of all students with ADHD do not qualify for educational services because their condition does not seriously affect their educational performance (CHADD, 2004).

DEFINITION

Table 2.5 gives the IDEA '04 and DSM-5 definitions of ADHD. As you review this table, think about what ADHD is and what it is not.

 ADHD

TYPES

ADHD is a complicated condition. Students with ADHD tend to fall into three main groups:

1. Those who do not qualify for special education
2. Those who qualify for special education
3. Those who have coexisting disabilities

Most students with ADHD approach learning differently from typical learners. They can have difficulty focusing intently on learning tasks, and many tend not to be motivated. They also lack the persistence to make the extra effort to learn when it is difficult for them (Carlson, Booth, Shin, & Canu, 2002). Teachers can make a real difference in the educational experience for students with ADHD by

- Providing structure to the classroom routine.
- Teaching academic content directly.
- Holding high expectations.
- Encouraging appropriate academic and social performance.

TABLE 2.5	DEFINITIONS OF ATTENTION DEFICIT/HYPERACTIVITY DISORDER (ADHD)
Source	**Definition**
IDEA '04[1]	ADHD is listed as one condition within the "Other Health Impairments" category. Other *health impairments* means having limited strength, vitality, or alertness, including heightened alertness to environmental stimuli that results in limited alertness with respect to the educational environment, that: i. Is due to chronic or acute health problems such as asthma, attention deficit disorder or attention deficit/hyperactivity disorder, diabetes, epilepsy, a heart condition, hemophilia, lead poisoning, leukemia, nephritis, rheumatic fever, sickle cell anemia, and Tourette syndrome; and ii. Adversely affects a child's educational performance.
DSM-5[2]	In its DSM-5 manual, the American Psychiatric Association (APA) calls ADHD "a persistent pattern of inattention and/or hyperactivity-impulsivity that interferes with functioning or development" (APA, 2013, p. 61). A. Several inattentive or hyperactive-impulsive symptoms were present prior to age 12 years. B. Several inattentive or hyperactive-impulsive symptoms are present in two or more settings (e.g., at school, work, or home). C. There is clear evidence that the symptoms interfere with, or reduce the quality of, social, academic, or occupational functioning. D. The symptoms do not occur exclusively during the course of schizophrenia or another psychotic disorder and are not better explained by another mental disorder (e.g., mood disorder, anxiety disorder, dissociative disorder, a personality disorder, or substance intoxication or withdrawal).

SOURCES: [1]U.S. Department of Education (2006, pp. 1263–1264); [2]APA (2013, p. 61).

Those students with ADHD whose educational functioning is seriously affected by the condition do qualify for special education services. Many experience problems in both academic achievement and social skills. These students' poor academic performance is often due to their distractibility and their inability to focus on assignments for long periods of time. Hyperactivity and poor social skills often lead to rejection and bullying by their peers, leaving these individuals lonely and without friends (Olmeda, Thomas, & Davis, 2003). They come to judge themselves as social failures and tend to engage in solitary activities such as playing computer games and watching television. This situation can contribute to alienation and withdrawal.

ADHD often coexists with other disabilities (National Institute of Mental Health [NIMH], 2005). For example, compare the characteristics of learning disabilities, found in Table 2.2, with those of ADHD, found in Table 2.6. In some cases the characteristics of ADHD are very similar to those of other disabilities, and in some cases the individuals involved have more than one disability, or they have **coexisting disabilities**.

ADHD is likely to be identified in boys with externalizing emotional or behavioral disorders (Reid et al., 2000). For example, a teenager who cannot control his reactions to highly charged situations, or who may misread social interactions, might engage in hostile and reactive behaviors. When ADHD and antisocial behaviors both occur, the combination can be dangerous (Gresham, Lane, & Lambros, 2000). Violent behaviors tend to be infrequent, so many of these students have not qualified for special services and therefore did not receive interventions to prevent serious misbehavior. The end result of this situation can be disastrous.

ADHD is now a separate condition included in the "other health impairments" category. However, determining when it is separate, when it coexists with other disabilities, and when its characteristics are merely similar to those found in other disabling conditions can be challenging to professionals. Whether spending the time and effort to make true distinctions matters for diagnosis and treatment is open to debate.

CHARACTERISTICS

The three main characteristics associated with ADHD follow:

1. Hyperactivity
2. Impulsivity
3. Inattention

The judgment about whether a certain level of a specific activity is too much, or "hyper," is often subjective, and this makes **hyperactivity** difficult to define. If, for example, we admire the behavior, we might describe the child as energetic or enthusiastic rather than hyperactive. Nevertheless, the DSM-5 gives some good examples about which there is considerable consensus (APA, 2013, pp. 59–60). Hyperactivity can be manifested by

- Fidgeting or squirming in a seat.

- Not remaining seated when expected to do so.

- Running or climbing excessively in situations where it is inappropriate.

- Having difficulty playing or engaging quietly in leisure activities.

- Appearing to be often "on the go" or as if "driven by a motor."

- Talking excessively.

Students with ADHD, and many with learning disabilities, are said to be impulsive. **Impulsivity** may explain why they are unable to focus on the relevant components of problems to be solved or tasks to be learned and why they often disrupt the learning environment for an entire class. The third characteristic teachers and researchers commonly observe is **inattention** (Mercer, 2004). Children who do not focus on the task to be learned or who pay attention to the wrong features of the task are said to be distractible. Table 2.6 provides specific examples of characteristics of ADHD.

TABLE 2.6	CHARACTERISTICS OF ATTENTION DEFICIT/HYPERACTIVITY DISORDER (ADHD)

Either inattention or hyperactivity-impulsivity must have persisted for at least 6 months. Either condition must be at a level that is both maladaptive and inconsistent with development and must include six (or more) of the following symptoms.

Inattention	Hyperactivity-Impulsivity
• Often fails to give close attention to details or makes careless mistakes in schoolwork, work, or other activities	• Often fidgets with hands or feet or squirms in seat
• Often has difficulty sustaining attention in tasks or play activities	• Often leaves seat in classroom or in other situations in which remaining seated is expected
• Often does not seem to listen when spoken to directly	• Often runs about or climbs excessively in situations in which it is inappropriate (in adolescents or adults, may be limited to subjective feelings of restlessness)
• Often does not follow through on instructions and fails to finish schoolwork, chores, or duties in the workplace (not due to oppositional behavior or failure to understand instructions)	• Often has difficulty playing or engaging in leisure activities quietly
• Often has difficulty organizing tasks and activities	• Is often "on the go" or often acts as if "driven by a motor"
• Often avoids, dislikes, or is reluctant to engage in tasks that require sustained mental effort (such as schoolwork or homework)	• Often talks excessively
	• Often blurts out answers before questions have been completed
• Often loses things necessary for tasks or activities (e.g., toys, school assignments, pencils, books, or tools)	• Often has difficulty awaiting turn
• Is often easily distracted by extraneous stimuli	• Often interrupts or intrudes on others (e.g., butts into conversations or games)
• Is often forgetful in daily activities	

SOURCE: Adapted from *Diagnostic and Statistical Manual of Mental Disorders*, Fifth Edition, Text Revision (Copyright 2013) (pp. 85–90). American Psychiatric Association.

Many students identified as having ADHD receive medication to control their behavior. Ritalin, Dexedrine, and Concerta do help some children with ADHD focus their attention on assigned tasks and reduce hyperactivity (Spencer, Biederman, & Wilens, 2010). They do not seem to have a positive effect on academic performance, however (Gotsch, 2002). Because of its time-release feature, which relieves school staff of the need to distribute and monitor the use of prescription drugs, medication is not always necessary and should be considered a last resort, used if behavioral techniques, direct and systematic instruction evaluated on a frequent basis, and highly motivating instructional materials have proved insufficient. In these cases, a combination of behavioral and medical intervention is most powerful in the treatment of ADHD (Fabiano et al., 2009).

PREVALENCE

As we have noted, obtaining precise indications of the number of students who are affected by ADHD is impossible. First, because ADHD is not a separate disability category, the federal government does not require separate reporting (students with ADHD are included in the count of students with "other health impairments"). Second, the government does not require a count of those students with ADHD who do not qualify for special education services but receive accommodations through Section 504. Third, the government does not require the states to report students' secondary conditions or disabilities. When a student's primary disability is learning disabilities and that student's secondary disability is ADHD, the student is reported only in the learning disabilities category.

Studies have shown that 70% of children with ADHD also have a learning disability (Mayes, Calhoun, & Crowell, 2000; Pierce, 2003). In another study, parents reported that 64% of students with emotional or behavioral disorders also had ADHD. Whether a student's ADHD is considered a primary or a secondary condition and whether it negatively influences educational performance, ADHD does result in special needs that can be met by perceptive and effective teachers.

WHAT ARE THE ATTRIBUTES OF STUDENTS WITH INTELLECTUAL AND DEVELOPMENTAL DISABILITIES?

As you will learn in the following sections, the field of intellectual and developmental disabilities has been in a state of transition for over a decade. In 1992 and again in 2002, two new definitions were developed. In 2007, the name of the disability was changed from *mental retardation* to *intellectual and developmental disabilities* by the field's oldest professional organization, which also changed its own name to reflect the new term. The American Association on Mental Retardation (AAMR) is now the American Association on Intellectual and Developmental Disabilities (AAIDD). In part, these changes seek to reduce the stigma and bias often associated with this disability (Luckasson & Schalock, 2013).

For some years to come, these changes may be a bit confusing. The definition supported by AAIDD was developed when this organization was called AAMR. IDEA '04 uses the term *mental retardation*, as do most states' regulations and statues. In this text, when we discuss this disability and its impact on the individuals and families involved, we use the term *intellectual and developmental disabilities*.

People often make many incorrect assumptions about intellectual and developmental disabilities. First, they assume the disability is infrequent and therefore a low-incidence condition. Second, they assume it is always severe. Here's what is true: Like all other disabilities, intellectual and developmental disabilities occur along a continuum ranging from mild to very severe conditions. In fact, the foundation for all of today's special education emanates from a likely case of intellectual and development disability. Recall the famous story recounted in Chapter 1 about Victor, the young boy found in the forest of southern France by farmers in 1799. That boy became known as the Wild Boy of Aveyron, and the Parisian doctor who cared for Victor, Jean-Marc-Gaspard Itard, is acknowledged as the father of the field of special education.

DEFINITION

In 2002, the American Association on Mental Retardation (AAMR), as it was then known, adopted the current definition of intellectual and developmental disabilities, the organization's 10th since 1921. That definition and its five assumptions are found in Table 2.7. How is this modern view different from previous orientations? Before 1992, definitions followed a deficit model, describing the limitations of the individual, such as "significantly subaverage general intellectual functioning." Today, the disability is conceptualized in terms of the adaptive behavior each individual possesses and the **intensity of supports** needed for him or her to function in the community as independently as possible (Luckasson & Schalock, 2013). "Adaptive behavior is the collection of conceptual, social, and practical skills that have been learned by people in order to function in their everyday lives" (AAMR, 2002, p. 73). Systems of supports enable us to function in everyday life and address the demands that face us. The intensity or level of these supports varies as a function of the needs and capabilities of each individual.

One defining feature of intellectual and developmental disabilities is that the individual has problems with *cognition* or *intellectual functioning*. The 2002 definition includes a cautious use of IQ scores, and caution is well-advised

TABLE 2.7	DEFINITIONS OF INTELLECTUAL AND DEVELOPMENTAL DISABILITIES
Source	**Definition**
IDEA '04[1]	*Mental retardation* (as it is called in this legislation) means significant subaverage general intellectual functioning, existing concurrently with deficits in adaptive behavior and manifested during the developmental period, that adversely affects a child's educational performance.
American Association on Intellectual and Developmental Disabilities[2]	Intellectual and developmental disabilities is a disability characterized by significant limitations both in intellectual functioning and in adaptive behavior as expressed in conceptual, social, and practical adaptive skills. This disability originates before age 18.
DSM-5[3]	Deficits in intellectual functions, such as reasoning, problem solving, planning, abstract thinking, judgment, academic learning, and learning from experience. Deficits in adaptive functioning that result in failure to meet developmental and socio-cultural standards for personal independence and social responsibility. Onset during the developmental period.

SOURCES: [1]U.S. Department of Education, 2006, p. 1263; [2]Luckasson et al., 2002, p. 1; [3]American Psychiatric Association (APA, 2013, p. 33).

because relying on such scores leads to many mistakes and erroneous assumptions about individuals' abilities. These individuals have cognitive abilities "significantly below average" or below levels attained by 97% of the general population. When a standardized test is used, the individual must score at least two standard deviations below the mean for that test. Recall our discussion of the normal curve in Chapter 1. Intelligence is regarded as one of those traits distributed among people in a predictable manner and reflected by a statistical distribution representing a bell-shaped curve, also called the normal curve. The majority of the population falls in the middle of the bell, at or around an **intelligence quotient (IQ)** score of 100, and fewer and fewer people fall at either end of the distribution, having very low or very high intelligence. IQ level is then determined by the distance a score is from the mean, or average, score. The 2002 definition uses a cutoff score of about 70 and below to designate intellectual and developmental disabilities. This disability is also classified according to levels of severity that can affect the individual's performance:

- Mild intellectual and developmental disabilities

  Outcomes: learning difficulties, able to work, maintain good social relationships, contribute to society

- Moderate intellectual and developmental disabilities

  Outcomes: marked developmental delays during childhood, some degree of independence in self-care, adequate communication and academic skills, require varying degrees of support to live and work in the community

- Severe intellectual and developmental disabilities

  Outcomes: continuous need of support

- Profound intellectual and developmental disabilities

  Outcomes: severe limitation in self-care, continence, communication, and mobility, continuous need of supports

Another defining characteristic of intellectual and developmental disabilities is adaptive behavior, which is what everyone uses to function in daily life, such as eating, dressing, using the toilet, having mobility, preparing meals, using the telephone, managing money, taking care of the house, and taking medication. People with intellectual and developmental disabilities, as well as many people without disabilities, can have difficulties with such skills that can impair their ability to function independently.

All of us also use systems of supports. We ask our friends for advice. We form study teams before a difficult test. We expect help from city services when there is a crime or a fire. We join together in a neighborhood crime watch group to help each other be safe. And we share the excitement and joys of accomplishments with family, friends, and colleagues.

For individuals with intellectual and developmental disabilities, systems of support are a means for promoting independence and bridging the gap between classroom expectations and the student's current levels of functioning. Supports have been defined as "resources and strategies that aim to promote the development, education, interests, and personal well-being of a person and that enhance individual functioning" (Schalock et al., 2010, p. 105). Seven support needs areas associated with school-age students follow (Thompson et al., 2008):

- Home Life Activities: pertain to an individual's personal care
- Community and Neighborhood Activities: relate to participating in community activities
- School Participation Activities: involve being an active member of class and school activities
- School Learning Activities: focus on being successful with school tasks and assignments
- Health and Safety Activities: pertain to maintaining healthy habits and keeping oneself safe
- Social Activities: involve skills associated with interacting with others in various settings
- Protection and Advocacy Activities: focus on self-advocacy

The primary goal of supports is to help the person meet the demands of life's various contexts. Because support needs have only recently found their way into the special education field, there are few support programs that have been proven effective by research. However, there is a growing body of research that has demonstrated that a combination of **assistive technology services** and **assistive technology devices** can help bridge the gaps between functional limitations and independent functioning (e.g., Bryant, Seok, Ok, & Bryant, 2012; Bryant, Shih, Bryant, & Seok, 2010; Fisher & Shogren, 2012; Wehmeyer, Tassé, Davies, & Stock, 2012).

Supports also can be offered at different intensity levels—intermittent, limited, extensive, pervasive—and can be of different types (Chadsey & Beyer, 2001; Kennedy & Horn, 2004):

- Natural supports: the individual's own resources, family, friends, and neighbors, as well as coworkers on the job or peers at school

- Nonpaid supports: neighborhood and community groups, such as clubs, recreational leagues, and private organizations

- Generic supports: public transportation, states' human services systems, and other agencies and services to which everyone has access

- Specialized supports: disability-specific services such as special education, special early intervention services, and vocational rehabilitation

TYPES

One way to consider the types of this disability is to think about causes. Some of these conditions are genetic in origin, others are environmental, and still others are caused by an interaction of biology and the environment. Today, more than 500 genetic causes of intellectual and developmental disabilities are known, and because of advances in medical research, more are being identified (The Arc, 2005). A condition identified in 1991 and now recognized as the most common inherited cause of intellectual and developmental disabilities is fragile X syndrome, which affects about 1 in 4,000 males and results from a mutation on the X chromosome (Taylor, Richards, & Brady, 2005). The associated cognitive problems can be severe, and it is believed that some 86% of fragile-X-affected males have intellectual disabilities and 6% have autism.

Another biological example caused by a chromosomal abnormality is Down syndrome. Certain identifiable physical characteristics, such as an extra flap of skin over the innermost corner of the eye, are usually present in cases of Down syndrome. The degree of cognitive difficulty varies, depending in part on the speed with which the disability is identified, the adequacy of the supporting medical care, and the timing of the early intervention (National Down Syndrome Society, 2006). Individuals with Down syndrome have a higher prevalence of obesity, despite typically consuming fewer than average calories (Roizen, 2001). Their reduced food consumption may explain why they are less active than their brothers and sisters and less likely to spend time outdoors. In turn, their opportunities for satisfying friendships, social outlets, and recreation are reduced. Teachers can help by encouraging them to be more active and to play sports with their peers during recess.

In the hereditary condition phenylketonuria (PKU), a person is unable to metabolize phenylalanine, an amino acid that then builds up in the body to toxic levels that damage the brain. If untreated, PKU eventually causes intellectual disabilities. Changes in diet, such as strictly eliminating certain foods that contain phenylalanine, such as milk, can control PKU and reduce its devastating impact. Here, then, is a condition rooted in genetics but brought on by the environment—by ingesting milk. Prompt diagnosis and parental vigilance are crucial to minimizing the associated problems. Teachers can help by monitoring these students' diets and ensuring that snacks and treats provided by classmates' parents for sharing do not include milk products that might be harmful. Now let's look at some toxins that do not have a hereditary link.

One well-recognized nonhereditary type of birth defect, considered by Congress to be the most common and preventable cause of intellectual and developmental disabilities, is fetal alcohol syndrome (FAS; U.S. Senate Appropriations Committee, 2004). This condition results from the mother drinking alcohol during pregnancy (The Arc, 2005). The average IQ of people with FAS is 79, which is relatively close to the cutoff score (about 70) for intellectual and developmental disability. These data explain why about 58% of individuals with FAS have intellectual and developmental disabilities, and why about 94% have a strong need for support assistance at school. Most also have problems in the areas of attention, verbal learning, and self-control (Centers for Disease Control, 2004). Estimates are that some 5,000 babies are born with FAS each year, and an additional 50,000 show symptoms of the less serious condition fetal alcohol effects (FAE; Davis & Davis, 2003).

CHARACTERISTICS

According to AAIDD, the three defining characteristics of intellectual and developmental disabilities follow:

1. Problems with cognition

2. Problems with adaptive behavior

3. Need for supports to sustain independence (Schalock et al., 2010)

Impaired cognitive ability has pervasive effects, whether the disability is mild or severe. Learning new skills, storing and retrieving information from memory, and transferring knowledge to either new or slightly different situations are challenges for these individuals. Short- and long-term memory are often impaired, making it hard to remember events or the proper sequence of events, particularly when the events are not clearly identified as important. Even when something is remembered, it may be remembered incorrectly, inefficiently, too slowly, or in inadequate detail. Teachers can help students with memory problems develop memory strategies and learn to compensate by having them create picture notebooks that lay out the sequence of steps in a task that needs to be performed, the elements of a job that needs to be done, or a checklist of things to do before leaving the house.

Through **explicit, systematic instruction** and the delivery of supports, adaptive behavior can improve. However, for these gains to happen, it is sometimes necessary for students to receive a separate curriculum that targets life skills, which are skills used to manage a home and job and engage in activities in the community. When goals for independent living become the target of instruction, students may then have reduced access to the general education curriculum and typically learning classmates.

The making of friendships between people with and people without disabilities has received considerable attention during the last decade, because friends are natural supports and sources of social interactions (AAMR, 2002). Research findings show that children of elementary school age with and without intellectual disabilities can become real friends who play together, express positive feelings for each other, and respond to each other reciprocally (Freeman & Kasari, 2002). However, as children get older, the odds of real friendships developing between typical students and classmates with disabilities seem to diminish (Hughes & Carter, 2006). During middle school, for example, children without disabilities tend to form friendships with others of similar backgrounds, age, gender, and interests.

Inclusion and friendships between individuals with and without disabilities have benefits beyond those that help the people with disabilities, however. The attitudes of students who attend school alongside students with disabilities are more positive and reflect a better understanding of the challenges they will face throughout their lives (Hughes & Carter, 2006; Kennedy & Horn, 2004).

PREVALENCE

According to the federal government, almost 1% (that is, not quite 1 of every 100) of U.S. students are identified as having intellectual and developmental disabilities as their primary disabling condition through IDEA '04. Recent data show that some 434,586 children with intellectual and developmental disabilities were served across the country. Most students with intellectual and developmental disabilities function at high levels and need few supports. In other words, most fall at the mild level.

WHAT ARE THE ATTRIBUTES OF STUDENTS WITH EMOTIONAL OR BEHAVIORAL DISORDERS?

The emotional or behavioral disorders category is the last of the high-incidence special education categories. Emotional/behavioral disorders (EBD) are very worrisome, because the connections between this disability and the criminal justice system, the commission of violence against self or others, and a life of unhappiness are well recognized (Walker, Ramsey, & Gresham, 2004). There is clear evidence that early intervention makes a real difference in the lives of these individuals. Unfortunately, such services are not delivered often enough to those who exhibit signs of troubling behaviors (Lane, 2004). Let's look more closely at this last high-incidence condition.

DEFINITION

IDEA '04 uses the term *emotional disturbance* to describe the characteristic of children to whom we refer as having behavioral or emotional disorders. Remember that this condition is expressed over a long period of time, is obvious to many observers, and adversely affects educational performance. Table 2.8 gives the IDEA '04 and National Mental Health and Special Education Coalition definitions of emotional or behavioral disorders.

TYPES

Emotional or behavioral disorders can be divided into three groups:

1. Externalizing
2. Internalizing
3. Low incidence

Students who exhibit externalizing and internalizing behaviors are the two main groups of students with emotional or behavioral disorders, but they do not account for all the conditions that result in placement in this special education category. **Externalizing behaviors** are characterized by an undercontrolled, acting-out style that includes behaviors we could describe as aggressive, arguing, impulsive, coercive, and noncompliant. These behaviors are expressed outwardly, usually toward other persons, and generally include some form of hyperactivity, including persistent aggression and a high level of irritating behavior that is impulsive and distractible. Many youngsters with this type of emotional or behavioral disorder engage in bullying and victimize their classmates (Hartung & Scambler, 2006). Some examples of externalizing behavior problems follow:

- Violates basic rights of others
- Has tantrums

- Is hostile or defiant, argues
- Ignores teachers' reprimands
- Causes or threatens physical harm to people or animals
- Intimidates, threatens
- Violates societal norms or rules
- Steals, causes property loss or damage
- Uses lewd or obscene gestures
- Is physically aggressive
- Demonstrates obsessive compulsive behavior
- Is hyperactive

TABLE 2.8	DEFINITIONS OF EMOTIONAL OR BEHAVIORAL DISORDERS
Source	**Definition**
IDEA '04[1]	*Emotional disturbance* means a condition exhibiting one or more of the following characteristics over a long period of time and to a marked degree that adversely affects a child's educational performance: • An inability to learn that cannot be explained by intellectual, sensory, or health factors. • An inability to build or maintain satisfactory interpersonal relationships with peers and teachers. • Inappropriate types of behavior or feelings under normal circumstances. • A general pervasive mood of unhappiness or depression. • A tendency to develop physical symptoms related to fears associated with personal or school problems. Emotional disturbance includes schizophrenia. The term does not apply to children who are socially maladjusted, unless it is determined that they have an emotional disturbance.
National Mental Health and Special Education Coalition[2]	The term *emotional or behavioral disorder* means a disability characterized by behavioral or emotional responses in school so different from appropriate age, cultural, or ethnic norms that they adversely affect educational performance. Educational performance includes academic, social, vocational, and personal skills. Such a disability • Is more than a temporary, expected response to stressful events in the environment; • Is consistently exhibited in two different settings, at least one of which is school-related; and • Is unresponsive to direct intervention in general education, or the child's condition is such that general education interventions would be insufficient. Emotional or behavioral disorders can coexist with other disabilities. This category may include children or youths with schizophrenic disorders, affective disorders, anxiety disorder, or other sustained disorders of conduct or adjustment when they adversely affect educational performance.

SOURCES: [1]U.S. Department of Education, 2006, p. 1262; [2]Forness and Knitzer, 1992, p. 13.

Young children who have serious challenging behaviors that persist are the most likely to be referred for psychiatric services (Maag, 2000). A pattern of early aggressive acts, beginning with annoying and bullying, followed by physical fighting, is a clear pathway to violence in late adolescence, particularly for boys (Archwamety & Katsiyannis, 2000). While still in high school, students with emotional or behavioral disorders are 13 times more likely to be arrested than other students with disabilities (OSEP, 2001). Some 30% to 50% of youth in correctional facilities are individuals with disabilities, and almost half of those have emotional or behavioral disorders (IDEA Practices, 2002).

Internalizing behaviors, the second type of emotional or behavioral disorders, are characterized by an overcontrolled and inhibited style that includes behaviors we would describe as withdrawn, lonely, depressed, and anxious (Kauffman, 2005). Anorexia, bulimia, depression, and anxiety are examples of internalizing behaviors. **Anorexia** and **bulimia** are serious eating disorders that usually occur during students' teenage years (Manley, Rickson, & Standeven, 2000), typically among girls and often because of their preoccupation with weight and body image, their drive for thinness, and their fear of becoming fat.

Often hard to recognize in children, depression includes components such as guilt, self-blame, feelings of rejection, lethargy, low self-esteem, and negative self-image. Children's behavior when they are depressed may appear so different from the depressed behavior of adults that teachers and parents may have difficulty recognizing it. Even so, a severely depressed child might engage in self-harm. Anxiety disorders may be demonstrated as intense response upon separation from family, friends, or a familiar environment, as excessive shrinking from contact with strangers, or as unfocused, excessive worry and fear.

Additional low-incidence conditions are included in the category of emotional or behavioral disorders. Some are very rare but are quite serious when they do occur. For example, schizophrenia is extremely rare in children, although approximately 1% of the general population over the age of 18 have been diagnosed as having the disorder. It usually includes bizarre delusions (such as the belief that your thoughts are controlled by the police), hallucinations (such as voices telling you what to think), "loosening" of associations (disconnected thoughts), and incoherence. Schizophrenia places great demands on service systems. Children with the disorder have serious difficulties with schoolwork and often must live in special hospital and educational settings during part of their childhood. Keep in mind that emotional or behavioral disorders are high-incidence disorders, but the category includes many different specific conditions, including many that are themselves low-incidence conditions.

CHARACTERISTICS

Social skills are the foundation for practically all human activities in all contexts—academic, personal, vocational, and community—and we use them to interact with others and to perform most daily tasks. Possibly more than any other group of children with disabilities, students with emotional or behavioral disorders present problems with social skills to themselves, their families, their peers, and their teachers (Kauffman, 2005). One related characteristic, antisocial behavior, seems to be a prime reason for these students' referrals to special education (OSEP, 2001). Antisocial behavior includes impulsivity and poor interpersonal skills with both peers and adults. These students' behavior patterns can be self-defeating, impairing their interactions with others in many negative ways. Most students with externalizing behavioral disorders exhibit at least some of the following behaviors *in excess*:

- Tantrums
- Aggression
- Noncompliance
- Coercion
- Poor academic performance

On the other hand, students with internalizing patterns tend to exhibit behaviors that reflect the following:

- Depression
- Withdrawal
- Anxiety

Fortunately, intervention can make a difference and improve the outcomes for students with externalizing or internalizing behaviors. For example, instruction in social skills can positively influence the development of social competence (Bullis, Walker, & Sprague, 2001). But such instruction and the use of positive behavioral instructional techniques should be initiated no later than first grade (Frey, Hirschstein, & Guzzo, 2000). Effective instruction is embedded within the general education curriculum and includes considerable demonstration and practice. Peers learn to help and provide support for each other, but getting peers to help these classmates can be challenging, because they tend to reject them (Bullis et al., 2001).

At the beginning of this chapter, we noted that all students identified through IDEA '04 as having a disability have problems with their educational performance. Here, too, even though emotional or behavioral disorders have their roots in social behaviors, the condition negatively affects academic performance. Regardless of intellectual potential, students with emotional or behavioral disorders typically do not perform well academically (Lane & Wehby, 2002). Clearly, being in personal turmoil affects our ability to attend to school tasks and to learn in general. Failure at academic tasks compounds the difficulties these children face not only in school but also in life. Their frustration with the educational system, along with its frustration with them, results in their having the highest dropout rates of all students (National Center for Educational Statistics [NCES], 2005). The outcomes of students who do not complete high school are not good. There is also evidence that when students are engaged in academic work, their disruptive behaviors decrease (Lane, 2004). Thus, in addition to helping these students with their behavior, it is constructive for teachers to address their academic skills.

iStock/BartCo

PREVALENCE

The federal government reports that slightly less than 1% of all schoolchildren have emotional/behavioral disorders, with some 373,154 public school students identified with this disability. Figure 2.1 shows that emotional disturbance accounts for 6.2% of all students ages 6 to 21 with disabilities. However, it is likely that these figures substantially underestimate the prevalence of these problems. Why might this be so? First, the definition is unclear and subjective. Second, because the label is so stigmatizing, many educators and school districts are reluctant to identify many children. Some believe the actual prevalence should be approximately 3% to 6% of all school-age students (Kauffman, 2005; Walker, Nishioka, Zeller, Bullis, & Sprague, 2001). Important factors in prevalence for this group of learners are gender and race.

Emotional/behavioral disorders are difficult to define. Important features of the condition are that it is expressed over a long period of time, is obvious to many observers, and adversely affects educational performance.

Most children identified as having emotional or behavioral disorders (about 74%) are male, and this is the highest ratio of boys to girls in all special education categories. The reason for this gender difference is not clear, but it is probably linked to boys' higher propensity to be troublesome and violate school rules, coupled with girls' tendency toward less disruptive, internalizing behaviors that are less likely to result in referral. Whereas Asian American and Hispanic students tend to be underrepresented in this special education category, African Americans are overrepresented: Twenty-nine percent of students identified as having emotional or behavioral disorders are Black, even though Blacks represent only about 14% of the student population (OSEP, 2006).

SUMMARY

The notion that the vast majority of the nation's students are typical learners is inaccurate. The special needs that many students present to their teachers and schools are considerable and varied. Students with disabilities are guaranteed an appropriate and individualized education, tailored to each of their exceptional learning needs, through IDEA. Other students with special needs are entitled to accommodations through Section 504. And many others require a special response to their unique learning challenges so that they can reach their potential and profit maximally from school.

Certainly, special needs arise from disabilities, but they come from a variety of other sources as well. Special learning needs result from conditions that are not disabilities but that still present considerable learning challenges and put students at risk for school failure, dropping out, or underachievement. What you should now understand is that the majority of America's students present an exciting mixture of learning strengths to each classroom situation.

REVIEW THE LEARNING OBJECTIVES

Let's review the learning objectives for this chapter. If you are uncertain and cannot talk through the answers provided for any of these questions, reread those sections of the text.

- **What are the categories for students with disabilities?**

  Some students with a disability and special needs are not special education students because their disability does not negatively affect their educational performance. For students who do qualify for special education services, frequently occurring disabilities are often referred to as high-incidence disabilities; low-incidence disabilities affect a very small proportion of students with disabilities.

- **How are disabilities organized for special education?**

  Three major schemes are used to group disabilities for the purposes of meeting educational needs. One classification system uses disability types or special education categories (learning disabilities, intellectual disabilities). Another groups students by the severity of the disability (mild, moderate, severe). And the third considers disabilities in terms of how often they occur (high incidence, low incidence).

- **What are the attributes of students with learning disabilities?**

  The largest special education category is *learning disabilities,* which can be severe, complex, pervasive, and lifelong. Learning disabilities are characterized as "unexpected underachievement" and as resistant to treatment. Learning disabilities are disorders that affect the ability to understand or use spoken or written expression, perform mathematical calculations, coordinate movements, or direct attention. Problems with reading and writing are the most common, yet a significant number of students with learning disabilities may also have mathematics learning disabilities.

- **What are the attributes of students with speech or language impairments?**

  Although they make up a single special education category, speech impairments and language impairments are really two separate but related disabilities. Speech or language impairments result in problems with communication, language, and/or speech. Speech impairments include articulation, fluency (stuttering), and voice problems. Many students with disabilities receive services from *both* special education teachers and SLPs. Language impairments are not the same as language differences, and their prevalence changes by age (the number lessens across the school years). Speaking English as a second language does not result in a disability, but some ELs may be slow in mastering their second language. Dialects of American English are also not impairments.

- **What are the attributes of students with attention deficit/hyperactivity disorder? (ADHD)**

  Attention deficit/hyperactivity disorder (ADHD) is a condition included in the IDEA '04 category of "other health impairments." Behaviors associated with ADHD (such as distractibility, hyperactivity) are also symptomatic of other disabilities, such as learning disabilities and emotional or behavioral disorders. Most students with ADHD approach learning differently from typical learners. About half of the individuals with this condition are eligible for special education because their educational performance is adversely affected by the condition; most of the other students with ADHD receive supports and accommodations through Section 504. It is estimated that more than half of all students with ADHD do not qualify for special education services because their condition does not seriously affect their educational performance.

- **What are the attributes of students with intellectual and developmental disabilities?**

  Intellectual and developmental disabilities result in problems with intellectual functioning, adaptive behavior, and independence. Individuals with intellectual and developmental disabilities have problems with *cognition* or *intellectual functioning* and demonstrate difficulties with adaptive

  behavior. Responses to intellectual and developmental disabilities include different intensities of supports (intermittent, limited, extensive, pervasive) and different types of supports (natural supports, nonpaid supports, generic supports, specialized supports). Also, seven systems of support needs areas should be focused on to promote success for individuals with intellectual and developmental disabilities with the demands of life's various contexts.

- **What are the attributes of students with emotional or behavioral disorders?**

  Emotional or behavioral disorders can be externalizing (aggressive, argumentative, impulsive, coercive, noncompliant), internalizing (overcontrolled, inhibited, withdrawn, lonely, depressed, anxious), or low incidence (such as schizophrenia). Internalizing behaviors (such as anorexia, bulimia, depression, anxiety) are less frequently identified early, and externalizing behavior disorders are highly associated with delinquency. Problems with social skills cause issues for the students themselves, their families, their peers, and their teachers. Evidence indicates that early intervention can make a difference in the lives of these individuals.

SAGE edge™ Test your understanding of chapter content. Take the practice quiz. edge.sagepub.com/bryant

REVISIT THE OPENING CHALLENGE •••••••••••••••••••••••••

Check your answers to the Reflection Questions from the Opening Challenge and revise them on the basis of what you have learned.

1. Do you think identifying students by specific disability is useful?

2. Why do you think Darren's special education label is being reconsidered at this point in his schooling?

3. Is Darren's situation unusual? Why or why not?

4. Will a change in category influence the way Ms. Clarkson teaches Darren?

5. Will it change the services Darren receives?

6. What do you think are some learning characteristics of the three students in Mr. Suarez's class?

7. What help might he be looking for from the special education teacher for these three students?

KEY TERMS

anorexia, 77

assistive technology devices, 72

assistive technology services, 72

bulimia, 77

coexisting disabilities, 66

English language learners (ELLs), 63

English learners (ELs), 63

explicit, systematic instruction, 74

externalizing behaviors, 75

high-incidence disabilities, 47

hyperactivity, 66

impulsivity, 67

inattention, 67

intelligence quotient (IQ), 70

intensity of supports, 69

internalizing behaviors, 77

language delays, 63

language different, 63

loudness, 61

low-incidence disabilities, 47

pitch, 61

pragmatics, 62

resistant to treatment, 55

semantics, 62

stuttering, 61

syntax, 62

unexpected underachievement, 55

$SAGE edge™ Review key terms with eFlashcards.
edge.sagepub.com/bryant

PROFESSIONAL STANDARDS AND LICENSURE

For a complete description of Professional Standards and Licensure, please see Appendix on page 569.

CEC Initial Preparation Standards

Standard 1: Learner Development and Individual Learning Differences

INTASC Core Principle

Standard 1: Learner Development

Standard 2: Learning Differences

Praxis II: Education of Exceptional Students: Core Content Knowledge

I. Understanding Exceptionalities: Human development and behavior

Review ➡ Practice ➡ Improve
Get the tools you need to sharpen your study skills. Access practice quizzes, eFlashcards, video, and multimedia: **edge.sagepub.com/bryant**

FIGURE 3.2 INCLUSION OF STUDENTS WITH HIGH- AND LOW-INCIDENCE DISABILITIES

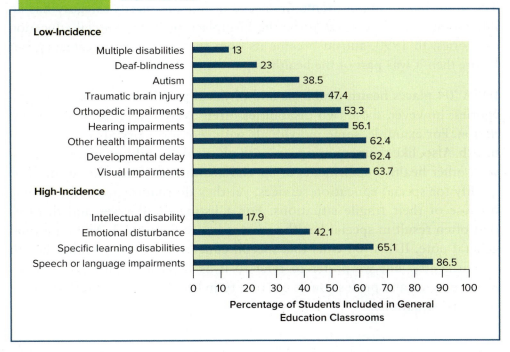

Low-Incidence

Disability	Percentage
Multiple disabilities	13
Deaf-blindness	23
Autism	38.5
Traumatic brain injury	47.4
Orthopedic impairments	53.3
Hearing impairments	56.1
Other health impairments	62.4
Developmental delay	62.4
Visual impairments	63.7

High-Incidence

Disability	Percentage
Intellectual disability	17.9
Emotional disturbance	42.1
Specific learning disabilities	65.1
Speech or language impairments	86.5

Percentage of Students Included in General Education Classrooms

SOURCE: U.S. Department of Education, National Center for Education Statistics (2013).

Each low-incidence disability is unique and presents an array of special needs. Teachers who understand these conditions make important differences in the lives of affected students and their families. Let's think about these disabilities in their order of prevalence.

WHAT ARE THE ATTRIBUTES OF STUDENTS WITH HEALTH IMPAIRMENTS OR SPECIAL HEALTH CARE NEEDS?

As we mentioned in Chapter 2, about 20 years ago the federal government, during one of its reauthorizations of IDEA (typically done every five years), identified ADHD as one condition in the other health impairments category. Before then, this category was very small, representing some 2% of students with disabilities and less than 0.1% of all students (U.S. Department of Education, 1996). We are confident that the disproportionately larger size of this formerly low-incidence category is due to the inclusion of students with ADHD. We have already discussed those students' special needs; in this section, we talk about students with other conditions in the other health impairments category. But first, let's identify several other general issues related to this special education category.

The **other health impairments** or special health care needs category has an interesting history. It seems to be the birthplace of future special education categories. In 1990, autism became its own special education category, but before then it was part of the health impairments definition.

IDEA '04 places health problems and physical problems into separate categories; however, these two disabilities often overlap and occur in combination. For example, some individuals with cerebral palsy also have fragile health. Also, like their counterparts with physical disabilities, many students with other health impairments or special health care needs do not need or qualify for special education services, yet they do require accommodations because of their fragile situations. For a listing of illnesses and diseases that often result in special health care needs, see Figure 3.3. And on a final general note, IDEA '04 calls this special education category "other health impairments," but we prefer to refer to it as "special health care needs." Many parents and professionals use that term because it better reflects these students' situations.

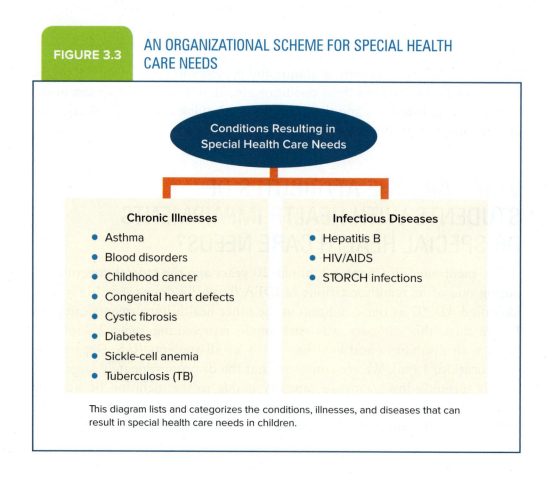

FIGURE 3.3 AN ORGANIZATIONAL SCHEME FOR SPECIAL HEALTH CARE NEEDS

Conditions Resulting in Special Health Care Needs

Chronic Illnesses
- Asthma
- Blood disorders
- Childhood cancer
- Congenital heart defects
- Cystic fibrosis
- Diabetes
- Sickle-cell anemia
- Tuberculosis (TB)

Infectious Diseases
- Hepatitis B
- HIV/AIDS
- STORCH infections

This diagram lists and categorizes the conditions, illnesses, and diseases that can result in special health care needs in children.

DEFINITION

The federal government uses the term "other health impairments" to describe, collectively, conditions and diseases that create special health care needs for children. The IDEA '04 definition is given in Table 3.1. Note that many specific health conditions are called out in this federal definition, but many other conditions—such as blood conditions, cancer, cystic fibrosis, tuberculosis, and STORCH infections (syphilis, toxoplasmosis, rubella, cytomegalovirus, Herpes)—are also included.

For many years the term **medically fragile** was used to describe all children with special health care needs, but it is now more selectively applied. Medically fragile is a status; it is not assigned to any specific condition but rather describes the individual's health situation noted in the aforementioned conditions. Because of advances in medical technology, students can survive health crises and move in and out of fragile status. In the past, many would have been too ill or not have lived long enough to go to school. Even though they are now stable enough to attend, they require ongoing medical management. Teachers must be familiar with emergency procedures for them; the "if, then" must be carefully planned in collaboration with doctors and the school's medical professional. Although steps for "worst-case scenarios" must be arranged, in most cases the accommodations required for these children are not terribly dramatic. (However, not having backup power for a child's ventilator could have disastrous results.)

TABLE 3.1	DEFINITION OF OTHER HEALTH IMPAIRMENTS
Source	**Definition**
Arkansas Department of Education Special Education Unit[1]	"Other health impairment" means having limited strength, vitality or alertness, including a heightened alertness to environmental stimuli, that results in limited alertness with respect to the educational environment that is due to chronic or acute health problems such as asthma, attention deficit disorder or attention deficit hyperactivity disorder, diabetes, epilepsy, a heart condition, hemophilia, lead poisoning, leukemia, nephritis, rheumatic fever, Tourette's Syndrome, and sickle cell anemia; and adversely affects a child's educational performance. The list of chronic or acute health problems included within this definition is not exhaustive. Children with attention deficit hyperactivity disorder (ADHD) and attention deficit disorder (ADD) may be classified as eligible for services under the "other health impairment" category in instances where the ADD/ADHD is a chronic or acute health problem that results in limited alertness, which adversely affects the child's educational performance resulting in the need for special education and related services. While it is recognized that the disorders of ADD and ADHD vary, hereafter, the term ADD will be used to encompass both disorders.

SOURCE: https://arksped.k12.ar.us/rules_regs_08/3.%20SPED%20ELIGIBILITY%20CRITERIA%20AND%20PROGRAM%20GUIDELINES%20FOR%20CHILDREN/PART%20I%20ELIGIBILITY%20CRITERIA%20AGES%205-21/H.%20OTHER%20HEALTH%20IMPAIRMENT.pdf

TYPES

In general, there are two major groups of students with special health care needs:

1. Those with chronic illness

2. Those with infectious diseases

Table 3.2 describes many of these conditions, some of which are very rarely seen in children. All children have episodes of illness during childhood, but most are brief and not very serious. For a small number of children, however, illnesses are chronic, lasting years or even a lifetime. Children with **chronic illnesses** often do not feel well enough to focus their attention on instruction. They are also absent often, causing them to miss a substantial part of their education.

TABLE 3.2 TYPES OF HEALTH CONDITIONS

Condition	Definition
Asthma[1]	*Asthma* is a chronic disease that affects your airways. Your airways are tubes that carry air in and out of your lungs. If you have asthma, the inside walls of your airways become sore and swollen. Children have smaller airways than adults, which make asthma especially serious for them. Children with asthma may experience wheezing, coughing, chest tightness, and trouble breathing, especially early in the morning or at night.
Cystic fibrosis[2]	*Cystic fibrosis* (CF) is an inherited disease of the mucus and sweat glands. It affects mostly your lungs, pancreas, liver, intestines, sinuses and sex organs. CF causes your mucus to be thick and sticky. The mucus clogs the lungs, causing breathing problems and making it easy for bacteria to grow. This can lead to problems such as repeated lung infections and lung damage. The symptoms and severity of CF vary widely. Some people have serious problems from birth. Others have a milder version of the disease that doesn't show up until they are teens or young adults.
Diabetes[3]	*Diabetes* is a disease in which your blood glucose, or blood sugar, levels are too high. Glucose comes from the foods you eat. Insulin is a hormone that helps the glucose get into your cells to give them energy. With Type 1 diabetes, your body does not make insulin. With Type 2 diabetes, the more common type, your body does not make or use insulin well. Without enough insulin, the glucose stays in your blood. You can also have prediabetes. This means that your blood sugar is higher than normal but not high enough to be called diabetes. Having prediabetes puts you at a higher risk of getting Type 2 diabetes.
Congenital heart[4]	*Congenital heart [condition]* is a problem with the structure of the heart. It is present at birth. Congenital heart [conditions] are the most common type of birth [problems]. The [conditions] can involve the walls of the heart, the valves of the heart, and the arteries and veins near the heart. They can disrupt the normal flow of blood through the heart. The blood flow can slow down, go in the wrong direction or to the wrong place, or be blocked completely.
Tuberculosis (TB)[5]	*Tuberculosis* (TB) is a disease caused by bacteria called Mycobacterium tuberculosis. The bacteria usually attack the lungs, but they can also damage other parts of the body. TB spreads through the air when a person with TB of the lungs or throat coughs, sneezes, or talks. If you have been exposed, you should go to your doctor for tests. You are more likely to get TB if you have a weak immune system.
Childhood cancer[6]	*Cancer* begins in the cells, which are the building blocks of your body. Normally, new cells form as you need them, replacing old cells that die. Sometimes, this process goes wrong. New cells form when you don't need them, and old cells don't die when they should. The extra cells can form a tumor. Benign tumors aren't cancer while malignant ones are. Malignant tumor cells can invade

Condition	Definition
	nearby tissues or break away and spread to other parts of the body. Children can get cancer in the same parts of the body as adults, but there are differences. Childhood cancers can occur suddenly, without early symptoms, and have a high rate of cure.
Blood disorders[7]	Your blood is living tissue made up of liquid and solids. The liquid part, called plasma, is made of water, salts and protein. Over half of your blood is plasma. The solid part of your blood contains red blood cells, white blood cells and platelets. Blood disorders affect one or more parts of the blood and prevent your blood from doing its job. They can be acute or chronic. Many blood disorders are inherited. Other causes include other diseases, side effects of medicines, and a lack of certain nutrients in your diet.
Infectious Diseases	
HIV and AIDS[8]	HIV stands for human immunodeficiency virus. It kills or damages the body's immune system cells. AIDS stands for acquired immunodeficiency syndrome. It is the most advanced stage of infection with HIV. HIV most often spreads through unprotected sex with an infected person. It may also spread by sharing drug needles or through contact with the blood of an infected person. Women can give it to their babies during pregnancy or childbirth. The first signs of HIV infection may be swollen glands and flu-like symptoms. These may come and go a month or two after infection. Severe symptoms may not appear until months or years later. A blood test can tell if you have HIV infection.
STORCH[9]	*STORCH* is an acronym for [a] disease group comprising syphilis, toxoplasmosis, other infections, rubella, cytomegalovirus infection, and herpes simplex; fetal infections that can cause congenital malformations.
Hepatitis B[10]	Your liver is the largest organ inside your body. It helps your body digest food, store energy, and remove poisons. Hepatitis is an inflammation of the liver. One type, *hepatitis B*, is caused by the hepatitis B virus (HBV). Hepatitis B spreads by contact with an infected person's blood, semen, or other body fluid. An infected woman can give hepatitis B to her baby at birth. If you get HBV, you may feel as if you have the flu. You may also have jaundice, a yellowing of skin and eyes, dark-colored urine, and pale bowel movements. Some people have no symptoms at all. A blood test can tell if you have it. HBV usually gets better on its own after a few months. If it does not get better, it is called chronic HBV, which lasts a lifetime.

SOURCES: [1]http://www.nlm.nih.gov/medlineplus/asthmainchildren.html; [2]http://www.nlm.nih.gov/medlineplus/cysticfibrosis.html; [3]http://vsearch.nlm.nih.gov/vivisimo/cgi-bin/query-meta?v%3Aproject=medlineplus&query=diabetes&x=0&y=0; [4]http://www.nlm.nih.gov/medlineplus/congenitalheartdefects.html; [5]http://www.nlm.nih.gov/medlineplus/tuberculosis.html; [6]http://www.nlm.nih.gov/medlineplus/cancerinchildren.html; [7]http://www.nlm.nih.gov/medlineplus/blooddisorders.html; [8]http://www.nlm.nih.gov/medlineplus/hivaids.html; [9]http://medical-dictionary.thefreedictionary.com/STORCH; [10]http://www.nlm.nih.gov/medlineplus/hepatitisb.html

Asthma is the most common chronic disorder of children. This pulmonary disease is the leading cause of school absences among all the chronic diseases (Asthma and Allergy Foundation of America, n.d.). A person with asthma usually has labored breathing that is sometimes accompanied by shortness of breath, wheezing, and a cough. Years ago, many people believed asthma was a psychological disorder. It is not; its origin is physical. Many allergen-related factors, such as classroom pets, chalk dust, dirt in the environment, dust mites, and pollen can trigger an asthma attack, as can nonallergen-related physical activity or exertion. "Triggers" vary for each individual with asthma. Many students who have asthma are unable to participate in sports or even in physical education activities. Few actually need special education, but they do need special accommodations so their illness does not hinder their learning.

Human immunodeficiency virus (HIV) is a potentially fatal viral infection transmitted primarily through exchange of bodily fluids in unprotected sex or by contaminated hypodermic needles. It is the virus responsible for the deadly acquired immunodeficiency syndrome (AIDS) and can be communicated to a child by an infected mother. Before blood-screening procedures were instituted, the virus was also transmitted through blood transfusions. The effects of the infection in children include central nervous system damage, additional infections, developmental delay, motor problems, psychosocial stresses, and death. HIV/AIDS is an infectious disease, but unlike most others, such as flu and the common cold, it is serious and life threatening. The disease is very uncommon in young children, but unfortunately it is more common in teenagers because of dangerous life choices such as drug use and unprotected sex. For many years, parents and educators were concerned that noninfected children could catch the disease from a classmate. It is now clear that this is highly unlikely. With proper precautions (such as using latex gloves when treating a child's scrape and following normal sanitary procedures), everyone at school is safe and will not catch this disease.

CHARACTERISTICS

The health care needs of some children are so consuming, requiring special accommodations and considerations, that everything else becomes secondary. The treatment goals for these youngsters are to stay strong, healthy, and active and to lead a life as normal as possible. Although education is a major part of their childhood, many face barriers to efficient learning, such as the following:

- Fatigue
- Absences
- Inconsistent ability to pay attention
- Muscle weakness
- Loss of physical coordination

Some symptoms are directly related to medications and treatment, and others are a function of the disease, illness, or condition. For example, children who are receiving cancer treatment go through periods of feeling too sick to profit from much of the instructional day, and during this time they may have frequent absences or even some long periods where they do not come to school. Instead they receive a special education option outlined in IDEA '04, **home-bound/ hospital instruction**, in which an itinerant teacher helps them maintain progress in the curriculum by coming to their home or to a hospital (USDE, 2014). Sometimes, technology helps students stay connected with their classmates.

For example, simple video options (e.g., Skype, FaceTime) now readily available through computers allow a student who cannot come to school to join class discussions about a social studies topic or watch a demonstration of a science experiment online. Clearly, opportunities for students with health challenges are much greater today than they were only a few years ago. Possibilities for participating in and accessing the general education curriculum from a distance should be available to all students who face such challenges.

For some students, their health situations require special accommodations and considerations. Their treatment goals are to stay strong, healthy, and active and to lead lives as normal as possible.

PREVALENCE

Between 2002 and 2010, the size of this category increased from 291,850 to 371,617 (Child and Adolescent Health Measurement Initiative, 2011). Why might this be so? As we noted in Chapter 2, the most probable reason is the inclusion of ADHD in the other health impairments federal special education category. ADHD, however, is not the only condition contributing to the increase in this group of students. For example, asthma is the leading cause of school absenteeism and the condition that affects the most schoolchildren. In the United States, about 40 million people have asthma—13.3% are adults and 13.8% are children (National Institute of Environmental Health Sciences [NIEHS], 2012). Most of them do not require special education, but they do need special accommodations and considerations.

Some other health conditions are not increasing because they are better controlled through medication. For example, approximately 1% of the general population has epilepsy, but substantially less than 1% of the school population has the condition; for some 70% of those affected, medication ends the occurrence of seizures (Epilepsy Foundation of America [EFA], 2014). The number of new cases of pediatric AIDS occurring in the United States has dropped over the past 20 years (U.S. Department of Health and Human Services, 2010). Considering Diversity features descriptive information about sickle-cell anemia and prevalence rates, which are highest among African American and Hispanic American individuals.

WHAT ARE THE ATTRIBUTES OF STUDENTS WITH AUTISM SPECTRUM DISORDERS?

Autism has been receiving considerable attention in the media in recent years (e.g., Kohnle, 2014; Park, 2009). The reasons for all this public attention are understandable: The condition is on the rise, the causes remain unknown, and it can be very severe.

Autism Spectrum Disorder

CONSIDERING *diversity*

SICKLE-CELL ANEMIA

One health condition in particular disproportionately affects African Americans: Approximately 1 in 12 has the trait. For Hispanic Americans, approximately 1 in 100 has the trait (National Human Genome Research Institute, 2014). Sickle-cell anemia is a hereditary, life-threatening blood disorder that causes the red blood cells to become rigid and take on a crescent, or sickle, shape. During what is called a "sickling crisis," this rigidity and the crescent shape of the cells do not allow blood to flow through the vessels, depriving some tissues of oxygen and resulting in extreme pain, swollen joints, high fever, and even strokes. Educators need to know that many of these children may be frequently absent from school. To reduce the stress they experience when they return to school knowing they have missed assignments and instruction, teachers should work together and develop strategies with the students and their families to compensate for missed school days. For example, a neighborhood child could serve as a peer tutor who brings assignments home to the student and explains important instructions provided during the school day.

IDEA '04 still refers to the single disorder of autism, but most parents and professionals have adopted a revised conception of this disability. Rather than autism being a single condition, it is thought that five related conditions make up a spectrum of disorders. The umbrella term *autism spectrum disorders* (ASD) is a fairly new way of thinking about similar, but different, conditions or syndromes (see Figure 3.4). The previous conceptual framework used the term *autism* as the name for different conditions or syndromes that share "autistic-like" symptoms and characteristics. However, in today's broader concept, ASD is the larger category and autism is just one disorder within it.

Most experts agree that more children are diagnosed with autism today than in the past. Why might this be so? There is probably no single answer to this question. One reason is better diagnostic procedures. Another explanation is the use of broader and more inclusive definitions of ASD and autism. Despite all the concern about the increased prevalence of ASD, educators should keep in mind that it is a low-incidence disability, affecting 0.6% of the school population (USDE, 2014). Most general education teachers are likely to have little or no opportunity to meet or work with children who have the disorders or conditions included in this spectrum. Let's take a closer look at ASD and how it affects individuals.

DEFINITION

The federal government has not yet acknowledged the five types of ASD in the IDEA law, and IDEA '04 describes only autism. However, thinking

| FIGURE 3.4 | AUTISM SPECTRUM DISORDERS (ASD) UMBRELLA |

 VIDEO CASE 3.2

Supporting Students With Autism

1. Kristen Lanning is a behavior analyst who works with students who have autism. What services does a behavior analyst provide in order to support the academic and behavioral success of these students?

2. What daily living skills does Ms. Lanning teach at home and in the community? How does she support the family in addition to supporting the child with autism?

about autism as part of a spectrum is clearly the trend. The DSM-5 (2013, pp. 50-51) definition of autism spectrum disorders does this and appears in Table 3.3.

TYPES

Until the DSM-5 (APA, 2013) was published in 2013, ASD typically was considered a broad category that groups together five types of specific disorders:

1. Autistic disorder, or autism

2. Childhood disintegrative disorder (CDD)

3. Asperger's syndrome

4. Rett syndrome

5. Pervasive developmental disorder—not otherwise specified (PDD-NOS)

DSM-5 changed the focus from types of ASD to three levels of severity, but many professionals and advocates continue to use terms like Asperger's syndrome and PDD-NOS. Severity levels are based on support needs, which we discuss later in this chapter. Table 3.4 lists and describes the DSM-5 categories of severity for ASD.

TABLE 3.3	DEFINITION OF AUTISM SPECTRUM DISORDERS

Source	Definition
DSM-5	A. Persistent deficits in social communication and social interaction across multiple contexts, as manifested by the following, currently or by history (examples are illustrative, not exhaustive, see text): 1. Deficits in social-emotional reciprocity, ranging, for example, from abnormal social approach and failure of normal back-and-forth conversation; to reduced sharing of interests, emotions, or affect; to failure to initiate or respond to social interactions. 2. Deficits in nonverbal communicative behaviors used for social interaction, ranging, for example, from poorly integrated verbal and nonverbal communication; to abnormalities in eye contact and body language or deficits in understanding and use of gestures; to a total lack of facial expressions and nonverbal communication. 3. Deficits in developing, maintaining, and understanding relationships, ranging, for example, from difficulties adjusting behavior to suit various social contexts; to difficulties in sharing imaginative play or in making friends; to absence of interest in peers. *Specify* current severity: **Severity is based on social communication impairments and restricted repetitive patterns of behavior** (see Table 3.4). B. Restricted, repetitive patterns of behavior, interests, or activities, as manifested by at least two of the following, currently or by history (examples are illustrative, not exhaustive; see text): 1. Stereotyped or repetitive motor movements, use of objects, or speech (e.g., simple motor stereotypes, lining up toys or flipping objects, echolalia, idiosyncratic phrases). 2. Insistence on sameness, inflexible adherence to routines, or ritualized patterns of verbal or nonverbal behavior (e.g., extreme distress at small changes, difficulties with transitions, rigid thinking patterns, greeting rituals, need to take same route or eat food every day). 3. Highly restricted, fixated interests that are abnormal in intensity or focus (e.g., strong attachment to or preoccupation with unusual objects, excessively circumscribed or perseverative interest). 4. Hyper- or hyporeactivity to sensory input or unusual interests in sensory aspects of the environment (e.g., apparent indifference to pain/temperature, adverse response to specific sounds or textures, excessive smelling or touching of objects, visual fascination with lights or movement). *Specify* current severity: **Severity is based on social communication impairments and restricted, repetitive patterns of behavior**. C. Symptoms must be present in the early developmental period (but may not become fully manifest until social demands exceed limited capacities, or may be masked by learned strategies in later life). D. Symptoms cause clinically significant impairment in social, occupational, or other important areas of current functioning. E. These disturbances are not better explained by intellectual disability (intellectual developmental disorder) or global developmental delay. Intellectual disability and autism spectrum disorder frequently co-occur; to make comorbid diagnoses of autism spectrum disorder and intellectual disability, social communication should be below that expected for general developmental level. **Note:** Individuals with a well-established DSM-IV diagnosis of autistic disorder, Asperger's disorder, or pervasive developmental disorder not otherwise specified should be given the diagnosis of autism spectrum disorder. Individuals who have marked deficits in social communication, but whose symptoms do not otherwise meet criteria for autism spectrum disorder, should be evaluated for social (pragmatic) communication disorder.

SOURCE: Reprinted from *Diagnostic and Statistical Manual of Mental Disorders,* Fifth Edition (Copyright 2013), (pp. 50–51). American Psychiatric Association (APA).

TABLE 3.4 ASD SEVERITY LEVELS

Severity Level	Social Communication	Restricted, Repetitive Behaviors
Level 3 "Requiring very substantial support"	Severe deficits in verbal and nonverbal social communication skills cause severe impairments in functioning, very limited initiation of social interactions, and minimal response to social overtures from others. For example, a person with few words of intelligible speech who rarely initiates interaction and, when he or she does, makes unusual approaches to meet needs only and responds to only very direct social approaches.	Inflexibility of behavior, extreme difficulty coping with change, or other restricted/repetitive behaviors markedly interfere with functioning in all spheres. Great distress/difficulty changing focus or action.
Level 2 "Requiring substantial support"	Marked deficits in verbal and nonverbal social communication skills; social impairments apparent even with supports in place; limited initiation of social interactions; and reduced or abnormal responses to social overtures from others. For example, a person who speaks simple sentences, whose interaction is limited to narrow special interests, and who has markedly odd nonverbal communication.	Inflexibility of behavior, difficulty coping with change, or other restricted/repetitive behaviors appear frequently enough to be obvious to the casual observer and interfere with functioning in a variety of contexts. Distress and/or difficulty changing focus or action.
Level 1 "Requiring support"	Without supports in place, deficits in social communication cause noticeable impairments. Difficulty initiating social interactions, and clear examples of atypical or unsuccessful response to social overtures of others. May appear to have decreased interest in social interactions. For example, a person who is able to speak in full sentences and engages in communication but whose to-and-fro conversation with others fails, and whose attempts to make friends are odd and typically unsuccessful.	Inflexibility of behavior causes significant interference with functioning in one or more contexts. Difficulty switching between activities. Problems of organization and planning hamper independence.

SOURCE: Reprinted from *Diagnostic and Statistical Manual of Mental Disorders,* Fifth Edition (Copyright 2013), (p. 52). American Psychiatric Association (APA).

CHARACTERISTICS

According to the National Institute of Mental Health (NIMH, 2014), all children with ASD demonstrate the following:

- Persistent deficits in social communication and social interaction across multiple contexts;
- Restricted, repetitive patterns of behavior, interests, or activities.

Further, NIMH specifies the following:

- Symptoms must be present in the early developmental period (typically recognized in the first two years of life); and,
- Symptoms must cause clinically significant impairment in social, occupational, or other important areas of current functioning.

  Source: http://www.nimh.nih.gov/health/topics/autism-spectrum-disorders-asd/index.shtml

Experts with NIMH report that most of these youngsters exhibit social challenges, including problems with social communication and repetitive and stereotypic behaviors. Social difficulties include making little eye contact, looking at and listening to people in their environment less than most children or failing to respond to others, refusing to share their toys or activities with other children, and responding differently when others are angry, distressed, or affectionate. With regard to communication skills, children with ASD

- Fail or are slow to respond to their name or other verbal attempts to gain their attention.

- Fail or are slow to develop gestures, such as pointing and showing things to others.

- Coo and babble in the first year of life but then stop doing so.

- Develop language at a delayed pace.

- Learn to communicate using pictures or their own sign language.

- Speak only in single words or repeat certain phrases over and over, seeming unable to combine words into meaningful sentences.

- Repeat words or phrases they hear, a condition called **echolalia**.

- Use words that seem odd, out of place, or have a special meaning known only to those familiar with the child's way of communicating.

  Source: http://www.nimh.nih.gov/health/topics/autism-spectrum-disorders-asd/index.shtml

All children with autism spectrum disorders have impairments in communication, impairments in social skills, and restrictied and repetitive behavioral patterns or range of interests. The skills of children diagnosed with autism spectrum disorders vary greatly.

The skills of children diagnosed with ASD vary greatly. Those who have problems with social interactions often appear to live in their own world and may not seek out the company of peers or adults. Many are said to use people as tools. For example, a child may lead an adult by the hand to the refrigerator and push the adult's hand toward the juice the child wants. In this way, the child with ASD is using the adult as a means to an end (Heward, 2010). Children with autism do not generally initiate social situations and do not engage in social turn-taking just for the pleasure of being part of a social interaction.

Individuals with ASD who have repetitive or odd patterns of behavior, stereotyped behaviors, unusual interests, or strange responses to the environment exhibit a variety of symptoms. For example, they may be attracted to specific aspects of a toy, tirelessly spinning the wheel of a toy car or wiggling the string of a pull toy. Many have rigid patterns of behavior. For example, one child might line up his or her toys in a specific way and insist on following the same routine every day. If these patterns of behavior are violated, a tantrum might result to protest the disruption.

We mentioned earlier that all students now face higher academic expectations, and all but 1% will be expected to pass a high-stakes test to demonstrate they are performing to grade-level expectations. Many high-functioning students with ASD, such as those previously labeled as having Asperger's syndrome, can meet these expectations as they work in inclusive settings. Lower-function students with ASD may be among the 1% who qualify for an alternate assessment, but many may not. Regardless of the severity of the ASD, collaborative partnerships between general and special educators can help students meet their IEP goals.

PREVALENCE

Many different prevalence rates for autism and for ASD are cited. For example, the Centers for Disease Control and Prevention (CDC, 2014) estimates the rate of occurrence of ASD as 1 individual in 68, or about 1.5%. Also, the federal Office of Special Education Programs (OSEP, 2006) reported that 455,349 schoolchildren between the ages of 6 and 17 received special education services in 2013 because of ASD—up from 181,758 in 2005 (USDE, 2014). This alarming growth is of great concern to parents, policymakers, and professionals, and it is also confusing. Has there truly been a dramatic increase in ASD? Or does the increase reflect a more inclusive definition? The answers to these questions are elusive. Here's what we do know today. In 2003, the CDC found that the rate of autism was greater than it was during the 1980s and early 1990s; in 2014, the CDC reported an even greater rise in the prevalence rate. But ASD remains a low-incidence disability (National Center for Education Statistics, 2013).

WHAT ARE THE ATTRIBUTES OF STUDENTS WITH MULTIPLE-SEVERE DISABILITIES?

Students with multiple-severe disabilities make up the largest group of those with low-incidence disabilities. Why? Many states assign nearly all children and youths who have more than one disability to this special education category. The combination of disabilities present need not be specified. Thus some students have poor vision and also cognitive disabilities, and others may have a severe hearing loss and substantial mobility issues. Possessing more than one major disability presents unique challenges to the individual and the family. For example, deaf children who also have another disability need teachers who are specialists in more than one area and who also understand the special problems resulting from a unique combination of disabilities.

Teachers need to avoid the temptation to describe these students in terms of deficits, rather than in terms of what they can do through a variety of supports across many of life's dimensions. The emphasis for students with multiple-severe disabilities is on developing skills that promote independence and community presence (Snell & Brown, 2010). Ironically, in some cases, that means teaching individuals how to depend on others to gain the supports they require to achieve maximal independence.

The current outlook for individuals with multiple-severe disabilities is very different from what it was only a few decades ago. Not long ago, adults with severe disabilities spent their lives in large residential institutions with no access to the community and no chance to participate in mainstream society. Today, they have more opportunities than ever before. Many live in **group homes,** community-based living arrangements with a small number of adults, or in apartments, and they hold jobs in the community. Their educational opportunities have also increased. Before IDEA was passed in 1975, many were excluded from school and had no opportunity to benefit from a special education complete with the related services they needed. For those who did find access to education, it was often in segregated settings. And it was not until the 1960s and 1970s that researchers began to turn their attention to developing and validating instructional procedures and services that are especially effective for these learners. In addition to access to the general education curriculum, their education now includes the following:

- Expressions of choice
- Self-determination
- Functional skills training
- Social skills training
- Community-based instruction
- Supports and planning for the transition to adult life

These individuals' inclusion in school and in the community is relatively recent. Knowledge about best practices and services is still being developed, so the outcomes for the next generations of these students will be even greater.

DEFINITION

The definition of multiple-severe disabilities is included in Table 3.5. Combinations of disabilities and conditions lead to unique special needs. For example, an individual with a cognitive disability might need supports to pay bills and manage a budget. If that individual also has a moderate hearing loss, she or he might need an assistant to facilitate communication at the doctor's office but might function at work with only natural supports from coworkers. Let's consider further how different conditions can occur together.

TABLE 3.5	DEFINITION OF MULTIPLE-SEVERE DISABILITIES
Source	**Definition**
U.S. Department of Education (IDEA), 2004	*Multiple disabilities* means concomitant impairments (such as mental retardation-blindness or mental retardation-orthopedic impairment), the combination of which causes such severe educational needs that they cannot be accommodated in special education programs solely for one of the impairments. Multiple disabilities does not include deaf-blindness.

TYPES

Each individual with multiple-severe disabilities is unique. The possible combinations of conditions are numerous, and the ways in which the symptoms associated with these conditions can manifest themselves make it impossible to group these students by type. So instead, let's spend a little time thinking about common characteristics they present to themselves, their families, and their teachers.

CHARACTERISTICS

Individuals with multiple-severe disabilities display a wide range of skills and abilities, as well as a wide range of problem areas in need of intensive instruction. According to the National Dissemination Center for Children with Disabilities (NICHCY, 2012), this group of individuals shares some common characteristics:

- Limited speech or communication
- Difficulty in basic physical mobility
- Tendency to forget skills through disuse
- Trouble generalizing skills from one situation to another
- A need for support in major life activities (e.g., domestic, leisure, community use, vocational)

Many individuals with multiple-severe disabilities also face other challenges, including medical problems such as seizure disorders, vision or hearing problems, heart disease, and cerebral palsy. Consequently, they and their families deal with many professionals and disciplines, all with different styles of interaction, terms and jargon, and approaches. Such multiple interactions can complicate an already difficult situation.

One common characteristic of severe disabilities is the response to the challenges to gain independence and participation in the community. Typically, in order for someone to accomplish these goals, intensive and pervasive supports from a wide range of individuals and systems must be in place. Technology is one of those supports (Bryant & Bryant, 2011). Technology can also help people with disabilities and their families address and compensate for their disabilities (Bryant,

Technology has opened up avenues of communication for many students who are unable to communicate with others through oral speech. What forms of alternative and augmentative communication are available for students with disabilities?

Seok, Ok, & Bryant, 2012). The federal government continues to make a considerable investment in technology, because it is clear it has improved outcomes for students with disabilities (Bryant & Bryant, 2011). The data on which the government bases these conclusions indicate that technology helps these individuals

- Communicate more effectively.
- Increase their levels of independence.
- Control their environments.
- Have greater mobility.
- Gain access to information.

Technology has opened up avenues of communication for many students who are unable to communicate with others through oral speech (Bryant & Bryant, 2011). Let's look at one example. **Augmentative and alternative communication devices (AAC)**, which include software and hardware devices for communicating, can be very beneficial to individuals with low-incidence disabilities (Fisher & Shogren, 2012). Whether in the form of simple devices, such as communication boards, or complicated speech synthesizers (see http://www.tobiidynavox.com/ for an example of different AAC devices) that actually speak for the individual, technology now allows individuals to make their needs known, express their feelings, and interact with others (Bryant & Bryant, 2011). In the most straightforward systems, words and/or pictures are placed on a flat surface or in books. The student communicates by pointing to the appropriate symbols. Symbols are customized to the individual; the words or symbols on the board reflect the individual and salient features of the environments in which he or she operates. Some boards are simple homemade projects; others use quite sophisticated technology. Your job as a teacher is to encourage the use of these techniques and help shape them into a reliable system of communication for the student. When your students have these communication tools, learning and social interaction can take place.

PREVALENCE

Relatively few U.S. students—only 0.23%—are included in the federal special education category of multiple disabilities, representing some 132,986 students ages 6 to 17 (USDE, 2014). Some states do not include in this category students who have learning disabilities and also a hearing problem; other states do. Some states include in the intellectual and developmental disabilities category students with a mild visual disability who also have substantial cognitive disabilities; other states report these students to the federal government as having multiple disabilities. Regardless, all students with severe problems are served by special education, and the overall goal for their education usually focuses on achieving independent living in the community.

WHAT ARE THE ATTRIBUTES OF STUDENTS WITH DEVELOPMENTAL DELAY?

A child who is not speaking by the age of 3 is likely to have a problem that could be a significant disability. But which disability? It could be an intellectual and developmental disability, ASD, a learning disability, or a speech or language impairment. Rather than forcing a diagnosis that might be incorrect, IDEA '04 allows preschoolers ages 3 to 5 and children up to age 9 who show a general delay in development to receive special education services under the nonspecific category **developmental delay**, created in 1991. Creating this label was actually the federal government's first move toward supporting a noncategorical approach to special education. It means that, unlike their counterparts without disabilities, some youngsters are entitled to a free appropriate education during the preschool and early elementary years without being identified with a specific disability. The main purpose of this special education category is to reduce the chances of misidentifying children as having one disability when in fact they have another.

DEFINITION

So as not to mislabel, or incorrectly identify, children with disabilities between the ages of 3 and 9, IDEA '04 allows states to provide special services to those who exhibit general developmental delays without also identifying them as having a specific disability. The IDEA '04 definition of this noncategorical identification, developmental delay, is found in Table 3.6. Approximately 2.2% of students ages 6 through 21 have developmental delays (USDE, 2014).

TYPES

Preschoolers with developmental delays have a wide range of disabilities, only some of which can be specifically classified during their early years. Many states therefore use the developmental delay option for qualifying these children for special education services between the ages of 3 and 5, but some states may choose to identify children as being "at risk" for developmental delays when they are infants or toddlers (National Infant & Toddler Child Care Initiative, 2010), and some states include children younger than 3 and older than 5 years. For example, while preschoolers with severe visual disabilities can be readily identified, children with general delays in language and motor skills may receive services but not be assigned a categorical identification (such as intellectual and developmental disabilities).

TABLE 3.6	DEFINITION OF DEVELOPMENTAL DELAY
Source	**Definition**
Commonwealth of Virginia Policies and Procedures for Part C of IDEA	1. Children who are functioning at least 25% below their chronological or adjusted age, in one or more of the following areas: a. *cognitive development*; b. *physical development (including* fine motor, gross motor, vision, and hearing*)*; c. *communication development*; d. *social or emotional development*; e.g., *adaptive development*. OR – 2. Children who manifest atypical development or behavior, which is demonstrated by one or more of the following criteria (even when evaluation does not document a 25% developmental delay): a. Abnormal or questionable sensory-motor responses, such as: (1) abnormal muscle tone; (2) limitations in joint range of motion; (3) abnormal reflex or postural reactions; (4) poor quality of movement patterns or quality of skill performance; (5) oral-motor skills dysfunction, including feeding difficulties b. Identified affective disorders, such as: (1) delay or abnormality in achieving expected emotional milestones; (2) persistent failure to initiate or respond to most social interactions; (3) fearfulness or other distress that does not respond to comforting by caregivers; 3. Behavioral disorders that interfere with the acquisition of developmental skills.

SOURCE: Infant & Toddler Connection of Virginia, http://www.infantva.org/documents/ovw-pguidestatedefinition.pdf

CHARACTERISTICS

The main characteristic of youngsters with developmental delays is that they have general delays in their development. Professionals use this designation for two main reasons: (1) They are hesitant to assign a potentially incorrect disability label to the child, or (2) they believe the child may just be developing slowly and will later catch up to peers on critical developmental markers (such as speech, motor skills, and social skills). Although the federal government allows noncategorical identification of students up to the age of 9, as children get older, the percentage in this category decreases dramatically (U.S. Department of Education, 2014).

PREVALENCE

The special education label *developmental delay* is most often applied to children between the ages of 3 and 5. Of the 730,558 students ages 3 to 5 served by IDEA, Part B, 37% (over 270,000) were identified as having developmental delays (USDE, 2014). At a young age, data may be insufficient to make an eligibility determination associated with a different disability (Virginia Department of Education, 2010).

WHAT ARE THE ATTRIBUTES OF STUDENTS WITH PHYSICAL DISABILITIES?

Many adults with physical disabilities received a very different education than today's students who face physical challenges. Typically, they were not allowed to join their brothers, sisters, and friends at their neighborhood school. They were bused to special schools equipped with state-of-the-art equipment like therapy pools and staffed with related services professionals such as physical and occupational therapists. But these facilities were segregated, and only students with disabilities attended. When these individuals grew up, many became disability advocates. They have fought hard to enlarge the educational options available to students with disabilities, and specifically, they have sought the closure of separate, center schools for schoolchildren with physical disabilities. The result of their efforts is that students with physical disabilities attend school alongside typical learners in inclusive school settings. Many receive therapy from related services professionals. For some, their only teachers are general educators who provide accommodations guided by special education professionals.

WORKING *together*

PROMOTING ACCESSIBILITY

Earlier you met Mr. Dehiya, a high school teacher whose students helped restructure his classroom to make it accessible for one of his students who had been injured in a car accident and who now used a wheelchair to move about. Mr. Dehiya chose to go online and gain information about how to make his classroom accessible and also to communicate with and help make Abooksigun as comfortable as possible in the classroom. What we failed to mention earlier was that, after reading the information he found online and making a "to-do" list, Mr. Dehiya contacted a friend of his, Ms. Tsabetsaya, a trained and licensed occupational therapist. Ms. Tsabetsaya often acted as a consultant for the district, usually in the form of serving on assistive technology (AT) team meetings to help with AT assessments designed to create a student-technology match that would allow students to access the general education curriculum. But Ms. Tsabetsaya was also trained in helping business associates develop accessible workplaces or help clients who had sustained injuries access daily living activities. She was very familiar with the needs of wheelchair users and had developed a keen eye for identifying what might or might not be the effective and efficient change in a room to allow for maximum accessibility. This was especially useful in Mr. Dehiya's classroom, where students engaged in small group activities. The two met for about two hours, going over Mr. Dehiya's list and going through the classroom and discussing the feasibility of his suggestions. Although Ms. Tsabetsaya found that the list contained many excellent suggestions, she offered a few more; Mr. Dehiya shook his head a few times, wondering how he had not thought of "that." There are many professionals employed by a school district, some as full-time staff (speech-language pathologists, physical therapists, for example) or some as consultants. Rural school districts in particular often hire itinerant specialists to travel from school to school, serving the needs of perhaps only one or two students in a school with a small student population, but needed as full-time employees to meet the needs of all students attending schools across a wide geographical area. In this case, Mr. Dehiya and Ms. Tsabetsaya were friends, so he was able to contact her directly. At other times, teachers may have to meet with someone from the district to set up a meeting with a specialist.

QUESTIONS

1. You have a student in your classroom who has missed several days because of asthma. Who might you meet with to identify challenges posed by lengthy absences and identify solutions to those challenges?

2. As a class, brainstorm a list of professionals (areas, not necessarily individuals) who may have helpful information concerning the numerous low-incidence areas discussed in this chapter. For low-incidence categories where none are found, divide the list among small groups and go online to find answers. What term(s) might you insert into a search engine to find these professionals?

DEFINITION

IDEA '04 uses the term **orthopedic impairments** to refer to conditions that we call physical disabilities and others call physical impairments. The definition used in the law is found in Table 3.7. Individuals with these conditions have problems with the structure or the functioning of their bodies. For such a student to be eligible for special education services, the physical disability must adversely affect educational performance.

TABLE 3.7	DEFINITION OF PHYSICAL DISABILITIES
Source	**Definition**
Arkansas Department of Education, Special Education Unit	"Orthopedic impairment" means a severe orthopedic impairment that adversely affects a child's educational performance. The term includes impairments caused by congenital anomaly (e.g., clubfoot, absence of some member, etc.), impairments caused by disease (e.g., poliomyelitis, bone tuberculosis, etc.), and impairments from other causes (e.g., cerebral palsy, amputations, and fractures or burns which cause contractures).

SOURCE: Arkansas Department of Education Special Education Unit. © 2014 The State of Arkansas.

TYPES

The two major groups of physical disabilities follow:

1. Neuromotor impairments

2. Muscular/skeletal conditions

Many conditions included in each group are listed in Figure 3.5 and described in Table 3.8. When the central nervous system, consisting of the brain and the spinal cord, is damaged, the result is a neuromotor impairment that limits muscular control and movement. Cerebral palsy (CP) and seizure disorders (such as epilepsy) are examples of neuromotor impairments, as are muscular dystrophy, polio, and spina bifida. Individuals with muscular/skeletal conditions usually have difficulty controlling their movements, but the cause is not neurological. Juvenile arthritis and limb deficiencies are examples of muscular/skeletal conditions. Regardless of the type of physical disability, some individuals need special devices and technology even to do simple tasks—walking, eating, or writing—that most of us take for granted. Let's think about each of these types of physical disabilities in turn.

Two specific neuromotor impairments teachers should know about because they are more prevalent than other conditions are cerebral palsy and seizure disorders or epilepsy. Epilepsy is the most common neuromotor impairment encountered at school. A person with epilepsy often has recurrent seizures

FIGURE 3.5   AN ORGANIZATIONAL SCHEME FOR PHYSICAL IMPAIRMENTS

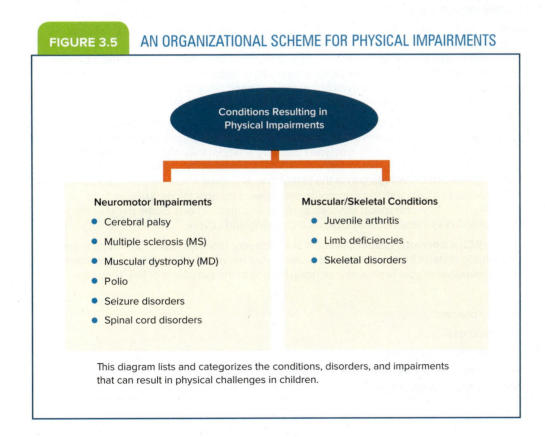

Conditions Resulting in Physical Impairments

Neuromotor Impairments
- Cerebral palsy
- Multiple sclerosis (MS)
- Muscular dystrophy (MD)
- Polio
- Seizure disorders
- Spinal cord disorders

Muscular/Skeletal Conditions
- Juvenile arthritis
- Limb deficiencies
- Skeletal disorders

This diagram lists and categorizes the conditions, disorders, and impairments that can result in physical challenges in children.

TABLE 3.8	TYPES OF PHYSICAL CONDITIONS
Condition	**Definition**
Neuromotor Impairments	
Epilepsy/ Seizure disorders[1]	Seizures are symptoms of a brain problem. They happen because of sudden, abnormal electrical activity in the brain. When people think of seizures, they often think of convulsions in which a person's body shakes rapidly and uncontrollably. Not all seizures cause convulsions. There are many types of seizures and some have mild symptoms. Seizures fall into two main groups. Focal seizures, also called partial seizures, happen in just one part of the brain. Generalized seizures are a result of abnormal activity on both sides of the brain.
Cerebral palsy (CP)[2]	Cerebral palsy is a group of disorders that affect a person's ability to move and to maintain balance and posture. The disorders appear in the first few years of life. Usually they do not get worse over time. People with cerebral palsy may have difficulty walking. They may also have trouble with tasks such as writing or using scissors. Some have other medical conditions, including seizure disorders or mental impairment.
Spinal cord disorders[3]	Your spinal cord is a bundle of nerves that runs down the middle of your back. It carries signals back and forth between your body and your brain. It is protected by your vertebrae, which are the bone disks that make up your spine. If you have an accident that damages the vertebrae or other parts of the spine, this can also injure the spinal cord. Other spinal cord problems include • Tumors • Infections such as meningitis and polio • Inflammatory diseases • Autoimmune diseases • Degenerative diseases such as amyotrophic lateral sclerosis and spinal muscular dystrophy Symptoms vary but might include pain, numbness, loss of sensation and muscle weakness. These symptoms can occur around the spinal cord, and also in other areas such as your arms and legs. Treatments often include medicines and surgery.
Polio[4]	Polio is an infectious disease caused by a virus. The virus lives in an infected person's throat and intestines. It is most often spread by contact with the stool of an infected person. You can also get it from droplets if an infected person sneezes or coughs. It can contaminate food and water if people do not wash their hands. Most people have no symptoms. If you have symptoms, they may include fever, fatigue, nausea, headache, flu-like symptoms, stiff neck and back, and pain in the limbs. A few people will become paralyzed. There is no treatment to reverse the paralysis of polio.
Muscular dystrophy (MD)[5]	Muscular dystrophy (MD) is a group of more than 30 inherited diseases. They all cause muscle weakness and muscle loss. Some forms of MD appear in infancy or childhood. Others may not appear until middle age or later. The different types can vary in whom they affect, which muscles they affect, and what the symptoms are. All forms of MD grow worse as the person's muscles get weaker. Most people with MD eventually lose the ability to walk. There is no cure for muscular dystrophy. Treatments can help with the symptoms and prevent complications. They include physical and speech therapy, orthopedic devices, surgery, and medications. Some people with MD have mild cases that worsen slowly. Other cases are disabling and severe.
Multiple sclerosis (MS)[6]	Multiple sclerosis (MS) is a nervous system disease that affects your brain and spinal cord. It damages the myelin sheath, the material that surrounds and protects your nerve cells. This damage slows down or blocks messages between your brain and your body, leading to the symptoms of MS. They can include • Visual disturbances • Muscle weakness • Trouble with coordination and balance • Sensations such as numbness, prickling, or "pins and needles" • Thinking and memory problems

Condition	Definition
	No one knows what causes MS. It may be an autoimmune disease, which happens when your immune system attacks healthy cells in your body by mistake. Multiple sclerosis affects women more than men. It often begins between the ages of 20 and 40. Usually, the disease is mild, but some people lose the ability to write, speak, or walk.
Muscular/Skeletal Conditions	
Juvenile rheumatoid arthritis[7]	Juvenile rheumatoid arthritis (JRA) is a type of arthritis that happens in children age 16 or younger. It causes joint swelling, pain, stiffness, and loss of motion. It can affect any joint, and in some cases it can affect internal organs as well. One early sign of JRA may be limping in the morning. Symptoms can come and go. Some children have just one or two flare-ups. Others have symptoms that never go away. JRA causes growth problems in some children. No one knows exactly what causes JRA. Scientists do know it is an autoimmune disorder, which means your immune system, which normally helps your body fight infection, attacks your body's own tissues.
Limb loss[8]	People can lose all or part of an arm or leg for a number of reasons. Common ones include • Problems with blood circulation. These may be the result of atherosclerosis or diabetes. Severe cases may result in amputation. • Injuries, including from traffic accidents and military combat • Cancer • Birth defects Some amputees have phantom pain, which is the feeling of pain in the missing limb. Other physical problems include surgical complications and skin problems, if you wear an artificial limb. Many amputees use an artificial limb. Learning how to use it takes time. Physical therapy can help you adapt.

SOURCES: [1]http://www.nlm.nih.gov/medlineplus/seizures.html; [2]http://www.nlm.nih.gov/medlineplus/cerebralpalsy.html; [3]http://www.nlm.nih.gov/medlineplus/spinalcorddiseases.html; [4]http://www.nlm.nih.gov/medlineplus/polioandpostpoliosyndrome.html; [5]http://www.nlm.nih.gov/medlineplus/musculardystrophy.html; [6]http://www.nlm.nih.gov/medlineplus/multiplesclerosis.html; [7]http://www.nlm.nih.gov/medlineplus/juvenilerheumatoidarthritis.html; [8]http://www.nlm.nih.gov/medlineplus/limbloss.html

resulting from the sudden, excessive, spontaneous, and abnormal discharge of neurons in the brain. The result can be loss of consciousness or changes in the person's motor or sensory functioning. The frequency of seizures may vary from a single isolated incident to hundreds in a day. Some children actually anticipate their seizures because they experience a **preictal stage**, or an **aura**, and have heightened sensory signals of an impending seizure, such as a peculiar smell, taste, vision, sound, or action. Others might experience a change in their behavior. Knowing about an aura pattern is helpful, because it allows an individual to assume a safe position or warn teachers and classmates before a seizure begins.

Cerebral palsy is a result of damage either before (prenatally), during (perinatally), or immediately after (postnatally) the child's birth, usually because of insufficient oxygen flow to the brain (Stern Law Group, 2015). The condition can also be acquired during the first three years of life. In these cases, it is usually caused by brain damage resulting from accidents, brain infections, or child abuse. Cerebral palsy is not a disease but rather a nonprogressive and noninfectious condition that results in severe motor impairments. Regrettably, once it has been acquired, it cannot be cured (at least as of today).

One of the most common muscular/skeletal conditions seen in children, **limb loss,** results from a missing arm or leg. Regardless of whether the impairment occurred before or after birth, it is a major impediment to normal physical activity and functioning. Emerging technology, particularly **robotics** or the use of robots, now provides much assistance to those with missing limbs. Artificial limbs make possible movements that only a few years ago were thought to be impossible.

A relatively common muscular/skeletal condition affecting joints and the function of muscles is juvenile rheumatoid arthritis. Although there are many different forms of this disease, it is typically chronic and painful. Juvenile arthritis usually develops in early childhood and can cause many absences from school. Children often need help keeping up with their classmates because they miss so much class instruction. Teachers must understand that their ability to move may be inconsistent (better or worse at different times of the day) and that sitting for extended periods of time can cause them to become stiff and experience considerable pain. These children need to be allowed to move around a lot. Those who have a high rate of absences probably need tutoring and extra help to keep up with their peers.

CHARACTERISTICS

Physical disabilities range from mild to severe and in many cases are only one of multiple conditions an individual must face. However, remember that physical disability and cognitive disability do *not* go hand in hand. Let's consider the characteristics of a few physical disabilities.

Some seizures are characterized by short lapses in consciousness, and it may be difficult to recognize that a student is experiencing anything out of the ordinary. Because some types of seizures are not dramatic, a teacher might wrongly assume that the child is merely daydreaming or not paying attention. In other types of seizures, the child may think the environment has become distorted and strange and that inexplicable events and feelings have occurred. Teachers might incorrectly believe the child is acting out, clowning around, or exhibiting bizarre behavior patterns. Of course, the most serious type of seizure, the one most of us think of first, is characterized by convulsions and loss of consciousness. The behaviors associated with these seizures may at first be frightening to the teacher and to other students in the class, but knowing what to expect and what to do in the event of a seizure reduces the stress (and the danger to the individual student). The school nurse, the student's parents, or the special education teacher can be a great resource when planning for the special needs of such students.

Individuals with cerebral palsy whose motor functioning is affected show the following characteristics alone or in combination: jerky movements, spasms, involuntary movements, and lack of muscle tone (refer back to Chapter 1 and reread the story about Paul who has cerebral palsy to give you a "human" perspective of this condition). Many have impaired mobility and poor muscle development. They may also need braces to help support the affected limbs and make them more functional or to prevent more problems and limitations on mobility. Proper positioning of the body also must be considered. Many children need wedges, pillows, and individually designed chairs and work tables so they can be comfortable, breathe more easily, avoid more problems, and participate in group activities. Although some degree of intellectual and developmental disabilities is present in about half these children, others are intellectually gifted. It is a tragic mistake to assume that cerebral palsy and intellectual and developmental disabilities always occur together.

The challenges facing students with physical limitations and their teachers are great. All schools must meet the special architectural codes required by the ADA law and must be barrier-free. Regardless, these students' worlds are often filled with physical barriers that must be overcome before they can achieve independence and a "normal" life. Surprisingly, students who use wheelchairs still face physical barriers at some schools. For example, classes are scheduled on the second floor although no elevator is available, bathrooms are not accessible, or passageways are too narrow to pass through (U.S. Department of State, Bureau of International Information Programs, 2013). These facts may explain why many individuals with a limb deficiency have difficulties adjusting to their situation. Eliminating barriers, even obvious physical ones, can be more difficult than you might think. Often, it is the student's teacher who must advocate for improvements to the bathroom, the lunchroom, the playground, the gymnasium, the music room, the library, and the bus. Remember, too, that barriers are not only physical, and integration may necessitate accommodations beyond the curb cuts, ramps, elevators, and bathroom alterations required by law. Most children will respond warmly and proudly to your subtle reminders that everyone enjoys being included in all aspects of school.

PREVALENCE

According to the USDE (2014), some 61,716 students, or about 0.12% of all schoolchildren, have physical disabilities requiring special education or related services. Let's look at the prevalence rates of a few specific conditions. About 1% of the general population has epilepsy, but substantially less than 1% of the school population has the condition, and from 70% to 80% of all cases are controlled by medication or surgical techniques (American Association of Neurological Surgeons, 2012). About 0.03% of

Some students with disabilities need to use special devices and technology to do basic physical tasks such as walking, playing, eating, or writing.

all children have cerebral palsy, and some do not require any special education services (cerebralpalsy.org, 2014). The prevalence of many diseases and conditions that seriously affect children continues to change across time. For example, some, like polio, are almost eradicated in the United States. Other conditions, like cerebral palsy, have remained stable for more than 40 years.

WHAT ARE THE ATTRIBUTES OF STUDENTS WHO ARE DEAF AND HARD OF HEARING?

The words *deaf* and *Deaf* both refer to individuals with severe and profound hearing losses, but they have very different implications. Possibly more than any other group of people with disabilities, Deaf individuals unite as a community. Their separate language and culture bind them together, and they feel much as people who live in different countries feel about each other and about those who do not share the same language, history, literature, and art (Hands and Voices, 2014). This group often interprets inclusion differently from those with other disabilities, believing it is undesirable and restrictive. They are also at the forefront of remarkable technological advances that will change many of their lives. However, not all people who cannot hear consider themselves Deaf and members of the Deaf community. The best indicator of how people think about themselves in this regard is whether they capitalize the "D" in *deaf*.

Perspectives on deafness differ. Some people with average hearing consider deafness a disability, a sad condition that isolates those affected from family and society. To many Deaf people, however, deafness is one aspect binding them together as a minority group rich in culture, history, and language (Hands and Voices, 2014). The language of the Deaf community is American Sign Language (ASL), a language that uses signs, has all the elements of other languages (grammar, syntax, idioms), and is not parallel to English in either structure or word order. ASL is not a mere translation of oral speech or the English language (as is signed English); it is a fully developed language. In fact, many states allow ASL as an option to meet the high school foreign language requirement, and the same is true at many colleges and universities. As the language of the Deaf community, ASL is used in all aspects of Deaf culture. For example, plays are written in ASL and performed by deaf theater groups around the world, and a base of folk literature has developed over the years. This community unites in many ways by coming together socially and by advocating against discrimination and for justice.

DEFINITION

There are two types of hearing problems that result in disabilities; these are identified in Table 3.9. Deaf students have a hearing loss so severe that, with or without help from a hearing aid or an assistive hearing device, it seriously affects

Students With Hearing Impairments

their ability to process spoken or auditory information by hearing. Clearly, these students' educational performance, their interactions with others, and their participation in the community are influenced by their hearing problems.

Students with hearing problems that are less severe—those whose hearing falls into the range considered hard of hearing—are also eligible for special education services. Most states do not specify a specific level of hearing loss that serves as a guideline for which students qualify for special education and which do not. Such states simply indicate that a student's hearing problems (whether permanent or fluctuating) must adversely affect educational performance. Experts vary in their definitions of hearing loss and in the point at which they believe it has educational significance. Although 18 states provide a cutoff score, usually including at least a 20-decibel loss in the speech range in the better ear, even a precise score on an **audiogram** cannot guide educators in assessing the significance of a hearing loss because individuals respond differently. Whether a student qualifies in the "deaf" or in the "hard of hearing" group, teachers should remember that all hearing losses are serious. Of course, at some point, the level of severity substantially influences the way in which students need to be taught and the degree to which they understand oral communication.

TABLE 3.9 DEFINITION OF HARD OF HEARING OR DEAFNESS

Source	Definition
U.S. National Library of Medicine	It's frustrating to be unable to hear well enough to enjoy talking with friends or family. Hearing disorders make it hard, but not impossible, to hear. They can often be helped. Deafness can keep you from hearing sound at all. What causes hearing loss? Some possibilities are • Heredity • Diseases such as ear infections and meningitis • Trauma • Certain medicines • Long-term exposure to loud noise • Aging There are two main types of hearing loss. One happens when your inner ear or auditory nerve is damaged. This type is usually permanent. The other kind happens when sound waves cannot reach your inner ear. Earwax build-up, fluid, or a punctured eardrum can cause it. Treatment or surgery can often reverse this kind of hearing loss. Untreated, hearing problems can get worse. If you have trouble hearing, you can get help. Possible treatments include hearing aids, cochlear implants, special training, certain medicines, and surgery.

SOURCE: http://www.nlm.nih.gov/medlineplus/hearingdisordersanddeafness.html

TYPES

The dimensions used to describe hearing problems follow:

- Type of loss
- Age of onset
- Degree of loss

The two general types of hearing loss are conductive and sensorineural. Conductive hearing loss is due to blockage or damage to the outer or middle ear that prevents sound waves from traveling (being conducted) to the inner ear. Generally, someone with a conductive hearing loss has a mild to moderate disability. Some conductive hearing losses are temporary; in fact, we have all probably experienced a conductive hearing loss at some point in our lives, for example, as a consequence of the change in air pressure when flying in an airplane or driving through the mountains. Children often experience head colds and ear infections that result in a temporary loss of conductive hearing. If the hearing loss was caused by a head cold, once the infection clears up, the hearing difficulties also disappear.

Other causes of conductive hearing losses can usually be corrected through surgery or other medical techniques. Damage to the inner ear or the auditory nerve results in a sensorineural hearing loss and is more difficult to improve through technology or medicine. Some people refer to this type of hearing loss as "nerve deafness." Individuals affected by a sensorineural loss are able to hear different frequencies at different intensity levels; their hearing losses are not flat or even. Sensorineural losses are less common in young children than the conductive types, but teachers need to understand that hearing aids can have mixed results with sensorineural losses.

The age when the hearing loss occurs, or age of onset, is important. Individuals who are born deaf or become deaf before they learn to speak and understand language are referred to as prelingually deaf. Genetic factors are considered the cause of over half of the incidents of congenital hearing loss in children (American Speech-Language-Hearing Association [ASHA], 2015). Their inability to hear language seriously affects their abilities to communicate with others and to learn academic subjects taught later in school. One in ten of those who are prelingually deaf has at least one deaf parent. Children in this group typically learn to communicate during the normal developmental period. However, instead of learning oral communication skills, many learn through a combination of manual communication (sign language) and oral language. One such approach, called the bilingual-bicultural approach, combines English as a second language (ESL) instructional methods and bilingual education, so that some young deaf children are taught ASL as their native language and learn English as their second language through reading and writing (Hoffmeister & Caldwell-Harris, 2014).

Those whose severe hearing loss occurs after they have learned to speak and understand language are called postlingually deaf. Many are able to retain their abilities to use speech and communicate with others orally.

Throughout this text, we have included notes about technology that can be used to help individuals in the classroom. In many instances, the technology is referred to as an assistive technology (AT) device. The Tech Notes feature that follows provides information about the importance of identifying the proper student-technology match.

TECH *notes*

FINDING THE RIGHT ASSISTIVE TECHNOLOGY DEVICE

Special education law defined an assistive technology device as "Any item, piece of equipment or product system, whether acquired commercially off the shelf, modified, or customized, that is used to increase, maintain, or improve the functional capabilities of children with disabilities" (IDEA, 2004). Making a student-technology match is usually the responsibility of an AT evaluation team, whose members may include the student's special education teacher, general education teacher, speech-language pathologist, physical therapist, occupational therapist, the student's family, the student, and/or whoever may be involved in the student's learning. In the case of students who are deaf or hard of hearing, the team convenes to identify any AT device that may be needed to help provide the students with access to the general education curriculum. As part of the process, a series of questions may be asked to better understand the students and their needs:

- How do the students utilize their residual hearing?

- What types of hearing technology are the students using or have been used in the past?

- Do they use sign language and/or an interpreter?

- Can they access what the teacher says at the front of the room, while the teacher walks around, or with the teacher's back turned to the class while writing on the board?

- Can they access what their peers say during class discussions or group activities or while in challenging environments?

- Do they have access to fire/tornado alarms? Announcements?

- Do they have a way to contact home in an emergency? Community supports?

- Are movies/videos shown in class? Do the students, families, and staff know how to access captioning?

- How do they communicate with others—family, peers, and community?

- Are the students able to take notes and watch the teacher/interpreter effectively?

- How do they access information during group activities—lectures, programs, or events?

Once these questions have been answered, the AT evaluation team can then consider the students and their learning context to identify AT devices that may help enhance learning. As a teacher, you will likely be a member of an AT evaluation team; it is best to attend the meeting knowing that your input is essential in helping make a student-technology match.

Although no precise cutoff exists to divide students with hearing problems into two groups, we distinguish between being hard of hearing and being deaf. Intensity, or loudness, of sound is measured in decibels (dB). Softer, quieter sounds have lower decibel measurements; louder sounds have higher decibel numbers. Decibel levels ranging from 0 to 120 dB are used to test how well an individual can hear different frequencies; a child with normal hearing should be able to perceive sounds at 0 dB. In the United States (other countries may not use the same terms), we associate hearing loss with different decibels levels. A mild hearing loss occurs at 26 to 45 dB. People with a mild hearing loss have some difficulty hearing speech, and even what might be considered a mild hearing loss can be serious for children who are still learning to talk. A moderate hearing loss occurs at 46 to 65 dB, which results in greater difficulty hearing speech. A severe loss (66–85 dB) results in considerable difficulty hearing speech, and a person with this level of hearing loss is usually considered "deaf" rather than hard of hearing. At 85 dB or more, a profound loss is evident, and even the most effective hearing aids may not help a person hear speech. At the profound level of loss, cochlear implants become an option for some.

For examples of what different decibel levels sound like, see Figure 3.6. Common sources of loud sounds or noise in our environment are also noted in this figure. Many are themselves dangerous and, with continued exposure, can cause hearing loss (American Speech-Language-Hearing Association, 2014). As a teacher, you can help your students come to understand the importance of being careful with sound. For example, students should know that listening to iPods and MP3 players with the volume turned up high will eventually result in hearing problems.

The pitch, or frequency, of sounds is measured in a unit called the hertz (Hz). The normal ear hears sounds that range from approximately 20 Hz to 20,000 Hz; speech sounds fall about in the middle of the human hearing range (between 250 Hz and 4,000 Hz). An audiogram is used to plot how well an individual hears at various combinations of hertz and decibels and also at various bands of pitch and loudness. Typically, the accommodations for and communication styles of these two groups of individuals differ. For example, students who are hard of hearing may need to sit closer to the teacher or have a classmate assist with note taking, whereas a student who is deaf may well need an interpreter to profit from lectures.

CHARACTERISTICS

Deaf and hard of hearing students are individuals with different learning styles and abilities, and teachers cannot make uniform judgments about the accommodations and services they require based on information about an individual student's amount or type of hearing loss. One student with a moderate loss might not profit from typical instructional methods (lectures, oral directions) alone, whereas another student with the same profile might function well without supports.

FIGURE 3.6 DECIBEL LEVELS OF NOISE IN AMERICAN ENVIRONMENTS

Hearing Level in Decibels	Examples of Common Sounds
140	Firecracker, nearby gunshot blast, jet engine
130	Live rock music, jackhammer
120	Jet plane taking off, car stereo turned all the way up
110	Shouting at close range, dance club, race car
100	Garbage truck, snowmobile
90*	Lawn mower, motorcycle
80	Hair dryer, alarm clock
70	City or freeway traffic, sewing machine
60	Normal conversation, air conditioner
50	Rainfall, refrigerator
40	Leaves rustling
30	Soft whisper, quiet library

*Levels 85 decibels and above are considered hazardous.

Another factor to consider is whether the individual has cognitive impairments along with hearing loss. In some conditions, these disabilities go hand in hand, and estimates are that nearly 25% of children with hearing loss have additional disabilities (U.S. Government Accountability Office [GAO], 2011). These may include visual disabilities, intellectual and developmental disabilities, learning disabilities, behavior disorders, and cerebral palsy and are often caused by the same disease or accident that caused the hearing loss. Students whose deafness is inherited, however, tend not to have multiple disabilities.

Two areas are of great concern to educators working with deaf students: academic achievement and speech ability. A long-term problem for individuals who are deaf is their academic achievement, particularly in the area of reading (Szymanski, Lutz, Shahan, & Gala, 2013). For example, by age 20, half the students tested read below the mid-fourth-grade level, leaving them unable to read most newspapers, which are written at least at the fifth-grade level.

Technology has changed the lives of many individuals with hearing problems. Whereas only 50 years ago students with mild to moderate hearing deficiencies could not hear teachers' instructions or classmates' discussions, improvements in surgery and in hearing aids and listening devices allow today's students to profit from education alongside their classmates without disabilities. Some do not even qualify for special education. More improvements are on the horizon. Medical technology holds the promise of both preventing and "curing" deafness at some point in the future. In 2000, deaf children as young as a year old were allowed to receive cochlear implants, assistive hearing devices designed to help those with sensorineural hearing loss gain useful hearing. By the end of 2012, about 38,000 children had received the implants (National Institute on Deafness and Other Communication Disorders, 2014). Although not a cure for deafness, implants hold great promise for many individuals with profound hearing loss. However, they remain controversial in the Deaf community, where deafness is accepted and celebrated and ASL remains the preferred communication mode for some.

PREVALENCE

Although many people have hearing problems, almost half are over 65. Despite this fact, hearing loss in children is one of the most common birth defects in the United States (ASHA, 2014). Approximately 1 in every 1,000 babies is born profoundly deaf, and another 2 to 3 have less severe hearing losses. Remember, estimates are that nearly 25% of deaf and hard of hearing children have additional disabilities (GAO, 2011). Typically, children who have multiple disabilities are not counted in the federal deafness or hard of hearing category, so we do not know precisely how many students have hearing problems. In 2014, the federal government reported 0.15% of the resident population, or 78,448 students, as those whose primary disability is related to their hearing (USDE, 2014). This number does not include students who do not need special education because hearing aids or assistive devices allow them to hear well enough to participate in typical classroom activities.

WHAT ARE THE ATTRIBUTES OF STUDENTS WITH VISUAL DISABILITIES?

Today, about 64% of students with visual disabilities spend over 80% of their school days in general education classrooms, most likely at their neighborhood school, and receive support from a resource specialist or itinerant teacher (USDE, 2014). These students participate in the general education curriculum with their sighted classmates and, if they do not also have multiple disabilities, tend to perform well academically. Most use aids, such as glasses or technology, that enlarge type to enhance their vision for accessing information and moving independently at school and in the community (Macular Degeneration Foundation, 2012).

DEFINITION

When people see normally, two important aspects of their vision are working well: acuity and peripheral vision. Problems can occur in one or both of these aspects of vision, resulting in a disability. **Visual acuity** measures how well a person can see at various distances. We measure normal visual acuity by testing how accurately a person can see an object or image 20 feet away. Normal vision is thus said to be 20/20. A person whose vision is measured at 20/40 can see at 20 feet what people who do not need visual correction (glasses or contact lenses) can see at 40 feet away. The width of a person's field of vision, or the ability to perceive objects outside the direct line of vision, is called **peripheral vision**. This aspect of vision helps people move freely through their environment.

How much impairment results in a disability? Look at Table 3.10 and the definition of blindness and loss of vision. Today, IDEA '04 and most states have adopted eligibility criteria that reflect a functional definition of visual disabilities, a concept initiated by researcher and advocate Anne Corn about 25 years ago. The basic premise is that a student has a visual disability when, even with correction, educational performance is adversely affected. In other words, the issue is how much **residual vision** a person has or can use to do well in school. States and school districts vary in the criteria they use to determine eligibility for special services.

TYPES

Many professionals talk about visual disabilities in four very different ways:

1. By identifying the reason for the visual loss

2. By considering the severity of the problem

TABLE 3.10	DEFINITION OF BLINDNESS AND LOSS OF VISION
Source	**Definition**
U.S. National Library of Medicine	Blindness is a lack of vision. It may also refer to a loss of vision that cannot be corrected with glasses or contact lenses.
	Partial blindness means you have very limited vision.
	Complete blindness means you cannot see anything and do not see light. (Most people who use the term *blindness* mean complete blindness.)
	People with vision that is worse than 20/200 with glasses or contact lenses are considered legally blind in most states in the United States.
	Vision loss refers to the partial or complete loss of vision. This vision loss may happen suddenly or over a period of time.
	Some types of vision loss never lead to complete blindness.

SOURCE: http://www.nlm.nih.gov/medlineplus/ency/article/003040.htm

3. By taking into account when the loss occurred

4. By determining whether the criteria for being considered legally blind are met

Numerous conditions can lead to visual loss that results in a disability. The conditions with which most of us are familiar are myopia (nearsightedness), hyperopia (farsightedness), and astigmatism (inability to focus), but many other conditions, only some of which can be prevented or corrected, can damage the eye, compromise its structure, and undermine its functioning.

Typically, persons with visual disabilities are divided into two subgroups:

1. Those with low vision

2. Those who are blind

Parents and professionals tend to employ functional definitions for these two subgroups. In other words, children with low vision use their sight for many school activities, including reading. Children who are blind do not have functional use of their vision and may perceive only shadows or some movement. These youngsters must be educated through tactile and other sensory channels.

Blindness can occur at any age, but its impact varies with age and with age of onset. Individuals can be

- Congenitally blind, with onset at birth or during infancy
- Adventitiously blind, with onset after the age of 2

This distinction is important because people who lose their sight after age 2, and hence are adventitiously blind, remember what some objects look like. Those who are congenitally blind were too young when the loss occurred to remember what things look like. The later the disability occurs, the more they remember. Visual memory is an important factor in learning, for it can influence our development of concepts and other aspects important to learning.

Although it is not related to how well a person can use his or her vision, another way to categorize people with visual problems is in terms of whether they meet the definition of legally blind. This designation allows individuals to receive special tax benefits and materials from the federal government and private agencies. Because the definition does not exclude people who have some functional use of sight, many individuals who are legally blind use print, not Braille, to read.

CHARACTERISTICS

The way individuals with visual disabilities access information sets them apart as a group, but the use of aids and technologies helps provide positive information outcomes (Macular Degeneration Foundation, 2012). Contrary to popular belief, the vast majority use vision as their primary method of learning and means of participating in the community. For many students, the amount of vision they have left—their residual vision—can be further developed through training and practice. The vision of some is static, remaining the same from day to day, whereas others find that their ability to see varies with the day, time of day, or setting (American Foundation for the Blind, 2014a). For some, higher or lower levels of illumination, or changes in distance and contrast, affect how well they can see, but for others, these make little difference. For most, optical aids such as glasses have a positive effect.

Because of the importance of literacy and the ability to read, IDEA '04 insists that instruction in the use of Braille be considered for every student who has severe visual loss.

Literacy development has long been a major objective for students with visual impairments, who need direct instruction in reading (American Foundation for the Blind, 2014b). Most read print, usually via enlarged type. Others read via Braille, and many others access printed materials by listening to books on tape or a personal reader, meaning someone who reads for others. Because it is so important to be able to read, IDEA '04 insists that instruction in the use of Braille be considered for every student who has severe visual loss (Jackson, 2014).

Although students with visual disabilities participate in inclusive classrooms at a very high rate, they must also learn skills related to being independent, such as accessing transportation, moving freely in their environment, and acquiring life skills such as cooking, doing laundry, cleaning the home, and so on. Therefore, orientation and mobility are major curriculum targets. Orientation is the mental map people have of their surroundings. Most of us learn landmarks and other cues to get from one place to another. As a teacher, you can assist a student with severe visual loss by helping her or him understand emergency evacuation procedures, recognize exit paths from the school buildings, and learn how to move safely through the school environment, which he or she should know well, both during normal school hours and in times of stress. Many schools and districts have designed emergency preparedness plans for students with disabilities (Marin County Office of Education, 2010). You can also make sure the student knows landmarks in the classroom environment so he or she is free to move around independently.

The ability to travel safely and efficiently from one place to another is called mobility. Most adults who are blind use the long cane, also called the Hoover cane, which is named after its developer, Richard Hoover. However, tapping the cane along a sidewalk or pavement of the street does not always help the individual avoid the many obstacles in modern society. For example, silent traffic signals, escalators, elevators, and public transportation, to say nothing of protruding and overhanging objects that are undetectable with mobility canes, can be very dangerous. Nor do canes tell users where they are or how to get to their next location. Guide dogs or service animals are another option. Although there are no definitive statistics available, the number of individuals who use guide dogs is relatively small. It has been estimated that only about 2% of people who are blind and visually impaired work with guide dogs (Guiding Eyes for the Blind, 2014). As a teacher, you can help students who are assisted by a service animal by helping classmates understand that the animal is not a pet and should be left to do the important job that took years of training for it to master.

Global positioning system (GPS) technology provides new orientation and mobility system advances for people with severe visual loss and may well become "the" mobility system of this century. Sometimes called "ambient technology" or "welfare technology" (Hill, Raymond, & Yeung, 2013), the GPS technology used by the navigational devices in cars and mobile devices can be used with long canes, and in some cases, with guide dogs as well (Cook & Polgar, 2012).

PREVALENCE

According to the World Health Organization (2014),

- About 285 million people are visually impaired worldwide; 39 million of them are blind.

- Throughout the world, most people with visual impairment are age 50 or older.

- About 90% of the world's visually impaired live in developing countries.

- The number of people blinded by infectious diseases has been greatly reduced by recent public health efforts, but age-related impairment is increasing.

- Cataracts remain the leading cause of blindness globally, except in the most developed countries.

- Correction of refractive errors could give normal vision to more than 12 million children ages 5 to 15.

- Globally about 80% of all visual impairment is avoidable.

    Source: http://www.who.int/mediacentre/factsheets/fs282/en/

Education Digest reports that 29,004 students with visual impairments are receiving special education services. This accounts for about 0.5% of those receiving special education services.

WHAT ARE THE ATTRIBUTES OF STUDENTS WITH TRAUMATIC BRAIN INJURY?

- The CDC (2014) noted that in 2010 in the United States, there were about 2.5 million emergency room visits, hospitalizations, or deaths associated with traumatic brain injury (TBI), either by itself or combined with other injuries; TBI contributed to the deaths of more than 50,000 people. A year earlier, almost 250,000 children (age 19 or younger) were treated in U.S. emergency rooms for sport- and recreation-related injuries that included a diagnosis of concussion or TBI.

Prior to the 1960s, most children whose brains were seriously hurt died soon after the trauma. Today's emergency procedures, imaging technology, surgical methods, and pharmaceutical treatments routinely save children's lives after serious accidents, although some survivors need long-term or short-term special education or special accommodations under Section 504 of the Rehabilitation Act. At some time during your career, you will probably work with at least one child with TBI.

DEFINITION

TBI became a separate special education category when IDEA was reauthorized in 1990. Because these students often exhibit memory deficits, attention problems, language impairments, and reduced academic performance, many are educated alongside their classmates with learning disabilities. Others, because of their head injuries, experience seizures and receive many of the same accommodations as children with epilepsy. The official IDEA '04 definition of TBI is found in Table 3.11.

TYPES

Like other disabilities, TBI ranges in severity from mild to severe (American Society of Neuroradiology, 2012–2013). Those with more severe head injuries receive home instruction, often for a year, before returning to school part time. In many cases the effects eventually disappear, but in some cases they are lifelong.

CHARACTERISTICS

Children with TBI and their families face great emotional turmoil during the time shortly after the injury. Educators must be alert to student conditions associated with concussions and TBI (e.g., appears dazed or stunned, is confused about events, answers questions slowly) and also be prepared to talk with students about their conditions (e.g., difficulty thinking clearly, difficulty concentrating or remembering, feeling more slowed down; CDC, 2010).

TABLE 3.11	DEFINITION OF TRAUMATIC BRAIN INJURY
Source	**Definition**
U.S. National Library of Medicine	Traumatic brain injury (TBI) happens when a bump, blow, jolt, or other head injury causes damage to the brain. Every year, millions of people in the U.S. suffer brain injuries. More than half are bad enough that people must go to the hospital. The worst injuries can lead to permanent brain damage or death. Half of all TBIs are from motor vehicle accidents. Military personnel in combat zones are also at risk. Symptoms of a TBI may not appear until days or weeks following the injury. A concussion is the mildest type. It can cause a headache or neck pain, nausea, ringing in the ears, dizziness, and tiredness. People with a moderate or severe TBI may have those, plus other symptoms: <ul><li>A headache that gets worse or does not go away</li><li>Repeated vomiting or nausea</li><li>Convulsions or seizures</li><li>Inability to awaken from sleep</li><li>Slurred speech</li><li>Weakness or numbness in the arms and legs</li><li>Dilated eye pupils</li></ul>

SOURCE: http://www.nlm.nih.gov/medlineplus/traumaticbraininjury.html

Alert teachers can be very helpful in early diagnosis and treatment of TBI (CDC, 2010). Many head injuries are the result of activities in which children commonly engage: riding a bicycle, using playground equipment, or even tussling in the schoolyard. Often, youngsters do not want to admit they fell or forgot to wear a protective helmet or were fighting on the playground. But when a student acts differently, becomes unable to pay attention, or seems unusually tired, seek help from the school nurse to be certain the child has not experienced a head injury. Symptoms may include blurred vision, loss of vision, change in hearing acuity, ringing in the ears, slurred speech, difficulty understanding spoken language, difficulty processing sensory input (via touch, smell, hearing), personality changes, loss of taste and/or smell, paralysis, lethargy, loss of bowel/bladder control, dizziness, inappropriate emotional responses (irritability, frustration, crying, or laughing), and seizures. Many of these conditions persist and can be mitigated somewhat by medications, but occasionally a condition (e.g., lethargy, inattention) may be demonstrated in the classroom.

PREVALENCE

In recent years, more than 150,000 children annually have been hospitalized due to a head injury; 1 in 10 of those children hospitalized will suffer moderate to severe impairments (Center for Head Injury Services, 2014). Most of these disabilities are mild. According to the federal government, 25,969 students with TBI were served by special education in the 2011 to 2012 school year (USDE, 2014).

WHAT ARE THE ATTRIBUTES OF STUDENTS WITH DEAF-BLINDNESS?

A great example of why we should not make assumptions about any person with a disability, even those with the most severe and complex problems, is a well-known person with deaf-blindness. Recall Helen Keller, mentioned earlier in the chapter, who graduated from Radcliffe with honors when few people *without* disabilities went to college, particularly women.

DEFINITION

Although every state acknowledges deaf-blindness, many define it differently. The definition of deaf-blindness is found in Table 3.12.

TYPES

When you hear the word *deaf-blindness,* you probably think of people who have no vision and no hearing abilities, whose lives must be severely restricted. Although this is true for some individuals with deaf-blindness, the majority do have some residual hearing and/or vision. Almost half have enough residual vision to read enlarged print, see sign language, move about in their environment, and recognize friends and family (Smith & Tyler, 2010). Some have sufficient hearing to understand certain speech sounds or hear loud noises. Some can even develop speech themselves. Others have such limited vision and hearing that they profit little from either sense.

In addition to their visual and hearing losses, most individuals with deaf-blindness also have other disabilities, such as intellectual and developmental disabilities, that further complicate their education. Most need considerable supports for their worlds to be safe and accessible; their educational programs must be carefully thought through and uniquely designed to ensure that each student meets his or her potential.

TABLE 3.12	DEFINITION OF DEAF-BLINDNESS
Source	**Definition**
Colorado Department of Education	The term "deaf-blind" may also be referred to as dual sensory impairment or dual sensory loss or spelled as deaf-blind. In Colorado, we use the term deaf-blind to connote it as a unique condition and not simply a disability of vision loss plus hearing loss.
	Deaf-blindness is a combination of vision and hearing loss. Deaf-blindness encompasses a spectrum from mildly hard of hearing plus mildly visually impaired to totally deaf and blind or combinations of the severity of vision and hearing loss. It is rare that an individual with deaf-blindness would be completely blind and completely deaf. Either the vision and/or the hearing loss can be present at birth or acquired.

SOURCE: http://www.cde.state.co.us/cdesped/SD-DB_WhoWhat.asp

CHARACTERISTICS

The world for children with deaf-blindness can be exceptionally restricted. For those whose hearing and vision losses are severe or profound, the immediate world may well end at their fingertips (Miles, 2008). They, their family members, and their teachers must address problems of isolation, communication, and mobility.

Possibly the greatest challenge facing individuals with deaf-blindness is learning to communicate (Miles, 2008). Many adults with this disability have developed outstanding communication skills, but this achievement does not typically come without considerable effort. Others communicate through touch (Miles, 2008). They use various forms of manual communication—sign language, body language, gestures—to express their needs and "talk" to others. Some use a special kind of sign language called hand over hand, in which two people use the palms of each other's hands to sign through touches. Earlier we mentioned Helen Keller; she and her teacher, Anne Sullivan, used this communication technique.

PREVALENCE

According to the federal government, fewer than 1,600 students across the nation fall into the deaf-blindness category (USDE, 2014). Why does such a large discrepancy exist? The reason is that the federal government insists that states report students' disabilities in only one area, and many deaf-blind students are reported in other categories because they have so many coexisting problems.

It is unlikely that you as a teacher will meet or work with a student with deaf-blindness. According to the Deaf-Blind Census, only about 430 students with deaf-blindness receive their education almost exclusively in the general education classroom (USDE, 2014). Regardless of their special education placement, students with deaf-blindness are few, and they need very special instruction and supports.

SUMMARY

Although less than 2% of all students have low-incidence disabilities, these disabilities include hundreds of discrete conditions. The federal government has designated eight disabilities, plus the flexible, noncategorical grouping "developmental delay" for children between the ages of 3 and 9, as being "low incidence." In this chapter, you learned that students with low-incidence disabilities exhibit complex and unique learning characteristics that challenge themselves, their families, and their schools. Their conditions and disabilities influence what they are taught and how they are taught to a greater degree than is true for many of their peers with and without disabilities. These students often require unique responses so that they can access the curriculum, participate fully in the school community, and be successful students. The types of supports, accommodations, and instruction must reflect the evidence-based practices you will learn about throughout this academic term. Despite the challenges and barriers many of these students face, they hold great promise of attaining remarkable accomplishments.

REVIEW THE LEARNING OBJECTIVES

Let's review the learning objectives for this chapter. If you are uncertain and cannot talk through the answers provided for any of these questions, reread those sections of the text.

- **What are the attributes of students with low-incidence disabilities?**

  Low-incidence disabilities have a low prevalence, so relatively few individuals and families are affected, but they often require intensive and unique responses to their very special needs. These unique responses include many, and sometimes complex, accommodations, as well as long-term interventions, instruction not typically included in the general education curriculum (such as Braille), and the inclusion of many different related services professionals (such as assistive technologists, physical therapists, and speech/language pathologists).

- **What are the attributes of students with health impairments or special health care needs?**

  The key features of most *health impairments* or *special health care needs* are fatigue, absences from school, inconsistent ability to pay attention, muscle weakness, and problems with physical coordination. Examples of health impairments include chronic illnesses (asthma, sickle-cell anemia) and infectious diseases.

- **What are the attributes of students with autism spectrum disorders?**

  The key features of *autism spectrum disorders (ASD)* are social challenges, including problems with social communication, and repetitive and stereotypic behaviors. There are three levels of severity within ASD, dependent on support needs.

- **What are the attributes of students with multiple-severe disabilities?**

  The key features of *multiple-severe disabilities* include the presence of more than one disability, goals that include independence and community presence, provision of supports that are ongoing and intensive, and problems with generalization, communication, memory, and life skills.

- **What are the attributes of students with developmental delay?**

  The key feature of *developmental delay* is that disability is noncategorically described (no disability label required). This means qualifying students for special education services is typically used for preschoolers between ages 3 and 5 but may include children up to the age of 9.

- **What are the attributes of students with physical disabilities?**

  The key features of *physical disabilities* vary with the condition that caused the physical disability. For example, orthopedic impairments, limb deficiencies, and juvenile arthritis result in problems with structure and functioning of the body; cerebral palsy (CP) can have multiple outcomes; and seizure disorders (epilepsy) can result in short episodes that briefly interrupt learning or major events that require major intervention.

- **What are the attributes of students who are deaf and hard of hearing?**

  The key features of the category *deaf and hard of hearing* vary by type (conductive or sensorineural), age of onset (prelingually or postlingually deaf), and degree of loss (hard of hearing or deafness). All these conditions usually result in problems with communication, academic achievement, and speech ability.

- **What are the attributes of students with visual disabilities?**

Low vision and blindness is typically categorized in terms of functional use of sight, age of onset (congenitally blind, adventitiously blind), and degree of loss (low vision, legally blind). Key issues for these individuals are attaining literacy (Braille or print), developing orientation and mobility skills, and developing maximal use of residual vision and sight for daily functioning. Those with blindness use touch and hearing as their primary means of accessing information; those with low vision use their sight.

- **What are the attributes of students with traumatic brain injury?**

Traumatic brain injury can be temporary, lasting about a year. In these cases, the symptoms are mild and are similar to those of learning disabilities. But in other cases, the conditions are severe, and many individuals experience hospital or home instruction for some period of time. For these people, the results can be long-lasting and require medications to help alleviate the conditions. In some instances, some conditions associated with TBI, such as inattention and lethargy, can be challenging to the student and teachers.

- **What are the attributes of students with deaf-blindness?**

Deaf-blindness is the occurrence of coexisting hearing and visual impairments; neither disability has to be severe or profound in nature. This exceptionally low-incidence disability results in problems with isolation, communication, and mobility.

$SAGE edge™ Test your understanding of chapter content. Take the practice quiz. edge.sagepub.com/bryant

REVIST THE OPENING CHALLENGE ·····································•

Check your answers to the Reflection Questions from the Opening Challenge and revise them on the basis of what you have learned.

1. Do you think Ms. Simpkin will need to plan for her new student differently than she has for other students with disabilities? If so, in what ways? If not, why not?

2. What learning characteristics might she have to consider as she makes initial plans for Josh?

3. How might her plans change after she learns what disabilities Josh has?

4. Provide Ms. Simpkin with five questions or issues she should discuss with her principal.

5. What do you think Mr. Dehiya figured out on his own, based on common sense, concerning classroom accessibility?

6. Why do you think Mr. Dehiya decided to have his students help restructure the classroom? Do you think this was a good idea?

7. Before clicking on the link that Mr. Dehiya found (http://www.cmccd .edu/getdoc.cfm?id=1044), what ideas do you think the information may include?

KEY TERMS

asthma, 93

audiogram, 115

augmentative and alternative communication devices (AAC), 104

aura, 111

chronic illnesses, 92

developmental delay, 105

echolalia, 100

group homes, 102

home-bound/hospital instruction, 94

limb loss, 112

medically fragile, 91

orthopedic impairments, 108

other health impairments, 90

peripheral vision, 121

preictal stage, 111

residual vision, 121

robotics, 112

sickle-cell anemia, 96

visual acuity, 121

SAGE edge™ Review key terms with eFlashcards.
edge.sagepub.com/bryant

PROFESSIONAL STANDARDS AND LICENSURE

For a complete description of Professional Standards and Licensure, please see Appendix on page 569.

CEC Initial Preparation Standards

Standard 1: Learner Development and Individual Learning Differences

INTASC Core Principles

Standard 1: Learner Development

Standard 2: Learning Differences

Praxis II: Education of Exceptional Students: Core Content Knowledge

I. Understanding Exceptionalities: Human development and behavior

Review → Practice → Improve
Get the tools you need to sharpen your study skills. Access practice quizzes, eFlashcards, video, and multimedia: **edge.sagepub.com/bryant**

4

OTHER STUDENTS WITH SPECIAL LEARNING NEEDS

With contributions by

The late Janette K. Klingner, *University of Colorado at Boulder*

Margarita Bianco, *University of Colorado at Denver,* and *Health Sciences Center, Denver, Colorado*

LEARNING OBJECTIVES

After studying this chapter, you will be able to answer the following questions:

- How are students with physical and cognitive needs protected under Section 504?

- How can we best meet the needs of students in our culturally and linguistically diverse classrooms?

- Who are students "at risk" and what should we know and do to help them achieve their full potential?

- What are the attributes of students with gifts and talents?

Helping Students With Other Special Learning Needs Access the Curriculum

ELEMENTARY GRADES Ms. Grelak has been teaching in the primary grades at Tyler Elementary School for 20 years, during which the school's population has changed a great deal from mostly White and middle class to a more culturally and linguistically diverse mix. This year she has 11 African American students and 19 Latino students, 9 of whom are English language learners at various levels of proficiency. She also has a new student from Korea who knows very little English. Most of her students qualify for free or reduced-price lunch. A resource teacher provides pullout English as a second language (ESL) support for Ms. Grelak's English language learners for 50 minutes a day, but it doesn't seem to be enough. Ms. Grelak feels frustrated about how best to meet her students' needs. Many seem to be struggling to keep up with grade-level material. She is especially concerned about Gabriel and Allen.

Gabriel's family moved to the United States from Mexico about a year and a half ago, and Gabriel was placed in a fourth-grade class. He knew very little English when he started school and is still at a beginning proficiency level. During his second-grade year he missed almost a month of school, some when he was ill and some when he and his family went to Mexico to visit relatives for Christmas. Now, in fifth grade, he seems to have made little progress and is reading only at a beginning first-grade level. He has trouble concentrating and appears to lack motivation. Ms. Grelak is unsure whether to recommend that he be retained; she suspects he might have a learning disability.

Allen has attended Tyler since kindergarten. He was retained after first grade and is now in the fifth grade. He is well-mannered, good-natured, and popular among his peers. Yet he struggles academically, and he is about two years behind in reading as well as math. Allen's mother is concerned about his lack of progress and works with him at home on practice activities that Ms. Grelak sends home for this purpose. She told Ms. Grelak that Allen is having much more

difficulty than either of his older sisters, and Ms. Grelak has decided to refer him for evaluation for possible placement in special education. She suspects he might have developmental delays.

Ms. Grelak thinks, *"I have so many students from diverse backgrounds, and many with special learning needs. I want to meet all their needs while trying to teach the curriculum for my grade level and also meet the needs of the other students in my class. I need to better understand how to help them all."*

SECONDARY GRADES Mrs. O'Malley is in her first year of teaching, having recently gone through the alternative certification program through her state's education agency. After her recent marriage, she and her husband moved from Maine to Arizona. She has a degree in chemistry but decided that, like her mother and father before her, she wanted to be a high school teacher. She was assigned to teach the general science class. As she looked at her student roster, she noticed that a high percentage of her students had Spanish surnames. Even though her certification coursework included some information about English language learners (ELLs), she was concerned that she might have difficulties meeting the needs of her Latino students. She called her mother, who suggested that she make an appointment with the district's ELL specialist to identify resources and receive advice on teaching techniques.

During the meeting, the ELL specialist directed Mrs. O'Malley to Arizona's Office of English Language Acquisition Services' website (http://www.azed.gov/ada-learners/eld_pd/), which contains a variety of learning strategies; she also stated that there would be a session titled "Meeting the Needs of ELLs in Content Classes" during the district's professional development training before the start of school. Mrs. O'Malley thanked the specialist after the meeting and went home and immediately looked up the information on the state's website. By the first day of school, Mrs. O'Malley felt that she had acquired enough information to feel reasonably comfortable working with her students.

REFLECTION QUESTIONS In your journal, write down your answers to the following questions. After completing the chapter, check your answers and revise them on the basis of what you have learned.

1. What should Ms. Grelak's next steps be with Gabriel?

2. Do you agree that Ms. Grelak should refer Allen for a special education evaluation? Why or why not?

3. In what ways does his level of English language proficiency seem to be affecting Gabriel?

4. What characteristics does Gabriel have that seem consistent with those of a gifted student? What characteristics does Gabriel have that seem consistent with those of English language learners?

5. What advice would you give Ms. Grelak about instruction for English language learners with learning problems?

6. Where might you go to look for information about teaching English language learners in your state? What specific questions might you like to have answered?

7. Do you share some of the same concerns as Mrs. O'Malley? Find the website of your home city's school system. Is there information pertaining to culturally and linguistically diverse student populations? What information is provided for parents and teachers?

As we learned in Chapter 1, special education services are available for students with identified disabilities according to criteria established in the Individuals with Disabilities Education Improvement Act of 2004 (IDEA). These students are entitled to the supports and services they need to benefit from instruction and participate with their peers in the least restrictive environment (LRE). Yet it is almost inevitable that you will have other students with special learning needs in your classroom who may not be eligible for special education services under IDEA but who require special attention in order to fully reach their potential in school. They need academic and other supports to ensure that they can benefit from instruction in the general education classroom. "Inclusive education" is a means to meet the full range of student needs in the classroom by implementing validated practices and providing support systems that help teachers reach all their students.

In this chapter, we discuss some of those other special needs that can affect educational outcomes of students in our classrooms. Understanding that the types of needs and life situations students bring with them are varied and numerous, we do not attempt to approach comprehensiveness in this discussion. Rather, we discuss some of the more critical and common needs and circumstances—health-related, cultural, linguistic, economic, social, and academic—and hope you will recognize that those students, too, require and deserve special attention in your instructional planning and implementation.

HOW ARE STUDENTS WITH PHYSICAL AND COGNITIVE NEEDS PROTECTED UNDER SECTION 504?

Section 504 of the Rehabilitation Act of 1973 is a civil rights law that prohibits discrimination against individuals with disabilities. It requires federal, state, and local governments to provide access to buildings and other public spaces to people with disabilities through such accommodations as alternatives to stairs (ramps and elevators) and barrier-free sidewalks (via curb cuts that allow wheelchairs to roll from sidewalk to street).

Section 504 also requires that teachers in publicly funded schools make accommodations and modifications for students with disabilities to ensure that they have equal access to an education. Because some students who receive services under Section 504 may not be in special education, it is the general education teacher's responsibility to make those accommodations and modifications for the non-special education students. Let's review how students qualify for services under Section 504 and the educational accommodations that are available to them.

QUALIFYING FOR SERVICES UNDER SECTION 504

There are students with special learning needs who are not covered under IDEA. However, they may qualify for services under Section 504 because the definition of disability is broader under Section 504 and extends beyond school age. To be eligible for protections under Section 504, the child must have a physical or mental impairment that substantially limits at least one major life activity. Major life activities include walking, seeing, hearing, speaking, breathing, learning, reading, writing, performing math calculations, working, caring for yourself, and performing manual tasks. The key is whether a person "has a physical or mental impairment which substantially limits one or more of such person's major life activities" (Yell, 2012, p. 96).

Tech Notes discusses AT needs for students and the range of available devices.

TECH *notes*

HIGH TECH VERSUS LOW TECH

When making decisions regarding assistive technology (AT) needs for students who qualify under Section 504, it is important to recognize that AT ranges from low tech (sometimes called lite tech) to high tech. It is often assumed that students require the latest, most advanced devices to meet their needs, but this

(Continued)

 Special Education Law

(Continued)

is not always the case. Let's consider one example, for Allen, mentioned in the opening challenges. He struggles with reading, and his teacher and test data indicate that he is reading about two years below his peers. A high tech alternative could involve purchasing a scanning machine to scan his textbooks and also text-to-speech computer software to have the computer read the text aloud, giving Allen access to the reading material. A lite tech alternative might involve having a classmate or older student volunteer to read the textbook into a digital recorder. Allen could take the digital information home each day to use when completing his homework. There could be other AT solutions that fall between these two options, such as purchasing digital textbooks that Allen can use in much the same way as the lower tech option. The point is, if you, as a teacher, are asked to serve on an AT evaluation team for Section 504 students, come to the evaluation meeting with the desire for the team to look at a continuum of AT options. Sometimes low tech (lite tech) options are the most viable. If, in subsequent follow-up meetings, the AT device is not meeting Allen's needs, a more high tech solution can be recommended.

If the student has a disability that adversely affects educational performance, the student is eligible for special education services under IDEA and would also be automatically protected from discrimination under Section 504. However, the opposite is not true: If a student has a disability that does not adversely affect educational performance, the student will not be eligible for special education services under IDEA, but the student will usually be entitled to protections under Section 504. For example, a student with AIDS, a student with ADHD, and a student with chronic asthma are all protected from discrimination under Section 504. Each of these students may also be eligible for special education services under IDEA (under the category "Other Health Impairments" described in Chapter 3), but those decisions would be based on the specific educational needs of each student (Wrightslaw, 2015). Students with conditions such as drug or alcohol addiction, temporary disabilities resulting from accidents, attention problems, or chronic health issues can qualify as having a disability under Section 504 (Vermont Department of Education, 2010). Although no funding is attached to this legislation, school districts and general education professionals are expected to implement measures to address any special conditions they believe would jeopardize a student's ability to learn.

PROVIDING EDUCATIONAL SERVICES UNDER SECTION 504

Under Section 504, students who qualify as having a disability are assessed, and a 504 plan is developed and monitored (see Figure 4.1 for an example). The plan includes accommodations and adaptations, identifies the person(s) responsible for implementation, and lists the procedures for monitoring the effectiveness of the plan. Accommodations and adaptations might include changes to the physical environment (specialized lighting, a quiet study place), adaptations to curriculum and instruction, accommodations in testing, and

Section 504

FIGURE 4.1 **SECTION 504 SAMPLE PLAN**

Sample Components of a 504 Plan for a Student with Diabetes

Student's Name: _____

Birth Date: _____ Grade: _____ Type of Diabetes: _____

Homeroom Teacher: _____ Bus Number: _____ Date: _____

Objectives/Goals of this Plan

The goal of this plan is to provide the special education and/or related aids and services needed to maintain blood glucose within this student's target range of _____ and to respond appropriately to levels outside of this range in accordance with the instructions provided by the student's personal health care team.

1. **Provision of Diabetes Care:** Designated individuals will receive training to be Trained Diabetes Personnel (TDP).

2. **Student Level of Self-Care and Location of Supplies and Equipment:** The student can perform the following diabetes care tasks without help at any time of the day and in any location _____. The student needs assistance or supervision with the following diabetes health care tasks _____. The student needs a TDP to perform the following diabetes care tasks _____.

3. **Snacks and Meals:** The school nurse, or TDP if the school nurse is not available, will work with the student and his/her parents/guardians to coordinate a meal and snack schedule in accordance with the attached Diabetes Medical Management Plan (DMMP) that will coincide with the schedule of classmates to the closest extent possible. The student shall eat lunch at the same time each day, or earlier if experiencing hypoglycemia. The student shall have enough time to finish lunch. A snack and quick-acting source of glucose must always be immediately available to the student.

4. **Exercise and Physical Activity:** The student shall be permitted to participate fully in physical education classes and team sports except as set out in the student's DMMP.

5. **Water and Bathroom Access:** The student shall be permitted to have immediate access to water and be permitted to use the bathroom without restriction.

6. **Checking Blood Glucose Levels, Insulin, and Medication Administration, and Treating High or Low Blood Glucose Levels:** Blood glucose monitoring will be done at the times designated in the student's DMMP, whenever the student feels her blood glucose level may be high or low, or when symptoms of high or low blood glucose levels are observed. Insulin and/or other diabetes medication will be administered at the times and through the means (e.g., syringe, pen, or pump) designated in the student's DMMP.

7. **Tests and Classroom Work:** If the student is affected by high or low blood glucose levels at the time of regular testing, the student will be permitted to take the test at another time without penalty. If the student needs to take breaks to use the water fountain or bathroom, check blood glucose, or treat hypoglycemia during a test or other activity, the student will be given extra time to finish the test or other activity without penalty.

Emergency Contact:

_____   _____   _____

Parent's/Guardian's Name   Home Phone Number   Emergency Phone Number

Approved and received:

_____   _____

Parent/Guardian   Date

_____   _____

School Representative and Title   Date

SOURCE: Adapted from http://main.diabetes.org/dorg/PDFs/Advocacy/Discrimination/504-plan.pdf

assistance with organizing time and activities (Friend, 2008). In addition to instructional programs, the plan can cover other academically related programs such as field trips and summer programs.

Some students with disabilities who qualify for Section 504 accommodations and adaptations may not be receiving special education services. For these nonspecial education students, the general education teacher is responsible for providing needed accommodations and adaptations.

HOW CAN WE BEST MEET THE NEEDS OF STUDENTS IN OUR CULTURALLY AND LINGUISTICALLY DIVERSE CLASSROOM?

Every one of us has a culture (or cultures), just as we all speak a language (or languages). So what do we mean when we say *culturally and linguistically diverse* (CLD) *students?* In the United States, this term has come to mean students with cultural, ethnic, and linguistic backgrounds different from the macroculture and language of the White majority (Standard English). Sometimes the term *people of color* or *students of color* is used instead. Any individual belongs not to just one culture or macroculture but to many microcultures (Gollnick & Chinn, 2012). We can think of a macroculture as a society that embraces overarching cultural factors. For example, democracy is one of those factors valued as part of our macroculture. A microculture is a group whose members share similar backgrounds such as age, class, geographic region, disability, ethnicity, occupation, and so forth (Neuliep, 2015). Thus, students in our classrooms represent a variety of microcultures, each with its own identity and perspectives. Our schools must be responsive to and respectful of the richness of diversity as the CLD population continues to increase.

Dual language programs are increasingly popular models that strive to help native English speakers develop proficiency in a second language, while helping students who speak a language other than English develop English proficiency.

We use numerous terms when discussing students whose primary language is other than English. To understand the differences among the terms, see Table 4.1.

Diversity in the United States is growing, as evidenced by increases in the size of various groups in the population (U.S. Census Bureau, 2010). And this increasing diversity in the general population means more CLD students. Figure 4.2 shows population percentages for racial and ethnic groups in the United States, beginning

| TABLE 4.1 | TERMS COMMONLY ASSOCIATED WITH STUDENTS WHOSE PRIMARY LANGUAGE IS NOT ENGLISH |

Term	Definition
Bilingualism	The ability to communicate successfully in two languages, with the same relative degree of proficiency. It is important to note that bilinguals are rarely perfectly balanced in their use of two languages; one language is usually dominant.
English Language Learner (ELL)	An individual who is in the process of actively acquiring English and whose primary language is one other than English. This student often benefits from language support programs to improve academic performance in English due to challenges with reading, comprehension, speaking, and/or writing skills in English. Other terms that are commonly used to refer to ELLs are *language minority students, English as a Second Language (ESL) students, culturally and linguistically diverse (CLD) students,* and *limited English proficient (LEP) students.*
Limited English Proficient (LEP)	A term used by the U.S. Department of Education to refer to ELLs who are enrolled or are getting ready to enroll in elementary or secondary school and who have an insufficient level of English to meet a state's English expertise requirements. However, the expression *English language learner (ELL)* has started to replace LEP, to avoid the implication that nonnative-English-speaking students are deficient (National Council of Teachers of English, 2008). The former term for LEP was *limited English speaking (LES)* and was used in the first authorization of the Bilingual Education Act (Title VII of ESEA, prior to NCLB) in 1968.
English as a Second Language (ESL)	A term often used to designate students whose first language is not English; it has become less common than the term ELL. Currently, ESL is more likely to refer to an educational approach designed to support ELLs.
Non-English Proficient	An ELL who has minimal or no proficiency in English.

SOURCE: Bardack (2010).

in 1980 with projected growth to 2050. The U.S. Census Bureau projects that by 2050, the White population will increase by 7% but at a lower rate than other ethnic groups and will therefore constitute an estimated 50.1% of the population, compared with the 72.4% reported in 2010 (Nieto & Bode, 2008; U.S. Census Bureau, 2011). The African American population is expected to increase from 12.3% in 2010 to 14.6% in 2050 (Nieto & Bode, 2008; U.S. Census Bureau, 2011). The Hispanic population will almost double, from 16.3% in 2010 to 24.4% in 2050 (Nieto & Bode, 2008; U.S. Census Bureau, 2011). Finally, the Asian population is expected to increase from 4.8% in 2010 to 8% in 2050 (Nieto & Bode, 2008; U.S. Census Bureau, 2011). Certainly, the rise in legal immigration and in the numbers of first-generation U.S. residents has contributed significantly to these figures. More than half of these residents are from Latin America, and one-quarter are from Asia (Nieto & Bode, 2008).

Changes in U.S. demographics are also reflected in our schools (Brown & Ortiz, 2014). There are now more than 4.4 million children who are ELLs in U.S. schools, meaning they are learning English as a second or even third language (National Center for Education Statistics [NCES], 2014; Nieto & Bode, 2008).

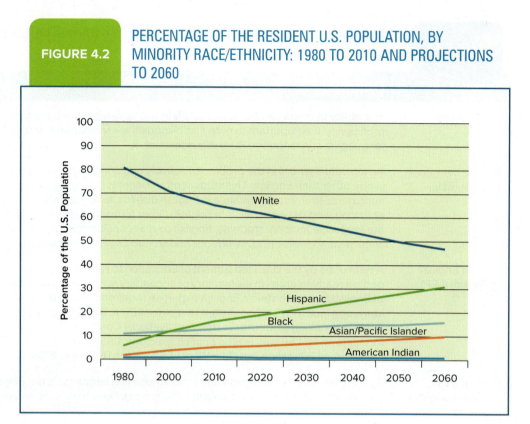

FIGURE 4.2 PERCENTAGE OF THE RESIDENT U.S. POPULATION, BY MINORITY RACE/ETHNICITY: 1980 TO 2010 AND PROJECTIONS TO 2060

SOURCE: U.S. Census Bureau (2012).

Among the more than 300 non-English languages spoken in the United States by individuals 5 years and older, Spanish is the first language of a little over 60% (Ryan, 2013).

Think back to the Opening Challenge. How are these changing demographic figures reflected in Ms. Grelak's classroom? Given the increasing diversity in our society and schools, educators are challenged to learn more about culture and how it influences our thinking, belief systems, values, and interactions. In other words, culture matters. Let's turn our attention to the definition of culture and to types of programs for CLD students.

DEFINITION OF CULTURE

What is culture? **Culture** is a way of perceiving the world and of interacting within it. Gollnick and Chinn (2012) noted that cultural norms influence our thinking, language, and behavior. Culture is shared; it includes the customs and values that bind us together. These customs developed over centuries in response to environmental conditions. And yet culture is not static; rather, it is dynamic, complex, and ever-changing. Our cultural identities evolve throughout our lives in response to political, economic, educational, and social experiences.

Cultural identity is learned as part of our ethnic group, but it is also developed as part of our religion, socioeconomic status, geographic region, place of residence (urban or rural), and gender, to name just a few microcultures. Our participation in some microcultural groups may take on more importance at different times in our lives. The interaction of these microcultures within the larger macroculture is also important. Schools and classrooms themselves develop their own patterns of behavior and are said to have a culture.

Culture is involved in all learning (Klingner, Boelé, Linan-Thompson, & Rodriguez, 2014). From the time we are quite young, we are socialized to learn in different ways. For example, in her classic study of children in three different communities, Shirley Brice Heath (1983) noted that only the middle-class White children started school accustomed to the ways of teaching and learning they encountered in their classrooms. They were not surprised when they were asked questions to which their teachers already knew the answers. They knew how to narrate stories in just the style expected by their teachers. Children from different backgrounds, on the other hand, were not accustomed to being asked questions designed to test their knowledge ("What shape is this?"). Some children had learned in their homes and communities to tell elaborate, complex stories that their schoolteachers did not value because they did not get to the point quickly enough. In other words, there was a mismatch between home and school cultures and between ways of teaching and learning. All the children in the communities Heath studied started school ready to learn, but their schools were not ready to teach all children. When Heath helped teachers understand these differences, they were able to instruct their students in ways that better capitalized on students' strengths and built on the knowledge and skills they brought to school.

In another classic study, Kathryn Au (1980) observed lessons while school staff in Hawaii implemented different reading programs that had been effective in other settings. It was not until the discourse of reading lessons became more like the style of day-to-day Hawaiian conversation that reading achievement improved. In other words, there had been a mismatch between the children's home culture and the culture of instruction in their schools. When the match between home and school improved, so did students' learning.

Teachers who are culturally responsive strive to match their instruction to their students. They make connections with their students as individuals, while understanding that there are many sociocultural influences on learning. What can teachers do to help CLD students learn and achieve to their potential? What lessons can Ms. Grelak in our Opening Challenge learn from the research we've discussed? Multicultural education is one approach to working with CLD students, including English language learners.

VIDEO CASE 4.1

Culturally and Linguistically Diverse Students

1. Why was the University of Texas Elementary School created eleven years ago? What is its purpose? How does Mia Tannous describe the efforts of her school to meet the needs of all students?

2. What methods do the teachers use to meet the needs of their students who are culturally and linguistically diverse? What advice does Lisa Sigafoos offer to new teachers to help them meet the needs of all their students?

MULTICULTURAL EDUCATION

We sometimes think of multicultural education as something added on to the curriculum, focusing on the holidays, traditions, and historical contributions of diverse ethnic groups. But multicultural education is much more than that. It is about making sure that schools are a place where all students feel welcomed, valued, and supported. Nieto and Bode (2008) define **multicultural education** as

> a process of comprehensive school reform and basic education for all students. It challenges and rejects racism and other forms of discrimination in schools and society and accepts and affirms the pluralism (ethnic, racial, linguistic, religious, economic, and gender, among others) that students, their communities, and teachers reflect. Multicultural education permeates the schools' curriculum and instructional strategies, as well as the interactions among teachers, students, and families, and the very way that schools conceptualize the nature of teaching and learning. Because it uses critical pedagogy as its underlying philosophy and focuses on knowledge, reflections, and action as the basis for social change, multicultural education promotes democratic principles of social justice. (p. 44)

Nieto and Bode emphasized that multicultural education should be a central part of comprehensive school reform movements designed to improve schooling for all students and to better prepare them for an increasingly diverse society.

Multicultural education is good for all students. All children benefit from "mirrors and windows"—that is, from seeing themselves reflected in the curriculum as well as from learning about others (Naidoo, 2014). All students benefit from learning there are multiple perspectives on any issue and from learning how to think critically about these issues. Instruction should build on students' experiences as a basis for further learning and should help them make connections with their own lives. Classrooms are a place of acceptance and mutual respect where no one is devalued. For example, during sharing time or storytelling, the teacher recognizes that students bring different ways of talking to school, and students are secure and comfortable risk-takers (Klingner et al., 2014). Linking episodes loosely or using a circular narrative structure is just as valid as relating a story in a more linear style. And when a student looks down rather than makes eye contact while the teacher is talking to her, the teacher considers that this might be a cultural norm and not a sign of disrespect. These also are examples of culturally responsive instruction.

ENGLISH LANGUAGE LEARNERS

Students who are not yet fully proficient in English are typically referred to as *English language learners* (ELLs) to emphasize that they are in the process of acquiring English. *Limited English proficient* (LEP) is another term used to mean the same thing and is the label preferred by the government. ELLs are a very diverse group (Brown & Ortiz, 2014). Although Spanish is the home language of the majority of ELLs, other languages (such as Vietnamese, Hmong, Cantonese, Korean, Haitian Creole, Arabic, Russian, Tagalog, and Navajo) are also well represented in U.S. classrooms. Subsets of ELLs are refugees or immigrants, with their own sets of needs (NCES, 2014). ELLs also vary in other ways, such as their socioeconomic status; nationality; generation in the United States; status as citizens, legal residents, or undocumented immigrants; and level of education in their home country, as well as the educational attainment of their parents (Hernández & Napierala, 2012). Some ELLs are already proficient readers in their native language; others are not. Thus, even though ELLs share some needs, such as the need to have their home language and culture valued and respected by their teachers, in other ways their needs vary. Each child is an individual.

WORKING *together*

In the Opening Challenge, you met Mrs. O'Malley, a first-year teacher who was concerned that she may not have had sufficient preservice training and experiences with ELLs to meet their needs in her science class. She met with a consultant from her school district, who offered state resources and identified an upcoming professional development session that might also provide useful information. Today, with increasingly complex standards being developed and implemented with the Common Core State Standards across the curriculum, it can be overwhelming for teachers to understand the standards and integrate them within their daily lessons. Consulting teachers who specialize in students whose first language is other than English are excellent resources who can assist teachers in areas such as (a) setting up the classroom, (b) being ready to teach ELLs from the first day of class, and (c) dealing with classroom management (https://www.heinemann.com/shared/onlineresources/E02682/Celic_websample.pdf). In addition, the consulting teacher can help teachers with their lesson plans, model how to administer lessons, and provide feedback after observing their teaching.

QUESTIONS

1. Before examining the website listed here (https://www.heinemann.com/shared/onlineresources/E02682/Celic_websample.pdf), think about ways in which your classroom can be designed to facilitate learning for ELLs. Review the information found online and compare your ideas to those mentioned. What did you think of the material and what did you identify that was not considered in the information presented?

2. Consider a lesson plan you have developed, either for a class in your program or to teach if you are a practicing teacher. Highlight sections of the lesson plan that are "ELL friendly," and underline sections that may need to be altered to meet the needs of students who struggle with English. What percentage of the lesson components were "ELL friendly," when compared with those that were not?

DISPROPORTIONATE REPRESENTATION OF CULTURALLY AND LINGUISTICALLY DIVERSE STUDENTS IN SPECIAL EDUCATION

CLD students are not any more likely than their peers to have true disabilities. Yet, despite the best intentions of their teachers and other school staff, they are overrepresented in special education programs relative to their percentages in the overall school-age population (Sullivan & Bal, 2013). Notably, CLD students are overrepresented only in the high-incidence disability categories (learning disabilities, intellectual and developmental disabilities, and emotional or behavioral disorders), not in the low-incidence disability categories (such as visual, auditory, or orthopedic impairment; U.S. Department of Education, Office of Special Education and Rehabilitative Services, Office of Special Education Programs [USDE], 2014). Medical doctors diagnose these latter disabilities, usually before a child starts school. On the other hand, school staff usually identify high-incidence disabilities after the child has started school. These are referred to as the judgmental categories, because the diagnosis relies so heavily on professional judgment (Sullivan & Bal, 2013).

Overrepresentation is most apparent among African American students when we look at nationally aggregated data (see Table 4.2), yet there are dramatic differences across states (NCES, 2014). The federal government reports two ways of calculating students' representation in special education categories: by risk indices and by risk ratios. We calculate the risk index by dividing the number of students in a given racial or ethnic group who are placed in a particular disability category by the total enrollment for that racial or ethnic group in the school population. The risk ratio is the risk index of one racial or ethnic group divided by the risk index of another racial or ethnic group. It provides a comparative index of the risk of being placed in a particular disability category and is the indicator of disproportionate representation preferred by the U.S. Department of Education, Office of Special Education Programs (OSEP).

Given that special education provides students with extra resources and specialized services, some researchers and educators wonder why so many people consider overrepresentation a problem. There are several reasons. Students in special education may have limited access to the general

| TABLE 4.2 | ETHNIC REPRESENTATION IN U.S. SPECIAL EDUCATION, 2012 (NATIONAL AGGREGATES IN PERCENTAGES) |

Disability	American Indian or Alaska Native	Asian	Black or African American	Hispanic/ Latino	Native Hawaiian or Other Pacific Islander	White	Two or more races
Autism	4.2	18.0	5.5	5.8	5.1	8.9	8.6
Deaf-Blindness	#	#	#	#	0.1	#	#
Developmental delay[a]	4.9	2.0	2.5	1.4	3.3	2.2	3.0
Emotional disturbance	6.3	2.5	8.8	3.9	4.8	6.4	8.5
Hearing impairments	0.9	2.9	0.9	1.4	2.3	1.1	1.0
Intellectual disabilities	6.8	7.6	10.5	6.8	5.9	6.4	60
Multiple disabilities	2.4	2.8	2.2	1.6	2.8	2.4	#
Orthopedic impairments	0.5	1.5	0.6	1.0	0.9	1.0	0.8
Other health impairments	11.1	7.9	12.8	8.9	10.1	15.6	149
Specific learning disabilities	46.4	26.7	41.8	49.0	52.9	36.0	35.6
Speech or language impairments	15.8	26.7	13.7	19.4	10.6	19.1	18.9
Traumatic brain injury	0.4	0.5	0.4	0.3	0.3	0.5	0.5
Visual impairments	0.4	0.8	0.4	0.4	0.9	0.5	0.4

Percentage was nonzero but less than 0.05 or 5/100 of 1%.

[a]States' use of the *developmental delay* category is optional for children ages 3 through 9 and is not applicable to children older than 9.

NOTE: Percentage was calculated by dividing the number of students ages 6 through 21 served under *IDEA*, Part B, in the racial/ethnic group and disability category by the total number of students ages 6 through 21 served under *IDEA*, Part B, in the racial/ethnic group and all disability categories, then multiplying the result by 100. The sum of column percentages may not total 100 because of rounding.

SOURCE: U.S. Department of Education, National Center for Education Statistics [NCES], Common Core of Data [CCD] (2012). These data are for the 50 states; Washington, DC; Bureau of Indian Education schools; Puerto Rico; the four outlying areas; and the three freely associated states. For actual data used, go to http://www.ed.gov/about/reports/annual/osep.

education curriculum. When students have been placed inappropriately, the services they receive may not meet their needs. Also, disability labels stigmatize students as inferior and abnormal; result in lowered expectations from their teachers, families, and even themselves; potentially separate them from peers; and lead to diminished educational and life outcomes (Hammer, 2012). Think back to the Opening Challenge. How does this information about overrepresentation influence your thinking about what Ms. Grelak should do about Allen?

What can we do to address overrepresentation? Change starts with each of us examining our own assumptions about how students learn and why they struggle and then considering what we each can do to improve learning opportunities for students. Too often, explanations for students' underachievement and inappropriate placement in special education have focused on perceived limitations in students' homes and communities. Ethnically diverse learners can and do excel in schools when culturally responsive and relevant teaching (CRT) is in place (Shealey, McHatton, & Wilson, 2011). CRT occurs when teachers utilize learners' culture, prior experiences, and performance styles to provide instruction that engages students intellectually, emotionally, socially, and politically.

MULTICULTURAL SPECIAL EDUCATION

Regardless of questionable special education referral, assessment, and placement practices, some CLD students *do* have disabilities and can benefit from appropriate services in special education programs. The field of multicultural special education offers the research base and expertise to guide educators in making well-informed decisions (Shealey et al., 2011). The goals of multicultural special education are to reduce inappropriate referrals, improve assessment procedures, and enhance instructional and support services.

The majority of ELLs with disabilities have learning disabilities; reading difficulties are the primary ones. Yet compared with ELLs without disabilities, ELLs with disabilities are more likely to receive fewer language support services and be instructed only in English. They also face many misconceptions (and realities); teachers should be aware of the associated implications (see Table 4.3).

One area that seems to be particularly problematic is distinguishing between learning disabilities and the process of acquiring English as a second language. There are many similarities, confusing even well-prepared experts. In Table 4.4, we compare and contrast the characteristics associated with learning disabilities, the process of acquiring a second language (L2), and cultural influences.

Whenever educators are trying to determine why a child is struggling, they should consider the learning context and environmental factors that might be

Diverse Families

TABLE 4.3 MISCONCEPTIONS AND REALITIES ABOUT THE LANGUAGE ACQUISITION PROCESS

Misconception	Reality	Implications
Bilingualism means equal proficiency in both languages.	Bilingualism rarely means equal proficiency in both languages.	1. ELLs are students with a wide range of proficiencies in their home language and English, with varying levels of bilingualism. 2. Bilingual students may be stronger in some areas in their home language and stronger in other areas in English.
Semilingualism is a valid concept and "non-non" classifications indicating children are limited in their home language and English (based on test results) are useful categories.	Semilingualism and "non-non" categories are the results of tests that do not measure the full range and depth of language proficiencies among ELLs acquiring two languages simultaneously.	1. The vast majority of children begin school having acquired the syntactic and morphological rules of the language of their community. 2. Current language assessment measures rarely capture the full range of skills that bilingual children bring to the classroom. 3. Classifying students as "limited-limited" or "non-non" is not useful because it does not guide teachers as to what students know or need to learn; instead, it promotes low expectations. 4. Other forms of authentic assessment should be used to determine language proficiency levels of ELLs, including natural language samples.
The more time students spend receiving English literacy instruction (being immersed in it), the faster they will learn to read in English.	Students who receive some home language literacy instruction achieve at higher levels in English reading than students who do not receive it.	1. Instruction in English and interactions with English speakers are important but not enough to provide the optimal support for ELLs to be able to fully participate in classroom learning and achieve to their potential. 2. Skills developed in students' native language transfer to English, particularly when teachers help students make connections across languages. 3. Students acquire English when they receive input that is understandable (i.e., by using language in context, providing background knowledge, using visual and context cues, clarifying vocabulary).
Errors are problematic and should be avoided.	"Errors" are a positive sign that the student is making progress, and are a necessary aspect of second language acquisition.	1. Overgeneralizing grammatical rules from one language to another is a natural, normal aspect of second language acquisition; this is referred to as interlanguage. 2. Errors such as confusion with verb tenses, plurals, possessives, word order, subject/verb agreement, and the use of articles are common among ELLs and should not be interpreted as signifying that a student has a disability. 3. Code-switching is common among bilingual individuals around the world and should not be considered a sign of confusion.
ELLs are not ready to engage in higher level thinking until they learn basic skills.	ELLs are equally capable of engaging in higher level thinking as their fully proficient peers.	1. Instruction and practice at every grade level must provide frequent opportunities for ELLs to engage in higher level thinking. 2. Instruction should ensure that ELLs of all proficiency levels have multiple entry points to access content.
All ELLs learn English in the same way at about the same rate; a slow rate of acquisition indicates a possible disability.	The length of time it takes students to acquire academic language in English varies a great deal, from four to seven years or more.	1. Many different variables affect the language acquisition process. 2. Even when ELLs appear to be quite proficient in English, they may not yet have acquired full academic proficiency. 3. The reasons for an ELL's struggles when learning to read are more likely to relate to the language acquisition process than to a disability.

SOURCE: Klingner (2014, pp. 6–7).

TABLE 4.4	SOME SIMILARITIES BETWEEN LEARNING DISABILITIES AND LANGUAGE ACQUISITION
Behaviors Associated With Learning Disabilities	**Behaviors When Acquiring a Second Language**
Difficulty following directions	Difficulty following directions because the directions were not well understood; it can be harder to remember directions in a second language.
Difficulty with phonological awareness	Difficulty auditorily distinguishing between sounds not in one's first language, or sounds that are presented in a different order.
Slow to learn sound-symbol correspondence	Confusion with sound-symbol correspondence when it is different than in one's first language. Difficulty pronouncing sounds not in the first language.
Difficulty remembering sight words	Difficulty remembering sight words when word meanings are not understood.
Difficulty retelling a story in sequence	Difficulty retelling a story in English without the expressive skills to do so, but the student might understand more than he or she can convey (i.e., receptive skills in English might be stronger than expressive skills).
Confusion with figurative language	Confusion with figurative language, idioms, pronouns, conjunctions, and words with multiple meanings.
Slow to process a challenging language	Slow to process a challenging language because it is not well understood.
May have poor auditory memory	May seem to have poor auditory memory if sounds or words are unfamiliar or not well understood.
May have difficulty concentrating	Learning in a second language is mentally exhausting; therefore, ELLs may seem to have difficulty concentrating at times.
May seem easily frustrated	Learning in a second language can be frustrating.

SOURCE: Adapted from Klingner (2014).

influencing learning. In the Considering Diversity feature, we present questions for instruction, assessment, and the learning environment as a means for thinking about whether children have had sufficient opportunities to learn before being considered for special education referral, which is discussed in Chapter 5.

EFFECTIVE MULTICULTURAL SPECIAL EDUCATION PROGRAMS

CLD students with special needs should be taught with validated instructional practices in culturally responsive, supportive learning environments (Shealey et al., 2011). This is a theme that resonates throughout the chapters in this book, where you will read about many validated practices to teach instructional content that supports the learning needs of CLD students.

CONSIDERING *diversity*

EQUAL OPPORTUNITY TO LEARN

Federal law stipulates that before children can be considered as having a disability, they must have received an adequate opportunity to learn. Thus, if they have missed too much schooling, they have not received enough instruction. Or, if they have attended school but the instruction has not been comprehensible or appropriate for their needs, they have not received an adequate opportunity to learn. The following questions can help make this determination:

Instruction

- Is the instruction at the appropriate level for the student—not too difficult or too easy?
- Is the instruction comprehensible—either provided in the student's native language or taught with sufficient supports to be understood?
- Is the instruction meaningful, motivating, and interesting for the student?
- Does the instruction explicitly help the student make connections between what he or she already knows and new learning?

- Are culturally relevant materials and culturally appropriate instructional practices used?
- When the student does not make progress, is he or she taught in different ways in a more intensive manner?
- Has the instructional model been validated with students who are similar to the student?
- Is the teacher implementing the instructional model with fidelity? If adaptations are made, are they consistent with research?
- Is the student's language acquisition supported?

Assessment

- Is the student's learning of what he or she has been taught assessed?
- Is the student allowed to demonstrate learning in multiple ways, including in his or her native language if appropriate?

- Does the assessment process inform instructional decisions?
- How does the student's rate of progress compare with the learning rates of his or her peers?
- Is the student reaching benchmarks?

Learning Environment

- Is the classroom learning environment a warm, supportive, and collaborative one, where students help each other and all students' contributions are valued?
- Does the teacher build positive, supportive relationships with students?
- Does the teacher work well with students' families and the community?
- Does the teacher help most culturally and linguistically diverse students succeed to high levels?

This last point deserves elaboration. In other words, if most of a student's peers are doing well but he or she is not, that is quite a different scenario from one in which most students in the class are struggling. If just one or two children are struggling, this reaffirms that they need additional support. If almost everyone is making little progress, the teacher should reexamine his or her instruction. Referring to the Opening Challenge, how can Ms. Grelak use the answers these questions yield to think about Gabriel's learning problems?

For example, Orosco and Klingner (2010) observed in Response to Intervention (RTI) classrooms and noted the value of aligning assessment and interventions. They also noted that one of the more successful teachers "provided direct and explicit native-language instruction that was socially and linguistically meaningful by connecting it to students' cultural and linguistic experiences" (p. 278). The most advantageous programs incorporate students' home cultures and include native-language instruction as well as a focus on English language development. It is this deliberate and intensive focus on *language* that makes bilingual special education distinct from generic special education (Klingner, 2014).

Linguistic Support

Language development should be an essential goal of instruction, whether in students' native language, in English, or in both. Students benefit from explicit instruction in vocabulary, through preteaching and ongoing reinforcement, using visuals and graphic organizers to bring words to life and make them meaningful for students. Instruction should also focus on developing students' higher order thinking and active problem-solving skills. Students should be provided with many and varied opportunities to practice and apply what they are learning (Bryant et al., 2014).

Brown and Ortiz (2014) noted that language develops along a continuum. The information found in Table 4.5 may be helpful as you develop linguistic supports for ELL students.

Validated Instructional Practices

Several instructional practices show promise when used with ELLs with disabilities. Vaughn and colleagues (2006) effectively provided ELLs with support in reading in their native language. Helpful interventions in English have included focused reading interventions coupled with language development activities, such as the use of repetitive language, modeling, gesturing, visuals, and explicit instruction in English language usage (Vaughn, Mathes, Linan-Thompson, & Francis, 2005).

Other instructional approaches promote students' reading comprehension and/or content learning. These include graphic organizers (Goldenberg, 2008) and collaborative strategic reading (CSR; Klingner, Vaughn, Boardman, & Swanson, 2012). CSR includes collaboration as an important instructional component, such as through peer tutoring and cooperative learning. You will learn more about these approaches in later chapters.

Curricular Modifications

Goldenberg (2008) noted the importance of providing culturally and linguistically diverse students with curricular modifications. Modifications might include the following:

TABLE 4.5	LANGUAGE PROFICIENCY CONTINUUM

Level	English language learner characteristics	How do ELLs gain language?	What do ELLs understand?	What can ELLs do?
1	Can be silent for an initial period; recognizes basic vocabulary and high-frequency words; may begin to speak with few words or imitate others	Multiple repetitions of language; simple sentences; practice with partners; use visuals and realia; model, model, model; check for understanding; build on cultural and linguistic history	Instructions such as "listen," "line up," "point to," "repeat color," "tell," "touch," "circle," "draw," "match," "label"	Use gestures; use other native speakers; use high-frequency phrases; use common nouns; communicate basic needs; use survival language (i.e., words and phrases needed for basic daily tasks and routines, e.g., *bathroom, no, yes*)
2	Understands phrases and short sentences; begins to use general vocabulary and everyday expressions; grammatical forms may include present, present progressive and imperative	Multiple repetitions of language; visual supports for vocabulary; preteach content vocabulary; link to prior knowledge	Present and past tense; school-related topics; comparatives/superlatives; routine questions; imperative tense; simple sequence words	Routine expressions; simple phrases; subject-verb agreement; ask for help
3	Increased comprehension in context; may sound proficient but has social, *not* academic, language; inconsistent use of standard grammatical structures	Multiple repetitions of language; use synonyms and antonyms; use word banks; demonstrate simple sentences; link to prior knowledge	Past progressive tense; contractions; auxiliary verbs/verb phrases; basic idioms; general meaning; relationship between words	Formulate questions; compound sentences; use precise adjectives; use synonyms; expanded responses
4	Very good comprehension; more complex speech and with fewer errors; engages in conversation on a variety of topics and skills; can manipulate language to represent his or her thinking but may have difficulty with abstract academic concepts; continues to need academic language development	Multiple repetitions of language; authentic practice opportunities to develop fluency and automaticity in communication; explicit instruction in the use of language; specific feedback; continued vocabulary development in all content areas	Present/perfect continuous; general and implied meaning; varied sentences; figurative language; connecting ideas	Range of purposes; increased cultural competence; standard grammar (USA); solicit information

(Continued)

TABLE 4.5 (CONTINUED)

Level	English language learner characteristics	How do ELLs gain language?	What do ELLs understand?	What can ELLs do?
5	Communicates effectively on a wide range of topics; participates fully in all content areas at grade level but may still require curricular adjustments; comprehends concrete and abstract concepts; produces extended interactions to a variety of audiences	May not be fully English proficient in all domains (i.e., reading, writing, speaking, listening); has mastered formal and informal language conventions; multiple opportunities to practice complex grammatical forms; meaningful opportunities to engage in conversations; explicit instruction in the smaller details of English usage Focus on gaps or areas still needing instruction in English; focus on comprehension instruction in all language domains	Analyze; defend; debate; predict; evaluate; justify; hypothesize and synthesize; restate; critique	May not yet be fully proficient across all domains; comprehends concrete and abstract topics; communicates effectively on a wide range of topics and purposes; produces extended interactions to a variety of audiences; participates fully in all content areas at grade level but may still require curricular modifications Increasing understanding of meaning, including figurative language; read grade-level text with academic language support; support their own point of view; use humor in native-like way

SOURCE: Adapted from Brown and Ortiz (2014).

- Providing taped textbooks.
- Highlighting textbooks and study guides.
- Using supplementary materials.
- Giving directions in small, distinct steps.
- Using written backup for oral directions.
- Using bilingual dictionaries.

As much as possible, however, the curriculum should emphasize enrichment rather than remedial activities.

CLD students with and without disabilities benefit from culturally responsive instruction in positive, supportive learning environments. Students thrive when they are valued and cared about, when their strengths are recognized and used in the service of their learning, when their achievement is carefully monitored, and when they are provided with appropriate instruction and effective, timely support when needed. For ELLs, instruction includes a strong oral language component. Thinking back to Gabriel in the Opening Challenge, how can Ms. Grelak improve instruction to meet Gabriel's needs?

Next, we discuss students who are at risk for school difficulties and who deserve special attention to ensure their learning needs are addressed.

WHO ARE STUDENTS "AT RISK" AND WHAT SHOULD WE KNOW AND DO TO HELP THEM ACHIEVE THEIR FULL POTENTIAL?

Students are considered *at risk* for school failure or underachievement if their family situations, personal conditions, and life events negatively affect their school lives. Although educators may not be able to influence some of the many factors that place students at risk, they can make a difference in these students' education by carefully identifying academic, behavioral, and social problems that can result from these factors and then implementing and monitoring plans to address them. Here we discuss the types of students who are at risk, possible conditions that contribute to risk, and ways to tackle the problems.

DEFINITION OF "AT RISK"

Students who are **at risk** have experiences, living conditions, or characteristics that contribute to school failure. Informal experiences such as interactions with other children, interactions with adults, and activities contribute to language and cognitive development in the early years of a child's life. Students who have limited life experiences, lower expectations, and fewer academic opportunities because of family situations, family income, and even geography lag behind their peers right from the start when entering school. Living conditions such as poverty, neglect, homelessness, physically and/or verbally abusive situations (including bullying), and drug or alcohol abuse contribute significantly to the risk.

Students who struggle with depression, exhibit suicidal tendencies, are coping with the death of a loved one, or are experiencing a divorce in their family may also have limited capacity to cope with the demands of the educational setting. Careful coordination and collaboration between the family and a team of professionals (such as social workers, school counselors, medical professionals, psychologists, and educators) are needed to tackle the challenges caused by these conditions. Students at risk benefit from academic and social support services and often respond to the same instructional practices that help students with high-incidence conditions learn the general education curriculum.

Many CLD students do well in school. However, some tend to underperform on measures of academic achievement in the United States (NAEP, 2013). During the 1970s and 1980s, the achievement gaps between African American and White students and between Hispanic and White students narrowed, but in the late 1980s and 1990s they widened again and are still large (NAEP, 2013). These gaps remain even when analysts statistically control for differences in parental income and housing value. A major educational goal is to close the performance gaps between groups of students.

The achievement gap is often characterized by substandard performance in reading, writing, and computing. Educational problems like these sometimes contribute to students' giving up and dropping out of school. Hispanic students have higher dropout rates than non-Hispanic students (NCES, 2014). Unfortunately, the economic and employment picture is bleak for students who drop out of high school because they lack the education and experience employers seek in the more competitive high-salary positions. Many educators suggest we should address these challenges by ensuring that CLD students receive an education more culturally and linguistically responsive to their needs (e.g., Shealey et al., 2011). In upcoming chapters, you will read about many ways to ensure such education.

SOME CONDITIONS THAT CONTRIBUTE TO RISK

Many conditions that contribute to risk affect students' performance in schools. In this section, we discuss several of these risk factors to help you better understand them as you work with children in inclusive settings. They are poverty, homelessness, migrant family factors, health influences, and the conditions of some schools.

Poverty

The link among childhood poverty, poor school outcomes, and disabilities is clear and well documented (DeNavas-Walt, Proctor, & Smith, 2012). The most important predictor of student success in school is readiness to learn to read. Unfortunately, many children from high-poverty homes enter school with limited readiness skills. Diverse students are overrepresented in the poverty category compared with their representation in the general population. Statistics for children under 18 living in poverty show that 39% of Black children, 36% of Native American children, and 33% of Hispanic children are poor, compared with only 13% of White children (U.S. Department of Commerce, 2013).

Homelessness

Not all children in poverty are homeless, but the relationship between homelessness and poverty is obvious. Homeless children and children of immigrants and migrant workers often experience disruption and dislocation—circumstances that can be challenging as they try to cope with frequent transitions from school to school (United States Department of Education, Office of Special Education and Rehabilitative Services, 2014). Children who live in shelters may be embarrassed or afraid they will be judged or stigmatized because they are homeless (National Center for Homeless Education [NCHE], 2014). These students often change schools every few months, breaking the continuity of their education and leaving gaps in their knowledge that result in reduced academic achievement. Educators must understand that their low academic performance occurs because of many factors, including fragmented education, absenteeism, and high risk for health problems.

On a positive note, between 2007 and 2013, unsheltered homelessness declined by 23% (U.S. Department of Housing and Urban Development [HUD], 2013). However, being homeless is difficult for children (NCHE, 2014). In one study, researchers tested children living in an urban shelter and found that 46% of them had a disability. The most common disability, affecting some 30% of these children, was emotional or behavioral disor-

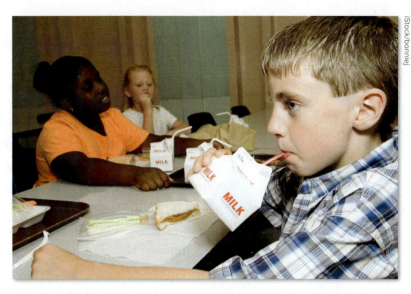

More than any other factor, poverty accounts for poor school performance. However, many school services available to students in poverty can make a real difference, such as free or low-cost meals.

ders. Because of the lack of social services and shelters, being homeless in rural areas is also challenging. Given the high percentage of homeless children who also have disabilities, IDEA '04 pays special attention to them and their unique needs (National Center for Homeless Education, 2007).

Migrant Status

Being from a migrant worker's family also places children at risk for poor school performance. An estimated 50% of migrant and seasonal farm workers are U.S. citizens or legal immigrants (Housing Assistance Council, 2011). These workers earn incomes below the federal poverty level. Most live in Florida, Texas, or California between November and April and move to find agricultural work the rest of the year. Approximately half a million migrant students live in the United States, and about 75% of them are Hispanic.

Lack of Health Care

The Children's Defense Fund (CDF, 2014) gives us some additional and alarming facts to consider when we think about the relationship between the conditions under which children live in the United States and their incidence of disabilities:

- More than one in five children, and almost one in four under age 5, were identified as poor in 2012.

- The median income of female-headed single-parent families was less than one-third of the median income of married-couple families and less than one-half of the median income of all families with children.

- In each state and the District of Columbia, a full-time minimum-wage worker cannot afford the monthly fair market rent (FMR) for a two-bedroom rental unit.

- In Fiscal Year 2011, 37 states and the District of Columbia had more than one in five children living in food-insecure households, which increases the risk of obesity. In 45 states and the District of Columbia, more than one in four children were overweight or obese.

- More than 21 million children received free or reduced-price school lunch in 2012, but only 2.3 million of them received meals during the summer of that same year.

- Despite substantial improvements in recent years, 1 in 11 (about 7.2 million) children under 19 were uninsured in 2012.

- The United States ranks 26th in immunization rates among industrialized countries.

There is no denying the lifelong impact of poor nutrition, limited or no access to health care (through being uninsured), and lack of timely immunizations during childhood (CDF, 2014). During the school year, the effects can be seen in learning and behavior problems. Across the life span, there are adverse effects on employment and life satisfaction.

At-Risk Schools

School environments can be rated as at risk for a number of reasons, including low performance. These schools tend to need major renovations, and the classrooms are crowded with too many students. Resources such as technology and instructional materials are typically limited, which means students do not have the same learning opportunities and experiences as their peers in better schools. Some teachers may be first-year instructors unprepared to handle the issues in an at-risk school, such as limited classroom resources, low standards and expectations for students, a high dropout rate, and discipline problems. Other teachers may be burned out from grappling with these issues and trying to teach at the same time (Starkes, 2013).

Although these issues are complex, they are not insurmountable. For example, the No Child Left Behind Act (2001) requires states to align state assessments with state standards. States must establish annual progress goals for improvement so all students can achieve proficiency. If goals are not achieved, schools must implement strategies to improve student performance. Moreover, assessment data must be disaggregated by group to determine how students with disabilities and CLD students are performing. Thus, the achievement gap is visible and the schools are accountable. School leaders must work strategically to establish appropriate interventions while keeping abreast of emerging research as they plan instruction at the elementary and secondary levels, especially in low-performing schools (Hassel & Hassel, 2010).

Students at Risk

Finally, well-prepared teachers and high-quality instruction are critical components in student learning. More attention is now focused on what we as educators are doing to help students learn. Research shows that activities such as providing explicit and systematic instruction with multiple opportunities for practice, differentiating instruction based on assessment results, adapting instruction to meet students' needs, and monitoring student progress improve students' academic outcomes (Bryant, Bryant, et al., 2014). What James M. Kauffman (1999) stated more than 20 years ago remains true today:

> If we are going to help students . . . we are going to have to change course. We cannot continue to avoid focusing on instruction! We cannot continue to suppose that consultation and collaboration [and structural changes] will somehow make up for the deficit in instruction. We cannot rely on substitutes for . . . intensive, relentless instruction. (p. 247)

Although Kauffman was referring to special education instruction, his advice is applicable to instruction for students at risk of school failure and for educators who teach in all schools.

PREVENTION OF RISK

The best way to help ensure that students are not at high risk of school failure is to make improvements in health care and educational practices.

Health Care

According to the Children's Defense Fund, the most effective and efficient way to make an enormous difference in the outcomes of children in poverty is to remove the risk variables by

- Improving these children and their families' access to health care.
- Removing bureaucratic barriers to existing health care options.
- Working hard to ensure every child has the healthy start necessary to survive and thrive in life (CDF, 2014).

Of course, effecting such sweeping social change is beyond any individual's capabilities, but alert educators can take certain actions to make a real difference in the lives of children. For example, even without guarantees that all workers will be insured, many free services are available to the poor and to people who live in urban centers. Unfortunately, however, families are often afraid of or unaware of them. Being knowledgeable about resources in your community and then increasing awareness of their availability is one way to help poor parents gain access to medical services that prevent some disabilities from occurring.

Educational Practices

Differentiating instruction to address specific learning needs of students in response to the tasks at hand is one example of an effective educational practice. Differentiating focuses on the tasks students must perform, their learning needs, and the adaptations that can be made to accommodate their individual needs. Thinking back to the ADAPT framework introduced in Chapter 1, you can adapt the way you deliver instruction in small groups and with extra instructional support. Specialized materials and adaptations in the content or activity are all ways to make learning more appropriate and individualized.

Another effective educational practice is universal screening to identify students who are performing in the risk category and then providing intervention to support the core or regular class instruction. For example, early identification and intervention to help students with learning and behavior difficulties in kindergarten through Grade 3 have received national attention in legislation such as IDEA and No Child Left Behind. The intent of early intervention is to prevent learning problems from escalating and to reduce inappropriate referrals to special education as a result of inadequate or poor instruction.

Screening and intervention are also necessary at the secondary level. Some students with learning problems manage to perform well enough to get by in the elementary grades. However, as the curriculum becomes more challenging, academic issues surface and require intervention. For example, students with reading problems may not successfully read and understand subject-area textbooks (history, science), or students with mathematics difficulties may lack the arithmetic and problem-solving skills needed for more advanced topics such as algebra. These are the students who are most at risk of dropping out of the educational system because of academic frustration.

Working collaboratively with other professionals and family members is yet another educational practice that responds to the special needs of students at risk. Multidisciplinary teams can generate solutions to problems teachers are encountering in the classroom when trying to work with a range of student needs. Team members can also provide in-class support to implement screening and intervention practices. Finally, connecting to families is critical to learning about their unique situations. The time spent in this endeavor will go a long way in identifying solutions to the problems and challenges families face.

In the next section, we discuss another group of students with special needs. Those with gifts and talents require specialized services to ensure their abilities are truly nurtured and enriched.

WHAT ARE THE ATTRIBUTES OF STUDENTS WITH GIFTS AND TALENTS?

Gifted and talented students do not necessarily face the same kind of challenges as most children who receive special education services. However, because of their unique needs, they confront other obstacles. Many gifted and talented learners are frequently stifled by educational approaches that do not challenge their cognitive abilities or help them achieve to their full potential. For these reasons, many parents, policymakers, and education professionals believe these students need special programs and services (National Association for Gifted Children [NAGC], n.d.).

IDEA does not offer gifted and talented students protections and rights as it does for students with disabilities. Although many states provide mandated services for gifted students, relatively few have laws or regulations that offer educational protections for gifted students similar to those found in IDEA for students with disabilities (NAGC, n.d.). Education for gifted and talented students is addressed in the Jacob K. Javits Gifted and Talented Students Education Act, initially enacted in 1988 (PL 100-297) and 2001. Let's examine the definition of giftedness, some traits that characterize it, the categories of students who are eligible for this identification, and teaching practices that address their unique needs.

DEFINITION

Why is it important to define giftedness? One reason is that the way a state or school district defines "gifted and talented" influences the identification process that determines who is eligible for special services. Many state departments of education rely on a federal definition of gifted and talented to come up with their own definition. These state definitions are then used as a guide to develop school district policies for identification and eligibility criteria (NAGC, 2014). Table 4.6 provides several commonly used definitions.

Defining giftedness is a complicated and often controversial task. There is no one universally accepted interpretation of what it means to be gifted and/or talented. Some definitions and identification procedures are more restrictive than others and emphasize test performance, including cutoff scores on intelligence and achievement tests. As a result, access to services for the gifted continues to be limited for many students who, despite their high abilities, may not perform well on these measures. Other definitions and identification procedures reflect a multidimensional view of gifted abilities with less emphasis on psychometric profiles. Adopting a broader perspective can "cast a wider net" and include students typically overlooked for consideration as gifted (Webb, Gore, Amend, & DeVries, 2007).

VIDEO CASE 4.2

Interview With a Parent of a Gifted Student

1. How does Anne Alvarez describe the characteristics of students who have gifts and talents? How did she see these characteristics in her own son?

2. What advice does Ms. Alvarez give to support the social and academic successes of children with gifts and talents? How can you incorporate these suggestions in the future, if you teach students who are gifted and talented?

Gifted Students

TABLE 4.6	DEFINITIONS OF GIFTED AND TALENTED
Source	**Definition**
U.S. Department of Education (Purcell, 1978, PL 95-561, Title IX, sec. 902)	The term "gifted and talented children" means children and, whenever applicable, youth, who are identified at the preschool, elementary, or secondary level as possessing demonstrated or potential abilities that give evidence of high performance capability in areas such as intellectual, creative, specific academic, or leadership ability or in the performing and visual arts and who by reason thereof require services or activities not ordinarily provided by the school. . . . [G]ifted and talented will encompass a minimum of 3 to 5 percent of the school population.
Jacob K. Javits Gifted and Talented Students Education Act of 1988 (PL 100-297)	Children and youth with outstanding talent [who] perform or show the potential for performing at remarkably high levels of accomplishment when compared with others of their age, experience, or environment. The children and youth exhibit high performance capability, or excel in specific academic fields. They require services or activities not ordinarily provided by schools. Outstanding talents are present in children and youth from all cultural groups, across all economic strata, and in all areas of human endeavor.
Federal government, No Child Left Behind Act of 2001 (PL 107-110)	Students, children, or youth who give evidence of high achievement capability in areas such as intellectual, creative, or leadership capacity, or in specific academic fields, and who need services or activities not ordinarily provided by the school in order to fully develop those capabilities.

TYPES

Howard Gardner's (1983) theory of multiple intelligences provides an excellent example of a broad perspective on intelligence and giftedness. In his book *Frames of Mind,* Gardner proposed that multiple dimensions of intelligence exist. This theory challenged the more traditional notion that giftedness can be defined, assessed, and identified only by standardized tests, which actually measure just a small sample of an individual's aptitude and abilities. Individuals with outstanding or unusual performance in any one of nine dimensions of intelligence—presented in Table 4.7—could be considered gifted under Gardner's scheme.

CHARACTERISTICS

What characteristics come to mind when you think of a gifted student? You may think of someone who is a natural leader, is an avid reader, has great mathematical aptitude, and excels in just about everything. Although some students can be considered "globally gifted," the majority of gifted students excel in some areas and not others. Students who are gifted are a heterogeneous group who differ from each other in abilities, interests, motivation, behavior, and needs. And yet they do share some characteristics. The

TABLE 4.7	GARDNER'S MULTIPLE INTELLIGENCES
Intelligence	**Definition**
Verbal-Linguistic	The ability to use languages effectively to accomplish certain goals.
Logical-Mathematical	The capacity to analyze problems using logical reasoning and problem solving.
Musical	Contains skill in performance and the emotional aspect of sound.
Kinesthetic	Entails one's body for both expressive [*sic*] and to solve problems.
Spatial	The ability to recognize and manipulate the visual aspects of the world.
Intrapersonal	The capacity to recognize one's own desires, fears, and capacities.
Interpersonal	The capacity to understand the intentions, motivations, and desires of other people.
Naturalist	Exhibits recognition for living and natural things.
Existential	The capacity to locate oneself with respect to the furthest reaches of the cosmos and the related capacity to locate oneself with respect to such existential features of the human condition.

SOURCE: Kutz, Dyer, and Campbell (2013, p. 2).

National Society for the Gifted and Talented identified these characteristics across six areas: creative thinking, general intellectual ability, specific academic ability, leadership, psychomotor ability, and visual/performing arts abilities (see Table 4.8).

Educators should be familiar with the characteristics of gifted learners for several reasons. First, recognizing how they learn best can help create an environment conducive to their success. For example, understanding that many students who are gifted learn quickly, have advanced interests, and become bored with drill and practice activities, teachers can differentiate instruction so that once students demonstrate mastery of the content being studied, they can explore topics in greater depth and in more creative ways.

Although many characteristics in Table 4.8 influence students to become highly focused and successful in and out of school, teachers need to understand how some traits, left unattended, can have a negative impact. For instance, sometimes the sensitivity, perfectionism, and intensity common among gifted students can become exaggerated and paralyzing for students, which causes a great deal of stress and contributes to underachievement. Dysfunctional perfectionism can lead to an inability to tolerate mistakes, avoidance of demanding tasks for fear of failure, and refusal to turn in assignments that are less than perfect (Fletcherm & Speirs Neumeister, 2012). Gifted students are also

TABLE 4.8	COMMON CHARACTERISTICS OF GIFTED AND TALENTED CHILDREN IN SIX AREAS
Area	**Characteristics**
Creative Thinking	• Independent thinker • Exhibits original thinking in oral and written expression • Comes up with several solutions to a given problem	• Possesses a sense of humor • Creates and invents • Challenged by creative tasks • Improvises often • Does not mind being different from the crowd
General Intellectual Ability	• Formulates abstractions • Processes information in complex ways • Observant • Excited about new ideas • Enjoys hypothesizing	• Learns rapidly • Uses a large vocabulary • Inquisitive • Self-starter
Specific Academic Ability	• Good memorization ability • Advanced comprehension • Acquires basic skill knowledge quickly	• Widely read in special interest area • High academic success in special interest area • Pursues special interest with enthusiasm and vigor
Leadership	• Assumes responsibility • High expectations for self and others • Fluent, concise self-expression • Foresees consequences and implications of decisions	• Good judgment in decision making • Likes structure • Well-liked by peers • Self-confident • Organized
Psychomotor	• Challenged by difficult athletic activities • Exhibits precision in movement • Enjoys participation in various athletic opportunities	• Excels in motor skills • Well coordinated • Good manipulative skills • High energy level
Visual/ Performing Arts	• Outstanding in sense of spatial relationships • Unusual ability in expressing self, feeling, moods, etc., through dance, drama, music, etc.	• Good motor coordination • Exhibits creative expression • Desire for producing "own product" (not content with mere copying) • Observant

SOURCE: National Society for the Gifted and Talented (retrieved from http://www.nsgt.org/giftedness-defined/).

often extremely sensitive to criticism while striving for unrealistic perfection. By understanding how these traits can manifest themselves in maladaptive ways, teachers can provide a flexible learning environment that challenges intellectual curiosity and is also safe for taking risks and accepting mistakes as a natural part of learning.

PREVALENCE

Because special education for the gifted is not mandated or guaranteed funding by IDEA, states are not required to report statistics about the prevalence of gifted students to the federal government. We can only estimate how many gifted and talented students are identified and receive special services.

Several subgroups of students are underidentified as gifted or talented, for several reasons. These students require special attention to help ensure that bias and different perceptions do not mask their giftedness and keep them from receiving an accelerated or enriched education. Let's turn our attention to three of these groups: culturally and linguistically diverse students, students with disabilities, and females.

Students with gifts and talents require special attention to help ensure that bias and incorrect perceptions do not keep them from receiving an accelerated or enriched education.

CULTURALLY AND LINGUISTICALLY DIVERSE GIFTED STUDENTS

Gifted and talented students can be found in every racial, ethnic, socioeconomic, and linguistic group; however, there is concern about the well-documented underrepresentation of CLD students among those identified as gifted and talented (Boulder Valley School District Office of Advanced Academic Services, 2010). As communities become more diverse, the change in the number of students identified as gifted and talented should mirror the demographic changes in the population, but that has not been the case. For example, recent data indicate that Black and Latino students represent 26% of the students enrolled in gifted and talented education programs, compared with their 40% enrollment figure in schools that offer such programs (U.S. Department of Education, Office for Civil Rights, 2014).

The problem of underrepresentation is compounded for students who have not acquired English language proficiency. Despite the fact that being able to speak two (or more) languages requires keen cognitive ability, bilingualism is frequently treated as a handicap in need of remedial efforts rather than as a strength that requires enrichment. Failure to identify and cultivate giftedness among our diverse student population is unfair to these students and to our society.

Several researchers and school systems have investigated characteristics associated with giftedness that may be common among certain CLD students. One such effort was conducted by the Boulder Valley School District Office of Advanced Academic Services (2010), where eight areas were identified as having potential for identifying students as gifted in the culturally, linguistically, and ethnically diverse student population. Some or all of the characteristics

163

shown in Table 4.9 may be sufficiently different from the dominant culture to be perceived as negative.

Teachers can help their CLD gifted learners to be successful in many ways. First, they should value students' cultures, languages, and experiences. They can often do this easily by building a connection among home, school, and community (such as inviting families to share their history). Teachers should also maintain high expectations for all students by providing rich content while incorporating multicultural education and instructional strategies that take advantage of students' strengths, such as problem solving, creativity, and primary-language abilities (Shealey et al., 2011).

GIFTED STUDENTS WITH DISABILITIES

Gifted students with disabilities—or twice-exceptional students—also require special attention. Students with disabilities are frequently overlooked when teachers are considering which of their students are gifted (Trail, 2011). Some teachers may have difficulty with the concept of a student both being gifted and having a disability.

Twice-exceptional students exhibit a complex array of abilities, weaknesses, and needs (Trail, 2011). Sometimes their disabilities mask their giftedness, making it difficult for teachers to recognize their strengths, or they may rarely show consistently high achievement, so they remain unidentified as gifted.

More than 30 years ago, Tannenbaum and Baldwin (1983) described gifted students with learning disabilities as "paradoxical learners." For example, these students may have advanced mathematical reasoning ability but have great difficulty with simple calculations; they may be extremely knowledge-able about many topics but be unable to remember simple facts; they may have excellent problem-solving skills but fail to master basic skills. Does this sound like a student you know?

Twice-exceptional students can display high levels of creative potential, exceptional analytic abilities, extraordinary spatial abilities, and superior vocabulary. They can be imaginative and creative with an advanced sense of humor, but despite these documented strengths, they have many character-istic behaviors that affect their learning and hamper their identification as gifted. Even if already identified as gifted, they may exhibit learning prob-lems in school and be considered underachievers (Montgomery County Public Schools, n.d.).

Frustration comes easily and quickly for students with disabilities who are gifted. Imagine how frustrating it must be to have a deep understanding of complex issues and not be able to express adequately or demonstrate this knowledge. Often these students give up on tasks quickly. They are afraid

TABLE 4.9 CHARACTERISTICS OF CULTURALLY AND LINGUISTICALLY DIVERSE GIFTED STUDENTS

Characteristic	Dominant Culture	Nondominant Cultures
Curiosity	Raises hand to ask question. Stays on task. Expresses self well. Expects shared experiences and common understandings. Curious about how things work more than about people.	May think questioning is rude. May be frustrated by not having the language necessary to ask questions. Does not have foundation of shared experiences. Curious about different experiences. May experience lack of understanding by teachers, peers and others. May enjoy questions with "shock value." More curious about people than things.
Task Commitment	Sticks with task. Confident in ability.	Stubborn. May have own priorities. May not see relevance in school work.
Sense of Humor	Begins with shared experiences and understandings. Uses dominant language with others. Uses subtleties with language.	May have difficulty showing humor in dominant culture's language. May be "smart alecky." May use language destructively, use put-downs. May be class clown. May demonstrate humor, tell jokes in one language and not the other.
Keen Interests	Good at many things. Enjoys learning new things. Enjoys collections. Enjoys book series.	Unable to make decisions. Makes decisions without regard for consequences. Appears random. Has trouble finding closure.
Use of Language	Expresses self well in formal register. Can elaborate well on others' ideas. Fairly even language profile.	Very expressive in casual register. Has trouble listening and staying attentive to others. Uneven in ability to speak, listen, read, write. Makes clever, silly or inappropriate responses. Opinionated, good talker but unable to support ideas or provide substance to ideas. Tells stories, enjoys listening to stories in own language, culture. Acquires new language quickly.
Self-Efficacy	Feels safe. Feels in control.	Feels unsafe, insecure. Feels like a victim.
Problem Solving	Good at solviing teacher problems. Applies learned rules to problem solving.	Good at solving "street" problems. Creative in fending for self. May not be interested in following rules.
Asynchronous Maturity	Taken care of by adults. Often protected from adult concerns.	May be responsible for younger siblings. May act as translator and interpreter for adults. May be needed, used in adult situations.

SOURCE: Boulder Valley School District Office of Advanced Academic Services (2010).

of taking academic risks, have difficulty with fine and gross motor skills, and have low self-esteem, frequently masked by inappropriate behaviors (Trail, 2011). As a consequence of the frustration caused by a unique combination of skills and deficits, twice-exceptional students can be some of the most disruptive in class. Teachers can make a real difference in their educational experience by making sure that their strengths are recognized and nurtured.

GIFTED FEMALES

You may be asking yourself why gifted females are being discussed as a separate group requiring special attention. Simply put, girls and young women who are gifted face their own set of challenges both in and out of school. A classic report more than 20 years ago from the American Association of University Women (AAUW, 1992) challenged the notion that girls and boys receive equitable treatment in our classrooms and outlined how gender bias shortchanges our young women. This seems particularly true for gifted females. For example, according to the AAUW report, teachers in all grade levels frequently select classroom activities that appeal more to boys' interests and are presented in formats in which boys typically excel. Another interesting finding suggests that boys are consistently given more instructional time, teacher attention, and praise and are called on more often than girls. These interaction patterns appear to be even more pronounced when teachers are dealing with high-achieving students (the top 10% to 20% of the school population) and in science and math classes.

Educators need to develop strategies for recognizing and encouraging gifted girls and for closing the gender gap that exists. One way teachers can help is by paying attention to their own behaviors with students and making sure there is no gender bias in their interactions. Other suggestions include using authentic learning, that is, applying science, math, engineering, and technology to solving real-world problems.

TEACHING STUDENTS WHO ARE GIFTED AND TALENTED

All gifted students should have a **differentiated curriculum** that offers learning experiences above and beyond those provided to typical learners through the general education curriculum. Educators can devise a differentiated curriculum in many ways, such as by modifying the standard curriculum's content, the learning environment, or the instruction provided. Gregory and Chapman (2013) provided a template for planning differentiated instruction (see Figure 4.3).

Many different models and instructional techniques are put into practice across the nation (Smith & Tyler, 2010). Services for students who are gifted and talented are delivered through a variety of placement options: general education

FIGURE 4.3 TEMPLATE FOR DIFFERENTIATED INSTRUCTION FOR GIFTED AND TALENTED STUDENTS

1. CORE STANDARDS: What should students know and be able to do?	Assessment tools for data collection: (logs, checklists, journals, agendas, observations, portfolios, rubrics, contracts)
Essential Questions:	
2. CONTENT: SKILLS: (concepts, vocabulary, facts)	
3. ACTIVATE: Focus Activity: Preassessment Strategy Preassessment Prior knowledge and engaging the learners	• Quiz, test • Surveys • K-W-L • Journals • Arm gauge • Give me • Brainstorm • Concept formation • Thumb it
4. ACQUIRE: Total group or small groups	• Lecturette • Presentation • Demonstration • Jigsaw • Video • Field trip • Guest speaker • Text
5. GROUPING DECISIONS: (TAPS, random, heterogeneous, homogeneous, interest, task, constructed) Apply formative assessments Adjust	• Learning centers • Projects • Contracts • Compact/Enrichment • Problem based • Inquiry • Research • Independent study
6. SUMMATIVE ASSESSMENT	• Quiz, test • Performance • Products • Presentation • Demonstration • Log, journal • Checklist • Portfolio • Rubric • Metacognition

SOURCE: Gregory and Chapman (2013).

classrooms, resource rooms or pullout programs, self-contained classes, and even special schools. Regardless of the method used, these key features define differentiated instruction for gifted learners as including the following:

- Problem-based learning
- Abstract thinking
- Reasoning activities
- Creative problem solving
- Content mastery
- Breadth and depth of topics
- Independent study
- Talent development

Acceleration and enrichment are two common educational approaches to teaching students who are gifted and talented. **Acceleration** allows students to move through the curriculum at faster rates than their peers who learn in more typical ways. **Enrichment** adds topics or skills to the traditional curriculum.

In a recent report by the AAUW, Hill, Corbett, and Rose (2010) urged that teachers (and administrators) in gifted and talented programs send the message that they value growth and learning:

> The danger of the "gifted" label is that it conveys the idea that a student has been bestowed with a "gift" of great ability rather than a dynamic attribute that she or he can develop. Talented and gifted programs should send the message that students are in these programs because they are advanced in certain areas and that the purpose of the programs is to challenge students in ways that will help them further develop and bring their abilities to fruition. Consider changing the name of talented and gifted programs to "challenge" programs or "advanced" programs to emphasize more of a growth mindset and less of a fixed mindset. (p. 36)

Acceleration

Acceleration can take many different forms. One form has students skipping to a grade ahead of their classmates of the same age. Grade skipping usually happens in the early elementary years, often at or during kindergarten when a child's giftedness is apparent because he or she can already read books, write stories, or solve mathematics problems. It also occurs with some frequency

iStock/Leadinglights

A differentiated curriculum can be achieved in many different ways. A field trip is one way to enrich the learning environment.

toward the end of high school, when students skip their remaining years and attend college through early-entrance programs. Another form of acceleration is advanced placement courses, which allow students to take classes that provide more in-depth course content and earn college credit for them. In ability grouping, another acceleration method, students of comparable abilities work together in courses or activities in which they excel. Finally, many high schools provide honors sections of academic courses as a form of ability grouping in which students must demonstrate superior academic performance for entrance.

Enrichment

One form of enrichment is independent study, through which a student studies a topic in more depth or investigates a topic that is not part of the general education curriculum. Independent study focuses on learning to be self-directed and to explore subjects in which the individual has an interest. Another form is mentorships, which pair students who have special interests with adults who have expertise in those areas. Mentorships need to be carefully arranged by teachers, but the benefits are both immediate and long term. Finally, internships are working assignments that allow gifted high school students who have expressed interest in a particular career to gain experience within that profession (Smith & Tyler, 2010). Effective programming, through educational approaches that are responsive to each student's unique needs, is possible and desirable for students who are gifted and talented.

SUMMARY

Students with other special learning needs encompass a broad range of characteristics and needs. We know that many of these students are protected under Section 504 and that their needs are met through the Section 504 plan, which focuses on their instructional program and on other academically related events such as field trips and summer programs. Students with a wide range of needs that are not covered under IDEA may qualify for services under Section 504.

The rapid demographic changes occurring in our nation are reflected in our culturally and linguistically diverse student population. With the numbers of ethnically and racially diverse students expected to grow significantly over the coming years, and with their strong current representation, educators must ensure that the educational system is responsive to the needs of all students. We must strive to understand linguistic and cultural differences so that no students are misdiagnosed as having a disability. Multicultural programs, bilingual programs, and bilingual special education programs are ways in which diverse students' needs are addressed.

Of great concern is the group of students who are at risk for school failure. This group of students is at risk because of experiences, living conditions, and/or specific characteristics that put them in the high-risk category. Educators should understand that students are at risk for many different reasons, such as poverty, homelessness, neglect, and abuse. They may also be at risk because of their status as a migrant student, refugee, or teen parent. Prevention via improved health care and educational practices can make a difference in the lives of these students who are underachievers and are at high risk for dropping out of school.

Finally, students who are gifted and talented are a unique group of students who have a variety of special learning needs. Teachers should understand the characteristics of these students and must ensure that students from all groups are considered for gifted and talented identification. Specialized programs must be in place for these students to ensure that they receive a rich educational experience to prepare them to maximize their potential.

REIVEW THE LEARNING OBJECTIVES

Let's review the learning objectives for this chapter. If you are uncertain and cannot "talk through" the answers provided for any of these questions, reread those sections of the text.

- **How are students with physical and cognitive needs protected under Section 504?**

The definition of disability is broader under Section 504 and extends beyond school age. For instance, any condition that greatly limits a major life activity, including the ability to learn in school, is defined as a disability. Students who qualify as having a disability under Section 504 are assessed, and a Section 504 plan is developed and monitored. The plan includes the accommodations and adaptations chosen, the person(s) responsible for implementing the plan, and the procedures for monitoring its implementation.

- **How can we best meet the needs of students in our culturally and linguistically diverse classrooms?**

Multicultural education should be a part of the school's curriculum, instructional strategies, and interactions. Bilingual education is instruction in two languages. Some programs help students maintain and develop full proficiency in their native language as well as in English. Others provide instruction in students' home language only temporarily, as a bridge to English, and phase quickly into English-only instruction. Dual-language programs help native English speakers develop proficiency in a second language while helping students who speak a language other than English develop English proficiency. Language support services and instruction in the native language are needed for English language learners with reading disabilities. Bilingual special education students require linguistic support, validated instructional practices, and curricular modifications.

- **Who are students "at risk" and what should we know and do to help them achieve their full potential?**

Students who are at risk have experiences, living conditions, or characteristics that contribute to school failure, such as poverty, homelessness, abuse, neglect, and poor instruction. They require specialized services to prevent negative outcomes. Health care services must be provided to reduce risk associated with a lack of regular medical attention. Educational practices such as differentiated instruction, screening and intervention, and collaborative partnerships can reduce risk and provide necessary support for these students.

At-risk students consistently have difficulties with achievement compared with their peer group; this condition is known as an achievement gap. They are also in the high-risk category for dropping out of school. Students who are culturally and linguistically diverse (CLD) tend to underperform on measures of academic achievement in the United States.

- **What are the attributes of students with gifts and talents?**

The majority of students with gifts and talents excel in some areas and not in others. Gifted and talented students can be found in every racial, ethnic, socioeconomic, and linguistic group, but CLD students are underrepresented among those identified as gifted or talented. Some students are twice-exceptional, that is, they have a disability as well as

a talent or gift. The key features of differentiated instruction for the gifted and talented are problem-based learning, abstract thinking, reasoning activities, creative problem solving, content mastery, breadth and depth of topics, independent study, and talent development. Acceleration helps students move through the curriculum more rapidly than their peers, whereas enrichment adds topics or skills to the traditional curriculum.

$SAGE edge™ Test your understanding of chapter content. Take the practice quiz. edge.sagepub.com/bryant

REVISIT THE OPENING CHALLENGE ....•

Check your answers to the Reflection Questions from the Opening Challenge and revise them on the basis of what you have learned.

1. What should Ms. Grelak's next steps be with Gabriel?

2. Do you agree that Ms. Grelak should refer Allen for a special education evaluation? Why or why not?

3. In what ways does his level of English language proficiency seem to be affecting Gabriel?

4. What characteristics does Gabriel have that seem consistent with those of a gifted student? What characteristics does Gabriel have that seem consistent with those of English language learners?

5. What advice would you give Ms. Grelak about instruction for English

language learners with learning problems?

6. Where might you go to look for information about teaching English language learners in your state? What specific questions might you like to have answered?

7. Do you share some of the same concerns as Mrs. O'Malley? Find the website of your home city's school system. Is there information pertaining to culturally and linguistically diverse student populations? What information is provided for parents and teachers?

KEY TERMS ....•

acceleration, 168

at risk, 153

culture, 140

differentiated curriculum, 166

enrichment, 168

multicultural education, 142

$SAGE edge™ Review key terms with eFlashcards. edge.sagepub.com/bryant

PROFESSIONAL STANDARDS AND LICENSURE

For a complete description of Professional Standards and Licensure, please see Appendix on page 569.

CEC Initial Preparation Standards

Standard 1: Learner Development and Individual Learning Differences

INTASC

Standard 1: Learner Development

Standard 2: Learning Differences

Praxis II: Education of Exceptional Students: Core Content Knowledge

I. Understanding Exceptionalities: Human development and behavior

II. Legal and Societal Issues: Federal laws and legal issues

III. Delivery of Services to Students with Disabilities: Background knowledge

Review ➡ Practice ➡ Improve

Get the tools you need to sharpen your study skills. Access practice quizzes, eFlashcards, video, and multimedia: **edge.sagepub.com/bryant**

PART II

PLANNING FOR EXCEPTIONAL LEARNERS

5

DEVELOPING COLLABORATIVE PARTNERSHIPS IN SCHOOLS AND WITH FAMILIES

CHAPTER OBJECTIVES

After studying this chapter, you will be able to answer the following questions:

- What are the characteristics of collaboration?

- What are critical prerequisite skills for effective collaboration?

- How can professionals work together collaboratively?

- How can professionals collaborate with paraprofessionals?

- How can professionals collaborate with families?

OPENING *challenge*

Collaborative Partnerships to Meet the Needs of All Students

ELEMENTARY GRADES Ms. Warren's inclusive fifth-grade classroom is made up of students with an array of strengths and special needs that are addressed collaboratively with assistance from professionals, her paraprofessional, and connections to the families of her students. Ms. Warren is committed to providing all her students with an appropriate education that is responsive to their needs. In her classroom, she is working with several students who are struggling with reading and mathematics. These students require interventions that support typical classroom instruction. She also has several students with emotional disturbance who need structured routines and management procedures so they will be ready to learn. Ms. Warren has several students who are English language learners (ELLs) and need extra instructional support in vocabulary development. One of her students receives services from the speech/language pathologist to correct articulation problems. Ms. Warren thinks about the related services providers and other individuals who work in the school community to help all students. *"How can I work collaboratively with all the people who are engaged with my students? I want to build strong partnerships with my colleagues and my students' families."* Ms. Warren finds herself in a situation that is very common. Developing and nurturing collaborative partnerships with many individuals, both families and service providers in inclusive classrooms, require certain skills and practice. These partnerships enhance the learning of all students and build helpful connections between students' home and school environments.

SECONDARY GRADES Ms. Bryant teaches 11th-grade English in a suburban high school. She has six classes each day with one prep. Ms. Bryant has been teaching for 27 years and has seen many changes in the services for students with disabilities and students who are gifted. This year she has a student who uses a wheelchair because of the effects of cerebral palsy and a tablet for accessing the literature texts required for class. The student also has a paraprofessional who assists him with assignments so that he can keep up with the rest of the class. Ms. Bryant collaborates with the paraprofessional by providing lesson plans each week; together they work with the special education teacher who visits the English class to ensure that the student is being successful in the class. Ms. Bryant wonders about how to work effectively with the paraprofessional besides providing lesson plans. *I think there must be more that I can do to support the paraprofessional when she is working with my student. I don't have much time during instruction to talk to the paraprofessional. I need to talk with the special education teacher about having a three-way meeting to be sure we are all together.*

REFLECTION QUESTIONS In your journal, write down your answers to the following questions. After completing the chapter, check your answers and revise them on the basis of what you have learned.

1. What professional collaborative practices can Ms. Warren use to help her students with special learning, behavior, and language needs succeed in the general education classroom?

2. How can Ms. Warren and Ms. Bryant collaborate effectively with their paraprofessional?

3. How can Ms. Warren effectively structure parent-teacher conferences and develop home-school communication effectively?

4. What should be the focus of the three-way meeting with Ms. Bryant, the special education teacher, and the paraprofessional?

We know that many students with special needs receive most, if not all, of their education in the general education classroom. For example, as you can see in Table 5.1, students with disabilities as a whole spend about 80% or more of their day in the general education classroom. Think about what you read in Chapters 1 and 5 about related services and the value of working collaboratively with those who provide them to deliver the services students with disabilities need to access the general education curriculum, such as assistive technology and speech/language therapy.

It is important to establish collaborative partnerships among professionals, paraprofessionals, and families to ensure that all students are receiving appropriate educational services in inclusive settings. (We use the term *families* to denote various family structures, such as extended families, children with guardians, single-parent families, and "blended" families.) **Collaboration** is an interactive process whereby individuals with diverse expertise choose to work together to provide high-quality services to all students in inclusive classrooms and their families (Idol, Nevin, & Paolucci-Whitcomb, 2000). It can be informal, as, for example, when two teachers meet to develop a plan together to help a student with special needs, or it can be formalized through a team approach, including related service providers. Collaboration also occurs when teachers work with paraprofessionals who are important members of the educational team. Finally, educators must utilize effective practices to collaborate with families, for they are the ones who know the most about the students we serve. In Chapter 7 we discuss ways in which peers can work collaboratively and teachers can help students build these collaborative relationships.

In this chapter, we provide information about the characteristics of collaboration and the foundation skills that are critical for establishing effective, collaborative partnerships. We also discuss models of professional collaboration and ways to develop collaborative partnerships with paraprofessionals and families. We include multicultural considerations when establishing collaborative partnerships and demonstrate how the ADAPT framework can be used during collaborative activities.

WHAT ARE THE CHARACTERISTICS OF COLLABORATION?

Collaboration is a key ingredient of the efforts of inclusive schools to meet the needs of all students in different settings and activities. For example, collaboration can occur when (a) a teacher works with parents on ways to improve their child's mathematics skills, (b) teachers are conducting prereferral or RTI

Collaboration in Education

| TABLE 5.1 | PERCENTAGE OF STUDENTS AGES 6 THROUGH 21 SERVED UNDER IDEA, PART B, WITHIN THE DISABILITY CATEGORY, BY EDUCATIONAL ENVIRONMENT FOR FALL 2012 |

| Disability | Percentage of day inside the regular class[a] | | | Other environments[c] |
	80% or more of the day[b]	40% to 79% of the day	Less than 40% of the day	
All disabilities	61.5	19.5	13.8	5.2
Autism	39.5	18.1	33.2	9.2
Deaf-blindness	21.5	11.5	34.0	33.1
Developmental delay[d]	62.4	19.5	16.5	1.6
Emotional disturbance	44.1	17.8	20.3	17.8
Hearing impairments	57.8	16.4	12.6	13.3
Intellectual disabilities	17.1	26.6	48.7	7.6
Multiple disabilities	13.1	16.2	46.2	24.5
Orthopedic impairments	54.8	16.2	21.6	7.4
Other health impairments	64.0	22.2	9.7	4.1
Specific learning disabilities	67.2	24.6	6.3	1.9
Speech or language impairments	86.6	5.5	4.3	3.7
Traumatic brain injury	49.0	22.3	20.1	8.6
Visual impairments	64.7	13.0	11.0	11.3

NOTE: Percentage was calculated by dividing the number of students ages 6 through 21 served under IDEA, Part B, in the disability category and the educational environment by the total number of students ages 6 through 21 served under IDEA, Part B, in the disability category and all educational environments for that year, and then multiplying the result by 100. The sum of row percentages might not total 100 because of rounding.

[a]*Percentage of day spent inside the regular class* is defined as the number of hours the student spends each day inside the regular classroom, divided by the total number of hours in the school day (including lunch, recess, and study periods), multiplied by 100.

[b]Students who received special education and related services outside the regular classroom for less than 21% of the school day were classified in the *inside the regular class 80% or more of the day* category.

[c]*Other environments* consists of *separate school, residential facility, and homebound/hospital environments, correctional facilities,* and *parentally placed in private schools.*

[d]States' use of the *developmental delay* category is optional for children ages 3 through 9 and is not applicable to children older than 9 years of age.

SOURCE: U.S. Department of Education, National Center for Education Statistics [NCES], Common Core of Data [CCD] (2012). These data are for the 50 states; Washington, DC; Bureau of Indian Education schools; Puerto Rico; the four outlying areas; and the three freely associated states. For actual data used, go to http://www.ed.gov/about/reports/annual/osep.

interventions to prevent inappropriate referrals to special education, (c) service providers are delivering related services, (d) a bilingual instructor and a special education teacher are developing a lesson plan together, (e) secondary school teachers are coteaching a science lesson, (f) the speech/language pathologist

VIDEO CASE 5.1

Collaboration and Coteaching

1. How do Jason Brown and Jeff McCann describe their cotaught, inclusive world history class? How has it changed throughout the school year? What strategies do the coteachers utilize to collaboratively support the needs of their students with disabilities?

2. In what ways is Mr. Brown and Mr. McCann's inclusive class similar to the other general education classes that Mr. McCann teaches? How is it different?

and general education teacher are team-teaching an instructional unit, or (g) general and special educators are consulting about a student with behavior problems. According to Idol et al. (2000), the collaborative process aims to successfully include all students in general education activities, to identify adaptations of content and materials, and to develop and implement specialized instruction as appropriate. The following characteristics of collaboration can ensure that the process will be successful.

SHARED PROBLEM SOLVING

Shared problem solving consists of identifying, implementing, and evaluating a plan to solve a chosen problem by making decisions together. The process can be complex, because different perspectives on how to address and resolve issues often arise and must be included (Friend & Cook, 2010). It is best accomplished when participants in the collaborative process (a) assess the current situation using specific criteria (such as behavior, time, situational factors, achievement information, nonverbal signals, or verbal comments); (b) identify together the specific behavior that is of concern (such as homework completion, reading comprehension, lateness to collaboration meetings, or following through on collaboration plans); (c) specify objectives for solving the problem; (d) develop a plan of action, including tasks, persons responsible, and time lines; and (e) evaluate the plan periodically (Idol et al., 2000).

SHARED RESPONSIBILITY

Each member of the collaborative team is equally responsible for ensuring that tasks are accomplished during the process. This usually entails dividing up the work in ways that promote parity among team members (Friend, Cook, Hurley-Chamberlain, & Shamberger, 2010). For instance, one person might be responsible for observing a student who is misbehaving in class, and another team member might contact the family to talk about how the student is performing in school. During coteaching, teachers assume shared responsibility for teaching and promoting positive behavior in the classroom. Teachers also share the function of grading assignments and planning instruction.

VOLUNTARY INVOLVEMENT

Collaboration is a process that individuals should volunteer to engage in, rather than being assigned by school or district-level administration. Research findings support the idea of voluntary participation. According to Scruggs, Mastropieri, and McDuffie (2007), who synthesized qualitative research on coteaching, educators believed coteaching should only be voluntary, not an assignment forced on those who do not want to participate. Collaboration will not naturally occur merely because someone is assigned to a team to address a situation, issue, or lesson. Ideally, individuals should be collaborating because they want to work together; however, in reality, situations will arise that warrant collaborative partnerships among people who would rather not collaborate for a variety of purposes (e.g., a team member is difficult to work with, an individual would rather "go it alone"). We can learn how to be more effective collaborators by developing important prerequisite skills to ensure effective collaborative partnerships.

WHAT ARE CRITICAL PREREQUISITE SKILLS FOR EFFECTIVE COLLABORATION?

Establishing collaborative partnerships with families, professionals, and para-professionals is a necessary component of effective schools. Partnership means working with people, and to do this well, teachers must be prepared in those critical prerequisite skills that foster collaboration. In this section, we discuss communication skills, conflict resolution skills, and multicultural and linguistic diversity considerations that can develop a foundation on which effective collaborative relationships can be built.

COMMUNICATION SKILLS

Heron and Harris (2000) conceptualized the communication process as consisting of a message that is encoded and transmitted, and a received message that is decoded and comprehended. For this process to occur successfully, the speaker and listener must possess effective listening skills, the ability to decode (or figure out) a message, and verbal encoding skills to convey their thoughts. Communication partners have to be aware of and interpret nonverbal signals in messages they send and receive.

Listening is an important skill to develop for decoding and improving communication. It calls for more than just politely hearing what someone else is saying before you speak (Vaughn, Bos, & Schumm, 2013); it requires maintaining appropriate eye contact, acknowledging the speaker's message with verbal feedback, and maintaining appropriate nonverbal signals. Deterrents to effective listening include being preoccupied and not listening, talking more than listening, second-guessing what the speaker will say and responding inappropriately, making judgments, being distrustful, using language not appropriate to the situation (too technical, for instance, or unmindful of cultural and ethnic values and perceptions), and giving way to fatigue or strong emotions (Friend et al., 2010).

One of the most effective types of listening is called **active listening** (Gordon, 1980). The purpose of active listening is to engage the listener in the message being sent, to demonstrate to the speaker that the listener is interested in the message, to enable the speaker to convey specific concerns, and to provide feedback to the speaker to ensure that the message was correctly received and perceived. Active listening can be used effectively in many types of interactions and, particularly, during conversations that may be emotionally charged.

Professional Collaboration

Although this type of listening was identified more than 30 years ago, it remains a key prerequisite communication skill to foster effective collaboration. There are six types of active listening:

1. *Acknowledging* tells the speaker you are listening and may include appropriate nonverbal signals and verbal comments.

2. *Paraphrasing* provides feedback to the speaker about the received, perceived message. The listener repeats to the speaker, in his or her own words, the message that was conveyed.

3. *Reflecting* tells the speaker the feelings he or she is verbalizing.

4. *Clarifying* asks for more specific information to help the listener better understand the message.

5. *Elaboration* asks the speaker to provide more information about an idea or about the whole message to broaden the content conveyed to the listener.

6. *Summarizing* requires the listener to reiterate the main ideas of the conversation and the actions that will be taken, if any. Summarizing gives closure to a conversation and provides feedback for all members about the key points discussed.

Besides having good listening skills, communication partners must be able to convey their message orally or in writing so it is correctly understood. We can analyze messages conveyed verbally in terms of the way the message is being received, what nonverbal language the listener is conveying, and how the listener is signaling accurate interpretation via feedback. Video technology has added another dimension to verbal communications with families, professionals, and paraprofessionals that used to be handled only through phone calls or face-to-face meetings. Through careful self-analysis and feedback from speakers, listeners can improve their skills so that more effective communication occurs. Idol et al. (2000) recommended the following procedures for facilitating effective verbal communication:

- Before speaking, organize your thoughts to be sure that they are relevant to the conversation and can be stated succinctly.

- Demonstrate good listening behaviors (discussed earlier) to show that you are indeed interested in the speaker's message.

- Use feedback to show that you are listening and understanding the speaker's message.

- Avoid being judgmental and evaluative.

- Be aware of extraneous factors (such as a receiver who doesn't feel well or who has a personal crisis, a parent who may be very angry at another professional yet unconsciously projects the anger onto you, a paraprofessional who feels that the tasks she or he is assigned are demeaning) that may interfere with the communication process.

- Avoid technical jargon that educators may use as convenient shorthand among themselves. Be specific without using acronyms that the speaker may not be familiar with.

Professionals communicate via social media such as Twitter and through e-mails, texts, blogs, newsletters, and notes. Although written communication reduces the need for face-to-face interactions, participants must be sure that written messages are conveyed appropriately to ensure accurate interpretation. For example, written messages containing spelling or syntactical errors make it clear the writer lacks some basic skills or has not proofread his or her work. The auto-correct feature of some electronic communications can be helpful or harmful and does not reduce the need to proofread carefully. Jargon should be limited, and brevity is best. Long, detailed messages lose their effectiveness simply because of their complexity and because recipients lack time to read them thoroughly.

Finally, written communication should include a signature, date, and request for a response (Idol et al., 2000). Reserve face-to-face or video technology for messages that could be misinterpreted or require opportunities for discussion and questions. Following are a few etiquette tips for various types of written communication:

- Respond to e-mails received during business days within 24 hours, if possible.
- Answer e-mails using the original thread. Avoid using "reply all" unless the response really needs to go back to everyone in the message.
- Even in a private text or e-mail, write only what is appropriate for multiple readers, given that electronic communication can be forwarded to others.
- Be concise.
- Edit for grammar and spelling errors.
- Avoid educational jargon and acronyms when communicating with families.
- Use punctuation and capitalization correctly.

Nonverbal communication is another aspect of communication that requires careful analysis to ensure that the speaker sends appropriate signals and that the listener understands the intended message. According to Heron and Harris (2000), this category includes facial expressions, body posturing and movement, use of space, and touch. Nonverbal messages are a powerful form of communication because they tend to be quite genuine, and they may be more easily conveyed than verbal messages that are emotionally laden.

There are several types of nonverbal communication. For example, facial expressions can be very informative about feelings, trust, and level of disdain or interest. Elevated eyebrows, lack of or regular eye contact, smiles, and frowns convey specific messages to speakers. Facing the speaker, crossing your arms, and sitting in a relaxed position all convey a subliminal message. A distance between speakers and listeners of 2 to 4 feet is an acceptable use of space when participants know each other and can interact comfortably. Touch is a form of communication that needs to be monitored carefully. Some people prefer that speakers or listeners not touch their arms or hug them, for instance.

The way we communicate with each other can enhance or impede successful collaborative partnerships. When working in diverse settings, individuals should take into consideration cultural and linguistic factors that are part of the communication process. For example, an interpreter should be available if family members do not speak or understand English. In some cultures, body posture such as nodding your head, smiling, and leaning forward convey openness, interest, and attentive listening. Teachers should learn about the values, perceptions, and culture of communication partners; this is especially true when working with families from diverse cultures. This information can go a long way in enhancing communication and establishing trust on which to build a collaborative partnership. Regardless of how hard we might try to be good communicators, conflict may arise. Thus, conflict resolution skills are another important prerequisite for collaboration. We now turn our attention to this critical area.

CONFLICT RESOLUTION SKILLS

In most collaborative partnership endeavors, a plan is developed for the benefit of a student. Very often professionals, paraprofessionals, and families are faced with complex problems that require careful consideration and action to help children; often issues arise that can lead to conflict. This conflict must be resolved so the partners can move forward with their plans.

Conflict is defined as the disagreement of interests or ideas (Heron & Harris, 2000). In a collaborative relationship, conflict may stem from differences in opinions about strategies, facts, perspectives, or values. Conflict may arise from any of the following situations:

- People perceive that they are forced into situations (working together, having students with disabilities in their classrooms full time, implementing a strategy for which no training occurred).

- Roles (special education teacher as consultant) are not clearly defined.

- Philosophies (humanistic, disciplinarian) clash.

- Levels of expertise and professional development do not match the demands of the situation (first-year teacher asked to chair a committee).

- Interpersonal styles (introvert, extrovert, direct, indirect) vary significantly.

- People are resistant to change (issues of "territory," power, and interest arise in trying new research-based ideas). (Heron & Harris, 2000)

For example, two professionals may be working on a plan they jointly developed for a student; however, one member falls short in completing his or her agreed-on tasks. Conflict could easily arise because the plan for the student is not being fully implemented. This issue would need to be addressed in a constructive manner that would facilitate progress toward implementing the plan. Because conflict is inevitable even in the best of circumstances, conflict-resolution skills are helpful. Following are helpful guidelines for conflict resolution:

- Do not expect the conflict to go away; it may diminish, but if problems and feelings are not discussed, they will emerge again at another time.

- Confront conflict when it occurs by stating your feelings using an "I-message" (refer to Chapter 9 for more information about I-messages). For example, "I'm feeling uncomfortable with this situation," "I'm sensing that maybe we're not on the same wavelength," or "What are your thoughts about how to proceed?" In essence, this is a reality check—an effort to determine whether your perceptions are accurate. If not, then promptly discussing the situation as you perceive it could prevent further misperceptions and possible problems.

- Avoid being judgmental or accusatory: "You're not listening," "You're late again," "That idea didn't work the last time and won't work this time."

- Use self-disclosure if appropriate: "I'm feeling really unsure about how to handle this problem and could use some assistance."

- Maintain open, ongoing communication even if it is just notes to other members. A major source of conflict is lack of communication between partners and the perception (or observation) that one person is moving ahead without talking the plan through with others.

- Use active listening: send I-messages, paraphrase, summarize, and clarify. These techniques can go a long way in developing a better understanding of how members feel and how they perceive situations.

- Discuss conflict at a time when members are not pressed to return to their classroom and are not in the midst of a situation that might interfere with the process of conflict resolution. Timing is an important consideration.

- Use problem-solving steps to reach consensus and identify a plan of action. This helps members to focus on a procedure that promotes communication, discussion, and resolution.

- Recognize that sometimes conflict may not be resolved and that partnerships may be terminated for the time being. Many reasons (including lack of interest, power, insecurity, bad timing, mistrust, and inability to establish congruent objectives) account for the inability of members to resolve conflict. Focus on letting go and finding an alternative, productive way to handle the situation if further action is required.

TECH *notes*

STUDENT RESPONSE SYSTEMS

Student response systems are educational tools that allow teachers to monitor their students' learning in real time using interactive software. Teachers can ask questions to check for student understanding and determine possible difficulties with the material. Using PowerPoint presentations, teachers generate questions about the content and students respond to interactive questions with devices such as "classroom clickers." The students' responses are displayed in the PowerPoint presentation in a graphical form for discussion where some students may need to rethink their answers. Teachers can monitor students' understanding about the content and adjust their instruction accordingly based on the students' responses.

AWARENESS OF MULTICULTURAL AND LINGUISTIC DIVERSITY

The cultural, ethnic, racial, and linguistic composition of U.S. society is changing dramatically, and this is reflected in our school-age population. Some students may qualify for a range of services, including bilingual programs, ESL (English as a second language) programs, and special education programs. Thus, it behooves educators to prepare for working with diverse populations so they can successfully and appropriately meet individual student needs, including special needs (Hoover, Eppolito, Klingner, & Baca, 2012).

We have already discussed several considerations for collaborating effectively with individuals from diverse cultural, ethnic, and linguistic heritages, such as recognizing diverse values and perceptions and communicating with people in their primary language. We also mentioned the need to be aware of different communication styles of collaborative partnerships.

Researchers (Garcia, 2002; Ortiz & Yates, 2001) have identified consultation competencies for educators who work with culturally and linguistically diverse students having special needs. These competencies include (a) reflecting on your own perspective—that is, your beliefs and values about students with special needs who are from diverse backgrounds and the professionals who work with them; (b) fully understanding the roles, values, perceptions, and beliefs of your collaborative partners; (c) improving your interpersonal, communicative, and problem-solving skills to promote successful collaboration; and (d) adopting appropriate assessment and instructional strategies (such as language and cultural considerations for assessment, specific strategies, and adapting curricula). For example, Garcia (2002) recommended that educators must examine their own cultural self-awareness and the influences of these cultural values on their behavior toward others. Understanding the roles in the collaborative process is another critically important competency, because conflict can arise when there are misunderstandings about roles and responsibilities. Regarding assessment strategies, Figueroa (2002; Klingner, Edwards, & Dunsmore, 2010) recommended that, when assessing ELLs, teachers should observe the student's behavior and performance across multiple contexts, observe over a period of time rather than drawing conclusions on the basis of one or two observations, and draw on the expertise of informed professionals in arriving at diagnostic decisions.

Finally, Nancy Cloud (2002) talked about culturally and linguistically responsive instruction that focuses on language differences and identifies disability needs and **cultural characteristics**, which are beliefs, norms, and customs that vary within and between groups. Teachers can integrate culturally and linguistically responsive instruction in the areas of curriculum and materials, classroom discourse (discussions), instructional techniques, management, and parent involvement.

In any discussion of diversity, keep in mind that culture permeates all of society and all interactions. We all belong to some cultural group that is distinguishable by its customs, traditions, beliefs, foods, and dress, as well as by a specific ethnicity, religious affiliation, or racial background. In schools, policies and procedures are influenced by "beliefs, values, and ideas about what our educational goals should be, and how schools should be organized to achieve them. We acquire these worldviews as part of our preparation and socialization into our profession as educators" (Garcia, 2014). Thus, educators must be aware of their own cultural values, the way they have been socialized professionally, and the cultural values of their collaborative partners (Garcia, 2002).

HOW CAN PROFESSIONALS WORK TOGETHER COLLABORATIVELY?

Many professionals, such as general and special education teachers, school psychologists, counselors, social workers, administrators, and speech/language, physical, or occupational therapists, are part of the school community that is responsible for working together to provide a quality education for all students. Because of the individual needs of students with special needs, a variety of professionals work together to plan and implement individualized education programs (IEPs). In Chapter 6 you will read about related services and the professionals who provide them. For example, speech/language pathologists provide services for the prevention and treatment of communication disorders. In this section, we talk about the need for collaborative professional partnerships and models of collaboration that promote inclusive practices.

THE NEED FOR COLLABORATIVE PARTNERSHIPS WITH PROFESSIONALS

As you know from Chapter 1, the Individuals with Disabilities Education Act (IDEA) of 2004 requires that students with disabilities be educated to

VIDEO CASE 5.2

Successful Collaboration

1. What elements of successful coteaching do Jason Brown and Jeff McCann identify? How are these practices beneficial to students with and without disabilities?

2. Mr. Brown and Mr. McCann describe the ways they collaborate together, both inside and outside of school. How do these collaborative experiences support their successful coteaching?

Collaborative consultation is an interactive process that enables groups of people with diverse expertise to generate creative solutions to mutually defined problems.

the greatest extent possible in the general education setting. Moreover, general education teachers are required to be part of the IEP team and are responsible for implementing the adaptations identified on the IEP to help students access and master the curriculum. Thus, there is a need for collaborative models among professionals to provide the support needed when educating all students in inclusive classrooms.

Collaborative models are prevalent in classrooms across the nation where educators are working together to ensure that all students can access the general education curriculum. For example, the "class within a class" model, developed by Dr. Floyd Hudson, promotes more academic interventions for students with learning problems in the context of the general education setting. In this model, the general education teacher provides grade-level curriculum knowledge and the special education teacher provides strategic adaptations and presentation techniques to facilitate understanding of the instructional content. Together these two professionals design lessons and activities to accommodate students with mild and moderate disabilities so that these students have access to the curriculum. Collaboration-consultation and coteaching are other models described in the next section. We also discuss collaboration considerations for ELLs.

MODELS OF COLLABORATIVE PARTNERSHIPS WITH PROFESSIONALS

There are several models of collaborative partnerships with professionals to help students with special needs function more successfully in the general education classroom. We provide an overview of collaboration-consultation and coteaching models.

Collaboration-Consultation

The collaboration-consultation model focuses on the partnership between the general education and special education teachers, tapping the expertise of both to provide appropriate services to students (Idol et al., 2000). In this model, collaboration includes planning, implementing, and evaluating student programs wherein teachers work together to meet the needs of all students. Intervention plans are developed that are typically implemented by general education teachers with ongoing support from the special education teacher. The expertise of both professionals, then, is applied in creating and evaluating plans. The intervention plans could be part of prereferral activities to prevent academic problems or could be developed to address the academic, behavioral, or social skills of students in inclusive classrooms.

Idol and colleagues (2000) identified six stages of the collaboration-consultation process.

STAGE 1: Gaining Entry and Establishing Team Goals

This stage consists of establishing rapport between or among participants and identifying specifically each member's goals, agenda, and outcomes for the collaborative process. Here it is important to ensure that each participant is clear about what he or she would like to see occur during the collaborative process and to identify what each member is capable of contributing to the partnership in terms of time, expertise, and commitment.

STAGE 2: Problem Identification

In this stage, participants engage in assessment practices (see Chapter 7 for information about assessment techniques) to identify the student's current level of academic performance, behavioral considerations, and affective/emotional status. Assessment data may be obtained from previously administered measures and behavioral rating scales, teacher observation, and current informal assessment measures. On the basis of available data, the participants develop a profile of the student's strengths and weaknesses and identify specific problems that may account for academic and/or behavior problems.

STAGE 3: Intervention Recommendations

Specific interventions are recommended for the problem(s) identified in Stage 2. An important aspect of this stage is identifying interventions that teachers can implement easily and that accommodate the special needs of the student. Other students for whom the intervention(s) may be appropriate and effective could be identified during this stage as well.

STAGE 4: Implementation of Recommendations

At this point, the intervention is implemented for the targeted problem. The special education teacher may be asked to model the intervention or provide feedback to the classroom teacher about the implementation process. The general education teacher may model an intervention for the special education teacher to learn, or both teachers may work together to implement a behavior management plan. There is room for flexibility in the way interventions are implemented and the way participants in the collaborative process work together to facilitate the plan's success.

STAGE 5: Evaluation

Monitoring student progress to determine the effectiveness of the intervention(s) is extremely important. Classroom teachers can administer evaluation measures that help participants in the collaborative process determine whether the intervention is effective.

WORKING *together*

AN EXAMPLE OF THE COLLABORATION-CONSULTATION PROCESS

Ms. Warren is concerned about how Felipe is progressing in developing oral reading fluency compared with the other students in her general education class. She has tried working individually with Felipe to practice reading, but she doesn't have enough time during the school day to meet his needs. Ms. Warren has collected and graphed data on Felipe's oral reading weekly for six weeks, and it is clear that he is not benefiting from instruction. She decides to initiate the collaboration-consultation process with Mr. Gonzalez, the special education teacher, to identify the next steps to take. Chapter 8 offers suggestions for data-based decision making, which is what Ms. Warren and Mr. Gonzalez are incorporating into the collaborative-consultation process.

Stage 1: The teachers agree to develop a plan for Ms. Warren to implement in the general education classroom to improve Felipe's oral reading performance. Ms. Warren says she needs an intervention that won't take too much more of her time because she is already working with Felipe and a few other students in a small group to improve their reading.

Stage 2: Ms. Warren shares Felipe's reading data; she and Mr. Gonzalez agree that Felipe is not responding sufficiently to small group reading instruction and that he needs an additional intervention to improve his reading fluency. The graphed data show the number of words Felipe read correctly each week, but his improvement is too slow for him to catch up to his classmates by the end of the school year. Ms. Warren also decides to share the reading data with Felipe's parents so they are aware of his progress and the need for an intervention.

Stage 3: Mr. Gonzalez and Ms. Warren discuss the possibility of taped assisted reading for Felipe. This intervention consists of taping reading passages and having Felipe practice the reading passages several times each day before he works in a small group with the teacher. Ms. Warren agrees to have her paraprofessional tape-record the passages, while she continues to collect weekly data on Felipe's reading performance. The taped reading practice along with the small group instruction are noted as a means of differentiating instruction in Tier 1 core instruction.

Stage 4: Mr. Gonzalez models for Ms. Warren and Felipe how to implement the tape-assisted reading practice. Ms. Warren continues the implementation process each day for four weeks. She has her paraprofessional oversee the process.

Stage 5: Data collection occurs, which in this case means recording the number of words read correctly during a one-minute timing each week. Ms. Warren collects the data to share at the follow-up meeting with Mr. Gonzalez.

Stage 6: Ms. Warren, her paraprofessional, and Mr. Gonzalez meet four weeks after the intervention began to review the data. At this time, they decide that Felipe's reading performance is much stronger with the tape-assisted intervention. They agree to continue the intervention and meet again in another four weeks. If the data do not continue to show adequate improvement, they agree they will reconvene sooner.

QUESTIONS

1. What is the purpose of each stage?

2. What planning is necessary for this partnership to work effectively to support Felipe?

3. Why is data collection an integral part of the process?

STAGE 6: Follow-up

Essential to an effective collaborative partnership for promoting student success are regularly scheduled meetings of participants to determine whether the intervention was effective and to identify additional potential problem areas that could be addressed during the collaborative process. During Stage 1, participants should commit to a meeting time that is convenient to all for discussing student progress. The following case study shows how collaboration-consultation might be successful where professionals work together to identify solutions for students who are having academic, social, and emotional difficulties.

Coteaching

Marilyn Friend (2006), one of the leading authorities on educational collaboration, defined coteaching as the following:

> A service delivery model in which two educators, one typically a general education teacher and one a special education teacher or another specialist, combine their expertise to jointly teach a heterogeneous group of students, some of whom have disabilities or other special needs, in a single classroom for part or all of the school day. (p. 140)

Both professionals take part in planning, teaching, and evaluating student performance. For example, in a coteaching situation that consists of a speech/language pathologist and a special education teacher, the language expertise of the speech/language pathologist can be combined with the special education teacher's expertise in instructional content to produce a lesson rich

In a coteaching classroom, both teachers take part in planning, teaching, and evaluating student performance.

© Jessica Miller/SAGE

COTEACHING APPROACHES

ONE TEACHES, ONE OBSERVES

One teacher leads the class in a lesson, and the other professional (school psychologist, special education teacher, counselor) collects academic, behavioral, or social data for a student or the class.

STATION TEACHING

Three stations are created for small group student rotation. Two teachers teach parts of a lesson in their respective stations. The third station is for students to work independently. Students rotate among the three stations during a designated instructional block of time.

PARALLEL TEACHING

Two teachers each instruct half the class on the same material. Student composition of each half is carefully considered. Instruction is differentiated depending on the needs of students in each group. A smaller group increases student participation opportunities.

ALTERNATIVE TEACHING

One teacher is responsible for teaching the class. The other teacher takes a small group for enrichment, remediation, or assessment.

TEAMING

Two teachers lead large group instruction by lecturing, debating, or individualizing for specific students' needs.

ONE TEACHES, ONE ASSISTS

One teacher leads the lesson and the other teacher circulates to work with individual students as needed.

Tech Notes (p. 184) illustrates how teachers in a coteaching model of "One Teaches, One Observes" can use real time to monitor students' understanding of the class material.

in language and content development. Or the special education and general education teachers can work collaboratively to plan, coteach, and evaluate a lesson presented in the general education classroom.

Coteaching is based on specific underlying assumptions about teaching and professionals' expertise. One assumption is that the coteaching team can bring to the classroom combined knowledge and expertise, which will greatly enhance instruction. Another is that team members can meet individual students' needs more effectively than one teacher (Walther-Thomas, Korinek, McLaughlin, & Williams, 2000).

There are many variations of coteaching partnerships, including teaming for one instructional period or block of time, teaming for the entire day, and assigning a special education and general education team to one class all year long (Villa, Thousand, & Nevin, 2008). Coteaching for one instructional period, especially at the middle and high school level, is most common. Also, coteachers may be general education teachers, special education teachers, counselors, bilingual/ELL teachers, and speech/language pathologists. The IEP team determines the coteaching members, the instructional content to be taught, and the student's academic, behavioral, and social needs the coteaching members will address. Friend et al. (2010) described six approaches for coteaching, which are noted in the Instructional Strategy 5.1 feature.

An example of how some of these coteaching approaches might work is presented in the ADAPT Framework feature below. Refer to Ms. Warren's opening challenge to see how she could use station and alternative teaching to provide additional support in her classroom.

In ADAPT in Action, Ms. Warren uses the ADAPT framework for planning station and alternative teaching time.

There are certain procedures that teachers should implement in a coteaching or teaming arrangement (Salend, Gordon, & Lopez-Vona, 2002). First, they must mutually define roles in the teaming relationship that pertain to instruction,

ADAPT *in action*

MS. WARREN USES STATION AND ALTERNATIVE TEACHING TECHNIQUES

(A) **Ask, "What am I requiring the student to do?"** Students must be able to complete mathematics assignments independently in stations.

(D) **Determine the prerequisite skills of the task.** Students must be able to perform the work independently. They need to be able to read word problems and complete them using the steps for word problem solving.

(A) **Analyze the student's strengths and struggles.** The student can attend to the task and work well with others in small groups during station time. The student has difficulty with reading the word problems and does not know the steps for solving the problems.

(P) **Propose and implement adaptations from among the four categories.** During station time, pair the student with a stronger reader who can help read the word problems. Use alternative teaching where the special education teacher can teach the word problem solving steps.

(T) **Test to determine whether the adaptations helped the student accomplish the task.** The student's work will be assessed for accuracy and completion of the task.

ADAPT *framework:* STATION AND ALTERNATIVE TEACHING

ASK "What am I requiring the student to do?"	**DETERMINE** the prerequisite skills of the task.	**ANALYZE** the student's strengths and struggles.		**PROPOSE** and implement adaptations from among the four categories.	**TEST** to determine if the adaptations helped the student accomplish the task.
		Strengths	Struggles		
Students must possess mathematics skills to work independently and successfully in stations.	1. Attend to and perform activities in the independent station.	1			
	2. Read word problems in the station to complete the tasks independently.		2	2. Instructional delivery: During *station teaching,* pair the student with a stronger reader to help read the word problems without teacher help.	2. Examine the finished product to determine student performance.
	3. Know the steps for solving word problems.		3	3. Instructional delivery: Use *alternative teaching* by having the special education teacher provide small group instruction on word problem solving strategies. Ms. Warren will work with the rest of the group to provide additional problem-solving activities.	3. Provide word problems for small group instruction. Assess accuracy.
	4. Work well with other students in the independent small group.	4			

behavior management, and evaluation. By identifying role responsibilities, teachers can prevent ambiguities and miscommunication. Second, team members need to spend time discussing instructional philosophies to determine whether a mutual, collaborative relationship can be established. This is important to the development of team rapport.

Third, teachers must explain what they hope to gain from a team effort instructionally and for students. Such disclosure can promote effective communication right from the start of a teaming relationship. Fourth, team members should convey to students the teachers' roles and explain how instruction and discipline will be handled in the classroom. Both teachers should maintain a similar level of authority when working with students. Finally, teachers need to meet regularly to work through problems, evaluate student progress, communicate with families, and plan further instruction. The Working Together feature provides examples for building and implementing the coteaching partnership.

WORKING *together*

COTEACHING

Mr. Sanchez and Mrs. Voress will use coteaching as a way to provide more support for students with special needs in Mr. Sanchez's class. Teaming can help them address the academic needs of students with learning disabilities and of other students who have similar academic difficulties. They decide to proceed by working through the following steps:

1. Establish a coteaching partnership.

   - Identify goals and expectations of the partnership.

   - Share beliefs and values about teaching, discipline, and expectations of students for learning.

   - Identify how the partnership will be communicated to parents and the principal.

   - Designate a workspace within the classroom for each teacher.

   - Identify roles and responsibilities. Here are possible questions to consider:

     o How will discipline be handled?

     o Whose materials will we use to teach lessons?

     o How will we manage progress monitoring and grading?

     o How will we coordinate team instruction?

2. Identify students' needs.

   - Identify each student's strengths and weaknesses.

   - Discuss IEPs for students with disabilities.

   - Consider adaptations needed for each student to benefit from instruction.

3. Develop an instructional plan.

   - Find time to plan. Try to have at least 45 minutes a week to coplan. Time for planning is the most frequently cited issue in coteaching. Work with your principal to establish time.

Coteaching

- Identify a classroom and behavior management system together.
- Identify student groupings. Group students on the basis of the specific goals and purpose of a lesson and/or the needs of the students. Balance homogeneous grouping with other grouping formats to implement flexible grouping.
- Select a coteaching model to suit the instructional purpose and students' needs.
- Develop a plan.

4. Monitor student performance together.

- Become familiar with standards and accountability for all students.
- Measure student progress regularly.
- Develop a record-keeping system.
- Make instructional-based decisions.
- Discuss and assign grades together.
- Conduct teacher-parent conferences together whenever possible.

QUESTIONS

1. How can teachers plan for coteaching to occur in inclusive classrooms?

2. What concerns might each of the teachers have about coteaching?

3. How can students benefit from coteaching?

Research on collaborative models suggests that teachers note many positive effects of working together. For example, in a three-year study of effective coteaching teams, Walther-Thomas (1997) found that general education and special education teachers reported increases in the following:

1. Academic and social gains for students with disabilities

2. Opportunities for professional growth

3. Professional satisfaction

4. Personal support

Other studies have shown that special education teachers have felt subordinate to the general education teacher and that time for planning was an issue (Murray, 2004). Careful planning, communication about roles and philosophies, and regular meetings are important. Weiss and Lloyd (2002) studied coteaching at the secondary level to discover whether it is possible for students with disabilities to receive the specialized education they need with this method. They also noted that building principals are responsible for ensuring that enough resources, time, and training are provided for coteaching to be successful. Finally, Murawski and Swanson (2001) conducted a review of literature on coteaching research and concluded that coteaching demonstrated strong effects in language arts, moderate effects in mathematics, and negligible effects for social student outcomes. They also noted that more research is needed to assess the effects of coteaching on achievement outcomes of students with disabilities.

COLLABORATION CONSIDERATIONS FOR ENGLISH LANGUAGE LEARNERS

Ortiz (2002) and Yates and Ortiz (2004) stressed the need for early intervention for students who are ELLs experiencing learning problems in the general education classroom. As soon as learning problems are identified, teachers should implement strategies to address special learning needs. Classroom teachers can collaborate with bilingual specialists who can provide assistance on effective instructional practices for ELLs. Ortiz and Yates and Ortiz recommended four strategies that build on the concept of prereferral interventions: the clinical teaching cycle, peer or expert consultation, the teacher assistance team process, and alternative programs and services for early intervention for struggling students.

The **clinical teaching cycle** consists of sequenced instruction, reteaching if necessary, and informal assessment procedures, including assessment of academic and conversational language proficiency (Ortiz, 2002).

Peer or expert consultation can include teachers observing their peers and providing interventions to ELLs who need supplemental instruction. Support can also be provided in consultation with an ESL teacher who can furnish information on how to integrate ESL strategies into academic instruction.

The **teacher assistance team process** (Chalfant & Van Dusen Pysh, 1989) can be another option to assist teachers in providing appropriate instruction for ELLs. In this model, Ortiz (2002) described a collaborative, team approach that discusses the problem, identifies possible interventions, and assists the teacher as needed in implementing strategies.

Finally, Ortiz (2002) provided ideas for alternative programs and services that teachers can implement in collaboration with colleagues and families.

Collaborative partnerships can provide services to students from diverse backgrounds. Ortiz (2002) provided intervention strategies with implications for collaborative partnerships for ELLs. Table 5.2 offers information about each of these strategies, which can also assist students exhibiting learning and behavioral problems.

TABLE 5.2

INTERVENTION STRATEGIES AND COLLABORATIVE PARTNERSHIPS FOR ENGLISH LANGUAGE LEARNERS

Issue	Strategy
Student experiences difficulty; implement clinical teaching cycle	**Clinical teaching cycle** • Teach skill or content. • Reteach using different strategies if student experiences difficulty. • Conduct informal assessments to identify difficulties. • Adapt instruction based on assessment results. • Monitor student response to instruction regularly.
Problem persists; request assistance from teacher assistance team	**Teacher assistance team process** • The teacher requests assistance from the team. • The team leader reviews the request and obtains additional information if necessary. • The leader arranges a classroom observation. • A team meeting is held. • The team designs an intervention plan. • The teacher implements the plan with assistance as appropriate. • A follow-up team meeting is held to determine student progress. • If the problem continues, the process is repeated.
Problem still persists; refer student to alternative general education programs and services	**Alternative programs and services** • One-to-one tutoring • Cross-age tutoring • Remedial programs • Student and family support groups • Family counseling

SOURCE: Ortiz (2002).

Next we discuss developing collaborative partnerships with paraprofessionals. These individuals are critical players in addressing the needs of students with special needs, especially students with more severe disabilities.

HOW CAN PROFESSIONALS COLLABORATE WITH PARAPROFESSIONALS?

Paraprofessionals, or paraeducators, are individuals hired to work with teachers in a supportive role under the supervision of licensed professionals (IDEA, 2004). Their titles vary across schools and districts; paraprofessionals may be called paraeducators, nonteaching assistants, classroom assistants, teaching assistants, or special support assistants, among other titles. Whatever their title, they are members of the instructional team in classrooms and other educational settings, and they often deliver direct services to students and their families (Werts, Harris, Tillery, & Roark, 2004).

At one time paraprofessionals spent most of their time performing clerical duties; monitoring the halls, playground, and cafeteria; and supervising students who were being disciplined for behavior problems. However, their role has evolved with rising awareness of the valuable contributions they can make in diverse and inclusive educational settings. Increased training opportunities have helped many develop important skills that can benefit educational teams. Paraeducators are increasingly being relied on to provide special education services to students with more severe disabilities. In addition to performing clerical tasks and providing student supervision, daily needs care, mobility support, and behavior support (Downing, Ryndak, & Clark, 2000; Minondo, Meyer, & Xin, 2001), they are often required to teach instructional lessons (Pickett & Gerlach, 2003).

Studies have shown that most paraprofessionals are women who live in the area served by the school in which they work (French, 2004). In many cases, paraprofessionals can bridge linguistic and cultural connections between the school and the community (Chopra et al., 2004). Thus, they can make connections between their schools and the families and community affiliated with their schools. The No Child Left Behind Act of 2001 indicates that paraprofessionals must have a high school diploma or its equivalent. Those who provide instructional support must also have

- Completed two years of study at an institution of higher education,
- Obtained an associate's (or higher) degree, or
- Demonstrated, through a formal state or local assessment, knowledge of, and ability to assist in, reading, writing, and mathematics instruction.

These criteria aside, researchers have noted that paraeducators' role has become one of serving a more diverse student population and supporting the inclusion of students with more significant disabilities in the general education classroom (Bernal & Aragon, 2004; French, 2004).

Paraprofessionals account for more than half of the nonteaching staff that provide services to students with special needs.

Paraprofessionals account for more than half of the nonteaching staff who provide services to students with special needs (White, 2004). Today, that demand continues as more students with disabilities receive their instruction in general education settings and sometimes require services beyond those that general educators can reasonably provide. In addition to working in special education and general education classes, paraprofessionals are needed to help implement community-based instruction for students with more severe disabilities. They may take public transportation with students to their job sites, assist students with disabilities in their job-site tasks, and participate with students and teachers in community activities designed to promote recreational and social skills.

Yet Giangreco and Doyle (2007) noted that "at present, there is no international consensus about the extent to which teacher assistants [paraeducators] should be utilized, circumstances that warrant their involvement, the duties they should appropriately perform, or what constitutes adequate training and supervision" (p. 437). Thus, as options expand for providing services and effective instruction to students with special needs, the need remains to establish roles and responsibilities and provide supervision and training. The next two sections address these areas.

ROLES AND RESPONSIBILITIES OF PARAPROFESSIONALS IN COLLABORATIVE PARTNERSHIPS

According to IDEA (2004), teachers are responsible for ensuring the delivery of services specified in the IEP. However, paraprofessionals have an important role to play in supporting the delivery of these services. Communication about roles and responsibilities helps everyone understand the expectations when providing services to students and their families. Clear job descriptions, specifying roles and responsibilities, can enhance communication between teachers and paraprofessionals and foster appropriate expectations. Paraprofessionals and teachers should know about one another's job descriptions so that each is familiar with the requirements of the positions. Typically, job descriptions include a definition of the job, general responsibilities, and specific hiring requirements (amount of education, contractual duty day, and length of school year). Because of the guidelines provided, reviewing job descriptions is a good place to begin a discussion about roles and responsibilities. The job description usually provides information that school district administrative personnel feel is important for particular roles; teachers and paraprofessionals must abide by the established job guidelines (Pickett & Gerlach, 2003).

Once job descriptions have been reviewed, teachers and paraprofessionals can work together to delineate specific roles and responsibilities, clarifying classroom roles and responsibilities and establishing the authority of the teacher as supervisor and evaluator in the paraprofessional-teacher relationship. For example, roles might include instruction, administration, behavior management, assessment, and communication with families and other professionals. Together, teachers and paraprofessionals can develop a responsibilities list for each role and identify areas for training, philosophical discussion, and further explanation. Teachers have the responsibility for developing, implementing, and evaluating their students' IEPs and for protecting the safety and well-being of the students. However, paraprofessionals can greatly assist in a collaborative way to support these responsibilities (Pickett & Gerlach, 2003). The following include examples of possible responsibilities for paraprofessionals:

- Assessment
  - Conducting curriculum-based assessments
  - Scoring curriculum-based assessments

- Behavior Management
  - Implementing behavior management programs designed with the classroom teacher
  - Awarding points to students for appropriate behavior
  - Monitoring of behavior in small or whole groups

- Instruction
  - Providing instructional adaptations for lessons taught by teachers
  - Monitoring student work in learning centers
  - Providing small group instruction to students who require more assistance

- Communication
  - Serving as a link between special education and general education teachers
  - Meeting regularly with the classroom teacher to discuss specific student needs, instructional programs, successes, and concerns
  - Facilitating communication with parents for whom English is not their primary language

- Clerical Support
    - Conducting tasks to maintain classroom organization and management
    - Developing instructional materials
- Student Support
    - Working with students in community job-related settings
    - Escorting students during hallway, recess, and lunch activities
- Professionalism
    - Attending professional meetings with teachers or with other paraprofessionals

Often the paraprofessional is older than the teacher, has been at the school longer, and may have strong community connections with families, businesses, and children. These dynamics in the relationship between them must be respected; however, they should not undermine the role of the teacher as supervisor and as the person contractually responsible for the education of the students. Through effective communication techniques, teachers can tap the valuable knowledge paraprofessionals possess through their connections with the school and community. They should also be sensitive to the needs of younger paraprofessionals who may lack experience and educational expertise.

It is important for teachers to invest time in establishing rapport and team-building behaviors so a truly collaborative partnership can be nurtured. Table 5.3 provides examples of possible barriers to the development of collaborative partnerships with paraeducators and solutions for removing the barriers.

Experienced paraprofessionals contribute important information to relationships between themselves and teachers. For example, Riggs (2005) presented a list of what paraprofessionals identified as important tasks for beginning teachers:

- Know the paraprofessional's name, background, and interests.
- Know about district policies for paraprofessionals.
- View the paraprofessional as a member of the professional team.
- Define roles and responsibilities.
- Supervise the paraprofessional.
- Communicate with the paraprofessional.
- Acknowledge the paraprofessional's experience and knowledge.
- Be respectful of paraprofessionals.
- Assume "ownership" of all students.

TABLE 5.3	BARRIERS AND SOLUTIONS FOR COLLABORATIVE PARTNERSHIPS WITH PARAEDUCATORS

Barriers	Solutions
Lack of time	Try to set aside 30 minutes before or after school several days a week to discuss students' progress.
Differing roles and responsibilities	Discuss roles and responsibilities clearly so each person knows his or her duties.
Differing years of experience	Tap the expertise of paraeducators who have been working at the school longer than the teacher; help build the self-confidence of new paraeducators.

SUPERVISION AND TRAINING OF PARAPROFESSIONALS

Teachers are typically responsible for supervising and evaluating paraprofessionals with whom they work. In some cases, principals may share in the supervisory and evaluative process, but usually teachers assume the greater part of this responsibility.

Ongoing communication is vital to any supervisory situation. Paraprofessionals, like any employee, should be given opportunities to work with their supervisors in choosing how they will be supervised and evaluated. Teachers and paraprofessionals must review job descriptions, roles, and responsibilities as a starting point in the supervisory process. Specific tasks and expectations must be communicated effectively to reduce role ambiguity and misinterpretations. At a minimum, weekly meetings are recommended to review the paraprofessionals' tasks and job performance. Paraprofessionals should be given feedback about their performance, both positive and negative, on a regular basis.

Teachers should examine their supervisory style to ensure they adopt practices that foster collegial relationships. An authoritarian style will not promote a spirit of collaboration, but a sharing, direct approach, in which the teacher and paraprofessional have an equal opportunity to reflect on situations, can facilitate a collaborative partnership. Paraprofessionals also should have an opportunity to discuss practices of their supervisors that either impede or foster communication and the fulfillment of role responsibilities (Pickett & Gerlach, 2003). Teachers can ask the following questions to promote communication and build a collaborative partnership:

- How do you think we are doing working together as a team?

- What can we do to make our team stronger, to help students more, or to work better with each other?

- What would you like to discuss with me about how our teaming is working?

- What is important to you to make our teaming work well?

- How would you describe our team to others?

- What advice would you offer to another teacher-paraprofessional team just beginning together?

Teacher training in effective supervisory practices and evaluation criteria makes it easier to serve in the role of supervisor and evaluator. If training is not available, teachers should seek assistance from their building principal and special education coordinators to identify ways to become an effective supervisor and to conduct employee evaluations. Often, school districts have career ladders for paraprofessionals in which promotion depends on positive evaluations. Therefore, it is in everyone's best interest for teachers to learn about (a) evaluation criteria, (b) ways to conduct an evaluation (providing feedback, stating strengths and weaknesses, encouraging problem solving and conflict resolution), and (c) techniques to foster professional development in areas where improvement is needed.

Training for paraprofessionals is a critical element of effective supervisory practices. It is not enough to tell someone about weaknesses without offering options for improvement. School district human resources offices could team with teachers to identify specific areas in which paraprofessionals might benefit from in-service training. Paraprofessionals may have effective interpersonal skills and a caring attitude but need to acquire skills specific to the populations with whom they are working. Many may be working for the first time with children who have disabilities; they may not possess the skills necessary to meet individual students' educational, health, medical, and/or language needs. School district administrators should consider training options for these critical team members. For instance, local community colleges can provide classes geared to developing skills that paraprofessionals will need to work in the public schools. School district and community college instructors could easily develop a curriculum to serve this training need. Also, through informal modeling, prompting, and taking advantage of "think-aloud" situations, teachers can instruct paraprofessionals in their classrooms as they work with children. Third, school district and university staff can collaborate to offer a menu of in-service training opportunities for paraprofessionals.

We now turn to collaborative partnerships with families.

HOW CAN PROFESSIONALS COLLABORATE WITH FAMILIES?

Families are an integral part of the school community; they know their children better than anyone and can provide critical information that can help teachers understand the students' individual needs. For years, families have been influential in the development of special education services; this influence continues as educational reform efforts at the elementary and secondary level (such as NCLB and IDEA) contribute to the modification and/or creation of service delivery options for students with special needs. In this section, we talk about the importance of developing collaborative partnerships with families and about situations in which this collaboration can be facilitated. Table 5.4 identifies potential barriers and solutions for collaborative partnerships with family members.

TABLE 5.4	BARRIERS AND SOLUTIONS FOR COLLABORATIVE PARTNERSHIPS WITH FAMILIES
Barriers	**Solutions**
Lack of time	Be sure to meet with parents at times that are mutually agreeable. This may necessitate early morning or late afternoon meetings to accommodate busy work schedules.
Language differences	Have an interpreter present during meetings for parents who do not speak English. Be sure written communication is in the parents' primary language.
Professional jargon	Avoid technical terms and acronyms that may be unfamiliar to parents.

THE NEED FOR COLLABORATIVE PARTNERSHIPS WITH FAMILIES

Families have been significant contributors to the establishment of special education as a field. They have formed organizations, raised revenue, initiated litigation, pushed for legislation, formed advocacy groups, and demanded a free appropriate public education in the least restrictive environment for all students with disabilities. They have clout, and they know their children. Collaboration with them is indispensable.

Collaboration with families should be a major goal of all schools. However, for it to be achieved, educators must better understand families and their dynamics. As Pugach and Johnson (1995) so aptly noted years ago, our "students are all members of families first and students second" (p. 225). We must recognize the powerful effect families have on the students with whom we work and nurture collaborative relationships with families and family members. Like all students, students with special needs cannot be viewed in isolation; they are members of the total school community, of the community at large, and of their families (Smith & Tyler, 2014). We must come to know our students' families and understand their dynamics; only then can we begin the process of developing effective collaborative partnerships.

Working With Families

MODELS OF COLLABORATIVE PARTNERSHIPS WITH FAMILIES

Using the critical prerequisite skills for effective collaboration discussed earlier in this chapter, teachers can nurture successful partnerships with families to build a strong, positive relationship between families and the schools. In the following section we discuss the family systems approach as a technique for focusing on school-home relationships within a framework that is responsive to families' needs. We offer tips for working with families from diverse backgrounds, and we suggest ways to facilitate successful parent-teacher conferences and home-school communication.

Family Systems Approach

Collaborative efforts with students' families can be developed through a **family systems approach** in which families' needs and support are defined according to resources, interactions, functions, and the life cycle (Turnbull, Turnbull, Wehmeyer, & Shogren, 2016). Families may have specific issues, such as reactions to a family member with a disability, economic needs, and future planning. Collaborative efforts can be greatly enhanced between home and school if teachers are aware of (a) the family unit (one- or two-parent family, extended family); (b) resources families need to function; (c) family interactions that may affect the children's mental health and school success; (d) the economic, vocational, and educational needs of families; and (e) the adult and child development cycles that influence how individuals cope with and respond to their environments.

As part of the family systems approach, educators must come to understand that families of children with disabilities will probably need support systems that change as the children mature. For example, children with learning problems may manage during the preschool years, but when they enter school, issues related to learning may surface for families. Teachers should be prepared to explain instructional programs and services. Some families may wonder what the future holds for their child's postsecondary education.

For families of children with behavior problems, school may be just another arena in which difficulties surface, misconduct occurs, and negative encounters with authorities result. These families may not view the schools as partners in their child's education if encounters focus on what the child is doing wrong rather than on how we can help the child. For families of children with severe disabilities, an array of services provided

iStock/MarcelaC

Families are important members of the school community. Home-school communication can be greatly enhanced by making families part of a positive communication network.

Family Collaboration

by various professionals may be offered across the grade levels. However, as these children become older, parents will want to know how their child's specific needs will continue to be addressed after high school. Aging parents will want to be assured that their child with severe disabilities will be served.

A coordinated effort among professionals is necessary to ensure that communication with families is seamless across services and that the families' evolving issues and concerns are addressed. By viewing collaborative partnerships through a family systems approach, educators can tailor their interactions with families to each family's unique configuration and needs. For example, families may have difficulty finding transportation or childcare services so that they can attend school meetings. They may be dealing with health or social issues that preclude their participation in school activities. School staff should identify the needs of their school community and provide necessary accommodations that promote family participation in school activities. The Considering Diversity feature offers suggestions for collaborating with families and the community.

Values and perceptions are additional areas of the family systems approach that professionals and paraprofessionals must address as they work with students and family members. A person's value system and ways of perceiving information are important factors that can impede or promote effective home-school communication and collaboration. Values and perceptions are learned from significant adults, home environments, peers, cultural and ethnic groups,

CONSIDERING *diversity*

WAYS TO INVOLVE THE FAMILY AND THE COMMUNITY

Smith and Tyler (2014) offered a helpful list of suggestions for family and community involvement:

- Develop an atmosphere of trust and respect.
- Be sure families and communities feel welcome.
- Select and involve community leaders to serve as representatives of both school and home.
- Identify families' preferred means of communication and use it effectively.
- Communicate on a regular, ongoing basis (not just when there is a problem).
- Use interpreters who are knowledgeable about schools and their programs for effective communication and participation.
- Incorporate materials that reflect the diversity of the community.
- Seek meaningful ways (e.g., actively sharing culture, art, music, and recreational activities) to involve families and communities (as they feel comfortable).
- Treat families with individual respect, and avoid stereotyping on any basis (race, ethnicity, language, or socioeconomic class).
- Hold meetings with families at times and places that are manageable for them. (p. 100)

and religious and social affiliations. Unfortunately, it is all too easy to fall into the trap of assigning negative or positive opinions to another person's value system and perceptions on the basis of misconceptions, stereotypes, miscommunication, and our own values and perceptions.

Students who represent a rich cultural and linguistic heritage attend today's schools, and like all students, they come from a spectrum of socioeconomic environments ranging from homelessness to considerable affluence. The challenge for educators is to become more sensitive to all types of diversity, to become better educated about differences in values and perceptions, and to focus on ways to promote collaborative relationships that tap the diverse ways of viewing home-school partnerships.

Teachers are challenged to build effective communication bridges that convey information about school activities and to take the initiative in speaking with families to demonstrate an interest in establishing collaboration. Collaborative partnerships can be developed with parents and other family members through parent conferences and home-school communication. Table 5.5 provides the

TABLE 5.5 STAGES AND STEPS OF PARENT-TEACHER CONFERENCES	
Stages	**Steps**
Preconference Stage	1. Notify families of the time, day, and purpose of the conference. Notification should be written in the primary language spoken at home. Provide options for conference times and days that are mutually convenient for parents as well as for teachers (and other professionals, such as counselors, who might be attending the conference). In many families both parents work, and in single-parent homes the parent is usually employed full time. Flexibility in conference times and days is important to increase the likelihood of parental participation.
	2. Review assessment data that describe how the child is progressing academically, socially, and behaviorally. Prepare a summary of important data and information that will help families understand their child's progress. Samples of work can be gathered as evidence of progress or of the need for remediation. Share with families the plans for promoting academic success and addressing instructional problems.
	3. Develop an agenda for the meeting, including the starting and stopping times, questions that will be asked, a statement of purpose for the meeting, and time to develop a plan if necessary. Ask family members what topics they would like to discuss as part of the agenda.
	4. Arrange the environment to foster a collaborative spirit, including chairs that are designed for adults (a problem at the primary level), the removal of barriers (such as tables with large spaces between families and teachers or teacher desks), and the elimination of distractions (such as intercom interruptions).
	5. Identify key professionals and paraprofessionals who can contribute important information to the conference. This is especially important if the child works with a speech/language pathologist or counselor. The challenge is to ensure that there are not too many professionals present, which might be intimidating to families. In some cases, an initial parent-teacher conference might be a good approach, followed by a second meeting with other professionals, as needed. The key is to create an initial meeting in which rapport and trust can be built.

Stages	Steps
	6. Make arrangements for an interpreter if English is not the primary language or if sign language is needed. In some school communities, a home-school liaison delivers the conference information so families can communicate with school staff right from the start.
Conference Stage	1. Provide a warm welcome; greet family members at the door and guide them to the conference meeting table. A warm greeting and comfortable environment pave the way for a positive start.
	2. Present the agenda, and be sure that parents' questions and concerns are readily noted for discussion. Specify the time limits, which are important to help keep the conversation on track.
	3. Begin with an explanation and display of the child's strengths. Showing work samples and describing positive situations can begin the establishment of rapport and trust.
	4. Apprise family members of their child's progress and of the instructional plan for the child. Talk to families about ways to support instruction at home and tips for developing effective study and homework habits.
	5. Provide opportunities for family members to discuss their concerns throughout the conference. Don't just leave the last few minutes for them to ask questions.
	6. Watch for nonverbal and verbal communication cues that might be signaling discomfort, anger, joy, and so forth. If feelings begin to escalate, acknowledge points and use the communication techniques discussed in this chapter.
	7. Jot down important points during the conference; however, check with families about this practice to be sure it does not hinder communication. Writing on carbonless paper provides copies of the notes for each participant and makes the process transparent for all. Taking notes is especially critical if a plan of action must be developed in which families and teachers agree on responsibilities for solving a problem.
	8. End on a positive note, summarizing issues, successes, and plans for improvement. This can foster trust and boost the likelihood of other successful conferences occurring.
Postconference Stage	1. Review any notes that were taken during the conference to see whether specific activities must be planned for the following school day. If an agreement is made that certain activities (such as moving the child's desk or talking to the child privately more often) will occur, be sure this action is taken the following school day.
	2. Discuss concerns about the child and a follow-up plan to address those concerns with other professionals as needed. This may require scheduling an additional conference or establishing stronger home-school communication.

SOURCE: Adapted from Rivera and Smith (1997).

stages and steps of parent-teacher conferences. There are three stages of an effective parent-teacher conference: preconference, conference, and postconference. Specific actions can occur during each stage to foster collaboration and communication (Pugach & Johnson, 1995). Parent-teacher conferences are a critical component of building collaborative relationships, and time must be invested in this endeavor to ensure success.

Parent-Teacher Conference

The parent-teacher conference is a regular forum for families and teachers to develop collaborative, communicative partnerships (Pugach & Johnson, 1995). It can serve as a time to establish rapport with family members, to convey information about class activities, to identify individual students' strengths and weaknesses for educational planning, and to discover values and perceptions that can be nurtured to promote collaboration and communication. According to Turnbull and colleagues (2016), there are four purposes for the parent-teacher conference:

1. To jointly share information about the child's educational progress

2. To work together in finding solutions to problems

3. To establish rapport and joint responsibility for the child's educational program

4. To exchange information that might contribute to a better understanding of the child's progress and individual needs

Home-School Communication

Home-school communication can be greatly enhanced by making families part of a positive communication network (Lavoie, 2008). Sometimes the initial contact with families focuses on a problem, like a disciplinary concern, truancy, or missing homework, that requires action. Teachers should therefore make attempts, at the beginning of the school year and throughout the year, to focus on the positive by sending good news about class activities, student progress, and behavior to build communication bridges that foster collaboration. Then, if a contact must be made regarding concerns, a positive foundation exists on which they can discuss current issues.

Lavoie (2008) and Turnbull et al. (2016) offered several suggestions for promoting communication. For example, teachers can send home weekly or monthly newsletters describing events, giving special student recognition, mentioning important dates, and so forth. Keep in mind that some students in all grades, and secondary school students in general, may not want to be singled out; recognizing *groups* of students might be one way to address this issue. Students can participate in the design, layout, and production of the newsletter as a language arts activity, especially with the many desktop publishing software programs now available for students of all ages.

Notes recognizing a child's accomplishments can be sent home periodically. This can be done quietly with the student to minimize public display (especially important at the secondary level). Experience has shown that many secondary school students do like special recognition; the key point is how the teacher handles it. Elementary school students usually can deal with public recognition.

Teachers can make telephone calls periodically to inform families of their child's progress. Calling families to say, "I just wanted to tell you the good news . . ." can help tremendously in building communication and trust.

Weekly samples of work, including good work and work that needs improvement, as well as improved work, can be collected by students and taken home to their families. These samples inform family members about how their children are progressing with the skills that were designated as areas to focus on for the semester or school year.

Teachers with several years' experience may be ready to begin a parent group that focuses on topics of concern for many families (finishing homework, establishing study skills, building self-esteem, promoting reading at home). The school's counselor can conduct the groups, ensuring that another qualified professional addresses issues beyond the teacher's area of expertise. When childcare is provided for such after-hours events, more family members can take advantage of parent group training and bonding.

Some teachers involve families in the classroom. There are many ways to do this. For instance, families can come to class on a regular basis just to read with students during reading time. They can share a special skill or information from a trip. Families can work as individual tutors (be sure to provide some initial training and be specific about their tasks). Holidays are a good time, in particular, to involve families who can bring cultural and ethnic traditions and customs to share. Families can help teachers make bulletin board displays and learning materials—have a designated night to explain these needs and see the wonderful items you get!

Weekly report cards that require a signature are another way to keep families informed, to signal areas of growth and concern, and to share a note about a special achievement. These regular report cards also give children an opportunity to discuss their progress with their families.

Developing communication bridges takes time and effort, and teachers must be aware of cultural and linguistic factors to consider when working with families. Frequent positive and informative communication, written in the parents' primary language, is important. In the long run, the benefits are usually great and promote the type of home-school communication that contributes to the children's progress.

SUMMARY

A cornerstone of the federal laws ensuring all infants, toddlers, preschoolers, and students with disabilities a free appropriate education in the least restrictive environment is the individualized education created through the special education process. IDEA '04 guarantees these individuals and their families a tailor-made education program, which is guided by uniquely created planning documents: the individualized family service plan (IFSP) and the individualized education program (IEP). The IEP is further supported, when necessary, by behavior intervention plans and the statement of transitional services. These plans bring together multidisciplinary teams of parents, general educators, special educators, and related service providers for the purpose of helping young children and students with disabilities reach their full potential and achieve community presence and independence as adults.

REVIEW THE LEARNING OBJECTIVES •••••••••••••••••••••••••••••••••••••

Let's review the learning objectives for this chapter. If you are uncertain and cannot "talk through" the answers provided for any of these questions, reread those sections of the text.

- **What are the characteristics of collaboration?**

  Successful collaboration includes shared problem solving, shared responsibility, and voluntary involvement. These characteristics imply that the individuals choose to share expertise, decision making, and involvement to promote effective inclusive practices for all students.

- **What are critical prerequisite skills for effective collaboration?**

  Communication and conflict resolution skills are important for promoting effective collaborative partnerships. Professionals must also be aware of the cultural, linguistic, and socioeconomic backgrounds of their students and must accommodate differences in values and perceptions.

- **How can professionals work together collaboratively?**

  Effective practices include collaboration, consultation, coteaching, and strategies for English language learners, such as the clinical teaching cycle, peer or expert consultation, the teacher assistance team process, and alternative programs and services.

- **How can teachers collaborate with paraprofessionals?**

  The establishment of roles, supervision and training, and teaming are some approaches that promote effective partnerships between professionals and paraprofessionals. Paraprofessionals should be given opportunities to express their issues and concerns.

- **How can professionals collaborate with families?**

  Professionals should use a family systems approach when working with families. This approach takes into consideration the range of needs that families have regarding their child's education and well-being. Professionals can also use parent-teacher conferences and home-school communication as opportunities to develop partnerships. Professionals should be mindful of cultural considerations as they work with families.

> **$SAGE edge™** **Test your understanding of chapter content. Take the practice quiz.**
> edge.sagepub.com/bryant

REVISIT THE OPENING CHALLENGE •••••••••••••••••••••••••••••••••••

Check your answers to the Reflection Questions in the Opening Challenge and revise them on the basis of what you have learned.

1. What professional collaborative practices can Ms. Warren use to help her students with special learning, behavior, and language needs succeed in the general education classroom?

2. How can Ms. Warren and Ms. Bryant collaborate effectively with their paraprofessional?

3. How can Ms. Warren effectively structure parent-teacher conferences and develop home-school communication effectively?

4. What should be the focus of the three-way meeting with Ms. Bryant, the special education teacher, and the paraprofessional?

KEY TERMS

active listening, 179

clinical teaching cycle, 195

collaboration, 176

conflict, 182

cultural characteristics, 185

family systems approach, 204

paraprofessionals, 197

peer or expert consultation, 195

teacher assistance team process, 195

$SAGE edge™ Review key terms with eFlashcards.
edge.sagepub.com/bryant

PROFESSIONAL STANDARDS AND LICENSURE

For a complete description of Professional Standards and Licensure, please see Appendix on page 569.

CEC Initial Preparation Standards

Standard 2: Learning Environments

Standard 6: Professional Learning and Ethical Practice

Standard 7: Collaboration

INTASC Core Principles

Standard 3: Learning Environments

Standard 7: Planning for Instruction

Standard 9: Professional Learning and Ethical Practice

Standard 10: Leadership and Collaboration

Praxis II: Education of Exceptional Students: Core Content Knowledge

II. Legal and Societal Issues: Federal laws and legal issues

III. Delivery of Services to Students with Disabilities: Background knowledge

Review ➡ Practice ➡ Improve
Get the tools you need to sharpen your study skills. Access practice quizzes, eFlashcards, video, and multimedia: **edge.sagepub.com/bryant**

6

DELIVERY OF APPROPRIATE SERVICES TO STUDENTS WITH SPECIAL NEEDS

LEARNING OBJECTIVES

After studying this chapter, you will be able to answer the following questions:

- What is response to intervention?

- What is the evaluation and identification process?

- Who are the members of the IEP team?

- How do special education multidisciplinary teams and services meet the needs of students with disabilities?

- What plans guarantee students with disabilities an appropriate education?
- When and how are existing individualized plans evaluated?
- What does IDEA '04 require during the IEP process?

OPENING *challenge* ··

How All These Special Education Services Come Together

ELEMENTARY GRADES Mr. Hernandez has been teaching fourth grade for several years, but he had not taught a student with complex disabilities in his general education program until now. All of his students with disabilities have had mild to moderate learning challenges, and he has always worked well with the special education teacher to meet those students' needs. It is November, and the school year is well under way. Students are now assigned to the right groups, and he has a good understanding of each student's strengths and struggles. A new student, Emily, joined his class several weeks ago. She just moved to River City from another state, and her existing individualized education program (IEP) came with her. Because she has complex learning needs, the school's support team decided to implement the IEP process, create an IEP team for Emily, and schedule an IEP meeting.

As Mr. Hernandez prepares materials and all the documents for the upcoming IEP meeting, he begins to wonder, *"How many education professionals will be assigned to Emily? Who will be at Emily's IEP meeting? How can I possibly meet all of her needs and still be sure that the rest of the students get the instruction they need?"*

SECONDARY GRADES Ms. Cohen is a 10th-grade history teacher at Independence High School. She has been teaching for seven years and has worked with students with learning disabilities; in her class one year she had a student who was blind. This year, Ms. Cohen has several students with learning disabilities and one student who has a mild intellectual disability; the students with LD are in one of two inclusion classes she teaches each day. All of these students have reading disabilities. Two of the students' IEPs are up for reevaluation, so Ms. Cohen will have to attend IEP meetings. She has not attended a reevaluation before so she is unsure what to expect. She knows that the students' assistive technology (AT) needs must be considered in the meeting, but she is confused about what this actually means. She is also concerned about the services her students might require and how this works in high school classes. As she plans her lessons for the first month of school, she thinks about her inclusion classes; she plans to make an appointment with the special education teacher to discuss her students' needs and how their IEPs can be implemented in her classes. She also needs guidance to prepare for the upcoming IEP reevaluation meetings. Ms. Cohen wonders, *"What is in each student's IEP that I have to be mindful of* *for my instruction? What does an IEP reevaluation meeting entail? How is AT "considered"? What services might be added to the IEPs and how will I be able to work with various professionals and teach my history classes? How is the special education teacher going to help me?"*

REFLECTION QUESTIONS In your journal, write down your answers to the following questions. After completing this chapter, check your answers and revise them on the basis of what you have learned.

1. Are Mr. Hernandez and Ms. Cohen overly concerned about being able to meet their students' needs? Why or why not?

2. What advice would you give them about working with special education teachers regarding the supports and services that may be specified in their students' IEPs?

3. What kind of help and assistance should Mr. Hernandez and Ms. Cohen expect from the IEP team members?

4. Is Mr. Hernandez justified in expressing concerns about the educational progress of Emily's classmates? Why or why not?

5. How can special education and related service professionals help Mr. Hernandez and Ms. Cohen support their students' needs and enable them to teach the rest of their class?

6. How does the response to intervention (RTI) model affect instruction in Mr. Hernandez's and Ms. Cohen's classes?

⑤SAGE edge™

Get the edge on your studies: edge.sagepub.com/bryant

- Take a quiz to find out what you've learned.
- Review key terms with eFlashcards.
- Watch videos to see teachers in action.

For an education program to be appropriate for each infant, toddler, and student with a disability, it must be individualized. When education is appropriate, the results can be astounding. It is clear to us that there is no single answer to the educational needs of all students with disabilities: no standard program, no single service delivery option, no single place where education is received, and no single curriculum. For these reasons, the expression first applied to students with disabilities more than 20 years ago, "one size doesn't fit all," has become a mantra of special education (Borthwick-Duffy, Palmer, & Lane, 1996). This idea is verified and validated time and time again as the process enacted to develop IEPs for each student with a disability is applied.

Let's think first about how general education should be the strong foundation of the educational experiences of all students, including students with disabilities, through the RTI model.

WHAT IS RESPONSE TO INTERVENTION?

Response to intervention (RTI) is a model for delivering scientifically based, schoolwide, multitiered systems of support (MTSS), which is designed to promote improved academic performance for all students and minimize

Response to Intervention

behavior problems. Through the RTI model, students who are identified as at risk for poor academic achievement are eligible to receive additional educational support. In terms of applying the RTI model to behavior, Positive Behavioral Interventions and Supports (PBIS) is commonly utilized in school districts to prevent behavior problems and to provide intensive interventions for the small group of students who require this support (Sugai, Horner, Fixen, & Blase, 2010; see Chapter 9 for additional information about PBIS).

Scientifically based or evidence-based instruction means that instructional practices employed in schools are based on findings from research studies that involved systematic, rigorous procedures using experimental or quasiexperimental research designs. The instructional practices should have been implemented with **fidelity**, which refers to following the protocol or lesson steps as developed for the instructional practice, and the research measures should have been valid and reliable. Also, experts should have examined the findings for the instructional practices, for example, through the peer-reviewed process for journals (Mastropieri & Scruggs, 2014).

RTI is also designed to provide evidence toward the evaluation for and identification of learning disabilities in the event that a special education referral is necessary because of continually low performance in spite of intensive instruction. According to IDEA '04, states must adopt criteria for determining the presence of a learning disability. As an alternative to the criteria of a severe discrepancy between intellectual ability and achievement, which was in vogue for many years as part of the identification process, states must now permit the use of the RTI model as part of the disability identification process.

RTI involves four fundamental components: universal screening, progress monitoring, data-based decision making, and high-quality, evidence-based, multitiered instructional support in relation to students' educational needs (http://www.rti4success.org). **Universal screening** is the schoolwide process of identifying students who are at risk for poor performance. **Progress monitoring** involves systematically monitoring student performance in relation to the delivery of intensive interventions. **Data-based decision making** is used to identify students who require additional instruction and to determine whether intensive intervention supports are effective. Data can be used to determine movement within the multitiered system and as part of the disability identification process (see Chapter 8 for a discussion of these three components of RTI).

Multitiered instructional support involves tiered levels of increasingly intensive intervention at the primary, secondary, and tertiary levels. Tier 1, the primary level, consists of high-quality, evidence-based core instruction for all students; approximately 80% of all students can benefit from this typical, core

VIDEO CASE 6.1

What Is Response to Intervention?

1. How are multi-systems of support, such as response to intervention, used to meet the needs of all students? In what ways are assessment data used in the planning process in order to fully meet student needs?

2. How does Mia Tannous describe Tier 2 and Tier 3 interventions? How are these levels of support provided at her school?

Response to Intervention

instruction. Tier 2, or secondary intervention, involves about 15% of students who have been identified through universal screening as at risk and in need of intensified instructional support. Tier 3, the tertiary level, is more intensified intervention and is appropriate for approximately 5% of students. This group of students continues to demonstrate poor performance in spite of receiving evidence-based instructional practices in Tiers 1 and 2. For some students who perform so poorly during universal screening, the Tier 3 level of support may be immediately necessary.

Figure 6.1 shows the three levels of the RTI model. Many school districts employ a three-tiered level of instructional support, although some districts offer four or more levels of instructional intensity. In this chapter, we focus on the three-tiered model, which is used to support reading and mathematics instruction at the elementary and secondary levels (Bryant et al., 2011; Bryant et al., 2014; Denton, 2012; Fuchs, Fuchs, & Compton, 2012; Vaughn et al., 2010; Vaughn & Fletcher, 2012; Vaughn et al., 2009).

TIER 1 (PRIMARY)

Effective general education core instruction is the foundation for all students and is typically aligned with state or national standards. High-quality core instruction for students with disabilities incorporates individualized plans and interventions, which increase access to the general education curriculum. Recall from Chapter 3 that about 66% of students with learning disabilities receive at least 80% of their education in a general education classroom. Therefore, high-quality core instruction must be responsive to the needs of all students.

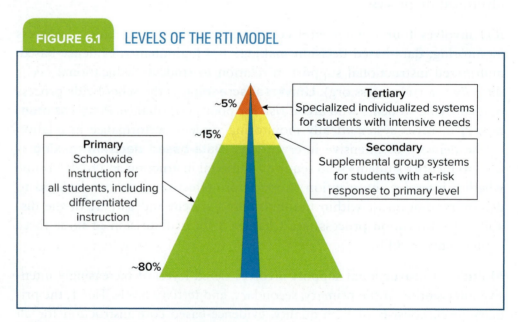

FIGURE 6.1 **LEVELS OF THE RTI MODEL**

SOURCE: Center on Response to Intervention at American Institutes for Research, http://www.rti4success.org.

Evidence-based effective practices, when integrated into the general education curriculum and teaching process, can and do make real differences for every student—those with and those without disabilities. We introduced many of these practices in Chapter 1, and we discuss them in more detail throughout this text as we talk about specific curriculum areas such as reading, writing, and mathematics. For now, we want to remind you about some evidence-based practices and ways of differentiating instruction to improve access to the general education curriculum for students with disabilities.

Evidence-Based Instruction

Evidence-based instruction offered to all students in the general education class is important for many reasons. Education that uses instructional procedures that have been validated through research is responsive to struggling students, prevents school failure, and reduces the number of referrals to special education (Fuchs & Vaughn, 2012; McMaster, Fuchs, Fuchs, & Compton, 2005). Because many believe that assignment to special education includes low expectations and locking students into a curriculum that prohibits them from achieving their real potential, prevention of inappropriate referrals is clearly an important role of general education in the lives of many students, particularly those from diverse backgrounds (Obiakor & Ford, 2002). However, when special education services are needed, and when general educators and school leaders (e.g., principals) support those services, the results for students with disabilities can be remarkable (Sataline, 2005).

Differentiating Instruction

For some instructional topics, students require an individualized change in how instruction is delivered. Differentiated instruction is designed to improve access to the general education curriculum by adapting instruction to each student's learning needs (Haager & Klingner, 2005; Hoover & Patton, 2004). In other words, instruction is adjusted in response to the individual's readiness, interests, strengths, and struggles (Tomlinson & Moon, 2013).

In Chapter 1, we introduced the mnemonic ADAPT to remind you about the five steps involved in using that framework to make appropriate instructional adaptations for differentiating instruction. The five steps in ADAPT are as follows: A—Ask, "What am I requiring the student to do?" D—Determine the prerequisite skills of the task. A—Analyze the student's strengths and struggles. P—Propose and implement adaptations from the four categories (instructional activity, instructional content, instructional delivery, and instructional materials). T—Test to determine if adaptations helped the student accomplish the task. Thus, different instructional methods might be employed for members of a class who are all learning the same content.

How might instruction be differentiated? Differentiation can be accomplished through the four categories of instructional adaptations. A different *instructional activity* might be provided to a small group of students to teach a skill when the original activity, using evidence-based practices, was not improving student learning. Sometimes, teachers need to adapt the *instructional content* by teaching a portion of the content related to the lesson's objective. Focusing initially on a smaller amount of information may help students be more successful in handling the quantity of information they need to learn. For example, if teachers are teaching the multiplication facts, the "times 5" facts might be taught separately and then combined with the "times 6" facts. Controlling the amount of instructional content gives students opportunities to focus their practice and then increase the amount as "chunks" of content are mastered.

Instructional delivery can be adapted by using flexible grouping practices to differentiate instruction (Haager & Klingner, 2005). Flexible grouping practices include same-ability groups and mixed-ability groups. Students with comparable abilities and achievement can be grouped so the pace of instruction can be different from that of other groups (Tomlinson & Moon, 2013). Or students can be assigned to heterogeneous groups where students complement each other's strengths and can help each other as they solve problems or complete assignments. In this way, flexible grouping practices allow teachers to group students based on the goals of the lesson. Instructional delivery can be adapted in terms of how teachers present instruction and how students practice their learning.

Finally, by selecting different types of materials or making adjustments to current materials, *instructional materials* can be adapted. For example, worksheets can be changed to include fewer practice items or they can be formatted differently to emphasize instructional information or directions. Technology can be used to support instruction, and manipulatives can be used to make math concepts concrete.

Throughout this text, we continue discussions about the ADAPT framework and provide specific examples of its implementation, because many students with disabilities require even more changes to their instructional programs to succeed in the general education program. The ADAPT in Action section and ADAPT Framework provide examples of how the process works. Refer back to the Opening Challenge with Ms. Cohen; she has a student with an intellectual disability who has reading disabilities. She is seeking information from the special education teacher about how to work with this student in her history class. In Chapter 7, you will learn more about differentiating instruction by using the ADAPT framework.

ADAPT *in action*

MS. COHEN SEEKS INFORMATION

(A) **Ask, "What am I requiring the student to do?"** Students must be able to read class materials, including the textbook and handouts.

(D) **Determine the prerequisite skills of the task.** Students must be able to read text and comprehend the material.

(A) **Analyze the student's strengths and struggles.** Ms. Cohen's student with an intellectual disability attends class every day and is able to work in small groups. Her student is able to read the materials but has difficulties comprehending the vocabulary and text provided each day in class.

(P) **Propose and implement adaptations from among the four categories.** The special education teacher proposes that she will teach the student a comprehension strategy and provide vocabulary study materials to help the student comprehend the textbook and handouts.

(T) **Test to determine whether the adaptations helped the student accomplish the task.** Ms. Cohen gives chapter tests weekly; these will be assessed to determine whether the adaptations are promoting comprehension.

TIER 2 (SECONDARY) AND TIER 3 (TERTIARY)

Students who are identified as at risk for having low academic performance during universal screening or through progress monitoring in the general education class qualify for more intensive intervention support. For these students, instructional features such as longer durations of instruction, smaller group size, adapted instruction (see the ADAPT Framework in Chapter 7), and frequent progress monitoring are essential. It should also be noted that in some states, Tier 3 means special education services, but this is not true for all states. Whether Tier 3 is reserved for students with identified disabilities, students who qualify for Tier 3 intervention demonstrate persistently low performance and require the most intensive services and instructional support. These students typically perform below the 10th percentile on academic curriculum-based measures (CBMs; see Chapter 8), which suggests that their ability to respond proficiently is limited. Adjusting instructional features and individualizing as needs dictate are critical for students in Tier 2 and particularly in Tier 3. Table 6.1 presents the components and instructional features of an RTI three-tiered model. Further discussion about instructional features occurs in Chapter 7.

ADAPT *framework:* MS. COHEN SEEKS INFORMATION

ASK "What am I requiring the student to do?"	**DETERMINE** the prerequisite skills of the task.	**ANALYZE** the student's strengths and struggles.		**PROPOSE** and implement adaptations from among the four categories.	**TEST** to determine if the adaptations helped the student accomplish the task.
		Strengths	Struggles		
Students must be able to read class materials, including the textbook and handouts.	1. Read text.	1			
	2. Comprehend the material.		2	2. Instructional delivery and instructional activity: The special education teacher will teach the student a comprehension strategy.	2. Weekly chapter tests will be assessed to determine whether the adaptations are promoting comprehension.
				2. Instructional materials: The special education teacher will provide vocabulary study materials.	

WHAT IS THE EVALUATION AND IDENTIFICATION PROCESS?

IDEA '04 mandates that an individualized program be delivered to every infant, toddler, and student who is identified as having a disability and is in need of special education. The purposes of these individualized programs are to ensure that each of these individuals

- Receives FAPE.
- Is provided an education in the LRE.
- Is specific to the student.
- Is provided services with the expectation of outstanding results.

Students' IEPs are the plans or road maps created to guide instruction and the delivery of services that are the foundation for an appropriate education.

TABLE 6.1 COMPONENTS AND INSTRUCTIONAL FEATURES OF RTI FOR A THREE-TIERED MODEL

RTI Components	Tier 1	Tier 2	Tier 3
Universal Screening	All students	All students	All students
Tiered Instruction	Evidence based, core—all students	Evidence based, supplemental, intensive interventions, standardized approach to instruction—some students	Evidence based, adapted, intensive interventions, individualized approach to instruction—few students
Curriculum	Grade level based on district, state, and/or national standards	Grade level based on district, state, and/or national standards; prerequisite knowledge and skills content; focused on smaller amount of content	May be grade level; focused on prerequisite knowledge and skills; more focused on smaller "chunks" of the curriculum
Instructional Grouping	Flexible	E: Homogeneous (similar instructional levels); 4 to 5 students: 1 teacher; S: Range of low ability, 12 to 15 students: 1 teacher	E: Homogeneous (similar instructional levels); 2 to 3 students: 1 reading or mathematics specialist or special education teacher; S: Very low ability, 5 to 10 students: 1 teacher
Instructional Duration (core instruction is required for students in Tiers 2 and 3)	E: Typical daily time allotted to instruction (e.g., 120 minutes for reading, 90 minutes for mathematics for elementary level); S: Typical class period of 45 to 60 minutes for secondary level	E: 30 to 45 minutes; after school sessions, 3 to 4 days a week; S: 45 to 60 minutes, block with two class periods devoted to a subject area	E: Daily 60 to 90 minutes; S: Daily 45 to 60 minutes, block with two class periods devoted to a subject area
Progress Monitoring	Monthly or fall, winter, spring	Bi-weekly/ diagnostic assessment if low response persists	Daily to weekly/diagnostic assessment if low response persists
Data-Based Decision Making	All students	All students	All students

NOTE: E = elementary; S = secondary (middle and high school).

Although some students with special needs receive accommodations for their special conditions through Section 504 of the Rehabilitation Act, only those with disabilities defined by IDEA '04 are required to have IEPs. Thus some students with a disability that does not require special education services (such as a limb deficiency that does not affect educational performance) do not require an IEP. Conversely, sometimes students without disabilities do have an IEP. For example, in some states, students who are gifted or talented are included in special education. Although education of these students is not included in the federal special education law, those states often take their lead from IDEA '04 and develop IEPs for students who are gifted or talented.

IEPs focus on students' strengths and on their individual needs. Parents and school districts' education professionals must agree on these plans for the delivery of special services. IDEA '04 is very specific about the requirements of IEPs and the process to be used in their development and implementation (U.S. Department of Education, 2006). The law spells out the minimum process or steps that are to be used when developing individualized programs offered under the auspices of special education. States often impose further requirements in addition to those that are outlined in IDEA '04 and monitored by the federal government. Because there are many local variations on the rules surrounding IEPs, we present here what the national law requires and do not address specific regulations that various states expect school districts and teachers to follow.

The formation of an individualized program can be organized into seven steps (see Figure 6.2), beginning with prereferral and ending with evaluation of a student's program:

1. Prereferral

2. Referral

3. Identification

4. Eligibility

5. Development of the IEP

6. Implementation of the IEP

7. Evaluation and reviews

FIGURE 6.2   THE SEVEN STEPS IN THE IEP PROCESS

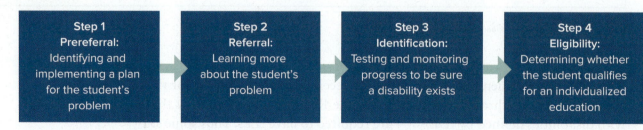

| Step 1
Prereferral:
Identifying and implementing a plan for the student's problem | Step 2
Referral:
Learning more about the student's problem | Step 3
Identification:
Testing and monitoring progress to be sure a disability exists | Step 4
Eligibility:
Determining whether the student qualifies for an individualized education |

Now let's look at these seven steps in more detail to get a better understanding of what each means and how they form the IEP process.

STEP 1: PREREFERRAL

At this step, the general education teacher and the school's support team ensure that the target student has received high-quality instruction and additional instructional assistance if necessary. During this step, the school's support team must become confident that neither "poor teaching" (the application of practices that are not evidence based) nor a need to learn the English language explains the student's inadequate performance. The team may be called a prereferral team, a multidisciplinary team, or an RTI team if the RTI model is utilized, whose purpose is to

- Document and explain how and when the student is struggling.
- Determine the effectiveness of classroom adaptations and additional assistance.
- Monitor the student's progress during the application of high-quality instruction.

For schools that are implementing an RTI model of assessment and interventions, prereferral activities include screening students for learning or behavioral difficulties, implementing evidence-based practices, and documenting student responses to these practices. In general, before any formal referral for special education services is made, teachers, school-based education professionals, and family members work together to determine whether the general education teacher alone can resolve a student's educational or behavioral difficulties. The assessments used during this step are intervention based and conducted in the student's general education class using direct measures of performance (McNamara & Hollinger, 2003). Teachers implement different validated teaching approaches and use assessment measures to document how students respond to this instruction (Barnett, Daly, Jones, & Lentz, 2004). They also systematically differentiate instruction more intensively to address individual learning or behavioral needs.

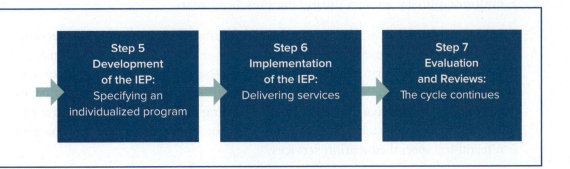

Step 5
**Development
of the IEP:**
Specifying an
individualized program

Step 6
**Implementation
of the IEP:**
Delivering services

Step 7
**Evaluation
and Reviews:**
The cycle continues

iStock/peepo

Teachers and families may be involved in the prereferral step. Prereferral activities are intended to address individual students' learning or behavior needs to prevent unnecessary referrals to special education.

Prereferral activities are intended to address individual students' learning or behavioral needs through the use of effective practices to prevent unnecessary referrals to special education, which are costly in time, money, and resources for formal assessments. You as a teacher may receive both assistance and consultation from specialists during this phase of the IEP process. Students whose learning remains challenged—those who continue to struggle—are referred to special education and the next step of the IEP process.

STEP 2: REFERRAL

Some students come to school already identified as having a disability and needing special education. Some of these students have already received special education services for many years. Why is this so? For infants, toddlers, and preschoolers, IDEA '04 stresses the importance of an activity called *child find,* wherein those with disabilities are actively sought (U.S. Department of Education, 2006). In these cases, referrals can come from parents, a social service agency, public health nurses, day care professionals, or a doctor. Young children who are at risk of having disabilities because of improper prenatal care, low birth weight, accident or trauma during infancy, or child abuse are referred for special services. Also, those with visible indications of a disability (such as a missing arm or leg or facial differences resulting from Down syndrome) or other signals of significant developmental delay (such as an 18-month-old child not walking independently or a 3-year-old not talking) are usually identified early and receive early intervention services during infancy or their preschool years. Typically, the referral process begins sooner for children with very severe disabilities, because their disabilities are obvious at birth or during infancy. As children grow older, other signs often trigger referrals. For example, a toddler who does not respond to loud sounds and is not walking by age 2 and a preschooler who has excessive tantrums are both candidates for early referrals. Such children and their families usually come to school expecting an individualized education because they have received multidisciplinary services during the preschool years.

Students identified as having disabilities during the elementary or secondary school years present different reasons for referral. For example, students whose academic performance is significantly behind that of their classmates are prime candidates for special education referrals. Also, those students who continually misbehave and disrupt the learning environment often draw the attention of their teachers and are targeted for intervention and (ultimately) referral for special education services.

STEP 3: IDENTIFICATION

Assessment is one foundation of the identification process. The purpose of this step in the IEP process is to determine whether a student has a disability, whether special education services are required, and what types of services are needed. Evaluations are conducted by multidisciplinary teams consisting of professionals who have expertise in each area of concern. Each member helps to evaluate the student's unique strengths and struggles. For example, if a student is suspected of having a language impairment, a speech/language pathologist (SLP) is a member of the team. If there may be a hearing problem, an audiologist participates, and so on. For students who are 16 years old or older, evaluation includes assessments related to the need for transition services for moving either from school to work or from secondary to postsecondary education (Madaus & Shaw, 2006).

Information can come from a broad range of sources, including the student's parents and family members. The professional who actually coordinates the identification process varies by state and district. In some states, the assessment team leader is a school psychologist, an educational diagnostician, or a psychometrician. In other states, a teacher from the student's school leads the team's efforts.

At this step, many different types of data are used to inform the team about the student's abilities. Medical history, information about social interactions at school and at home, adaptive behavior in the community, educational performance, and other relevant factors are considered. Evaluations include an array of assessment instruments and procedures. Information should be collected from the student and family. Formal tests—tests of intelligence, of academic achievement, and of acuity (vision and hearing)—are usually part of the information used to make decisions about students and their potential special education status.

Less formal assessments—assistive technology evaluations, school observations of classroom and social behavior, examples of academic assignments, direct measurements of academic performance, CBMs of reading and mathematics skills being taught, and portfolio samples of classroom performance—are also important pieces of evidence used in this step of the IEP process. Together, data from the formal and informal assessments are used to develop a profile of the student. One result of the evaluation step of the IEP process can be a determination that the individual does not have a disability. In these instances the IEP process is discontinued. For those individuals who do have disabilities, this phase of the process results in a baseline of performance data to guide the development of the individualized education program and, later, help judge the program's effectiveness.

STEP 4: ELIGIBILITY

The information from the assessment step is used to identify students who actually have a disability and qualify for special education services. For those students, the IEP team then determines what components of the full range of special education and related services are needed so that an appropriate education can be planned and ultimately delivered. The education of those students who do not meet the eligibility requirements remains the sole responsibility of general educators; the education of those students with disabilities who are eligible for special education services becomes the shared responsibility of general education teachers and administrators, special education teachers and administrators, and the appropriate related service professionals. The Considering Diversity feature provides guidance about the issue of confusing linguistic diversity with a learning disability.

CONSIDERING *diversity*

DON'T CONFUSE LINGUISTIC DIVERSITY WITH LEARNING DISABILITY

Culturally and linguistically diverse (CLD) students are disproportionately represented in special education classes. Inappropriate placements of this sort often occur because educators may have limited preparation in providing early interventions to remediate existing underachievement problems. Educators may also have limited preparation in discerning the characteristics of linguistically diverse students from the characteristics of students with language and learning disabilities. However, professionals must provide early intervention to students who are exhibiting achievement difficulties. Documentation of the student's response to this intervention is also required. When these efforts are not successful with individual students, a referral to special education for a comprehensive assessment may be appropriate. According to IDEA '04, limited English proficiency cannot be a reason for determining that a student has a disability. Educators may be unfamiliar with questions that can be asked to help determine whether a referral for special education

assessment is appropriate. Yates and Ortiz (2004) provided guidelines that school-based teams can use as part of the referral process and to eliminate factors besides a disability as the reason for academic underachievement:

- Have the difficulties been noted by a variety of professionals, such as the general education teacher, parents, and the remedial teacher?

- To what extent do the difficulties exist across contexts, such as in classrooms, in "specials or electives" (art, music), and at home?

- What are the student's reading abilities in the native language and in English?

- Are the difficulties evident in the native language as well as in English?

- How is the student progressing compared with other students who had or have a similar level of English language proficiency?

- What concerns have family members expressed about language difficulties?

- Has the student received consistent native language instruction?

- What evidence suggests that difficulties can be explained by factors other than disability, such as cultural differences, school attendance issues, teacher bias or expectations, and teachers not prepared to teach CLD students?

- What evidence suggests issues related to assessment, such as measures that are not normed for English language learners (ELLs), language proficiency of the student that does not match the language in which the assessment was conducted, and results that conflict with documentation about response to intervention?

- What efforts are being made to determine whether the student's language characteristics, such as pronunciation, oral language, and comprehension difficulties, are a result of learning a second language or a language disability?

Professionals must ensure that CLD students who go through the disability identification process (a) have received effective remedial interventions prior to referral and (b) have been thoroughly reviewed to rule out limited English proficiency as the reason for the problem.

STEP 5: DEVELOPMENT OF THE IEP

After thorough completion of the prereferral, referral, identification, and eligibility steps of the IEP process, it is time to develop the actual individualized plan—an individualized family service plan (IFSP) for infants and toddlers, an IEP for preschoolers and schoolchildren, and a transition component of the IEP for those students with disabilities who are 16 years old or older. If behavior is a concern, a behavior intervention plan will be written for the individual student as well. We discuss the development of the IEP in more detail later in this chapter, but for now, it is important for you to know that parents and the education professionals who are all part of the student's IEP team make important decisions about what services and placements constitute an appropriate education for this individual at this step of the IEP process. The assessment results are used to help make these decisions. It is at this point that the IEP team begins its work to outline the individualized education needed by the student. Collectively, the team members, who include parents and the student (if appropriate), now use the knowledge they have gained to identify resources needed for that student to access the general education curriculum, determine the appropriate goals for improvement, and then craft a good education program for the student. Of course, goals must include greater success with the general education curriculum or independence and a community presence later in life. It is at this point that the services and supports that become part of the student's appropriate education are specified.

STEP 6: IMPLEMENTATION OF THE IEP

Once the IEP is developed, the student's services and individualized program begin. The IEP has laid out what constitutes an appropriate education for the student, the extent to which the student participates in the general education curriculum, the accommodations the student receives both for instruction and for assessment, and the array of multidisciplinary services from related service providers that supports the student's educational program. For students who are participating in a different curriculum or whose goals differ from those of the general education curriculum, the IEP has specified alternate assessment procedures as well.

Minor adjustments in students' goals or in the benchmarks that indicate attainment of those goals do not signal a need for a new IEP or another IEP meeting; services continue. However, major changes in goals, services, or placement do require parents to be notified in writing. Some changes, particularly if they involve a more restrictive placement, may necessitate a meeting of the IEP team and the parent or guardian. Most often, this situation arises when issues surrounding discipline are the reason for the change in placement or services. Later in this chapter, you will learn more about behavior intervention plans, which must be developed as part of students' IEPs when serious behavioral infractions (such as bringing guns or drugs to school, fighting, or being out of control) occur. Also, in Chapter 9, you will learn about effective interventions that should help resolve behavior issues that affect both the individual and his or her classmates when rules are violated.

STEP 7: EVALUATION AND REVIEWS

IDEA '04 requires accountability for each IEP developed. In most states, students' IEPs are reviewed annually. Under an IDEA '04 pilot program, which is attempting to reduce paperwork and administrative burdens on educators, 15 states conduct these reviews every three years. The purpose of the IEP review meetings is to ensure that students are meeting their goals and making educational progress. Because accountability measures determine whether the student is making progress, educators are careful to describe expectations for tasks and skills the student needs to learn in terms that can be evaluated. Whether the IEP process is for an infant or toddler (an IFSP) or for a schoolchild (an IEP and possibly a transition component), the expectation is that frequent assessments of the individual's performance will occur, even if major IEP reviews occur once a year or only every three years.

The No Child Left Behind Act of 2001 (NCLB) and IDEA '04 require that all students participate in annual state or district-wide testing or in alternate assessments. Because of the importance of these assessments and of each school's collective adequate yearly progress (AYP)—whereby all its students demonstrate their attainment of high levels of achievement—we devote an

IEP Meetings

entire chapter to assessment issues (see Chapter 8). For now, it is important to understand that assessment adaptations are allowed for many students with disabilities while taking these tests. For example, students who use enlarged print or Braille to read classroom materials receive these assessment adaptations in the testing situation as well.

For some students, alternate assessments are made available. For example, students who are learning English as their second language and students with disabilities whose IEP goals focus less on accessing the general education curriculum and more on skills related to independence, life skills, and community presence may participate in alternative assessments if these are specified in the students' IEP. Remember, in addition to annual assessments, students with disabilities frequently receive less formal evaluations of their progress. Sometimes these assessments are made weekly or even daily. The purpose of such measurements of progress is to guide instruction and to ensure that scheduled interventions are effective.

WHO ARE THE MEMBERS OF THE IEP TEAM?

IDEA '04 is very clear about membership in IEP teams (Office of Special Education Programs [OSEP], 2006a). The exact language of the regulations is found in Table 6.2, but it is important for you as a teacher to remember that each IEP team is individually determined according to the specific needs of the student and his or her disability.

As a teacher attending an IEP meeting for one of your students, you can be most helpful in ensuring that the right people are participating and contributing to the development of a meaningful IEP for your student. Review Table 6.2 and consider a student who faces motor challenges resulting from cerebral palsy. Emily is a very bright fourth grader, but she has difficulty engaging in class discussions because her speech is slow, deliberate, and difficult to understand. She uses a walker and finds it challenging to hold a pencil, but she can use a computer's keyboard. IDEA '04 is specific about the minimum representation of those members who make up IEP teams for students with disabilities. Who are those essential members? For Emily, IDEA '04 also allows for the inclusion of more multidisciplinary professionals. What additional members would be appropriate for Emily's IEP team? To answer these two important questions, it might be helpful to know more about the roles of IEP team members. Some of those roles and responsibilities are highlighted next.

ROLES OF EDUCATION PROFESSIONALS

All education professionals working at every school are crucial to positive experiences for students with disabilities. As we mentioned at the beginning of Chapter 1, it is surprising to us that after some 30 years of including more and

TABLE 6.2	MEMBERS OF THE IEP TEAM

According to the IDEA '04 regulations, the public agency must ensure that the IEP Team for each child with a disability includes:

- The parents of the child

- Not less than one general education teacher of the child (if the child is, or may be, participating in the general education environment)

- Not less than one special education teacher of the child, or, where appropriate, not less than one special education provider of the child

- A representative of the public agency (who has certain specific knowledge and qualifications)

- An individual who can interpret the instructional implications of evaluation results (this person may also be one of the other listed members)

- At the discretion of the parent or the agency, other individuals who have knowledge or special expertise regarding the child, including related service personnel as appropriate

- Whenever appropriate, the child with a disability

  o The public agency must invite a child with a disability to attend the child's IEP Team meeting if a purpose of the meeting will be consideration of the postsecondary goals for the child and the transition services needed to assist the child in reaching those goals.

SOURCE: OSEP (2006a, pp. 2–3).

more students with disabilities in general education classes, many teachers, principals, and other education professionals still report that they feel ill-prepared to accept responsibilities associated with the education of these students (Fisher, Frey, & Thousand, 2003; Futernick, 2006). Those who harbor such attitudes (particularly if they are uneasy with, or even reject, students with disabilities) can negatively influence outcomes for these students (Cook, 2001; Cook, Tankersley, Cook, & Landrum, 2000). Such negative attitudes are often subtly expressed in the ways in which inadequately prepared educators talk about students with disabilities and the adaptations they need for successful participation in the general education curriculum (Salend, 2010). We also know that well prepared educators can and do make a real difference in the lives and the educational achievements of their students (Darling-Hammond, 2005, 2006a, 2006b). We are confident that you, as a teacher thoroughly prepared with knowledge about effective interventions and the ADAPT framework, will positively influence the lives of your students with disabilities.

The school principal is a key person in the collaborative effort at every school (Praisner, 2003; Rodríguez, Gentilucci, & Sims, 2005). Because principals often coordinate management efforts at their site, they can be most helpful in developing and ensuring the delivery of special education services (particularly for large-scale assessments), in monitoring the array of services indicated on every student's IEP, and in ensuring the coordination of services throughout the school and across the district. Effective principals also set the tone for positive attitudes crucial to all students' success. They welcome and facilitate the efforts of the many different professionals who are itinerant, coming to their school to work with individual students such as Emily, whom we described at the beginning of this section. For example, students with challenges similar to Emily's typically receive services from SLPs, physical therapists, experts in assistive technology, and possibly occupational therapists. These members of Emily's multidisciplinary team are not permanent or full-time members of the school staff. Their schedules are complicated and often hard to coordinate because each of them travels from school to school, sometimes long distances, to work with individual students and their teachers who need their services. Also, these professionals often find themselves in crowded schools where they do not have sufficient space or appropriate places to work with individual students or to store their equipment. Principals can lead their school's staff to solve complex coordination issues that itinerant multidisciplinary team members often present, smoothing the way for efficient delivery of related services.

Neither IDEA '04, individual states' regulations, nor school districts' guidelines have established definitive roles for each profession's IEP team member. Teams must determine each member's role and responsibility when they collaborate as members of IEP teams and work together to plan for the delivery of an effective and appropriate education for each student with a disability. In part, this lack of uniformity exists because no single or uniform action can reflect what special education services any particular student needs. Also, government officials do not want to dictate how groups of professionals elect to work together. For example, at one school, the principal and IEP teams might assign duties differently than the principal and team members at another school (Praisner, 2003). At one school, the school counselor coordinates the entire schedule; at another, a special education teacher schedules related services for all students with disabilities, and the principal's assistant develops the other teachers' and students' schedules. In short, the way in which these professionals collaborate is partially determined by how they are organized at each school.

The IEP process, the development of responsive IEP teams, and the inclusion of students with disabilities require true partnerships among those who share responsibilities for the education of students with disabilities. Fisher and his colleagues (2003) help us think about how both general and special education teachers could share responsibilities that typically arise in providing an appropriate education to students with disabilities. Some of their ideas are presented in Table 6.3.

ROLES OF FAMILIES

IDEA '04 stresses the importance of involving families of students with disabilities in the IEP process and as members of their child's IEP team (U.S. Department of Education, 2006). The IEP process can help develop partnerships among

VIDEO CASE 6.2

Roles of Special and General Education Teachers

1. How does a special education teacher support the needs of students with disabilities who are included in the general education classroom? What types of services might a special education teacher advocate for their students?

2. In what ways do general education teachers support the needs of all their students in an inclusive classroom? How do they collaborate with other professionals to ensure that all their students are successful?

TABLE 6.3	ROLES OF GENERAL AND SPECIAL EDUCATORS IN THE EDUCATION OF STUDENTS WITH DISABILITIES	
	Special Educators	**General Educators**
Prereferral and Referral	• Assist with data collection • Test effectiveness of educational modifications and accommodations	• Conduct prereferral assessments • Use tactics of varying intensity • Provide instruction under different conditions
Instruction	• Individualize instruction (1:1; 1:3) • Apply instruction to small groups • Adapt materials and instruction • Consult with, and provide assistance to, other educators	• Apply instruction to whole class and small groups • Ensure maximal access to the general education curriculum by implementing adaptations and accommodations • Train and supervise peer tutors
Assessment	• Monitor progress frequently • Determine appropriate adaptations and accommodations	• Develop and maintain portfolios • Implement adaptations and accommodations for testing situations
Communication	• Foster parent partnerships • Communicate with school personnel about needed accommodations	• Communicate with parents and families • Work in partnership with special education personnel
Leadership	• Train and supervise paraprofessionals • Advocate for each student with a disability • Coordinate students' related services • Conduct in-service training sessions about access to the general education curriculum	• Work with paraprofessionals • Participate in IEP meetings • Facilitate the scheduling and delivery of related services • Maintain anecdotal records
Record Keeping	• Develop the IEP • Maintain records of accommodations and IEP progress	• Keep records of accommodation use and effectiveness

parents and extended family members, schools, and professionals (Sopko, 2003). This purpose should be actively fostered, for the importance of these partnerships cannot be overestimated (Dabkowski, 2004).

When parent involvement is high, student alienation is lower and student achievement is increased (Brown, Paulsen, & Higgins, 2003; Dworetzky, 2004). Educators need to recognize, however, that many parents believe schools control the special education process. As a result, many families feel disenfranchised or confused about rules, regulations, and the purpose of special education (Cartledge, Kea, & Ida, 2000). Most parents want to participate in their children's education, but sometimes they do not understand the educational system.

Often, families need help to participate effectively in IEP meetings and in the resulting individualized programs (Tornatzky, Pachon, & Torres, 2003). Here are some tips that teachers can give parents to help them better prepare to participate in IEP meetings (Buehler, 2004):

Make a list of important questions to ask IEP team members. Examples: What is my child's daily schedule? How is my child doing in school? Does my child have friends? How well does my child behave? What problems is my child having?

- Outline points to make about your child's strengths.

- Bring records regarding your child's needs.

- Ask for clarification.

- Be assertive and proactive but not aggressive or reactive.

- Listen and compromise.

- Remain involved with the professionals on the IEP team.

- Know about placement and service options, and explore each with the team.

For families who do not speak English well enough to understand the complicated language used to talk about special education issues, participation may seem impossible (Hughes, Valle-Riestra, & Arguelles, 2002). In such instances, schools must welcome family members and people from the community who are fluent in the family's native language and also knowledgeable about the special education process and procedural safeguards guaranteed to families through IDEA '04. The law encourages the family's maximal participation, so it requires schools to find interpreters to the fullest extent possible. Remember, it is the obligation of educators to include and inform parents and students about the efforts that will be made on their behalf.

ROLES OF STUDENTS

Review Table 6.2 and remember the importance that IDEA '04 places on students participating on their own IEP teams, particularly when adolescents are about to transition out of high school. The law stresses student involvement because it has found that many students are unfamiliar with their IEPs and do not know the goals established for them. One result is a lack of "ownership" in the school program especially designed for them. Involving students has many benefits (Test et al., 2004). Particularly if students are active participants, they can learn important skills needed in life. Here are two examples. Self-determination is the ability to identify and achieve goals for oneself. Self-advocacy consists of the skills necessary to stand up and advocate for what one needs to achieve those goals. These two skills are interrelated and can be fostered during the IEP process when students are involved (Wood, Karvonen,

iStock/Terry J. Alcorn

IDEA law stresses the importance of student involvement in their IEPs because, surprisingly, many students are unfamiliar with the content and the goals established for them within their IEPs. Involving students in the process has many benefits.

Test, Browder, & Algozzine, 2004). Here are some ways in which older students can contribute to their IEP meetings:

- Describe personal strengths, weaknesses, and needs.

- Evaluate personal progress toward accomplishing their goals.

- Bring a list of adaptations and explain how each is helpful.

- Communicate their preferences and interests.

- Articulate their long-term goals and desires for life, work, and postsecondary schooling.

HOW DO SPECIAL EDUCATION MULTIDISCIPLINARY TEAMS AND SERVICES MEET THE NEEDS OF STUDENTS WITH DISABILITIES?

Although evidence-based instruction and differentiated instruction are important components of general education's foundation for individualized special education services, students with disabilities typically need more intensive interventions and supports to achieve independence and success. The multidisciplinary teams and the services they deliver are what make special education truly special for students with disabilities and their families. Let's turn our attention to the professionals and services that can be specified for students with disabilities through the individualized education guaranteed by IDEA '04.

HIGHLY QUALIFIED SPECIAL EDUCATORS

A special educator might be a resource specialist, an itinerant teacher, a special education classroom teacher, a job coach, a home or hospital teacher, or an administrator. The skills needed by special educators are many. They must have in-depth knowledge about differentiating instruction, implementing practices validated through rigorous research, monitoring students' progress, understanding the requirements and expectations of IDEA '04, and ensuring that every student with a disability receives an appropriate education and achieves to the greatest degree possible. Special educators' jobs are complex and require skills that are honed by knowledge and practice.

NCLB, which is the reauthorization of the federal Elementary and Secondary Education Act, requires all general education teachers to be "highly qualified." NCLB expects teachers to hold a credential, have a degree, or demonstrate competency in every content area in which they teach. When IDEA was reauthorized in 2004, language was included affirming that special education teachers also must be highly qualified. Because of these requirements, coteaching is gaining in popularity, particularly at the middle and high school levels where it is not possible for individual teachers to meet the requirements of every core subject area that special educators teach. Blending the expertise of general education professionals (e.g., math, science, history, English) and special educators through coteaching arrangements can make the education that students with disabilities receive truly special (Magiera, Smith, Zigmond, & Gebauer, 2005). This new requirement for highly qualified special education teachers creates many opportunities for middle and secondary teachers to work together, to create wonderful learning opportunities, and to consider the special needs of all students, not just those with disabilities. In Chapter 5, we discuss coteaching as one way to promote effective collaborative professional partnerships between general and special educators.

Clearly, general educators and special educators are two of the important ingredients of an effective education for students with special needs. But the recipe for success may also include the expertise of professionals who come from different disciplines. It is the IEP process that brings together experts who have unique skills to meet the individual needs of students with disabilities. Let's think about related services and the professionals who provide them.

RELATED SERVICES AND PROVIDERS

Many students with disabilities need help beyond that given through the partnership of general and special education. As you learned in Chapter 1, related services are typically beyond what general and special education teachers can provide (Etzel-Wise & Mears, 2004; Neal, Bigby, & Nicholson, 2004). Related services are definitely a unique feature of special education, offering a wide range of services and expertise to students and their families. These experts facilitate the attainment of LRE and FAPE.

The three most commonly used related services are speech therapy, physical therapy, and assistive technology. IDEA '04 does not provide a precise list of related services, because its authors did not want to be too prescriptive; these services are to be determined by the exact needs of the individual (Downing, 2004). As Table 6.4 shows, related service professionals may include those who provide assistive technology, audiology, occupational therapy, physical therapy, school health services, speech/language therapy, or other services needed by the student. Unfortunately, particularly for students with high-incidence disabilities (such as learning disabilities), IEP teams (educators who meet to develop the IEP) often fail to fully consider students' needs for related services (Mitch Yell, as quoted in Earles-Vollrath, 2004). It is important for all teachers to understand that students, regardless of their disabilities, are guaranteed needed related services by IDEA '04.

With exceptions for very young children in some states, related services are provided at no cost to the student's family. However, in some cases, costs for

TABLE 6.4	EXPLANATION OF FREQUENTLY PROVIDED RELATED SERVICES SPECIFIED IN IDEA '04

Related Service	Explanation	Provider
Adaptive physical education (therapeutic recreation)	Assesses leisure function; provides therapeutic recreation and leisure education	Recreational therapist
Assistive technology	Assists with the selection, acquisition, or use of any item, piece of equipment, or product system used to enhance functional capabilities (assistive technology device)	Assistive technologist
Audiology services	Identifies and diagnoses hearing loss; determines proper amplification and fitting of hearing aids and other listening devices	Audiologist
Counseling services/ rehabilitative counseling	Provides psychological and guidance services, including career development and parent counseling; develops positive behavior intervention strategies	School counselor, social worker, psychologist, guidance counselor, vocational rehabilitation counselor
Diagnostic and evaluation services	Identifies disabilities	School psychologist, diagnostician, psychometrician
Occupational therapy	Improves, develops, or restores the ability to perform tasks or function independently	Occupational therapist (OT)
Orientation and mobility training	Enables students who are blind or have low vision to move safely and independently at school and in the community	Orientation specialist, mobility specialist
Physical therapy	Works to improve individuals' motor functioning, movement, and fitness	Physical therapist (PT)
School health services	Provides health services designed to enable a student with a disability to participate in FAPE	School nurse
Social work	Mobilizes school and community resources and works in partnership with family members to resolve problems in a child's living situation that affect school adjustment	Social worker
Speech/language therapy	Provides services for the prevention and treatment of communicative disorders	Speech/language pathologist (SLP)
Transportation	Assists with travel to, from, between, and within school buildings, typically using specialized equipment (e.g., special or adapted buses, lifts, ramps)	Orientation specialist, mobility specialist

SOURCE: Adapted from U.S. Department of Education (2006, pp. 1257–1258, 1284–1294).

related services are paid for by agencies other than schools (such as Medicare or private insurance companies). Some medical services are considered related services. Here's a guideline to whether a medical service is also a related service: If a school nurse can provide the medical services the student needs, they are likely to be related services. If, however, the services need to be performed by a physician, they are not (Bigby, 2004; National Association of School Nurses [NASN], 2004).

Assistive technology is a unique and critical component of many effective programs (Bryant & Bryant, 2003). For these reasons, we highlight such technology in the remaining chapters of this text. For now, remember that assistive technology is both equipment and a related service. Assistive technology is often what allows students with disabilities to access general education, interact with their friends, participate in class discussions, and complete their schoolwork more easily. Like evidence-based practices and differentiated instruction, assistive technology often is an important component of general education's foundation for effective special education services.

As stipulated in IDEA '04, the IEP team must consider a student's need for assistive technology and services so that the student can receive FAPE in the LRE (U.S. Department of Education, 2006). The Tech Notes feature lists some of the questions that IEP team members consider when specifying what AT services and devices are to be included in a student's IEP. When identified in a student's IEP, a device or specific type of equipment becomes part of the student's educational program. However, not every device you can think of is considered AT by IDEA '04. For example, IDEA '04 clarified for school districts and families that cost for the maintenance of surgically implanted medical devices, such as cochlear implants, are not the responsibility of the schools (Kravetz, 2005). The expertise of assistive technologists can be critical to ensure that the latest in technology is available to resolve challenges that some individuals face. In Chapter 7, we present additional information about AT.

TECH *notes*

SELECTION OF ASSISTIVE TECHNOLOGY DEVICES AND SERVICES

Following are questions IEP team members ask themselves as they consider what AT services and devices to include in a student's IEP:

1. How can AT devices and services help the student receive a free appropriate public education?

2. How can AT devices and services help the student receive an education in the LRE?

3. How can AT devices and services help the student access the general education curriculum and achieve IEP goals successfully?

4. How do the features of the AT device match the strengths and struggles of the student and the tasks of the environment?

5. How will the use of AT devices and services be monitored to ensure successful implementation as well as benefits to the student?

SOURCE: Adapted from Chambers (1997).

Many students with disabilities need help beyond that given through the partnership of general and special education. This student requires physical therapy from a related services provider.

You have learned that at the heart of special education are the professionals who join with families to collaborate and provide multidisciplinary services and supports to students with disabilities. These teams are unique because they are individually determined and their membership reflects the individual needs of the student. These multidisciplinary teams of experts not only deliver critical services to students with disabilities and their families but also are valuable resources to teachers as they strive to meet the needs of each student. You as a teacher should always remember that these professionals are available to help you as well as your student. When everyone works together, IEP teams ensure more than the protection of basic rights guaranteed by IDEA '04: They orchestrate the best education possible. When each individually arranged IEP team develops partnerships, so that students' programs are coordinated, the results are remarkable, allowing individuals to overcome challenges caused by disabilities.

Now let's think about the process and plans that guide everyone's actions to make these programs a reality.

WHAT PLANS GUARANTEE STUDENTS WITH DISABILITIES AN APPROPRIATE EDUCATION?

Four tools, or plans for individualized programs, serve to coordinate and document what constitutes the appropriate education for each infant, toddler, and student with disabilities. The tools that guarantee an appropriate education to those with disabilities follow:

1. The individualized family service plan (IFSP)—for infants and toddlers

2. The individualized education program (IEP)—for preschoolers through high school students

3. An additional statement of transitional services—initiated at age 16 to help those students who require special education services to make successful transitions to independence, community living, and work

4. A behavior intervention plan—for those students with disabilities who commit serious behavioral infractions

Let's examine each of these plans in turn.

INDIVIDUALIZED FAMILY SERVICE PLANS (IFSPS)

Infants or toddlers (birth through age 2) who have disabilities or who are at great risk for disabilities were originally guaranteed the right to early intervention programs through PL 99-457, which was passed in 1986. That right continues today through IDEA '04. (For a review of IDEA legislation, see Chapter 1 and Table 1.3.) IFSPs are written documents that ensure that special services are delivered to these young children and their families. The IFSP is the management tool that guides professionals as they design and deliver these children's special education programs. Service managers are the professionals who provide oversight and coordination of the services outlined in IFSPs. The key components of these early education management plans follow:

- The child's current functioning levels in all relevant areas (physical development, cognitive development, language and speech development, psychosocial development, and self-help skills)

- The family's strengths and needs in regard to the development of their child

- The major outcomes expected, expressed in terms of procedures, evaluation criteria, and a time line

- The services necessary and a schedule for their delivery

- Projected dates for initiation of services

- The name of the service coordinator

- A biannual (every six months) review, with the child's family, of progress made and of any need for modifications in the IFSP

- Indication of methods for transitioning the child to services available for children ages 3 to 5

To many service coordinators and early childhood specialists, the IFSP is a working document for an ongoing process in which parents and specialists work together, continually modifying, expanding, and developing a child's educational program. Children and families who participate in early intervention programs often find these years to be an intense period, with many professionals offering advice, training, guidance, and personalized services, as well as care and concern. Also, the transition to preschool at the age of 3 can be particularly difficult and frightening. One reason is that services that were delivered primarily at the family's home now will be delivered at a preschool. Therefore, IFSPs include plans for these youngsters and their families to transition from very intensive and individually delivered interventions to more traditional classrooms. IDEA '04 allows states to give families the option of delaying entrance into school-based preschool programs by keeping their child in an early intervention program, but making this decision sometimes results in the family having to pay for some or all of the services (U.S. Department of Education, 2006).

INDIVIDUALIZED EDUCATION PROGRAMS (IEPS)

IEPs are the documents that describe the special education and related services appropriate to the needs of students with disabilities who are 3 to 21 years of age. These management tools are the cornerstones of every educational program planned for preschoolers (ages 3 to 5) and students (ages 6 to 21) with disabilities (OSEP, 2006a). IDEA '04 delineated what the IEP must contain at the very least, and it is important that every educator know these key components:

- Current performance: The student's present levels of academic achievement and information about how the student's disability influences participation and progress in the general education curriculum

- Goals: Statement of measurable goals related to participation in the general education curriculum or to meeting other educational needs resulting from the disability

- Special education and related services: Specific educational services to be provided, including accommodations, program modifications, or supports that allow participation in the general education curriculum and in extracurricular activities

- Participation with students without disabilities: Explanation about the extent to which the student will not participate in general education classes and in extracurricular activities alongside peers without disabilities

- Participation in state and district-wide testing: Description of assessment accommodations needed for these assessments, or, if the student will not be participating, a statement listing reasons for nonparticipation and explaining how the student will be alternately assessed

- Dates and places: Projected dates for initiation of services, where services will be delivered, and the expected duration of those services

- Transition service needs: A transition component for those students (beginning at age 16) whose goals are related to community presence and independence that is included in the IEP to identify postschool goals and to describe transitional assessments and service needs

- Age of majority: A requirement to inform students, beginning at least one year before they reach the age of majority, of those rights that transfer to them

- Measuring progress: Statement of how the student's progress toward achieving IEP goals will be measured and how parents will be informed about this progress

Individualized Education Program

To stress the importance of including all of these components in each student's IEP, the federal government provided a template for school districts to use as a model (OSEP, 2006b). The IEP is a written document that is developed for each eligible child with a disability. Part B regulations specify the procedures that school districts must follow to develop, review, and revise the IEP for each child. Table 6.5 sets out the IEP content that those regulations require.

IEPs must be written for each student with a disability, so each IEP will be different from the next. Remember Emily, who was described earlier in this chapter? She needs services from several related service professionals, such as a SLP, a physical therapist (PT), and an assistive technologist. Some students, such as in Ms. Cohen's classes, may need help only from a special education teacher or a paraprofessional. Other students may require assistance from many more members of a multidisciplinary team. Academic areas may be reflected, but so may areas not typically part of educational programs for students without disabilities (e.g., fine and gross motor skills and life skills). Services indicated on the IEP must be provided, and they cannot be traded for other services, such as more time in the general education classroom. Services not being readily available (including AT devices and services) is no reason for omitting them from an IEP: If the student needs the service, it must be delivered. In other words, if a student needs the services of an assistive technologist and requires some special equipment, those services and devices must be made available. In addition, any changes in placement, related services specified in the IEP, or annual goals necessitate another IEP meeting and mutual approval by the family and the school district.

The contents of a student's IEP must be available to all educators who work with the student (U.S. Department of Education, 2006). IEPs are meant to be a communication tool. Surprisingly, it is not uncommon for teachers to be unaware of the goals, objectives, and services required by their students' IEPs. This situation leads one to ask how an appropriate education can be delivered when the educators who interact with students with disabilities do not understand what the students' education should comprise. The answer is obvious: An appropriate education cannot be delivered under these circumstances.

TRANSITION COMPONENTS OF IEPS

When IDEA was reauthorized in 1997, plans to help students transition from school to postsecondary experiences became a special education requirement. At that time, such a plan was a separate document—a mini-IEP of its own— for students age 14 and older and was called an individualized transition plan (ITP). Since the 1997 reauthorization of IDEA, these plans for assessments and services to prepare for postschool life, or statements of transitional services, are a part of the students' IEPs; they are not stand-alone documents. IDEA '04 increased to 16 the age for initiation of the transition component of students'

TABLE 6.5 INDIVIDUALIZED EDUCATION PROGRAM

Statements

A statement of the child's present levels of academic achievement and functional performance including:

- How the child's disability affects the child's involvement and progress in the general education curriculum (i.e., the same curriculum as for nondisabled children) **or** *for preschool children,* as appropriate, how the disability affects the child's participation in appropriate activities.

A statement of measurable annual goals, including academic and functional goals designed to:

- Meet the child's needs that result from the child's disability to enable the child to be involved in and make progress in the general education curriculum.
- Meet each of the child's other educational needs that result from the child's disability.

For children with disabilities who take alternate assessments aligned to alternate achievement standards (in addition to the annual goals), a description of benchmarks or short-term objectives.

A description of:

- How the child's progress toward meeting the annual goals will be measured.
- When periodic reports on the progress the child is making toward meeting the annual goals will be provided such as through the use of quarterly or other periodic reports, concurrent with the issuance of report cards.

A statement of the *special education and related services* and *supplementary aids* and *services,* based on peer-reviewed research to the extent practicable, to be provided to the child, or on behalf of the child and *a statement of the program modifications or supports* for school personnel that will be provided to enable the child:

- To advance appropriately toward attaining the annual goals.
- To be involved in and make progress in the general education curriculum and to participate in extracurricular and other nonacademic activities.
- To be educated and participate with other children with disabilities and nondisabled children in extracurricular and other nonacademic activities.

A statement of any individual appropriate accommodations that are necessary to measure the academic achievement and functional performance of the child on State and district wide assessments.

If the IEP Team determines that the child must take an alternate assessment instead of a particular regular State or district wide assessment of student achievement, a statement of why:

- The child cannot participate in the regular assessment.
- The particular alternate assessment selected is appropriate for the child.

An explanation of the extent, if any, to which the child will not participate with nondisabled children in the regular classroom and in extracurricular and other nonacademic activities.

The projected date for the beginning of the services and the anticipated frequency, location, and duration of *special education and related services* and *supplementary aids and services* and *modifications and supports.*

Transition Services

Beginning not later than the first IEP to be in effect *when the child turns 16, or younger if determined appropriate by the IEP Team,* and updated annually thereafter, the IEP must include:

- Appropriate measurable postsecondary goals based on age-appropriate transition assessments related to training, education, employment, and, where appropriate, independent living skills.
- The transition services (including courses of study) needed to assist the child in reaching those goals.

Rights That Transfer at Age of Majority

- Beginning not later than one year before the child reaches the age of majority (which is 18 years of age in most states) under State law, the IEP must include a statement that the child has been informed of the child's rights under Part B of the IDEA, if any, that will, consistent with 34 CFR §300.520, transfer to the child on reaching the age of majority.

SOURCE: OSEP (2006b).

IEPs. Transitional planning is very important for high school students with disabilities, because these individuals' postschool outcomes have much room for improvement.

Although more students with disabilities graduate from high school with a standard diploma (about 64%), too many still drop out of school (OSEP, 2006c). Some 28% of students with disabilities recently exited high school with no diploma or certificate of completion (Wagner, Newman, Cameto, Levine, & Garza, 2006). Completion rates vary greatly by type of disability. For example, 95% of students with visual or hearing disabilities and 85% of those with autism and physical disabilities complete high school. However, only 56% of those students identified as having emotional or behavioral disorders finish high school. How do these statistics compare with those for students without disabilities? Not well. Almost 90% of all students complete high school, and this average takes into account the dismal completion rate of Latino/a students, only 75% of whom complete high school (National Center for Education Statistics [NCES], 2006).

Of course, high school completion rates influence participation rates in postsecondary opportunities. Students with disabilities participate in postsecondary programs at about half the rate of their peers without disabilities; about 20% of students with disabilities attend community colleges or four-year colleges and universities (Sanford et al., 2011). All of these reasons contribute to the fact that individuals with disabilities earn less than their counterparts without disabilities and more often find themselves in jobs that do not provide benefits such as health insurance.

It is also important for teachers who participate in transition planning to understand that as adults, these individuals tend to engage in active leisure activities less than individuals without disabilities. They participate in organized community groups at a rate much lower than would be expected, and they also get in trouble with the law more often than their typical peers (Wagner et al., 2006). Helping students set goals for themselves, gain work experience, and develop skills needed for independent living can be critical to the life satisfaction experienced by adults with disabilities (Neubert, 2003).

The transition component supplements and complements the IEP, and as you can tell, it has the potential of being very important to the long-term results of your students. Whereas the IEP describes the educational goals and objectives that a student should achieve during a school year, the transitional services part of the IEP focuses on the academic and functional achievement of the individual to prepare for adult living (National Center on Secondary Education and Transition [NCSET], 2005). Transition components are designed to facilitate the process of going from high school to any of several postschool options: postsecondary education, vocational education, integrated employment (including supported employment), adult services, or community participation (de Fur, 2003). The last years of school can be critical to the achievement of special education outcomes and to these learners' smooth and successful transition to adulthood. Look back at Table 6.5 to determine the components on the transition plan.

BEHAVIOR INTERVENTION PLANS

When any student with a disability commits serious behavioral infractions, IDEA '04 requires that a behavior intervention plan, which is like an IEP but addresses the behavioral infraction, be developed (U.S. Department of Education, 2006). Because inappropriate behavior is so often at the root of special education referrals, of teachers' dissatisfaction with working with students who have disabilities, and of lifelong challenges, we devote an entire chapter (see Chapter 9) to behavior management, development of good social skills, and interventions for serious and persistent behavior issues. Here, we will introduce the plans that IDEA '04 requires for students who have an IEP and also engage in seriously disruptive or violent behavior.

Why did behavioral plans for students who have major behavioral issues become part of students' IEPs? One reason reflects concerns of Congress and the public about violence, discipline, and special education students. Although students without disabilities can be expelled for breaking school rules (for bringing guns to school, for example, or engaging in serious fighting), some students with disabilities cannot. These students can, however, be removed from their current placement and receive their education away from their assigned classroom(s) in what is called an interim alternative educational setting (IAES) for up to 45 school days. Continued progress toward the attainment of IEP goals must be one intention of the IAES placement. Students who cannot be expelled are those whose disruptive behavior was caused by their disability. Under the older versions of IDEA, this protection was called the "stay put" provision. Through a process called manifestation determination, educators figure out whether the disability caused the infraction. All students with disabilities who are violent or "out of control" must have behavior intervention plans developed for them. These plans focus not only on the control or elimination of future serious behavioral infractions but also on the development of positive social skills.

To develop behavior intervention plans, educators use a process called functional behavioral assessment (FBA), which clarifies the student's preferences for specific academic tasks and determines when the undesirable behavior is likely to occur (Kern, Delaney, Clarke, Dunlap, & Childs, 2001). We discuss FBA in some detail in Chapter 9. This assessment process was originally developed for students with severe disabilities. IDEA '04 suggests a broader application of the procedure and emphasizes its use when students with any disability face disciplinary actions. The FBA process leads teachers directly to effective interventions with socially validated outcomes (Barnhill, 2005; Ryan, Halsey, & Matthews, 2003). FBAs help determine the nature of the behavior of concern, the reason or motivation for the behavior, and under what conditions the behavior does and does not occur (Hanley, Iwata, & McCord, 2003).

The goal of the assessment is to determine what activities are associated with problem behaviors and to identify the student's interests and preferences (Shippen, Simpson, & Crites, 2003). Instructional activities are then modified to incorporate the student's "likes" into activities where problems typically occur. Here's how it works: Ethan's behavior during activities that require him to write is highly disruptive. However, he likes to use the computer, so he is allowed to complete written assignments using a word processing program on a computer. The double benefit is that his academic performance is improving and his disruptive behavior has decreased. There is a major caution, however. These assessments often miss behaviors that occur rarely, and this is a real problem because many low-frequency infractions (hitting a teacher, setting a fire, breaking a window) are the most dangerous and serious. Because of the propensity of students with emotional or behavioral disorders to exhibit behavior problems, FBAs are used with most of these students. Therefore, more details about FBA and effective interventions that address problem behaviors are found in Chapter 9. As a teacher, you will need to become proficient in using FBAs and understanding their results.

WHEN AND HOW ARE EXISTING INDIVIDUALIZED PLANS EVALUATED?

Assessments of students' performance have many different purposes. The first purpose of assessments, identifying and qualifying students with disabilities, is an important part of the initial IEP process. Those assessments are conducted before the IEP is developed. The data gathered and judgments made are used to shape the IEP process and help the student's IEP team determine what services are necessary for an appropriate education. However, once an IEP is developed, there are three primary purposes of evaluating the student's performance:

- Evaluate the student's progress toward IEP goals.
- Evaluate the effectiveness of services or supports.
- Monitor progress.

Students with disabilities are tested and evaluated more than any other group of learners. As we just mentioned, these individuals experience many different kinds of assessments during the IEP process. In addition, students with disabilities participate in assessments

- To determine whether the school is making AYP.
- To monitor their individual progress toward academic and social targets.
- To monitor the school's progress toward AYP.

Like their classmates without disabilities, nearly all students with disabilities participate in state and district-wide assessments (Ziegler, 2002). For improved school accountability, NCLB and IDEA '04 require all students to participate in annual assessments. Only a very small percentage—some 2%—of all students with disabilities can be excused from these tests, and they receive an alternate assessment. The other group excused from tests consists of those students just learning English as their second language (U.S. Department of Education, 2006). Because the overall results from individual schools—their AYP—are used to "grade" a school's effectiveness, affect student promotion, and sometimes impact the school's funding, these yearly assessments are often referred to as high-stakes testing. The ultimate expectation is that all students will achieve proficiency in reading and math, and if students' test scores indicate they have not reached those levels, the schools they attend will experience significant disincentives (penalties). All students with disabilities must participate in their school district's accountability system. Those who are participating in the general education curriculum may take tests with accommodations, if such accommodations are called for in the student's IEP (Shriner & Destefano, 2003). Students whose curriculum targets life skills and community presence most often participate in alternate assessments, which evaluate students' progress toward meeting benchmarks for targeted achievement of skills that are not part of the general education curriculum (OSEP, 2006b; Thompson, Lazarus, Clapper, & Thurlow, 2004). Very few students with disabilities receive alternate assessments, because IDEA '04 allows states to give this option to only 2% of all students with disabilities (U.S. Department of Education, 2006).

Although it is important to monitor the overall achievement of a school and how well its students are mastering the general education curriculum, yearly tests do not provide teachers with enough information about the progress of individual students to guide instruction. Other types of assessments are better suited to monitoring students' progress and adapting instruction accordingly. Careful and consistent progress monitoring is important to avoid wasting instructional time by using a tactic that is ineffective. Teachers need to document these students' improvement in academic achievement, behavior, or attainment of life skills. They use results from these evaluations both to guide their instruction and to communicate with the IEP team. We provide more details about direct assessment systems in Chapter 8, but to put these procedures in context, we introduce them here.

All students experience assessments of their classroom performance. Weekly spelling tests, math tests, exams after the completion of social studies units, and history papers are all examples of students' classroom work that is graded. Such evaluations of students' work are authentic assessments, because they use the work that students generate in classroom settings as the evaluation measurements (Layton & Lock, 2007). Results on students' class assignments, anecdotal records, writing samples, and observational data on behavior are examples of authentic assessments. In other words, evaluation is made directly from the curriculum and the students' work. Teachers often collect more authentic assessments for students with disabilities than they do for their students without disabilities (Fuchs, Fuchs, Hosp, & Jenkins, 2001).

Authentic assessments can be comprehensive and include ongoing, systematic evaluations of students' performance. Portfolio assessment is an example of authentic assessment that includes samples of a student's work, over a period of time, to show her or his growth and development (Layton & Lock, 2007). This evaluation process involves students in both instruction and assessment because they select the exhibits of their work to include. A portfolio may include prizes, certificates of award, pictures, dictated work, photographs, lists of books read, and selections from work done with others. It may also include reports, written by the teacher or by others who work with the child, about challenging situations or patterns of behavior that should be a focus of concern.

Authentic assessments use work that students generate in classroom settings as evaluation measurements. Teachers often collect more authentic assessments for students with disabilities than for their students without disabilities.

Considered both a self-correcting instructional method and an evaluation system, curriculum-based measurement (CBM) is a detailed data collection system that frequently measures how well a student is learning specific instructional targets. With CBM, teachers quickly know how well their students are learning and whether the chosen instructional methods are effective (Vaughn & Fuchs, 2003). For example, a teacher instructing a student in math keeps a record of the number or percentage of problems correctly solved across time. Using this system, teachers can track the percentage of words spelled correctly, the number of new arithmetic facts memorized, the number of words correctly read per minute (reading fluency), or the number or percentage of topic sentences included in writing assignments. These records help teachers judge whether the instructional methods selected are both efficient and effective. CBM is often part of the evaluation system used during the prereferral stage of the IEP process, particularly for students suspected of having learning disabilities (Bradley, Danielson, & Hallahan, 2002; Fuchs, Fuchs, & Powell, 2004).

CHANGE IN SERVICES OR SUPPORTS

Remember, IDEA '04 guarantees students with disabilities and their families a continuum of services. However, the intention is not for these services to be offered in a fixed sequence. Rather, they are to be a flexible constellation, invoked when supports need to be increased because a student's progress has slowed, or phased down when they are no longer necessary. In other words, the needs of individual students are not fixed but, rather, change across time. A student with a reading disability might, for some period of time, need intensive instruction outside of the general education classroom for some portion of the school day. There, intensive instruction would be delivered to a very small group of learners, all struggling with the task of learning how to read, and all receiving individualized instruction. However, when the reading difficulty is resolved, that student may well move immediately back to the general education setting, where continued progress in reading is monitored every several weeks and then every month or so.

When changes in placement, either more or less restrictive, are considered, the IEP team, including the family (and, in some cases, the student), must be in communication (U.S. Department of Education, 2006). In some cases, the whole IEP team, which includes the parents, holds a meeting. In other cases, only selected members of the team who have expertise related to a particular portion of the student's individualized program need to meet. IDEA '04 requires schools to notify parents in writing about changes being made to the student's program. Regardless, for correct decisions to be made about whether a student's services need to be more or less intensive, information must be current and precise. Typically, authentic assessments are used for such decisions.

WHAT DOES IDEA '04 REQUIRE DURING THE IEP PROCESS?

IDEA '04 includes many requirements for the IEP process and students' IEPs. For example, the law is very specific about these issues:

1. IEP team membership
2. Parent participation
3. Attendance of IEP team members at IEP meetings
4. When meetings must be held
5. Transition components of IEPs
6. Blending of IFSP and IEP content in plans for children between the ages of 2 and 3
7. Access to IEP content
8. Transfer of the IEP when a student relocates

As we have noted, states often add steps to the IEP process by expanding components or features of IEPs as they are implemented at the state or district level. Such additional requirements extend beyond what the federal government requires that school districts, schools, and teachers provide to students with disabilities and their families. Federal officials felt that each of the issues listed here needed to be addressed in IDEA '04, so let's think about each of them in turn.

You have already learned about what IDEA '04 says about who must serve on IEP teams (review Table 6.2). You learned that each IEP team is a multidisciplinary team of experts who come together to plan an individually designed program to meet the unique needs of each student with a disability. IDEA '04 requires that every team have members from the following groups: the student's parent(s) (or guardian), at least one general education teacher, at least one special educator, a representative of the school district, someone (such as a school psychologist) who can interpret the student's test results, related service providers in each area of need, and the student (when appropriate).

The participation of parents in the IEP process can be a key element in the success of each student's education. However, it can be difficult to schedule and coordinate everyone's time. Parents' work schedules may conflict with the school's schedule. Some parents may not have transportation to get to and from school at specific times, or they may not be able to arrange baby sitters, or they may feel uncomfortable with the education system. Every effort must be made to assist parents and encourage their participation in the IEP process and IEP team meetings. As a way to facilitate participation, IDEA '04 now allows for these meetings to be held through different means: conference calls, video conferences, and possibly even e-mails. Many suggest that extended family members also be included, but what is most important is that the schools welcome parents and families of all students with disabilities (Smith, 2007).

IDEA '04 does not require that every member of the IEP team be present at each and every meeting about the student's educational program (OSEP, 2006a). For example, if an IEP meeting is being held to discuss only the student's speech or language problems, the school psychologist on the team might not have much to contribute. However, that professional may be excused only if both the parent(s) and the school district officially agree in writing.

Unless he or she is part of a pilot program operating in 15 states, every student with a disability must have the IEP reviewed at least annually. However, if major changes are not going to be made, the parents and school district can agree not to hold an official meeting. The IEP team needs to meet more often than once a year if the student's progress mastering the general education curriculum is less than expected or if unanticipated needs surface. Also, if a major change in the student's services or placement is to occur, a meeting must be called. For example, if the student violates school rules by bringing a gun to campus and a change in placement is to occur, an IEP meeting must be called.

On another note, and addressing a common concern about IEPs, IDEA '04 reaffirms that IEPs are to be open to every education professional who works with the student. However, special education records are confidential, and only those directly involved in administering services described on the IEP have legal access to them. It is important that everyone who works with the child benefit from the collaborative work of the team that developed the IEP. For the same reason, IEPs move with the student. When a family moves to another school, school district, or state, the new education team should benefit from all of the work that went into development of the IEP. Therefore, IDEA '04 stresses the importance of quickly transferring records of students who are relocating.

The Working Together feature provides an example of how IEP team members come together to ensure that Emily's IEP is serving her needs as her education continues.

WORKING *together*

Reviewing Emily's Progress

Professionals representing related services in addition to the required IEP team members work together to fine-tune Emily's IEP. The focus of the meeting is to conduct an annual review of Emily's performance in school and to determine what changes to her IEP may be necessary to ensure an appropriate education. The IEP team consists of Mr. Hernandez, Emily's fourth-grade teacher, Emily's art teacher, the special education teacher, the principal, Emily's parents, the special education coordinator, and the diagnostician. Also, because of Emily's speech/language and motor needs, the speech/language pathologist, recreational therapist, assistive technologist, occupational therapist, and physical therapist participate on this IEP team. Different members of the IEP team have obtained Emily's input about her needs during an interview and observations. All individuals involved in this process should be prepared to discuss Emily's academic, behavioral, social, motor, and language needs from their own perspective. The IEP team members will bring their summaries about Emily's progress and questions for the team to address. Based on their discussions, Emily's IEP can be adjusted to more appropriately address her needs to ensure successful inclusion in the fourth-grade class.

Here are some tips that can help ensure the success of this collaborative process:

1. Mr. Hernandez should be prepared to discuss how Emily is performing compared with her peers and what techniques he is using to make environmental and instructional adaptations for her. He should also describe how well the computer works as an accommodation to help her do her work and how well Emily is socializing in his class.

2. The art teacher should describe how Emily is progressing based on any adaptations that were made to the materials or content.

3. The special education teacher should explain how she teams with Mr. Hernandez to support Emily and how Emily's learning needs are also being addressed during the twice-weekly pullout sessions with the special education teacher.

4. The parents should have an opportunity to express their concerns at home with schoolwork and any other issues that are important for the IEP team to discuss and resolve.

5. The speech/language pathologist can provide an update on therapy sessions to help Emily develop her speech. A discussion about how Emily is doing with her oral language communication in class should also occur.

6. The recreational therapist should update the IEP team on how Emily is performing in adaptive physical education (PE) and provide guidance about how to include Emily in general PE classes.

7. The assistive technologist should work with the occupational therapist to reevaluate Emily's use of the computer as an alternative to using a pencil. Discussion about other assistive devices or adaptations to the keyboard may be necessary.

8. The physical therapist should evaluate Emily's use of the walker in various school environments and bring this information to the meeting. Issues related to transportation and mobility should be addressed. A discussion with Emily about how the walker helps her mobility can inform discussion in the meeting as well.

QUESTIONS

1. How can these services be coordinated to benefit Emily and to help Mr. Hernandez with his teaching?

2. What advice can you offer Mr. Hernandez about collaborating with professionals from the content in Chapter 5?

Finally, IDEA '04 included language to help students who are transitioning from early childhood programs to school-based programs. This transition period is a very difficult time for many families. For example, for infants and toddlers under the age of 3, service providers often work with both the child and the family at home and in "natural environments," such as community play groups. When children are age 3 or older, education is typically provided at schools. Also, for children under the age of 3, goals and benchmarks of programs planned through IFSPs are not comparable to the education described in IEPs. IFSPs address targets such as school readiness, emerging language, developing motor skills, and preliteracy. IEPs focus more on access to the general education curriculum. To assist in the transition from early childhood programs to school-based programs, the law mandates that the service manager or representative from the early intervention program participate in the young child's initial IEP meeting.

SUMMARY

A cornerstone of the federal laws ensuring all infants, toddlers, preschoolers, and students with disabilities a free appropriate education in the least restrictive environment is the individualized education created through the special education process. IDEA '04 guarantees these individuals and their families a tailor-made education program, which is guided by uniquely created planning documents: the individualized family service plan (IFSP) and the individualized education program (IEP). The IEP is further supported, when necessary, by behavior intervention plans and the statement of transitional services. These plans bring together multidisciplinary teams of parents, general educators, special educators, and related service providers for the purpose of helping young children and students with disabilities reach their full potential and achieve community presence and independence as adults.

REVIEW THE LEARNING OBJECTIVES

Let's review the learning objectives for this chapter. If you are uncertain and cannot talk through the answers provided for any of these questions, reread those sections of the text.

- **What is response to intervention?**

  Response to intervention (RTI) is a model for delivering scientifically based, school-wide, multitiered systems of support (MTSS). Through the RTI model, students who are identified as at risk for poor academic achievement are eligible to receive additional educational support. RTI is also designed to provide evidence toward the evaluation for and identification of learning disabilities in the event that a special education referral is necessary because of continually low performance in spite of intensive instruction. RTI involves four fundamental components: universal screening, progress monitoring, data-based decision making, and high-quality, evidence-based, multitiered instructional support in relation to students' educational needs.

- **What is the evaluation and identification process?**

  IDEA '04 mandates that an individualized program be delivered to every infant, toddler, and student who is identified as having a disability and is in need of special education. The purposes of these individualized programs are to ensure that each of these individuals receives FAPE, is provided an education in the LRE, is specific to the student, and is provided services with the expectation of outstanding results. IDEA '04 requires that these steps, at a minimum, be included in the IEP process:

  1. Prereferral, 2. Referral, 3. Identification, 4. Eligibility, 5. Development of the IEP, 6. Implementation of the IEP, and 7. Evaluation and reviews.

- **Who are the members of the IEP team?**

  IDEA '04 is very clear about membership in IEP teams (OSEP, 2006a). The parents, general education and special education teacher of the child, and a representative from the public agency are members of the team, along with a person who can interpret the instructional implications of evaluation results. In addition, the team can include, at the discretion of the parent or the agency, other individuals who have knowledge or expertise, such as related services professionals and, whenever possible, the child with a disability.

- **How do special education multidisciplinary teams and services meet the needs of students with disabilities?**

  The multidisciplinary teams and the services they deliver are what make special education truly special for students with disabilities and their families. A special educator might be a resource specialist, an itinerant teacher, a special education classroom teacher, a job coach, a home or hospital teacher, or an administrator. Related services are definitely a unique feature of special education, offering a wide range of services and expertise to students and their families. Related service professionals may include those who provide assistive technology, audiology, occupational therapy, physical therapy, school health services, speech/language therapy, or other services needed by the student.

- **What plans guarantee students with disabilities an appropriate education?**

  The plan that guarantees an appropriate education to infants and toddlers (i.e., individuals from birth up to the age of 3) is called the Individualized Family Service Plan (IFSP); the plan for preschoolers and schoolchildren is called the Individualized Education Program (IEP). IEPs may have additional components, such as a transition component for students age 16 or older and a behavior intervention plan for students with disabilities who violate schools' conduct codes.

- **When and how are existing individualized plans evaluated?**

  Once an IEP is developed, there are three primary purposes of evaluating the student's performance:

  ○ Evaluate the student's progress toward IEP goals.

  ○ Evaluate the effectiveness of services or supports.

  ○ Monitor progress.

- **What does IDEA '04 require during the IEP process?**

  IDEA '04 mandates that an individualized program be delivered to every infant, toddler, and student who is identified as having a disability and is in need of special education. IDEA '04 includes many requirements about the IEP process and students' IEPs.

  For example, the law is very specific about these issues:

  1. IEP team membership

  2. Parent participation

  3. Attendance of IEP team members at IEP meetings

  4. When meetings must be held

  5. Transition components of IEPs

  6. Blending of IFSP and IEP content in plans for children between the ages of 2 and 3

  7. Access to IEP content

  8. Transfer of the IEP when a student relocates

$SAGE edge™ Test your understanding of chapter content. Take the practice quiz. edge.sagepub.com/bryant

REVIST THE OPENING CHALLENGE

Check your answers to the Reflection Questions from the Opening Challenge and revise them on the basis of what you have learned.

1. Are Mr. Hernandez and Ms. Cohen overly concerned about being able to meet their students' needs? Why or why not?

2. What advice would you give them about working with special education teachers regarding the supports and services that may be specified in their students' IEPs?

3. What kind of help and assistance should Mr. Hernandez and Ms. Cohen expect from the IEP team members?

4. Is Mr. Hernandez justified in expressing concerns about the educational progress of Emily's classmates? Why or why not?

5. How can special education and related service professionals help Mr. Hernandez and Ms. Cohen support their students' needs and enable them to teach the rest of their class?

6. How does the response to intervention (RTI) model affect instruction in Mr. Hernandez's and Ms. Cohen's classes?

KEY TERMS

data-based decision making, 215

fidelity, 215

progress monitoring, 215

universal screening, 215

SAGE edge™ Review key terms with eFlashcards. edge.sagepub.com/bryant

PROFESSIONAL STANDARDS AND LICENSURE

For a complete description of Professional Standards and Licensure, please see Appendix on page 569.

CEC INITIAL PREPARATION STANDARDS

Standard 1: Learner Development and Individual Learning Differences

Standard 2: Learning Environments

Standard 3: Curricular Content Knowledge

Standard 4: Assessment

Standard 6: Professional Learning and Ethical Practice

Standard 7: Collaboration

INTASC CORE PRINCIPLES

Standard 1: Learner Development

Standard 2: Learning Differences

Standard 3: Learning Environments

Standard 4: Content Knowledge

Standard 6: Assessment

Standard 7: Planning for Instruction

Standard 9: Professional Learning and Ethical Practice

Standard 10: Leadership and Collaboration

Praxis II: Education of Exceptional Students: Core Content Knowledge

I. Understanding Exceptionalities: Basic concepts in special education

II. Legal and Societal Issues: Federal laws and legal issues

III. Delivery of Services to Students with Disabilities: Background knowledge

SAGE edge™

Review ➡ Practice ➡ Improve
Get the tools you need to sharpen your study skills. Access practice quizzes, eFlashcards, video, and multimedia: **edge.sagepub.com/bryant**

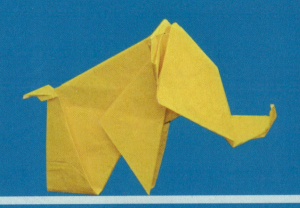

7

PROMOTING ACCESS TO THE CURRICULUM

LEARNING OBJECTIVES

After studying this chapter, you will be able to answer the following questions:

- What is universal design for learning?

- What is the ADAPT framework?

- What are effective instructional practices?

- How can instructional grouping practices promote effective instruction?

- What guidelines should be followed for textbooks and instructional materials?

- What are assistive technology devices and services for promoting access to the general education curriculum?

Planning and Delivering Instruction

ELEMENTARY GRADES Mrs. Bell is an experienced and effective fifth-grade teacher with 26 students in a large, urban, public school district. In Mrs. Bell's school, 72% of the students qualify for free or reduced-cost lunch, and 25% are English language learners (ELLs). Mrs. Bell's class includes two students with reading, writing, and mathematics learning disabilities (LD), who are performing about two years below grade level. Her four ELL students speak Spanish or Vietnamese and attended bilingual classes in the primary grades. The Language Support Team (LST) in Mrs. Bell's school agreed that the four were ready to move into English instruction classes; however, one requires pullout services from an ELL specialist. Mrs. Bell also has her first student, Paul, who has cerebral palsy (CP). Paul uses a wheelchair and has good communication skills but struggles with motor tasks such as writing with a pencil. Mrs. Bell reflects about her class: *"I have a range of abilities and needs this year. In reviewing the fall academic assessment scores, I see that about one-third of my class requires extra help with reading, writing, and mathematics. I also have to be sure that I am addressing the needs of my students who are ELLs and students with LD and CP. Differentiating instruction is critical for the success of all my students."*

SECONDARY GRADES Ms. Mendez is a ninth-grade biology teacher at a high school in the same school district as Mrs. Bell with similar demographics. Of her six class periods, three are "inclusion classes" with a larger proportion of students with disabilities, including some with LD and a high-functioning student with autism. The special education teacher now joins the weekly science teachers' meetings to identify how best to meet individual students' needs. As she prepares for an upcoming team meeting, Ms. Mendez reflects on her instructional practices: *"The range of reading, writing, and mathematics abilities is challenging, particularly when students read text in class and for homework. Judging from performance on science tests, some students have not mastered the mathematical concepts and skills required for science instruction, and the writing skills of some are also weak. I know I should make adaptations to differentiate instruction, but I am not sure where to begin. My training is in the sciences, not in basic academics, so I will have to rely on the special education teacher, Ms. Reid, to support the inclusion students and me."*

REFLECTION QUESTIONS In your journal, write down your answers to the following questions. After completing the chapter, check your answers and revise them on the basis of what you have learned.

1. How can Mrs. Bell and Ms. Mendez implement the principles of universal design for learning into their instructional practices?

2. How can Mrs. Bell and Ms. Mendez use the ADAPT framework to differentiate instruction for their students?

3. How can Mrs. Bell and Ms. Mendez differentiate instruction for their multicultural and ELL students?

4. What instructional and grouping practices might help them provide effective, differentiated instruction for their students?

5. How can Mrs. Bell and Ms. Mendez ensure that the textbooks and instructional materials they use are appropriate for all of their students?

6. How can assistive technology help Mrs. Bell's students with disabilities access the general education curriculum?

nclusive schools use a variety of practices to ensure that all students have opportunities to learn and thrive in a supportive, responsive school environment and to have access to the general education curriculum.

Having **access to the general education curriculum** means being able to (a) learn the knowledge and skills we expect all students to learn; (b) benefit from evidence-based instruction that is designed, delivered, and evaluated for effectiveness; and (c) use materials, facilities, and labs that facilitate learning. For many at-risk students and students with disabilities, mastering the critical academic knowledge and skills is difficult because of learning challenges such as sensory, memory, communication, motor, behavioral, and cognitive problems. Differentiating instruction, then, is critical to helping them become successful learners.

Differentiating instruction is instruction that is responsive to the diverse needs of all students, with a focus on curriculum, instructional adaptations, services, and instructional intensity. Figure 7.1 illustrates how most of the student population can benefit from less differentiation in order to successfully access and master the general education curriculum. Some students require differentiation, however, and it can take various forms depending on the student's individual needs. For example, we can differentiate the intensity of instruction by offering small groups increased time for more individualized or alternative instructional intervention. Specialized staff, including special educators, can also deliver more intensive, adapted instruction. Differentiation can occur in different settings, too, such as the general education classroom, a resource room, or a self-contained classroom. In some cases, a change in the curriculum emphasizing more life skills may be required. Student progress with lesson objectives is also carefully monitored (National Center on Intensive Intervention [NCII], 2014). Think back to Chapter 6 regarding the RTI model. It is easy to see how the three levels in Figure 7.1 corresponds to a multi-tiered approach to instruction and intensified intervention instruction for some students.

In this chapter, we discuss ways to differentiate instruction, including using the principles of universal design for learning (UDL) and the ADAPT framework. We provide information about multicultural and linguistic considerations when differentiating instruction. We also discuss effective instructional practices that help students access and master the curriculum, ways to adapt instructional materials, and assistive technology devices and services.

WHAT IS UNIVERSAL DESIGN FOR LEARNING?

Universal design for learning (UDL) is a means for differentiating instruction for all students, including learners with disabilities. It is a framework that provides ways to remove or minimize barriers to learning and promote

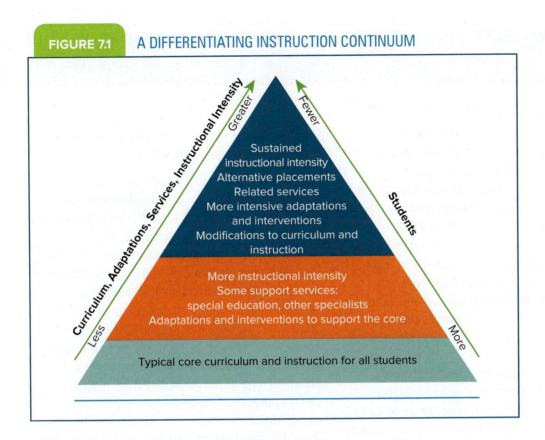

FIGURE 7.1 A DIFFERENTIATING INSTRUCTION CONTINUUM

accessibility to curricula and **pedagogy,** or teaching practices, for all learners, including students with and without disabilities and English language learners (CAST, 2011). The goal is to foster learners' ability to achieve mastery of the curricula within a flexible environment that features various ways content can be conveyed to account for individual differences (CAST, 2011). According to the Higher Education Opportunity Act (2008), universal design for learning

> (A) provides flexibility in the ways information is presented, in the ways students respond or demonstrate knowledge and skills, and in the ways students are engaged; and

> (B) reduces barriers in instruction, provides appropriate accommodations, supports, and challenges, and maintains high achievement expectations for all students, including students with disabilities and students who are limited English proficient.

UDL is an outgrowth of the concept of universal design (UD), which has its roots in the field of architecture (King-Sears, 2009). Let's take an example of UD as it relates to the ADA law, which requires that the physical environment be made accessible for individuals with disabilities. Curb cuts enable people who use wheelchairs to use sidewalks, cross streets, and move independently as they shop or get from a parking lot to a restaurant. But curb cuts also help parents with strollers and people with shopping carts as they walk through neighborhoods or shopping centers. Removing barriers allows people with disabilities to

TECH *notes*

UDL DIGITAL MEDIA

Digital media offer an excellent example of how the universal design principle "Multiple Means of Representation" can promote access for students with different needs, such as adaptations in learning, seeing, hearing, moving, and/or understanding English (Rose et al., 2006). Current technology and partnerships with textbook publishers now make electronic versions of texts readily available, so print is not the only way to access books. For the student with CP and motor problems in Mrs. Bell's class and the student with LD in Ms. Mendez's class who has difficulty reading, the computer can be used to immediately provide auditory access by translating print to audio so a book can be heard instead of read, facilitating access for both students. In another example, by using the same electronic version of the book, the computer can convert print into Braille for tactile access by a student with severe visual disabilities. These types of access to print should be noted in the IEP. UDL allows the broadest spectrum of learners to access the curriculum: students with varying learning needs, those with disabilities, and those with other special needs.

UDL guidelines can also be applied to teaching students from culturally and linguistically diverse backgrounds. For example, for the "Provide Multiple Means of Representation" principle, teachers can adjust their level of English vocabulary to the student's level of understanding (UDL Checkpoint 2.1) and support instructional language by repeating, rephrasing, and extending the student's language (UDL Checkpoint 2.4). They can use nonverbal cues such as gestures, pictures, objects, and other instructional materials to facilitate understanding (UDL Checkpoint 2.5). Teachers can also preview new content by teaching key vocabulary, asking questions to stimulate thinking about the new content, and making linkages among students' experiences (UDL Checkpoint 3.1).

The Considering Diversity feature offers ways to differentiate instruction for English language learners. Then, we turn our attention to the ADAPT framework.

participate in daily life, but it also helps people without disabilities (see http://www.ncsu.edu/ncsu/design/cud/about_us/usronmacespeech.htm for an inspirational speech by Dr. Ron Mace, who coined the term *universal design*).

Now, let's translate this concept of UD access to education. Universally designed curricula and pedagogy reflect three principles (Rose, Harbour, Johnston, Daley, & Abarbanell, 2006). First, there are **multiple means of representation;** in other words, information is presented in various formats to reduce sensory and cognitive barriers. For example, written text can be accompanied by audio for students who are blind, and graphics can enhance the content for students who are deaf or have learning problems. Closed captions on video are another option.

The second principle, **multiple means of action and expression,** refers to the ability of students to respond in a variety of ways. For example, voice recognition software, scanning devices, and switches help students with physical disabilities access the computer to complete computer-based activities. The third principle, **multiple means of engagement,** consists of actively engaging

UDL and Its Applications

students in activities and making available more than just a single mode of representation and expression to address their needs and interests. Using the computer is an example of providing different ways to engage students in the learning process.

Each principle is comprised of three guidelines and several checkpoints. For example, in Table 7.1, the principle "Provide Multiple Means of Representation"

TABLE 7.1 UNIVERSAL DESIGN FOR LEARNING GUIDELINES		
1. Provide Multiple Means of Representation	**2. Provide Multiple Means of Action and Expression**	**3. Provide Multiple Means of Engagement**
1: *Provide options for perception*	4: *Provide options for physical action*	7: *Provide options for recruiting interest*
1.1 Offer ways of customizing the display of information	4.1 Vary the methods for response and navigation	7.1 Optimize individual choice and autonomy
1.2 Offer alternatives for auditory information	4.2 Optimize access to tools and assistive technologies	7.2 Optimize relevance, value, and authenticity
1.3 Offer alternatives for visual information		7.3 Minimize threats and distractions
2: *Provide options for language, mathematical expressions, and symbols*	5: *Provide options for expression and communication*	8: *Provide options for sustaining effort and persistence*
2.1 Clarify vocabulary and symbols	5.1 Use multiple media for communication	8.1 Heighten salience of goals and objectives
2.2 Clarify syntax and structure	5.2 Use multiple tools for construction and composition	8.2 Vary demands and resources to optimize challenge
2.3 Support decoding of text, mathematical notation, and symbols	5.3 Build fluencies with graduated levels of support for practice and performance	8.3 Foster collaboration and community
2.4 Promote understanding across languages		8.4 Increase mastery-oriented feedback
2.5 Illustrate through multiple media		
3: *Provide options for comprehension*	6: *Provide options for executive functions*	9: *Provide options for self-regulation*
3.1 Activate or supply background knowledge	6.1 Guide appropriate goal-setting	9.1 Promote expectations and beliefs that optimize motivation
3.2 Highlight patterns, critical features, big ideas, and relationships	6.2 Support planning and strategy development	9.2 Facilitate personal coping skills and strategies
3.3 Guide information processing, visualization, and manipulation	6.3 Facilitate managing information and resources	9.3 Develop self-assessment and reflection
3.4 Maximize transfer and generalization	6.4 Enhance capacity for monitoring progress	
⬇	⬇	⬇
Knowledgeable learners	Strategic, goal-directed learners	Purposeful, motivated learners

is comprised of "Provide Options for Perceptions," a guideline, and "Offer Ways of Customizing the Display of Information," a checkpoint for that guideline and principle.

The three principles of UDL are featured in the UDL guidelines (CAST, 2011). Applying the principles of UDL to curricula and pedagogy means adapting goals, strategies, materials, and tests to enable access for all and to remove or minimize barriers to learning. The intent is to make the curriculum and instruction flexible enough to accommodate the diverse learning needs evident in most classrooms (CAST, 2011; Rao, Ok, & Bryant, 2014). Table 7.1 provides a visual representation (see http://cast.org/udl/index.html for additional information).

UDL is supported in the field of education and included in the IDEA legislation as a means for promoting access to the curriculum and instruction for all learners. However, it's important to know about the evidence that supports these practices (Edyburn, 2010). Fortunately, research studies on the effects of utilizing the principles of UDL on student performance are emerging, and preliminary findings are promising (Hall, Cohen, Vue, & Ganley, 2014; Kennedy, Thomas, Meyer, Alves, & Lloyd, 2014; King-Sears et al., 2014). In Tech Notes on page 260, UDL examples are shown for how the UDL "Multiple Means of Representation" principle can be operationalized in the classroom.

CONSIDERING *diversity*

STRATEGIES FOR DIFFERENTIATED INSTRUCTION FOR ENGLISH LANGUAGE LEARNERS (ELLS)

Think about how the UDL guidelines connect with these strategies.

Scheduling Strategies

- Chunk instruction into shorter segments to allow for time to check work.

- Expand assignments over a longer period.

- Extend wait time for oral responses.

- Plan challenging tasks and subjects earlier in the day or period—or other best time for the student.

Setting Strategies

- Seat ELLs close to speaker, screen, or reader.

- Assign support staff to work with ELLs in addition to the classroom teacher.

- Provide small-group instruction.

- Pair or group ELLs with "buddies" who will assist with modeling and explaining tasks.

- Work one-to-one with students.

- Introduce and develop new vocabulary visually by using a picture dictionary and other visual aids.

Presentation Strategies

- Provide ample repetition of language: repeat, restate, rephrase, reread.

- Keep language consistent when describing or explaining; synonyms, idioms, and metaphors may be confusing at first; gradually introduce figurative language to expand language development.

- Keep explanations and directions brief and concise—focus on key concepts and vocabulary.

- Highlight and explicitly teach key vocabulary needed to accomplish the assigned task.

Response Strategies

- Encourage and allow for nonverbal responses such as pointing, nodding, drawing pictures, using manipulatives, and completing graphic organizers.

- Adjust expectations for language output (e.g., student speaks in words and phrases, simple present-tense statements).

- Allow shortened responses.

- Require fewer assignments (focus on the quality of a reduced number of instructional objectives).

- Use bilingual dictionaries during reading and writing assignments in order to clarify meaning when possible.

- Adapt texts by shortening or simplifying language to make the content more accessible.

- Use technology and multimedia (software such as Inspiration®, books on tape) and graphic organizers.

- Enhance oral presentations with visual and written support, graphic organizers, and modeling.

- Allow students time to check and discuss their understanding of directions and material with peers.

- Present material through multiple modes, using audiovisual and other technology (books on tape, instructional software, visuals on the overhead projector, presentation software).

- Encourage and allow for nonverbal responses through the use of pictures, manipulatives, and graphic organizers.

- Pair ELLs with strong speakers and writers (buddies).

- Encourage "buddies" to take a dictated response during pair work where ELLs explain concepts.

- Allow ELLs to dictate responses into a tape player as evidence of completion of assigned written work.

SOURCE: Adapted from Price and Nelson (2003).

WHAT IS THE ADAPT FRAMEWORK?

We can also differentiate instruction by adapting the activities used to teach objectives, content being taught, procedures for delivering instruction, and materials that support instruction. Adaptations share three characteristics. They are *individualized,* focusing on the strengths of the individual; they are *relevant* to the objective being taught to all students; and they must be *effective* to ensure that students learn the objectives. If our first attempt at making an adaptation does not help the student benefit from instruction, then we continue to make adaptations until performance improves. Student performance on tasks is a good indicator of the effectiveness of the chosen adaptations. By using the ADAPT framework, educators can make decisions about adaptations that are individualized for the student's strengths and needs and relevant to the task, such as reading and completing homework. It should be noted that the ADAPT framework and the principles of UDL fit nicely together. Think about UDL broadly as the principles apply to instruction for all students and benefit students with various learning needs, whereas the ADAPT framework is intended for students who are at risk or who have disabilities and require adaptations to instructional delivery, materials, content, and activities. The UDL principles are the "bigger picture" for all and the ADAPT framework is a "smaller picture" for some.

The ADAPT framework consists of five steps to guide your decision making about selecting and evaluating the effects of the adaptations:

1. **A**sk, "What am I requiring the student to do?"

2. **D**etermine the prerequisite skills of the task.

3. **A**nalyze the student's strengths and struggles.

4. **P**ropose and implement adaptations from among the four instructional categories—content, materials, delivery, and activity.

5. **T**est to determine whether the adaptations helped the student accomplish the task.

We examine each step to illustrate how to apply the ADAPT framework in your class with students who have special learning needs. Throughout the remaining chapters, you will read about specific ways to use ADAPT in academic, social, and behavioral areas.

ADAPT STEPS

The first step is *Ask, "What am I requiring the student to do?"* For example, in second grade, students are expected to learn basic academic skills, demonstrate the ability to get along with others, and listen to the teacher. In high school, students are required to take notes in class, complete their homework, learn from textbooks, conduct and write about research, and pass end-of-semester exams.

These "setting-specific demands" are typical of the **core curriculum**—content that is taught to all students in the general education setting (Lenz & Deshler, 2004). Students who have difficulty with these requirements are opportunities for teachers to use the ADAPT framework.

The second step is *Determine the prerequisite skills of the task.* This means identifying what students must be able to do to meet teachers' expectations, "pulling apart" the task to identify those specific prerequisite skills. For example, to add two numbers (9 + 3 = ?), students must be able to (a) identify and understand the numerical value of the numerals 9 and 3, (b) identify and know the meaning of + and = symbols, (c) use a strategy (such as "Count on 3 from 9") to arrive at the solution, and (d) write the numeral 12 correctly (not 21). All these steps should be performed rather quickly so students can keep up with instruction.

Older students may be required to take notes in class. Think for a minute about yourself as a learner in your college course. What prerequisite skills related to taking notes are necessary for you to be successful? You understand the second step if you said any of the following: listening, identifying important information, writing, summarizing the notes, and studying them for a test. Identifying prerequisite skills is an important step in the ADAPT framework because it forms the basis for addressing the remaining steps.

The third step, *Analyze the student's strengths and struggles,* means identifying each prerequisite skill of a task (from Step 2) as a strength or struggle for an individual student. You can use assessment techniques or your knowledge of the student. For example, in thinking about our addition problem (9 + 3 = ?), teachers can use **active process assessment,** interviewing students as they solve the problem out loud (see Chapter 8) to see they do it. By having the students "think aloud," the teacher can figure out whether the steps for arriving at the answer reflect strengths or struggles. For example, if a student reads the numerals and symbols correctly, then these prerequisite skills can be listed as strengths for this task. If a student starts with 1 and counts up to 12 rather than starting with 9 and counting up 3 to get 12, the teacher suspects the "Start big and count on" strategy is a struggle.

The teacher can also use observation to determine whether numerals are written correctly, which is a strength. If 12 were written as 21, then writing numerals correctly is a struggle. Referring to our note-taking task, teachers can ask for a copy of a student's notes to analyze them for the prerequisite skills of identifying and recording the important information and summarizing the information.

In the fourth step, *Propose and implement adaptations from among the four categories,* the teacher considers the student's strengths and struggles to identify appropriate instructional adaptations. In the ADAPT framework, there are four adaptation categories: (1) instructional activity, (2) instructional content, (3) instructional delivery, and (4) instructional material. Each is described here.

Returning to our addition problem example (9 + 3 = ?), the teacher identifies the need to reteach the "Start big and count on" addition strategy. She decides to work with a small group of students (instructional delivery), all of whom need to be retaught the strategy. She uses easier facts (instructional content), such as 3 + 2, and then increases to more difficult facts, such as 8 + 2 and 9 + 3; reviews the concept of greater than (instructional content) to be sure students know which number in a problem is the larger of the two; and uses chips (instructional material) so students can keep track of the "counting on" number (for 8 + 2, there are two chips to move as the student starts big, at 8, and counts on 2 to get 10).

In our note-taking example, several adaptations come to mind. The teacher can provide a skilled student with carbonless paper (instructional material) to take notes and then share a copy of these notes with the student who struggles with the task. The student can record the lecture (instructional material) and then record key ideas. Or a note-taking strategy (instructional activity) such as Note Shrink, discussed in Chapter 12, can be taught to a small group of students who can benefit (instructional delivery).

The fifth step, *Test to determine whether the adaptations helped the student accomplish the task,* focuses on monitoring student progress. For example, returning to our addition problem 9 + 3, during curriculum-based assessment or one-minute timed assessments, the teacher can check to see whether problems that can be solved with "Start big and count on" are answered correctly. In the note-taking example, a final copy of the notes can be graded, and the exam on which the notes are based can be examined for evidence of the key information in the student's answers.

Bryant and Bryant (1998) originally identified four adaptation categories from which educators can choose when selecting adaptations that are individualized for the student and relevant to the task:

- **Instructional activity** is the actual lesson used to teach and reinforce skills and concepts. Sometimes, a different instructional activity is needed if students do not benefit from the original lesson delivered by the teacher.

- **Instructional content** consists of the skills and concepts that are the focus of teaching and learning, the curriculum that state and local school districts require educators to teach. Content can be located in standards, district documents, and the teachers' guides that accompany textbooks and other materials. For example, the Common Core State Standards (CCSS; National Governors Association Center for Best Practices, Council of Chief State School Officers, 2010) provide information about concepts and skills that should be part of each school district's curriculum where the CCSS have been adopted.

- **Instructional delivery** describes the way the activity is taught, including grouping practices, instructional steps, presentation

Making Instructional
Adaptations

techniques, practice techniques, and student activities. Systematic, **explicit instruction** is included in instructional delivery and includes the following: (a) **modeling,** in which teachers provide a demonstration of steps and examples for solving a problem; (b) "**thinking aloud,**" in which teachers make their thinking processes transparent to students by saying out loud the steps they are taking while solving a problem; (c) **prompts or cues,** with which teachers provide visual or verbal assistance to increase the likelihood of correct responses; (d) **error correction,** or immediate feedback to correct error responses; (e) **guided practice,** or multiple opportunities for students to respond and practice; and **pacing,** in which teachers provide instruction at an appropriate rate to keep students engaged in learning and understanding. These practices are well-grounded in the literature as critical for struggling students (Bryant, Bryant, Porterfield, et al., 2014; Coyne, Kame'enui, & Carnine, 2011; Gersten et al., 2009; Swanson, Hoskyn, & Lee, 1999).

- **Instructional materials** are aids such as textbooks, kits, hardware, software, and manipulatives. In any subject area, there are multiple types of instructional materials that teachers can use to address various learning needs. You will read about many examples in later chapters.

Recall from the Opening Challenge that Ms. Mendez has students with learning disabilities. She is concerned about their ability to read and understand the science text. She knows adaptations are needed, so she uses the ADAPT framework in action to make instructional decisions. As you read about how she does so, think back to the three characteristics of adaptations and consider whether each adaptation is individualized for the student, relevant for instruction, and effective.

In the remaining chapters, you will encounter many examples of the ADAPT framework in action and you will see applications that illustrate quickly and simply how ADAPT can be implemented. Look for these features as you read.

WHAT ARE EFFECTIVE INSTRUCTIONAL PRACTICES?

In this section, we discuss two important components related to instructional practices. Planning instruction is considering what you will teach and how you will go about teaching it so all students in your class can benefit from your instruction. Delivering instruction means adopting specific practices for conveying information and ensuring appropriate student responses.

PLANNING FOR INSTRUCTION

We discuss four areas that teachers should plan as they prepare to teach lessons. For the first, we provide information about *types of knowledge and critical think-*

ADAPT *in action*

STUDENTS WITH LEARNING DISABILITIES IN READING

Ms. Mendez's ninth-grade students with LD in reading are required to read science text in class or for homework. Comprehending text requires many skills, including figuring out difficult words and monitoring your understanding of the science text. Ms. Mendez is alarmed at how poorly these students did on a recent quiz she gave on the science text material. She decides to work with the special education teacher to implement ADAPT to help her choose appropriate adaptations to improve these students' reading comprehension. She shares her thinking about her students using ADAPT.

(A) **Ask, "What am I requiring the student to do?"** "My students need to read the science text in class and at home. Text may be in a book or a handout for small group work. Lab assignments often require reading and following instructions that students must comprehend."

(D) **Determine the prerequisite skills of the task.** "Students need to be able to read the text, identify important information from multiple paragraphs, organize this information to facilitate comprehension, see relationships among important ideas, and pass quizzes that test their understanding."

(A) **Analyze the student's strengths and struggles.** Ms. Mendez knows several of her students have reading comprehension difficulties. They appear motivated to succeed, participating in small group activities and enjoying the lab assignments. Text reading and understanding are her main concerns. She works individually with the students to analyze difficulties by asking them to read several paragraphs out loud, identify important information, talk about the relationships among these important ideas, and organize the information in a way that enhances learning and retention. She finds the students can read many of the words and have strategies for figuring out harder words. They can tell her the important ideas but cannot discuss the relationships among these ideas or organize them in a way that promotes understanding. For example, she gave them a news story about global climate change, and they were unable to structure information that focused on cause and effect.

(P) **Propose and implement adaptations from among the four categories.** Ms. Mendez decides to try **graphic organizers (GOs)**, which are visual aids (instructional material) that help students organize, understand, see relationships, and remember important information. GOs can structure different types of information, including causes and effects and similarities and differences. In a small group of her students with reading difficulties, Ms. Mendez models by thinking aloud how to use the graphic organizers as she is reading text (instructional delivery). She gives the students a short paragraph, and together they read the material and complete the GO. She sets aside 20 minutes to conduct this minilesson (instructional activity), while the other students in her class work in small groups (instructional delivery) on a review exercise.

 Test to determine whether the adaptations helped the student accomplish the task. Ms. Mendez will review the information included in the graphic organizer as one way to determine the effectiveness of the adaptation. She will also provide a quiz on the material to see how the students understood the content. Can you identify how the adaptation is individualized, relevant, and effective?

ADAPT *framework:* FOR STUDENTS WITH LEARNING DISABILITIES IN READING

ASK "What am I requiring the student to do?"	**DETERMINE** the prerequisite skills of the task.	**ANALYZE** the student's strengths and struggles.		**PROPOSE** and implement adaptations from among the four categories.	**TEST** to determine whether the adaptations helped the student to accomplish the task.
		Strengths	Struggles		
The students will read science text.	**1.** Figure out difficult words by breaking them apart.	1			
	2. Identify important information.	2			
	3. Organize information to understand and recall.		3	**3.** Instructional Activity: Conduct a minilesson on using graphic organizers (GOs). Instructional Delivery: Model using "thinking aloud" and show students how to use GOs. Instructional Material: Provide GOs to be used in class and for homework.	**3.** Assess student use of GOs and mastery of content through correct completion of GOs and accuracy on quizzes.

ing and instructional techniques for teaching this information. For the next, *types of questions,* we provide examples of questioning techniques. Next is *stages of learning,* where we include information about how students' performance may be affected by their level of acquaintance with the content being taught. How we teach students at different stages varies. Finally, we discuss *instructional components,* including steps for delivering instruction.

Types of Knowledge and Critical Thinking

Different types of knowledge and critical thinking for different content areas are applicable across the grade levels. They include discrimination, factual knowledge, procedural knowledge, conceptual knowledge, and metacognitive knowledge. Critical thinking refers to reasoning abilities (Mastropieri & Scruggs, 2014).

Discrimination

Discrimination is the ability to distinguish one item (such as a letter, number, letter sound, math sign, state, or piece of lab equipment) from another. It occurs during the early stages of learning when students are first learning new information and requires the ability to identify and pay attention to the relevant features of an item. Students with learning difficulties may have problems discriminating among items. Teachers should teach the relevant features of items and then present similar items among which discrimination is necessary. For example, students can learn that 12 has a 1 and 2 where the 1 can be color-coded or made larger to emphasize the relevant feature that 1 is first in 12. The same can be done for 21. Once students can identify each number separately, teachers can present the numbers together for them to name. Students should be given multiple opportunities to practice discriminating among items such as similar letters (b, d, m, w, p, q) and numbers (6, 9, 21, 20, 102, 120), words with similar sounds (pet, pit, pig, big), symbols (+, −, ×, =), and concepts that are similar (types of plants). For older students, discrimination learning occurs, for instance, when they are required to identify pieces of lab equipment before instruction begins or mathematics tools such as a compass or protractor before a geometry lesson.

Factual Knowledge

The ability to memorize, retain, and recall information is factual knowledge, which is fundamental to school. Examples include math facts, vocabulary definitions, historical events and dates, parts of speech in English or a foreign language, parts of a plant, and parts of the brain and their functions. Students with special learning needs may have difficulties learning factual information because of problems with encoding, retaining, and recalling the information. They benefit from strategies that teach them how to memorize and recall information (Swanson, Cooney, & O'Shaughnessy, 1998). Students must learn numerous facts across the content areas so they can apply information to their learning.

Procedural Knowledge

Learning a set of steps that must be followed to complete a task involves procedural knowledge. Examples include the steps to solve an arithmetic problem, conduct a lab experiment, develop a historical time line, and follow a strategy to read difficult words or to comprehend text. Students with special learning needs may have difficulty with procedural knowledge because it requires memorization of the steps in the correct sequence and the ability to perform each step. It may also be necessary to teach prerequisite knowledge. For example, if students are following a series of steps to multiply 32×64, they must know the steps and the prerequisite knowledge of 4×2, 4×3, 6×2, regroup, and 6×3. Modeling, practice, and error correction are examples of ways to teach procedural knowledge. Cue cards containing the steps of the procedure can also be useful for students to refer to until they learn the steps.

Conceptual Knowledge

Knowledge about principles, models, and classifications entails conceptual knowledge. In essence, **concepts** are categories of knowledge. They range in level of abstractness. For instance, the concept of a table is concrete and easy for most students to understand, and it can be easily represented. The concept of democracy, however, is very abstract and requires multiple examples.

Visual displays can help students understand concepts. For instance, the concept *table* can be described using the categories "dimensions," "function," and "types of construction." Students can create collections of words and pictures that represent a concept. For instance, pictures of different types of tables can be assembled, and descriptive words can be identified to describe the concept (*claw-legged table*). Price and Nelson (2003) recommend that teachers conduct a concept analysis of content to be taught prior to instruction. The concept analysis should include the following:

- Identification of the critical concepts to be taught as part of a unit or chapter
- Definitions of the concepts
- List of attributes or characteristics of the concepts
- List of noncritical attributes that are not essential for understanding the concept
- List of examples
- List of "nonexamples"
- List of related concepts

Metacognitive Knowledge

Metacognition is often described as thinking about the strategies we use to tackle tasks. It is knowledge about how people learn and process information

VIDEO CASE 7.1

Planning Effective Instruction

1. The teachers in the video discuss a variety of instructional practices that they find to be useful for planning effective instruction. Why do they find these practices to be highly effective and how do they support student learning? Do you notice similarities and differences between the practices used by teachers at the elementary and high school levels?

2. Which types of instructional grouping arrangements are shown within the video? What strategies do the teachers use to plan cooperative groups that promote effective instruction? What are the similarities and differences in how grouping practices are used to support student learning at the elementary and secondary levels?

or tasks, such as the nature of the task and the processing demands on the individual. Students need to understand how they learn and process information so they can develop a plan for accomplishing a given learning task, monitor their comprehension when reading text, and evaluate their progress toward the completion of a task (Pintrich, 2002).

Instructional Techniques

For students to learn information from their content instruction, information must instead be presented in a meaningful way to aid memory (Schumaker & Deshler, 2006). Instructional techniques that promote meaningful associations of knowledge include clustering, elaboration, and mnemonic devices (Mastropieri & Scruggs, 2014; Schumaker & Deshler, 2006).

Clustering

Clustering involves categorizing information in a meaningful way. For example, when teaching about states, cluster the states according to the category of geographic region (New England states, West Coast states). Students have a better chance of learning the information when you (or they) reduce the amount of information to learn all at once and organize it in a meaningful way. Information can also be organized and presented in visual displays such as semantic maps and relationship displays (Vaughn & Bos, 2011). Examples of semantic maps and relationship displays are provided in Chapters 10 and 12.

Elaboration

Adding more details to facts to aid in memorization, retention, and recall constitutes elaboration. According to Mastropieri and Scruggs (2009), elaboration helps students remember information. Students can identify what they know about a topic to help them make elaborative sentences. Take the following list of animals: giraffe, elephant, lion, and leopard. Students might create the elaborative sentence "The giraffe and elephant fear the lion and leopard" to help them remember it.

Mnemonic Devices

These devices are techniques for aiding memory by forming meaningful associations and linkages across information that appears to be unrelated (Mastropieri & Scruggs, 2014). Mnemonic devices help students learn content-area vocabulary, memorize lists of factual information, and read multisyllabic words (Bryant & Bryant, 2003; Schumaker & Deshler, 2006).

The **keyword method** is one type of mnemonic device. It links information, such as a word, with response information, such as the word's definition (Schumaker & Deshler, 2006; Mastropieri & Scruggs, 2009). In Chapter 12, we discuss the keyword method as a technique to assist students in learning vocabulary meanings.

Acronyms and acrostics are mnemonic devices that aid in recalling lists of information. An **acronym** is a word made from the first letters of the words to be learned. For example, the acronym HOMES refers to the Great Lakes (Heron, Ontario, Michigan, Erie, and Superior). Students must learn and remember not only the acronym, HOMES, but also what each letter represents. An **acrostic** is a sentence wherein the first letters of the words stand for the items to be remembered *and* their correct order. For example, the first letters in "Every good boy deserves fudge" stand for the notes represented by the lines on a musical staff: E, G, B, D, F.

Mnemonic devices are techniques for aiding memory by forming meaningful associations and linkages across information that appears to be unrelated. How could mnemonic devices help these students memorize the planets in the solar system?

Critical Thinking

Critical thinking involves reasoning to learn new concepts, ideas, or problem solutions (Mastropieri & Scruggs, 2014). Examples of the use of critical thinking include reasoning about how to resolve a social issue, explaining the ending of a novel, determining how to solve a problem, and explaining historical events and their impact on society and the world. Students with learning needs may experience difficulties with critical thinking because they have not been taught how to think critically, they lack the prior knowledge and background that would help them understand issues, and their earlier instruction may have focused more on factual and procedural knowledge.

One way to ensure instruction is responsive to the need for critical thinking is to incorporate activities that tap domains of cognitive taxonomies that foster critical thinking (Anderson et al., 2001; Bloom, Engelhart, Furst, Hill, & Krathwohl, 1956). Table 7.2 provides helpful information about how to do so. It identifies and describes cognitive domains in column 1 (remembering, understanding, applying) and provides examples of verbs relevant to each domain in column 2. These can be translated into class assignments (column 3) and activities (column 4). Think about how you could design a lesson by incorporating activities addressing the various cognitive domains that promote critical thinking. It is easier to develop critical thinking skills by drawing from the higher order domains (numbers 3–6) on the list. However, these domains encompass knowledge taught through the lower order domains. So, there is a place in instruction for each domain.

Types of questions. Posing various types of questions can help students think critically about what they are learning. Students can demonstrate their knowledge about a topic by answering convergent questions. **Convergent, lower order questions** usually have one answer and start with *who*, *what*, or *when*.

TABLE 7.2 CRITICAL THINKING ACTIVITIES

Critical Thinking Activity (arranged lowest to highest)	Relevant Sample Verbs	Sample Assignments	Sample Sources or Activities
1. **Remembering** Retrieving, recognizing, and recalling relevant knowledge from long-term memory, for example, find out, learn terms, facts, methods, procedures, concepts.	Acquire, Define, Distinguish, Draw Find, Label, List, Match, Read, Record	1. Define each of these terms: encomienda, conquistador, gaucho 2. What was the *Amistad?*	Written records, films, videos, models, events, media, diagrams, books
2. **Understanding** Constructing meaning from oral, written, and graphic messages through interpreting, exemplifying, classifying, summarizing, inferring, comparing, and explaining. Understand uses and implications of terms, facts, methods, procedures, concepts.	Compare, Demonstrate, Differentiate, Fill in, Find, Group, Outline, Predict, Represent, Trace	1. Compare an invertebrate with a vertebrate. 2. Use a set of symbols and graphics to draw the water cycle.	Trends, consequences, tables, cartoons
3. **Applying** Carrying out or using a procedure through executing, or implementing. Make use of, apply practice theory, solve problems, use information in new situations.	Convert, Demonstrate, Differentiate between, Discover, Discuss, Examine, Experiment, Prepare, Produce, Record	1. Convert the following into a real-world problem: velocity = dist./time. 2. Experiment with batteries and bulbs to create circuits.	Collection of items, diary, photographs, sculpture, illustration
4. **Analyzing** Breaking material into constituent parts, determining how the parts relate to one another and to an overall structure or purpose through differentiating, organizing, and attributing. Take concepts apart, break them down, analyze structure, recognize assumptions and poor logic, evaluate relevancy.	Classify, Determine, Discriminate, Form generalizations, Put into categories, Illustrate, Select, Survey, Take apart, Transform	Illustrate examples of two earthquake types. Dissect a crayfish and examine the body parts.	Graph, survey, diagram, chart, questionnaire, report
5. **Evaluating** Making judgments based on criteria and standards through checking and critiquing. Set standards; judge using standards, evidence, rubrics; accept or reject on basis of criteria.	Argue, Award, Critique, Defend, Interpret, Judge, Measure, Select, Test, Verify	1. Defend or negate the statement: "Nature takes care of itself." 2. Judge the value of requiring students to take earth science.	Letters, group with discussion panel, court trial, survey, self-evaluation, value, allusions
6. **Creating** Putting elements together to form a coherent or functional whole; reorganizing elements into a new pattern or structure through generating, planning, or producing. Put things together, bring together various parts, write theme, present speech, plan experiment, put information together in a new and creative way.	Synthesize, Arrange, Blend, Create, Deduce, Devise, Organize, Plan, Present, Rearrange, Rewrite	1. Create a demonstration to show various chemical properties. 2. Devise a method to teach others about magnetism.	Article, radio show, video, puppet show, inventions, poetry, short story

SOURCE: Anderson et al. (2001).

Answers to these questions are essential to show student understanding about a topic. **Divergent, higher order questions** tap critical thinking skills because they require students to make inferences, to analyze or synthesize information, and to evaluate content. These questions may start with *What could happen . . . ? What if . . . ? What do you think caused . . . ? Why do you think . . . ?* or ask *How were the characters alike and different?* and *How could events be changed to affect the outcome?* Critical thinking must be developed through divergent questioning strategies and coaching. Consider how these types of questions relate to the cognitive domains. Table 7.3 provides examples of instructional techniques for different types of knowledge and critical thinking.

Stages of Learning

All learners experience stages of learning as they learn new skills. As an example, think about a young student learning how to ride a bike. She gets on the bike and starts to pedal, perhaps at first with a parent holding on to the seat to provide support and stability. Shakily, she peddles. As she builds confidence and learns balance, she is able to peddle on her own. She becomes a proficient bike rider, navigating tight areas and making turns with ease. As you read about the stages of learning, think about how this youngster learned to ride her bike.

Knowing about your students' stage of learning can help you plan instruction and make adaptations to accommodate all their learning needs. Researchers have shown that knowledge of students' stages of learning is important for selecting appropriate instructional interventions. For example, in two classic studies, Ayllon and Azrin (1964) and Hopkins (1968) learned that rewards are not always effective—there had to be some level of correct response before reinforcement could take place. In another classic study about the stages of learning, Smith and Lovitt (1976) found that students had to learn how to solve computational arithmetic problems before reinforcement was effective.

Acquisition stage of learning. In this stage, the learner may not know how to perform the skill, so the aim is for the individual to learn to perform it accurately. After a period of instruction, some learners demonstrate that they can perform the task or skill with 90% to 100% accuracy; at this point, they have passed through the acquisition stage of learning. Other students, such as those with special learning needs, may require further instruction and adaptations.

Proficiency stage of learning. In this stage, the aim is for the learner to perform the skills fluently; the focus is on accuracy and speed of responding. Examples of skills that should be learned proficiently are answering basic arithmetic facts, saying the letters of the alphabet, writing letters, and identifying instruments used in a science lab.

There are some very important reasons why proficient levels of performance are necessary goals. If students can write the letters of the alphabet correctly but too slowly, they will not be able to complete writing tasks in a timely manner and keep up with their peers. Writing a report and taking a spelling test are examples of skills that require proficiency in forming letters.

Computing basic facts accurately and quickly is another example; here, proficiency is important for more difficult skills such as multiplying multidigit problems. Students need to be able to perform many tasks fluently so they can work as proficiently but also as quickly as their peers. Students should be able to perform lower-level cognitive skills automatically so that more emphasis can be placed on those higher level skills (such as problem solving, comprehending text, and writing reports) that extend knowledge and learning.

Maintenance stage of learning. The goal for the maintenance stage is for the mastered skills to remain at the same performance level as during the proficiency stage. Retention of learning is important. For some students with special learning needs, this is a challenging stage because they may forget factual knowledge, rules, or procedures for solving different types of problems. When students do not retain information at the desired levels of performance, teachers must include in their planning instructional time for reviewing and evaluating what has been taught to promote maintenance of learning. An example is to teach multiplying by factors of 9 ($9 \times 3, 9 \times 2$) to mastery, such as computing 20 facts correctly in a minute, and then building into mathematics instruction 10 minutes every Friday to review all the mastered multiplication facts.

Generalization stage of learning. This stage means that the mastered skills should occur across all appropriate situations. For many students, skills learned in the classroom do not automatically occur in other settings, with other people, or with various materials without explicit instruction. For example, a student may learn a strategy in English class that helps in the writing process but does not apply the strategy in history class when asked to write a report. Another student may have demonstrated the ability to regroup when subtracting two digits minus one digit but may not be able to regroup when subtracting two digits minus two digits. For these students, generalization must be taught (see the classic paper by Stokes & Baer, 1977, for more information about teaching for generalization). In fact, some researchers (Schumaker & Deshler, 2006) recommend that the concept of generalization be introduced to students during the acquisition stage and specifically promoted following demonstration of skill mastery (when students have passed a quiz, for example). A good way to promote generalization during the acquisition stage is to ask students where they can use the new strategy in other classes. For instance, if they are going to be taught a writing strategy in English, they can identify other classes and situations in which they can use it.

Application stage of learning. The application stage requires the student to use learning and extend it to new situations. For example, students learn

TABLE 7.3 INSTRUCTIONAL TECHNIQUES FOR KNOWLEDGE AND CONCEPTS

Types of Knowledge and Critical Thinking	Instructional Techniques
Discrimination	Model how to identify the relevant features. For example, point out the lower part of the "b" and say that by adding a similar part to the top you make a "B." Small "b" is in big "B." Present a "d." Point out the lower part of the "d" and say that by adding a similar part to the top you do not make a big "B." So, "d" is not "b." Provide practice and error correction on discrimination activities. Prompt students if they require additional help making discriminations. For example, "Can you put a similar part on the top of 'b'?" What letter did you make? What letter is this 'b'?" Initially, teach letters, numbers, and sounds that are dissimilar; then introduce items that are similar and focus on the relevant distinguishing features. For example, a 3 only has one side compared to an 8. Put a line under 6 and 9 to help students distinguish where the circle part of the number appears.
Factual knowledge	Present information in categories rather than in long lists. Have students use visual displays to organize the factual knowledge. Reduce the amount of information to be learned. For instance, focus on multiplication facts ×7, then ×8, and finally ×9 before mixing the facts. Teach strategies to aid in remembering, such as counting strategies for math facts. Starting Big and Counting On and Counting Back are good strategies for specific facts (see Chapter 11). Provide concrete and pictorial examples of content-area factual knowledge. Show videos that depict the factual knowledge. Take field trips that focus on the information to be learned. Provide multiple opportunities for students to engage with content actively and in ways that aid memory associations (such as categorization, visual displays, and mnemonics; see Chapter 12).
Rules	Teach content knowledge and behavior rules. Have students repeat the rules. Provide examples of how the rules "look" in use and what happens when the rules are broken. Provide practice opportunities to help students recall the rules, especially at the beginning of the school year or after a break such as winter or spring break.
Procedural knowledge	Model using "think aloud" to demonstrate how to use a series of steps to solve a problem. Provide repetition and opportunities to practice each step. Chunk instruction so that students learn just a few steps at a time. Coach students through the use of the steps. Allow students to watch a peer use the steps.
Conceptual knowledge	Name and define the concept. Teach the critical and noncritical attributes of the concept. Have students find examples that illustrate the concept. Provide multiple examples of concepts. Provide nonexamples for students to discriminate from examples. Use concrete and pictorial examples. Have students explain in their own words the meaning of the concept. Have students keep a concepts dictionary.
Critical thinking	Ask divergent questions regularly to provide practice for thinking critically. Model how to answer divergent questions using factual and conceptual knowledge. Provide problem situations for student groups to work together to solve.

SOURCE: Adapted from Mastropieri and Scruggs (2014).

strategies for solving word problems. They then apply these strategies to real-life situations in which they have to solve problems such as determining how much money to take when going to a movie. Students need to be flexible as they apply their learning to new situations. Table 7.4 provides examples of teaching techniques for the stages of learning. Instructional Strategy 7.1 offers an illustration of how students progress through the stages of learning and how teaching techniques vary accordingly.

TABLE 7.4	EXAMPLES OF TEACHING TECHNIQUES FOR THE STAGES OF LEARNING
Stage of Learning	**Instructional Techniques**
Acquisition	1. Teach each subskill of a task analysis. 2. Pace the rate of instruction slower than the other stages. 3. Keep materials and types of responses consistent. 4. Use prompts and cues such as color, size, and verbal cues to focus student attention. 5. Use "think aloud" to show the steps. Have students imitate the process. 6. Teach the prerequisite skills for the tasks. 7. Tell what the response should look like. 8. Ask a question or show a fact, and provide wait time for a response. Shorten the wait time. 9. Provide multiple practice opportunities. 10. Focus on error correction; have students practice just the problems that need extra work.
Proficiency	1. Increase the pace of instruction. 2. Provide timed activities as appropriate (writing letters or numbers, naming information, computing facts). 3. Use reinforcement (praise, tokens) to reward increases in fluent responding. 4. Provide goals or benchmarks for students to achieve. 5. Graph weekly fluency scores.
Maintenance	1. Provide weekly, biweekly, and monthly reviews. 2. Provide reinforcement for accuracy. 3. Provide minilessons on parts of instruction not retained. 4. Assess cumulative knowledge regularly.
Generalization	1. Provide specific activities across environments, requiring students to generalize their learning. 2. Use role playing and think aloud to teach generalization. 3. Have students work with different people (peers, a paraprofessional) to practice skills. 4. Change the response mode from oral to written. 5. Change the materials, such as showing math facts vertically and horizontally.
Application	1. Provide situations for role-playing. 2. Give real-life problems that require the use of skills already taught.

Instructional Components

Research findings have identified specific instructional components that produce positive learning outcomes for students with special learning needs (Coyne, Kame'enui, & Carnine, 2011; Swanson & Deshler, 2003). These components are based on direct instruction and strategy instruction. **Direct instruction** is teacher directed and focuses on the teaching of skills using explicit, systematic procedures such as modeling, practice opportunities, pacing, error correction, and progress monitoring. **Strategy instruction** focuses on the process of learning by using *cognitive strategies* (steps for facilitating the learning process) and *metacognitive* (self-regulatory) cues (Wong, 1993). For example, cognitive strategies for comprehending material from a textbook include activating background knowledge, predicting, and paraphrasing; metacognitive strategies include asking, "Can I make connections between my background knowledge and what I am reading?" "Were my predictions accurate?" and "Does my paraphrase contain the most important information and is it in my own words?"

In a major classic study on the effectiveness of interventions to teach students with learning disabilities, Swanson et al. (1999) found using instructional components from direct and strategic instruction were the most effective. They labeled these instructional components as the combined model and suggested using the following instructional components when planning instruction.

- Sequencing: breaking down the task, providing step-by-step prompts

- Drill-repetition-practice: daily testing of skills, repeated practice

- Segmentation: breaking down skills into parts and then synthesizing the parts into a whole

- Directed questioning and responses: asking process or content questions of students

- Control of task difficulty: sequencing tasks from easy to difficult, teaching prerequisite skills

- Technology: delivering instruction via computer or presentation software

- Teacher-modeled problem solving: demonstrating processes or steps to solve a problem or explaining how to do a task

- Small group instruction: delivering instruction to a small group

- Strategy cues: reminding students to use strategies, modeling the "think aloud" technique

- Instructional Strategy 7.1 illustrates the different stages of learning for Marcus, who is learning how to solve word problems.

DELIVERING INSTRUCTION

Here we review several instructional steps and techniques designed to help all students access and master the curriculum. They include use of an advance organizer, presentation of information, practice, closure, and progress monitoring.

Advance Organizer

An **advance organizer** consists of activities to prepare students for the lesson's content (Lenz & Deshler, 2004; Schumaker & Deshler, 2006). Advance organizers tell students the purpose of the lesson (objectives), motivate students

STAGES OF LEARNING

Marcus is a fifth-grade student in Mrs. Bell's class identified as having a learning disability in mathematics. His IEP specified annual goals in mathematics, including solving word problems. Mrs. Bell gives a curriculum-based assessment to determine which types of word problems Marcus can solve and which types require instruction. Assessment data show zero percent accuracy for solving two-step word problems using whole-number computation. That is, Marcus is in the acquisition stage of learning for this skill. He can solve one-step word problems but does not generalize his knowledge to two-step problems.

Mrs. Bell uses explicit instruction to teach Marcus a strategy for solving two-step word problems. She discusses with him the importance of solving two-step problems, pointing out that problem solving is used in many daily activities (promoting the occurrence of generalization). Marcus continues to build fluency with basic facts because facts are part of the word problem calculations (proficiency stage for facts). It takes Marcus four days to reach mastery (90% accuracy) for learning how to solve two-step word problems using the strategy Mrs. Bell taught him. Mrs. Bell has Marcus work in a cooperative learning group with his peers to solve one-step (maintenance stage) and two-step (generalization stage) word problems. The group works together for a week, at which point she determines through curriculum-based assessment that the students can solve two-step problems proficiently. Mrs. Bell then has student groups write their own problems based on situations in the school, at home, or in the community (application stage). The groups share their problems so that different groups solve all the problems. She plans to provide periodic reviews (maintenance stage) of one- and two-step word problems to ensure continued mastery of the skills required for solving them.

by sparking their interest, and activate background knowledge by reviewing related information. Such a review helps students "warm up" for the lesson, promotes active responding, and provides teachers with information about students' current levels of understanding before new material is introduced. In planning advance organizers, teachers should consider their students' background knowledge, experience, and ability with prerequisite skills for the new task, the vocabulary to be learned, and the level of abstraction of the new learning (Price & Nelson, 2003). Examples of advance organizers include the following:

- Writing the objective on the board and explaining how it will be taught.

- Explaining the importance of learning the objective and asking students to provide examples of how they can use the new information.

- Providing an active technique such as role-playing, seeing a video clip, or taking a field trip before instruction.

- Having students map or tell what they know about the content to be studied.

- Providing a review of related information for students to make connections.

An advance organizer consists of activities to prepare students for the lesson's content. Here, students prepare for a lesson by watching an overview of the topic on a video.

Presentation of Subject Matter

In this step, teachers present instructional content related to the instructional objective, such as rules (spelling, phonics, mathematics), strategies (reading strategy, paragraph-writing strategy), and concepts (place value, science vocabulary, health). When presenting facts, rules, and procedures, teachers should *model,* or demonstrate, the correct responses and the appropriate thinking processes by using "think aloud." Students can imitate the modeled responses orally, in written form, or motorically (by manipulating objects). If students are in the acquisition stage of learning, modeling is particularly important.

Teachers can ask questions to promote discussion and engage students in the lesson. They should ask different types of questions (what, why, how) and provide sufficient wait time (3 or 4 seconds) between asking a question and calling on a student to answer it. Asking a question and then calling on a student by name maintains a moderate **level of concern,** which is student interest in the instruction, and promotes **on-task behavior,** which means students are working on the task that is assigned. Calling on a student by name first and then asking a question allows other students to tune out, so the level of concern and on-task time may be diminished.

Examples should be provided to illustrate new information, and nonexamples can help too. For instance, an example of democracy is the right to vote; a nonexample of democracy is being told who will control the government.

Finally, teachers should keep the instruction moving along so that students remain engaged in learning and to promote on-task behavior. Ideal pacing is demonstrated when the amount of content does not overwhelm and frustrate students (Coyne et al., 2011). Keeping up with other students is often a problem for students with special learning needs. Teachers can provide them with extra practice on chunks or smaller segments of information. For example, math facts can be chunked into segments (×6 facts, ×7 facts), vocabulary word lists can be segmented, and the number of questions to answer can be reduced.

Practice

We can think of practice in several ways. First, there is guided practice, which engages students in practicing what they have learned, usually under the teacher's direction, and checking their understanding. There are several techniques.

Students with special learning needs benefit from multiple opportunities to practice, or **massed practice;** active-participation activities can provide these opportunities. Active participation also promotes engaged time and on-task behavior. **Engaged time** is the amount of time students are actively learning. Students are making some type of response (oral, written, constructing) or exhibiting behavior (demonstrating eye contact, paying attention) that suggests they are paying attention, listening, and engaged. Figure 7.2 provides examples of active-participation activities for guided practice.

Checking for understanding (CFU) means periodically determining whether students are learning the content. For instance, CFU can be conducted after subject matter is presented or during guided practice. It is necessary to ensure that all students respond. Teachers can use the following techniques to check for student understanding (Price & Nelson, 2003):

- Present information that was taught (factual, rule, procedure) and ask students to show, by signaling thumbs up or thumbs down, whether the information is correct.
- Use response cards for students to indicate their response to the teacher's statement or question.
- Have students show their responses using materials such as manipulatives in math.
- Have students write their responses to be turned in for checking.
- Have students write their responses on white boards.

Error-correction procedures should be implemented to correct mistakes and to provide feedback, ensuring that students do not practice mistakes or learn information incorrectly. Error-correction procedures include stopping the student if an error is made, modeling the correct response, and having the student repeat the correct response.

FIGURE 7.2 EXAMPLES OF ACTIVE-PARTICIPATION ACTIVITIES

1. Use Jigsaw (Slavin, 1991) as a technique to engage all students in learning and sharing information (see the section on cooperative learning on page 289).

2. Use Think-Pair-Share-Write (students work with a partner to share their response to a question; students turn in their own written responses).

3. Use "Numbered Heads Together" (Kagan, 1990) (students in groups discuss the response to an answer; each student has a number; the teacher calls on one number to provide the answer). This works really well to review the meanings of concepts and terms.

4. Have students brainstorm responses to questions; call on students randomly to provide answers.

5. Require students to take notes.

6. Use peer pairs for practice (see the discussion of small groups in the section on grouping structures).

7. Have students find pictorial representations for content being learned (students can make time lines with significant events pictured or drawn along the time line).

8. Use response cards. Card 1 can be used when questions require a yes/no or true/false response. Words can be color-coded so that teachers can quickly scan the students to be sure the correct color (word) is displayed. Cards 2 and 3 are pinch cards. The teacher can present a definition and the student "pinches" the answer (puts thumb and forefinger next to the answer). Students should be told, "Hold your response card at chest level. I will give you a question (or definition). I will say 'think,' and then you show me. Hold up your card with the correct answer or pinch the correct answer."

| **Card 1**
 Yes/No or
 True/False Card

 Yes
 True

 No
 False | **Card 2**
 Pinch Card
 Rectangle

 • Pyramid
 • Cylinder
 • Isosceles trapezoid
 • Parallelogram
 • Triangle | **Card 3**
 Pinch Card

 • Length
 • Area
 • Volume
 • Perimeter |

Questioning continues to be an important instructional technique to monitor student comprehension of the instructional objectives. Teachers can also use the Response-Dependent Questioning Strategy, which has remained viable for years, shown in Table 7.5, to help students arrive at the correct answer to a question.

Independent practice is a type of practice that occurs in the classroom or as homework and implies that students have demonstrated a good understanding of the skill (as determined during progress monitoring) and are ready for activities that do not require direct teacher supervision or guidance. For example, students can practice in small groups or independently at their desks. They can also be assigned homework as another opportunity for practice. Independent practice activities should be related directly to the instructional objective introduced during the presentation of information, and students can be capable of high

TABLE 7.5	RESPONSE-DEPENDENT QUESTIONING STRATEGY		
Steps	**Questioning Strategy**	**Example**	**Response**
Step 1: Opening Question	Teacher asks question about subject being presented.	*Example:* Asks student to make the sound of the digraph EE.	*Response:* Student makes correct sound; if incorrect, proceed to Step 2.
Step 2: Constructed Response	Teacher seeks correct response by prompting student to focus on specific knowledge or information from which a correct response can be constructed.	*Example:* Think about the rule we have learned for two vowels together.	*Response:* Student makes correct sound; if incorrect, proceed to Step 3.
Step 3: Multiple Choice	Teacher provides choice of two responses; one of the responses is correct.	*Example:* Is the sound "ee" (makes long "e" sound) or "e" (makes short "e" sound)?	*Response:* Student selects correct sound; if incorrect, proceed to Step 4.
Step 4: Restricted Alternative	Teacher eliminates the incorrect response from Step 3 but does not provide the answer.	*Example:* EE (points to letters on chalkboard) does not make the "e" (makes short "e" sound) sound. What is the correct sound of EE?	*Response:* Student provides correct response; if incorrect, proceed to Step 5.
Step 5: Complete Model	Teacher provides correct response.	*Example:* Teacher points to EE on chalkboard and makes "ee" sound.	*Response:* Student imitates correct response.

SOURCE: Adapted from Stowitschek, Stowitschek, Hendrickson, and Day (1984).

levels of success working independently. **Distributive practice**, which is practice opportunities presented over time on skills that have been taught, ensures that students continue to get some level of practice (in the maintenance stage of learning, for example) so their learning of new skills remains intact. Distributive practice on taught skills can be done during independent practice and as part of homework.

Closure

During closure, which occurs at the end of a lesson and may take only a few minutes, teachers and students review the instructional objective, review the lesson's activity, relate learning to other contexts, and discuss follow-up plans. Closure activities can be brief, but they are an important part of the lesson and need to be considered when time is allotted for instructional planning.

Progress Monitoring

In **progress monitoring**, teachers must evaluate students' understanding of the lesson and their ability to perform the skill. We discuss progress monitoring in Chapter 8 and provide examples of this important instructional step throughout the remaining chapters.

INSTRUCTIONAL STEPS

Ms. Mendez is teaching a new unit on global warming. She spent several days one week probing her students' knowledge about the concept to determine what they already know from media coverage. She determines her students' stage of learning by assessing overall student performance on key vocabulary and important ideas pertaining to causes and effects and solutions to problems. On the basis of her assessment information, Ms. Mendez decides to use explicit instruction to teach key vocabulary as the beginning of her unit on global warming.

ADVANCE ORGANIZER

Ms. Mendez tells the students the purpose of instruction. She has them work with a partner to write down their ideas about the meaning of global warming. After several partner pairs share their ideas, which she puts on the chalkboard, she presents five key vocabulary words and explains that to learn more about global warming, they must understand the meanings of these words.

PRESENTATION OF INFORMATION

Ms. Mendez reads the list of five words and their definitions, which are presented in two columns and projected for the entire class to see. She covers up one column (the definitions column). She reads one of the words and asks students to state the definition. She reveals the definitions column and covers up the other column (vocabulary words). She has a student read one of the definitions and asks another student to state the word. Next, she uses one word in a sentence and then asks students for examples of the other words in sentences.

PRACTICE

Ms. Mendez has the students stand. With the list of words and definitions concealed, she says a word and gently tosses a Koosh ball to one student, who must define the word. Having defined the word, the student returns the Koosh ball to Ms. Mendez, who repeats this process with the remaining words and different students. She provides error correction for any student who is unable to define the word by showing the definition. She also uses this procedure for saying a definition and asking students to supply the word.

Next, she has students work with a partner to match the words and definitions. She gives each pair two envelopes, one with the words and another with the definitions, for them to match. After the timer sounds, each pair turns to a neighboring pair to share their matches.

Finally, Ms. Mendez gives the students a passage about global warming that contains the new words. She asks them to underline the words and to explain how the words are used in the sentences.

CLOSURE

At the end of the lesson, Ms. Mendez asks students to explain the purpose of the lesson and what they learned. She describes the activities in the unit on global warming that the students will complete over the next few weeks.

PROGRESS MONITORING

Ms. Mendez gives the students a matching exercise to check their accuracy in selecting the definitions. She also has them use the new words in sentences.

The instructional steps are illustrated in Instructional Strategy 7.2 with an example regarding Ms. Mendez's science instruction.

Table 7.6 offers questions to help teachers reflect on their practices during the steps.

TABLE 7.6   REFLECTIVE QUESTIONS TO GUIDE INSTRUCTIONAL DECISION MAKING

Instructional Step	Reflective Questions
Advance Organizer	• Do I have the students' attention? • Is the instructional objective stated specifically? • Do students appear to be interested in the lesson? • Is there sufficient review of background or related content? • Is there vocabulary that needs to be reviewed? • Are students making connections across skills?
Presentation of Information	• Are students comprehending the lesson? • Is modeling effective? • Do I need to provide more examples? • Do students understand after error correction?
Guided Practice	• Are all students engaged actively in learning? Do I need to provide more examples? • Are more practice opportunities necessary? Do I need to give more prompts? • Do students understand after error correction? Is the grouping practice effective for instruction? • Are there vocabulary words that require further instruction? • Are the instructional materials and textbooks appropriate? • Are the practice opportunities appropriate?
Independent Practice (can also be homework)	• Are students ready for independent practice? • Is the grouping practice effective in promoting practice on the instructional objective? • Are students capable of completing activities independently? • Are students achieving high levels of accuracy on independent practice activities? • Am I providing feedback for activities?
Closure	• Do I allow enough time for closure? • Do all or most of the students have opportunities to engage in closure activities? • Do I still have students who do not understand the instructional objective? • Are students able to relate the lesson's objective to other learning?
Progress Monitoring	• Have students demonstrated mastery of the skill presented in the lesson? • Do I need to reteach or model the skill? Was my instructional intervention effective? • Is the skill appropriate for students? • Do I need to task-analyze the skill further to meet individual needs of students?

HOW CAN INSTRUCTIONAL GROUPING PRACTICES PROMOTE EFFECTIVE INSTRUCTION?

There are a variety of instructional grouping practices, including whole group instruction, flexible small groups, and one-to-one teaching. Peer tutoring is another grouping practice that supports students who can benefit from more opportunities to practice their skills. Finally, teachers have used cooperative learning structures for years to enrich practice in student-centered instruction. Consider how to use these practices when planning and delivering instruction.

INSTRUCTIONAL GROUPING PRACTICES

Whole Group Instruction

In whole group instruction, the teacher presents a lesson to the entire class. This grouping practice works well where common instructional objectives are identified, the teacher delivers the lesson, and students respond orally or in writing. Whole group instruction is often chosen to teach content-area subjects, such as science, social studies, and health, and it is common at the secondary level. Examples of activities for whole groups include direct, explicit instruction on new information (vocabulary, rules, concepts), read-alouds, and presentations.

Researchers have shown that whole group instruction can be effective for students of varying abilities (Gersten, Carnine, & Woodward, 1987). It allows them to hear responses from peers, and it also lets the teacher pace instruction to maintain academic engaged time and work individually with students following instruction. The disadvantages include limited error correction, which is problematic for students with special learning needs, a pace that may be too fast for some, and the use of instructional objectives that may not be appropriate for everyone. Teachers must be sure the objectives are appropriate for most of the students and allocate time for those who require further individualized instruction.

Flexible Small Groups

Flexible small groups consist of three to five students and can include those of the same or different abilities. The purpose varies according to instructional level and students' individual needs.

Same-Ability Groups

Identified through assessment, all the students in **same-ability groups** are performing comparably on a particular skill and require extra or accelerated instruction. For struggling students, extra practice on curricular objectives is often necessary. For students who are high achieving, gifted, or talented, same-ability groups can provide enrichment activities.

Research supports the efficacy of this grouping practice. Small group instruction yields better academic outcomes for students with disabilities than whole group instruction (Schumm, Moody, & Vaughn, 2000; Vaughn, Hughes, Moody, & Elbaum, 2001). Its major advantage is the opportunity to provide students with more modeling, prompting, and error correction, and pacing better tai-

VIDEO CASE 7.2

Working in Groups

1. What instructional grouping practices do the teachers in the video suggest in order to promote effective instruction? What practices help older and younger students to work collaboratively in small groups or pairs? How are these practices used to support student learning throughout the video?

2. What are the benefits of having older students assist younger students? What are the benefits of having students of the same age work cooperatively together? Describe how both of these effective instructional practices are used within the video.

Students performing at varying levels both academically and socially can learn from one another in mixed-ability groups.

lored to their individual needs than in whole group instruction. The challenge is to ensure that the rest of the class is actively engaged in meaningful tasks. Having backup tasks ready for those students who require teacher assistance when it is not available, and for those who finish their tasks before small group instruction concludes, can help ensure that all students are actively learning.

Mixed-Ability Groups

This instructional grouping practice consists of students, identified through assessment, who are performing at various levels on skills. This grouping practice can allow students to work on projects and to make presentations. The advantage is that they can learn from each other. Little evidence exists that **mixed-ability groups** adversely affect the learning of students who are gifted and talented (Tieso, 2005).

One-to-One Teaching

In one-to-one groupings, teachers provide instruction to individual students on the basis of their specific learning and behavioral needs. For example, a student may need prompts, feedback, or directions to begin working on or mastering an instructional objective. A student's behavior may warrant individualized instruction away from other students in the classroom. Tutorial assistance might be necessary when preparing for an exam in a content-area class, or individualized assistance might be necessary to correct errors on a homework assignment.

One-to-one instruction has been shown to help students avoid frustration and cope with instructional demands. The advantage is that individual students receive assistance that promotes their learning. On the other hand, teachers must plan tasks so other students are engaged as well. Furthermore, one-to-one instruction may not be easy to achieve in general education classrooms because of the number of students and time constraints.

PEER TUTORING

Peer tutoring is an instructional grouping practice wherein pairs of students work on assigned skills, usually for extra practice. Peer tutoring models that have remained viable instructional grouping practices include Classwide Peer Tutoring (Delquadri, Greenwood, Whorton, Carta, & Hall, 1986) and Peer-Assisted Learning Strategies (PALS; Fuchs, Fuchs, Mathes, & Simmons, 1997). Research on peer tutoring models has shown that peer tutoring can improve the academic achievement of tutees as well as increase the amount of time students spend on school tasks (Heron, Villareal, Yao, Christianson, & Heron,

2006). Based on years of research, peer tutoring has been shown to increase active student involvement and students' opportunities to respond, review, and practice skills and concepts.

In peer tutoring, there is a tutor-tutee relationship, which consists of instruction and feedback to provide efficient teaching to students with disabilities and students who are at risk for academic difficulties (Heron et al., 2006). In reading, for example, a higher performing peer can be paired with a student who is reading at a somewhat lower level and needs additional instructional support. The partners take turns serving as reading coach and reader. The reading coach reads the designated reading passage for a short time period; the reader then reads the same passage for the same time period. The partners provide error correction as needed and praise for good reading. Often this passage reading is followed by comprehension questions. These same procedures can be applied in mathematics, vocabulary development, and spelling.

The advantages of this grouping practice include the opportunity for students to develop academic skills, form cooperative relationships, and gain extra instructional support for learning and behavioral problems. Among the challenges are allocating time to teach tutors their role responsibilities, matching students appropriately, monitoring the pairs, and assessing progress. Moreover, there is a group of students with disabilities who do not necessarily benefit from the peer tutoring model in reading (McMaster, Fuchs, & Fuchs, 2006). Students whose reading skills are significantly lower than the rest of the class likely will require explicit, systematic instruction.

COOPERATIVE LEARNING

Cooperative learning allows mixed-ability small groups to focus on academic and social skills. According to some of the pioneer researchers on cooperative learning, the purposes of this type of learning are for students to work collaboratively to achieve common academic and social goals and to be accountable to the team for their individual efforts (Johnson, Johnson, & Holubec, 1994).

Extensive research on cooperative learning has been conducted in various academic areas (mathematics, reading, social studies) with students who have disabilities, students who are typically achieving, and students who come from diverse backgrounds. In most cases, a classic review of the research literature showed that students tend to derive academic and social skills benefits from this instructional arrangement (Slavin, 1991).

Several models of cooperative learning are popular in classrooms. The techniques share similar characteristics: group academic and social goals, arrangement of heterogeneous student groups, task structure, cooperation, and individual and group accountability. Table 7.7 provides information about cooperative learning models.

Differentiate
Your Grouping

TABLE 7.7 SELECTED MODELS OF COOPERATIVE LEARNING

	Teams–Games–Tournaments	Learning Together	Jigsaw
Steps	1. Teacher presents material to be studied. 2. Students work in teams to learn material. 3. Students compete in tournament games with peers of similar ability, answering questions about the material practiced in teams. 4. Points are awarded on the basis of performance in tournaments. 5. Team (original cooperative learning team) scores are obtained from points that members accrue in tournament games. 6. Team standings are announced weekly.	1. Teacher explains academic task, cooperative goal structure, and criteria for success to group teams. 2. Students are responsible for learning material and making sure group members learn material as well. 3. Students provide encouragement and assistance to team members. 4. Teacher monitors group work and intervenes to provide task assistance or teach collaborative skills. 5. Student work and group functioning are evaluated. 6. Students are arranged to promote face-to-face interaction. 7. Teams construct one group product.	1. Teaching material is divided into parts and assigned to group members. 2. Students learn how to communicate with and tutor other students. 3. Subgroups of students with the same material meet, learn, and then share their material with the original team members. 4. All members of the team must learn all parts of the material. 5. Teachers monitor groups, providing assistance, encouragement, and direction.
Goals	1. Students learn academic material. 2. Students help team members learn material.	1. There is an academic task goal. 2. There is a cooperative/collaborative/social goal.	1. Students learn a part of the material and then teach this to other team members.
Student Groups	1. They are heterogeneous, diverse groups. 2. There are four to five students per team. 3. Everyone must learn concepts.	1. They are heterogeneous, diverse groups. 2. There are two to six students per team.	1. They are heterogeneous, diverse groups. 2. There are four to seven students per team.
Task Structure	1. There is group-paced instruction. 2. Teams work together to study material.	1. There is group-paced instruction. 2. Teams work together to study topic/concept/material/problem—"We all sink or swim together." 3. Everyone must learn concepts and participate. 4. Student roles may be assigned. 5. Only limited materials are provided, thus necessitating interdependence.	1. The structure is cooperative/interdependent. 2. Students learn a section of material pertaining to a topic and then teach that material to group members.

	Teams–Games–Tournaments	Learning Together	Jigsaw
Cooperation	1. Students help each other to learn material so members will do well in tournaments.	1. Students help each other learn material. 2. Students demonstrate collaborative/social group skills (e.g., providing feedback, elaborating, sharing, staying on task, doing one's share of the work).	1. All students must work together to learn all the material on a topic.
Accountability/ Evaluation	1. Everyone is responsible for his or her own learning. 2. Everyone is responsible for ensuring that other team members learn concepts. 3. Each member's tournament contributes to a group score.	1. Everyone is responsible for his or her own learning. 2. Everyone is responsible for ensuring that other team members learn concepts. 3. Members may be asked to explain group answers, take a test, or edit another person's work.	1. All students are accountable for learning all the material.
Group Processing		1. Group members evaluate their ability to work as a team according to set criteria at the conclusion of their work. 2. Group members determine group skills that should be worked on to promote better collaboration.	

In preparing for cooperative learning, consider the following questions:

- What are the academic and social skills objectives?
- What task or activity structure can be used to teach the objectives?
- How can the elements of cooperative learning be promoted?
- How will student groups be formed?
- What environmental factors must be considered?
- What management techniques will be used?
- What is the teacher's role during group activities?
- How will individual and group progress with instructional objectives be monitored?
- What difficulties might students with special needs encounter in cooperative learning groups?

Findings from the review of the research literature identified advantages of cooperative learning. First, there are opportunities for students to work together toward common goals, thus necessitating some degree of collaborative behavior. Second, group work requires verbal interactions, creating opportunities to develop language skills. Third, cooperative learning means students, rather than teachers, are responsible for solving problems. Fourth, it promotes social interactions and peer acceptance (Slavin, 1991).

Cooperative learning activities require extensive planning and preparation. Teachers must ensure that all students—regardless of their group assignment—participate fully. The bulk of the work should not fall on the shoulders of only a few students. Finally, teachers must be sure students are capable of performing instructional objectives successfully with group members and individually. The Working Together feature shows how professionals can collaborate to determine how to differentiate content, instructional approach, grouping, and materials for students who are having difficulties—in this case, during a mathematics lesson.

WORKING *together*

COLLABORATING TO DIFFERENTIATE INSTRUCTION

Mrs. Bell is teaching her fifth-grade students different ways to represent fractions and wants them to compare and order fractions according to fractional parts. She provides a review of different fractions and key vocabulary. Mr. Rivera, the math specialist, has encouraged the classroom teachers to provide students with number lines and fraction strips to represent fractional parts, so Mrs. Bell has incorporated these into her instructional practice. She has the students work in small, mixed-ability groups to compare and order fractions before they apply this factual knowledge to problem solving. Ms. Chavez, the special education inclusion teacher, works with the students with mathematics learning disabilities to provide more specialized instruction on fractions. As Mrs. Bell circulates among the small groups, she listens to group discussions and notices that several students seem confused. She sits with them and asks questions to check their understanding of the assignment, the vocabulary, and the use of the number lines and fractions strips for comparing and ordering fractions. She decides to model the procedure once more and watches students complete the next example; she also provides error correction as needed. She instructs the students to complete the next few problems as she circulates among the other groups and makes notes about student progress in her assessment notebook. During the fifth-grade teachers' planning period, Mrs. Bell, the other two fifth-grade teachers, Mr. Rivera, and Ms. Chavez discuss the progress monitoring data from the fractions lessons. They discuss how Mr. Rivera and Ms. Chavez can help students who are struggling during mathematics instruction and support the teachers. Having Ms. Chavez working with struggling students in small groups and Mr. Rivera providing tips for effective

Promoting
Effective Grouping

instruction on fractions are viewed by the fifth-grade teachers as effective collaborative practices for now. The teachers have agreed to stagger their math instruction time so that Ms. Chavez can work in all of the classes.

QUESTIONS TO CONSIDER

1. How can Mr. Rivera help Mrs. Bell better understand the difficulties struggling students are having learning fractions?

2. What cooperative learning model can Mrs. Bell and Ms. Chavez use to maximize Ms. Chavez's support of struggling students?

3. How can Mr. Rivera and Mrs. Bell team-teach a lesson on fractions?

WHAT GUIDELINES SHOULD BE FOLLOWED FOR TEXTBOOKS AND INSTRUCTIONAL MATERIALS?

TEXTBOOKS

Basals are textbooks usually adopted by school districts to serve as a primary source for subject-area content. They are a good source of instructional content but often raise challenges for struggling students:

- The reading level of the textbook probably exceeds the ability of the student with reading difficulties. For students to benefit from reading a textbook, the material should be at their **instructional reading level,** the level at which they have 90% to 94% word recognition and 90% to 100% comprehension.

- The organization or structure of the text content may be hard for students with reading difficulties to follow. The text may lack, or the student may not be familiar with, key words that signal different types of text organization (cause/effect, compare/contrast). Recognizing how text content is organized helps readers comprehend the material.

- Basals usually do not include enough direct, explicit instruction to help struggling students learn content. For example, there may not be sufficient practice opportunities or examples.

In Chapter 10, we provide additional information about textbooks for students with reading difficulties. In Chapter 12, we offer suggestions for selecting and using content-area textbooks with struggling readers, especially at the secondary level.

INSTRUCTIONAL MATERIALS

Guidelines for selecting and using instructional materials should address (a) the student and (b) the content and methodology.

Student

- What are the student's present levels of educational performance?
- Can the instructional material be used to meet IEP goals?
- Does the student seem to be motivated to accomplish tasks and under what conditions?
- Does the student remain focused and persist with tasks? When does the student appear to lose focus and persistence?

Teachers can consult the IEP to identify a student's reading level as they make decisions about the need to adapt instructional materials that require the ability to read. They can also identify a student's reading level by conducting an informal reading inventory, discussed in Chapter 8. Finally, it's important to determine a student's interest in content and materials and identify where in the learning process the student stops trying. Motivation is a key ingredient of successful learning, and knowing their students' level of persistence helps teachers understand learners' needs more fully.

Instructional Content and Methodology

- Is the content age-appropriate?
- Does the content address state standards and core curriculum?
- Does the instructional material specify a sequence of skills?
- Is information about teaching strategies included?
- Are there sufficient opportunities for practicing new skills?
- Are generalization and maintenance activities included?

Age-appropriateness of instructional materials is a primary concern in the selection process. For example, high-interest/controlled vocabulary materials can be used with older students who have limited reading vocabularies. These materials focus on topics that appeal to older students, such as current events, sports, and entertainment personalities, yet are written with grade-specific vocabulary to take into account limited word recognition and reading abilities. Equally important is the relationship between the materials and the curricular expectations from the school district and state. Teachers are held highly accountable through state assessments to teach the content on which students will be assessed, so materials selected for instruction must reflect this content, which has been specified as appropriate for all students.

Teachers can adopt a sequence for teaching skills and then be sure the instructional materials match this sequence. For example, if math instruction focuses on addition facts (6 + 9, 7 + 3), then the instructional material should include problems that match this skill. Subtraction math facts should not be included. The next skill in the sequence may include subtraction math facts and materials that focus on these types of problems.

Instructional materials might include review activities (for maintenance), teaching strategies, practice opportunities, and enrichment activities (for generalization purposes). Teachers must examine the materials to determine how the instructional material can best be used in a lesson and what adaptations are needed, if any.

Very often, teachers need to modify instructional materials to meet an individual learner's needs. Some instructional materials offer suggestions, such as extension exercises or alternative methodologies. Other adaptations might include adding more practice options, using only portions of the material, rewording complex directions, and breaking instructional components down into smaller instructional activities.

ADAPTATIONS FOR CURRICULAR MATERIALS

Textbooks and instructional materials are important components of instruction and must be selected wisely. Textbooks may be assigned to teachers, but those teachers must still analyze them critically to see what difficulties students might encounter when reading the material. Instructional materials are used when concepts are first presented, during guided practice, and as part of independent practice activities. For example, students can use math manipulatives as part of place value instruction, complete reading comprehension sheets during independent seatwork, or use a scale as part of a cooperative learning activity on measurement. These materials must also be chosen carefully to augment instruction. Table 7.8 provides examples of ways to adapt instructional materials.

WHAT ARE ASSISTIVE TECHNOLOGY DEVICES AND SERVICES FOR PROMOTING ACCESS TO THE GENERAL EDUCATION CURRICULUM?

Advances in technology have benefited most of society, but it could be argued that for people with disabilities, technology has provided a means to an end, which is independence. Assistive technology (AT) allows students access to the curriculum in inclusive settings and environments at school. By focusing on an individual's functional capability, it promotes independence for students with disabilities by enabling them to communicate and socialize with their peers; participate across settings such as the playground, classroom, cafeteria, and library; and demonstrate their learning of the curriculum. **Functional capability** refers to those abilities—such

| TABLE 7.8 | EXAMPLES OF ADAPTATIONS FOR INSTRUCTIONAL MATERIALS |

Task/Instructional Materials	Student Struggles or Challenges	Material Adaptation
Reading directions or instructions/workbooks, worksheets	Reading or understanding written directions or instructions	Have students underline important words (circle, underline, draw). Rewrite directions or instructions using easier words. Explain the directions or instructions to the student. Say, "Tell me what you need to do first." "What do you need to do next?" Reduce the number of directions or instructions.
Reading books and word lists/textbooks, literature	Reading words	Put the text on tape for the student to listen to the reading (electronic books). Use high-interest/low-vocabulary materials.
Comprehending text	Comprehending material	Provide graphic organizers (see Chapters 10 and 12). Provide questions for students to answer after reading a few paragraphs.
Completing worksheets	Completing items on worksheets	Provide more time. Reduce the number of items. Reformat using borders to separate important information. Use color to highlight important information.
Reading text or worksheets	Seeing the material	Enlarge font size. Use a font that has simple lettering. Provide a magnifier. Use screen magnification software (see the following section on assistive technology). Use color. Contrast the foreground with the background.
Computing mathematical problems using workbooks or worksheets	Identifying symbols (=, +, ×).	Have students circle the symbol and state its meaning. Have students highlight the symbol with color before proceeding. Provide a cue sheet with the symbols and their meaning. Enlarge the font size of symbols to make them more readily visible.

as vision, hearing, communication, mobility, cognition, and motor control—that are used to help individuals compensate for struggles that are disability related. For example, an individual who has good hearing but is blind might want to read a chapter in a textbook. Listening to the chapter in an electronic book provides access to that material. When selecting AT devices, *we focus on strengths* to select devices that help individuals access their environments.

ASSISTIVE TECHNOLOGY DEVICES

An **assistive technology device** is the unit itself, which can be an item (a Hoover cane to help a person who is blind with mobility), a piece of equipment (a motorized wheelchair to help an individual with physical disabilities move about), or a product system (a computer with speech output software that reads the text on the screen). The intent is to promote access and independence for individuals with disabilities by enhancing their functioning. Therefore, an assistive technology device is anything bought or made that helps a person with a disability accomplish tasks that would otherwise be difficult or impossible (Bryant & Bryant, 2003).

AT devices can be viewed along a continuum from low-tech to high-tech. Most of us identify as "high-tech" those devices that are usually electronic. Computers with their multiple capabilities, talking calculators, electronic books, screen reader and voice recognition software, and powered wheelchairs fall at the "high-tech" end of the continuum. Grips for pencils, different font sizes for text, a grab bar in the shower, and a magnifier are at the "low-tech" end. Thus, for a student who has a mathematics learning disability (LD), a calculator may be identified in the IEP as an AT device to help the student compute basic facts when solving word problems. For students who do not have a math LD and who use calculators to check their arithmetic, the calculator is an instructional material rather than an AT device.

Assistive technology service was defined by the Tech Act as "any service that directly assists an individual with a disability in the selection, acquisition, or use of an assistive technology device" (Assistive Technology Act of 2004). Services include the following:

- Purchasing and/or leasing AT
- Selecting, designing, and fitting AT
- Coordinating and using other therapies or interventions
- Training or providing technical assistance for an individual with disabilities or the family
- Training or providing technical assistance for a professional

How are the terms *assistive technology device* and *assistive technology service* related? The answer is simply that they go together. A device of some sort (such as a wheelchair, a computer, a Braille text, or an FM listening system) may be necessary for a person with a disability to meet challenges related to impaired mobility, cognitive function, or sensory function. But the services associated with such assistive technology devices must also be carefully considered. How will the device be purchased? Who will assess whether the device and the person are a good match? Who will train the student to utilize the device properly? How will teachers, other professionals, family members, and

Importance of
Assistive Technology

others with whom the AT user interacts learn how to provide personal and educational supports, in and out of the classroom? And how will these people and their services be coordinated? These questions must be answered successfully for devices and services to be effective.

For more information about assistive technology devices and services to support students' special learning needs, refer to http://www.closingthegap.com. Tech Notes, below, provides information about Dragon Dictate, which is voice recognition software and will be used by Mrs. Bell to help Paul write in his electronic reading journal.

We can group AT devices into categories that reflect their purpose and function. These categories include positioning and seating, mobility, communication, adaptive toys and games, adaptive environments, computer use, and instructional aids (Bryant & Bryant, 2003).

Positioning and seating devices encourage the best posture and seating arrangement for a particular function and time period. Students might move from one place to another using a wheelchair, sit during conversation and instruction, and have help while eating. Physical and occupational therapists are key professionals who work with positioning.

Mobility is the act of movement. When most people think of mobility AT devices, they think of wheelchairs, but mobility devices also include scooter boards, vehicular modifications, and white canes. Rehabilitation engineers, physical therapists, and orientation and mobility specialists are important team members with whom to discuss mobility issues.

Communication devices help people compensate for expressive language (speaking) difficulties by focusing on their capabilities to understand language and to convey their thoughts, ideas, and needs. **Augmentative and alternative**

TECH *notes*

DRAGON DICTATE

Dragon Dictate is a voice input and voice output program for Mac users. Individuals with upper extremity or vision disabilities, LD, or spinal cord injury are the target groups for this software. It provides a hands-free operation, so individuals can speak naturally and control applications with voice commands to move the cursor or click on the screen. The software was designed to enable writing, editing, and proofreading capabilities. It includes recognition training so that the software can learn how the user speaks and comes with a USB headset microphone and Bluetooth wireless capabilities (manufacturer: Nuance Communications, Inc., http://www.nuance.com).

communication (aug com) devices are included in the communication category. Aug com devices can supplement vocalizations when speech is not understood by a particular communication partner and can provide a way for an individual to speak. The speech/language pathologist is a key member of the IEP team when aug com decisions are to be made.

Adaptive toys and games (recreation) give children with disabilities an opportunity to play with toys and games to help them develop cognitive skills and to socialize with their peers. They might include devices with a sound so children who are blind can discriminate among them. Game board markers might have large tops so children with motor problems can grasp and hold them. Early childhood specialists work with assistive technologists and occupational therapists to design features that enable all students to interact with toys and games.

Adaptive environments (control of the environment) are devices and approaches that enable a person to manipulate the environment to allow for daily living, working, schooling, playing, and so forth. For instance, remote control units can be used to turn lights on and off, respond to the doorbell, open doors, or turn a computer on and off in the home, school, or workplace. In the classroom, something as simple as widening aisles can enhance mobility for a student who uses a motorized wheelchair. Other adaptive environment devices include curb cuts; Braille words for restroom, elevator, and room numbers; grab bars in showers; and automatic door openers. Occupational therapists help make decisions about ways to adapt the environment.

Computer access devices include keyboard overlays (templates that lie on the keyboard to define the key space for responding), pointers, and screen reader and voice recognition software. For example, by using voice recognition software, a student whose upper body control is limited but whose speech is a "functional capability" can speak into a microphone and tell the computer what functions to employ. For people who are blind and whose hearing is a "functional capability," alternative output devices for computer use, such as screen reader software, are necessary. Screen reader software reads the text displayed on the computer screen. Educators, occupational therapists, and rehabilitation specialists typically assist with computer access.

Finally, instructional aids provide access to the curriculum, instruction, and instructional materials. Access to information can come via a screen reader program that allows access to the World Wide Web for research for a student who is blind, and remediation can come from math or reading instructional software.

Instructional software can provide students with extra practice on academic and problem-solving skills. However, students must continue to receive instruction from the classroom teacher.

Figure 7.3 provides guidelines for evaluating and selecting instructional apps and software.

FIGURE 7.3 GUIDELINES FOR SOFTWARE AND APPS EVALUATION AND SELECTION

A. Basic Information

Name of software or app _____

Publisher _____ Cost _____

Hardware/mobile device requirements _____

B. Description

Grade level(s) _____ Reading level of text (if applicable) _____

Instructional area(s) _____

Purpose _____

Type: _____ Tutorial _____ Drill and practice _____ Simulation _____ Game

Instructional Objectives _____ yes _____ no

List objectives if stated _____

How is information presented? (check all that apply) _____ Speech _____ Music

_____ Graphics (pictures) _____ Text (words) _____ Animation

How do the visuals look? (check all that apply) _____ Screen is too busy

_____ Graphics enhance, rather than distract from, purpose _____ Print is legible

_____ Print size age-appropriate

What is the quality of the sound? (check all that apply)

_____ Sound is clear/audible _____ Speech is audible _____ Sound is distracting _____ Rate of speech is appropriate

C. Instructional Design

Directions are clear, easy to read, and short _____ yes _____ no

Examples or models are provided _____ yes _____ no

Pacing is appropriate _____ yes _____ no

Practice opportunities are provided _____ yes _____ no

Error correction is provided _____ yes _____ no

Difficulty level can be individualized _____ yes _____ no

Reinforcement (visual and/or auditory) is present _____ yes _____ no

A recordkeeping/evaluation option is available _____ yes _____ no

D. Content

Appropriate to stated objectives _____ yes _____ no

Factual and accurate _____ yes _____ no

Free of gender, cultural, or racial bias _____ yes _____ no

Relates to school's curriculum _____ yes _____ no

Relates to student's IEP _____ yes _____ no

E. Technical Considerations

User Demands (respond to any that apply) Academic _____

Physical/motor _____

Computer or mobile device knowledge _____

Technical vocabulary _____

Functions (check all that apply) _____ Save work in progress _____ Print in progress _____ Alter sound _____ Return to main menu at any point in program _____ Change pace

Teacher Demands (respond to any that apply) Amount of instruction to students for using software _____ _____

Installation procedures _____

Level of student monitoring _____

Preparation needed before using software _____

SOURCE: Adapted from Bryant (2015).

Classroom teachers can work with assistive technologists and special education teachers to decide which instructional aids are most suitable to help students with disabilities access the curriculum (Bryant & Bryant, 2003). Table 7.9 provides examples of AT devices students with disabilities can use, in accordance with their IEPs, to access and benefit from instruction and function successfully in various environments.

TABLE 7.9   EXAMPLES OF AT DEVICES

Use of Device	AT Device
For Students to Access Reading	
To enlarge text screen magnifier software, screen magnifier	Large-print books, larger font size, hand-held magnifier, closed-circuit television
To enhance text and graphics	Eyeglasses, color contrast, pictures, Braille text
To convert text to speech	Screen reader software, talking dictionaries, electronic books
For Students to Access Writing	
To increase use of writing tools	Pencil grips, writing paper with colored lines, writing templates
To enhance writing productivity	Electronic/talking spell checker/dictionary, voice recognition software, talking word processor software (WriteOutloud, CoWriter), voice dictation input
To use alternative writing tools	Computer, keyboard enhancements (keyguard, repeat rate adjustments ["stickie keys": key remains depressed for longer time]), electronic notetakers (with Braille), pointing device to access keyboard, alternative keyboards (Intellitools, on-screen keyboard), switches and scanning devices

(Continued)

TABLE 7.9 (CONTINUED)	
Use of Device	**AT Device**
For Students to Access Mathematics	
To support calculation	Calculator with print output, "talking calculator," calculator with large keypad, on-screen calculator, graph paper for problems with writing and aligning
To support measurement	Measuring devices with tactile output, measuring devices with speech output, talking thermometers
To support time telling	Talking watches, watches with large faces, watches with tactile output
For Students to Access Study Skills	
To help with time management	Talking watches, calendars as planners with pictures if necessary, speech output devices to remind about dates
To support memory and organization	Hand-held recorders (e.g., mobile devices) to input important times, dates, and things to do; visual organizers (color-coded folders)
For Students to Be Able to Listen/Communicate	
To listen in class	Hearing aids, assistive technology systems (FM)
To communicate	Communication boards (electronic and nonelectronic), speech amplifier, TTY/TTD (teletype devices), mobile devices (smartphones, tablets)
To listen to multimedia	Closed captions on videotapes and TV, computer-generated speech output
To promote safety	Signaling systems (telephone ring signal, door knock signal, smoke alarm with strobe light)
For Students Who Require Mobility Support	
To enhance orientation and mobility	Eyeglasses, grab bars, white cane, tactile signage, power or manual wheelchairs, motorized scooter

SOURCE: Adapted from Technology and Media (n.d.).

AT devices will be necessary to help Paul, Mrs. Bell's student with cerebral palsy, benefit from instruction. She decides to use the ADAPT framework to make adjustments to a reading comprehension activity, which involves writing, for Paul.

ASSISTIVE TECHNOLOGY SERVICES

According to the Assistive Technology Act of 2004, several AT services must be provided to ensure that devices are properly identified and used. For example, the selection of appropriate AT devices based on an evaluation of the individual is an important service. Assistive technologists, diagnosticians, audiologists, occupational therapists, speech/language pathologists, and special and general education classroom teachers may participate in an AT evaluation of a student, depending on the student's needs. Each professional contributes information

ADAPT *in action*

READING, WRITING, AND ASSISTIVE TECHNOLOGY

Mrs. Bell has students read sections from a chapter and answer comprehension questions in their reading journal for part of the class period. She then has students share their responses to the questions to check their understanding and to promote class discussion. Paul has good reading and comprehension abilities and can readily participate in discussions. Paul is adept at using a computer to do his work and is familiar with its word processing and spell-check features. He has an electronic reading journal to ease difficulties associated with holding a pencil and writing. A laptop computer has been customized to fit on the tray of his motorized wheelchair. The computer keyboard has been equipped with a keyguard, which is an overlap placed on top of the keys to minimize keys being accidentally hit during typing. However, Mrs. Bell notices that Paul seems to tire when working on his reading journal and falls behind the other students in answering all of the questions. She decides to consult the assistive technologist, Ms. Parette, to identify further assistive technology adaptations to address Paul's needs.

(A) **Ask yourself, "What am I requiring the student to do?"** "I want my students to be able to read text and answer comprehension questions and share their answers."

(D) **Determine the prerequisite skills of the task.** "I want my students to answer comprehension questions in their journal about a section of the chapter from a social studies textbook. They need to be able to discuss their answers with the whole class."

(A) **Analyze the student's strengths and struggles.** Paul's reading comprehension skills are good and he is able to engage in discussions about the material. However, he has motor problems that make turning pages in a textbook and writing difficult. Although he is using a computer for writing, he seems to have problems when doing multiple typing assignments and turning pages in his textbook. He is not keeping up with his peers.

(P) **Propose and implement adaptations from among the four categories.** After conducting several observations of Paul engaging in the reading and writing tasks, Ms. Parette recommends an electronic page turner and Dragon Dictate voice recognition software for writing assignments, and she will teach Paul and Mrs. Bell how to use them.

(T) **Test to determine whether the adaptations helped the student accomplish the task.** Mrs. Bell will monitor whether Paul is completing all of the reading comprehension questions in his electronic journal and how well the page turner seems to be helping him read his section of the textbook. Ms. Parette will conduct observations as well and compare notes with Mrs. Bell.

ADAPT *framework:* READING, WRITING, AND ASSISTIVE TECHNOLOGY

ASK "What am I requiring the student to do?"	**DETERMINE** the prerequisite skills of the task.	**ANALYZE** the student's strengths and struggles.		**PROPOSE** and implement adaptations from among the four categories.	**TEST** to determine whether the adaptations helped the student accomplish the task.
		Strengths	Struggles		
The students will write answers to reading comprehension questions on a section of a chapter from a social studies textbook.	**1.** Is able to read the textbook with understanding and respond to questions.	1			
	2. Is able to turn the pages in the textbook.		2	**2.** Instructional material provides an automatic page turner.	**2.** Observe to see whether the device is working properly.
	3. Uses a computer to write answers to comprehension questions.		3	**3.** The student already uses a computer to complete written assignments. Needs voice recognition software, Dragon Dictate.	**3.** Observe to see how the software works to help the student answer all of the questions and keep up with his peers.

about how the student is performing in relation to academics, communication, motor development, vision, or hearing. One evaluation example is the *Functional Evaluation for Assistive Technology* (Raskind & Bryant, 2002), which enables professionals to rate the performance of a student on listening, speaking, academics, memory, organization, motor tasks, and behavior. Each discipline (such as occupational therapy, speech/language, and audiology) has its own criteria for evaluating student performance.

For example, when AT is being considered during an IEP meeting for a student with an identified reading disability, the AT technologist works with classroom teachers to determine reading strengths and areas of difficulty when completing classroom activities. Classroom teachers may be asked specific questions about reading requirements in the classroom and about the student's performance on these tasks. The AT technologist consults a speech/language pathologist if language difficulties are also noted. Together, professionals can make decisions about devices that can help the student with reading tasks. The evaluation process is ongoing; changes may occur in a student's environment or setting, strengths and struggles, and maturity (Bryant & Bryant, 2003; Raskind & Bryant, 2002).

Training is another example of an AT service (Rieth, Colburn, & Bryant, 2004). Training on AT devices should be provided to the students or users of the devices, their families, and professionals such as classroom teachers, speech/language pathologists, and occupational therapists. Professionals must be trained to know how devices work, how to integrate them when working with students, how to troubleshoot if a device malfunctions, and how to evaluate students to make an appropriate match between device and needs. Training must be an ongoing priority to ensure that both users and professionals remain informed. It is conducted in teacher preparation programs and as a part of ongoing inservice training (Rieth et al., 2004). Paraprofessionals too must become competent in the use of AT devices to work effectively with their students who rely on them.

Finally, because devices can often go home with students, family members must know how to use them properly. If electronic devices prove overwhelming, more training may be required for successful implementation (Lemons, 2000).

It is crucial to include families in selecting AT devices and to listen to their viewpoints (Bryant & Bryant, 1998). Team members must consider family viewpoints about disability and how services that are intended to be helpful may be interpreted. The family's experience and comfort level with technology are very important, especially if they are helping their child use the technology at home. Finally, family members should know what outcomes educators hope to achieve by having the student use a particular AT device. These outcomes should reflect the family's interest and values in promoting their child's independence.

ASSISTIVE TECHNOLOGY INTEGRATION

As teachers design instruction, they can think about the curriculum and objectives students will be taught and the way instruction will be delivered (using grouping, modeling, guided practice). They must also consider the strengths and needs of their students with IEPs and how AT devices can promote their active participation in lessons (Bryant & Bryant, 2003; Rieth et al., 2004). Finally, they should also consider the environmental requirements for the devices, such as whether they produce potentially distracting sound or require electricity. Students may be able to use headphones with devices such as talking calculators, speech output, and tape recorders. The location of electrical outlets will dictate where devices that require electricity can be set up. Other devices may require batteries, often preferable when mobile environments are part of the setting.

During instruction, teachers should monitor how easy it is to use the device and whether further training is required. Teachers should monitor their students' ability to keep pace with their peers in completing the tasks. Practice with the nuances of the device may be necessary so students can achieve the maximum benefits from using it.

Finally, teachers should not overlook the fatigue factor when using the device. Some devices, such as keyboarding with computers, may be tiring and hinder productivity. Evaluating the effectiveness of integrating assistive technology requires the input of professionals, family members, and students. We now consider using the principles, guidelines, and checkpoints of UDL in a lesson as another example of how teachers can make the curriculum accessible for all learners in an RTI model.

UDL *in action*

Universal Design for Learning Lesson

Note: This UDL-based lesson was developed, in part, using an adapted version of the CAST UDL Lesson Builder (http://udlexchange.cast.org/home).

Title: World War I

Subject: Social Studies: American History

Unit Description: This lesson is part of a group of lessons that focus on World War.

Unit Goals: The purpose of this unit is to understand the sociopolitical issues and causes of World War I.

Lesson Goals: The purpose of this lesson is to provide background about the events that led to

World War I through the perspective of the U.S. presidents in power at the time.

Methods: Advance Organizer: Tell the student(s) that the purpose of the day's lesson is to help them become familiar with events that led to World War I. A video from a special series about the Roosevelts will be used to address perspectives about the war from U.S. presidents in power at the time (http://www.pbs.org/kenburns/the-roosevelts).

Introduce and Model New Knowledge:

1. Show a clip of President Theodore Roosevelt that portrays his perspectives surrounding world events that eventually caused

the United States to enter World War I (*Checkpoint 5.1—Use multiple media for communication*). Give students questions to answer following the clip to check their understanding of the video's content. Have students share their responses with a partner (*Checkpoint 8.3—Foster collaboration and community*).

2. Give each pair of students an opportunity to share one idea from the video. Return to sections of the video that support these ideas (*Checkpoint 3.3—Guide information processing, visualization, and manipulation*).

Provide Guided Practice:

1. Have students work in cooperative learning groups to read information from their social studies text on the causes of World War I by relating this content to the video clip.

2. Have student groups create a graphic organizer of the causes of World War I (*Checkpoint 3.2—Highlight patterns, critical features, big ideas, and relationships; Checkpoints 3.3 and 8.3*).

3. Have a representative from each group display their graphic organizer to the whole class and explain the group's thinking (*Checkpoint 5.1—Use multiple media for communication*).

Provide Independent Practice:

1. At the end of the lesson, have students answer a set of questions about the causes of World War I.

SUMMARY

Access to the general education curriculum is critical for *all* students. Differentiating instruction to meet the special learning needs of students helps to ensure that students benefit from instruction and learn the curriculum. UDL is an effective way to promote access and differentiation for all students through the principles, guidelines, and checkpoints. The ADAPT framework is a tool that can help teachers differentiate instruction that is responsive to the individual needs of students. As teachers plan, deliver, and evaluate instruction, they can identify effective practices from the adaptations categories (instructional activity, content, delivery, and materials) to address specific student learning needs. We know that adaptations should be individualized to the learner, relevant to the curriculum, and effective in order to improve learning outcomes. We know a great deal about what constitutes effective instructional practices for students with special needs. These practices focus on planning and delivering instruction, teaching different types of knowledge, and employing techniques that take the stage of learning into account. Grouping practices such as whole group and small group instruction are a critical component of effective instruction. As part of quality instruction, teachers adapt instructional materials to accommodate learning needs. Finally, assistive technology devices and services hold great promise in helping students with disabilities be active, independent participants in the educational setting.

REVIEW THE LEARNING OBJECTIVES ························

Let's review the learning objectives for this chapter. If you are uncertain and cannot talk through the answers provided for any of these questions, reread those sections of the text.

- **What is Universal Design for Learning?**

  UDL is a means for differentiating instruction for all students, including learners with disabilities. The principles, guidelines, and checkpoints of UDL provide ways to remove or minimize barriers to learning and promoting accessibility to curricula and pedagogy, or teaching practices, for all learners, including students with and without disabilities and English language learners. The goal is to foster the development of learners to achieve mastery of the curricula within a flexible environment that features various ways content can be conveyed to account for individual differences.

- **What is the ADAPT framework?**

  The ADAPT framework consists of questions that relate to the ADAPT mnemonic:

  - **A**sk, "What am I requiring the student to do?"

  - **D**etermine the prerequisite skills of the task.

  - **A**nalyze the student's strengths and struggles.

  - **P**ropose and implement adaptations from among the four categories.

  - **T**est to determine if the adaptations helped the student accomplish the task.

  There are four categories of adaptations: instructional activity, instructional content, instructional delivery, and instructional materials.

- **What are effective instructional practices?**

  Effective instructional practices include planning for and delivering instruction. In the course of planning, teachers consider types of knowledge (discrimination, factual,

rules, procedural, conceptual, or metacognitive) and critical thinking; types of questions; stage of learning (acquisition, proficiency, maintenance, generalization, or application); and instructional components of direct, explicit instruction and strategy instruction. In delivering instruction, teachers should include the following instructional steps and techniques: an advance organizer, presentation of information, practice, independent practice, closure, and progress monitoring.

- **How can instructional grouping practices promote effective instruction?**

  Grouping practices include whole group, flexible, small group, and one-to-one grouping structures. Other effective grouping practices include peer tutoring and cooperative learning. The whole group format works well where common instructional objectives are identified, the teacher delivers the lesson, and students respond orally or in writing. Flexible, small groups include same-ability groups and mixed-ability groups. Teachers use same-ability groups to provide extra instruction and support to those students who are most in need of additional assistance. Mixed-ability groups can be used for students to work on projects and to make presentations. One-to-one instruction enables teachers to tailor instruction to individual students and their specific learning and behavioral needs. In tutoring via peer partners, pairs of students can work on assigned skills, usually for extra practice.

- **What guidelines should be followed for textbooks and instructional materials?**

  For textbooks and instructional materials, consider the student and the instructional content and methodology. Regarding the student, identify the student's present levels of educational performance when selecting materials, and consider whether the material can be used to meet IEP goals. Regarding content and methodology, decide whether the material is age-appropriate. Determine whether it includes a sequence of skills and teaching strategies. Ensure that there are sufficient opportunities to practice new skills and that generalization and maintenance activities are included.

- **What are assistive technology devices and services for promoting access to the general education curriculum?**

An assistive technology device is anything that is bought or made that helps a person with a disability accomplish tasks that would otherwise be difficult or impossible. AT devices can be grouped into categories, including positioning and seating, mobility, communication, adaptive toys and games, adaptive environments, computer use, and instructional aids.

Assistive technology services are those activities that ensure adoption and maintenance of appropriate devices. One such service is evaluating the functional capabilities and struggles of individuals with disabilities to aid in the selection of appropriate devices to promote access and independence. Another service is the training of professionals, paraprofessionals, families, and users. Training should include how devices work, how to integrate devices into settings, how to troubleshoot if a device malfunctions, and how to evaluate students to determine an appropriate match between device and needs.

$SAGE edge™ Test your understanding of chapter content. Take the practice quiz. edge.sagepub.com/bryant

REVISIT THE OPENING CHALLENGE

Check your answers to the Reflection Questions from the Opening Challenge and revise them on the basis of what you have learned.

1. How can Mrs. Bell and Ms. Mendez implement the principles of universal design for learning into their instructional practices?

2. How can Mrs. Bell and Ms. Mendez use the ADAPT framework to differentiate instruction for their students?

3. How can Mrs. Bell and Ms. Mendez differentiate instruction for their multicultural and ELL students?

4. What instructional and grouping practices might help them provide effective, differentiated instruction for their students?

5. How can Mrs. Bell and Ms. Mendez ensure that the textbooks and instructional materials they use are appropriate for all of their students?

6. How can assistive technology help Mrs. Bell's students with disabilities access the general education curriculum?

KEY TERMS

access to the general education curriculum, 258

active process assessment, 265

assistive technology device, 297

assistive technology service, 297

augmentative and alternative communication (aug com), 298

basals, 293

checking for understanding, 282

concepts, 271

convergent, lower order questions, 273

cooperative learning, 289

core curriculum, 265

differentiating instruction, 258

distributive practice, 284

divergent higher order questions, 275

elementary grades, 257

engaged time, 282

functional capability, 295

graphic organizers (GOs), 268

$SAGE edge™ Review key terms with eFlashcards.
edge.sagepub.com/bryant

PROFESSIONAL STANDARDS AND LICENSURE

For a complete description of Professional Standards and Licensure, please see Appendix on page 569.

CEC Initial Preparation Standards

Standard 1: Learner Development and Individual Learning Differences

Standard 2: Learning Environments

Standard 3: Curricular Content Knowledge

Standard 5: Instructional Planning and Strategies

Standard 6: Professional Learning and Ethical Practice

Standard 7: Collaboration

INTASC Core Principles

Standard 4: Content Knowledge

Standard 7: Planning for Instruction

Standard 8: Instructional Strategies

Praxis II: Education of Exceptional Students: Core Content Knowledge

II. Legal and Societal Issues: Historical movements/trends

III. Delivery of Services to Students with Disabilities: Background knowledge

$SAGE edge™

Review ➡ Practice ➡ Improve

Get the tools you need to sharpen your study skills. Access practice quizzes, eFlashcards, video, and multimedia: **edge.sagepub.com/bryant**

AP Photo/The Patriot-News, John C. Whitehead

8

ASSESSMENT AND DATA-BASED DECISION MAKING

LEARNING OBJECTIVES

After studying this chapter, you will be able to answer the following questions:

- Why do we assess students?

- How do we assess students with special needs?

- How do we adapt and modify assessments for students with special needs?

Determining What Students Know

ELEMENTARY GRADES Ms. Thompson is a third-year, fourth-grade teacher. One of her students, Kim, excels as a reader but has difficulties in mathematics. She barely passed her third-grade high-stakes mathematics test, but in the fourth grade she is experiencing difficulty with more advanced skills and concepts. She is a hard worker but has difficulty with basic computation and struggles with mathematics vocabulary. Now that she is working on fractions and algebra readiness skills and concepts, she gets easily confused and frustrated. Ms. Thompson met with the school's Response to Intervention (RTI) teacher, Mr. Peters, to discuss Kim's progress. At the start of the school year, Kim met the district benchmark for mathematics on the beginning-of-year universal screener, but only by one point. Mr. Peters administered the middle-of-year test and Kim failed to meet the benchmark. As a result, Mr. Peters provided supplemental instruction, as Ms. Thompson continued to provide Kim with core mathematics instruction from the district-adopted basal textbook.

After 10 weeks, Kim continued to struggle and again failed to meet the benchmark to exit the program. Rather than having Kim undergo another round of supplemental instruction, Mr. Peters and Ms. Thompson decided to refer Kim for a special education evaluation to determine whether she has a mathematics learning disability (MLD). A variety of tests were administered, as dictated by district policy. Her standardized mathematics tests showed that Kim was performing very poorly compared with her peers; other test scores in reading and writing were above average when compared with those of her classmates. Based on the accumulated evidence, it was determined that Kim did have MLD, and she is now receiving special education support in her inclusion classroom with Ms. Thompson.

SECONDARY GRADES Mr. Gomez has been teaching for four years. His state has recently revamped its state standards and high-stakes tests. Mr. Gomez's students will be taking the test in the spring to determine whether they will move on to Grade 7.

Mr. Gomez has a diverse classroom, and the achievement levels range from very low to very high. He is confident that some of his students could take the test now and do quite well. Others in his classroom are so low-achieving that he questions whether he can teach them the skills they need to pass. He has decided to implement progress monitoring for his entire class. He will collect data on his students' progress in reading, math, and science, the three areas being assessed in the spring. He will tailor his instruction to their needs and monitor their achievement throughout the school year.

Two students in particular concern Mr. Gomez. *"Sonya is new to the school and has serious reading problems. She is unable to decode words and has very little comprehension of written materials. Dondra, my other challenging student, has attention issues. She is very bright and capable but has difficulty paying attention and sitting still."*

Although Mr. Gomez has worked with students who have attention problems, he indicated the following: *"None of my former students compare to Dondra. Her condition is exacerbated by muscle control issues. She has fine motor problems that cause her to struggle when she has to grasp, pick up, or use small objects."*

REFLECTION QUESTIONS In your journal, write down your answers to the following questions. After completing the chapter, check your answers and revise them on the basis of what you have learned.

1. How could Ms. Thompson set up a progress monitoring procedure?

2. How could she set goals and chart her students' progress?

3. How can Mr. Gomez teach Sonya science and test her abilities when she cannot read?

4. What measures are available to identify Dondra's attentional difficulties and Kim's mathematics struggles?

5. How can assessments be used to identify student strengths and struggles?

In education, **assessment** is any method by which teachers and other professionals gain information about students. Students can be assessed to measure academic performance, intelligence level, behavior tendencies, or emotional stability. Often, people equate assessment with testing. Tests are one form of assessment but not the only one (Taylor, 2008). When working with students who have special needs, teachers use a variety of techniques, including but not limited to testing, to gain information about their work and abilities.

Teachers gather assessment information every time they watch children and adolescents do things such as play together or complete an assignment. In assessment terminology, this "watching" is called conducting **observation**, and it includes not only watching students do something but also thinking about what they are doing, why they are doing it, and what the "doing" means to the students and those around them. Teachers' observations occur over time and are ongoing, which makes them a valuable tool for recording behavioral or academic changes (Bryant et al., in press; Flower, McKenna, Muething, Bryant, & Bryant, 2013). Teachers can also gain information by questioning the student, the student's other teacher(s), and the student's parents or classmates, through interviews or a questionnaire or survey. Assessments help teachers gain valuable information, but only if the results are valid—that is, only if they truly represent the abilities of the students being assessed.

WHY DO WE ASSESS STUDENTS?

PURPOSES OF ASSESSMENT

There are several reasons why we assess students with special needs. Here we discuss a few key purposes.

Identifying Strengths and Weaknesses

A major purpose of assessment across various areas like reading, writing, mathematics, and classroom behavior is to gather information about what a student with special needs can do well (strengths) and what he or she struggles with (weaknesses). For example, Sonya, in Mr. Gomez's class, has difficulty reading,

Early Childhood Assessment

and Dondra has attentional issues. Often, teachers use assessments called diagnostic measures, not because these measures, in and of themselves, diagnose a particular condition, but because they assess a student across a variety of skill areas. Those areas can be within a construct (for instance, several different reading skills), or they can be more global (reading, writing, *and* mathematics).

Get the edge on your studies:
edge.sagepub.com/bryant

- Take a quiz to find out what you've learned.
- Review key terms with eFlashcards.
- Watch videos to see teachers in action.

When teachers make comparisons among an individual student's abilities, they are performing an intraindividual comparison. These comparisons are important because they enable us to identify what needs to be worked on to help improve any problem areas that might be discovered.

Determining Relative Standing

In contrast to making intraindividual comparisons, teachers can compare a student's performance with that of others. In this case, the teachers are making interindividual comparisons. Many school districts administer an achievement test in the spring of each year. This test—perhaps the *Iowa Test of Basic Skills,* the *Stanford Achievement Test,* or some similar test—measures students' skills, such as reading, math, and writing. Professionals at the test publishing company, where the tests are scored, assign normative scores that reflect each student's standing relative to that of other students across the country (that is, a national average) and/or to those within the school district (a district average). Sometime a month or two thereafter, the school is sent the test results. Those results, along with a booklet explaining what they mean, are shared with parents, and the results are placed in each student's cumulative folder, the school's record of each student's academic activity. District superintendents and principals also use the test scores to identify how the schools within the district compare with one another and how a particular district compares with others across the country.

Informing Instruction

One of the first questions teachers should ask when reviewing assessment results is, "What does the assessment tell me about what I should be teaching my student?" This is an example of using assessment data to inform instruction or guide instructional efforts.

For example, when administering a reading test to Sonya, whether it is a standardized test or an informal reading inventory, Mr. Gomez can observe how Sonya responds to different text features. He may conduct a miscue or error analysis to see what words she misses as she reads and to make judgments about her word identification skills. If Sonya continuously leaves off suffixes or inflectional endings, those skills could be targeted for instruction. If she can correctly respond to literal comprehension questions but misses a sizable proportion of inferential questions, Mr. Gomez may decide to focus reading instruction on making inferences.

VIDEO CASE 8.1

Why and How Are Students Assessed?

1. Which informal assessment methods are mentioned in the video? How do the teachers use the results of these informal assessments to guide their instructional planning on a daily basis?

2. What formal assessment measures do the teachers identify and how are they used to measure student learning? How do the teachers prepare their students for standardized assessments?

Determining Program Eligibility

In some cases, assessment data are used to identify exceptionalities (such as intellectual and developmental disabilities, learning disabilities, emotional or behavioral disorders, and giftedness) and to determine that students are eligible to receive special program services. These programs may be special education, Section 504 programs, or dyslexia services, to name but a few. There is no test for exceptionalities per se. Instead, assessment professionals (usually psychologists or educational diagnosticians) administer a battery of tests, make observations, and conduct interviews (in other words, perform a number of assessments), and they then look at the results with certain criteria in mind. There are established procedures for diagnosing exceptional conditions, and a team of people (including classroom teachers) talk about the results of the assessments and decide whether the student qualifies as having a particular disability or exceptionality.

The role of the classroom teacher in this process cannot be overemphasized. Teachers are the educational professionals who know the student best, and theirs is an important voice that lends credibility to the assessment findings that shape the decision-making process. For instance, Ms. Thompson referred Kim to the IEP team for having potential learning disabilities in mathematics. After conducting the assessments, the school psychologist recommended that Kim be identified as having a reading learning disability but not a mathematics learning disability. The assessment data did not show a math disability but they did show a reading disability. Ms. Thompson, having worked with Kim for months, had never noticed a reading problem. In fact, the teacher had always been impressed with the student's abilities as a strategic reader. If Ms. Thompson does not speak out during the meeting and provide contrasting evidence, there is a good chance that the student may be misdiagnosed as having a reading learning disability. Test data alone should not be used to make eligibility decisions. Data should come from a variety of sources, including daily work samples, which in this case would show that Kim is an accomplished reader in class.

Grading

Perhaps the most common form of assessment that teachers encounter is assessing students for grading purposes—that is, assigning a numeric or letter index based on a student's performance within a specified academic calendar period (usually a semester). To see whether students learned their spelling words, teachers typically administer a spelling test at the end of the week and record the percentage correct in the grade book. An end-of-chapter test might be administered after completion of a science unit. Often these tests have been prepared by the textbook publisher, but many teachers choose to create their own tests. Whichever approach is used, test grades are assigned and constitute a portion of each student's final grade for the course.

Whenever teachers grade students' products, there is always the possibility of bias. Reynolds, Livingston, and Willson (2009) noted several sources of error that can affect grading students' work, especially when subjective scoring occurs (such as for essays or reports). The *halo effect* occurs when teachers are influenced by a student's positive or negative attributes that are unrelated to the product being graded. For example, if a student pays attention to the teacher and is eager to please, the teacher may be inclined to view his or her work more favorably and let those positive attributes affect scoring.

Leniency errors occur when teachers tend to score all papers positively and provide high scores. Conversely, severity ratings occur when teachers tend to score all papers negatively and provide consistently low scores. Central tendency errors occur when teachers tend to score all papers in the average range, limiting high scores and/or low scores.

Personal bias errors can occur when teachers tend to let stereotypes influence student ratings. A teacher may score a paper higher because "Jimmy has a disability, and he tries hard." Conversely, a teacher may score a paper lower because of preconceived notions of what students with disabilities can accomplish in the classroom.

Finally, *logical errors* may occur when teachers tend to associate one characteristic with another. For example, teachers may grade papers higher for those students who demonstrate high academic aptitude and give lower scores when the opposite is true.

This is not to say that all teachers make these types of errors. But these errors do occur, and teachers should be on the lookout for them.

Determining Annual Yearly Progress

According to No Child Left Behind legislation, educators must ensure that all students make **adequate yearly progress (AYP)**, so it is important for teachers to collect assessment data to determine whether students are making progress toward their end-of-year goals (Smith & Tyler, 2010).

Teachers want students to be performing at a certain level by the end of the school year. These end-of-year assessments are sometimes called **high-stakes assessments**, because districts and schools use the results to monitor the effectiveness of their teaching efforts. Test results also may determine whether students advance to the next grade or graduate from high school; in other words, the stakes for some students are really high.

High-stakes testing has become more rigorous over the past decade or so, as states have raised the bar of expectations. Students now are being held to higher standards than ever before, and with the increasing demands of the Common Core curriculum being adopted across the country, student accountability has never been higher. High-stakes tests are being written to assess the Common Core State Standards (CCSS), and such groups as the Partnership for Assessment of Readiness for College and Careers (PARCC) and Smarter Balanced Assessment Consortium (SBAC) have led the way in constructing and field-testing reliable measures that produce valid results for assessing AYP. Many states differ in the way they determine AYP and what tests are used to measure it. We urge you to visit your state education agency's website to look up the expectations for your state, but if you are currently teaching or if you soon will be, you may already have attended meetings about your school and district requirements. In these meetings, you can find out what your district is doing to align current textbooks to the new standards, because the transition to the CCSS or any set of higher standards is changing the way texts are written and instructional plans are carried out. Because textbook purchases are made fairly infrequently (they require considerable effort and expense on the part of schools and districts), it could be years before all texts in use are in line with current standards. Also, standards change periodically, so teachers constantly face challenges keeping their materials up to date.

Documenting Progress

Progress monitoring is particularly important in RTI programs. In fact, progress monitoring is considered one of RTI's "nonnegotiables," meaning that no RTI program should be without it. In our RTI work, we typically use four types of progress monitoring that cut across some of the areas we have already discussed. As you can see in Table 8.1, progress monitoring measures are designed to answer specific questions relating to measurement. Benchmark checks are used as a universal screener and designed to answer these questions: "Where does the student stand in comparison to his or her peers?" and "Does the student qualify for intervention?"

Universal screeners in RTI are usually administered three times each year, at the beginning, in the middle, and at the end of the school year. A benchmark (that's why it is called a *benchmark check*) is that score on the test that determines qualification for intervention (what we earlier called *determining program eligibility*). Students who score at or above the benchmark are seen as doing well in the subject matter being tested and therefore do not qualify for the RTI intervention. Students who score below the benchmark are seen as needing the intervention.

We look at benchmark check scores as falling within three categories: A, B, and C (these stand for levels of performance on the benchmark check, not letter grades). We call those who score above the 35th percentile A students; the A stands for "All ahead full," which means teachers should continue to do what they are doing with these students because it is working—the students are learning what is being taught. Students who score between the 25th

TABLE 8.1	DESCRIPTION OF PROGRESS MONITORING TOOLS

Progress Monitoring Tool	Purpose	Administration	Examples
Benchmark check	To answer these questions: "Where does the student fall in comparison to his or her peers," and "Does the student qualify for intervention?"	Benchmark checks are given to all students in the fall, winter, and spring of the year.	Four, 2-minute timed tests assessing number and operation skills (e.g., magnitude comparisons, number sequences, place value, addition/subtraction combinations), which are summed to form a total score.
Daily check	To answer the question "Did the student meet the objective of the day?"	Daily checks are administered only to students receiving intervention at the end of each day's lesson.	Several items that assess the content of the lesson. Administered as part of independent practice, the daily check total score should allow for one mistake yet still achieve mastery (e.g., for a five-item daily check, mastery is set at 80% correct).
Unit check	To answer these questions: "Has the student mastered the content of the unit/chapter as presented across a two-week (or so) period?" and "Has the student maintained daily learning across an elongated time frame?"	Unit checks are administered only to students receiving intervention at the end of the two-week intervention unit or chapter.	Ten to twenty items that assess the content taught during the unit/chapter. Tests can be a pregenerated component of the commercial or research intervention, or unit checks can be created using items from the daily checks. With at least 10 items, mastery can be set at 90%.
Aim check	To answer the question "Is the student making progress toward his or her intervention goal?"— which is usually the next benchmark.	Aim checks are administered twice per week to students receiving intervention. Some teachers choose to administer aim checks to all students once every week or two weeks.	Aim checks should be alternate forms of benchmark checks. It is best to create four or five forms of the aim check to ensure that students do not remember answers from a single form.

SOURCE: Cuillos, SoRelle, Kim, Seo, & Bryant (2011).

percentile (our benchmark) and the 35th percentile are B students, meaning "Be alert." Students who score at the B level percentile have met the benchmark but not by much. Teachers should be alert while teaching these students, because they are potential candidates for falling below the benchmark during the next round of testing. Do they struggle with new skills and concepts? Do they require additional help when they struggle? Do scaffolds need to be introduced to help them learn these new skills and concepts?

VIDEO CASE 8.2

Progress Monitoring

1. How does Mia Tannous describe progress monitoring in reading at her school? What progress monitoring methods does Tema Khieu mention? How are the results from ongoing progress monitoring used to enhance student learning?

2. Why does Ms. Tannous say that the math specialists at her school are creating new math assessments? What characteristics will the new assessments include and how can the data be used by the teachers?

Finally, those who score below the benchmark—that is, below the 25th percentile—are C students, and C stands for "Change." These students qualify for the RTI program, so their teachers change what they are doing by providing supplemental instruction (referred to as Tier 2 instruction in Chapter 6) in addition to their core instruction (Tier 1).

When the next round of testing occurs, students receiving supplemental instruction may reach the benchmark, leave Tier 2, and remain in Tier 1 full time. Some students who met the benchmark in the previous round of testing may now miss it. These students (very often the B students from round 1) now qualify for Tier 2 intervention, which supplements their Tier 1 instruction.

The next type of progress monitoring measure is given only to students receiving Tier 2 or Tier 3 instruction (see Chapter 6 for Tier 3). The question being asked with the daily check is, "Did the students meet the objective of the day's lesson?" Daily checks are given at the end of each lesson, often in the form of independent practice items. They are important because if students fail to meet the lesson's objective and continue to fail to meet other lessons' objectives, the odds they will do well on the next benchmark check are slim—they simply will not have learned enough. If a student does poorly on two or three daily checks, the intervention teacher will have to make some kind of change in the student's teaching. For example, the student may have to be moved to a different group that is functioning at a lower level than the current group. Or perhaps the student will be part of a smaller group, one that allows the intervention teacher to check for understanding more often, add additional scaffolds, or adapt instruction more often or in different ways.

The third measure in progress monitoring is called a unit check, which is similar to the end-of-chapter test found in many textbooks. Unit checks, like daily checks, are administered only to intervention students. The questions being asked here are, "Has the student mastered the content taught of the unit/chapter as presented across a two-week (or so) period?" and "Has the student maintained daily learning across an elongated time frame?"

Many RTI interventions are composed of lessons that are combined into a unit or module. The unit check is composed of representative items across the lessons that compose the unit or module. Often, these items are selected from daily checks; so, for example, if a unit is composed of 20 lessons, a unit check may be composed of 20 items, one item from each lesson. Experienced teachers often note that students seem to be learning just fine, as might be the case when the student meets the objective by scoring well on all daily checks. But when a unit check is given, for some reason a student might perform poorly—he or she has forgotten what was taught earlier and has not maintained learning across the time spent on the unit. Can you imagine how frustrating that must be for the teacher—and the student?

The final check in this progress monitoring system, the aim check, is designed to answer this question: "Is the student making progress toward his or her intervention goal?" Most often the intervention goal is to score at or above the benchmark on the next benchmark check (the next administration of the universal screener). The aim check should be four or five measures that are alternate forms of the benchmark check. Often the Aim Check is administered every two weeks during intervention, but sometimes it can be administered more often; aim check performance is graphed or charted to show growth and movement toward the benchmark.

See Figure 8.1 for an example. Here, Min's initial benchmark check score is plotted on the graph (she answered 16 items correctly). The next benchmark check will be given 10 weeks later, and to meet it, Min must score 42 points, so that score is plotted on the chart. A line is drawn from the first score to the goal; this line is called an aim line, which is where the term aim check comes from. Min scored 20 points on her first aim check two weeks later, which is plotted on her graph. (By the way, students often do their own chart-

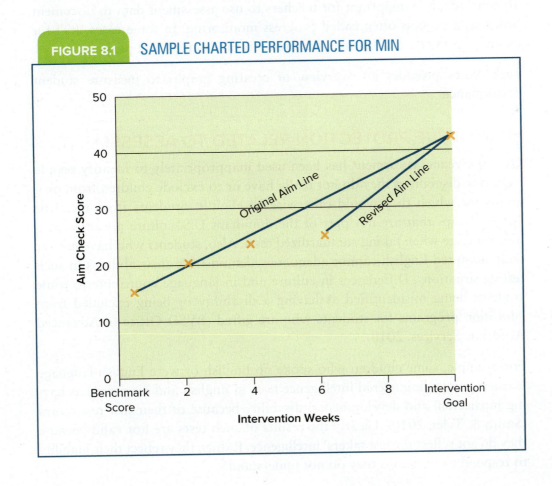

FIGURE 8.1 **SAMPLE CHARTED PERFORMANCE FOR MIN**

Perhaps the most common form of assessment teachers encounter is assessing students for grading purposes.

ing, which gives them ownership of the process while allowing them to see their own growth.) Two weeks later, Min scored 22 points, and two weeks after that, 22 points.

Can you see what is happening? Min's score is increasing but not at a rate that will allow her to meet her goal. At some point, the teacher must use what is called a "decision rule" to make some kind of change in the intervention. As we mentioned before, this decision might be to move Min to another group or to a smaller group where the teacher can more closely observe her during instruction. Let's say Min is now working with two other students instead of four. When the change is made, a new aim line is drawn, which shows the new slope, or trajectory, that must be accomplished to meet the intervention goal. Note that the new aim line is steeper than the original, which shows that Min must make more and faster progress than she had to initially. The hope is that the new grouping will work and Min's aim checks will show successful movement toward her objective.

To conclude, it is important for teachers to use assessment data to document progress, a process often called progress monitoring. In some cases, RTI for example, progress monitoring measures can vary in type and purpose.

Tech Notes provides an overview of creating graphs to measure student performance.

LEGISLATIVE PROTECTION RELATED TO ASSESSMENT

Over the years, assessment has been used inappropriately to identify people as having disabilities they do not really have or to exclude children from programs for which they would otherwise be eligible. Students from racial or ethnic groups that are not part of the dominant U.S. culture are often at a disadvantage when taking standardized tests. Also, students who have not yet truly mastered English cannot adequately demonstrate their abilities in such testing situations. Differences in culture and in language contribute to some students being misidentified as having a disability or being excluded from education programs for students who are gifted (BVSD Office of Advanced Academic Services, 2010).

For example, some children who spoke no English or were English language learners were administered intelligence tests in English and diagnosed as having intellectual and developmental disability because of their low test scores (Smith & Tyler, 2010). Clearly the results of such tests are not valid because they do not reflect the test takers' intelligence. Rather, they reflect their inability to respond to questions they do not understand.

TECH *notes*

GRADING CHARTS

When monitoring progress, it is typical to create a graph of student performance that includes the results of an initial assessment, usually in the form of a pretest; and a goal, a point total that the student is supposed to score at the end of the intervention (usually a benchmark of some kind). A line is drawn from the initial test score to the goal, and that line presents a path to success—the results of periodic testing should continue to improve and mirror the aim line (or that is the hope). As each periodic test is given, the score is plotted on the graph to present a visual depiction of progress.

Although graphs and charts can be drawn by hand, Microsoft Excel provides a means to do so electronically. To create a graph, open Excel and save the document as something like "Progress Monitoring Chart for Juan." On the first line, write Date, Session, Score, and Aim in the first four columns. Under date, enter the dates in each row that you will be collecting data (for example, Jan 4, Jan 6, Jan 11, Jan 13 for collected data twice a week beginning on January 4th). Under Session, write 1 to 20 (for 20 data collection sessions over a 10-week period). Under Score and Aim, write the pretest score (for example, 22). Now enter the next benchmark under Aim on the same line as the last

session. In our case, the benchmark is 56, so write 56 in the Aim column in the same row as Session 20. Then subtract the pretest score from the benchmark score (56 − 22), giving the difference of 34 points—the student must increase his pretest score 34 points to reach the benchmark at the end of the intervention. Next, divide 34 by the number of sessions; minus 1 (20–1), or 34/19. The quotient is 1.7895. Click on line 3 in the Aim column. Then, in the formula box (next to fx), enter = D2+1.7895 and press the "Enter" or "Return" key. The number 21.7895 will appear. Copy that box and paste it into the remaining boxes down to the last Aim number entered (56). You will then see numbers fill in the previously empty boxes. Now, highlight the Score and Aim boxes from the first to the last, and go to the Chart icon at the top of the Excel sheet. Click on Chart and several options will appear. Click on Line, then Marked Line. A chart will then appear on the Excel sheet, with an Aim Line created. As you enter each subsequent Score after progress monitoring testing, performance will be added to the graph. Save the document and you are good to go! Note: If you get stuck, simply type the following into your search engine: "Create an aim line in Excel YouTube"—several demonstration video options should appear. Enjoy!

To stress the importance of nonbiased evaluations, IDEA '04 requires that nondiscriminatory testing be established in each state. Assessment authorities have provided numerous procedures that test authors can undertake to reduce bias and therefore create measurement instruments that are nondiscriminatory (Salvia, Ysseldyke, & Bolt, 2010; Taylor, 2008). Before selecting tests for use with students who are culturally and/or linguistically different, teachers, school psychologists, educational diagnosticians, and other assessment professionals should consult the tests' technical manuals to see whether procedures were undertaken to reduce test bias. The manuals should provide empirical evidence, in the form of research studies and statistical analyses, supporting the tests' use in nondiscriminatory assessment.

HOW DO WE ASSESS STUDENTS WITH SPECIAL NEEDS?

Over the years, many terms have been used to describe the types of assessments used to measure student knowledge. For example, tests have been considered to be standardized or nonstandardized, formal or informal, or summative or formative, depending in large part on how the results of the tests were used. Earlier we discussed the purposes of assessment. Here we discuss the types of tests that are given and how they differ from one another.

TECHNICAL ADEQUACY

Whatever they are, test measures must be technically sound or adequate. Two important aspects of technical adequacy are **reliability** and **validity**.

Reliability means the test must yield consistent results (Salvia et al., 2010). There are several types of reliability. *Internal consistency reliability* tells us whether items of a test consistently measure the same thing (spelling, addition). Results achieved on a measure one day should match results achieved if the assessment is conducted again a short time later; this is called *test-retest reliability*. When tests have multiple forms, such as Form A, Form B, and Form C (this is common in progress monitoring), *alternate forms reliability* demonstrates that each form provides similar scores. *Interscorer agreement* or *interobserver reliability* demonstrates that scorers or observers are all seeing the same thing when they score a measure (such as a writing rubric) or observe a student in the classroom. The less reliable a measure is, the less confident we can be in the results of a test, observation, or scoring system.

Measures must also yield valid results; in other words, scores must reflect performance on the construct the test claims to be assessing (Miller, Linn, & Gronlund, 2013). A spelling test that consists of addition and subtraction items is not a spelling test, obviously, and the test's scores would never be considered a valid performance estimate of spelling abilities. But spelling test authors must go further than simply creating a measure that *looks* like it is assessing spelling. They must demonstrate that the items have *content validity* or come from a legitimate source and meet basic statistical criteria, have *criterion-related validity* and so produce results similar to those of established spelling tests, and have *construct validity*, meaning they produce results associated with the construct being measured. Test authors can demonstrate their test's construct validity by showing that the measures produce results related to other written language skills, that students get higher test scores as they get older and become better spellers, and that the test differentiates known poor spellers from known good spellers.

Teachers should be mindful of technical adequacy when they administer tests, when tests are administered by others such as school psychologists or

Coteacher Assessment

diagnosticians, or when they attend meetings such as IEP meetings. Most test publishers provide evidence of technical adequacy in their test manuals, but when attending meetings about tests that are not known to them, teachers can inquire about the technical adequacy of the measures administered. It is critical that decisions about students based on test results should be made only when tests are technically sound.

NORM-REFERENCED TESTS

Norm-referenced tests interpret a person's performance by comparing it to that of his or her peers. We discussed this earlier when we talked about benchmark checks. In school, norm-referenced tests answer the question "How does my student compare to others of the same age or grade?" This comparison can be made by comparing students with others in their classroom, with others in their school or district, or, most commonly in nationally standardized tests, with others across the country.

When interpreting students' results on a norm-referenced test, we need to know what the reported test scores mean. Most tests report results using raw scores, standard scores, percentiles, age equivalents, or grade equivalents.

Before we discuss the scores, we need to spend a little time talking about normative samples. A *normative sample* consists of the people who were given the test to develop an average score against which to compare the scores we are to report. If the test reports national norms, the test has been administered to many students across the country. Many tests have normative samples wherein thousands of people were tested at each age. Whatever the numbers, these scores are used to create the national average that serves as a comparison score for a particular student.

Thanks to sophisticated software, test publishers can quickly and accurately provide district norms as well, and the district superintendent may request these. Then, a student is compared not only with a national average but also with a more local average. National scores tell teachers how their students compare with those from around the country; they also show principals how their schools compare with those from around the nation and tell superintendents how their students, schools, and districts compare with those from around the country. District norms, sometimes called local norms, allow teachers to compare their students' scores with each other and help a principal and superintendent see how the schools compare with one another within the district. That is the power of a normative sample.

Test publishers report their normative sample's demographic characteristics (what percentage of the sample is Black, White, Hispanic, and so on), how many are male and how many female, how many in the sample are from urban schools and how many from rural schools, what states the sample was drawn from, and so forth. This important information is called a normative sample's *representativeness.* Teachers should ask, "How representative is this measure's normative sample? Does the sample 'look like' the students in my class?" Fortunately, most major measures used in school systems have representative normative samples (Salvia et al., 2010). Now let's look at the scores that tests yield.

Raw scores are simply the total number of points a person is awarded. In a test where the student has to spell 30 words and gets 20 correct, a raw score of 20 is recorded. On a rating scale that has a Likert-style rating system (for instance, a behavioral rating scale with behaviors listed, in which the rater is asked how often a student exhibits that behavior and selecting 1 for never, 2 for sometimes, 3 for frequently, or 4 for always), the raw score is the total number of points for the ratings. By themselves, raw scores mean little. Think about one test that contains 30 items and another that contains 70 items. Raw scores of 25 on these tests mean different levels of understanding, even though the numbers are the same. Raw scores are best translated into one or more of the derived scores described below.

Norms for many tests are presented in terms of standard scores, derived scores that have an average score, or mean score, and a set statistical standard deviation. Table 8.2 depicts the relationship of several standard scores typically reported in tests. Standard scores are valuable because they allow teachers both to make interindividual comparisons (that is, to determine how a student compares with the national or local average) and to assess intraindividual differences (strengths and weaknesses a person exhibits across test scores). We said before that when a student scores 25 raw score points on two different tests that contain different numbers of items, we cannot compare the two raw scores. But we *can* compare standard scores with one another. For example, if a test reports standard scores having a mean of 100 and a standard deviation of 15, we know that a reading score of 125 and a math score of 80 demonstrate a considerable performance advantage in reading over math. Likewise, reading and math scores of 110 and 108, respectively, mean the student demonstrated similar abilities in both areas.

Percentiles are also provided for most norm-referenced tests. Percentiles, or percentile ranks, as they are often called, are convenient and popular because they are so easy to understand. Percentiles range from 1 to 99, and they represent where the person would rank when compared with 99 of his or her peers. If a student achieves a percentile of 59 on a math test, it means that only 40 people scored as well as or better than he or she did on the test.

A percentile rank of 59 does not mean a student got 59% of the items correct on a particular test. This is a common misconception. A percentile indicates a person's standing relative to that of his or her peers based on test performance, not the percentage of items he or she got right on a test.

Age equivalents are provided for many test scores. These values indicate the age level from the normative sample that corresponds to the student's raw

| TABLE 8.2 | COMPARISON OF STANDARD SCORES TO ONE ANOTHER AND PERCENTILE RANKS AND DESCRIPTORS | | | | |

Standard Score	Percentile Rank	Scale Score	T-Score	Z-Score	Description
145	99.9	19	80	+3.0	Very Superior
140	99.6	18	77	+2.67	Very Superior
135	99	17	73	+2.33	Very Superior
130	98	16	70	+2.00	Very Superior
125	95	15	67	+1.67	Superior
120	91	14	63	+1.33	Above Average
115	84	13	60	+1.00	Above Average
110	75	12	57	+0.67	Average
105	63	11	53	+0.33	Average
100	50	10	50	0.00	Average
95	37	9	47	−0.33	Average
90	25	8	43	−0.67	Average
85	16	7	40	−1.00	Below Average
80	9	6	37	−1.33	Below Average
75	5	5	33	−1.67	Poor
70	2	4	30	−2.00	Poor
65	1	3	27	−2.33	Very Poor
60	0.4	2	23	−2.67	Very Poor
55	0.1	1	20	−3.00	Very Poor

SOURCE: Adapted from Dumont-Williams (n.d.).

score on each of the tests. For instance, for a fifth-grade student who was administered an intelligence test, an age equivalent of 3 years, 4 months simply means that students of that age in the normative sample scored the same raw score as the fifth grader. Be cautious: This result does *not* mean the older student has the same intelligence (or mental age, as it is sometimes inappropriately called) as a 3-year-old.

Grade equivalents also may be assigned to test scores, especially achievement tests. Similar to age equivalents, these values indicate the normative grade level that corresponds to a raw score made by a student on each of the tests or subtests administered.

Grade equivalents are reported frequently in achievement testing, but they are often misinterpreted. When a reading test reports a grade equivalent of 3-2 (third year, second month of school), it does not necessarily mean the student reads like a third grader. It means simply that the student achieved the same raw score as children in the third grade, second month of the school year when they took the test.

Informal reading inventories (IRIs) are unique tests that report scores in terms of grade equivalents (McLoughlin & Lewis, 2008). They typically consist of a graded word list that students are given to read (a list of first-grade words, a list of second-grade words, and so forth). The highest level of word list read at 90% or 95% provides a grade equivalent index. For instance, if an eleventh grader reads a graded word list and can successfully read only words on the sixth-grade list, reading the seventh- and eighth-grade lists at less than 90% accuracy, he or she has a grade equivalent index, *based on that inventory,* of the sixth grade. That does not mean the student reads like a sixth grader; it simply means he or she couldn't read words at a higher level *on that list.* The inventory may stop there, or it may have the student then read graded passages, usually from the kindergarten level up to the Grade 12 level. When the student can no longer read 90% to 95% of the words correctly, the examiner stops and assigns a grade-equivalent "reader level" index for the student.

PROGRESS MONITORING TESTS

As we mentioned earlier, schools today place a particular emphasis on monitoring students' progress. This is due jointly to the AYP requirement of No Child Left Behind legislation and to the progress monitoring requirements of RTI. Curriculum-based measures (CBMs) are ideally suited for monitoring progress because they are closely aligned with what is being taught in the classroom. We present more on CBMs in a later section of this chapter.

CRITERION-REFERENCED TESTS

Unlike norm-referenced tests that compare performance against that of peers, criterion-referenced tests compare performance to mastery of the content being tested (Taylor, 2008). The most common reason for evaluating students is to determine whether they have learned what has been specifically taught. For example, imagine a teacher has given a daily lesson on adding two-digit numerals to three-digit numerals and then follows up by giving a quiz. If the students get most of the quiz items correct, the assumption is that they have mastered the subject matter. If a student answers only half the items correctly, there is little doubt he or she has not mastered the content and reteaching is needed.

Mastery can be determined only when the student has had a sufficient number of opportunities to demonstrate competence. Response to a single item is not sufficient because it is no guarantee the student who fails to answer correctly would not answer the next 99 items correctly if given the opportunity. Likewise, answering the item correctly is no guarantee that the student wouldn't miss the next 99 opportunities. As a rule of thumb, only when a student can correctly answer 80% to 90% (or better) of the items can we assume mastery has been achieved. It would be unwise to base mastery on fewer than five items; a student with at least five items can slip up on one yet still demonstrate mastery by answering the others correctly. Assessing for mastery should include the opportunity to make a careless mistake without making a misleading interpretation inevitable.

Let's look at one way in which teachers can make their own criterion-referenced test for mathematics. Examine the scope-and-sequence chart example from a basal math textbook and identify skills to be assessed (see Figure 8.2). For our purposes, we'll keep our example brief and select only six skills.

Remember, children should be given an opportunity to miss one item and still demonstrate mastery. Because we have set our mastery level at 80%, we can write five items per skill (see Figure 8.3). We would write 10 items for each skill if 90% were the mastery level.

Finally, administer and score the test, and check for mastery. For each row of items, did the student get at least four correct? If so, we can assume the student has mastered the skill. If not, assume that the student has not mastered the skill and continue teaching the skill. Teachers should review each skill periodically to ensure students have maintained their mastery. Students need ongoing practice to maintain their skill sets.

TESTING FOR STUDENTS' STRATEGIES

Teachers often ask themselves, "How did José come up with that answer?" or "What was Lizzy thinking?" Some assessments are intended to identify strategies students use when they are problem-solving. Students rarely arrive at a

---

FIGURE 8.2   SAMPLE SCOPE-AND-SEQUENCE CHART

This scope-and-sequence chart for addition is representative of what can be found in elementary mathematics teacher's edition textbooks. We provide it as an example of content criterion reference measures.

Addition of two 1-digit numbers to 10, horizontal alignment

Addition of two 1-digit numbers to 10, vertical alignment

Addition of two 2-digit numbers (no renaming)

Addition of two 3-digit numbers (no renaming)

Addition of two 2-digit numbers, zero in addend (no renaming)

Addition of two 3-digit numbers, zero in addend (no renaming)

FIGURE 8.3	SAMPLE ITEMS BASED ON THE MATH SCOPE-AND-SEQUENCE CHART IN FIGURE 8.2

2+3=	5+1=	4+4=	2+8=	0+9=
3 +6	0 +4	2 +5	8 +1	2 +3
13 +25	43 +52	28 +50	57 +21	64 +33
183 +215	637 +121	843 +126	241 +530	389 +410
25 +50	61 +20	48 +30	27 +60	85 +10
243 +305	727 +102	631 +250	814 +105	174 +620

solution haphazardly; there is almost always a reasonable explanation of how they derived it. One of the most challenging yet interesting purposes for assessing math performance, for example, is to target the strategies a student employs during computation or problem solving. It is intriguing to find out why a student generates a correct or incorrect response.

We believe no mathematics assessment, for instance, is complete without what we term *process assessment*. Simply put, the goal of process assessment in mathematics is to identify the manner in which students derive a particular answer when solving a problem. More often than not, students solve math problems conventionally by utilizing standard school methods (algorithms). At times, however, they are unable to grasp the taught algorithm, so they design alternate means to derive the answer.

By way of illustration, consider the problem $43 - 27 = x$. The correct difference, 16, can be derived by (a) understanding the conceptual nature of place value and applying proper regrouping techniques, (b) failing to grasp the nature of place value conceptually yet knowing how to apply regrouping techniques, or (c) knowing nothing about either place value or regrouping but using an invented procedure (for instance, *counting on* from 27 to 43 and writing down the number of counts made along the way).

Process assessments allow us to identify the strategies by which students arrive at their answers. We provide two procedures here—passive assessment and active assessment. Teachers can conduct a passive process assessment by looking at a completed worksheet and analyzing a student's answer to a given problem. For example, consider the problem $43 - 27 = x$ again. A student's incorrect answer of 24 could well be the result of a regrouping miscue: The student probably thought something like, "Three minus seven . . . can't do it because you have to subtract the smaller number from the larger one, so seven minus three is four . . . four minus two is two . . . 24." Although this answer commonly results from overgeneralizing the basic rule that numbers of lesser values must be subtracted from numbers of greater value, we cannot be certain it was indeed the student's strategy. Perhaps instead the student counted on from 27 but forgot how many counts it took to get to 43. Memory failure is a common source of error in counting on to higher numbers. The obvious disadvantage with passive process assessment, therefore, is the uncertainty that exists when examining errors for defective strategy employment.

The second procedure, active process assessment, generally employs some form of flexible interviewing, whereby the student discusses aloud what she or he thought during computation. For instance, a student may be asked to "think out loud" while doing a math problem. By listening to the student's explanation, we can identify the strategies employed. The teacher generally asks follow-up questions to further probe the student's strategies. To illustrate, consider a student who calculates $43 - 27$ and states, "Three minus seven can't be done, so I borrow one from here (tens place) and put three, then I put one next to three (ones place), and 13 minus 7 is 6, three take away two is one . . . 16." A follow-up question might be "Okay. Tell me why you crossed out the four and put three above it." Based on the student's response, the teacher can gain insight into the student's knowledge of place-value concepts.

SCREENING TESTS

Sometimes teachers wish to identify quickly and efficiently who is struggling in a particular area and who is not. Usually, teachers can identify their students who are having problems just by working with them, but administering a screening measure helps validate those impressions. Although the most efficient screeners are group administered because good group tests provide valid scores in a short time, individual tests can be given. The screening process often leads to more diagnostic, comprehensive testing, but as is the case with RTI and its universal screening component, it qualifies students for supplemental instruction.

Various types of screening instruments are available, some highly standardized and others less so. Torgesen and Bryant's (2005) *Test of Phonological Awareness* (TOPA-2+) is an example of a highly standardized instrument for screening students for phonological awareness and phonics skills. The test is group administered to kindergarten, first-grade students, or second-grade children, and those who score below a set benchmark are in need of more comprehensive testing.

But not all screening needs to be highly standardized. For example, teachers know their students well enough to complete rating scales about their abilities and provide valid and reliable information for screening purposes. Teachers who have had a month or two to observe and work with their students can be asked simply to rate each student's performance along a five-point continuum from Poor to Superior or a more detailed rating scale that spans academic and behavioral areas.

DIAGNOSTIC ASSESSMENTS

Diagnostic measures are like survey tests in that they survey, or assess, numerous different areas. They provide more in-depth assessment than screening measures and take longer to administer. For that reason, screening measures are used to limit the number of students who need to be administered diagnostic measures. For example, students who do not meet benchmarks might then be administered the second edition of the *Comprehensive Test of Phonological Processes* (CTOPP-2; Wagner, Torgesen, Rashotte, & Pearson, 2013) to identify strengths and weaknesses across phonological awareness abilities. Or they might be given the most recent edition of the *Test of Word Reading Efficiency* (TOWRE-2) (Rashotte, Torgesen, & Wagner, 2012) to assess in-depth phonics skills.

Schools typically use two types of diagnostic measures. The first is a global achievement measure that examines a variety of areas. The *Woodcock Johnson IV Test of Achievement* (WJ-IV; Schrank, McGrew, Mather, & Woodcock, 2014), for example, contains more than a dozen subtests that examine reading, writing, mathematics, and other areas of achievement. By administering all WJ-IV subtests, examiners obtain a comprehensive overview of a student's skills across subject matter.

The *Woodcock Reading Mastery Test*, third edition (WRMT-III; Woodcock, 2011), is a second type of diagnostic measure. This test examines only reading, but it does so by studying many subcomponents of reading, such as comprehension and basic skills. Comparing and contrasting scores within the measure provides for an intraindividual analysis of reading strengths and weaknesses. Many such tests provide detailed analyses of strengths and weakness across mathematics, writing, and other academic skills.

Diagnostic measures also exist for assessing behavior, attention, anxiety, adaptive behavior skills, and other areas related to school success. With these scales, "diagnostic measure" takes on a subtly different meaning. Not only are the measures broad-based in their content, but they may actually be used to diagnose a condition. One of the most popular scales used for assessing attention problems is the *Conners Rating Scale—3rd edition* (Conners-III; Conners, 2008). Because ADHD must be observed across several settings, this rating scale is completed by parents and teachers, who report on the child's behaviors at home and in the classroom. Such a procedure allows for an ecological assessment, because it looks at behavior across settings and locations and collects data from multiple sources—in this case, the parents and one or more teachers. With the Conners scale, the teacher (or parent) reads a list of student behaviors and rates the extent to which each behavior is present for a particular child. The more behaviors the student exhibits that correspond to those who have ADHD, the greater the likelihood the student has ADHD.

Before we continue, recall that diagnostic tests are not so named because they "diagnose" conditions. Although usually true, this statement requires clarification. The results of diagnostic tests may lead to a diagnosis of a disability by special education team members. The team is typically composed of the student's parents, psychologists, diagnosticians, teachers, a representative from special education, and the principal and other professionals. Team members examine the data provided by diagnostic tests, observations, work samples, and so on and come to a decision about a person's eligibility for special education services. Although test scores are key contributors to the process, it is important to remember this oft-cited dictum: "Tests don't diagnose; people diagnose" (Wiederholt & Bryant, 2012).

OBSERVATIONS

Yogi Berra, one of baseball's greats, once said, "You can observe a whole lot just by watching." On the surface, this statement seems redundant; watching and observing are seemingly the same. But this is not necessarily true. Rather, people watch so they can observe. Watching is seeing. Observing is seeing *and* learning *and* making decisions about what you are seeing.

Teacher observations thus provide valuable data that should be combined with the data from other assessments to make educational decisions. Teachers can observe students and make performance judgments in many ways (see Chapter 9 on behavior). Here, we provide an example that yields objective data on students as they work by examining a target student (the student you are concerned about) and his or her peers. Design a rating scale that examines the behaviors of interest—in this simple case, object noise and out of place—while your observation form can examine any behavior of concern (hitting, off-task, unsolicited talking out). Create an observation tool that looks at the behaviors over a 20-minute time span (see Figure 8.4).

The approach is quite simple. Determine beforehand which students in the class will serve as the peer observants (for instance, two students in a row). Then observe the target student for 30 seconds. If the student is observed doing the behavior (say, out of place) at any time during the 30 seconds, record a slash mark (/) in the box. Then observe the first peer student for 30 seconds, recording the behavior (if present) in the same way. Observe the target student

FIGURE 8.4 — SAMPLE OBSERVATION FORM

Behavior (Target Student)	1	2	3	4	5	6	7	8	9	10	11	12	13	14	15	16	17	18	19	20	Total
Object Noise	/		/		/				/	/			/		/		/	/	/		10
Out of Place	/					/		/						/							4

Behavior (Peers)	1	2	3	4	5	6	7	8	9	10	11	12	13	14	15	16	17	18	19	20	Total
Object Noise	/		/		/							/						/			5
Out of Place		/	/						/		/									/	5

Object Noise 10/5 = 2.0

Out of Place 4/5 = 0.8

again, then the second peer student, and so on until forty 30-second intervals have passed (20 for each student).

Peer performance is important because it serves as a basis for comparison. To arrive at an assessment of performance, simply divide the target student's total number of slashes by the number of slashes for the peers. The resulting quotient provides an index of observed behavior. In our example, the target student was observed as making object noise twice as much as the peers (2.0). But for out of place, the target student was actually in place more often that the peers (0.8). By comparing the student with peers, we can identify whether the behavior is student specific or is actually being done by other students in the class as well.

Teacher observations made during instruction can yield considerable worthwhile information. Effective instruction calls for checking for understanding throughout a lesson, which means more than simply asking, "Any questions?" or "Do you understand?" Most students, especially struggling students, will not ask questions or admit to not understanding. So they remain silent, having little or no idea what was taught. Teachers should question students directly to check for understanding and observe student responses to determine whether their students "get it" or not. For example, if the topic pertains to a story being read, ask "Why" or "What of it" questions, or questions such as "What is the author trying to say here?" to gauge student understanding. Students' answers provide a wealth of information about their level of understanding, and such questions can be asked across content areas.

INTERVIEWS

Teachers can obtain a great deal of important information about the children they teach from the students' parents or guardians. When developing a diagnostic profile of a student, evaluators ask parents or guardians questions

AP Photo/Denis Poroy

Teachers can obtain a great deal of important information about the development of a child from their students' family members.

about their child's birth, developmental milestones, illnesses, social skills, and interests. This case history can provide basic information that helps the teacher or educational diagnostician better understand the child's overall development. However, because recall of developmental history may be sketchy or not totally accurate, try not to rely too heavily on this information. Rather, interpret it, along with information obtained from other teachers and from the students themselves, within the total context of assessment data.

Teachers and students can also be interviewed. Overton (2011) suggested that teachers are in a unique position to consider several important characteristics of their students. For example, how prepared is the student each day? How does the student begin assignments during class? If distracted, how does the student perform? Does the student complete his or her homework assignments? Does the student respond in class? Such questions provide the interviewer with a sense of the student's behaviors that may not be noted during a particular observation.

Think-aloud interviews are a type of process assessment aimed at identifying the cognitive strategies students use to solve mathematics problems, comprehend reading material, explore a social studies scenario, conduct a science experiment, and so forth (McLoughlin & Lewis, 2008). In the think-aloud interview, the teacher asks a student to think out loud as he or she performs a task. Interview questions might include the following: (a) "What are you thinking?" (b) "How will you solve this task or problem?" (c) "What is another way to solve the problem?" (d) "What do you think the answer might be and why do you think that?" and (e) "How would you explain this problem to another student?"

Several factors must be present for the think-aloud interview to be used appropriately. First, the interviewer must be a good observer of student performance. Second, the person must be knowledgeable about the scope and sequence of the curriculum being used. Third, the interviewer must be familiar with cognitive strategies the student may be employing (McLoughlin & Lewis, 2008). For example, if a student is asked to explain (think out loud about) how to add a group of four blocks to a group of five blocks, and the student puts the two groups together and then starts counting from one to arrive at the answer, further questions are needed to determine the extent of her or his knowledge of numbers and groups and of her or his ability to use the "count on" addition strategy. These questions might include "What is an easier way to count all the blocks besides starting with one?" and (given five blocks) "What different arrangements can you make with the blocks to show five?"

Through the think-aloud interview, it is possible to gain an understanding of how a student approaches the problem or task and of what strategies are being used. This information may lead to the development of new instructional objectives or to a change in the intervention. The interview information, along with other data, can help teachers better understand the processes their students use to solve problems or tasks and the effectiveness of these processes.

Although "thinking out loud" can be effective, many children with learning problems have difficulty expressing their thoughts aloud and require a different interviewing method. We have found that role-playing can be very effective in identifying what students are thinking as they work. In this instance, the student plays the role of teacher and the teacher assumes the student's role. As an example, you might tell your student, "I have an idea. You be the teacher and show me how to subtract 17 from 35." The following dialog may take place (T is the Teacher; S is the student):

S. First write down 35 on your wipe board.

T. (writes 35) Like this?

S. Yes, very good. Now below the 35, write 17, and make a line under it and put a minus sign in front of the 17.

T. (writes 17, but the alignment is off) Okay, what's next?

S. That's close, but you have to make sure the 1 is in the tens place below the 3 and the 7 is in the units place below the 5. You sort of have it mixed up. Watch me (models correct placement).

T. (erases the incorrect alignment and writes the proper way) Oh yeah, I forgot.

S. It's very important that the numbers line up. Now the next thing is to subtract the numbers in the unit column. You can't go 5 minus 7 because you always have to subtract the smaller number from the bigger number. So I can't do 5 minus 7, I have to do 7 minus 5. 7 minus 5 is 2, so write the 2 below the line in the units column.

The process continues, but you already have found that the student has a subtract misconception. Simply by looking at the student's work (what we called *passive process assessment* earlier), one might be able to draw this conclusion; but this approach confirms the misconception.

Both interviewing methods serve the same purpose. Teachers may choose one to use consistently or may alternate the methods for the sake of variety. The key is to use some form of interview to identify efficient and inefficient strategies students are employing.

RATING SCALES AND CHECKLISTS

Rating scales and checklists are valuable sources of information that can be used as part of the assessment process (Reynolds et al., 2009). Typically, rating scales and checklists provide a listing of skills or abilities, and the rater provides responses indicating how well a person performs each skill. Sometimes the responses are dichotomous—that is, the skills are either present or absent. Dichotomously scored rating scales are really checklists. Other scales offer a range of responses and use a Likert-type response format. Figures 8.5, 8.6, and 8.7 provide examples of these types of scoring options.

Figure 8.5 demonstrates the use of a dichotomous checklist to examine early childhood behaviors. Figures 8.6 and 8.7 are rating scales that examine writing. The first figure provides a holistic evaluation of writing and the second provides an analytic approach.

RUBRICS

Rubrics are increasingly being used to evaluate writing samples (see Table 8.3). Here we see another way to evaluate a writing sample. Rubrics are very similar to rating scales; they are important to understand because they are often used in tests that measure state standards in writing. Our sample rubric is one similarly used when assessing the Common Core writing standards for ninth and tenth graders writing a narrative text. As you can see, it examines five areas: exposition, narrative techniques and development, organization and cohesion, style and conventions, and conclusion. Criteria are provided for five scores, ranging from exceptional (worth 5 points) to inadequate (1 point). Scorers usually read and reread each student passage several times with these areas and scoring criteria in mind.

FIGURE 8.5 EXAMPLE OF A CHECKLIST USED WITH PRESCHOOL CHILDREN

Directions: Circle Yes or No to indicate whether each skill has been demonstrated.

Self-help skills

Yes	No	Attempts to wash face and hands
Yes	No	Helps put toys away
Yes	No	Drinks from a standard cup
Yes	No	Eats using utensils
Yes	No	Attempts to use the toilet
Yes	No	Attempts to dress self

Language development

Yes	No	Follows simple directions
Yes	No	Verbalizes needs and feelings
Yes	No	Speech can be understood most of the time
Yes	No	Speaks in sentences of three or more words

Basic skills development

Yes	No	Can count to 10
Yes	No	Recognizes numbers to 10

Can name the following shapes

Yes	No	Circle
Yes	No	Square
Yes	No	Triangle
Yes	No	Star

Can identify the following colors

Yes	No	Red
Yes	No	Blue
Yes	No	Green

Understands the following concepts

Yes	No	Up and down
Yes	No	Big and little
Yes	No	Open and closed
Yes	No	On and off
Yes	No	In and out

Social development

Yes	No	Plays independently
Yes	No	Plays parallel to other students
Yes	No	Plays cooperatively with other students
Yes	No	Participates in group activities

FIGURE 8.6 **EXAMPLE OF A HOLISTIC SCORING RUBRIC**

Essay item: Compare and contrast communism and fascism. Give examples of the ways they are similar and the way they differ.

Classification	Description	Rating
Excellent	The student demonstrated a thorough understanding of both concepts and could accurately describe in detail similarities and differences and give examples. This is an exemplary response.	5
Good	The student demonstrated a good understanding of the concepts and could describe similarities and differences and give examples.	4
Average	The student demonstrated an adequate understanding of the concepts and could describe some similarities and differences. Depth of understanding was limited and there were gaps in knowledge.	3
Marginal	The student showed limited understanding of the concepts and could provide no more than vague references to similarities and differences. Some information was clearly inaccurate. Examples were either vague, irrelevant, or nor applicable.	2
Poor	The student showed very little understanding of the concepts and was not able to describe any similarities or differences.	1
Very Poor	The student showed no understanding of the concepts.	0

SOURCE: C.R. Reynolds, R.B. Livingston, & V. Willson, V. (2009). *Measurment and assessment in education* (2nd ed.). Boston: Allyn and Bacon, p. 235.

FIGURE 8.7 **EXAMPLE OF AN ANALYTIC SCORING RUBRIC**

Essay item: Compare and contrast communism and fascism. Give examples of the ways they are similar and the ways they differ.

Area	Poor (0 points)	Average (1 point)	Above Average (2 points)	Excellent (3 points)
The student demonstrated an understanding of communism.				
The student demonstrated an understanding of fascism.				
The student was able to compare and contrast the concepts.				
The student was able to present relevant and clear examples highlighting similarities and differences.				
The response was clear, well organized, and showed a thorough understanding of the material.				

SOURCE: Reynolds et al. (2009, p. 235).

TABLE 8.3   NARRATIVE SCORING RUBRIC

Description	5 Exceptional	4 Skilled	3 Proficient	2 Developing	1 Inadequate
Exposition: The text sets up a story by introducing the event/conflict, characters, and setting.	The text creatively engages the reader by setting out a well-developed conflict, situation, or observation. The text establishes one or multiple points of view and introduces a narrator and/or complex characters.	The text engages and orients the reader by setting out a conflict, situation, or observation. It establishes one or multiple points of view and introduces a narrator and/or well-developed characters.	The text orients the reader by setting out a conflict, situation, or observation. It establishes one point of view and introduces a narrator and/or developed characters.	The text provides a setting with a vague conflict, situation, or observation with an unclear point of view. It introduces a narrator and/or under-developed characters.	The text provides a setting that is unclear with a vague conflict, situation, or observation. It has an unclear point of view and underdeveloped narrator and/or characters.
Narrative Techniques and Development: The story is developed using dialogue, pacing, description, reflection, and multiple plot lines.	The text demonstrates sophisticated narrative techniques such as engaging dialogue, artistic pacing, vivid description, complex reflection, and multiple plot lines to develop experiences, events, and/or characters.	The text demonstrates deliberate use of narrative techniques such as dialogue, pacing, description, reflection, and multiple plot lines to develop experiences, events, and/or characters.	The text uses narrative techniques such as dialogue, description, and reflection that illustrate events and/or characters.	The text uses some narrative techniques such as dialogue or description and merely retells events and/or experiences.	The text lacks narrative techniques and merely retells events and/or experiences.
Organization and Cohesion: The text follows a logical sequence of events.	The text creates a seamless progression of experiences or events using multiple techniques— such as chronology, flashback, foreshadowing, suspense, etc.— to sequence events so that they build on one another to create a coherent whole.	The text creates a smooth progression of experiences or events using a variety of techniques— such as chronology, flashback, foreshadowing, suspense, etc.— to sequence events so that they build on one another to create a coherent whole.	The text creates a logical progression of experiences or events using some techniques— such as chronology, flashback, foreshadowing, suspense, etc.— to sequence events so that they build on one another to create a coherent whole.	The text creates a sequence or progression of experiences or events.	The text lacks a sequence or progression of experiences or events or presents an illogical sequence of events.

Description	5 Exceptional	4 Skilled	3 Proficient	2 Developing	1 Inadequate
Style and Conventions: The text uses sensory language and details to create a vivid picture of the events, setting, and characters.	The text uses eloquent words and phrases, showing details and rich sensory language and mood to convey a realistic picture of the experiences, events, setting, and/or characters.	The text uses precise words and phrases, showing details and controlled sensory language and mood to convey a realistic picture of the experiences, events, setting, and/or characters.	The text uses words and phrases, telling details and sensory language to convey a vivid picture of the experiences, events, setting, and/or characters.	The text uses words and phrases and telling details to convey experiences, events, settings, and/or characters.	The text merely tells about experiences, events, settings, and/or characters.
Conclusion: The text provides a conclusion that follows from the course of the narrative. The conclusion provides a reflection on or resolution of the events.	The text moves to a conclusion that artfully follows from and thoughtfully reflects on what is experienced, observed, or resolved over the course of the narrative.	The text builds to a conclusion that logically follows from and reflects on what is experienced, observed, or resolved over the course of the narrative.	The text provides a conclusion that follows from and reflects on what is experienced, observed, or resolved over the course of the narrative.	The text provides a conclusion that follows from what is experienced, observed, or resolved over the course of the narrative.	The text may provide a conclusion to the events of the narrative.

SOURCE: iParadigms, LLC (2012). Retrieved from http://www.schoolimprovement.com/docs/Common%20Core%20Rubrics_Gr9-10.pdf (p. 5).

Unlike many rating scales, rubrics have lengthy descriptions of the scoring criteria, making scoring decisions somewhat less subjective. However, it takes considerable time and practice to learn to use rubrics to score writing passages. Teachers often attend lengthy workshops where they learn how to score passages using rubrics, and they practice scoring passages with other teachers and compare their scores. It is not uncommon to find considerable differences of opinion early on during the training, but as discussion and further practice sessions are conducted, closer agreement is reached. It is critical that whoever scores a rubric arrives at a similar score. In assessment language, this is called interscorer reliability, which we discussed earlier in the "Technical Adequacy" section.

WORK SAMPLES

Work sample analysis is a procedure that helps teachers assess academic skills by looking at students' permanent products (McLoughlin & Lewis, 2008) to identify types and frequencies of errors. This information can help teachers establish instructional objectives or select a new intervention.

The most common type of work sample analysis is error analysis, which is fairly easy to conduct. The teacher (a) identifies the objective of the assignment, (b) spells out the mastery criteria for the work, (c) examines work sample products, (d) documents error types, (e) asks students to explain how they arrived at an erroneous solution, and (f) makes instructional recommendations. For instance, in mathematics, the teacher could (a) establish that students are expected to complete 10 word problems at 90% accuracy, (b) examine the story problems completed by students, (c) record the percentage correct, (d) examine each problem to identify the types of errors made (for instance, erroneous computation, incorrect diagram to depict information, incorrect use of "key word" technique), (e) ask students to explain how they solved the problems, and (f) identify additional instructional objectives, based on the error types and student explanations, to rectify the problems. In oral reading, the teacher could record error types (such as substitutions, omissions, additions) and the number of errors. If the number of incorrect responses is significant, the teacher can institute a remedial plan.

The error analysis procedure can yield good information for designing the instructional program. It is important to ask students to explain their answers. Through careful analysis of work samples, coupled with student explanations, teachers can pinpoint faulty conceptual or procedural knowledge that they can then remediate.

SCHOOL RECORDS

Teachers glean information about their children from a variety of sources, such as the measures we described earlier. But they can also find information in students' cumulative folders (or cumulative records or files, as they are also called), which contain academic and behavioral history data.

School records can be a valuable source of information about student academic and social progress. Records of attendance, achievement test scores, curricular materials used during instruction, anecdotal notes, and student work provide a composite overview of the student's progression through the grades. Teachers can use this information to document particular problems that might have been evident in earlier grades, attendance patterns, techniques that were implemented earlier, classroom and behavioral interactions, and teacher concerns. Again, although this is important information, some pieces (such as anecdotal notes) may need to be interpreted cautiously because of reliability concerns. That is, people may be inconsistent in their interpretation of information found in the records.

PORTFOLIO ASSESSMENTS

Portfolio assessment is a means of monitoring student learning and evaluating the effectiveness of instructional programs and decision making. Portfolios contain student-selected work samples and sometimes student notes about how the samples were created and edited or improved. Portfolio assessment can compare student progress to curricular objectives and instructional methods, focus our evaluation on process rather than just on product, measure student academic achievement and classroom learning more directly, and assist in evaluating the effectiveness of instruction.

Reynolds et al. (2009) noted that portfolios are typically scored using evaluation rubrics. These rubrics should specify all evaluation criteria that needs to be considered when evaluating the students' work products, provide explicit qualifications for performance levels for all criteria, and indicate whether the criteria are applied holistically or analytically.

For students with learning and behavior problems, portfolio information should be related to curricular goals included in the IEP. Obviously, such information typically would include academic and social skills, but information can also be provided about behavior and adaptive functioning, academic and literacy growth, strategic learning and self-regulation, and language and cultural aspects that can be linked to the IEP.

Students with learning and behavior problems typically lack specific academic skills and effective cognitive strategies that promote efficient learning. Therefore, portfolio assessment should include examples of completed products (for instance, math problems or writing samples), with analyses that document the types of strategies employed during problem solving or drafting/editing. Notes taken during writing conferences can accompany writing samples.

Frequent measures of student progress can help teachers monitor learning and implement decision-making criteria. For example, it is possible to measure fluency in oral reading twice a week to determine the effect of the instructional intervention: Collect rate data and analyze student growth, implement decision rules regarding rate of student progress, and store graphs in the portfolio until the next timing. The important point about the time line used for collecting and assessing portfolio items is frequency. For students with learning and behavior difficulties, monitor progress regularly to determine whether instructional techniques are indeed promoting student academic growth.

BEHAVIORAL ASSESSMENTS

All students go through periods in their lives that affect their behavior and personality. Events at home or with their peers can cause children to act out or to become depressed or anxious. Typically, these periods do not last long, and the students bounce back. For some students, however, behavior problems occur for a long time and are systematic. For these students, assessments can help identify emotional problems that are symptomatic of disabilities.

Earlier we mentioned that the Conners-III has a parent and teacher rating component. This allows for an ecological evaluation, that is, one that considers multiple ways to collect information, such as across people or settings. Across the scales, the responses to one or two items may not be indicative of a serious behavior problem. But students whose ratings are consistently problematic across settings when observed by different people may well have serious behavioral or emotional conditions. The advantage of using ecological assessments, whether gathered in one scale or across several measures, is that they allow teachers and others to determine whether the problems occur in just one setting or are pervasive across multiple settings and people. We provide several examples of less standardized assessment procedures in Chapter 9 on behavior concerns. All the techniques contribute to identifying problem behaviors and ameliorating them.

CURRICULUM-BASED MEASURES

Progress monitoring relies on collecting data periodically and using it to make instructional decisions. Curriculum-based measures (CBMs) have gained in popularity as a technique for monitoring student performance while considering curricular goals and instructional techniques. Accordingly, CBMs are typically the assessments of choice for monitoring student progress over time. Professionals use assessment measures that determine how students are performing not only in relationship to the peer group but also in relationship to the curriculum and instruction presented daily. Recently, progress monitoring has also become a critical feature of learning disability identification procedures that employ the RTI procedure. See the Working Together feature for information about how general education teachers collaborate with special educators to establish a multitiered service delivery system for RTI implementation.

WORKING *together*

RTI IMPLEMENTATION

With the passage of IDEA '04, school districts can now use the RTI procedure to help in the learning disability identification process. This procedure may use a multitiered approach to identify early those students who may be at risk for having learning disabilities and to intervene in kindergarten, Grade 1, or Grade 2 to help reduce the likelihood that students will be misidentified as having an LD.

General education teachers work closely with special educators to help set up a multitiered system wherein young children are given curriculum-based assessments (CBAs) in the fall of the school year. Those students who fall below preset benchmarks, usually set at the 25th or 16th percentile, are targeted for small group supplemental instruction in the second tier. Students receiving the supplemental instruction continue to receive regular class instruction in the core curriculum but also are provided additional, small group instruction using validated practices designed to help them increase their skill levels to those of their peers.

Special educators can help general education teachers identify reliable CBMs that yield valid results and can also help teachers identify research-based supplemental instructional procedures. Every two weeks or so, CBMs are readministered and provide an index of growth for each student receiving supplemental instruction. If the students are making progress, no changes are made to the supplemental program. However, instruction for students who are not making sufficient progress is modified to better meet student needs. After 8 to 12 weeks of supplemental instruction, midyear testing is used to determine whether the students can exit the second tier of intervention or need to continue such instruction for an additional 8 to 12 weeks. After spring testing, students who do not make sufficient progress may be identified as having an LD if they meet additional, federally prescribed criteria.

Clearly, assessment plays a critical role in the RTI process. Additional testing using highly standardized tests may also be administered in the determination of a learning disability, but CBA is at the heart of the assessment process.

QUESTIONS

1. What types of questions might a general education teacher ask a special educator as they discuss RTI-related issues.

2. Put yourself in the position of the general education teacher. How might you find information about your school's RTI program? What questions might you need to have answered?

3. Why are assessments important during the RTI process?

To assist educators in designing, implementing, and evaluating instruction to meet the needs of an increasingly diverse student population, assessment procedures must be versatile yet valid. With CBM, the content of the curriculum and the content found in the assessment are the same. The teacher uses material from the students' curricula to determine where students should be placed, what their instructional objectives should be, and how they are progressing. In this section, we describe (a) the purposes of CBM, (b) ways to design CBAs, (c) data collection and analysis procedures, and (d) procedures for pairing instruction and evaluation. (See the literature on CBMs and precision teaching; both use graphing, decision-making rules, and intervention recommendations to guide the instructional process.) As you read each section, think about a student you may know or have observed who has a disability. What considerations should occur at each step to help reduce the need for later adaptations based on the test's and the student's characteristics?

Curriculum-based measurement has several purposes:

- To measure directly the curriculum being taught

- To establish a link between students' IEPs and classroom instruction

- To provide a means for monitoring student progress and evaluating the effectiveness of the intervention being used to teach the instructional objective

- To obtain data during the prereferral stage about students' progress in the general education setting without special education services

- To provide a more "culture fair" or "culture neutral" means of assessing the progress of youngsters from culturally and linguistically diverse backgrounds

- To determine initial placement in a task analysis of skills

Thus, curriculum-based measurement offers an alternative to standardized testing as a means for teachers to place, monitor, and evaluate instructional programs and student progress.

DESIGNING CURRICULUM-BASED MEASURES

CBMs can help identify the initial instructional objective placement and measure students' progress with the identified instructional objective. Before identifying instructional placement within the designated curriculum, teachers should refer to the IEP and identify the goals designated for instruction. By examining these goals, teachers can begin to develop an idea of the content and skill areas that require instruction. The next step is to design the placement CBA. Taylor (2008) listed five steps to follow when constructing CBMs for instructional placement purposes.

STEP 1: Identify the goal to be assessed.

Examine the student's goals on the IEP. An example of a goal might be, "The student will compute whole numbers."

STEP 2: Identify the instructional objectives (task analysis).

Break down Step 1 into smaller steps that can become instructional objectives. Instructional objectives for the goal identified in Step 1 might include the following: two-digit + one-digit numbers with no regrouping, two-digit + two-digit with no regrouping, three-digit + two-digit with no regrouping, three-digit + three-digit with no regrouping, two-digit + one-digit with regrouping, two-digit + two-digit with regrouping, three-digit + two-digit with regrouping, and three-digit + three digit with regrouping to the tens and hundreds place. Each of these steps could be treated as an instructional objective, depending on the student's ability level.

STEP 3: Develop test items for each instructional objective.

Develop sufficient items (four or five) for each objective to ensure the student has enough opportunities to respond in the time frame allowed. Develop several versions of the CBA for testing across several days.

STEP 4: Set standards of performance (mastery levels).

Identify a performance standard for each objective. The criterion can be stated in terms of percentage correct (80% or 90% accuracy) or rate (100 words per minute correct); data collection procedures are discussed later. To select an appropriate performance standard or criterion, (a) have students in the general education classroom perform the skill and take the average of those scores as the criterion, or (b) use a "percentage-correct" criterion or fluency criterion based on the type of skill being assessed (acceptable percentage-correct criteria usually range from 80 to 100, depending on the skill; fluency depends on the skill), or (c) use the school district's performance standards.

STEP 5: Administer and interpret the instrument.

Have students take the CBM several times; one administration is not sufficient to give an accurate picture of students' instructional abilities. Analyze test item results for each instructional objective; the scores can be averaged to arrive at the student's instructional levels of performance. Instructional objectives with results that fall below the criterion level are targeted for instruction. Students should know the time limits in which they will work and the standards that apply (for instance, work quickly, skip problems you don't know, reduce fractions, show your work, finish all the pages).

A major component of CBMs is the collection and evaluation of data for determining placement and progress in an instructional sequence. A data collection system that accurately measures the targeted skill is selected, and teachers implement specific data analysis procedures to determine whether their intervention is indeed making a difference with the students.

Teachers can incorporate charting into their progress monitoring using CBM data. An example appears in Figure 8.8. Here, a student has been given 40 addition and subtraction facts to calculate in one minute. The number of items answered correctly in that time span (calculations correct per minute or CCPM) is graphed on a sheet of paper. The students can do this themselves to see their own progress. In our sample, the student's scores were graphed weekly. Through Week 3, the student was making progress toward his end-of-semester objective (marked with an X). But then, for three consecutive weeks, the student's scores plateaued. We have drawn an arrow to show how much progress is needed in the short time remaining before the end of the semester. The arrow demonstrates that changes must be made in the program to ensure sufficient progress toward the student's goal.

HOW DO WE ADAPT AND MODIFY ASSESSMENTS FOR STUDENTS WITH SPECIAL NEEDS?

Assessment adaptations include any change in administration, scoring, and interpretation procedures we make specifically because of a test taker's ability. Their purpose is to level the playing field, meaning each test taker has the same chance as any other student to succeed, whether the assessment is a high-stakes test or Friday's spelling quiz.

We begin our discussion of assessment adaptations by exploring universal design as it applies to assessment. We then discuss briefly the role of parents in making test adaptations or accommodations. Then we introduce different adaptation categories. We conclude our discussion of assessment adaptations by examining two specific applications where assessment adaptations may or may not be warranted: high-stakes testing and grading. We also briefly discuss alternative assessments. Many of the adaptation procedures described in the section can be generalized to any number of additional scenarios related to assessments.

FIGURE 8.8 SAMPLE CHART DEPICTING CORRECT CALCULATIONS PER MINUTE (CCPM)

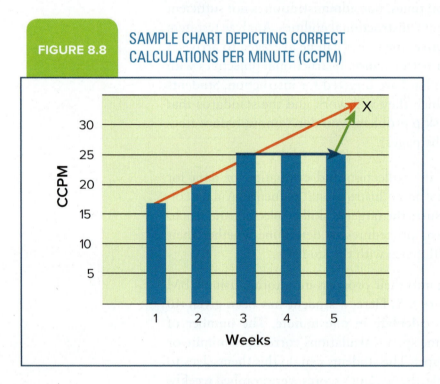

UNIVERSAL DESIGN FOR ASSESSMENT

As described in Chapter 7, the term **universal design** refers to barrier-free systems that meet the needs of everyone, including people with disabilities (Smith & Tyler, 2010). Initially used in conjunction with accessible housing for people with and without disabilities, universal design has expanded to teaching and testing. The premise is that curricula and assessments should be made accessible to all students by "remov[ing] barriers to accurate measurement of learner knowledge, skills, and engagement" (CAST, 2011, p. 8).

With regard to universal design for assessment, more than 10 years ago Thompson, Johnstone, and Thurlow (2002) provided some suggestions for making tests more accessible to all students that are still relevant today:

- **Select an inclusive assessment population.** When developing items, think about all students who will participate in the assessment. Ideally, examinees would be afforded equal opportunity to prepare for a test.

- **Precisely define test content.** Define what is to be tested so that irrelevant cognitive, sensory, emotional, and physical barriers can be removed.

- **Choose accessible, nonbiased items.** Build accessibility into items from the beginning, and use bias review teams to ensure that quality is retained in all items.

- **Be amenable to accommodations.** Test design must facilitate the use of need accommodations (for instance, all items can be communicated in Braille).

- **Provide simple, clear, and intuitive instructions and procedures.** Make sure students are easily able to follow the directions for taking a test.

- **Ensure maximum readability and comprehensibility.** For example, use plain language strategies and other approaches that reduce ambiguity and increase understandability.

- **Ensure maximum legibility.** Characteristics that ensure easy decipherability are applied to text, tables, figures and illustrations, and response formats.

PARENTAL INVOLVEMENT

Parents are (or should be) active participants in all aspects of their children's education, including testing. They should be aware of, and sign off on, testing accommodations that have been suggested for their child. In addition, parents can request testing accommodations the district should consider. PARCC (2013) has written a parental guidebook that outlines roles and responsibilities (see http://www.parcconline.org/resources/parent-resources). You can type into your server, Expanding Accessibility: Accessibility Features for All Students and Accommodations in PARCC Assessments—A Parent's Guide, to download a copy of the guide.

One section of the guide is titled "What Parents Can Do to Support Their Child." Here is what PARCC offers to parents:

- Familiarize yourself with the Common Core State Standards. Talk to your child's teachers about what he or she is learning.

- Learn about the PARCC assessments—their purpose, what they measure, and how the results will be used.

- Learn about PARCC accessibility features and accommodations. Identify those that your child may need or find helpful to use at home, in the classroom, and on the PARCC assessments.

- Find out how your child's teachers are preparing for the new assessments and how they are helping your child get ready.

To make assessments accessible to all students, teachers should give simple, clear, and intuitive instructions and ensure that students are easily able to follow the directions.

- Talk to your child about the accommodations he or she already uses on tests. Discuss whether or not your child thinks they are helping him or her. Share this information with your child's teachers—or encourage your child to share his or her ideas with teachers.

- Share information about your child's strengths and needs related to using computers for work assignments with educators. Include information about the types of strategies your child uses routinely to complete homework assignments and other tasks in the home and the community.

- Encourage your child to use the accessibility features and/or accommodations identified in his or her IEP or Section 504 plan at home, if possible.

- Ask about the technology your child will be using for the PARCC assessments. Ask about how your child can practice using the technology during school.

- Make sure your child is willing to use the accommodation(s) and/or accessibility feature(s). Inform his or her teacher if your child is having difficulty using an accommodation.

- Research possible state and/or regional technology centers for information on matching student needs with allowable assistive technology. (p. 3)

As a teacher, you will likely be the first person parents contact with questions about their student's testing. Check with your district to see whether a parental handbook is available that can provide useful information. If there is one, provide parents with a copy, but at the same time explain its content. If there is no handbook available, create one and have it checked with your district assessment office. In any case, remember that not all parents understand education language, and even though these handbooks are typically written with parents in mind, no two parents are alike. Many will need the material presented in a way they can understand, and they trust you with that task.

ADAPTATION CATEGORIES

Adaptations tend to cluster around four basic areas: input adaptations, output adaptations, time and/or schedule adaptations, and location adaptations. We add a fifth area, academic qualifications, which deals more with curriculum issues than with testing adaptations.

Input Adaptations

Input adaptations adjust the way students access test stimuli and questions. More than 20 years ago, Hammill, Brown, and Bryant (1992) identified three testing input formats that remain relevant today for assessment adaptations: listening (the test taker listens to instructions and/or test questions), reading print (words and numbers), and looking at stimuli, such as spatial tests that have the student look at a one-dimensional, unfolded drawing and ask what the object would look like if folded into a three-dimensional object. The input of test items should suit the needs of all students, including those who have a disability. For example, a student with a reading learning disability is unlikely to do well on a science test if he or she has to read the question. In this instance, recognizing student needs allows teachers to adapt the test input to allow the student to demonstrate acquisition of science knowledge.

One of the key considerations for input adaptations deals with the content that is being assessed by the test. Think about Sonya, a student we met earlier in Mr. Gomez's class. In two weeks, she is going to take two tests, back-to-back, that require reading paragraphs and responding to multiple-choice questions. The first test is a measure of reading comprehension, and the second test assesses knowledge of science concepts. Because Sonya has a learning disability in reading, she struggles with both test formats, so she decides to speak with Mr. Gomez about possible input adaptations.

Sonya will probably not be allowed to use an adapted input format for the reading comprehension test, but she is likely to receive adaptations for the science test. Why? The content of the reading test is *reading*. Adaptations that remove reading from the task defeat the purpose of the test; in other words, changing the input format changes the content being measured. This is one litmus test of any assessment adaptation. If the content being measured by the assessment is altered, the adaptation proposal is likely to be unsound.

Science content, on the other hand, would not be altered if we remove reading as the input format. The test uses reading as an efficient way to test large numbers of students' understanding of science, because the assumption is that all (or at least most) test takers can read the paragraphs and questions. But reading ability itself is not being tested. Thus, because the content of the assessment is not being changed, altering the input format to speech would be legitimate.

Output Adaptations

Output adaptations adjust the way a test taker records responses to test questions. Output formats include speaking, minor (providing a one- or two-word response); speaking, major (responding with sentences); manipulating objects (such as blocks or coins); marking an answer sheet (the familiar "fill in the bubble," for example); pointing; drawing; and writing print. If a test's output format interferes with its ability to provide valid scores for a student who has a disability, output adaptations can be made.

Consider Dondra from the chapter's opening example, who has a neurological impairment that affects her fine motor skills. As a result of this disability, Dondra has trouble grasping a pencil, and when she finally controls it, she has difficulty using the pencil to write or make identifiable marks. Dondra is studying to take a social studies exam in three days. This exam requires students to read multiple-choice questions and respond by filling in bubbles of a Scantron sheet. Thus, the test's output format will make it nearly impossible for Dondra to mark the answer sheet (completely filling in a bubble without going outside the bubble). Clearly, the test's content has nothing to do with filling in bubbles on an answer sheet; it is measuring social studies skills. Therefore, it is likely that Mr. Gomez will alter the test's output format for Dondra to allow her to better respond to the test questions.

Time and/or Schedule Adaptations

When appropriate, teachers may extend testing time and may also change the way the time is organized. Extended time is a common test adaptation. The idea is that people with reading disabilities, even if they are able to read the text, do so at a much slower rate than their peers without disabilities. Thus, the slow readers will not have the same opportunity to complete the test as their peers without disabilities.

Most tests have time limits. As a rule of thumb, students are expected to complete about 75% of the test in the prescribed time allocation, and/or 80% of the students are expected to have an opportunity to respond to all items. Students with disabilities may not be able to complete the test in the allotted time, so time adaptations may be made. In addition, a test may be organized to provide 25 minutes for one test to be taken, give students a five-minute break, and then call for a second test to be administered after the break. Some students, by the nature of their disability, may be fatigued and require a longer break between test administrations. Depending on the circumstances, the students may be allowed to wait longer before completing the rest of the test. Such an adjustment is a schedule adaptation.

Location Adaptations

Location adaptations may change the setting in which a test is administered or the conditions of the test setting. Some students have disabilities that affect their ability to perform when distractions occur around them. For these students, a conventional testing setting, such as the classroom, may be

Assessment Technology

inappropriate, and an isolated setting may be an appropriate location adaptation. In addition, some students with behavior issues may need to be tested in a situation that minimizes the effects of their behavior on others.

Academic Qualifications

Although they are not really adaptations in the true sense of the word, academic qualifications are used to identify whether a person should take the test in the first place. Most students with disabilities, by law, participate in the general education curriculum, so they will take the same tests as their nondisabled peers. However, some students with severe disabilities have IEPs that focus on special academic areas such as life skills. In this instance, alternate assessments would be deemed more appropriate than a test that measures mastery of content the students haven't been taught.

ADAPTATIONS FOR HIGH-STAKES TESTING

Most states have adopted the Common Core State Standards (National Governors Association Center for Best Practices & Council of Chief State School Officers, 2010). For the first several years of the CCSS, there was no standard high-stakes assessment that measured performance on the standards. States that had adopted the CCSS were left to either adjust their state's high-stakes tests to conform to the new standards or continue to test the non-CCSS content that had been assessed by the previously administered instruments. To remedy the situation, the Smarter Balanced Assessment Consortium and the Partnership for Assessment of Readiness for College and Careers wrote and field-tested a standard assessment. States not adopting the CCSS will continue to use their own high-stakes tests.

Curricular Content

Usually, a team of experts meets and creates, for each subject area, a list of skills they want taught to their state's students. Essentially, they are telling teachers across the state what it is important for all students in their classrooms to learn in kindergarten, Grade 1, and so on through high school. Through this process, state departments of education tell their teachers and population, "This is important for all children in _____ (insert any state here). We care enough about our children's education that we have created a set of skills all children should have before they go on to the next grade." Supposedly, when students have learned everything they should know in the third grade, they are ready to learn the material in the fourth grade, and so on until graduation.

Assessment Issues

Once the curriculum skills have been set, a team of experts creates a test to measure those skills, and these state exams form the basis for most states' high-stakes testing. Think about the logic behind the testing. It begins with "These are the skills that all students in the state of _____ need in order to graduate from high school." Then it moves to "If students need to know this information by the end of high school, what skills do they need at the end of the ninth grade? We'll create a test of those skills, which students will take at the end of ninth grade. If they fail the test, they have to repeat the ninth grade until they are ready for the tenth grade." Most states do not test at every grade level; they pick key grades for testing, usually two or three years apart. For most students in states with this policy, high-stakes testing can begin as early as the third grade.

High-stakes testing has a dramatic effect on teachers and students. First, teachers have to teach the skills the state has specified. Fortunately, most publishers of basal textbooks understand this, so they work to ensure a correspondence between these enumerated skills and the skills that are taught in textbooks. If there are gaps, teachers are responsible for filling them.

As we have already noted, not all students have to participate in high-stakes testing. If a student has a disability, the student's IEP may state that he or she is **exempt** from such testing. However, states are increasingly devising alternate tests for students with disabilities. This approach stems from the belief that all students should be accountable for learning.

Adaptation Issues

If a student with a disability is going to take a high-stakes test, test adaptations may be made to compensate for the student's disability. The decision to do so is not made haphazardly. Usually, states and districts have set policies governing the choice; teachers may wish to consider the following six-step procedure. (*Note:* Throughout this section, we deal with disability-related adaptations for high-stakes testing. For adaptations related to English language learners, see the Considering Diversity feature.)

STEP 1: As the IEP committee, discuss whether the student should participate in state and district assessment.

This step has three components:

1. Examine a student's IEP goals and the content of the educational program or the state's curriculum.

2. Examine the purpose of the state and district-wide assessments and the content of the assessments.

3. Measure the match between the student's educational program and the content of the assessment.

If there is no match between the student's educational program and the content of the assessment, the student may be exempted from the testing. If there is a match, the next step in the process is to determine whether adaptations are warranted.

STEP 2: As a committee, discuss the student's need for test adaptations.

IEP committees should examine the input and output formats of the state and district-wide assessments and the IEP and student work samples to determine whether the formats of the assessment will yield valid results.

If the committee agrees that the formats match the student's abilities, there is probably no need for adaptations. If, however, the formats preclude achieving valid results because they do not allow for the student's limitations (for example, Sonya's inability to read precludes using reading as an input format that yields valid results), adaptations may be needed.

STEP 3: As a committee, identify test adaptations that respond to the student's needs identified in Step 2.

Earlier, we described several areas where adaptations typically take place. To review, do input concerns preclude obtaining valid results in a typical setting? Does the output format need to be altered to ensure that the student can complete the task? Or, if he or she reads slowly because of the disability, is more time needed to complete the task? If the student is easily distracted, is a different testing location needed?

STEP 4: As a committee, document your decision in the IEP. If the IEP committee decides the student should not participate, members should recommend an appropriate alternate assessment.

STEP 5: As a committee, collect data and develop procedures for monitoring the effectiveness of adaptations.

What type of data should teachers collect? Usually, there are four sources of data. First, collect student scores on two versions of the same test, with and without adaptations. Remember that it is entirely possible the student will fail the test because he or she does not know the answers to the test items. Adaptations don't guarantee success; they are designed to guarantee only that the results are valid. If the student doesn't know the content and, with adaptations, demonstrates that lack of knowledge, then the results are valid.

Interview the student after testing to gauge his or her reactions. Did the adaptations work? What other issues may have arisen during testing that you need to know about?

Teachers also must be interviewed. This interview can be conducted at any time to learn about the student's academic characteristics, but it is important to know whether test adaptations have been used successfully in class. Ideally, each teacher will be a member of the committee and will provide input during each stage of the process.

CONSIDERING *diversity*

ADAPTATIONS FOR HIGH-STAKES TESTING OF ENGLISH LANGUAGE LEARNERS

Frequently Provided Accommodations/Adaptations for English Language Learners	Permitted by NAEP [†]
Native language version of test	No
Bilingual version of test (Spanish/English)	No (except for mathematics and science)
Bilingual word lists or glossaries (Spanish/English)	No (except for science)
Bilingual dictionary without definitions	Yes* (except for reading)
Directions translated aloud into native language or presented by audiotape	No
Student's oral or written responses translated into written English	No
Passages, other stimulus materials, or test questions read aloud in English or presented by audiotape	Yes (except for reading)
Directions read aloud in English or presented by audiotape[†]	Yes
Passages, other stimulus material, or test questions translated aloud into native language or presented by audiotape[‡]	No
Small group	Yes
One-to-one (tested individually)	Yes
Extended time	Yes
Preferential seating	Yes

*Not provided by the NAEP, but the school, district, or state may provide this after fulfilling NAEP security requirements.

[†]Standard NAEP practice; not considered an accommodation.

[‡]For Spanish/English bilingual mathematics and science, this would be standard NAEP practice; not allowed otherwise.

SOURCE: Adapted from http://nces.ed.gov/nationsreportcard/about/inclusion.asp (2014).

STEP 6: Finally, interview the student's parents. What are their perceptions of the testing process and the way it affects their son or daughter? Parents will be dramatically affected by the results of the high-stakes assessment, so they need to have input throughout the process, and their reactions to the committee's findings and the testing process should be documented. Ideally, they too have been members of the committee, but that is seldom the case.

ADAPT *in action*

SONYA: ADAPTING TEST INPUT

Earlier we introduced you to Sonya, a student in Mr. Gomez's class. Sonya is new to the school and has serious reading problems. She is unable to decode words and has very little comprehension of written materials. Mr. Gomez has just completed a science unit and is about to administer a paper-and-pencil, multiple-choice test to his students. Think about Sonya and the problems such a test might present. Use the ADAPT framework to find a way to test Sonya's knowledge of the science unit that produces valid results.

(A) **Ask, "What am I requiring the student to do?"** Sonya must read test items and select a response from four choices, a typical multiple-choice test.

(D) **Determine the prerequisite skills of the task.** Sonya must be able to listen to instructions, read the test items and each response choice, recall her science knowledge to identify the answer to each question, and circle her answer, A, B, C, or D.

(A) **Analyze the student's strengths and struggles.** Mr. Gomez recognizes that Sonya will struggle with reading the test items and each response choice.

(P) **Propose and implement adaptations from among the four categories.** For "reading the test items and each response choice," Mr. Gomez can reduce the number of test items by sampling the material and selecting the items that best differentiate between successful and unsuccessful readers (*instructional content*). He can also give Sonya a digital player to listen to the test questions and response choices (*instructional material*). Mr. Gomez can also choose to read Sonya the items aloud; she can either circle her answers on the scoring sheet or state her answers (*delivery of instruction*).

(T) **Test to discover whether the adaptations helped the student accomplish the task.** Mr. Gomez will examine the test to determine student performance with the adaptations.

ALTERNATE ASSESSMENTS

Although states differ in the options they make available to students with disabilities in high-stakes testing, all states have some sort of alternate testing plan available. No Child Left Behind legislation has dictated that no more than 1% of students may be assessed using alternate assessments. As a result, such assessments are usually administered only to students with severe cognitive disabilities or those whose disability requires alternate means for testing.

The National Center on Educational Outcomes (NCEO) suggests three approaches that states may use when conducting alternative assessments. Alternative assessments based on alternative achievement standards (AA-AAS)

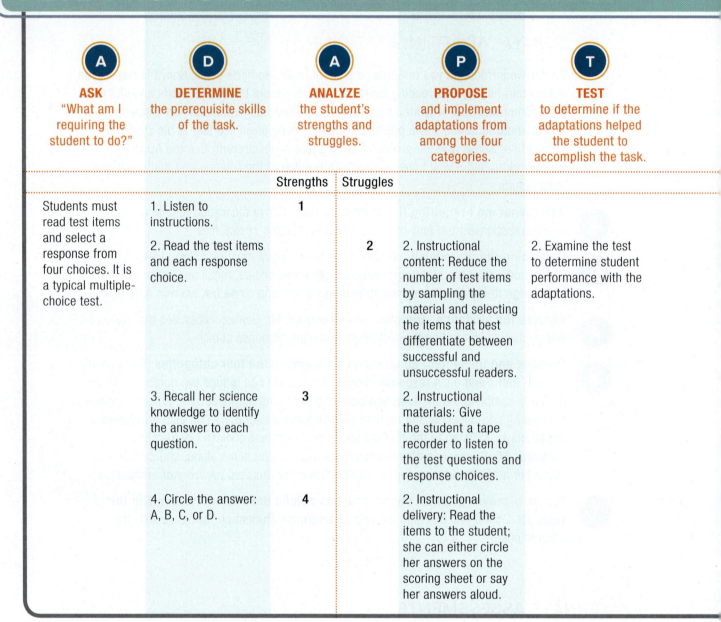

ADAPT *framework:* ADAPTING TEST INPUT

	A	D	A	P	T
	ASK "What am I requiring the student to do?"	**DETERMINE** the prerequisite skills of the task.	**ANALYZE** the student's strengths and struggles.	**PROPOSE** and implement adaptations from among the four categories.	**TEST** to determine if the adaptations helped the student to accomplish the task.
			Strengths / Struggles		
	Students must read test items and select a response from four choices. It is a typical multiple-choice test.	1. Listen to instructions.	1		
		2. Read the test items and each response choice.	2	2. Instructional content: Reduce the number of test items by sampling the material and selecting the items that best differentiate between successful and unsuccessful readers.	2. Examine the test to determine student performance with the adaptations.
		3. Recall her science knowledge to identify the answer to each question.	3	2. Instructional materials: Give the student a tape recorder to listen to the test questions and response choices.	
		4. Circle the answer: A, B, C, or D.	4	2. Instructional delivery: Read the items to the student; she can either circle her answers on the scoring sheet or say her answers aloud.	

are used with students with the most severe cognitive limitations. "These assessments are based on the grade-level content covered by the typical assessment used with all students, but they do so at reduced depth, breadth, and complexity. These assessments describe achievement based on what a state determines is a high expectation for these students" (NCEO, 2013, para. 3).

Alternative assessments based on modified achievement standards (AA-MAS) can be administered to those students with disabilities who are accessing the general education curriculum that is covered by the general assessment but who may need more time to take the test. According to NCEO (2013, para. 4), "these assessments measure a student's mastery of grade-level content but are less difficult than grade-level achievement standards." States that use the AA-MAS are in the process of discontinuing this option.

Alternative assessments based on grade-level achievement standards (AA-GLAS) "include the same grade-level content as the general assessment and describe achievement in the same way as the general assessment" (NCEO, 2013, para. 5). The AA-GLAS is for those students with disabilities who require alternate testing formats or procedures that typically are not included as part of the general assessment or are not addressed with use of accommodations.

Some organizations, such as the National Center and State Collaborative, and the Educational Testing Service, have been working with selected states and groups for years to construct and field-test reliable alternative assessments that yield valid results. Much of this work is aligned with the CCSS. Other states are taking it upon themselves to create their own alternative assessments, particularly those that have chosen not to adopt the CCSS. In these cases, the alternate assessments focus on individual state standards.

SUMMARY

This chapter presents techniques for promoting positive behavior and facilitating social skills. Both of these areas can greatly influence a teacher's success in promoting an atmosphere for learning. Identifying specific behavioral and social tasks will help teachers plan effective adaptations and interventions that can provide students with skills to use not only in the classroom but also schoolwide and in the community.

By utilizing assessment practices, teachers will realize quickly how successful their adaptations and intervention programs are in promoting an environment that is conducive to learning. Implementing practices discussed in this chapter will help students with disabilities become more involved in the classroom and be better accepted by their peers.

REVIEW THE LEARNING OBJECTIVES

Let's review the learning objectives for this chapter. If you are uncertain and cannot talk through the answers provided for any of these questions, reread those sections of the text.

- **Why do we assess students?**

There are several reasons for assessing students. One reason is to identify strengths and weaknesses. Another reason is to determine the student's relative standing in class compared with the other students. Informing instruction, documenting progress, and determining program eligibility are yet other reasons. Finally, grading and determining annual yearly progress are reasons for assessing students.

- **How do we assess students with special needs?**

Norm-referenced tests compare a person's performance with that of his or her peers.

Criterion-referenced tests measure abilities against a mastery standard. And non-referenced tests examine the strategies that a person uses when problem solving. Curriculum-based measures provide information that is curriculum specific, and performance-based assessments allow for authentic information gathering that cannot be obtained using conventional assessments.

- **How do we adapt and modify assessments for students with special needs?**

Assessment adaptations include any change in administration, scoring, and interpretation procedures we make specifically because of a test taker's ability. Their purpose is to level the playing field, meaning each test taker has the same chance as any other student to succeed, whether the assessment is a high-stakes test or Friday's spelling quiz.

> **$SAGE edge™** Test your understanding of chapter content. Take the practice quiz. edge.sagepub.com/bryant

REVISIT THE OPENING CHALLENGE

Check your answers to the Reflection Questions in the Opening Challenge and revise them on the basis of what you have learned.

1. How could Ms. Thompson set up a progress monitoring procedure?

2. How could she set goals and chart her students' progress?

3. How can Mr. Gomez teach Sonya science and test her abilities when she cannot read?

4. What measures are available to identify Dondra's attentional difficulties and Kim's mathematics struggles?

5. How can assessments be used to identify student strengths and struggles?

KEY TERMS

adequate yearly progress (AYP), 317

assessment, 314

exempt, 354

high-stakes assessments, 317

norm-referenced tests, 325

observation, 314

reliability, 324

universal design, 348

validity, 324

> **$SAGE edge™** Review key terms with eFlashcards. edge.sagepub.com/bryant

PROFESSIONAL STANDARDS AND LICENSURE

For a complete description of Professional Standards and Licensure, please see Appendix on page 569.

CEC Initial Preparation Standards

Standard 1: Learner Development and Individual Learning Differences

Standard 3: Curricular Content Knowledge

Standard 4: Assessment

INTASC Core Principle

Standard 2: Learning Differences

Standard 4: Content Knowledge

Standard 6: Assessment

Praxis II: Education of Exceptional Students: Core Content Knowledge

III. Delivery of Services to Students with Disabilities: Assessment

Review ➡ Practice ➡ Improve

Get the tools you need to sharpen your study skills. Access practice quizzes, eFlashcards, video, and multimedia: **edge.sagepub.com/bryant**

PART III
ADAPTATIONS TO MEET INDIVIDUAL LEARNER NEEDS

9

PROMOTING POSITIVE BEHAVIOR AND FACILITATING SOCIAL SKILLS

This chapter was written with the assistance of **Dr. Andrea Flower.**

LEARNING OBJECTIVES

After studying this chapter, you will be able to answer the following questions:

- What practices can be used to foster student relationships and communication?

- What ways can be used to communicate effectively with students?

- What are effective classroom arrangement practices?

- What are the goals of misbehavior?

- How can problem behaviors be assessed?
- What instructional strategies are available for behavior problems?
- What is social competence?
- How can safer schools be promoted?

OPENING *challenge* ···

Addressing Behaviors and Social Problems

ELEMENTARY GRADES Ms. Watson is midway through her tenth year of teaching and in her third year of teaching second grade. Three weeks ago a new student, Sandy, joined her class after moving from another state. Sandy was diagnosed as having autism spectrum disorder (ASD) as a preschooler and has been in inclusive settings throughout her schooling. Ms. Watson has never had a student diagnosed with ASD and, because Sandy is new to her class, she did not have a chance to attend professional development (PD) sessions about Sandy's challenging behaviors. Sandy is a friendly student who is eager to please, but she presents social and behavioral challenges that Ms. Watson has not confronted before. For example, when Marianne, a classmate, came to school with a new haircut, Sandy blurted out, "Ewwww, that's ugly," causing Marianne to start crying and other classmates to yell at Sandy, resulting in a meltdown. Sandy speaks without thinking at times; because of the statements she makes, her classmates sometimes see her as a bully. Sandy also demands to go first in activities, does not respond well to changes in routine, and screams when she does not get her way or is frustrated.

For three days per week for half a day, a special education teacher comes into the classroom to provide support. She works with Sandy as Ms. Watson teaches lessons. The special education teacher rephrases Ms. Watson's instructions at times to make the lessons more accessible, and she also serves to calm Sandy when she gets frustrated or upset. Once each week, the special education teacher meets with Ms. Watson during her planning period to provide PD on how to meet Sandy's unique demands.

SECONDARY GRADES It is October of Ms. Martinez's second year of teaching eighth-grade English, and she is planning lessons for the upcoming week. She connects her lessons to the Common Core State Standards (CCSS) and the district's curricula. She makes sure that there are activities that keep her students engaged. Depending on the lesson, she pairs students with disabilities with students who have stronger skills. However, things are not going very well for her students with disabilities. Ms. Martinez is puzzled about three students who seem to challenge her day in and day out. She has read their school folders, but she feels that she doesn't know them well.

One student, Sam, is identified as having ADHD. She studied this condition in her teacher-preparation program and even worked with one student with ADHD during student teaching, but having a student with ADHD in her class all day long is wearing her out. Ms. Martinez begins to question her ability to work effectively with Sam: *"How can I get him to pay attention? How can I help him get organized? He forgets what to do and can't remember to return homework. Why does he have so few friends? Am I really prepared to help this child learn?"*

Her second student, Eric, is identified as having a mild emotional or behavioral disorder. He was retained in fifth grade. Ms. Martinez worries about Eric: *"I don't really understand his disability. Why is he so defiant? He seems to do things on purpose just to be disruptive and get everyone's attention. What can I do with him so that he will stop interfering with my teaching? Why does he bully the other children? Shouldn't he be in a special education classroom?"*

Finally, Ms. Martinez turns her thoughts to Luisa, who has a learning disability in reading and writing: *"She seems so lost during group instruction and spends way too much time fiddling with things in her desk, sharpening her pencils, and being off task. Why can't she work with the other students? What's wrong?"*

Ms. Martinez asks herself the following: *"How can I help these students behave? What can I do about their social skills? How do I know whether my teaching practices are working?"*

REFLECTION QUESTIONS In your journal, write down your answers to the following questions. After completing the chapter, check your answers and revise them on the basis of what you have learned.

1. If you were Ms. Watson, in what areas would you seek PD help from the special education teacher?

2. How might Ms. Watson be able to identify specific challenges that Sandy presents?

3. What advice would you offer Ms. Martinez about getting to know her students better?

4. How can Ms. Watson and Ms. Martinez foster student relationships and communication?

5. How can both teachers help their students with their behavior?

6. How can both teachers facilitate their students' social skills?

7. How can both teachers determine whether student behavior and social skills are improving?

8. How can Ms. Watson and Ms. Martinez use the ADAPT framework to promote positive behavior and facilitate social skills?

The classroom is a social environment in which academic instruction must thrive. For teaching to be successful, teachers must create, nurture, and manage a classroom environment that supports student learning and interactions, minimizes situations that contribute to the occurrence of problem behaviors, and addresses those unacceptable behaviors that interfere with teaching and learning. For example, consider Sam, Eric, and Luisa in the Opening Challenge. Practices are readily available that teachers can employ to help students with their behavior and social problems. Some of these practices are presented in this chapter. Research has confirmed that teacher attention to nurturing and managing the classroom, student behavior, and social aspects of learning involving behavior management and applied behavior analysis contribute significantly to promoting an environment that is conducive to teaching and learning (American Psychological Association, 2014; Wolfgang, 2008).

This chapter presents practices that teachers can use to improve student relationships and communication. You will learn about ways to promote appropriate behavior and to facilitate the social skills of all students. You will also learn about interventions that may be necessary for a small number of students so that they can succeed in inclusive settings. Assessment techniques will help you identify behaviors and social skills that require intervention and determine if these interventions are effective. Finally, you will learn about positive behavioral supports, a process supported by the Individuals with Disabilities Education Improvement Act (IDEA; U.S. Department of Education, 2004), and also about ways to promote safer schools. The ADAPT framework will be implemented throughout the chapter so that you can learn how to use the framework to promote positive behavior and to facilitate social skills in your classroom.

Get the edge on your studies:
edge.sagepub.com/bryant

- Take a quiz to find out what you've learned.
- Review key terms with eFlashcards.
- Watch videos to see teachers in action.

WHAT PRACTICES CAN BE USED TO FOSTER STUDENT RELATIONSHIPS AND COMMUNICATION?

There are a number of practices you can adopt to cultivate good relationships with—and among—the students you teach.

GET TO KNOW YOUR STUDENTS

Students' attitudes, beliefs, experiences, and backgrounds influence their perceptions of school and learning and how they approach their relationships with their teachers. Teachers who get to know their students quickly can structure their teaching according to students' interests, background experiences, and attitudes. By doing so, teachers show they care about their students and make connections between their students and teaching. Getting to know students by taking time to talk with them (before school, between classes, during a conference, and in small groups) is one of the most powerful techniques for fostering positive relationships and creating an effective learning community.

How can teachers learn more about their students with disabilities? A good place to begin is by examining students' individualized education programs (IEPs; for a complete discussion on IEPs, see Chapter 6) to determine their academic and social goals. IEPs can provide helpful information about those areas in which the students need support. Such areas might actually be prerequisite skills for those behavior and social skills tasks that teachers expect from their students. For example, students are expected to follow classroom directions. If the student's IEP states that assistance is needed to help the student

Student Relationships

VIDEO CASE 9.1

Getting to Know Your Students

1. What methods does Melissa Wood-Glusac use to learn about her students? How does she incorporate a get-to-know-you activity into the English curriculum?

2. How does Ms. Wood-Glusac use knowledge about her students as readers and writers to plan effective instruction and meet the needs of all students in her class? What are other advantages of getting to know your students?

follow directions, then the teacher may need to adapt the delivery of directions for that student by shortening the length of directions and including cues and reminders. With practice, these simple adaptations can be implemented very naturally and without much effort. Oftentimes, simple adaptations benefit many students in the classroom, including those who have IEPs.

Teachers can also get to know their students through a variety of activities. For example, students can complete an **interest inventory**, which consists of a series of questions geared for a particular age-group. It can help teachers find out more about their students' backgrounds, interests, and perspectives. Questions that help teachers get to know students better include the following:

- "How many brothers and sisters do you have?"
- "What is your favorite movie and why?"
- "What was the name of the last book you read that you enjoyed?"
- "What is your favorite sport?"
- "What do you like to do after school?"
- "What do you like to do on the weekends?"
- "What is your favorite television show?"
- "Who is your hero and why?"
- "How do you know if someone is your friend?"
- "How can we help people who are mean to other people?"
- "If you could change one thing about school, what would it be and why?"
- "What do you like most about school?"
- "How do you spend time with your family?"
- "If you could change one thing in your life, what would that be?"

Answers to these sample questions, obtained orally or in writing, can provide teachers with information about their students. Information from the interest inventory can be used to initiate discussions, help decide which books to select for the reading center or for class literature groups, or identify a topic for group work and research. Interest inventory answers also can provide important information about students' cultural backgrounds and experiences (Zakrzewski, 2012).

USE MOTIVATIONAL PRACTICES

Implementing practices to motivate students is another way that you can foster positive student relationships. When designing or implementing instruction, it is important to focus on what motivates students to perform well, whether academically, behaviorally, or socially. For example, at times students may be bored or frustrated with the academic materials presented to them. Those who have been identified as gifted and talented may not be challenged sufficiently in inclusive settings with the core curriculum. Enrichment activities provided in instructional materials or in basal textbooks (i.e., those used to teach subject-area content) can be good sources of extra stimulation needed by those students who are gifted and talented. In contrast, students with learning and behavior difficulties have experienced varying degrees of success and failure with academic and social interactions during their school years. These successes and failures influence their motivational levels for classroom activities and assignments.

Later in this chapter, information about functional behavioral assessment (FBA) is presented. This process can help teachers determine possible reasons why students are not motivated to do their best in class. Identifying specific reasons through FBA can influence how teachers approach teaching. For example, if some students are reluctant to work on a research project, giving them more instruction in the steps for doing research or in getting online to locate research materials may increase their motivation to complete a research project.

Older students, in particular, may present challenging behavior that is often driven by a lack of motivation for tackling tasks that continue to frustrate them. For example, older students with reading difficulties have spent years struggling with textbook reading. As the demands of the classroom shift from "learning to read" to "reading to learn," older students may exhibit problem behavior that is a manifestation of their frustration. Given that older students may legally drop out of school, teachers of older students with academic and behavioral problems are challenged to implement effective techniques for motivating them.

When working with students of all ages, it is important to distinguish between students with a skill deficit (i.e., the student has not mastered specific skills) and those with a performance deficit (i.e., the skill or behavior is not consistently exhibited even though it is in the student's repertoire). For students who exhibit a skill deficit, teachers should spend time teaching them new skills. Oftentimes, learning new skills is motivating for some students who may have spent years struggling. Empowering students with new knowledge and the recognition that they *can* do it can go a long way toward providing motivation and creating a positive learning community. In contrast, students who exhibit performance deficits require different procedures. These are students who have learned the skill but lack the motivation to perform under certain circumstances or with certain people. For these students, some of the following motivational techniques may be helpful for fostering a positive learning community:

1. Know your students' names and use their names as often as possible.

2. Plan for every class; never try to wing it.

Fostering Positive
Relationships With Students

3. Pay attention to the strengths and limitations of each of your students. Reward their strengths and strengthen their weaknesses.

4. If possible, set your room in a U-shape to encourage interaction among students.

5. Vary your instructional strategies; use lectures, demonstrations, discussions, case studies, groups, and more.

6. Review the learning objectives with your students. Be sure students know what they are expected to learn, do, know, etc.

7. Move around the room as you teach.

8. Make your classes relevant. Be sure students see how the content relates to them and the world around them.

9. Be expressive. Smile.

10. Put some excitement into your speech; vary your pitch, volume, and rate.

11. Give lots of examples.

12. Encourage students to share their ideas and comments, even if they are incorrect. You'll never know what students don't understand unless you ask them.

13. Maintain eye contact and move toward your students as you interact with them. Nod your head to show that you are listening to them.

14. Provide opportunities for students to speak to the class.

15. Be available before class starts, during break, and after class to visit with students.

16. Return assignments and tests to students as soon as reasonably possible. Provide constructive feedback.

17. Be consistent in your treatment of students.

18. Make sure that your exams are current, valid, and reliable. Tie your assessment to your course objectives.

19. Plan around 15- to 20-minute cycles. Students have difficulty maintaining attention after a longer period of time.

20. Involve your students in your teaching. Ask for feedback. (University of Nebraska–Lincoln, Office of Graduate Studies, n.d.)

Some students see little reason for tackling the academic activities of the day. They may not see the relevance of the tasks or be interested in the way in which activities are presented. To increase motivation, activities must be presented in a meaningful way. What are some examples of meaningful activities? Meaningful activities relate learning to students' interests and encourage them to become actively involved in learning. **Student-centered learning** is a type of learning that engages students actively in the learning process through the use of hands-on tasks, discussions, and decision making. It is widely supported as an effective means for teaching and learning (Powel, 2013). Creating exciting learning experiences, such as class plays, group assignments, mock TV news productions of historical events, and field trips, encourages student involvement. Actively engaging students in the learning process and helping them make connections to real-life situations increases their motivation for participating in and completing activities (Neo, Neo, & Tan, 2012).

BE RESPONSIVE TO CULTURAL DIFFERENCES

Demographic changes within our society mean that today's classrooms include students from diverse linguistic, ethnic, racial, and socioeconomic backgrounds (U.S. Census Bureau, 2010). This rich heritage of diversity, coupled with a wide range of familial experiences, serves as a strong foundation for classroom instruction and has created a new context for teaching (Hernandez, 2001). Teachers should be informed about the social and behavioral norms of various cultural, ethnic, and racial groups. Teachers should examine their curricula and classroom literature to determine if students can see themselves reflected in the lessons and can learn about themselves and others. Fostering positive student relationships requires educators to be sensitive to the diverse norms brought to classrooms so that they can understand the behavior of different groups and be responsive to these cultural variations (Klingner, Boelé, Linan-Thompson, & Rodriguez, 2014). For example, in some cultures (e.g., Native American, Hawaiian), the spirit of cooperation is contrary to the focus on competitiveness that is found in other cultures and in many of today's classrooms (Smith & Tyler, 2010).

It is important for teachers to understand behavioral patterns that are socially acceptable in certain cultures so that they can avoid the risk of misidentifying students as possibly having behavioral disorders. For example, students who exhibit behavioral interactions that are counter to "mainstream" behavior could be mistakenly identified as having emotional or behavioral disabilities. The potential long-term and negative effects on school achievement when students are misidentified as having disabilities are both obvious and well-documented (Sullivan & Bal, 2013). The misdiagnosis of a disability and inappropriate placement in special education can be disastrous for a student. The results can be reduced expectations from parents and teachers, low self-esteem, and feelings of inferior achievement.

For example, in Chapter 4 you read about the disproportionate representation of African American and Hispanic students in special education. Some parents, educators, and policymakers believe that one reason for these students' disproportionate representation may rest in a conflict between teachers' perceptions and expectations and students' cultural identity. Take a few moments to read the example in the Considering Diversity feature on the potential conflict between a teacher's perceptions and a student's cultural identity.

How can teachers better understand the cultural values and norms in today's diverse classrooms? How can they plan and implement practices that are responsive to cultural and ethnic norms? Teachers can learn more about their students through observation, questionnaires, and student-teacher conferences. They can ask students how they like to work (alone or in a group), how large a group they prefer, how they seek adult feedback, how they feel about being praised publicly and privately, how they respond to rewards, and how they are disciplined. Student input will help teachers create student-centered activities. Teachers can learn how students from diverse

CONSIDERING *diversity*

MIXED MESSAGES?

One expression of cultural identity among African American male adolescents is a walking style that many educators consider "nonstandard." The *stroll*, as it is sometimes called, is characterized as a deliberately swaggered or bent posture, with the head held slightly tilted to the side, one foot dragging, and an exaggerated knee dip. This raises interesting questions about making assumptions on the basis of behaviors related to cultural identity. For instance:

- How can a student's walk contribute to a teacher's perceptions about individual student achievement, aggression, or need for special education?
- How might a teacher's perceptions about students' behavior influence referrals to special education?

Some answers to these questions come from research. Based on students' styles of walking,

teachers made the following decisions about middle school boys:

- Boys who stroll, regardless of race or ethnicity, are more likely to be judged by teachers as having lower achievement than those who use standard walking styles.
- Those who stroll are viewed as being more aggressive and deviant.

Without information about academic achievement, these boys are also thought of as being in need of special education. In other words, teachers are likely to mistake cultural differences, such as walking style, with cognitive and behavioral disabilities, placing those students at risk for underachievement, inappropriate referrals to special education, and misidentification as students with disabilities.

SOURCE: Belgrave and Brevade (2014).

backgrounds perceive the rules and expectations imposed by the teaching staff and the school. Additionally, it is important for teachers to understand how families perceive school environments and the discipline of their children. Teachers can strive to integrate these values and norms into a more cohesive learning community.

CONDUCT STUDENT MEETINGS

More than 40 years ago, William Glasser (1969) presented the *classroom meeting* as a way for teachers and students to confront problems and issues constructively as a group. Through group participation and ownership of issues, a positive climate can be created and positive relationships with students can be fostered. Glasser described three types of meetings that are still widely conducted today:

- The open-ended meeting is for students to discuss how they would deal with possible problems and take a "What would you do if . . ." approach to problem solving. This gives teachers a chance to discuss hypothetical problems to help students think about possible resolutions before problems come up.

- The educational/diagnostic meeting determines what students know and what they do not know about a topic to be studied. "What is . . . ?" and "Why is that a problem?" are examples of questions for learning about students' knowledge of a topic.

- The problem-solving meeting focuses on a problem exhibited in class that may be related to the handling of materials, class procedures, or a specific student. Students are asked to explain the problems they see, their effects, and possible solutions. The meeting concludes with an agreed-upon plan.

For older students, a peer-forum technique was first implemented more than 25 years ago by Lewandowski (1989) as a means for students to discuss issues and resolve problems. The peer forum is a panel of students who have had trouble in school; these students have agreed to talk with their peer group about how they handled these difficulties. Panel members discuss problems they encountered in school and offer positive advice about how they handled their problems. Additionally, panel members discuss strategies for being successful in school, such as study techniques, counseling, and how to access additional resources. By engaging in conversation with older students who have dealt with these types of problems, students demonstrate problem-solving skills, enhancing the opportunity for a more positive community approach to learning and problem resolution. Next, we discuss ways to promote effective communication with students.

WORKING *together*

ASSISTANCE WITH BEHAVIOR MANAGEMENT: LEARNING READY

Ms. Watson does small group, Tier 2 instruction as part of her RTI responsibilities. She has been having difficulties with managing the behavior of some of the students in her small groups. She met with the special education teacher, Mr. Asad, to identify a strategy to help the students remain engaged during her reading, writing, and mathematics interventions. Mr. Asad suggested that she use Learning Ready, a strategy that can be applied to whatever content is being taught. During mathematics, he calls it Math Ready; when applied to reading, he calls it Reading Ready. He presented a picture of a hand that shows the components of Math Ready (see Figure 9.1). Each digit represents something that the students should be doing to remain engaged during a lesson. He places the Math Ready graphic on the table where instruction is taking place. On the first instructional day, he goes over each component and provides examples and nonexamples of each. Students practice being Math Ready before the lesson begins. Periodically, if he notes a student or two not being Math Ready, he simply states "Math Ready," and his students usually reengage.

FIGURE 9.1   DEPICTION OF MATH READY

1. Eyes on activity! Students' attention should be on the teacher or on the worksheet/materials being used in the lesson.

2. Mouth quiet! It is difficult to speak and listen at the same time, so the idea is to have students speak when appropriate but be quiet when the teacher or peers are talking.

3. Hands on table! Children often slouch when they are seated, and we want them to be in a position where they can write with proper posture. Having hands on the table also reduces the likelihood that children's hands will be on one another.

4. Ears listening! This is the yang to Mouth quiet's yin. During instruction, the teacher often provides and verbally explains multiple examples. Students listen to the instruction and respond to questions designed to check for understanding. Listening is a critical piece of the engagement puzzle.

5. Ready to learn! If the students are engaged by adhering to the previous four guidelines, they are ready to learn.

Mr. Asad added that intermittent checks for Learning Ready are useful. He sets a vibrating timer at different times, 30 seconds, 2 minutes, and so forth, for a total of eight checks over the course of a 30-minute lesson. When the timer vibrates, he checks the students for being Math Ready. If they are, he places a token in a jar. At the end of the day, if they accumulate at least seven tokens as a group, they receive a sticker.

QUESTIONS

1. Think about your observations of or experiences with teaching small groups. What types of challenging behaviors did you encounter? How might Mr. Asad's suggestions be helpful?

2. In a small group in class, practice Mr. Asad's strategy. How long does it take to feel comfortable observing the "students," managing the timer, and employing the token system?

VIDEO CASE 9.2

Communicating Effectively With Students

1. In what ways do the elementary teachers in the video use praise and other rewards to motivate their students? How do the students respond to these practices?

2. How does Jan Evans support her students' success by communicating clearly with them? What advice does she give to other teachers about communicating with students?

WHAT WAYS CAN BE USED TO COMMUNICATE EFFECTIVELY WITH STUDENTS?

In addition to using techniques that promote a positive learning community, managing *teacher* behavior can facilitate the accomplishment of expected behavioral and social skills tasks by all students.

COMMUNICATE CLEAR AND CONSISTENT MESSAGES

Communication is a critical component of any classroom learning community. Poorly articulated behavioral and social expectations and inconsistent ways of handling the results of mixed messages detract from a positive tone in any classroom. Behavioral and social expectations, and the consequences for following (or not following) them, should be communicated to students. Consequences, both positive and negative, must be consistent if students are to take teachers' messages seriously. For example, if tardiness is an unacceptable behavior, it should be addressed each time it occurs. Ignoring the problem sometimes and addressing it at other times sends mixed messages to students about expected behavior and social skills.

Sometimes, despite clearly communicated expectations for behavioral and social tasks, students continue to struggle. Thomas Gordon's (2003) *Teacher Effectiveness Training* program, which remains widely used today, helps teachers understand how to handle some of these problem situations. Gordon's approach is based on the work of Carl R. Rogers, who conducted research on emotional and self-concept development. Rogers believed that people respond to an emotionally supportive approach that includes openness and understanding. According to Gordon, if a problem behavior infringes on either the teacher's or the other students' rights, or if it is a safety issue, the teacher should own the problem (Wolfgang, 2008). Teachers can respond to such problems by using text messages to communicate feelings to students about the effects of their behavior. With an I-message, the teacher tells students his or her feelings without blaming the students. Let's compare a good I-message and a poor one, both offered to address the same problem.

> Problem: Several students interrupt the teacher when she is explaining assignments.

> Good I-message: "When students interrupt (*problem behavior*) me when I am speaking, I have to repeat what I just said (*effect of the behavior*), and that frustrates me (*feelings*)."

This example tells the students the problem, its effect, and the feelings of the person sending the I-message.

> Poor I-message: "I want you to stop interrupting me. If you do that again, you'll have to stay after school."

This example orders the students to stop a behavior and uses a threat to curb it. The teacher is in a position of power. According to Gordon, practices such as ordering, threatening, and warning are roadblocks to effective communication (Wolfgang, 2008; see Table 9.1 for examples of 12 roadblocks to communication).

Gordon acknowledges the need for teachers to use strong directives such as ordering, but only if danger is present (Wolfgang, 2008). Gordon stresses that overusing commands can result in conflict between the teacher and students. Clearly communicated behavioral and social skills tasks, delivery of consequences, and the use of I-messages all contribute to effective communication (Wolfgang, 2008).

EXPLAIN THE RULES AND CONSEQUENCES

Rules are a necessary part of society; this is true for the classroom as well. Rules provide parameters, structure, and predictability. Rules set the limits! Without rules, students are left to their own devices to determine the

TABLE 9.1	TWELVE ROADBLOCKS TO COMMUNICATION
Response	**Example**
Some typical responses that communicate nonacceptance:	
1. Ordering, commanding, directing	"Stop whining and get back to work."
2. Warning, threatening	"You had better get your act together if you expect to pass my class."
3. Moralizing, preaching, giving "should" and "ought"	"You should leave your personal problems out of the classroom."
4. Advising, offering solutions or suggestions	"I think you need to get a daily planner so you can organize your time better to get your homework finished."
5. Teaching, lecturing, giving logical arguments	"You better remember you only have four days to complete that project."
These next responses tend to communicate inadequacies and faults:	
6. Judging, criticizing, disagreeing, blaming	"You are such a lazy kid. You never do what you say you will."
7. Name-calling, stereotyping, labeling	"Act your age. You are not a kindergartner."
8. Interpreting, analyzing, diagnosing	"You are avoiding facing this assignment because you missed the directions due to talking."
Other messages try to make the student feel better or deny there is a problem:	
9. Praising, agreeing, giving positive evaluations	"You are a smart kid. You can figure out a way to finish this assignment."
10. Reassuring, sympathizing, consoling, supporting	"I know exactly how you are feeling. If you just begin, it won't seem so bad."
This response tends to try to solve the problem for the student:	
11. Questioning, probing, interrogating, cross-examining	"Why did you wait so long to ask for assistance? What was so hard about this worksheet?"
This message tends to divert the student or avoid the student altogether:	
12. Withdrawing, distracting, being sarcastic, humoring, diverting	"It seems like you got up on the wrong side of the bed today."

teacher's expectations and guidelines for appropriate behavior and social skills. Sometimes, teachers assume that students know how they are supposed to act in class. The codes of school conduct often are implied and not communicated carefully. Unfortunately, in some school situations, students learn about the rules only when they break them and are punished for their infractions. How can teachers communicate rules so that students can meet the behavioral and social expectations of the classroom? Teachers can use a class meeting to

When students exhibit minor problem behavior, teachers can intervene by giving instruction on how to behave appropriately.

involve students in establishing classroom rules by asking them, "What rules do we need so that I can teach and you can learn in a safe classroom?" Here are a few tips for selecting rules (Canter, 2010):

- Four to six rules are enough; having too many rules makes it difficult to monitor compliance.

- State rules in a positive manner, such as "Follow directions."

- Select observable rules that apply throughout the day. "Be respectful" is difficult to observe, is too vague, and may require the teacher to take instructional time to ask, "Is that respectful?" A more specific rule, such as "Raise your hand to speak in group discussion," is more effective.

- Involve students in setting the rules. This is especially important for older students so that they feel they have a voice in the decision-making process.

Once rules are selected, they should be shared with the principal and students' families. The rules should also be posted. Rules should come with both positive recognition and consequences. When students follow the rules, praise, special notices, privileges, and other types of positive recognition provide helpful reinforcement (Canter, 2010).

When rules are broken, consequences must follow. Here are some items to consider when deciding on consequences:

- The consequence should match the infraction; that is, the consequence must make sense for the misbehavior or broken rule. For example, the consequence for being late to class once should be different from that for being late four days in a row.

- The consequence should be something that the teacher can manage. If the consequence is "stay after school," the teacher may have to give up planning time at the end of the day.

- Consequences should be applied consistently and as soon as possible after the infraction. If consequences are applied inconsistently, students get mixed messages about following the rules.

- Consequences need to be communicated clearly to students. They should know what will happen when rules are broken and when they are followed.

Is it necessary to teach rules? Yes! Rules must be explained, reinforced, and reviewed regularly. Teachers should work closely with special education colleagues regarding enforcement of rules and logical consequences for students with disabilities. For instance, a student with mild emotional or behavioral disabilities may have an IEP with certain guidelines for rules. Likewise, students who lack the ability to shift among different settings and teachers may need extra guidance in remembering the rules as situations and teachers change during the day.

EXPLAIN THE DAILY SCHEDULE

Most people like to be informed about the schedule of events so that they know what to expect during the course of the day, week, or even vacation period. By communicating a schedule to students, teachers can prepare them for what to expect each day; they will know what is going to happen and be prepared for it. A classroom schedule establishes routines and communicates to all students the activities of each day.

The teacher can develop a classroom schedule and post it for students to review throughout the week. Several routines can be part of one week. For example, one routine can be used on two days and a different routine on three days. The teacher can help students by reviewing the schedule for the day or for the class period.

For students who struggle with certain academic subjects or tasks, problems might occur during specific times of the day associated with those subjects or tasks. For instance, if reading is a demanding activity for a student, it is not surprising that the student might get out of his or her seat, start talking to a friend, or take extra time to go to the reading table for instruction. Think back to Luisa in the Opening Challenge. Luisa has a learning disability in reading and writing. Her teacher identified problems with her remaining on task and getting her work done.

What can a teacher do about this academic problem, besides adjusting the work? The Premack Principle is a highly effective technique for motivating students to accomplish tasks (Education Portal, 2015). With this method, activities that are more demanding or challenging (such as reading and writing for Luisa), and thus less preferred, are conducted earlier in the day or class period. Less demanding and more preferred activities are scheduled for later in the day or class period so that students have something to work toward. In some cases, earned or free time (i.e., designated time during the school day that is provided for students who have completed their work) can be scheduled later in the day. Some parents use the Premack Principle to get their children to eat: "When you finish your dinner you can have dessert!" Astute teachers have used the Premack Principle for years to help students accomplish classroom tasks.

PROVIDE GOOD DIRECTIONS

What does it mean to provide good directions? If students understand what they are supposed to do, remember the directions, and follow them, then the teacher probably has provided good directions. Here are some tips for providing good directions and communicating them effectively:

- Be concise; too many words may confuse students or be difficult to remember. Two or three single-step actions are sufficient.

- State directions right before the activity.

- Check student understanding of the directions. For example, consider the following directions: "In pairs, I want you to first (*use a visual signal showing one finger*) read the paragraph together; second (*showing two fingers*), underline words you don't know; and third (*showing three fingers*), write two sentences about the paragraph." The teacher does a quick check for understanding by asking students what they are supposed to do.

DESCRIBE TRANSITION PROCEDURES

Why is transition time so important? **Transition** is the time when students are changing activities or classes. Often it is a less structured time, so transition can be a challenging time for students who need structure as part of their routine. Students may struggle with shifting from one activity to another either in the classroom or across settings in the school. When students complete small group work, the expectation is that they can return to their desks without problems. Unfortunately, this is not always the case.

Difficulties with transition times occur for a variety of reasons. Sometimes, teachers do not pay enough attention to student movement in the classroom during transitions. At other times, the teacher has not clearly communicated expectations for student behavior during transitions. Also, the procedures that teachers use to make transitions may not be the most effective ways for students to change activities. For example, asking all students to line up for lunch or move into group work at the same time may invite problems.

How can teachers communicate effectively during transition times? Here are several transition suggestions:

- Signal to students that it is time to finish their work because soon they will be moving to the next activity. Providing a verbal reminder, "Finish up what you are doing because the bell will ring in 10 minutes," signals how much time students have to complete their work and get ready for the next activity or class.

- Gain student attention prior to the transition to provide directions for the transition. Teachers can use their proximity (e.g., standing at the front of the classroom), a visual signal (e.g., flickering the lights), or a verbal signal (e.g., counting backward from five to one) to gain students' attention. Then, directions for the transition to another activity in the classroom or to another location, such as the next class or the cafeteria, can be provided. One teacher shared her strategy for gaining student attention: "All eyes on me." Her students were taught to reply in unison, "All eyes on you." It works!

- Communicate the transition plan and behavioral expectations. For instance, younger students could be told that they need to meet in their spelling groups at the carpet area and that they should walk to the mat quietly. Older students could be told that they should return to their seats and gather their belongings to get ready for the bell to change classes.

- Praise students who follow the transition plan and meet behavioral expectations. Provide specific praise, thank students for following the directions given, and demonstrate the appropriate behavior if convenient. For example, announcing "The Red group went to the mat quietly with their spelling materials; thank you for following the directions" or "The group working on computers did a nice job of logging off and returning to their desks quietly" tells students specifically what they did appropriately that related to following transition directions.

USE SPECIFIC PRAISE JUDICIOUSLY

Specific praise is complimenting or verbally rewarding students for their accomplishments. Providing specific praise is a very simple way to communicate behavior and social expectations. Praise can serve as a reward for proper behavior and social interactions and as a reminder about expectations for students. Specific praise is a form of attention and feedback that has been studied for many years, and it has been shown to be very powerful in bringing about positive behavior in classrooms (Haydon & Musti-Rao, 2011). Although easy to implement, specific praise is underutilized in many classroom settings. Thus, one of the easiest interventions for managing behavior remains untapped in many classrooms. Think back for a moment to Sandy in the Opening Challenge; recall her problems with saying hurtful things without thinking. Ms. Watson gives her a card with a happy face (*instructional material*) to remind her to make positive statements and provides specific praise (*instructional delivery*) when she "catches" her giving a compliment to a classmate. She can also conduct periodic role-playing with small groups to facilitate positive social communication.

What guidelines are important to consider when using specific praise to promote positive behavior?

- Make the praise specific. For example, a teacher who wants students to raise their hands to speak during group discussions can acknowledge a student who demonstrates this task by saying, "Thank you, Eric, for raising your hand to speak instead of shouting out." This praise is specific to the task of raising a hand, which the teacher expects students to demonstrate during class discussions. This praise also gives Eric positive attention.

- Consider the age of the student or students being praised. For instance, teachers cannot praise tenth-grade students in the same way they do first graders. Older students may not respond favorably to a teacher who praises them publicly, but a private word can mean a great deal.

- Use praise judiciously. This means that teachers should focus on the behavior or social skill that they want students to demonstrate. Excessive praise loses its reinforcing value.

Next, we describe classroom arrangements that can address problem behaviors.

WHAT ARE EFFECTIVE CLASSROOM ARRANGEMENT PRACTICES?

Your classroom is the stage on which the educational experience unfolds. It pays to plan the setting thoughtfully.

PHYSICAL ARRANGEMENTS

The physical arrangement of the classroom is an important component of effective classroom management. What are some considerations for designing the environment? Arranging activity-based centers in less distracting parts of the room can minimize problems. For example, in elementary classrooms, the reading, writing, and listening centers could be placed next to one another, assuming that students are using headphones in the listening center. The art center, however, should be placed away from students' seats and quieter centers. At the secondary level, instructional supplies and materials for students could be stored away from students' desks. Computers can be arranged in another section of the room.

TRAFFIC PATTERNS

Traffic patterns, the paths students take to move about the classroom, are another issue to consider. How can traffic patterns make a difference? The arrangement of furniture and the location of instructional materials (e.g., pencil sharpener, computers, books, lab instruments) may influence how students move about the classroom as they go from large group to small group instruction and from independent seatwork to the pencil sharpener. The following tips can help manage classroom traffic patterns:

- Separate instructional areas.
- Provide adequate movement space.
- Provide access to the most-frequented areas. (Emmer & Evertson, 2008; Evertson & Emmer, 2012)

Emmer and Evertson (2008) recommended that teachers simulate student movement about the classroom to determine possible problem areas. For instance, a student who uses a wheelchair will require more navigational space in the classroom; the room arrangement will require wider spaces to accommodate the student's movement about the room.

SEATING ARRANGEMENTS

How students' desks are arranged is yet another consideration. The types of activities and desired interactions should influence desk arrangements and seating patterns, such as rows and groupings. In addition, specific student behavioral needs will influence how the desks are arranged and where certain students' desks are located in proximity to the teacher and other students. For instance, students who are distracted easily or who like to socialize will require preferential seating (i.e., closer to the teacher or with students who can ignore "talkers"). A student who is easily distracted should sit in an area that is less traveled by peers, rather than in an area (such as by the pencil sharpener) that is frequented during the day.

WITH-IT-NESS

Teachers must be able to see all of the students all of the time to be aware of interactions; this is referred to as **with-it-ness** (Pressman, 2011). Why is

With-it-ness

with-it-ness so important? A lack of teacher awareness of classroom activities and student behavior can contribute to misbehavior and social problems. Nooks and crannies may offer students "private space," but they limit teachers' abilities to be aware of classroom activities. In addition, teachers who position themselves in the classroom where visibility is limited are inviting problems that they cannot see or stop. Teachers must have "eyes in the back of their heads" and let students know such is the case. Designing the classroom's physical environment to maximize visibility of all students makes it possible to prevent behavioral and social problems or to address them as situations warrant.

CLASSROOM OBSERVATION

Taking time to observe the environment, including traffic patterns, seating arrangements, and student interactions, will provide information about changes that may be needed. Through observation, teachers can reduce behavioral problems and increase student involvement with those students who tend to be quiet or uninvolved with their peers. Asking students, particularly older ones, about environmental factors such as temperature, noise, furniture, and arrangements can also inform decision making about creating an environment that is conducive to learning, managing behavior, and facilitating social interactions.

This section presented practices that teachers can use to help all students understand and accomplish behavior and social skills tasks in the classroom. We know there is also a group of students who exhibit difficulty managing their behavior. For these students, it is helpful to understand the "goals" of misbehavior and to be familiar with interventions that can address problem behavior.

WHAT ARE THE GOALS OF MISBEHAVIOR?

For many years, researchers have studied student behavior to better understand why problem behaviors occur and to identify ways to promote positive behavior. Differing viewpoints about the causes of inappropriate behavior have influenced the development of approaches and systems for managing it. For example, inspired by Alfred Adler's work on the relationship of behavior to social acceptance, Rudolph Dreikurs (1968) and Dreikurs and Cassel (1972) believed that people's behavior, including misbehavior, is goal driven—specifically, that it is performed to achieve social acceptance. If students are not successful in achieving social acceptance, misbehavior occurs that can be annoying, hostile, destructive, or helpless. But students who believe that inappropriate behavior will garner an adult's positive attention are mistaken. The attention they get is negative. These students are desperately seeking positive acceptance but do not know how to achieve it. They need to learn appropriate **prosocial behaviors**—behaviors that are positive and that build relationships—to achieve the acceptance they are seeking.

Teachers can help students recognize their misguided goals and can offer alternatives for social acceptance (Wolfgang, 2008). When teachers understand the goals of misbehavior, an appropriate intervention plan can be implemented to support positive behavior and to decrease or eliminate inappropriate behavior. Table 9.2 provides information about the goals of misbehavior and offers examples of techniques for handling mistaken goals. Additional instructional strategies are provided in the next section.

HOW CAN PROBLEM BEHAVIORS BE ASSESSED?

How can positive behaviors and problem behaviors be described when they occur? What behaviors are acceptable? How can the occurrence of problem behaviors be assessed? Teachers must be able to describe behaviors that are desirable as well as those that are intrusive to teaching so that they can design and assess intervention plans.

TABLE 9.2   GOALS AND TECHNIQUES FOR HANDLING MISBEHAVIOR

Goal	Description of Misbehavior	Techniques
Attention getting	The student engages in behavior that demands excessive praise or criticism.	Ignore the behavior. Give an I-message. Lower your voice. Change the activity. Praise appropriately behaving students.
Power and control	The student tries to manage situations, get his or her own way, or force himself or herself on others.	Leave the scene. Have the student repeat the desired behavior. Remove the student from the group. Change the topic.
Revenge	The student engages in hurtful and malicious behavior.	Implement a time-out. Take away a privilege.
Inadequacy	The student does not cooperate or participate and avoids or escapes situations.	Adapt instruction. Break tasks down into smaller steps. Provide more praise. Showcase successes. Teach positive encouraging talk, such as "I can do it."

SOURCE: Adapted from Wolfgang (2008).

BEHAVIOR IDENTIFICATION

Teachers must be able to describe problem behavior. An identified behavior should be observable, measurable, consistent over time, and of great concern (e.g., interfering with teaching or learning). For example, "calling out" can be observed, and it can be counted for a designated period. "Calling out" is a behavior that, although not serious, interferes with class discussions and can be labeled as rude and relatively disruptive. Returning to the Opening Challenge, "How many times Eric 'calls out' during a 15-minute discussion after viewing the film" tells us that "calling out" is the behavior that is being observed for 15 minutes. Ms. Martinez can measure it consistently over time by using a tally system to record how many times Eric calls out. Information on the identified behavior can help Ms. Martinez describe the problem behavior (calling out during a discussion), determine how often it occurs (measuring the behavior for a time period), and know if the behavior (calling out) is decreasing and if a desirable behavior (hand raising) is increasing when an intervention plan is implemented.

Identified behavior can be stated in the form of behavioral objectives that include a condition, a behavior, and a criterion for improvement. The following examples include these three components and relate to our three students from the Opening Challenge.

- In the reading group (*condition*), Luisa will stay in her seat (*behavior*) for 20 minutes (*criterion*).

- During the daily 10-minute whole class morning discussion (*condition*), Eric will raise his hand (*behavior*) each time (*criterion*) he wishes to participate.

- For writing activities (*condition*), Sam will have his pencil (*behavior*) each day (*criterion*) to complete the writing assignments.

OBSERVATIONAL TECHNIQUES

For students who engage in minor infractions, simply recording observations of positive behavior and problematic behavior anecdotally in a notebook or on lesson plans may suffice to keep track of how they are progressing with behavior intervention programs or to identify possible issues. However, in many cases systematic observational systems can provide information helpful in the design, implementation, and evaluation of behavior programs.

Observational systems can determine how frequently or how long a problem behavior occurs. Table 9.3 provides observational systems that can be used to gather data about the identified behavior and to assess the effectiveness of

TABLE 9.3	SYSTEMS FOR OBSERVING AND ASSESSING BEHAVIOR
System	**Description and Example Behaviors**
Event recording	Number of occurrences of the identified behavior is recorded using a count or tally (e.g., 1111 = 4).
	Session time period (and hence opportunities to respond) is held constant.
	Example behaviors: hand raising, talk-outs, tardiness, pencil sharpening, tattling.
Interval recording	Number of intervals in which the identified behavior occurs or does not occur is counted.
	Session time period is divided into small intervals (e.g., 10-minute group time is divided into 10-second intervals).
	Occurrence of the identified behavior *during any portion* of the interval is noted by a plus (+); nonoccurrence is noted by a minus (−).
	Each interval has only one notation; percentage of occurrence of the identified behavior for the session time period is calculated by dividing the number of intervals in which the behavior occurred by the total number of intervals and multiplying by 100. It can be challenging to record occurrences of behavior and teach at the same time, but this method provides a more accurate picture of the occurrences of a behavior than time sampling.
	Example behaviors: out of seat, talking with neighbors.
Momentary time sampling	Number of intervals in which the identified behavior occurs is counted.
	Session time period is divided into larger intervals (e.g., 1-hour group time is divided into 10-minute intervals).
	Occurrence of the identified behavior *at the end* of the interval is noted by a plus (+); nonoccurrence is noted by a minus (−).
	Each interval has only one notation; percentage of occurrences of the identified behavior for the session time period is calculated by dividing the number of intervals in which the behavior occurred by the total number of intervals and multiplying by 100. In momentary time sampling, it is easier to record occurrences of behavior and teach, but it provides a less accurate picture of the occurrences of behavior than interval recording.
	Example behaviors: out of seat, talking with neighbors, not working on an assignment.
Duration recording	How long a high-rate or continuous behavior occurs is noted.
	Session time period can be a short period of time, a day or a week; at the onset of the identified behavior, a stopwatch is started to record the cumulative time.
	Example behaviors: out of seat, temper tantrums, staying with one's group.

the intervention plan. Think about behaviors you have seen in classrooms and select the observational system you would use to measure that behavior. Keep in mind that the system should be sensitive to the behavior. For example, if a student continuously and rapidly taps a pencil on the desk, it would be hard

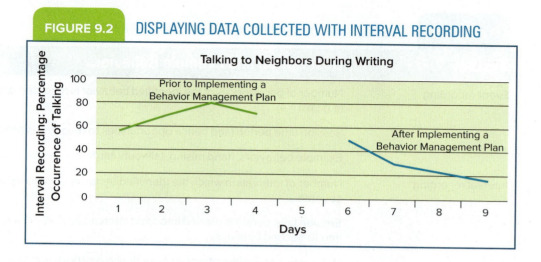

FIGURE 9.2 DISPLAYING DATA COLLECTED WITH INTERVAL RECORDING

to use event recording to capture each occurrence of this distracting behavior. Rather, interval recording would be a more appropriate system to use to get a sense of the occurrence of the behavior.

Oftentimes, it is helpful to display data. Figure 9.2 shows one way to depict data collected on an identified behavior. Data displays provide an easy way to see what is happening. In this example, the teacher was concerned about Patricia's talking with her neighbors when she was supposed to be writing independently in her journal for 10 minutes each day. The teacher chose the interval recording system to collect data. Prior to implementing a behavior management plan, the teacher collected the first four data points. As shown in the figure, Patricia's percentage of talking was quite high. However, a dramatic decrease in talking (the remaining four data points) is noted with the introduction of a behavioral intervention. What intervention from those discussed in this chapter would you use to reduce the inappropriate talking behavior?

Events that occur either before or after the behavior may contribute to its occurrence. Descriptive observation of these events can reveal important clues about how to manage the behavior. The Antecedent Behavior Consequence (ABC) log is a good tool for recording observations. "A" stands for events that occur before the behavior of concern, "B" is the behavior of concern, and "C" stands for the events that happen after the behavior occurs. The ABC log can be used for gathering data about what is going on with the student and the environment. These data can help the teacher make informed decisions about why problem behavior is occurring. An example is provided in Figure 9.3. Review the data and try to determine what is triggering or maintaining the behaviors. Based on your idea, what would you do next? For example, Luisa's reading abilities can be assessed with the possibility of providing more intensive reading intervention to help her learn to read better.

FIGURE 9.3 ABC LOG

Date/ Time	Antecedent Events or Situations	Behaviors	Consequences
12/01 10:30	**1. Teacher (T):** "Luisa, Sarah, and Ben come for reading."	**2. Luisa:** "I need to sharpen my pencil." Luisa sharpens her pencil. She stops and talks to Ricardo. Luisa pokes Stephanie with her pencil. Stephanie hits Luisa. **4.** Luisa wanders around the room.	**3. T:** "Okay, stop that." The teacher goes over to the students and separates them. Stephanie cries. **5.** The teacher sends Stephanie to the nurse and has a private conference with Luisa, who loses recess for the day.

The team hypothesized that Luisa's pencil sharpening and poking served the purpose of avoiding the reading task because of her difficulties with reading. The incident has attracted the attention of the whole class. And although she was given detention that day, she had the tecaher's undivided attention, negative as it was, during the class time.

The ABC log technique can be easily adapted to a format that offers students the opportunity to self-evaluate and self-manage their own behavior. Ms. Martinez plans to use the strategy to help Luisa be prepared for class.

SOURCE: Adapted from *Preventing School Failure: Tactics for Teaching Adolescents*, by T. Lovitt, 2000, 2nd ed., Austin, TX: PRO-ED.

ADAPT *in action*

LUISA: ABC

Ms. Martinez thinks about Luisa as she prepares to teach the lesson. Ms. Martinez decides to implement the ADAPT framework to identify how Luisa can avoid antecedents that trigger her negative behavior.

 A Ask, **"What am I requiring the student to do?"** Ms. Martinez notes, "The students will learn how to complete and implement an ABC Log."

 D Determine the prerequisite skills of the task. Ms. Martinez realizes that students have to learn what each letter (A, B, and C) means. As she provides examples of antecedents, behaviors, and consequences from real-life experiences, students have to

(Continued)

(Continued)

provide their own examples. Students have to think about what triggers their actions, both positive and negative, so that they can see the connection between antecedents and consequences. Students have to discriminate between antecedents that trigger positive behavior and those that trigger negative behavior and what happens to them after positive and negative behaviors occur. Students then have to identify a plan to deal with the antecedents that trigger negative behaviors. For example, if the trigger is "time to work on reading," having pencils already sharpened and avoiding conflict would be positive behaviors rather than having to sharpen the pencil and poke a fellow student, which would cause the students to receive disciplinary action. Finally, students select one of their own behaviors to change. Students can keep a record of the behavior in a journal.

 Analyze the student's strengths and struggles. Ms. Martinez reflects on Luisa's skill set with regard to the lesson: "She knows what triggers the behavior, reading instruction, and she knows what she does and that poking a classmate gets her in trouble, so she can identify that as needing to be worked on. What she struggles with is coming up with a solution and implementing a plan to change her behavior. She'll need help with that. Also, she has trouble writing, so she'll need help completing her ABC log."

 Propose and implement adaptations from among the four categories.
Ms. Martinez knows that she will have to meet with Luisa to help her identify an action plan. They determine together that Luisa will begin her day by sharpening five pencils and then going directly to her desk and placing them in a box. This simple step (A Delivery of Instruction adaptation) will ensure that she has a pencil when her small reading group meets. When it is time to meet, she will bring the box of pencils and not open it until seated, which will reduce the likelihood of her poking a classmate on the way to her group. Ms. Martinez then helped Luisa complete her ABC log using the computer. Luisa's teacher had created a table similar to that found in Figure 9.3 using Don Johnston's Write:OutLoud. Luisa simply spoke into a microphone and words appeared onscreen. In this way, she could "write" by speaking to complete the ABC log. Ms. Martinez and Luisa signed a contract stating that (a) if Luisa kept her ABC log current, and (b) Luisa came to her reading group with sharpened pencils inside the box and refrained from poking others, she would be given 15 minutes at the end of the week to play games on Ms. Martinez's iPad.

 Test to determine if the adaptations helped the student accomplish the task.
After the activity was over, Ms. Martinez kept a running record of the times Luisa came to the activity with her pencil box full of sharpened pencils. She also recorded the number of times Luisa got through the activity without poking her classmates with the pencil. Finally, at the end of each day, Ms. Martinez would check the ABC log to make sure it was current and complete.

ADAPT *framework:* FOR LUISA

ASK "What am I requiring the student to do?"	DETERMINE the prerequisite skills of the task.	ANALYZE the student's strengths and struggles.	PROPOSE and implement adaptations from among the four categories.	TEST to determine whether the adaptations helped the student to accomplish the task.

		Strengths	Struggles		
The students will learn how to complete and implement an ABC log.	1. Provide their own examples of antecedents, behaviors, and consequences.	1			
	2. Think about what triggers their actions, both positive and negative, so that they can see the connection between antecedents and consequences.	2			
	3. Discriminate between antecedents that trigger positive behavior and those that trigger negative behavior and what happens to them.	3			
	4. Select one of their own behaviors to change.	4			
	5. Identify a plan to deal with the antecedents that trigger negative behaviors.		5	5. Instructional delivery: Teacher meets with student to develop a plan.	5. Teacher determines whether pencils are sharpened and student refrains from poking fellow students.
	6. Keep a record of the behavior in a journal after positive and negative behaviors occur.		6	6. Instructional materials: Student uses Write:OutLoud to create and complete the ABC chart.	6. Teacher checks the ABC log for accuracy.

Reviewing existing records is another source of data. Records can include office referrals, attendance records, counselor information, and cumulative school folders. Also, interviews of family members and support personnel can yield important clues about the events that trigger or maintain problem behavior. We review instructional strategies for positive behavior next.

WHAT INSTRUCTIONAL STRATEGIES ARE AVAILABLE FOR BEHAVIOR PROBLEMS?

Sometimes, specific interventions must be implemented to promote positive behavior in the classroom.

PLANNED IGNORING

Planned ignoring, sometimes referred to as the *ignore strategy,* is the planned, systematic withdrawal of attention by the individual from whom the attention is sought. This individual could be the teacher but could also be a classmate.

Planned ignoring is an appropriate intervention if the behavior is a minor infraction that poses no threat of harm to others (Evertson & Emmer, 2008). Behaviors such as threatening others or fighting will probably not be influenced quickly enough by ignoring and should be dealt with quickly and directly. The landmark research that clearly demonstrated the power of adult attention on nursery school children's behavior was conducted more than 50 years ago (Allen, Hart, Buell, Harris, & Wolf, 1964). Results showed the correlation between behavior and the application and withdrawal of teacher attention.

What guidelines apply to planned ignoring? First, the person who is doing the ignoring must be the individual whose attention is being sought. It is important to know whose attention a student is seeking. How can a teacher determine this? Adult attention is extremely important to younger children, which is why teachers see immediate and often dramatic changes when they praise or ignore younger students. However, as students get older, the attention of the peer group increases in importance, and the teacher's influence lessens. This is why ignoring older students when they are off task probably will not be effective. Second, planned ignoring must be implemented consistently, even if the behavior of concern increases. It is common for inappropriate behavior to escalate when planned ignoring is first introduced. Notably, some students will purposefully exhibit inappropriate behavior to gain the teacher's attention. However, planned ignoring can quickly become an effective intervention when implemented consistently, even during the brief escalation period (Corrol, Tynan, & Lines, 2009). As experienced teachers have noted for years, when a student's behavior fails to achieve the desired effect, the behavior will usually stop. However, teachers should become aware of students who engage

Problem Behaviors

in attention-seeking behavior and provide them with positive attention for appropriate behavior as much as possible.

REDIRECT INAPPROPRIATE BEHAVIOR

Redirection is the process of informing a student that an error was made and asking the student to describe the appropriate behavior. The student is provided an opportunity to demonstrate the appropriate behavior with reinforcement. Redirection is an effective way to help a student stop a problem behavior and receive further instruction on appropriate behavior in a relatively short amount of time. Much like specific praise and planned ignoring, redirection is a helpful intervention if the behavior is relatively minor and stems from the need to remind students about appropriate behavior.

When students exhibit minor problem behaviors, the teacher can intervene by giving instructions on how to behave appropriately. Students should be told the desired behavior and provided with positive support for demonstrating the appropriate behavior. With a focus on the positive, a reprimand—a negative response to problem behavior—is avoided. A reprimand does not provide the student with the opportunity to practice the correct behavior and receive reinforcement. For example, if a student calls out rather than raises his hand during discussion, the teacher can talk privately with the student, stating that calling out is inappropriate and asking the student to explain what he should have done during discussion (raise his hand to contribute). Then, in further class discussion, contingent on hand raising, specific praise could be provided for the appropriate behavior. Redirection is a positive intervention and helps students become aware of and practice the desired behavior. In thinking back to Eric from the Opening Challenge, who calls out and may be seeking Ms. Martinez's attention, she can redirect his calling out by privately having him explain to her what he can do besides calling out and by praising him with positive attention each time he raises his hand.

CONTINGENT OBSERVATION

Sometimes problem behavior occurs during small group work or an activity when peers may be reinforcing the student's misbehavior. Peer reinforcement may result in increased levels of the problem behavior. Contingent observation is a form of time-out whereby a disruptive student is removed from an activity but is still allowed to observe the proceedings. Contingent observation can be implemented in such situations if it appears that the peer group is contributing to the problem behavior. The advantage of this intervention is that the student can observe others participating appropriately in the group work, which can reduce the loss of instruction. It is important to ensure that the contingent observation period is long enough to make a difference but not so long that interest is lost in rejoining the group.

Managing Classroom Behavior

Classroom rules should be posted. Rules should come with both positive recognition and consequences. When students follow the rules, praise, special notices, privileges, and other types of positive rewards may be earned.

CRITERION-SPECIFIC REWARDS

With criterion-specific rewards, students earn privileges only as they reach desirable levels of the target behavior. This intervention is used widely in schools. Rewards are given to students who achieve designated levels of improvement (the criterion level) for a specific academic, behavioral, or social skill. Rewards may include the following:

- Tangible items, such as food, trinkets, or prizes.

- Token reinforcers, such as happy faces, stickers, or points toward a "payoff."

- Social reinforcers, such as praise, positive notes, or positive calls to parents.

- Activity reinforcers, such as a one-night no-homework pass, 10 minutes of extra recess time, or earned time to select a desired activity in the classroom (listening to a tape).

It should be noted that a reward for one student might not have the same appeal for another; therefore, it is necessary to find out from students what rewards are most desirable to them. Also, something that is rewarding in September may not be appealing to students in November. Rewards will probably lose some of their value to students over time, so they must be changed to achieve results. Table 9.4 provides a list of suggested rewards for elementary and secondary students.

Think back to the Opening Challenge; Ms. Martinez is reflecting about Sam. Recall that he has been identified as having ADHD. He has difficulties staying organized and being prepared to work. See how Ms. Martinez uses a certificate as a reward when Sam achieves the desired goal of an organized desk, which in turn helps him be prepared for class.

CONTRACTING

Contracting involves setting up a written agreement between two parties that designates a targeted behavior that needs improvement. This technique is sometimes necessary for students whose problem behaviors do not seem to respond to other interventions. Alberto and Troutman (2012) suggested that contracts can be an effective intervention for teachers to implement because the conditions for reinforcement are written down, which can help busy teachers remember how behavior for certain students will be managed.

TABLE 9.4	SUGGESTED REWARDS FOR ELEMENTARY AND SECONDARY STUDENTS
Type of Reward	**Examples**
Academic Activities	• Go to the library to select a book. • Help a classmate with an academic assignment. • Help the teacher to present a lesson (e.g., by completing sample math problem on blackboard, reading a section of text aloud, assisting cooperative learning groups on an activity). • Invite an adult "reading buddy" of student's choice to classroom to read with student. • Listen to books-on-tape. • Play academic computer games. • Read a book of his/her choice. • Read a story aloud to younger children. • Read aloud to the class. • Select a class learning activity from a list of choices. • Select a friend as a "study buddy" on an in-class work assignment. • Select friends to sit with to complete a cooperative learning activity. • Spend time (with appropriate supervision) on the Internet at academic sites.
Praise/Recognition	• Be awarded a trophy, medal, or other honor for good behavior/caring attitude. • Be praised on school-wide announcements for good behavior or caring attitude. • Be praised privately by the teacher or other adult. • Design—or post work on—a class or hall bulletin board. • Get a silent "thumbs up" or other sign from teacher indicating praise and approval. • Have the teacher call the student's parent/guardian to give positive feedback about the student. • Have the teacher write a positive note to the student's parent/guardian. • Post drawings or other artwork in a public place. • Post writings in a public place. • Receive a "good job" note from the teacher.

SOURCE: Intervention Central (n.d.).

The following are simple guidelines for implementing contracts:

1. The desired behavior and a reward that is meaningful to the student must be identified.

2. The conditions for earning the reward must be stipulated as part of the contract, including the desired behavior and the time frame.

3. The contract should contain an *If . . . then* statement and include the behavior, condition, criterion, and reinforcer (Alberto & Troutman, 2012).

4. The teacher and the student should sign the contract. A sample contract is shown in Figure 9.4.

ADAPT *in action*

SAM: PREPARING FOR CLASS

Ms. Martinez thinks about Sam as he participates in class. He really tries to get his work done and seems to understand instruction, as indicated by his responses on written work. However, Sam lags behind his classmates in getting to work and finishing on time. Ms. Martinez observes that he spends too much time managing his materials and getting organized. Ms. Martinez decides to implement the ADAPT framework to identify a positive reinforcement system to help Sam be prepared for class.

(A) Ask, "What am I requiring the student to do?" Ms. Martinez notes, "I expect all of my students to be prepared for class so that we can focus on the lessons at hand."

(D) Determine the prerequisite skills of the task. Ms. Martinez realizes that, in part, being prepared means that her students have supplies and materials readily available in their desks and that they are organized for learning.

(A) Analyze the student's strengths and struggles. Ms. Martinez reflects on Sam's preparation for class: "He lost his pencil four times last week and left his homework at home twice. Sam said he knew he was supposed to have a pencil and bring back his homework. When I asked him where he put his pencil, he couldn't seem to remember. He said he forgot his homework but that he did it. His desk is a mess; it's a wonder he can find anything. I have to stop my small group work to help him get organized so that he can do his work. What can I do to help him be more prepared?"

(P) Propose and implement adaptations from among the four categories. Ms. Martinez thinks that Sam may have difficulty organizing his space enough to keep track of his pencils and that he may have problems organizing himself at home to remember to return his homework. She decides to implement a behavior management system with Sam. First, she and Sam clean out his desk and develop an organization system (*instructional delivery adaptation*). She views the organization system as an instructional delivery adaptation because being prepared is really a prerequisite for instruction. She tells Sam that once a week she will do a "desk check" with him to see if the books and supplies are organized. If so, he will earn a "Being Prepared" certificate (*instructional material adaptation*) to take home. Ms. Martinez also sends home a chart (*instructional material adaptation*) for Sam to look at before leaving the house to go to school. The chart simply asks, "Do you have your homework?" Sam's mom says that she will tape the chart to the door as a reminder.

(T) Test to determine if the adaptations helped the student accomplish the task. As the days progress, Ms. Martinez notes that Sam remembers to bring his homework to school. She praises him for being so good at remembering to do this. The "desk checks" are also beginning to work. At first, she finds herself quietly reminding him about his desk organization, but by the second week he is developing the habit of organizing his books and storing supplies, including his pencil, in the box in his desk. He confided that things were going better for him because he could find his pencil when he needed it. With a little extra effort, Ms. Martinez helped Sam develop better organization skills and the ability to remember his homework, which seems to improve his preparation for class.

ADAPT *framework:* FOR SAM

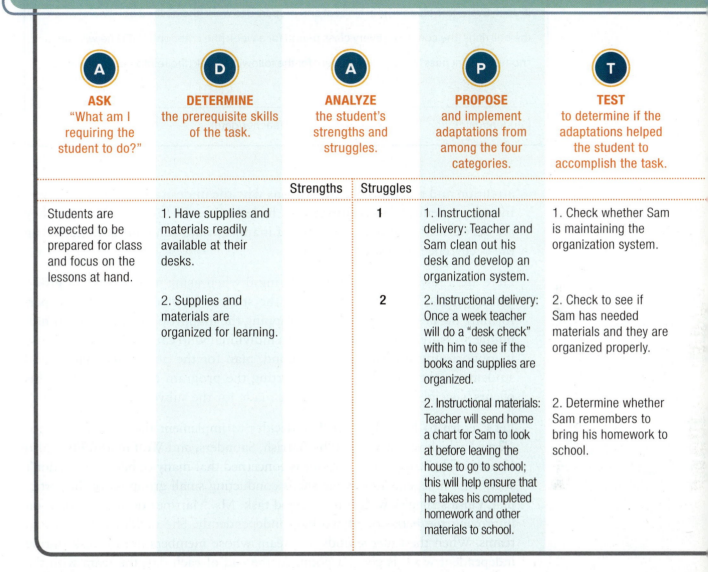

(A) ASK "What am I requiring the student to do?"	(D) DETERMINE the prerequisite skills of the task.	(A) ANALYZE the student's strengths and struggles.		(P) PROPOSE and implement adaptations from among the four categories.	(T) TEST to determine if the adaptations helped the student to accomplish the task.
		Strengths	Struggles		
Students are expected to be prepared for class and focus on the lessons at hand.	1. Have supplies and materials readily available at their desks.		1	1. Instructional delivery: Teacher and Sam clean out his desk and develop an organization system.	1. Check whether Sam is maintaining the organization system.
	2. Supplies and materials are organized for learning.		2	2. Instructional delivery: Once a week teacher will do a "desk check" with him to see if the books and supplies are organized.	2. Check to see if Sam has needed materials and they are organized properly.
				2. Instructional materials: Teacher will send home a chart for Sam to look at before leaving the house to go to school; this will help ensure that he takes his completed homework and other materials to school.	2. Determine whether Sam remembers to bring his homework to school.

INTERDEPENDENT GROUP CONTINGENCIES

Students and teachers respond well to group contingency interventions because they are typically arranged as classroom games (Flower, McKenna, Muething, Bryant, & Bryant, 2013). They take a little more time on the teacher's part to manage, but they can be effective for dealing with problem behaviors that are resistant to other interventions, such as planned ignoring and redirection. With **interdependent group contingencies,** students earn reinforcement when they achieve a goal that has been established for the group. Group contingencies focus on using the peer group as a resource to encourage positive changes in behavior. Interdependent group contingencies are effective for all age-groups, particularly when the peer group's

FIGURE 9.4	SAMPLE BEHAVIOR IMPROVEMENT CONTRACT

IF John Evans [the student] is in his seat and prepared to work [the desired behaviors] when the bell rings [the condition] every class period for a week [the criterion], THEN he will earn a "no-homework pass" for one assignment for the following week [the reinforcer, or reward].

_____   _____

(Student/date)   (Teacher/date)

attention and reactions are the reasons why the undesirable behavior occurs. Interdependent group contingencies have been used for years because they are very effective in reducing rates of inappropriate behavior and increasing the occurrence of desired behaviors.

Here are a few guidelines to keep in mind when using interdependent group contingencies. First, be certain that the student involved is capable of performing the desired behavior and stopping the inappropriate behavior. If not, undue pressure could be placed on an individual who causes the group to lose its opportunity for the reward. Second, plan for the possibility that several students might actually enjoy subverting the program for the group. If this occurs, special arrangements must be made for the subversive students.

Let's return to Ms. Martinez. She decides to implement the "Good Behavior Game," which was developed by Barrish, Saunders, and Wolf in 1969 (see also Flower et al., 2013). Ms. Martinez is concerned that many of her students don't work well independently while she is conducting small group work. In particular, Luisa struggles with this expected task. Ms. Martinez decides to focus on improving the behavior of working independently. She divides the class into teams. When the timer sounds, the team whose members are on task during independent work is given a point. At the end of each day, the team with the most points earns 10 minutes to work on an activity of their choice (something the class values as important). The members of the other team who haven't earned enough points have to continue with their independent work. Eventually, Ms. Martinez sets a criterion of five points as the goal for earning the reward.

SELF-REGULATION

Self-regulation occurs when individuals monitor their own behavior. Using self-regulatory techniques, individuals attempt to avoid situations that lead to inappropriate behavior or stop problem behavior if it has already started. Self-regulation is a type of self-management (i.e., the implementation of specific interventions by the targeted student to manage his or her own behavior). Studies have shown that self-management techniques (or self-mediated techniques, as they are sometimes called) are effective for both elementary and secondary students (Ryan, Pierce, & Mooney, 2008). Self-management techniques are appealing because they actively involve the individual in the learning process and promote independence and decision making. Examples of self-regulation techniques include "counting to 10," using self-talk to work through a problem, and walking away from a potentially problematic situation. Obviously, these techniques require the teacher to help the student know how to recognize a problem situation and when to use the appropriate technique.

Let's examine some guidelines for implementing the self-regulation intervention. Modeling and role-playing are good ways to help students learn self-regulation techniques. It will be necessary to determine which techniques are more appropriate for younger or older students. The students' use of self-regulatory techniques will increase as they receive reinforcement and see the effects of the techniques. Figure 9.5 is an example of a "Countoon." Students can use the Countoon to self-regulate by recording occurrences of a desired behavior, such as "raising hand during class discussions," and the problem behavior, such as "calls out." The technique of self-recording to monitor one's own behavior can lead to increases in the desired behavior and to decreases in the problem one. In the following section, we offer instructional strategies for more serious behavior.

Sometimes, students may exhibit problem behaviors that require more intensive interventions. We provide examples of interventions that you can use to reduce or eliminate these problem behaviors.

Self-management techniques are appealing because they actively involve the individual in the learning process. These techniques require the teacher to help the student know how to recognize a problem situation and when to use the appropriate technique.

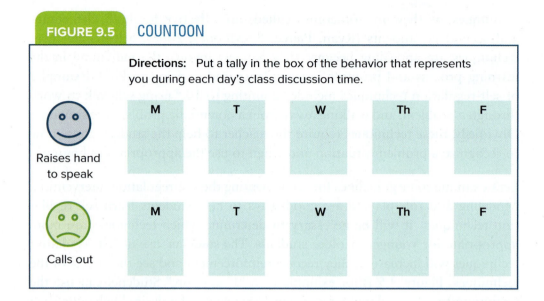

FIGURE 9.5 COUNTOON

Directions: Put a tally in the box of the behavior that represents you during each day's class discussion time.

Raises hand to speak | M | T | W | Th | F

Calls out | M | T | W | Th | F

Time-out and Seclusion Time-out

Time-out is an intervention that removes the student from a situation that is reinforcing the inappropriate behavior. Seclusion time-out, in which the pupil is placed in an isolated room, is used for severe, out-of-control behavior. With seclusion time-out, the student is removed from a situation that is encouraging and maintaining the problem behavior and placed in a neutral environment. Usually, the neutral environment is a small room where the student is isolated for a designated period of time (Alberto & Troutman, 2012). Seclusion time-out has gained in popularity because it offers the student a chance to calm down, think about what happened, and rejoin the group in a short time period. However, the Council for Children with Behavior Disorders (2009) cautioned that "seclusion to control behavior should be used only under the following emergency circumstances and only if all three of these elements exist":

- The student's actions pose a clear, present, and imminent physical danger to him/her or to others;
- Less restrictive measures have not effectively de-escalated the risk of injury; and
- The seclusion should last only as long as necessary to resolve the actual risk of danger or harm or while awaiting the arrival of law enforcement or crisis intervention personnel such as when the student has possessed a weapon or committed a crime. (p. 10)

In-School Supervision

In-school supervision is recommended only for severe behavior problems and only after other positive interventions have been tried but failed over a period of time. Because students miss class, this intervention is usually reserved for major disruptive acts, such as fighting (Emmer & Evertson, 2008). School privileges are suspended, and students must spend their time completing schoolwork in a quiet environment. Students should not consider in-school supervision a better place to be than in class. The advantage of this intervention for teachers is that they do not have to miss their lunch breaks or planning periods to supervise disorderly students; rather, someone is assigned to supervise the in-school suspension room. The advantage for students is that they are required to complete schoolwork and are in school rather than out on the streets. The in-school supervision procedure serves as a deterrent to future disruptive behavior. Let's look at how problem behaviors can be assessed.

IDEA (2004) requires the use of positive behavioral interventions and supports and functional behavioral assessment for students with disabilities who exhibit challenging behavior. To meet this federal mandate, many schools now utilize three-tiered models or multitiered systems of support (MTSS) to prevent and respond to challenging behavior. You probably have thought of tiered systems with regard to RTI and academics; tiered systems can also be used to deal with behavior as well. For example, MTSS for behavior provide classwide and schoolwide supports at the core level (Tier 1); targeted, preventive, small group interventions at the secondary prevention level (Tier 2); and individualized support at the tertiary level (Tier 3; Sugai & Horner, 2009). The core level facilitates appropriate behavior for all students by establishing behavioral expectations and procedures. Students who do not appropriately respond to core supports may require more intensive, frequent supports that are provided at the secondary level. The Tier 2 intervention level addresses students with at-risk behaviors who can benefit from instructional interventions focused on reducing harm, such as social skills interventions (Lane, 2007). As with academic supports for RTI, some students may still require more intensive, frequent, and supportive interventions than provided at the secondary level. Tertiary, or Tier 3 level interventions typically support individual students through individualized interventions such as functional behavioral assessment and function-based interventions (Sugai & Horner, 2009).

Schoolwide positive behavior support (SWPBS) is an example of MTSS through which core, secondary, and tertiary supports can be utilized along a continuum. SWPBS is a framework, not a curriculum, intervention, or program. As such, it can be tailored to meet the needs of the students with whom it is being implemented. As Sugai and Horner (2009) suggested, it is an approach that should lead to "sustained use of evidence-based practices related to behavior and classroom management" (p. 309) that are accurately implemented.

MTSS for behavior is dynamic, that is, it is continually developing and evolving. Recent advances in this field have included SWPBS at the core level. SWPBS addresses schoolwide social cultures while providing behavioral supports for students with challenging behavior, including those with emotional/behavioral disorders (Sugai & Horner, 2009). For students with emotional/behavioral

VIDEO CASE 9.3

Positive Behavior Supports

1. How is SWPBS used at Mia Tannous's school? What methods are used to ensure that it is working effectively in each classroom and across the school?

2. How does SWPBS help students to feel safe in school? How does it support students' learning?

disorders, the prevention elements of MTSS may be critical for addressing their complex academic and behavioral challenges to intervene early when student behavior is most easily changed (Lane, 2007).

The continual evolution of MTSS for behavior is an important component of students' education. Researchers and practitioners must not only understand the current evidence-based practices that promote improved behavioral outcomes but also continually search for ways to facilitate improved outcomes for learners who exhibit multiple, challenging risk factors. With more than 18,000 U.S. schools implementing MTSS for behavior (http://www.pbis.org), researchers are needed to study the critical features of each level of MTSS. Teachers just beginning their careers should become well-versed in using MTSS to help them manage behavior in their classrooms. School and district leaders must be able to support teachers as they implement behavior supports.

Functional Behavior Assessment

Simply put, functional behavior assessment (FBA) is "a systematic set of strategies that is used to determine the underlying function or purpose of a behavior, so that an effective intervention plan can be developed" (The National Professional Development Center on Autism Spectrum Disorder, n.d., para. 1). Individuals engage in behavior because it gets them something they want (e.g., teacher attention) or helps them avoid something they do not want (e.g., time-out). Thus, the behavior has a function, goal, or purpose. Conditions in the environment also can cause behaviors to occur. FBA is used to determine what the individual is doing and under what conditions.

The goals of the FBA are as follows:

- Describe the problem behavior and the conditions that trigger and reinforce its occurrence.
- Generate hypotheses or educated guesses of why the behavior is occurring.
- Identify goals for decreasing the problem behavior.
- Develop an intervention plan.

The ABC log, student and parent interviews, and review of school records and documents are examples of ways to collect data as part of the FBA and to write the behavior intervention plan.

Behavior Intervention Plan

Teachers who can explain the function or purpose of problem behavior can respond more effectively to students by planning appropriate interventions. A behavior intervention plan provides teachers with a road map for changing

CREATING A BEHAVIORAL INTERVENTION PLAN (BIP)

INSTRUCTIONAL OBJECTIVE

Students will be provided with a BIP to improve their behavior in school.

INSTRUCTIONAL CONTENT

Behavior

INSTRUCTIONAL MATERIAL

Student's functional behavior assessment (FBA), BIP chart

INSTRUCTIONAL DELIVERY

Grouping: Individual

TEACHING PROCEDURES

1. Meet with a behavioral intervention team and with the student and/or parent(s).

2. From the student's FBA, identify antecedent events, problem behaviors, and consequences.

3. Generate a hypothesis as to the cause(s) of the problem behavior that will result from the BIP.

4. Determine the goal of the BIP.

5. Create the BIP, including the intervention, person responsible, and the assessment.

BEHAVIOR INTERVENTION PLAN

Student: Mark Friar

School: Fairview Middle School, Grade: 6 (language arts and reading)

General Education Teacher: Mrs. Franklin; Special Education Teacher: Mr. Garcia

RESULTS FROM THE FBA

Antecedent Events (A): Request by the teacher to work in a small group; small group involves students with average reading abilities; small group tasks involve reading aloud.

Problem Behaviors (B): Student refuses to move to and work with the small group.

Consequences (C): Teacher attention (redirection, reprimands); instructional time lost because of lack of compliance for working in small groups.

Hypotheses: Because of low reading skills and the setting demands of the small group, the student may have feelings of inadequacy and thus is engaging in behavior to avoid the reading tasks. He may seek acceptance through attention-getting behavior and isolating himself from the group.

INTERVENTION GOAL

The intervention goal is to increase compliance for working in small groups on literacy tasks.

Intervention	Person Responsible	Assessment
• Have the student practice the reading passages that will be used in small groups.	• Special education teacher during resource time	• Observation: Student is reading aloud in the group.
• Provide the passages on tape for the student to practice at home.	• Special education teacher	• Observation: Student is reading aloud in the group.
• Change the group membership to be more heterogeneous.	• General education teacher	• Observation: Student works with group members.
• Give the student a strategy for letting the teacher know when the reading material is too difficult and thus will cause embarrassment.	• School counselor	• Conference between counselor and teacher to assess when the student is using the strategy.
• Provide specific praise (in note format) for using the strategy.	• General education teacher	• Observation: Student uses the strategy.

inappropriate behavior and teaching new, appropriate skills. The behavior intervention plan is developed on the basis of findings from the FBA.

Classroom teachers can expect other school personnel, such as the special education teacher, school psychologist, and counselor, to work together to conduct the FBA and to write, implement, and evaluate the behavior intervention plan. An example of how professionals collaborate to conduct the FBA and to write the behavior intervention plan is shown in the Working Together feature below. Take a moment to read this example.

We now discuss social skills and how teachers can facilitate the development of these skills in their classroom through the ADAPT framework. Good social skills are extremely important for peer group acceptance. The social skills of some students with disabilities and at-risk students may not be adequate to promote peer acceptance. Thus, it is essential to devote attention to ways teachers can facilitate social skills in inclusive settings.

Now, let's examine social skills. We begin with a description of social competence.

WHAT IS SOCIAL COMPETENCE?

Social competence means that a person uses social skills well enough to obtain positive reactions and to reduce the likelihood of negative reactions from others. Being socially competent means that an individual has the ability to perceive when and how to use social skills depending on the situation and social context. The result contributes to acceptance by others. Unfortunately, research studies suggest that many individuals with special needs tend to have difficulty with an array of social behaviors, including, for example, choosing appropriate social behaviors for different situations, predicting behavioral consequences, reading social cues, and adapting their behavior in social situations.

WORKING *together*

THE FUNCTIONAL BEHAVIOR ASSESSMENT AND BEHAVIOR INTERVENTION PLAN

The process of conducting an FBA and developing a BIP is a team effort that can involve the special education teacher, general education teacher, counselor, speech/language pathologist, and other professionals, as appropriate. Consider the following example to learn about possible roles for each professional and the student.

Mrs. Evans, the eighth-grade social studies teacher, was concerned about the behavior of one of her students with a diagnosed emotional or behavioral disability. She has tried several interventions to address the misbehavior, to no avail. She called together the school support team to work with her on the next step. The team decided that the needs of the student warranted an FBA.

Mrs. Evans indicated that she could use the ABC log to collect data on the situational events prior to and following the behavior of concern. She agreed to do this for a week. The special education teacher agreed to collect quantitative data using an observational system so that the frequency could be identified. The counselor agreed to interview the student's mother, which might help shed light on events at home that could help the team understand the student's behavior. Finally, the counselor agreed to review school records and interview the student.

After the FBA was finished, the data analyzed, and the hypotheses generated, the team wrote the BIP together. Collectively, they identified the interventions that could reasonably be implemented to teach the student more appropriate behavior and to reduce the misbehavior. They agreed to give the plan two weeks and then reevaluate.

QUESTIONS

1. How can the ABC log be implemented in the classroom during the instructional day?

2. What is important for Mrs. Evans to remember when she observes the "B" part of the ABC log?

3. Pretend you are the counselor. What questions would you ask the student's mother?

Think about the three students—Sam, Eric, and Luisa—from the Opening Challenge. Review their social skills issues. Table 9.5 provides examples of social skills tasks and prerequisite skills. How do Sam, Eric, and Luisa's social skills problems compare with this list of social skills tasks that teachers expect in the classroom?

CURRICULUM

Social skills curricula have been developed for elementary, middle, and high school students. Social skills can be categorized into a variety of domains, such as communication skills, problem-solving skills, getting along with others, and coping skills. Figure 9.6 includes sample social skills curricula for elementary and secondary students. Take a moment to review this information. Using Figure 9.6, which social skills activities would you recommend for Sam, Eric, and Luisa? If you said "getting-along skills" for Sam, "negotiation" and "coping skills" for Eric, and "conversation" for Luisa, then you're on track for matching interventions to struggles with prerequisite skills for social skills tasks.

The Tech Notes feature discusses communication devices.

TABLE 9.5	EXAMPLES OF SOCIAL SKILLS TASKS AND PREREQUISITE SKILLS THAT FACILITATE TEACHING AND LEARNING

Social Skills Tasks	Prerequisite Skills
Gets along with others	• Is able to compromise • Is polite • Accepts others' points of view • Is helpful • Knows how to share
Converses appropriately	• Initiates conversation • Uses an appropriate tone • Listens to others • Can maintain a conversation • Takes turns in conversation • Can end a conversation appropriately
Makes and keeps friends	• Makes an effort to talk with others • Cooperates • Has good hygiene • Is loyal
Gives feedback	• Offers feedback in a positive manner • Is able to express own needs • Can use I-messages to give feedback • Can say "no" to peer pressure
Solves problems	• Can identify the problem • Can initiate solutions • Can generate solutions • Can evaluate the effects of solutions
Exhibits self-control	• Recognizes situations that are provoking • Can self-monitor behavior • Initiates action to remain calm • Is able to resolve conflict • Can evaluate the effects of actions • Accepts consequences

Now let's consider ways to assess social skills. Assessing social skills provides information about students' social behavior and how interventions are working. Several techniques can be used to assess social skills. For example, the ABC log described elsewhere in this chapter can be used to determine what social skills are problematic and what events and individuals may be triggering or increasing the occurrence of the inappropriate social behavior. Rating scales found in many social skills curricula can be used to determine which

FIGURE 9.6 SAMPLE SOCIAL SKILLS CURRICULA AND PROGRAMS

The ACCEPTS Program: A Curriculum for Children's Effective Peer and Teacher Skills

By H. M. Walker, S. McConnell, D. Holmes, B. Todis, J. Walker, and N. Golden

ACCEPTS is a curriculum for teaching classroom and peer-to-peer social skills to children with or without disabilities in grades K through 6. Different instructional groupings can be used. Included is a 45-minute videotape that shows students demonstrating the social skills that ACCEPTS teaches. The curriculum includes the following social skills:

- **Classroom skills:** Listening to the teacher, doing your best work, and following classroom rules
- **Basic interaction skills:** Eye contact, using the right voice, listening, answering, taking turns
- **Getting-along skills:** Using polite words, sharing, following rules, assisting others
- **Making-friends skills:** Grooming, smiling, complimenting, and friendship making
- **Coping skills:** When someone says no, when you express anger, when someone teases you, when someone tries to hurt you, when someone asks you to do something you can't do, and when things don't go right

ASSET: A Social Skills Program for Adolescents

By J. S. Hazel, J. B. Schumaker, J. A. Sherman, and J. Sheldon

ASSET consists of eight teaching videotapes that contain four vignettes, which focus on specific social skills areas. The curriculum includes the following social skills:

- **Giving positive feedback:** Thanking or complimenting others
- **Giving negative feedback:** Expressing criticism or disappointment in a calm, nonthreatening manner
- **Accepting negative feedback:** Listening calmly to criticism, asking permission to tell your side of the story
- **Resisting peer pressure:** Saying no, giving a personal reason, suggesting alternative activities
- **Problem solving:** Identifying problems, considering consequences, determining possible solutions
- **Negotiation:** Resolving conflicts with others, suggesting solutions, asking for alternatives, learning to compromise
- **Following instructions:** Listening carefully, acknowledging, clarifying, following through
- **Conversation:** Interacting with others, introducing yourself, initiating and maintaining a conversation

The ACCESS Program: Adolescent Curriculum for Communication and Effective Social Skills

By H. M. Walker, B. Todis, D. Holmes, and G. Horton

ACCESS is a curriculum for teaching social skills to students at the middle- and high-school levels. The program teaches peer-to-peer skills, skills for relating to adults, and self-management skills. The curriculum includes the following social skills:

- **Relating to peers:** Listening, greeting others, having conversations, offering assistance, complimenting, making and keeping friends, interacting with the opposite sex, negotiating, being left out, handling group pressures, expressing anger, and coping with aggression
- **Relating to adults:** Getting an adult's attention, disagreeing with adults, responding to requests, doing quality work, working independently, developing good work habits, following classroom rules, and developing good study habits
- **Relating to yourself:** Taking pride in your appearance, being organized, using self-control, doing what you agree to do, accepting the consequences of your actions, coping with being upset or depressed, feeling good about yourself

TECH *notes*

COMMUNICATION DEVICES

Poule at en.wikipedia

Melissa is a 14-year-old student who is a ninth grader in the local high school. Melissa was born with a severe form of spastic cerebral palsy that makes it difficult for her to produce intelligible speech. For mobility she uses a motorized wheelchair, which can be operated with a joystick. She is able to keep up with the work in general education classes with appropriate adaptations and modifications. To communicate, Melissa uses an electronic communication device as a means to express her needs, to interact with teachers and friends, and to function in her classes.

Because of Melissa's cognitive and receptive language strengths, the communication device contains features that provide a range of communicative interactions. A scanning system is used that searches by row and column an array of communicative choices. When the choice is highlighted, Melissa activates a switch that emits the oral response. Switch-activation capabilities are appropriate for Melissa because of her motoric challenges.

The use of the communication device is a good start for enhancing social interactions because it gives the user a tool for expressive language. However, communication partners should exhibit patience by giving the user a chance to manipulate the device (motor control) and by allowing time for the rate of communication utterances (electronic emission) to occur. Students are likely to be intrigued by this tool, and if appropriate, the operator may enjoy "being the expert" and showing them how it works.

students are exhibiting poorer skills than their peers. Also, sociometric surveys and sociograms can be used to identify peer relationships in the classroom.

Sociometric Survey

Sociometrics, or peer-nominating techniques, help teachers learn about peer relationships. Through the use of a sociometric survey—a set of questions answered by students regarding their perspectives on their peers—teachers can learn which students may be popular, which may be rejected, and which may be isolated within the classroom or peer group. The sociometric survey can be conducted by asking students to respond to several of the following questions:

- Who would you most like to eat lunch with?
- Who are your top three choices to sit next to?
- Who do you not want to sit next to?
- Who would you invite to your birthday party?

- Who do you get together with during the weekend?
- Who would you not want to be in your working group?

Some of these questions relate to relationships within the classroom and others relate to afterschool activities. By asking these types of questions and having students record their responses confidentially, teachers can learn a great deal about students who are popular and students who are disliked. Teachers also can learn which students may be isolated. This information can help teachers plan social skills training and instructional groupings to foster better peer relationships in the classroom.

Sociogram

Drawing a sociogram—a graphic depiction of peer relationships—of the information gleaned from the sociometric survey can help a teacher see quickly what relationship patterns are evident in the classroom. A sociogram is shown in Figure 9.7 to graphically display students' answers to the first question from the sociometric survey. See if you can figure out the relationships in this classroom.

We now examine ways to teach social skills. Each of the following procedures can be effective in teaching social skills. With a little practice, students can improve their social skills in the classroom and with peers.

Role-Playing

Role-playing is an activity in which students practice the desired behaviors under the guidance of their teacher or counselor. Role-playing includes

FIGURE 9.7   SOCIOGRAM

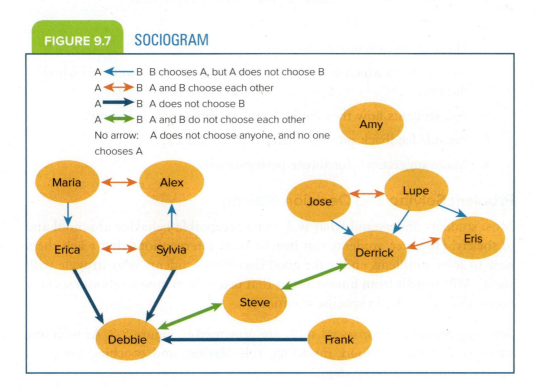

a combination of effective teaching practices to teach skills and provides an opportunity for students to practice with guidance. You can construct contrived situations in which students role-play particular behaviors. How can role-playing be used to teach social skills?

- The teacher can model the appropriate social interaction skills. By "thinking aloud," students learn the steps and thinking process used to initiate the social interaction skills successfully.

- The teacher can provide examples of the appropriate use of the target skills and examples of failure to exhibit them. This step helps students see how the interaction *should* look and how it *should not* look.

- Students should practice the desired social interaction behaviors in contrived situations while the teacher prompts the desired behaviors.

Coaching

Coaching focuses on encouraging appropriate behaviors through modeling and feedback. Coaching can be used to teach many different social skills (Brooks, 2011). It is an interactive process that facilitates self-directed learning by teachers or other coaches providing guidance and feedback on appropriate social behaviors in natural settings.

How does coaching work? Coaching involves the use of direct verbal instructions, followed by the opportunity for students to rehearse or practice the target skill in a nonthreatening situation. Use the following steps in a coaching situation:

1. Present the rules or standards for the target behavior.
2. Model the desired behavior.
3. Have students rehearse the skill.
4. Ask students which behaviors in their opinion went well and which did not.
5. Ask students how they could do things differently next time.
6. Provide feedback on the rehearsed performance.
7. Make suggestions for future performances.

Problem Solving and Decision Making

Most students understand what is deemed acceptable behavior at school and in society. However, students can benefit from interventions that teach them how to solve problems and make good decisions. Students who struggle with social skills benefit from interventions that teach them how to choose socially acceptable behaviors in specific situations.

Teaching procedures for social skills are presented in Figure 9.8. As with any social skill, thinking aloud, modeling, role-playing, and coaching are good interventions to teach the steps.

LISTENING TO OTHERS

INSTRUCTIONAL ACTIVITY

Listening to others

INSTRUCTIONAL OBJECTIVE

Students will understand the skills associated with listening to others during communication.

INSTRUCTIONAL CONTENT

Social skills: Communication

INSTRUCTIONAL MATERIALS

- Cards or sheets of paper with the following purpose statements (one for each student, incorrectly ordered):
  - I should look directly into someone's eyes while they are talking so that we both feel "connected" to the conversation.
  - I should acknowledge what someone is saying by nodding or making a comment so that the other person knows that I understand what is being said.
  - I should look at the face of the person that is talking to me so that he or she feels that I am listening to him or her.
  - I should stand facing toward someone so that I can hear him or her clearly and let him or her know that I am paying attention.
- Blank sheet of paper or overhead transparency
- Blank "Listening to Others" chart (Figure 9.8)

INSTRUCTIONAL DELIVERY

Grouping: Whole class or small groups

TEACHING PROCEDURES

1. Brainstorm and record on a piece of paper (or blank transparency) some important reasons for "listening" to other people when they are talking.

2. Give each student a blank "Listening to Others" chart that presents the four skills relating to being a good listener:
   - When someone is talking to me, I should stand facing him or her.
   - When someone is talking to me, I should look at his or her face while he or she is speaking.
   - When someone is talking to me, I should look directly into his or her eyes from time to time.
   - When someone is talking to me, I should acknowledge him or her by nodding my head or making a comment about what he or she is saying.

3. Give students the card or sheet that contains the purpose statements. Have them match each purpose statement to "The Skill" and write the purpose in the adjacent, matching purpose box.

4. Model each of the four skills from the "Listening to Others" chart for the students. Have them determine which skill you are modeling and state the purpose for the behavior.

5. Have your students model the behavior to get a "feel" for how it should be done.

6. Videotape their "performance" and let them watch it back and critique themselves to improve for next time.

SOURCE: Adapted from Do2Learn (2013).

411

FIGURE 9.8   LISTENING TO OTHERS FORM

"Listening to Others"

The Skill	The Purpose
When someone is talking to me, I should stand facing him or her.	
When someone is talking to me, I should look at his or her face while he or she is speaking.	
When someone is talking to me, I should look directly into his or her eyes from time to time.	
When someone is talking to me, I should acknowledge him or her by nodding my head or making a comment about what he or she is saying.	

SOURCE: Adapted from Do2Learn (2013).

Table 9.6 provides an example of how teachers can take steps in their classroom to make decisions and solve problems.

Cohen (2011) developed a social skills program that uses coaching to help young adults who have social anxiety. Students are matched with a coach to work with throughout the program. Social coaches offer helpful guidance through three scenarios.

First, **job interviews** are conducted to prepare for and practice potential job interviews. During this time, social coaches discuss possible jobs that students might be interested in and provide helpful tips on how best to answer possible interviewer questions while also serving as interviewers in mock sessions and providing helpful comments.

Bookstore conversations take place in bookstores and involve the coach and student observing customers as they browse through books and interact with employees. Students are taught to "read the room" for people who may be receptive to talking about the books that are available.

Finally, coaches observe students as they make and participate in telephone calls to and with their friends. The coaches work with their students to create a script of what to do before making the call, how to initiate the conversation, and how to respond to the person on the other end of the call. The coaches also provide emotional support when needed. In the next section, we discuss ways to make our schools safer, an issue that has become paramount.

HOW CAN SAFER SCHOOLS BE PROMOTED?

Recent events in some high schools across the country are vivid reminders of the importance of making connections with our youth and identifying potential problems before they become serious.

Teaching problem-solving and decision-making skills is an important part of the social skills curriculum at all grade levels. What social skills are needed to help these students complete their group assignment?

GUIDELINES FOR SAFER SCHOOLS

Educators are looking at ways to address violence and aggressive acts to help make schools safer. According to Smith and Tyler (2010), adhering to the following guidelines makes for safer schools:

- Consistent rules, expectations, and consequences across the entire school
- Positive school climate
- Schoolwide strategies for conflict resolution and dealing with student alienation
- High level of supervision in all school settings
- Cultural sensitivity

TABLE 9.6	DECISION-MAKING AND PROBLEM-SOLVING STEPS	
What Is the Step?	**What Is Involved?**	**What Intervention Can I Use?**
STEP 1: Gathering information	Identify information needed to make a decision and solve the problem.	Hold a class meeting. Conduct a brainstorming session. Have students collect data. Use the ABC log process. Involve the school counselor.
STEP 2: Problem identification	State the precise nature of the problem in observable, measurable terms.	Have students identify the problem; use the criteria—observable and measurable—to evaluate the wording. Take a vote to obtain consensus about the problem.
STEP 3: Solution generation	Describe specific solutions to the problem.	Brainstorm solutions with students. To help students generate solutions, have them answer the following questions: • What happens when the problem does not occur? • What does our classroom look like when this problem does not occur? • Who needs to help solve this problem? • What would happen if . . . ?
STEP 4: Decision-making criteria	Establish criteria for selecting the best solution.	Use data from the ABC log to help guide solution generation. Have students describe the resources needed for each possible solution. Rule out those solutions that require unrealistic resources (e.g., too much time, too many people, money). Rank-order possible solutions with 1 = best idea.
STEP 5: Action plan	Develop a specific plan using the solution, including who does what, by when.	Write the action plan using either a class meeting or a designated team of students. Post the action plan.
STEP 6: Evaluation	Meet to determine whether the action plan is working and whether the problem has been solved.	Conduct a class meeting to assess the action plan. Revise if necessary. Set another time line for reevaluating.

• Strong feelings by students of identification, involvement, and bonding with their school

• High levels of parent and community involvement

• Well-utilized space and lack of overcrowding

BULLYING

Bullying has received national attention as educators strive to address this critical issue in schools. As White and Loeber (2008) noted, "bullying can create a climate of fear and discomfort in schools and communities" (p. 380). Bullying is intent on harming the victim and is one of the most significant health risks to children (Raskaukas & Scott, 2011). Bullying can be physical, verbal, or psychological and occurs at all grade levels. The person doing the bullying attempts to assert power and control over the person being bullied. Bullying most often occurs in Grades 6 through 10, with about 3 in every 10 students being involved in bullying, as either the bully or the victim (http://www.bullyingstatistics.org). Limited research on bullying and disabilities suggests that students with disabilities have a greater chance of being bullied than their nondisabled peers (Raskaukas & Scott, 2011; Saylor & Leach, 2009). Examples of bullying include physical attacks on the playground or after school, verbal intimidation, and exclusion from social networks.

Boys are noted as asserting more physical types of bullying, whereas girls tend to exhibit more psychological types of bullying, such as excluding and gossiping about the victim. Both boys and girls report being victimized by bullies.

In examining student traits, individuals who engage in bullying and victims of bullying share several characteristics. Both exhibit problems with social and psychological adjustment, as shown in demonstrated difficulties with friendships and reported feelings of isolation. It has been suggested that some students with disabilities who bully others may have social information processing deficits; that is, "a lack of social skills may be related to the lack of assertion, a lack of self-control, or both" (Rose, Swearer, & Espelage, 2012, p. 4).

What can teachers do about this critical problem? Remember that in the Opening Challenge, Ms. Watson noticed that some students thought that Sandy was a bully because of the mean things she would sometimes say. One could question whether Sandy is intentionally bullying her classmates, but bullying is a major issue in schools today and any perceived threat should be dealt with. Strategies for all students can be implemented to address the bullying problem:

Teaching problem-solving and decision-making skills is an important part of the social skills curriculum at all grade levels. What social skills are needed to help students interact more appropriately with their peers?

- Make bullying prevention and intervention part of the curriculum. Students should understand that there are bullies, victims, and bystanders who reinforce the bullying behavior. Provide information about the types of bullying—physical, verbal, and psychological—including examples. Students may want to describe examples of bullying as well.

- Involve school administrators, teachers, families, and the community. School procedures for preventing and responding to bullying should be developed and shared with students and families.

- Work with the school counselor to identify effective strategies to handle and report acts of bullying. Have the school counselor conduct age-appropriate discussions with students about power, aggression, and control. Ask the school counselor to meet privately with students to conduct individual or small group discussions about feelings related to self-concept, social relationships, and other situations in school or at home that may be problematic.

- Sociograms can reveal students who are viewed less favorably by many classmates (note Amy and Debbie on the sociogram in Figure 9.6). Although sociogram results should be interpreted cautiously, evidence should be gathered to support possible problems with social relationships. For example, the teacher can observe students' behavior toward one another in class and note students who are frequently withdrawn from the group.

Although most attention to bullying has been regarding student-to-student bullying, attention also needs to be paid to violence against teachers. In a 2011 study conducted by the American Psychological Association Task Force on Violence Directed Against Teachers (APA, 2013), 80% of the 2,998 K–12 teachers surveyed reported at least one instance of victimization in the previous 12 months. Teachers reported being victimized not only by students but by their parents as well. Although little research has been conducted in preventing violence against teachers, Espelage et al. (2013) suggested that at the student level, teachers employ functional assessment-based interventions that target the reasons why such behaviors occur and work to avoid situations that lead to aggressive student behavior. They also suggested that teachers clearly state classroom and school rules, model and reward positive behavior, and avoid public confrontations. Finally, teachers should provide their students with clear expectations and demonstrate appropriate social and behavioral skills that students can use to manage anger, resolve conflict, and improve the classroom environment. Clearly, more research is needed to identify effective practices, and attention needs to be paid to violence against educators in both preservice and inservice teacher training programs.

UDL *in action*

Universal Design for Learning Activity

Note: This UDL lesson was developed, in part, using the CAST UDL Lesson Builder (http://lessonbuilder.cast.org/create.php?op=new).

Refer to the UDL information in Chapter 7 to determine which checkpoints are addressed in this lesson.

The UDL framework (version 2.0) is comprised of three main principles (I. Representation, II. Action and Expression, and III. Engagement). Each principle has three guidelines and several checkpoints that define them further. In this lesson plan, we delineate how various instructional strategies meet the UDL checkpoints.

TITLE: Playing Together

SUBJECT: Other

GRADE LEVEL(S): 3–5

DURATION: 20 minutes

UNIT DESCRIPTION: This lesson is part of a unit that teaches students to initiate interactions with peers during school recess and/or playtime.

UNIT GOALS: The goal of this unit is to increase social skills.

LESSON DESCRIPTION: This lesson teaches prerequisite skills: ability to communicate verbally, make requests, and ask for information.

LESSON GOALS: The purpose of this lesson is to teach students to initiate interactions with peers during school recess and/or playtime.

METHODS:

Anticipatory Set: Tell students that the purpose of the day's lesson is to help them play better with their classmates. State that, although it is fun to play alone, it is also fun to play with others. In fact, some games or activities require more than one person. But playing with others isn't always easy, and today's lesson will help them learn some of the "rules" that help people play together.

INTRODUCE AND MODEL NEW KNOWLEDGE: Have a student select a toy, game, or activity and decide whom he or she wants to play with. Then model how to ask peers to play with him or her. Show a short film clip of, or show pictures depicting, examples and nonexamples (multiple means of representation). Model appropriate and inappropriate volume during communication (e.g., using quiet and loud voices to say, "Will you play ___ with me?"). Explain why using appropriate and inappropriate initiators will encourage or discourage others to become play partners. Continuously check for understanding and provide reinforcement and/or error correction as appropriate. Provide scaffolds as needed (multiple means of presentation; e.g., have games/toys available that are appropriate only for individuals and those that are appropriate only for multiple players—have students select those suited for multiple players; show a clip of students playing well together and students arguing during play—which students would be better play partners?). Consider collaborating with colleagues to have older students create and videotape example and

(Continued)

(Continued)

nonexample scenarios that can be used during instruction as a multiple means of representation during this instructional phase or during guided or independent practice.

PROVIDE GUIDED PRACTICE: Tell students that you will practice together. Role-play, demonstrating appropriate and inappropriate initiators. Have students practice appropriate game selection (What games/toys/activities are suited to playing together?), identify a potential play partner (Who do you know who likes this game/activity? Who would you like to play with? Who plays well with others?), and practice initiating contact. Allow students to communicate in the way that is most effective (multiple means of action and expression; e.g., phrases rather than complete sentences, pointing). Continuously check for understanding and provide reinforcement and/or error correction as appropriate.

PROVIDE INDEPENDENT PRACTICE:

- Day 1: At the end of the lesson, provide four or five examples of appropriate and inappropriate selection of games/toys/activities, potential play partners, and initiators. Have students select whether each example is appropriate or inappropriate. If scenarios have been created depicting examples and nonexamples, these can be used during independent practice.

- Day 2: During the play period, present a verbal prompt whenever one minute passes without the student initiating interaction with a play partner. (Sample prompt: "Remember how we worked on asking someone to play with you? Go ask _____ to play with you." Provide the prompt in a quiet voice.

Adapted from Licciardello, Harchik, and Luiselli (2008).

SUMMARY

This chapter presents techniques for promoting positive behavior and facilitating social skills. Both of these areas can greatly influence a teacher's success in promoting an atmosphere for learning. Identifying specific behavioral and social tasks will help teachers plan effective adaptations and interventions that can provide students with skills to use not only in the classroom but also schoolwide and in the community.

By utilizing assessment practices, teachers will realize quickly how successful their adaptations and intervention programs are in promoting an environment that is conducive to learning. Implementing practices discussed in this chapter will help students with disabilities become more involved in the classroom and be better accepted by their peers.

REVIEW THE LEARNING OBJECTIVES

Let's review the learning objectives for this chapter. If you are uncertain and cannot talk through the answers provided for any of these questions, reread those sections of the text.

- **What practices can be used to foster student relationships and communication?**

There are a number of practices you can adopt to cultivate good relationships with—and among—the students you teach, including getting to know your students, using motivational practices, being responsive to cultural differences, and considering student meetings.

- **What ways can be used to communicate effectively with students?**

  Managing teacher behavior can facilitate the accomplishment of expected behavioral and social skills tasks by all students. Some techniques include communicating clear and consistent messages, explaining the rules and consequences, explaining the daily schedule, providing good directions, describing transition procedures, and using specific praise.

- **What are effective classroom arrangement practices?**

  There are several practices. Examine the physical arrangement and observe traffic patterns. Consider seating arrangements and maintain with-it-ness.

- **What are the goals of misbehavior?**

  Lack of social acceptance contributes to the goal of misbehavior. Other goals are attention getting, power and control, revenge, and inadequacy.

- **How can problem behaviors be assessed?**

  Teachers must be able to describe behaviors that are desirable as well as those that are intrusive to teaching so that they can design and assess intervention plans. Observational techniques and the ABC log can be used to assess problem behaviors.

- **What instructional strategies are available for behavior problems?**

  For less serious behavior, several strategies are available, including planned ignoring, redirecting inappropriate behavior, providing contingent observations, providing criterion-specific rewards, contracting,

planning interdependent group contingencies, and implementing self-regulation techniques. For more serious behavior, there are several strategies, including time-out, seclusion, and in-school supervision.

- **What is social competence?**

  A person uses social skills well enough to obtain positive reactions and to reduce the likelihood of negative reactions from others. Several techniques can be used to assess social skills including the ABC log, rating scales found in many social skills curricula, and sociometric surveys and sociograms, which can be used to identify peer relationships in the classroom. There are a variety of instructional strategies that can be used to teach social skills. Role-playing, coaching, and problem solving and decision making are examples.

- **How can safer schools be promoted?**

  A variety of techniques can be used, including the following:

  o Consistent rules, expectations, and consequences across the entire school

  o Positive school climate

  o Schoolwide strategies for conflict resolution and dealing with student alienation

  o High level of supervision in all school settings

  o Cultural sensitivity

  o Strong feelings by students of identification, involvement, and bonding with their school

  o High levels of parent and community involvement

  o Well-utilized space and lack of overcrowding

SAGE edge™ Test your understanding of chapter content. Take the practice quiz.
edge.sagepub.com/bryant

REVISIT THE OPENING CHALLENGE

Check your answers to the Reflection Questions from the Opening Challenge and revise them on the basis of what you have learned.

1. If you were Ms. Watson, in what areas would you seek PD help from the special education teacher?

2. How might Ms. Watson be able to identify specific challenges that Sandy presents?

3. What advice would you offer Ms. Martinez about getting to know her students better?

4. How can Ms. Watson and Ms. Martinez foster student relationships and communication?

5. How can both teachers help their students with their behavior?

6. How can both teachers facilitate their students' social skills?

7. How can both teachers determine whether student behavior and social skills are improving?

8. How can Ms. Watson and Ms. Martinez use the ADAPT framework to promote positive behavior and facilitate social skills?

KEY TERMS

interdependent group contingencies, 397

interest inventory, 368

job interviews, 412

planned ignoring, 392

prosocial behaviors, 384

specific praise, 381

student-centered learning, 371

text, 376

traffic patterns, 383

transition, 380

with-it-ness, 383

$SAGE edge™ Review key terms with eFlashcards.
edge.sagepub.com/bryant

PROFESSIONAL STANDARDS AND LICENSURE

For a complete description of Professional Standards and Licensure, please see Appendix on page 569.

CEC Initial Preparation Standards

Standard 1: Learner Development and Individual Learning Differences

Standard 2: Learning Environments

Standard 3: Curricular Content Knowledge

INTASC Core Principles

Standard 1: Learner Development

Standard 2: Learning Differences

Standard 3: Learning Environments

Standard 4: Content Knowledge

Standard 6: Assessment

Standard 8: Instructional Strategies

Standard 9: Professional Learning and Ethical Practice

Praxis II: Education of Exceptional Students: Core Content Knowledge

I. Understanding Exceptionalities: Human development and behavior

III. Delivery of Services to Students: Curriculum and instruction

Review ➡ Practice ➡ Improve

Get the tools you need to sharpen your study skills. Access practice quizzes, eFlashcards, video, and multimedia: **edge.sagepub.com/bryant**

10 TEACHING LITERACY

After studying this chapter, you will be able to answer the following questions:

- What issues are related to written communication instruction?

- What are the five components of reading?

- What are the stages of the writing process?

- How can teachers provide effective instruction and adaptations for reading and writing?

ELEMENTARY GRADES Mr. Nu is reviewing results of the screening assessment that was administered as part of the RTI initiative in place in his urban school district. The district's policy requires teachers in kindergarten through third grade to assess all their students in the fall, winter, and spring to identify those at risk for reading and/or writing difficulties and to monitor their academic progress throughout the school year. The demographics of the district reflect a rich cultural diversity, and many students are eligible for free or reduced-price meals.

Mr. Nu taught kindergarten for four years and is now in his fifth year teaching third grade. In his class of 21 students, three are at risk for reading difficulties and five are at risk for writing difficulties. In examining the reading results, Mr. Nu reflects, *"These students have problems with word identification. They lack ways to identify words in a list or in their reading passage. Decoding results show that some of the students lack basic skills to figure out unknown words. Some have difficulty identifying individual phonemes and can't seem to blend or segment sounds to form words. I'm concerned that this problem may affect their decoding and spelling skills. All these students exhibit difficulty with oral reading. Their reading is choppy because they don't know the words by sight. Problems with reading fluency affect their ability to understand the text. I'll have to provide them with extra reading support in addition to my regular reading and writing instruction for the entire class."*

In examining the writing results, he reflects, *"The students exhibited problems across the board. In the mechanics portion of the test, they spelled poorly and failed to follow capitalization and punctuation rules. In their writing passage, the word counts were very low, they tended to write using simple sentences, and there were numerous agreement errors. And I had a very difficult time reading their passages because of poor handwriting. We have no formal assessment data that deal with the stages of the writing process per se, but we teach the writing process at our school and I have many student writing samples that I can examine as part of an informal writing assessment. I can see by the results of these writing samples that some of my students have really struggled with some or all of the stages of the writing process."*

In thinking about the results of the assessments, Mr. Nu realizes that most of his students are doing well, but several aren't. He will have to spend time teaching reading and writing skills as part of his core curriculum while also providing small-group supplemental instruction to his struggling students. During core instruction, Mr. Nu will be guided by the UDL principles as he creates and delivers his reading and writing lessons.

SECONDARY GRADES Mrs. Sago is in her third year of teaching 11th-grade English, literature, and reading in a small, rural high school. In her school district, all students are required to take at least two years of English composition. Across her five classes, the number of students ranges from the smallest class size of 11 to the largest class of 21. During the summer, Mrs. Sago attended several workshops on the writing process. In applying what she learned, she noticed that most of her students were adept at brainstorming and topic selection and could produce a first draft. For the most part, students were able to adjust their writing to the purpose of the passage and to the hypothetical audience who would be reading their works. Some students, however, had considerable difficulty in this regard. Nearly all students had some level of difficulty in organization, but a few of her students continued to write disjointed paragraphs even after guidance from her. Spelling, capitalization, and punctuation were not problematic for most of her students, but a small group of students produced errors across the board and were ill-equipped to edit their work for errors. She reflects on her efforts: *"I have to admit that it was a frustrating experience at first. I divided each class into groups of five students, who were to brainstorm about a topic of their choosing. One group decided to write letters to admissions directors at their favorite colleges to inquire about scholarships and academic opportunities. They went online to the website of their school of choice and to the guidance counselor's office to get some brochures. Each created a rough draft of his or her letter. When I met individually with them in a writing conference to discuss the revision, editing, and publishing stages, two students were completely lost. They didn't understand why their letter couldn't just go out "as is." For the two reluctant students, each stage presented its own challenge. Their revised letters looked almost identical to their originals, with the same disorganization, simple sentence construction, and immature vocabulary as their first draft. Editing proved extremely difficult. They simply could not spell and struggled correcting their errors. Capitalization and punctuation were not problem areas, because every sentence began with a capital letter and ended with a period or a question mark. There were no other punctuation marks or capital letters because of the simplicity of their sentences. I really struggle with how to help them."*

Although teaching at opposite ends of the education spectrum, Mrs. Nu and Mrs. Sago both have students who "get it" and students who don't. Although Mr. Nu is teaching early writing skills and Mrs. Sago is having her students apply skills they supposedly learned many years earlier, they both were faced with the challenge of helping their students put words on paper in a meaningful way.

REFLECTION QUESTIONS In your journal, write down your answers to the following questions. After completing the chapter, check your answers and revise them based on what you have learned.

1. What specific difficulties might students in Mr. Nu's class exhibit in idea generation, grammar/syntax, vocabulary/semantics, capitalization, punctuation, spelling, and handwriting/legibility?

2. What specific difficulties might Mr. Nu's students exhibit in phonological awareness, word identification, reading fluency, reading vocabulary, and reading comprehension?

3. How might students benefit from writing conferences in Mr. Nu's class as they move through the five stages of the writing process?

4. How can Mrs. Sago provide the adapted lessons to students who require additional instruction while keeping the rest of the class engaged in relevant work?

5. How can Mrs. Sago integrate reading and writing instruction?

6. How can Mrs. Sago monitor her students' progress or response to intervention?

Most students enjoy learning to read and write, and many young children enter kindergarten with some, and maybe even considerable, literacy skills. This head start is due in large part to the literacy-rich environment full of books, writing utensils, and communication in which they grow up. But some children are not so fortunate. Their homes do not have these literacy advantages, or they were unable to attend preschool, or because of disability-related conditions they are unable to benefit from their environmental advantages. These students may struggle with learning to read and write, and they require special attention and instructional efforts to become literate. This chapter examines key features of reading and writing instruction and provides examples of effective literacy instruction that have been proven useful to teachers who work with struggling students.

In 2000, the National Reading Panel, commissioned by Congress to evaluate the evidence for early reading instruction, published *Teaching Children to Read: An Evidence-Based Assessment of the Scientific Research Literature on Reading and Its Implications for Reading Instruction*. This report documented the importance of explicit reading instruction, including instruction in phonological awareness, phonics, reading fluency, reading comprehension, and vocabulary.

Figure 10.1 depicts these five components of reading and illustrates their relationship to good reading instruction. According to the National Reading Panel (2000), reading instruction must occur for each component. Good readers use skills from each component effortlessly and in combination as they read a variety of texts, such as novels, magazines, newspapers, and textbooks.

Although no comparable group has been gathered to address writing instruction, we have learned much over the years via research and practice, most of which centers on the "recursive" process of writing. The recursive writing process has five stages: prewriting, drafting, revising, editing, and publishing. In a later section, we review the stages by describing what each stage means, showing how some students may struggle with the tasks in each stage, providing instructional guidelines for each stage, and showing how lessons within each stage can be adapted based on struggling students' needs. Here, we begin by presenting the various issues in effective written communication instruction.

FIGURE 10.1   READING COMPONENTS

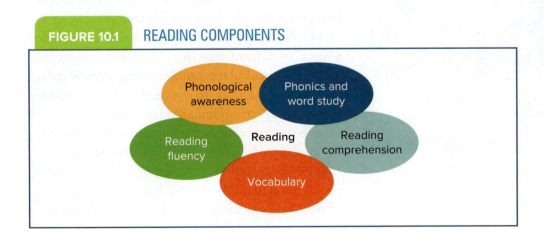

WHAT ISSUES ARE RELATED TO WRITTEN COMMUNICATION INSTRUCTION?

It is estimated that one in four students has difficulty learning to read. Of those who exhibit problems learning to read by the end of first grade, about 85% will continue to struggle through the fourth grade and beyond (U.S. Department of Education, 2002). Results from the National Assessment of Educational Progress (2013) indicate that approximately 40% of all fourth graders read below grade level. The percentages among students from diverse backgrounds and students who live in poverty or have disabilities are even higher.

Research has identified specific difficulties demonstrated to varying degrees by students who are struggling readers (Wanzek & Roberts, 2012). Some may have trouble discriminating sounds in rhyming activities or identifying sounds in words. Further deficits may be noted in the ability to connect sounds to letters and letter combinations. Some students may show adequate abilities with phonological awareness skills but struggle to learn sound-symbol relationships (or letter-sound correspondences, as they are sometimes called) and have limited sight vocabularies. Reading fluency may be slow and choppy; problems with fluency hamper the ability to comprehend text because students spend so much mental energy identifying words that they find it difficult to also concentrate on the meaning of what they are reading. Students who find reading laborious and difficult often don't read independently for pleasure. Yet extensive reading is one of the best ways to increase reading vocabulary. Thus, vocabulary development may be affected because of limited reading exposure.

Older students may also exhibit reading difficulties that remain uncorrected from the elementary years. They may have limited strategies for figuring out words with multiple syllables and lack techniques for breaking words apart, sounding out the parts, and blending the parts together to read the word. Secondary teachers often note that their students with reading difficulties have problems comprehending text and are hampered by a limited vocabulary (Bryant et al., 2011). In classes where the textbook is the major source of information for students, comprehension and vocabulary problems can greatly affect the student's ability to succeed at the secondary level. Many struggling readers who would not otherwise attend colleges or universities can continue their education at the postsecondary level thanks to community colleges. If their reading problems remain, however, they experience many of the same challenges they faced in high school.

iStock/monkeybusinessimages

Reading skills are fundamental for success in school. How can you provide appropriate reading instruction and adaptations for all your students?

Many students who have reading problems also experience difficulties in writing tasks. Over the past decade, written communication instruction has attained a prominent role in all classroom settings. Spurred by national interest in improving academic skills, research findings in cognitive psychology, and the renewed emphasis on writing in postsecondary settings and adult life, written communication instruction warrants teachers' attention across all academic subjects (Graham & Perin, 2007). As a result, more instructional time has been allotted to writing, and increased written communication competency testing has been implemented nationwide (Harris et al., 2012).

Elementary and secondary students with learning problems are unable to express themselves successfully in written communication. For example, compared with their typically achieving peers, students with learning problems write fewer, shorter, less cohesive narrative story compositions and include fewer story elements (Lane et al., 2011). Students with learning problems typically lack effective writing strategies (Graham & Harris, 2005), spell poorly because they do not associate letters with sounds (Moats, 2005/2006), require explicit instruction to edit effectively (Graham & Harris, 2011), revise ineffectively (Graham, Harris, & Larson, 2001), and write using fewer different words and fewer sentences. Clearly, writing instruction is necessary for elementary and secondary students with learning difficulties to improve their skill in written communication.

Foundational skills such as spelling and handwriting are also critical. The reader will likely view a paper that contains rich ideas and vocabulary and is written in an engaging manner negatively if it contains numerous mechanical errors and is barely legible (Santangelo & Graham, 2014).

Some students with reading and writing problems are identified as having dyslexia or dysgraphia, respectively. **Dyslexia,** a language-based reading disability thought to affect 15% of school-age students, is a lifelong condition found in people from all backgrounds. It tends to run in families (Honig, Diamond, & Gutlohn, 2008) and affects the following areas to varying degrees, depending on its severity:

- Learning to speak

- Decoding unknown words

- Recognizing words

- Learning letter-sound associations

- Memorizing facts

- Comprehending

- Spelling

- Writing

Creating a Climate
to Motivate Readers

- Discriminating sounds
- Learning a foreign language

Bryant, Bryant, Hammill, and Sorrells (2004) identified the following research-based characteristics associated with dyslexia:

- Sound–letter association errors when reading aloud
- Poor memory for letters and words
- Slow oral reading
- Slow silent reading
- Substitution of words of similar meaning while reading aloud (e.g., substitutes *thermos* for *flask*)
- Substitution of phonetically similar words while reading aloud (e.g., substitutes *chair* for *cheer* or *then* for *when*).
- Oral reading with flat, disjointed, or nonmelodic (dysrhythmic) intonation
- Does not remember letter sequences in printed syllables
- Interchanges short words, especially articles (e.g., substitutes *a* for *the*) when reading orally
- Omits inflectional endings (such as *-s, -ed, -ing*) when reading aloud
- Cannot break a word into syllables
- Cannot combine syllables into words
- Reverses sounds (e.g., *pan* as *pna*) when reading aloud
- Reads as though each word is encountered for the first time
- Cannot call pseudowords (e.g., *nim, klep*).
- Calls words correctly but does not know their meaning
- Adds words when reading aloud
- Cannot retell what has been read
- Cannot comprehend a passage without reading it more than once

Appropriate instruction and the implementation of instructional adaptations can help most struggling readers learn to read. Teachers must focus on teaching the skills of the five components of reading shown in Figure 10.1 and help students apply these skills to various types of text.

Dysgraphia is a writing disorder that causes problems with handwriting, spelling, and composition. In a review of the research and intervention literature, Hammill and Bryant (1998) found that students with writing disabilities are reluctant to write at all. When they do, they write awkwardly and slowly and with limited output (i.e., their essays are too short, and they write relatively few words and sentences). They spell poorly, omit or repeat letters, add letters, reverse them (such as using *b* for *d*), put them in the wrong sequence (for example, *htnig* for *thing*), confuse vowels, and either do not attempt to spell phonetically or misspell words by attempting to spell phonetically. Some students misspell so badly their words are indecipherable (*camelu, huete*). Some use unconventional pencil grips, write in mirror fashion, and form letters correctly but slant the line upward across the page.

From a syntactic and semantic perspective, students with dysgraphia use too many short words, omit word endings, omit words from sentences, write the wrong words (e.g., *hotel* for *house*), produce sentence fragments, and avoid complex sentences. Qualitatively, some write wordy but content-empty passages and sequence ideas improperly when writing a paragraph. Not all students with writing disabilities or difficulties exhibit all these characteristics. But if you have had the chance to observe writers, you have probably observed several of these behaviors. In fact, you could form a checklist of these behaviors and use it to screen for students who either may be developing poor writing habits or may already have dysgraphia. For these students, help with the stages of writing is critically important.

WHAT ARE THE FIVE COMPONENTS OF READING?

Teaching struggling students is hard work and requires patience and perseverance. It is frustrating to sometimes find that students who seem to be progressing appear to have forgotten everything they learned over the past few weeks of instruction. Fortunately, researchers and practitioners have identified a number of teaching strategies to help students become better readers and writers. In this section, we present information about the areas of reading and the stages of writing, including examples of lessons that can be used to teach important literacy skills and concepts.

PHONOLOGICAL AWARENESS

Phonological awareness describes a variety of listening skills, including rhyming, blending, and segmenting. Although technically a skill that requires listening and speaking, phonological awareness has long been studied in relation to reading, initially as **auditory discrimination,** which is the ability to identify speech and other sounds, such as environmental sounds. When auditory discrimination includes only speech sounds, it is the same as phonological awareness.

One type of phonological awareness, phonemic awareness, is the ability to segment, blend, and manipulate individual phonemes, which are the smallest units of sound that influence the meaning in words. Phonemic awareness is considered

VIDEO CASE 10.1

Components of Reading

1. The students and teacher in the video discuss three of the five main components of reading. How do the students and teacher describe the components of fluency, comprehension, and vocabulary? How do these components work together during the reading process to enhance students' reading success?

2. In the video, you see a variety of effective practices that are used to support fourth-grade students' reading of the novel *Holes*. What instructional strategies does the teacher use to teach the components of reading, and how does she implement them in an inclusive classroom? How are these practices used throughout the video to support student learning?

the most important type of phonological awareness because it is related to phonics instruction, spelling, the ability to read, and the alphabetic principle—the recognition that letters of the alphabet represent sounds in language.

Characteristics of Students Who Struggle With Phonological Awareness

It is not uncommon for beginning readers to have difficulty with the following tasks (Bryant, Wiederholt, & Bryant, 2012):

- Recognizing or producing words that rhyme
- Blending or segmenting syllables
- Blending or segmenting onset-rimes
- Recognizing that two words begin or end with the same sound or different sounds
- Recognizing that two words contain the same or different medial, or middle, sounds
- Segmenting or blending a word's individual sounds
- Manipulating sounds to identify a new word when a sound is deleted or substituted in a word

Strategies for Teaching Phonological Awareness

There are myriad ways to teach phonological awareness skills. Teachers can have students play games like Simon Says, wherein the teachers says, "Simon says, 'Blend the sounds together to form a word: /m/ /a/ /n/.'" At some point, do not say, "Simon Says." Say, "Blend the sounds together to form a word: /t/ /a/ /p/." If the student responds, she or he is out of the game.

Other activities include arranging the students in a circle and having them pass around a bag containing objects with consonant-vowel-consonant, often called CVC, names (such as rock, can, tape). Students identify the object, then segment the word into individual sounds (/r/ /o/ /k/) before passing the bag along to others. The game can be modified to have the next student say the word, say a new word that ends or begins with a different sound ("sock"), and then segment the word (/s/ /o/ /k/) before the next person continues the game.

These students are listening to a book on tape while also reading the book in print. What reading skills are these students practicing? What other activities may reinforce these skills?

PHONICS AND WORD STUDY

Phonics is the teaching of letter-sound patterns so that students can identify unknown words they encounter in text. The ability to read words quickly and effortlessly lets students recognize words on sight. Good readers also possess effective decoding strategies to decipher unknown words. Word identification instruction consists of teaching sight word recognition and decoding skills.

Characteristics of Students Who Struggle With Phonics and Word Study

Teaching students to recognize sight words and to decode unfamiliar words are important parts of word identification instruction. Struggling readers at the elementary and secondary level often possess a limited sight word vocabulary and have difficulty recalling words automatically, even after instruction. For these students, constant practice and review of sight words, along with reading the words in text, is a critical component of daily instruction. The guidelines for sight word instruction in the next section offer ways to provide the extra practice struggling readers need.

Phonic analysis difficulties vary among students with reading problems. Many students are able to identify letter-sound correspondences and know how to say letter combinations in isolation. For these students, the problem often lies in blending letter sounds together to read words. This difficulty is especially apparent as they try to decode pseudowords (such as *zim*) used to assess phonic analysis skills. Conversely, good readers have developed such automaticity in reading words that it is impossible to tell whether words are in their sight vocabularies or they are rapidly and effortlessly applying their phonics skills.

Strategies for Teaching Phonics and Word Study

The following guidelines for sight word instruction provide helpful tips for effective teaching in an area that typically requires practice and review for mastery and retention. They should be implemented regularly and will help teachers plan their instruction (Honig et al., 2008).

Assessment: Use a sight word list to determine which words should be targeted for intervention.

Instructional content: Teach targeted words that most commonly occur in informational text, literature, and basal readers that students encounter during reading. Teach the words before students read text containing these words.

Instructional content: Teach irregular words with common parts and similar sound patterns as word families, such as *would, could,* and *should;* and *other, mother,* and *brother.*

Instructional content: Teach separately words that have visually similar patterns. Words such as *though, thought,* and *through; was* and *saw;* and *were* and *where* should not be taught together.

Instructional content: Teach a limited number of new words in each lesson.

Instructional materials: Use flash cards for instruction and review. Color-code parts of words that require more attention (color green the *w* in *was* and the *s* in *saw* to focus student attention on the initial sound of the word).

Instructional delivery: Focus student attention on all the letters and sounds of irregular words, including letters or letter combinations that do not follow common English sounds or spellings.

Review/maintenance: Include a cumulative review of key high-frequency words (two to three minutes daily).

Fluency: Build fluency once words have been learned. Have students read groups of sight words on flash cards. Show the flash card and ask, "What word?" Students should respond correctly within three seconds. Put unknown words in a separate pile for further instruction.

Progress monitoring: Daily, at the conclusion of the lesson, review the words taught to determine which were learned. Review previously taught words on a weekly basis. Put words not remembered back into the instructional content pool of words.

Teaching phonic analysis is an important part of early reading instruction. Students must establish a strong understanding of letter-sound correspondence and combinations. They must also be able to identify word parts such as phonograms, or rimes, which are parts of a word to which consonants or blends are added to make a word (*an, ip, un*). The following practices can help struggling readers learn to decode using phonic analysis skills (Cunningham, 2013).

Instructional content: Teach letter-sound correspondence in a logical order. Most useful initially are the consonants *b, c, d, f, g, h, k, l, m, n, p, r, s,* and *t,* and the vowels. Present continuous letter sounds (e.g., *s* and /sss/, *m* and /mmm/, *n* and /nnn/) before stop letter sounds (*p* and /p/, *k* and /k/). Select letters that represent sounds found in decodable text students will read.

Instructional content: Introduce the most common sounds of the letters first. Lowercase letters should be taught before uppercase ones.

Instructional content: Teach the letter combinations that most frequently occur in text.

Instructional content: Avoid teaching letter-sound correspondence and letter combinations that sound similar and may confuse students. For instance, /m/ and /n/ and /sh/ and /ch/ should not be taught together. Letter combinations with the same sound, such as /ir/ and /ur/ and /ee/ and /ea/, can be taught at the same time.

Instructional content: Teach phonograms containing letter-sound correspondences that have been introduced. Phonograms or rimes such as *ap, at, ip, it, un,* and *et* paired with initial consonants or onsets provide opportunities to segment and blend sounds to make words. These words should be featured in the decodable text students will read. **Decodable texts** contain words with the sounds and patterns you have previously taught and students have mastered

Instructional delivery: Teach students to blend the letter sounds together in a seamless fashion. For instance, students should be taught to say *mmmaaannn* rather than separating the sounds /m/ /a/ /n/.

Instructional materials: Have students read decodable texts.

Connections to spelling: Have students spell the words so their phonics instruction can be reinforced. Spelling and reading are closely related skills. Here are some examples of ways to make connections to spelling:

- Introduce letter-sound correspondences for spelling as they are being introduced and taught in reading.

- Have students sort words into spelling patterns.

- Have students identify words from their text with patterns that match what they are learning in phonics.

The following are guidelines for English language learners:

- Discuss letters that may have pronunciations in English that differ from those in the student's first language (the letter *h* in Spanish is silent). Correct differences of speech sounds carefully.

- Where appropriate, add pictures of words (such as on the back of word cards) to help students associate words and meanings and to learn vocabulary.

- Use charts and word banks to categorize words according to patterns.

- Teach rules for decoding words with letters that do not make their most common sound (silent-*e* words, double-vowel words).

READING FLUENCY

Reading fluency is the ability to read text accurately, quickly, and with expression. The ability to read with "speed and effortlessness" is what fluency is all about.

There are two types of reading fluency. Oral reading fluency is the combination of rate, or how fast someone reads, and accuracy, or how many words he or she correctly identifies. For oral reading, fluency may also include expression or *prosody*, which means altering pitch, tone, and so forth. Silent reading fluency is a combination of rate and comprehension.

PHONICS ANALOGIES

INSTRUCTIONAL CONTENT: Initial, middle, and final phonemes

INSTRUCTIONAL MATERIALS: Elkonin mat and boxes, Chips

TEACHING PROCEDURE

1. Give students a mat with blank boxes and chips.

2. Place a picture at the top of the mat (e.g., *man*).

3. Ask students to identify and say the word.

4. Tell them that the three boxes stand for each sound in *man*.

5. Say the first sound in man (/m/) and have the students repeat the sound as they place the chip in the first box.

6. Say the middle sound in can (/a/) and have the students repeat the sound as they place the chip in the second box.

7. Say the final sound in can (/n/) and have the students repeat the sound as they place the chip in the third box.

8. Tell them to blend the sounds together to form the word while sliding their pointer finger left to right under the boxes. /m/ /a/ /n/

9. Have them say the word . . . *man*.

Error Correction: If students make an error, say, "Stop. Listen as I model the procedure." Model another word. Have students repeat. Then continue with guided practice.

Guided Practice: Provide several words for the students to work on in groups of three or four. As they work, circulate and provide error correction and feedback.

Independent Practice: Give each student several words to do alone. Tell the other students to sound out each letter, blending them and then saying the word quickly.

PROGRESS MONITORING: After the lesson, give the students 10 words to identify using their blending skills; check for mastery.

To connect the phonics analogies activity to the alphabetic principal after they have mastered the phonics analogies activity, exchange the child with letters (m a n) and repeat the activity. Say, "Put the letter that represents the /mmm/ sound in the word *man* in the correct box. What sound? (/mmm/). What letter? (m). What location? (beginning). Put the letter that represents the /nnn/ sound in the word *run* in the correct box. What sound? (/nnn/). What letter? (/n/). What location? (end). Put the letter that represents the /a/ sound in the word *rat*. What sound? (/a/). What letter? (a). What location? (middle).

Despite its importance, most teachers do not spend a lot of instructional time building students' fluency. Some spend *no* time. However, time spent on fluency building is time well spent.

Reading fluency is an important skill for older readers who have to read large quantities of material for school assignments. We suspect that you, as a student and a teacher, understand the importance of fluency and how it affects the amount of time you allocate to completing your reading. Repeated reading, the process of developing fluency through multiple readings of the same passage, increases reading accuracy, reading rate, and comprehension. Researchers have found repeated reading to be very effective in developing the reading fluency and reading comprehension abilities of students with reading difficulties (Kim, Bryant, & Bryant, 2015).

Fluency is influenced by numerous factors, such as content and purpose for reading, and the fluency expectations for oral and silent reading differ. Findings from a study that examined oral reading fluency rates for first grade (beginning in winter) through eighth grade are presented in Table 10.1 (Hasbrouck & Tindall, 2005).

Characteristics of Students Who Struggle With Reading Fluency

Beginning readers read more slowly and make more oral reading errors than mature readers, read with very little prosody, and struggle with silent reading comprehension. More specifically, beginning and struggling readers

- Exhibit problems with accuracy and speed.
- Present basic word reading difficulties.
- Have a small sight vocabulary.
- Read word by word.
- Rarely self-correct their errors during their reading.
- Have difficulty reading aloud in ways that reflect a misunderstanding of the text and are unable to engage listeners.

Strategies for Teaching Reading Fluency

Students need to read fluently so they can focus on reading comprehension (Kim et al., 2015). To build fluency, they should have opportunities to practice reading words in isolation (such as sight words) and text at their independent level. The following practices can help develop fluency.

TABLE 10.1	READING RATES FOR ORAL READING (IN WORDS PER MINUTE)		
Grade	**Fall**	**Winter**	**Spring**
1		23–81	53–111
2	51–106	72–125	89–142
3	71–128	92–146	107–162
4	94–145	112–166	123–180
5	110–166	127–182	139–194
6	127–177	140–195	150–204
7	128–180	136–192	150–202
8	133–185	146–199	151–199

SOURCE: From *Oral Reading Fluency: 90 Years of Assessment* (BRT Technical Report No. 33), by J. Hasbrouck & G. Tindall, 2005, Eugene, OR: Author. Reprinted with permission.

Instructional content: Select appropriate text. Fluency instruction is best accomplished using materials at the students' independent reading level, where they recognize many words at sight and identify unknown words quickly. Students should concentrate on reading with an increased rate and not worry about decoding unknown words. Instructional-level materials can be used, but avoid frustration-level texts. Beginning readers can practice building their fluency by reading decodable texts. In addition, texts for fluency building should be of interest to the students.

Instructional delivery: Model fluent reading or have a fluent reader do so.

Instructional delivery: Teach students word identification skills to build automaticity and obtain a core sight word vocabulary. Help build fluency with isolated words, phrase reading (reading three or four word phrases, such as "in the tree" and "on the large ball"), and connected text.

Progress monitoring: Assess students' oral reading ability at least biweekly. Graph the number of words per minute that are correct. Compare progress to the benchmark fluency rates presented in Table 10.1. Students must make steady progress on each assessment so they will reach the winter and spring benchmarks.

READING VOCABULARY

Vocabulary is knowledge of the word meanings. A person's **reading vocabulary** is his or her understanding of words, or word comprehension. When readers understand individual words, they are better able to understand phrases and sentences. This, in turn, can help them understand new words with the help of context clues, or surrounding text, particularly when a word has more than one meaning. Once readers comprehend sentences, they can better understand paragraphs and finally achieve passage comprehension, the ultimate goal of reading.

Characteristics of Students Who Struggle With Reading Vocabulary

Considerable research has sought to identify the vocabulary differences between struggling and good readers. Good readers have a deep understanding of words. They use background knowledge to understand the meaning of unknown words, and they can select from multiple meanings the correct definition of a word in context. Good readers understand word origins and know that many words are based on Greek and Latin words. They know word parts (base words, prefixes, and suffixes), and they understand both denotative and connotative definitions of words. Good readers are able to apply context clues, and if they still do not know the definition of a word, they can use reference materials such as a dictionary or a thesaurus. Finally, they are confident in their ability to identify word meanings using a variety of strategies.

Struggling readers are deficient in all these skills. They lack confidence to apply context clues, or they don't know the clues to begin with. They struggle

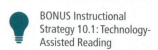

BONUS Instructional Strategy 10.1: Technology-Assisted Reading

with using dictionaries and often lack the reading ability to use guide words to access unknown words in the dictionary. As we have seen in word identification, beginning readers struggle with identifying prefixes and suffixes, so it stands to reason they have difficulty understanding word parts. Their knowledge of word origins is virtually nonexistent. Finally, beginning readers may be able to apply denotative meanings to words, but they rarely understand connotative meanings. All in all, beginning readers not only have difficulty identifying words but also struggle with word meanings.

Strategies for teaching reading vocabulary. Vocabulary instruction that produces in-depth word knowledge and increases reading comprehension is important for all students. Instructional practices must focus on enhancing retention of new vocabulary to help students comprehend text. Students must learn strategies for independently developing a deeper understanding of the meanings of words that often constitute vocabulary found in content-area text. The following practices can help focus more attention on vocabulary learning.

Instructional content: Teach students to use context clues to figure out meaning in conjunction with other vocabulary instructional approaches. Like the dictionary approach, context clues alone are insufficient for struggling readers. For example, they may not fully understand the meaning of the word *magnanimous* in the sentence "The philanthropist's donation to the Girl Scouts of America was a *magnanimous* gesture," but they can use the context of the sentence to know it's probably a good thing to be *magnanimous*.

Instructional delivery: Integrate vocabulary instruction within the context of a reading lesson. Have students use graphic organizers to map meanings of words. Teach them to use word parts, such as prefixes and suffixes, to understand word meanings. Identify a few words to preteach before the lesson, especially if they are technical words. When possible, combine the definition and contextual approaches for identifying word meanings. Review word meanings after reading by playing games with words and definitions (such as *Jeopardy* and *Concentration*) and by creating or elaborating on semantic maps.

Instructional delivery: Provide students with multiple opportunities to practice using words they know. Researchers have noted that it takes multiple exposures to words to understand them well enough to incorporate them into our vocabulary (Butler et al., 2010).

Instructional material: Teach students to use reference materials. Make this one, but not the *only*, strategy for finding word meanings. Show students how to choose which meaning to apply in a particular context. Have them make connections between their background knowledge and word meaning.

BONUS Instructional
Strategy 10.2: Contextual
Searching

WORD MEANING/PICTURE ASSOCIATIONS

INSTRUCTIONAL OBJECTIVE: The students will learn how word associations with synonyms, antonyms, and visuals can facilitate their learning and enhance retention of word meanings.

INSTRUCTIONAL CONTENT: Vocabulary

INSTRUCTIONAL MATERIALS: Word Association Chart

INSTRUCTIONAL DELIVERY

Grouping: Whole class or small group

TEACHING PROCEDURE

1. Give students a copy of the chart and a vocabulary word. Have them write it in the top left-hand box of the chart (see table that follows).

2. Have students draw a picture that depicts the word in the picture box.

3. Tell students to write a synonym (or example) and an antonym (or "nonexample"; tells what the word does *not* mean) in the boxes.

4. Have students write a definition of the word using the meaning from the picture and the synonym and/or antonym.

5. Direct the students to write a sentence that uses the word and is personally meaningful.

6. Have students work in small groups to complete the same activity for the next vocabulary word.

7. The students can make posters of their words, share their charts, or create a *Jeopardy*-type game with the words.

PROGRESS MONITORING: Have students define the words in a quiz or group project.

ADAPTATIONS

- Instructional content: Provide fewer words for students to define.

- Instructional materials: Eliminate one or two boxes on the chart initially.

- Instructional delivery: Have students make posters of their charts showing variations in pictures, synonyms, and antonyms (nonexamples) for vocabulary words.

NAME

Vocabulary word	Picture of word
Associate: Synonym, or example	Associate: Antonym, or nonexample
Write the definition in your own words.	

READING COMPREHENSION

Reading comprehension requires interacting with text and extracting meaning from stories or passages (Honig et al., 2008). Literal comprehension deals specifically with the material on the printed page; inferential comprehension focuses on what is "behind the scenes" (that which is not directly stated). Someone with literal comprehension can read a passage on Mount Vesuvius and recall factual information obtained in it (for instance, Vesuvius destroyed the city of Pompeii; there were no known survivors). Inferential comprehension requires the reader to go beyond the facts stated in the passage and project his or her own ideas to imagine the writer's thoughts and feelings or those of the people affected by the volcano.

Enhancing Reading Comprehension Instruction

Characteristics of Students Who Struggle With Reading Comprehension

Much has been written about the struggles students face as they try to comprehend what they are reading. Beginning readers do not understand the multiple purposes for reading; either they have little background knowledge about the topic of the passage or they don't know how to activate the knowledge they have. When their understanding breaks down, they continue to read without monitoring their reading. They have great difficulty creating mental images of what is going on in the passage and struggle to identify the main ideas and the way they are supported by specific details. When asked to summarize what they read, they either produce a blank stare or repeat the story verbatim as well as they can. They may be able to answer literal questions, at best.

Conversely, good readers are strategic readers. They demonstrate the ability to use effective strategies before, during, and after reading to enhance comprehension. They possess strategies to access and understand text, and they can generalize their strategies to all kinds of reading materials.

Strategies for Teaching Reading Comprehension

Reading comprehension strategy instruction plays an important role in helping students become strategic readers. It focuses on teaching them to construct meaning *before*, *during*, and *after* reading by integrating text information with their background knowledge (Honig et al., 2008). Students who can activate and apply whatever background or prior knowledge they have regarding a topic are more likely to understand a passage than those who cannot.

Comprehension strategy instruction has proved especially helpful for promoting the learning opportunities of students with reading disabilities. Consider one type of comprehension strategy instruction, *collaborative strategic reading (CSR)*.

CSR consists of four reading strategies—preview, click and clunk, get the gist, and wrap up. These strategies are combined with cooperative learning to teach students how to comprehend what they are reading. Before they read, students activate their prior knowledge by *previewing* the text. They brainstorm what they know about the topic and then predict what they will read about based on the text's features (such as illustrations and headings). Making predictions is an important activity for strategic readers because it gets them engaged and gives them a reason for reading ahead. Will their prediction turn out to be right or wrong? Compare this with someone who is reading simply to be able to turn the page and get closer to the end of an assignment.

Next, students read short segments of the text, such as a paragraph or two, during what is called *click and clunk*. They read along (click) until they come to a word they do not know. They are taught to use fix-up strategies, written on clunk cards, and vocabulary strategies, such as context clues, to determine the meaning of unknown words, concepts, or phrases, which are called *clunks*. For each paragraph, *get the gist* (or find the main idea) requires students to tell *who*

VIDEO CASE 10.2

Instructional Adaptation Strategies

1. In the video, the teacher shares a variety of instructional adaptations that make Shakespearean text more accessible for her students. What specific strategies does she mention, and why does she use them? How do these strategies help her students to understand *Romeo and Juliet*?

2. Shakespearean text contains language that may be unfamiliar and daunting to high school students. What methods does the teacher use to enhance her students' understanding of the vocabulary found in the prologue of *Romeo and Juliet*? How does understanding the vocabulary used at the beginning of the play establish context for the students and support their comprehension of the plot?

Working in cooperative groups can help increase student success in reading comprehension.

or *what* they read about and the most important information about the "who" or "what" in 10 or fewer words. Finally, students *wrap up* by summarizing key concepts and asking questions like "who?" "what?" "why?" and "how?" to reflect on important information in the reading passage. Students record their predictions, clunks, gists, and wrap-up questions on a graphic organizer called a *learning log.* They complete the four strategies in cooperative groups to learn from each other and to resolve questions about vocabulary and concepts.

CSR should be taught in two stages. In stage 1, the teacher uses think-aloud and modeling to introduce the four strategies, followed by students practicing the strategies for several days. During stage 2, students learn cooperative learning roles and then are divided into small groups to implement CSR with minimal adult assistance.

Struggling students, including those with disabilities, can experience difficulty in any or all of the five areas of reading. Often but not always, students who struggle with reading also struggle with writing, because many of the skills related to reading affect writing acquisition. For example, a student who has little knowledge of phonics skills will likely be a poor speller. Likewise, students with limited reading vocabularies may find it difficult to select mature words as they write.

WHAT ARE THE STAGES OF THE WRITING PROCESS?

We now turn our attention to the expressive side of literacy—writing. Before discussing the writing process, or the stages students go through as they put their ideas on paper and revise and edit their product, we present a few ideas about the work of Karen Harris and Steve Graham, which deals with the complexity of writing and the reasons some students may struggle.

INSTRUCTIONAL DESIGN FEATURES THAT PROMOTE SUCCESS

Harris and Graham have spent many years developing strategies for struggling students, including those with LD, to become effective writers. Their application of the Self-Regulated Strategy Development (SRSD) approach to writing has been proven effective for helping students become better writers (Harris & Graham, 2013).

Their six phases of writing instruction provide a framework within which teachers can guide students through the writing process, as they align closely with the five stages of the writing process. To their list we have added the

BONUS Instructional Strategy 10.3: Story Mapping for Narrative Text writing conference, which can integrate all Harris and Graham's framework elements throughout the stages of the writing process.

Develop and Activate Background Knowledge

We have already discussed the importance of background knowledge as it pertains to reading comprehension, but having prior knowledge of a topic is just as important in writing. In Harris and Graham's SRSD approach to writing instruction, background knowledge also includes "critical vocabulary and understandings students need to successfully understand, learn, and apply writing and self-regulation strategies" (Harris & Graham, 2013, p. 75). As teachers apply the SRSD approach, they also take note of student aversions to writing, including any doubts about whether they can undertake the task successfully. As most experienced teachers will attest, success breeds success, so it is important that students begin to experience success in writing as early as possible.

Discuss It

In this case, "it" stands for what good writers do. Teachers discuss with students how good writers go about finding something to write about, learning more about the topic, creating an initial draft, and revising and editing their product. Another goal in this step is to have students recognize that the writing process, while challenging at first, becomes enjoyable as they see their works develop into thoughtful pieces; in other words, writing can be fun! Teachers introduce strategies as "tricks" students can use to improve their writing.

Model It

Once the concepts have been introduced, teachers model strategies and ways to implement them. Think of this as interactive modeling or modeled practice, because students are active participants in the process. This form of modeling has two purposes. First, it keeps the students engaged. Second, it provides the teacher with a way to check for student understanding. Having the students do what the teacher models reveals whether the students understand the procedures to that point. If a problem occurs, the teacher can introduce a scaffold or provide additional examples.

Memorize It

Many strategies in the SRSD approach use memorization, for instance, mnemonics such as POWTREE. Even if a mnemonic is not presented, however, students must memorize the strategy so they can call on it automatically when needed. You have probably used a mnemonic at some point in your life, such as for learning the colors of the rainbow (Roy G Biv helps us remember the colors red, orange, yellow, green, blue, indigo, and violet).

Support It

Teachers support students as they write by carefully monitoring student progress as they plan, draft, revise, and edit. Through experience, teachers learn to recognize

Creating a Climate
for Writing

Support from teachers is critical for all students as they work to expand their writing abilities.

telltale signs of misunderstanding (crinkled noses, sighs, hands covering the face, or even tears) and know when to introduce scaffolds to get students beyond the troubling spots. Even though scaffolds fade over time as students become more independent in their writing, students tend to remember them and can apply them independently when problems arise or know when to ask teachers for help. Experienced teachers recognize early that struggling students tend to quit when they experience problems during writing, whereas typical students are challenged by difficulties and endeavor to work through them on their own or with the help of a peer, or, of course, ask the teacher for assistance. In other words, good writers self-monitor throughout the writing process.

Perform Independently

Independent writing is the goal of effective writing instruction. Throughout the writing process, teachers encourage students to apply what they have learned thus far not only to novel writing experiences but also to their other classes. For example, if writing is taught in the English or language arts class, students are encouraged to apply their writing skills to their work in science, social studies, or mathematics classes. As students mature, writing becomes an important aspect of their coursework, and their ability to generalize their strategies to all their classes becomes very important.

Engage in Writing Conferences

Throughout the writing process, students can work together or with the teacher to plan, draft, and revise their written product. Known as writing conferences, such collaborations provide a means to generate ideas, identify the audience for whom the written work is intended, choose the form and tone of what is to be written, and revise and edit the various drafts. All the writing strategies presented in this chapter can take place during such conferences.

PREWRITING STAGE OF WRITING

We have often compared writing to a competition between the mind and the blank piece of paper (or computer screen) that sits before the writer. Many times, the writer has plenty of ideas but struggles to get them onto the page. Soon, the blankness of the page begins to win out; what was in the mind begins

Strategies for
Teaching Prewriting

to disappear, and the mind itself becomes the blank page! The prewriting stage can serve to help the writer win the competition by allowing the student to do some constructive planning before he or she puts pen to paper (or fingers to keyboard) to write a first draft. During the prewriting stage, the student has to select a topic, gather research or information about the topic, determine who the audience will be (i.e., who will read the paper), and so on. Many consider the prewriting stage (or planning stage, as it is sometimes called) the most important stage in the writing process. Proper research, planning, and organizing set the stage for what is to come and save a lot of time and energy "down the writing road."

Characteristics of Students Who Struggle With Prewriting

Hammill and Bryant's (1998) research has significant relevance to the prewriting stage, as the behaviors exhibited by students with learning disabilities show us. As you read each characteristic, think about how it would affect students as they brainstorm, select a topic, conduct research, organize their paper, and so forth—all key features of the prewriting stage. When they tackle the prewriting stage of a writing task, struggling students

- Do not move from one idea to another.
- Approach complex problems in a concrete way.
- Veer from the subject at hand to pursue some minor detail.
- Are inconsistent in thinking and make illogical arguments.
- Have difficulty learning abstract concepts (such as *freedom, pronoun,* and *nation*).
- Have difficulty organizing, grouping, and forming concepts.
- Do not see cause/effect relationships.
- Organize time poorly.
- Are rigid and resistant to changes in thought.
- Lack "stick-to-it-iveness," or persistence.
- Are unable to generate worthwhile ideas.
- Cannot organize ideas into a cohesive plan of action.
- Jump to premature conclusions.
- Show poor judgment.

Strategies for Teaching Prewriting

Numerous activities can help guide students through the prewriting stage of the writing process. We present a few here.

Using Self-Writing. *Self-writing* encourages writing about the student's own experiences. Students try to capture five or six incidents from their past as briefly but as realistically as possible. Have them

- Recall morning activities, remember something that happened, and write it down.

- Go back in time one to two weeks, remember an event, and write it down.

- Go back in time one to two months, recall an event, and write about it, focusing on as many details as can be recalled.

- Go back in time as a young child, recall a fun activity or event, and write about it.

Making Lists. Students can make many different lists to find a topic to write about. Nancie Atwell (2010) suggested that students keep lists of past and potential purposes, audiences, topics, and genres. They can also keep lists of events and subjects that interest them, as well as favorite belongings or accomplishments. The teacher can give a general topic such as accidents, courage, or school, modeling by first listing one or two personal events that have to do with that topic. Students then develop lists of their own experiences and share those lists. Sharing often helps trigger memories for those who are having difficulty. Teachers then need to model how to choose the best topic from the list.

Writing Literature. After reading a story, novel, play, or poem, have students brainstorm the themes of the piece and then plan an original work using one of the themes. Or the student could write a story using one of the characters or a setting from the literature or compare/contrast a character in one story with a character in another. Literature, especially children's books, can also be used to trigger memories and promote personal applications.

Brainstorming. Brainstorming is a way to generate ideas. Johnson (2008) noted that most students do not know how to brainstorm, and brainstorming rules must be taught explicitly and modeled.

1. All ideas must be accepted. No criticizing or evaluation is allowed. At this stage, bad ideas are just as important as good ideas.

2. Freewheeling is celebrated. Creative, bizarre, unusual, and silly ideas are welcomed.

3. The goal of brainstorming is quantity. The more ideas generated, the greater the opportunity to find a solution.

4. Hitchhiking is welcome. Hitchhiking occurs when students add to ideas that have already been stated or combine multiple ideas into a single thought (adapted from Johnson, 2008 pp. 191–192).

BONUS Instructional Strategy 10.4: Planet Wright (Plan-it Right)

CONSIDERING *diversity*

WRITING ASSISTANCE FOR CULTURALLY AND LINGUISTICALLY DIVERSE STUDENTS WITH SPECIAL NEEDS

Culturally and linguistically diverse students who have special learning needs, such as writing difficulties, can benefit from the following suggestions:

1. Designate adequate time for writing. Thirty minutes each day should be allotted to writing instruction and opportunities for students to practice under the teacher's guidance and with feedback.

2. Provide a variety of writing topics, including those with which students are most familiar. Students who are learning to write in a second language and have writing difficulties should be allowed to select topics that are related to their background knowledge and experiences. Allowing students to choose their own topics at first can enhance success, because students will probably select topics with which they are most comfortable.

3. Establish a "writing environment." Teachers can create positive associations with writing by engaging students in different types of writing (informational, lists, directions, journals) throughout the school day. Students should view writing as a natural means of expression, with links to academic areas such as reading, mathematics, and social studies. Conferencing with students regularly reinforces their writing efforts by providing enthusiastic feedback about written work, as well as suggestions for improvement.

4. Incorporate culturally diverse materials. Surround students with books and materials that depict various cultural heritages. Teachers can use these materials (pictures in the books, for example) as story starters. For older students, global and national current events can serve as topics for students to write about.

5. Include technology. Students should learn keyboarding skills and have access to computers with word processing programs, spell-check tools, and specialized assistive technology (text-to-speech, voice recognition) to facilitate the writing process.

6. Provide explicit instruction during the writing process. Model and "think aloud" the steps involved in each stage of the writing process. Provide many opportunities for students to hone their writing skills. Carefully assess their progress, and use the results to inform further instruction.

7. Facilitate vocabulary development. For students who are learning new vocabulary, provide word walls and instruction on vocabulary building. Teachers can use the vocabulary strategies discussed in the chapter on reading to help students develop their written vocabulary.

SOURCE: Adapted from Bos and S. Vaughn (2006).

DRAFTING STAGE OF WRITING

Most people have heard of the "first draft," which is the goal of drafting—a first attempt to put ideas into print. During the drafting stage, the intent is for writers to simply translate their ideas into written form. Improving the draft comes later.

Characteristics of Students Who Struggle With Drafting

When preparing students to make initial drafts of their work, remember the differences between struggling writers and their same-age peers (Hammill & Bryant, 1998). Struggling writers typically

- Write without considering the purpose for their work, who will read what they write, or the form their writing should take.

- Focus too little attention on meaning, concentrating instead on mechanics and writing "rules."

- Have little knowledge about the elements of text structure, such as word order and vocabulary.

- Avoid taking risks.

Strategies for Teaching Drafting

There are many useful ways to help writers generate effective sentences. See the Considering Diversity feature for ways to provide writing assistance for bilingual students.

Instructional delivery: Use examples and nonexamples to demonstrate effective text structure—and the lack of it.

Instructional delivery: Provide students with multiple opportunities to practice writing effective sentences.

Instructional delivery: Model how to write a variety of sentences in a paragraph. Check for student understanding, and provide corrective feedback.

During the drafting stage of writing, students put their prewriting ideas into a written draft form. Bryant and Bryant (2011) described how word prediction programs support the writing process by helping students select related words to complete their thoughts (see this chapter's Tech Notes feature).

REVISING STAGE OF WRITING

During the revising stage, the focus shifts from the writer to the reader. How do students revise what they have written so that it will be easy for the reader to understand and will fully demonstrate the writers' knowledge of the topic using the most appropriate form and tone?

Characteristics of Students Who Struggle With Revising

Struggling writers have difficulty revising their work because they lack the appropriate skills. Their approach to the revision process is quite different from the approach used by their same-age typical peers (Hammill & Bryant, 1998). Struggling writers

- Have little knowledge about how to improve their writing.

- Have trouble recognizing errors in word order and vocabulary use that might affect meaning.

- Lack strategies and skills for correcting errors in their work.

- Make revisions that do not address the errors they have made, so the overall quality of their draft remains the same.

BONUS Instructional Strategy 10.5: Supported Writing

TECH *notes*

WORD PREDICTION PROGRAMS

Originally developed to help students with physical impairments to reduce the number of keystrokes needed to write, word prediction programs are often used by struggling writers to select words. The student begins to type, and the word prediction program offers alternatives that can be used to help write a sentence; the writer then selects the word and continues typing as new words come into view. Word prediction programs often include speech synthesis to read the text and the various word options that appear on the screen. Bryant and Bryant described two popular word prediction products that are widely used:

- *Co:Writer* (Don Johnston Inc.) was designed to add word prediction,

grammar, and vocabulary to word processing programs. In addition to word prediction described earlier, the grammar feature corrects grammatical errors and helps students practice their writing skills.

- *WordQ 2* (Quillsoft) is also used with word processing programs as described previously; the writer selects a word with either a mouse click or keystroke. Once each sentence is written, *WordQ 2* reads the sentence aloud. An interesting feature of this program involves the use of a temporarily disappearing word prediction box that allows the writer to work through the document without distraction.

Strategies for Teaching Revising

As students look at each section of their paper during the revising stage, have them participate in peer revision conferences. Before the conferences, writers can examine their own work for possible improvements.

Instructional content: Have students ask themselves the following questions:

- Has the author written for a specific audience?
- Is the purpose for writing clear?
- Is the information presented in a logical sequence?
- Does the writer stay on topic?
- Are there topic sentences with supporting details?
- Is there a strong conclusion?

As students answer these questions, they should highlight the parts of their text that relate to them.

Instructional activity: Select several sentences from a passage. For each sentence, delete a word and provide three options. The student selects the option that best fits the sentence syntactically and semantically.

Instructional delivery: Model ways to ask the questions and revise a paper on the basis of the answers.

447

PEER REVISION

INSTRUCTIONAL ACTIVITY: Peer revision

INSTRUCTIONAL OBJECTIVE: Revising documents

INSTRUCTIONAL CONTENT: Revising of whole passage

INSTRUCTIONAL MATERIALS: None

INSTRUCTIONAL DELIVERY

Grouping: Students in pairs

TEACHING PROCEDURE

1. Have the students divide into pairs.

2. Model how to consider questions before giving the paper to a peer reviewer.

   - Does the paper fulfill its intended purpose?

   - Will the audience understand what you have written?

   - Does the form of the paper fit the purpose and intended audience?

   - Is the paper interesting?

   - Is there anything that can be done to make the paper more interesting?

   - Are there enough details or examples in the content of the paper?

   - Does it "read right"?

3. Teach students explicitly how to make revision symbols during peer revisions. Provide examples and nonexamples, and provide multiple opportunities to practice (Haager & Klingner, 2005).

4. Have peer reviewers also answer the questions in procedure 2. Model appropriate interactions between peer reviewers and writers, such as providing constructive criticism and avoiding caustic remarks. Give examples and nonexamples of appropriate comments.

5. Give exactly the same passage to all student pairs. Direct each pair to role-play and practice peer revision. Check for student understanding, and provide praise or corrective feedback as warranted.

6. Have students revise their own drafts and then exchange papers with a peer for a peer review. Periodically check for understanding, and provide praise and corrective feedback. Ensure that students are staying on task and taking this revision process seriously. If need be, stop the process and model once again how to provide constructive criticism.

PROGRESS MONITORING: As you check for understanding during guided practice, provide error correction or praise. Meet with the students in a conference after they have revised their papers following peer revision. As you participate in this conference, examine the actual edits and see how the students have revised their papers on the basis of the revision suggestions. After the final paper has been turned in, be sure to grade in terms of what was taught during the revision process. It does little good to teach revising skills if students are not held accountable for errors that "slip through."

To add words, insert ^ between the words and write the added word above the ^.	big Tom had a ^ dog.
To take words out, draw a line through the word to be omitted.	Marcy didn't ~~not~~ think she could help.
To change the order of two consecutive words, draw a ⌒ around the words.	Pedro and ⌒sister his⌒ went shopping for new school clothes.

As a reminder to add ideas, use this mark: ✓	tell which dog ↘ The dog is furry and friendly.
To insert a space between run-on words, use a / and the # sign.	# Marcus enjoyed/playing football with his teammates.
When a lowercase letter needs to be uppercase, use a triple underline: ═══	Tom likes <u>mary</u> a lot. (triple underline)

Throughout the writing process, teachers can have students collaborate with one another during writing conferences. Such conferences allow students to share their work with their peers (or the teacher) to receive critical feedback. Even though conferences occur frequently during the revising and editing stages, they can be held during the prewriting or drafting stages as students share and discuss their ideas and first drafts. Other possibilities include having a display area for students' writing, modeling writing, thinking aloud while working through the writing process, using the overhead projector to generate compositions showing the writing process, establishing a post office, designing activities around students' interests, and having students write, write, write!

EDITING STAGE OF WRITING

After students have revised their drafts and fully developed the meaning of what they have written, they move to the editing stage, where they focus on ensuring that the written piece is grammatically and mechanically correct. To produce a paper that contains as few errors as possible, they should look for inconsistencies in mechanics and grammar choices, such as lack of subject-verb and pronoun-antecedent agreement and the appearance of sentence fragments or run-ons.

Some writing experts differentiate between editing and proofreading, but we see them as similar and interrelated. Editing requires a variety of strategies that must be explicitly taught to help writers become competent at finding and correcting their mistakes. As writers become better editors, they can often correct grammar and mechanical errors during the revising stage. In fact, they may begin to make fewer common errors during the drafting process.

iStock/track5

Editing requires a variety of strategies that must be explicitly taught to help writers become competent at finding and correcting their mistakes.

449

During the editing stage, students can first edit their own papers and then share their papers with at least one other person. This opportunity to practice makes writers/editors better at finding mistakes in their *own* writing, thus helping them create drafts with fewer errors.

Characteristics of Students Who Struggle With Editing

We considered the characteristics of students with writing disabilities earlier in this chapter; many are particularly relevant for students who struggle during the editing stage. To review, these students

- Spell poorly.
- Use too many short words.
- Omit words in sentences.
- Omit endings of words.
- Write the wrong words.
- Write sentence fragments.
- Avoid writing complex sentences.
- Sequence ideas improperly when writing a paragraph.

Strategies for Teaching Editing

A number of instructional routines are available to students when editing.

Instructional materials: Have the writers use checklists while they act as the first editor of their own work. They should ask themselves the following:

- Did I express myself clearly? Will the reader understand what I wrote?
- Did I write any sentence fragments?
- Did I capitalize the first word in each sentence?
- Did I capitalize proper nouns?
- Did I end each sentence with the correct punctuation mark?
- Did I spell all the words correctly?
- Did I use semicolons in the right places?
- Did I use proper verb tenses?
- Did I use apostrophes correctly?
- Did I vary the length of my sentences?
- Did I capitalize "I" whenever I used it?
- Did I use commas when I wrote lists?

Instructional delivery: Model editing strategies and teach students to check their work against their checklist.

Instructional delivery: Explicitly teach one editing skill at a time.

Instructional delivery: Teach students how to proofread others' work and provide corrective, supportive feedback.

PUBLISHING STAGE OF WRITING

At the end of the writing process, we arrive at the publishing stage, where we determine that the paper is finished. Of course, minor changes might need to be made, because in writing there are always a number of possible revisions and edits that *can* be made. But at some point we have to tell the students their work is done. They are now ready to publish their work, which consists of creating a written product that is easy for the reader to read. If it is handwritten, it should be neat and legible.

WORKING *together*

TAKING ON TECHNOLOGY

Many teachers are uncomfortable working with technology, especially sophisticated technology such as speech-to-text or text-to-speech. We encourage you to get to know and collaborate with your assistive technology (AT) specialist. Not every school has an expert in assistive technology in the building. Many school districts or regional service centers hire itinerant professionals, who move from school to school and provide consultant services with classroom teachers and special educators. If you need help with assistive technology devices or services, contact the AT specialist and arrange for a meeting to discuss your students who have special needs.

Skills. Teachers should be able to rate the student (weak, average, or strong) in the following skills:

- Applies capitalization rules.

- Spells correctly.

- Writes neatly with little difficulty.

- Uses appropriate grammar.

- Edits/proofs well.

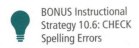

BONUS Instructional Strategy 10.6: CHECK Spelling Errors

- Writes well conceptually.

- Applies a sense of audience effectively.

- Demonstrates overall writing skills.

Setting demands. The teacher should also share the extent to which the following tasks are accomplished in the classroom:

- Writes test answers.

- Writes papers (reports, term papers).

- Writes stories/essays/poems.

- Copies from the chalkboard/text (words and numbers).

- Takes notes.

- Spells words (in isolation and in continuous text).

Having this information available will give the AT specialist some of the information he or she requires to help you work with your students who have special needs. You will probably be asked many more questions. Also, be sure to ask questions that *you* have regarding how AT devices and services can help you meet the needs of your struggling students. Together, you can examine the student ratings and the writing requirements of the classroom setting.

QUESTIONS

1. Think about students you have worked with or observed. What are their AT needs, if any, and what resources might you use to learn more about AT devices and services? Knowledge about AT will help you discuss your students' needs with the AT specialist.

2. Role-play with a classmate a conversation concerning a hypothetical student. One of you will be the teacher, the other the AT specialist. What questions would be asked? What information would you require to answer the questions?

Characteristics of Students Who Struggle With Publishing

Penmanship is important for handwritten work, but it can be a struggle for some students. Cecil Mercer and Paige Pullen (2004) described a variety of handwriting difficulties:

- Slowness

- Incorrect direction of letters and numbers

- Too much or too little slant

- Inconsistent spacing

- General messiness

- Inability to stay on a horizontal line

- Too much or too little pencil/pen pressure
- Mirror writing
- Closed letters
- Closed top loops that should be open (forming *e* like *i*)
- Open loops that should be closed (forming *i* like *e*)
- Omission of parts of letters

Strategies for Teaching Publishing

Graham (2009–2010) stressed the importance of handwriting in writing improvement, noting that "early handwriting instruction improves students' writing. Not just its legibility, but its quantity and quality" (p. 20).

Instructional content: Establish desirable habits such as short daily learning periods.

Instructional content: Do not accept poorly written work.

Instructional delivery: Have students **overlearn** skills, that is, continue to practice them beyond mastery. Apply this strategy to letter formation and alignment in isolation and then use the skills in meaningful contexts and assignments.

Instructional delivery: Have students evaluate their own handwriting.

Instructional delivery: Teach handwriting skills explicitly.

HOW CAN TEACHERS PROVIDE EFFECTIVE INSTRUCTION AND ADAPTATIONS FOR READING AND WRITING?

Reading and writing can be taught separately, of course. But opportunities exist to dovetail them as part of integrated literacy lessons. For example, teachers can have students create a story map (see Figure 10.2) as part of reading comprehension and prewriting instruction. The components of the map become a writing outline that describes the story elements.

Another example teaches word identification, reading comprehension, and drafting or revising instruction. The teacher can select a passage from the text, delete certain words, and create a maze for students to complete. By providing three word choices, only one of which fits the sentence semantically and syntactically, the teacher offers the student instruction in word selection,

Publications That
Feature Student Writing,
Poetry, and Art

ADAPT *in action*

MARK: ORAL READING FLUENCY

Mark is a 12-year-old sixth grader reading on a third-grade level who attends Mr. Williams's reading class. He is a hard worker and eager to please, with a sight vocabulary of several hundred words and good letter-sound correspondence skills. He needs instruction on vowel teams (*ee, oa, ai*), especially consonant digraphs (*sh, th, wh*) and diphthongs (*ou, ow*), and with structural analysis and multisyllabic word recognition skills to decode harder words. He reads in a word-by-word manner and lacks expression as he reads aloud. Mr. Williams plans on implementing a whole-class (peer-mediated) reading fluency program, because many of his students can benefit from fluency building. BONUS Instructional Strategy 10.7 presents paired reading, which is modeled after classwide peer tutoring and uses repeated reading.

While circulating during graphing time, Mr. Williams notices that Mark's and several other students' graphs are not showing an upward trend in the number of words read during "best read." Mr. Williams decides to use the ADAPT framework.

(A) **Ask, "What am I requiring the student to do?"** Mr. Williams wants Mark and other students who need help to become more fluent readers. He knows this is critical so that Mark can read his textbooks more easily and focus on comprehension.

(D) **Determine the prerequisite skills of the task.** Mr. Williams knows that to read fluently, students must be able to quickly recognize words (on sight) and decode difficult ones. In paired reading (*task*), students must be able to practice with a partner, read the passage, and read quickly.

(A) **Analyze the student's strengths and struggles.** Mr. Williams notices that Mark has difficulty keeping up with his partner and reading the passage when it is his turn.

(P) **Propose and implement adaptations from among the four categories.** Mr. Williams decides he will provide Mark with a shorter selection of text (*instructional content*), use easier material (*instructional material*), and serve as Mark's partner (*instructional delivery*).

(T) **Test to discover whether the adaptations helped the student accomplish the task.** Mr. Williams will continue to monitor progress as specified in the paired reading lesson.

an important skill in drafting or revising. Using the preceding sentence as an example, we have the following:

> By _____ (provide, provided, providing) three word
> choices, only one of which _____ (fitting, fits, fitted) the

BONUS Instructional Strategy
10.7: Paired Reading

ADAPT *framework:* FOR MARK

ASK
"What am I requiring the student to do?"

DETERMINE
the prerequisite skills of the task.

ANALYZE
the student's strengths and struggles.

PROPOSE
and implement adaptations from among the four categories.

TEST
to determine whether the adaptations helped the student accomplish the task.

ASK	DETERMINE	Strengths	Struggles	PROPOSE	TEST
I want Mark and other students who need help to become more fluent readers.	**1.** Quickly recognize words (on sight) and decode any difficult words.		1	**1.** Instructional content: Provide Mark with a shorter selection of text. Instructional material: Use easier material. Instructional delivery: Teacher will serve as Mark's partner.	1 and 2: Monitor progress as specified in the paired reading lesson.
	2. Be able to practice with a partner, read the passage, and read quickly.		2	**2.** Instructional delivery: Mark will be paired with another student before the small group work to help him understand the semantic features they will be discussing and to help him stay on task.	
				2. Instructional materials: The day before the work is to be done, Mrs. Hiroshito will make sure Mark records in his "schoolwork diary" that he needs to bring his history book to class.	
				2. Instructional content: Mark will work on only one battle at a time.	

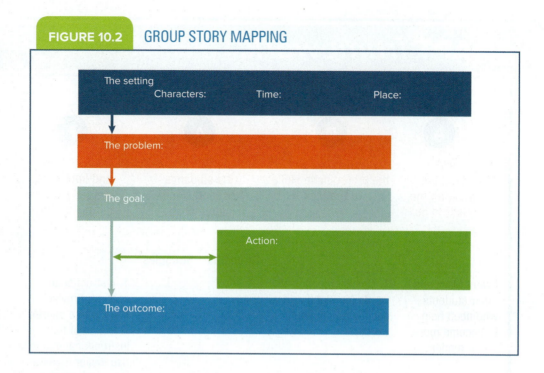

FIGURE 10.2   GROUP STORY MAPPING

sentence semantically and syntactically, the teacher offers the student _____ (illusion, instruction, illustrate) in word selection, an important skill in drafting or revising.

Finally, the same maze procedure can promote fluency and editing at the same time. Instead of providing three syntactic/semantic word choices, the teacher can provide three spellings of the missing word. The students select the word that is correctly spelled for as many of the missing words as they can in a one- or two-minute time span. Again using the previous sentence, we have the following:

The students _____ (silekt, select, sullect) the word that is correctly _____ (spelt, spelld, spelled) for as many of the missing words as they can in a one- or two-minute _____ (time, tyme, tiem) span.

Integrating reading and writing instruction helps to save instructional time and provides opportunities to demonstrate to students the important link between reading and writing. In the case of the story map and outline, the activity also demonstrates the importance of organization in writing. Outlining is a difficult skill for many students, and using a graphic organizer such as the one provided for the story map simplifies the process considerably.

BONUS Instructional Strategy
10.8: HINTS Identifying
Multisyllabic Words

UDL *in action*

Using UDL Principles to Design and Integrate Literacy Lessons

Note: This UDL-based lesson was developed, in part, using the CAST UDL Lesson Builder (http://lessonbuilder.cast.org/create.php?op=new).

The UDL framework (version 2.0) is comprised of three main principles (I. Representation, II. Action and Expression, and III. Engagement). Each principle has three guidelines and several checkpoints that define them further. In this lesson plan, we delineate how various instructional strategies meet the UDL checkpoints.

TITLE: Reading Lesson: Character Map: Fern Arable

SUBJECT: Reading Comprehension

GRADE LEVEL: 4

DURATION: 45 minutes

UNIT DESCRIPTION: This lesson is designed to identify characteristics of a main character in *Charlotte's Web.*

LESSON DESCRIPTION FOR DAY: The students need the following prerequisite skills: ability to communicate verbally and attend to a short video clip and work collaboratively.

UNIT GOALS: The purpose of this unit is to understand the roles that characters play in the story.

LESSON GOALS: The purpose of this lesson is to teach students to complete a character map for one of the characters in the story, *Charlotte's Web.*

METHODS:

Anticipatory Set: Tell the student(s) that the purpose of the day's lesson is to help them understand how characters in stories help us understand why events in stories occur. They will be working with print and digital copies of E. B. White's classic story *Charlotte's Web,* as well as the film version that came out in 1973.

INTRODUCE AND MODEL NEW KNOWLEDGE

1. Introduce Fern Arable to the class as someone who will play an important role in the story. Explain that Fern is 8 years old at the beginning of the story and will grow up as the story progresses. State that students will be working on discovering the traits that Fern possesses.

2. Read the section of *Charlotte's Web* that deals with her saving Wilbur's life and promising her father that she will take care of the young piglet. Project a copy of the passage onto the whiteboard.

3. Play a short clip of the movie *Charlotte's Web* (*Checkpoint 1.3—Offer alternatives for visual information*) that covers the material that was read.

4. Have students work in small groups to talk about Fern and to describe her physical and personality features and to plan their character map (*Checkpoint 6.2—Support planning and strategy development*).

5. Have them create a character map using paper and pencil, overhead transparency, or *Kidspiration* or *Inspiration* (*Checkpoint 5.1—Use multiple media for*

(Continued)

(Continued)

communication). A useful resource for initial training for *Kidspiration* can be found at http://www2.needham.k12.ma.us/mitchell/technology/how_to/kidspiration.pdf.

6. Provide scaffolds as needed (*Checkpoint 6.3—Facilitate managing information and resources*).

   a. Demonstrate to students how they alter the displays of information using features from *Kidspiration* (*Checkpoint 1.1—Offer ways of customizing the display of information*).

   b. Have students label their map using key terms such as *physical traits, personality development, teen challenges,* and so forth (*Checkpoint 2.1—Clarify vocabulary and symbols*).

   c. For struggling students, provide a digital copy of *Charlotte's Web* with screen reader software, so that the story can be read aloud as the student follows along (*Checkpoint 2.3—Support decoding of text, mathematical notation, and symbols*).

PROVIDE GUIDED PRACTICE

(*Checkpoint 5.3—Build fluencies with graduated levels of support for practice and performance*):

1. Provide print, digital, and video versions of *Charlotte's Web*.

2. Select a chapter that will be the focus of the activity.

3. Have students work in small groups to create their character map (*Checkpoint 8.3—Foster collaboration and community*). Allow them to choose groupings for learning activities.

4. Allow students to choose what they will produce.

   a. Create the character map presentation using the medium of their choice.

   b. Conduct a role-playing interview of Fern for a *Charlotte's Web* blog. A character map will accompany the interview.

   c. Create a newspaper article discussing how Fern comes to Wilbur's rescue as her father prepares to slaughter him. A character map will be part of the article.

   d. Other (as approved by teacher).

5. Be prepared to model, for example, PowerPoint or interview procedures.

6. Check for understanding and provide corrective feedback as needed.

7. Support self-regulation skills by assisting students in setting and monitoring learning and behavioral goals (*Checkpoint 9.2—Facilitate personal coping skills and strategies*).

PROVIDE INDEPENDENT PRACTICE

1. At the end of each day, students answer questions related to the new information as they leave the classroom (e.g., What feelings did Fern experience as she grew older?).

2. When student projects are completed, they will be evaluated using a scoring rubric designed for the product type. Alternative progress monitoring will be available based on discussions with and requirements for individual students (*Checkpoint 6.4—Enhance capacity for progress monitoring*).

UDL Guidelines are available at http://www.udlcenter.org/aboutudl/udlguidelines/downloads.

SUMMARY

A successful reading program must consider the phonological awareness, word identification, reading fluency, reading vocabulary, and reading comprehension abilities of individual students and the development of instruction tailored to individual needs. A comprehensive and effective reading program must include a balanced approach to instruction. Students demonstrate a variety of reading characteristics in the five components of reading as they develop reading skills. Effective reading instruction includes features that encompass delivery of instruction and what should be included, such as strategy training and opportunities for students to read good literature. Guidelines for teaching each component of reading were provided and should be used when planning and delivering instruction. Finally, instructional adaptations make it possible to teach these reading components to all struggling readers, including those who have reading or other disabilities.

REVIEW THE LEARNING OBJECTIVES

Let's review the learning objectives for this chapter. If you are uncertain and cannot talk through the answers provided for any of these questions, reread those sections of the text.

- **What issues are related to written communication instruction?**

Students may have trouble discriminating sounds in rhyming activities or identifying sounds in words. Further deficits may be noted in the ability to connect sounds to letters and letter combinations. Some students may show adequate abilities with phonological awareness skills but struggle to learn sound-symbol relationships and have limited sight vocabularies. Reading fluency may be slow and choppy; problems with fluency hamper the ability to comprehend text. Older students may have limited strategies for figuring out words with multiple syllables and lack techniques for breaking words apart, sounding out the parts, and blending the parts together to read the word.

- **What are the five components of reading?**

Phonological awareness, word identification, reading fluency, reading vocabulary, and reading comprehension.

- **What are the stages of the writing process?**

Prewriting, drafting, revising, editing, and publishing.

Prewriting: Review the purposes for writing and ways to select from the various purposes; discuss audience sense, the process for determining the probable reader; and review the way the purpose and audience will affect form and tone. *Drafting:* Present a sentence pattern (beginning with simple sentences and moving to compound sentences, complex sentences, and then compound-complex sentences), use examples and nonexamples to illustrate the critical features of a particular sentence pattern, and provide students opportunities to practice identifying parts of sentences and the associated sentence patterns. *Revising:* Students should decide whether their writing tells the reader what the writing is about, whether the purpose is clear, and whether any part of the writing does not help achieve the purpose. *Editing:* Have the writer serve as the first editor of his or her own work, using checklists and other strategies. Model editing strategies and teach the students to make appropriate comments, and then have the students use peers as editors. Briefly edit students' writing and confer with students about one or two editing skills. *Publishing:* Teach handwriting skills explicitly, establish desirable habits in short daily learning periods, and have students overlearn skills in isolation and then apply them in meaningful contexts and assignments.

- **How can teachers provide effective instruction and adaptations for reading and writing?**

The ADAPT framework can help make instructional adaptations to ensure that students attain the instructional reading and writing objectives. Teachers can examine the instructional task of the lesson and any prerequisite skills students need and, if students lack one or more prerequisites, make lesson adaptations such as providing an alternate activity, changing the instructional content or materials, or using flexible grouping strategies. Once the adapted lesson has been taught, teachers conduct lesson-related assessments to ensure the student attained the instructional objective, that is, learned what was taught.

> **$SAGE edge™**   **Test your understanding of chapter content. Take the practice quiz.** edge.sagepub.com/bryant

REVISIT THE OPENING CHALLENGE

Check your answers to the Reflection Questions from the Opening Challenge and revise them on the basis of what you have learned.

1. What specific difficulties might students in Mr. Nu's class exhibit in idea generation, grammar/syntax, vocabulary/semantics, capitalization, punctuation, spelling, and handwriting/legibility?

2. What specific difficulties might Mr. Nu's students exhibit in phonological awareness, word identification, reading fluency, reading vocabulary, and reading comprehension?

3. How might students benefit from writing conferences in Mr. Nu's class as they move through the five stages of the writing process?

4. How can Mrs. Sago provide the adapted lessons to students who require additional instruction while keeping the rest of the class engaged in relevant work?

5. How can Mrs. Sago integrate reading and writing instruction?

6. How can Mrs. Sago monitor her students' progress or response to intervention?

KEY TERMS

auditory discrimination, 429

decodable texts, 433

dysgraphia, 428

dyslexia, 427

overlearn, 453

phonological awareness, 429

reading fluency, 433

reading vocabulary, 436

> **$SAGE edge™**   **Review key terms with eFlashcards.** edge.sagepub.com/bryant

PROFESSIONAL STANDARDS AND LICENSURE

For a complete description of Professional Standards and Licensure, please see Appendix on page 569.

CEC Initial Preparation Standards

Standard 1: Learner Development and Individual Learning Differences

Standard 3: Curricular Content Knowledge

Standard 4: Assessment

Standard 5: Instructional Planning and Strategies

INTASC Core Principles

Standard 1: Learner Development

Standard 2: Learning Differences

Standard 4: Content Knowledge

Standard 6: Assessment

Standard 7: Planning for Instruction

Standard 8: Instructional Strategies

Standard 9: Professional Learning and Ethical Practice

Praxis II: Education of Exceptional Students: Core Content Knowledge

I. Understanding Exceptionalities: Characteristics of students with disabilities

III. Delivery of Services to Students: Curriculum and instruction

COMMON CORE STATE STANDARDS

Reading

- Literacy
- Craft and Structure
- Integration of Knowledge and Ideas
- Range of Reading and Level of Text Complexity

Writing

- Text Types and Purposes
- Production and Distribution of Writing
- Research to Build and Present Knowledge
- Range of Writing

Review ➡ Practice ➡ Improve

Get the tools you need to sharpen your study skills. Access practice quizzes, eFlashcards, video, and multimedia: **edge.sagepub.com/bryant**

iStock/SimmiSimons

11 TEACHING MATHEMATICS

LEARNING OBJECTIVES

After studying this chapter, you will be able to answer the following questions:

- What are the attributes of students with mathematics difficulties?

- What is early number development and how is it taught?

- What are arithmetic combinations and how are they taught?

- What is place value and how is it taught?

- What is whole-number computation and how is it taught?

- What are rational numbers and how are they taught?

- What is algebra and how is it taught?

- What is problem solving and how is it taught?

OPENING *challenge* ·····································

Helping Struggling Students Access the Mathematics Curriculum

ELEMENTARY GRADES Ms. Hart is a third-grade teacher in a large urban school district. Her class of 23 is culturally and linguistically diverse (CLD) and includes several students who have reading and mathematics problems. Three—from Eastern Europe, Chile, and Taiwan—are bilingual. After administering the district's curriculum-based assessment in mathematics, Ms. Hart learns that one-third of her students do not perform at the competent level on end-of-second-grade skills and concepts; several are performing closer to the first-grade level in fundamental concepts and skills such as numeration. Third grade is the year her students take the state's assessment in reading and mathematics. She realizes she must focus extra attention on the Common Core State Standards for Mathematics (CCSSM, 2010), the part of the curriculum that presents the greatest challenges for her students. *"I have to begin teaching the third-grade mathematics curriculum to all my students. But I must provide extra instruction on fundamental skills and concepts to my struggling students to give them the support they will need to learn more advanced mathematics. I'll use word problems to reinforce student use of the basic number and operation skills so they can apply what they learn to a problem situation. I know what I need to do, but how am I going to find time for the extra instruction in mathematics and reading? How can I use peer-mediated strategies to support my teaching? What should I do about monitoring the students' progress in mathematics?"*

SECONDARY GRADES Mrs. Reid is reviewing her sixth-grade students' papers from today's quiz on problem solving. She is using a problem-based approach to teaching the CCSSM (2010) required by her school district. She starts lessons with a quick vocabulary assignment, a review of what was taught the previous day, and an introduction of materials for the day's exercises. Her students work in small groups to generate solutions to problems that require the use of measurement, geometry, and prealgebra skills and concepts. Mrs. Reid reflects on the quiz results. *"Most of my 140 students got the majority of the problems correct. They used different strategies to solve the problems, which suggests that their group work helps them identify ways to solve problems correctly. But I have 32 papers in which most of the answers are incorrect. Many mistakes are due to inaccurate calculations and faulty strategies. I've spent weeks on problems that focus on specific skills, yet some of my students aren't getting it. I am stumped about what to do next."*

Ms. Hart and Mrs. Reid share a similar concern—a significant number of students in their classes lack prerequisite skills to perform grade-level mathematics. These teachers must decide how to provide extra intervention for their students, what interventions to implement, and how to monitor student progress to determine whether the interventions are working.

REFLECTION QUESTIONS In your journal, write down your answers to the following questions. After completing the chapter, check your answers and revise them on the basis of what you have learned.

1. What mathematical learning characteristics might be contributing to the students' learning difficulties?

2. How can Ms. Hart and Mrs. Reid use the features of effective mathematics instruction to structure their lessons?

3. What instructional adaptations can be implemented to help students access the mathematics curriculum?

4. What suggestions do you have on ways in which these teachers can monitor student progress?

Mathematical literacy is the ability to use skills and concepts to reason, solve problems, and communicate about mathematical problems in the classroom and in everyday life (National Mathematics Advisory Panel [NMAP], 2008). According to the National Council of Teachers of Mathematics (NCTM, 2000) in their *Principles and Standards for School Mathematics,* "the need to understand and be able to use mathematics in everyday life and in the workplace has never been greater and will continue to increase" (p. 4). NCTM noted, "those who understand and can do mathematics will have significantly enhanced opportunities and options for shaping their futures. A lack of mathematical competence keeps those doors closed" (p. 5). The development and application of mathematical competence are important educational goals for all students. The CCSSM provide guidance for many states and school districts in their development of mathematics curricula, instruction, and assessment. States, school districts, researchers, higher education teacher preparation faculty, and textbook publishers have acknowledged the importance of the CCSSM nationally. You can find the standards at http://www.core standards.org/Math/.

We know mathematics instruction should include approaches, activities, and interventions to teach mathematical skills and concepts that promote mathematics literacy for all students. Adaptations help students with mathematical difficulties and disabilities participate in classroom discussions and learn mathematical skills and concepts emphasized in the CCSSM (2010).

In this chapter, you will learn about these students and about ways to provide effective mathematics instruction using the ADAPT framework. We begin with information about students with mathematics difficulties.

WHAT ARE THE ATTRIBUTES OF STUDENTS WITH MATHEMATICS DIFFICULTIES?

About 5% to 8% of school-age students are identified as having a mathematics disability (Geary, 2011), and some have difficulties in both reading and mathematics instruction. About 5% to 10% of school-age students have persistent low achievement in mathematics; these difficulties could have long-term consequences as students move through the grades with increasingly more difficult curriculum (Bryant, Bryant, Kethley, et al., 2008; Jordan, Glutting, & Ramineni, 2009; Murphy, Mazzocco, Hanich, & Early, 2007). Clearly educators and researchers need to pay attention to the mathematical needs of these students.

As early as preschool, parents, educators, and researchers notice that some students have problems learning simple mathematics ideas such as counting, telling how many are in a group, and naming numbers. Even though this may sound very basic, these students may be exhibiting problems with **number sense**. Number sense is an awareness and knowledge of concepts related to numbers, measurement, data, and algebraic thinking, for example (Berch, 2005). You may have worked with a student whose answer to an arithmetic problem was wildly off the mark. Through

Research findings have shown that 5% to 8% of school-age children are identified as having a mathematics disability.

multiple opportunities to use representations to show and talk about numbers, students can develop number sense to help them reason mathematically. Now, we examine mathematics difficulties and disabilities.

MATHEMATICS DIFFICULTIES AND DISABILITIES

According to the Individuals with Disabilities Education Act of 2004, a learning disability can be identified in mathematics calculation and/or mathematics problem solving. Sometimes, mathematics difficulties are referred to as **dyscalculia**, which refers to problems in learning mathematics skills and concepts. However, the terms *learning disabilities in mathematics* and *mathematics disability* are more widely used today.

Students with mathematics calculation difficulties may demonstrate problems with some or most of the following skills:

- Identifying the meaning of signs (e.g., $+$, $-$, $\times$, $<$, $=$, $>$, %, Σ)

- Remembering answers to basic arithmetic combinations (e.g., $8 + 9 = ?$, $7 \times 7 = ?$)

- Using effective counting strategies to calculate answers to arithmetic problems

- Understanding the commutative property (e.g., $5 + 3 = 8$ and $3 + 5 = 8$)

- Solving multidigit calculations that require regrouping

- Misaligning numbers

- Ignoring decimal points

Difficulty solving word problems can be observed in any of the following skills:

- Reading the problem
- Understanding the meaning of the sentences
- Understanding what the problem is asking
- Identifying extraneous information that is not required for solving the problem
- Developing and implementing a plan for solving the problem
- Solving multiple steps in advanced word problems

Mathematics difficulties appear to be persistent and evident across elementary and secondary levels and into adulthood; they are cumulative and worsen across the grade levels (Jordan, Glutting, & Ramineni, 2009).

LEARNING CHARACTERISTICS

Gersten, Jordan, and Flojo (2005) examined the results of a series of studies comparing the abilities of young students in kindergarten through Grade 2 who exhibited mathematics difficulties as compared with the abilities of their typically achieving peers. Learning problems were noted in arithmetic combinations (basic facts), counting strategies (counting all, counting on), and number sense (basic counting techniques, understanding of size of numbers, number relationships). Gersten and colleagues found that over a period of time, limited mastery of arithmetic combinations (basic facts) was a "hallmark of mathematics difficulties" (Gersten et al., 2005, p. 296). They suggested that difficulties learning arithmetic combinations seem to be a characteristic of a developmental difference that hinges on memory or cognitive problems (Geary, 2011).

In another study on mathematics difficulties, Bryant, Bryant, and Hammill (2000) asked a group of teachers who taught students with learning disabilities and mathematics difficulties to rate the frequency at which specific mathematical skills were problematic for their students. These mathematics skills were then analyzed statistically to determine whether they actually predicted mathematics difficulties. Table 11.1 shows the results of this analysis of mathematics skills, which were most predictive of mathematics difficulties of second- through eighth-grade students.

For students receiving Tiers 2 and 3 mathematics intervention in an RTI model and students with mathematics disabilities, evidence-based instructional practices can teach most mathematics concepts and skills. First, the concrete-semiconcrete-abstract (CSA) instructional routine is a way to help students understand the abstract nature of mathematics and to develop conceptual understanding. It was originally studied as a way to teach place value (Peterson, Mercer, & O'Shea, 1988) and arithmetic combinations (Miller & Mercer, 1993; Miller, Mercer, & Dillon, 1992), and a solid body of evidence

TABLE 11.1	MATHEMATICS SKILLS THAT ARE MOST PREDICTIVE OF MATHEMATICS DIFFICULTIES

- Has difficulty with multistep problems
- Makes "borrowing" (i.e., regrouping, renaming) errors
- Cannot recall number facts automatically
- Misspells number words (writes 13 as *threeteen,* 20 as *twoty*)
- Reaches "unreasonable" answers
- Calculates poorly when the order in which digits are presented is altered
- Cannot copy numbers accurately
- Orders and spaces numbers inaccurately in multiplication and division
- Does not remember number words or digits

SOURCE: Bryant et al. (2000).

supports its use. Students learned the skills to the criterion level, suggesting that CSA is highly effective for students with mathematics difficulties. The technique has also been applied to the teaching of rational numbers such as fractions (Butler, Miller, Crehan, Babbitt, & Pierce, 2003) and more recently to algebraic expressions (Strickland & Maccini, 2013). Table 11.2 shows the steps of the CSA instructional routine.

The following instructional procedures should be used when implementing the CSA instructional routine.

The CSA teaching procedures begin with the teacher providing an advance organizer about the purpose of the lesson. Next, the teacher models how to solve the problem, while verbalizing the steps ("thinking aloud"). The teacher asks questions, such as "What is the first thing I do?" Then guided practice

TABLE 11.2	CONCRETE-SEMICONCRETE-ABSTRACT INSTRUCTIONAL ROUTINE

Steps of the Concrete-Semiconcrete-Abstract Instructional Routine	
STEP 1. *Concrete*	Use manipulatives to physically represent a number concept or skill being taught, such as whole-number computation of addition with regrouping. Refer to Figure 11.1 for examples of manipulatives and materials for mathematics instruction.
STEP 2. *Semiconcrete*	After several lessons where students achieve 90% accuracy on problems using manipulatives, change the representation to semiconcrete. Use pictorial representations such as tally marks or pictures of base-10 materials for several lessons.
STEP 3. *Abstract*	After several lessons where students achieve 90% accuracy on problems using pictorial representations, change the representation to abstract. Have students solve problems that employ only numbers but are otherwise similar to those presented in Steps 1 and 2. Again, expect 90% accuracy for the problems presented.

is implemented. Students work on several problems, and the teacher provides prompts and cues. A prompt might go something like this: "You have the correct number of blocks for the first number. Now which number do you look at?" Corrective feedback and assistance are provided immediately. Finally, students work independently to complete 10 problems. To solve problems during guided practice, students use manipulatives in the concrete phase and tallies in the semiconcrete phase; in the abstract phase, students are instructed to solve the problem using only numerals.

Following are evidence-based intervention practices and instructional routines:

- Instruction during the intervention should be explicit and systematic. This includes providing models of proficient problem solving, verbalization of thought processes, guided practice, corrective feedback, and frequent cumulative review.

- Interventions should include instruction on solving word problems that is based on common underlying structures.

- Intervention materials should include opportunities for students to work with visual representations of mathematical ideas, and interventionists should be proficient in the use of visual representations of mathematical ideas.

- Interventions at all grade levels should devote about 10 minutes in each session to building fluent retrieval of basic arithmetic facts.

- Progress monitoring should be employed, with students receiving supplemental instruction if they appear to be at risk.

- Motivational strategies should be included in Tiers 2 and 3 interventions.

- Students should receive help in recognizing that fractions are numbers and that they expand the number system beyond whole numbers. Number lines can be used as a central representational tool in teaching this and other fraction concepts.

- Students should be assisted in understanding why procedures for computations with fractions make sense.

- Students' conceptual understanding of strategies for solving ratio, rate, and proportion problems should be developed before they are exposed to cross-multiplication as a procedure to solve such problems.

SOURCES: Gersten et al. (2009), Siegler et al. (2010).

For students with autism spectrum disorder (ASD) and students with intellectual disability (ID) ranging from mild to severe, different mathematics profiles appear. Some researchers feel some students may have average mathematics abilities (Wei, Christiano, Yu, Wagner, & Spiker, 2015), while others have observed that about 25% of students with ASD have a mathematics LD (Williams,

Coteaching
Mathematics

Goldstein, Kojkowski, & Minshew, 2008). Difficulties in learning-related social skills in ASD have been found to relate to academic difficulties (Blair & Razza, 2007). Also, repetitive and/or restricted interests and activities may challenge students to remain engaged with academic tasks (Rispoli et al., 2011; Stasolla, Perilli, & Damiani, 2014). Depending on their intellectual cognitive profile and mathematics difficulties, interventions could be designed for students with ASD, similar to those for students with mild to severe cognitive disabilities or LD (Gevarter et al., 2015).

Students with severe cognitive disabilities typically are taught mathematics concepts and skills that we commonly think of as functional skills, which means skills they need to engage in basic living activities. Many relate to money, purchasing, basic calculations, time, and measurement (Browder, Spooner, Ahlgrim-Delzell, Harris, & Wakeman, 2008). Although most of these skills are identified in the CCSSM, purchasing is not; it is a functional skill students must learn.

Table 11.3 shows a sampling of behavioral strategies that were part of research studies focusing on students with either ASD or severe cognitive disabilities.

FACTORS CONTRIBUTING TO MATHEMATICS DIFFICULTIES

Several factors contribute to mathematics difficulties. First, language difficulties can interfere with reading and understanding the vocabulary of the curriculum. For instance, students must understand the meaning of terms and symbols related to mathematics instruction. Years ago, Wiig and Semel (1984) referred to mathematics as "conceptually dense," which means that students must understand the meaning of each mathematical symbol and word because context clues, such as those that appear in reading, are limited or nonexistent. Wiig and Semel's idea is important because students must identify and understand the meaning of abstract symbols such as $=$, Σ, σ, π, and $\geq$ to solve problems. Take $4 < 9$, for example. The student must understand each symbol to decide whether this number statement is true or false. Or consider solving $6 \times 8 =$. Many students with mathematics difficulties interpret the equal sign ($=$) as an operational symbol meaning "I have to find the answer" (Powell & Fuchs, 2010). But the equal sign is a relational symbol, meaning both sides of the equation must be the same or there is a relationship between them. So, $6 \times 8 = 48$, $48 = 6 \times 8$, $6 \times 8 = 40 + 8$, and so forth (Powell, 2014). Teachers can spend time during mathematics lessons teaching and reviewing this symbolic language. Posting the symbols with a brief explanation is a good reference tool for students. The Considering Diversity feature on language and symbols of mathematics provides other ideas for teachers to think about as they work with students from CLD backgrounds, including those from other countries.

| TABLE 11.3 | BEHAVIORAL STRATEGIES FOR TEACHING MATHEMATICS TO STUDENTS WITH ASD OR SEVERE COGNITIVE DISABILITIES |

Skills	Students With ASD	Students With Severe Cognitive Disabilities	Mathematics Material
Calculations	x	x	Manipulatives, virtual manipulatives, TouchMath
Prompting: Verbal, gestural, or physical assistance given to learners to assist them in acquiring or engaging in a targeted behavior or skill. Reinforcement: An event or activity occurring after a learner engages in a desired behavior that leads to the increased occurrence of the behavior in the future.			
Money	x	x	Coins and bills
Prompting: Verbal, gestural, or physical assistance given to learners to assist them in acquiring or engaging in a targeted behavior or skill. Reinforcement: An event or activity occurring after a learner engages in a desired behavior that leads to the increased occurrence of the behavior in the future.			
Purchasing	x	x	Items to purchase
Prompting: Verbal, gestural, or physical assistance given to learners to assist them in acquiring or engaging in a targeted behavior or skill. Constant time delay: A learner engages in a behavior or skill; a brief delay occurs between the opportunity to use the skill and any additional instructions or prompts.			
Word Problems	x		Problems
Reinforcement: An event or activity occurring after a learner engages in a desired behavior that leads to the increased occurrence of the behavior in the future. Task analysis: An activity or behavior is divided into small, manageable steps to assess and teach the skill. Video self-modeling reinforcement: A visual model of the targeted behavior or skill is provided via video recording and display equipment to assist learning in a desired behavior or skill.			

SOURCES: Browder et al. (2008); Gevarter et al. (2015); Wong et al. (2013).

Think back to Ms. Hart's concerns about her students from CLD backgrounds in the Opening Challenge. She needs ideas for helping her students learn the language of mathematics. Table 11.4 provides examples of the language or vocabulary associated with mathematics curricula. For struggling students,

CONSIDERING *diversity*

FOCUSING ON THE LANGUAGE AND SYMBOLS OF MATHEMATICS

Although mathematics may be called the "universal language," there are some important differences among cultures with respect to terminology, algorithms, and solving strategies. We must not assume that learners have a low level of mathematical proficiency if they are interpreting terminology, performing algorithms, and using strategies that are different from those used in this country, because they may be mathematically correct. For example, in Chinese, 14 is "ten four." In Eastern Europe, the numeral 3,076 corresponds to the numeral 3.076 in the United States (Sorto, 2012).

The linguistic and symbolic features of mathematics have "tricky spots" because words may be used in unfamiliar ways (*odd* and *even*), structural relationships between words and syntax must be discerned (relationship of adjectives and nouns in sentence structure), and algorithmic formats (reading from left to right or from top to bottom) may be different. Therefore, teachers must be sure that *all* students have the necessary semantic, linguistic, and symbolic understanding of the mathematics concepts and skills presented for instruction.

Language difficulties can occur when solving word problems, for instance, because this requires understanding what the problem is asking and the sentence structure and identifying extraneous information (Van de Garderen & Scheuermann, 2014). Difficulties with syntax and word meaning can affect students' ability to solve problems successfully.

The language and symbolism of mathematics must be taught directly as part of a mathematics lesson. This is especially true for secondary students, who are often faced with abstract mathematical concepts, such as algebra and geometry that require a solid foundation of mathematical skills (equations, formulae, mathematical properties) and language. Teaching ideas include the following: (a) identify prerequisite symbols, syntactic language, and word meanings for the lesson; (b) assess current student understanding of this language; (c) provide explicit instruction to teach the language; and (d) include sufficient practice and review.

the preview and review of new terms are critical. Consider using the instructional ideas for teaching vocabulary found in Chapters 10 and 12 for teaching the language of mathematics.

Second, problems with memory and executive functioning contribute to mathematics difficulties. **Working memory** is the function by which we process and store information simultaneously. **Long-term memory** is the function that permanently stores information. **Executive functioning** is the ability to self-monitor by using working memory, inner speech, attention, and recall of recent information (Swanson & Jerman, 2006). Students who have memory problems and who process information slowly (Geary, 2011) lack the automatic ability to remember arithmetic combinations or facts. Memory difficulties can also influence the child's ability to recall the steps needed to solve more difficult word problems

Working Memory

TABLE 11.4	EXAMPLES OF VOCABULARY TERMS FOR MATHEMATICS INSTRUCTION			
Addend	Equivalent	Logarithmic	Positive	Square
Area	Estimate	Least common denominator	Product	Square root
Circle	Exponent	Magnitude	Proper fraction	Sum
Circumference	Expression	Matrix	Proportion	Symmetry
Coefficient	Fraction	Minus	Pyramid	Theorem
Commutative	Function	Minute	Ratio	Tomorrow
Coordinate	Greater than	Month	Rational	Triangle
Decimal	Greatest common factor	Negative	Rectangle	Variable
Denominator	Improper fraction	Notation	Regrouping	Vectors
Diagonal	Integer	Numerator	Relationship	Volume
Diameter	Inverse	Pattern	Remainder	Yesterday
Dividend	Isosceles	Percent	Right angle	Zero
Divisor	Length	Perimeter	Round	
Equal	Less than	Place value	Second	
Equation	Linear	Polynomial	Sort	

in the upper grades (Bryant et al., 2000), to recall the steps in solving algebraic equations, or to remember what specific symbols mean. It is common to hear a teacher say, "He knew the math facts yesterday, but he just can't seem to remember them today." Memory difficulties play an important role in how successfully students can perform mathematical operations (Shin & Bryant, 2015).

Finally, mathematics difficulties can be attributed to instructional issues. One issue is the insufficient development of fundamental understandings of whole numbers, the relationships among the four operations, and whole number properties. Another issue is lacking an understanding of the arithmetic properties. Students may have a limited understanding of the commutative ($A + B = B + A$; $A \times B = B \times A$) and associative ($[A + B] + C = A + [B + C]$; $[A \times B)] \times C = A \times [B \times C]$) properties of addition and multiplication and of the distributive property ($A \times [B + C] = [A \times B] + [A \times C]$). Knowledge about these properties can help students solve more accurately ($5 \times 3 = 3 \times 5$) and more effectively derive answers for more difficult problems ($4 \times 8 = 4 \times 6 + 4 \times 2 = 24 + 8 = 32$; National Research Council, 2009).

A third instructional issue is insufficient opportunities to learn, practice, and master effective and efficient strategies. Teachers must include important validated principles of instructional delivery including scaffolding instruction (Coyne et al., 2011; Doabler & Fien, 2013). Refer to Chapter 7 for additional instructional delivery practices that should be included in an RTI model.

In each of the following sections, we present mathematics content that stems from the CCSSM. We use the four categories of the ADAPT framework to provide ideas for making adaptations to instruction. We use assessment ideas from Chapter 8 and understanding of the learning characteristics of individuals with mathematics difficulties and disabilities. Finally, we offer ideas related to the stages of learning and types of knowledge presented in Chapter 7. First, we look at early number development.

WHAT IS EARLY NUMBER DEVELOPMENT AND HOW IS IT TAUGHT?

Early number development describes a variety of skills and concepts that typically emerge and are taught in preschool, kindergarten, first grade, and second grade (Chard et al., 2008). Many activities can bolster students' understanding of numbers and using this to make sense out of mathematics. For example, the ability to count is a crucial skill many young children develop well before they enter formal schooling in kindergarten. Through informal experiences at home, on the playground, and in the grocery store, they are frequently exposed to counting principles (Bryant, Roberts, Bryant, & DiAndreth-Elkins, 2011). In their classic work on children's understanding of numbers, Gelman and Gallistel (1978) presented five counting principles important for early number development: (a) one-to-one correspondence, (b) stable order (counting words are stated in a consistent order), (c) cardinality (the last counting word indicates the number of objects in a given set), (d) abstraction (any group of objects can be collected to count), and (e) order irrelevance (counting objects in any sequence does not alter the count).

Along with basic knowledge about counting, young children acquire the vocabulary that describes mathematical relationships. They use "more" to ask for another cookie and "all gone" when the cookies are finished. They may hear an adult ask, "Do you want another cookie?" or "Do you want one more cookie?" Their experiences with objects teach the early language of mathematics via physical representations that children come to understand. Finally, young children often know how to read and write some numerals, such as 1, 2, and 3.

Parents and teachers can pair numbers with objects in sets so children are counting objects, saying how many, and selecting the numeral that represents the count. Although their writing may be rudimentary at the early stage, children are hearing, representing, seeing, and writing numbers (they can be asked to write the number 1). It is through these types of informal experiences with their environment, the media, other children, and adults that young children

Early Number
Development

Experience with objects, such as the manipulatives these students are using, teaches the early language of mathematics through physical representations that children understand.

develop the early understanding about mathematical concepts from which more formal instruction evolves.

The magnitude of numerals is another important concept for students to learn for later mathematical content. For example, students should be able to tell that 51 is greater than 48 and 19 is less than 20. The ability to make these judgments resides in understanding quantity but also knowing that 5 tens is more than 4 tens and 1 ten is less than 2 groups of ten. This ability relies on understanding place value or the **base ten** system, which is the decimal numeral system that has 10 as its base.

Let's take a look at difficulties with early number development.

DIFFICULTIES WITH EARLY NUMBER DEVELOPMENT

Research results have shown that students with early mathematics problems exhibit difficulties understanding number sense as demonstrated in number knowledge and relationship activities (magnitude, sequencing, base ten). They struggle to achieve conceptual understanding of counting principles, which can affect their use of more advanced counting strategies (such as counting on: $8 + 2 = 11$) to solve arithmetic combinations (Geary, 2004). Counting up and back two or three numbers from a given number and understanding "bigger than" and "less than" in number magnitude are other important skills that may be problematic (Jordan, Kaplan, Ramineni, & Locuniak, 2009). Number reversals may persist long after instruction in writing numbers has occurred. Reading, writing, and representing the teen numbers are consistently problematic for struggling students (Bley & Thornton, 2001). Consider that 11 and 12 sound very different than 13, 14, 15, and so forth. This difference can be difficult in terms of how to identify these numerals. Finally, Jordan, Kaplan, Ramineni, and Locuniak (2009) found that over time, students with mathematics difficulties scored lower on place value tasks than average students. Taken together, these findings suggest that students with mathematics difficulties require sustained instructional time on number knowledge, counting principles, and place value concepts in the early grades (Bryant, Bryant, Kethley, et al., 2008; Fuchs et al., 2010).

TEACHING EARLY NUMBER DEVELOPMENT

We begin with some general notes on teaching early number development and then look more closely at several specific skills.

Number Sense

- **Diagnosis:** Conduct an informal assessment asking students to read and write numerals, count objects, identify which numeral or group has more quantity, and tell how many are in a group. Use the results to help you determine early number skills and focus beginning instruction in early number development.

- **Instructional content—Comparing and grouping objects:** Provide many opportunities for students to show set equivalency, to make groups based on problems, and to decompose (take apart) larger numbers into smaller sets. Use word problems for students to form and manipulate sets. Pair number symbols with groupings to reinforce the connection between concrete representations and abstract symbols.

- **Instructional content—Reading and writing numerals:** Pair instruction on reading numerals with writing numerals. Writing proficiency may take longer to master as young children learn how to hold the pencil correctly and make correct stroke formations. Provide models of correctly written numerals, including directional arrows for stroke formation. Do not allow messy work, because if you do, it will persist throughout the school years.

- **Instructional materials—Place value and the ten-frame:** Use the ten-frame frequently to help students make and see the concept of 10. Use two ten-frames to build the teen numbers. Use a five-frame initially for students who struggle with the ten-frame.

- **Instructional materials:** Use counting cubes, number lines, ten-frames, and objects for counting, comparing, grouping, and decomposing activities, number magnitude, number sequencing, and number recognition. Refer to Figure 11.1 for examples of manipulatives and materials.

- **Language:** Provide multiple opportunities for students to use the language of mathematics. Refer back to Table 11.4 for examples of the language to emphasize. Model the use of these terms, such as *same, equal, more,* and *less,* in early number development activities.

- **Proficiency and progress monitoring:** Build fluent responding for number recognition and number writing. Use flash cards for "fact numbers," where students see the number and respond within three seconds ("look and say"). Focus instruction on numbers students cannot quickly name. Use "quick write," in which students write numbers in sequence, beginning with 0, for one minute. Count the number of correctly formed numerals. Then focus instruction on those numerals that are not in order or are not written correctly.

Counting

Develop basic counting skills. Conduct warm-ups by giving students a number and having them count up "two more" or count back "two less." Have students tap the count or show fingers so they get the count right. This builds counting skills and reinforces the concepts of more and less. Give students two

FIGURE 11.1 EXAMPLES OF MANIPULATIVES AND MATERIALS FOR MATHEMATICS INSTRUCTION

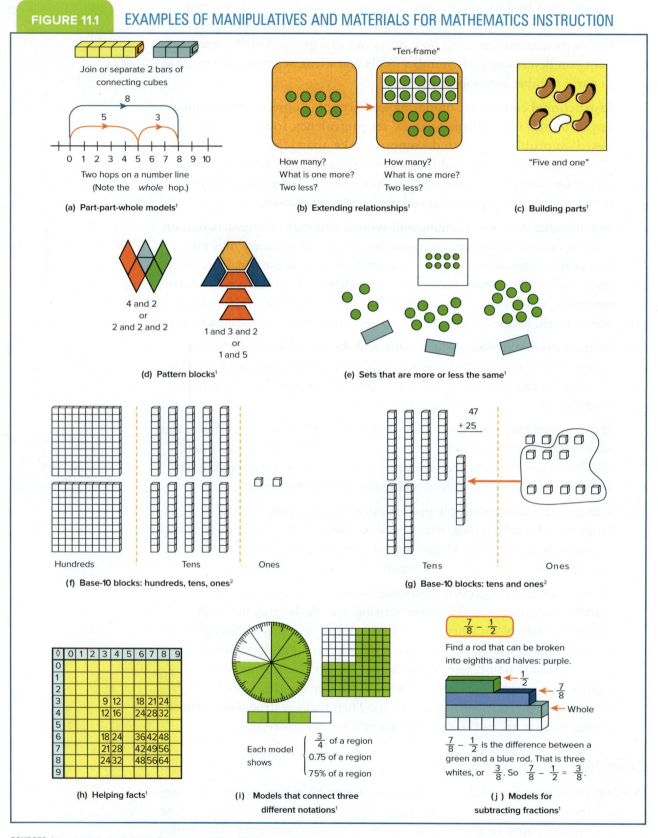

(a) Part-part-whole models[1]

(b) Extending relationships[1]

(c) Building parts[1]

(d) Pattern blocks[1]

(e) Sets that are more or less the same[1]

(f) Base-10 blocks: hundreds, tens, ones[2]

(g) Base-10 blocks: tens and ones[2]

(h) Helping facts[1]

(i) Models that connect three different notations[1]

(j) Models for subtracting fractions[1]

SOURCES: [1]Van de Walle et al. (2012); [2]Hudson and Miller (2006).

groups of objects. Have them count the first group and place it in a cup. Then, beginning with the last number named in the cup, have them count on the second group of objects. This develops the counting on strategy. Have students count groups of objects and then ask, "How many?" This builds the counting principles of one-to-one correspondence and cardinality.

Teen Numbers

Teach 14, 16, 17, 18, and 19 first by emphasizing that you say the second number first, such as four-teen. Try "fast numbers" with these five numbers; that is, the student looks and says the number quickly (within three seconds). Once students know these numbers, move to 13 and 15. Tell students how to read thir-teen and fif-teen. Once students know these two numbers, mix them with the other five numbers. Next, teach 11 and 12. They are not teen numbers but fall in the 10 to 20 number range. Tell students they just have to learn these numbers by sight. Once they know them, mix them with the other teen numbers. Pair the reading and writing of the teen numbers with making the numbers in the ten-frame during instruction. Have students name the numbers out of order and write them when dictated. Conduct magnitude comparison activities (discussed next) with these numbers.

Magnitude Comparison

Give students two numbers and have them tell which number is bigger, smaller, greater than, less than, more than, or less than the other number. At first, provide numbers that are somewhat far apart, such as 3 and 8, 22 and 36, or 105 and 116. Then provide numbers that are closer together, such as 9 and 11, 28 and 30, or 111 and 115. Focus on the teen numbers and on numbers with 0, such as 50, 106, and 207. For smaller numbers, have students use cubes to make trains or use the number line to show magnitude. For larger numbers, have students use the hundreds chart to explain number magnitude. Connect magnitude comparison with place value activities (discussed later).

Numeral Recognition: Fast Numbers

Show students the number cards 0 through 5. Model "Look and Say" quickly. Correct errors if needed and provide the correct response right away. Put correctly named number cards in one pile and incorrectly named number cards in another pile. Spend more time on the incorrect pile. Have students say numbers quickly for 30 seconds to see how many they can get right. Increase the range of numbers gradually. Keep numbers done correctly in a special pile and present them once a week to be sure students can still name them quickly.

Number Writing: Quick Write

Have students write numbers, beginning with zero, for one minute. After the timing, have students count the number of numerals written. Numerals that are

VIDEO CASE 11.1

Teaching Arithmetic Combinations

1. Jan Evans describes a variety of ways to use children's books to help students learn about math concepts and vocabulary. Which of these strategies do you see in the subtraction lesson in the video? How do these practices develop students' math skills?

2. What other strategies does Ms. Evans mention that help students to learn math concepts and vocabulary? How does she create concrete learning experiences for her young students?

written backward, are very messy, or are not in sequence are considered errors. Correct errors by providing a number line for students to see how numerals are written correctly. Have students graph the number of numerals they can write correctly in one minute. This is a good warm-up activity and can be done several times a week.

Reversals

Reversals may occur with single-digit numerals, such as 6 for 9, and with multidigit numbers, such as 24 for 42. Give students many opportunities to practice writing numerals correctly using a variety of materials. Use stencils for tracing, models of correctly formed numerals, and models with directional cues showing where to start making the numeral and in what direction to go. Have students correct reversals.

Part-Part-Whole Relationships

Identifying ways to compose and decompose numbers is a foundation skill that helps students think about the concept of numbers. The part-part-whole and missing-parts relationships are the building blocks for learning arithmetic combinations and solving word problems. It is important for students to develop an understanding of these relationships. For example, have students show the parts of a number such as 5. Model the commutative property, showing $4 + 1 = 1 + 4$ by using colored cubes and the five-frame. Make 5 with $4 + 1$; then turn the frame around so students see that $1 + 4$ also equals 5. Use the five-frame to determine other "parts" of 5, such as $3 + 2$, $2 + 3$, $0 + 5$, and $5 + 0$. These activities can be done with other number quantities and should be an integral part of instruction.

Arithmetic combinations are often difficult for students. In the next section we examine ways to teach this important foundation skill.

WHAT ARE ARITHMETIC COMBINATIONS AND HOW ARE THEY TAUGHT?

Instruction in arithmetic combinations (sometimes called basic facts) consists of developing declarative and procedural knowledge and conceptual understanding. In the elementary grades, students are taught strategies for learning these arithmetic combinations, so most remember the answers automatically. These students demonstrate computational fluency, which consists of knowing and using efficient methods for accurate computing (NCTM, 2000). Geary (2004) identified researched strategies typically developing students use for solving arithmetic combinations. When students are first learning addition, they use finger counting or verbal counting strategies (Siegler & Shrager, 1984). The counting all and counting on strategies are most commonly used (Fuson, 1982; Groen & Parkman, 1972).

The counting all strategy means taking the quantity of each addend and then counting both quantities (2 + 3 is 1, 2 + 1, 2, 3 = 1, 2, 3, 4, 5). The counting on strategy means taking the larger addend and counting on by the other addend (3 + 2 is 3 + 1, 2 = 3, 4, 5). The decomposition strategy means that students break down a fact into a partial sum and then add or subtract 1, for example (5 + 6 = 5 + 5 = 10 + 1 = 11 or 6 + 6 = 12 − 1 = 11). The direct retrieval strategy assumes students have learned the facts and can now retrieve the answer automatically. Eventually, as students master facts, the strategies they use become more memory based. However, for students who find mathematics challenging, computational fluency remains a persistent problem (Geary, 2004; Jordan, Hanich, & Kaplan, 2003).

DIFFICULTIES WITH ARITHMETIC COMBINATIONS

Difficulty with learning and remembering arithmetic combinations is a typical problem among students who struggle with mathematics and students who are identified as having mathematics disabilities. Problems in retrieval of arithmetic combinations seem to inhibit the ability to grasp the more complex algebraic concepts taught in later years (Bryant, Bryant, et al., 2011; Geary, 2004). Lack of efficient and effective counting strategies is another problem commonly associated with arithmetic combinations and students who struggle with mathematics (Bryant, Bryant, Gersten, Scammacca, & Chavez, 2008; Gersten et al., 2005). These students require instruction to develop both conceptual understanding of arithmetic combinations and procedural knowledge to figure out the answers. We know that instruction for struggling students is most enhanced through the use of physical, visual, and abstract representations of arithmetic combinations.

TEACHING ARITHMETIC COMBINATIONS

Let's begin with general notes and then look more closely at some specific skills.

- **Diagnosis:** Assess to identify which arithmetic combinations students know as "fast facts" and which they do not. Use observation and clinical interviews to identify what strategies (for example, counting on fingers) the students use to solve facts when a quick response is not provided. The think aloud procedure is used to examine a student's knowledge of and thinking about how to solve problems (McLoughlin & Lewis, 2008).

- **Instructional content—Sequence:** Teach arithmetic combinations systematically. Although there is no "best" sequence, you should generally teach easier strategies first (count on + 0, + 1, + 2, + 3; count back or down − 0, − 1, − 2, − 3; doubles − 4 + 4). Then teach turnaround combinations (for example: 1 + 4 = 4 + 1, also known as the commutative property) for addition. Teach fact families (5 + 3, 3 + 5, 8 − 3, 8 − 5) once students have mastered some addition facts.

- **Instructional content—Decomposition:** Present multiple opportunities for students to practice decomposition of numbers to solve arithmetic problems. For example, students can use the "doubles + 1" strategy to arrive at the answer for 7 + 8: What double is in 7 + 8? 7 + 7. What is double + 1? 7 + 7 + 1 = 15, so 7 + 8 = 15.

- **Acquisition:** For students learning facts, practice is an important component of instruction and should occur for about 10 minutes daily. Teachers such as Ms. Hart in the Opening Challenge, who are looking for ways to give students more practice, can use apps to provide it. Recall from Chapter 7 the key features—such as multiple examples and response opportunities—to look for when making decisions about downloading educational apps.

- **Proficiency:** Conduct one-minute timings ("fast facts") on arithmetic combinations to build fluency. Show flash cards with combinations and give students up to three seconds to say the answer (no fingers). Facts that are not answered quickly remain in the practice pile.

- **Generalization:** Promote generalization by having students answer problems with mixed signs and whole-number computational problems.

Table 11.5 presents a list of strategies and gives examples of arithmetic combinations for each strategy.

Returning to our Opening Challenge, recall the issues Ms. Hart faces with some of her students with mathematics. Now, you will see how she adapts instruction to address their needs. In ADAPT in Action, Ms. Hart uses the ADAPT framework to help students who have difficulty with some addition combinations.

For many students, place value is a challenging concept. In the next section we discuss how to teach it.

WHAT IS PLACE VALUE AND HOW IS IT TAUGHT?

The base-ten system is an important component of mathematics instruction that students must fully grasp (Van de Walle et al., 2012). Understanding place value helps students understand numerical relationships and the "how" and "why" of procedures used to solve problems. Yet evidence also suggests that students do not learn place value concepts sufficiently to understand procedures for multidigit calculations (Jordan, Kaplan, et al., 2009). For example, they might see the numeral 63 as a single numeral rather than seeing each individual digit representing specific values in the number. Yet instruction in place value

TABLE 11.5 ARITHMETIC STRATEGIES AND COMBINATIONS

Addition Strategies	Addition Combinations
Facts with zero Zero rule: "Any number + 0 is the same number."	(0, 1, 2, 3, 4, 5, 6, 7, 8, 9) + 0 and the commutative facts
Count on: +1 One more than	(0, 1, 2, 3, 4, 5, 6, 7, 8, 9) + 1 and the commutative facts
Count on: +2 Two more than	(0, 1, 2, 3, 4, 5, 6, 7, 8, 9) + 2 and the commutative facts
Count on: +3 Three more than	(0, 1, 2, 3, 4, 5, 6, 7, 8, 9) + 3 and the commutative facts
Doubles Count by 2's	(3 + 3, 4 + 4, 5 + 5, 6 + 6, 7 + 7, 8 + 8, 9 + 9)
Near doubles Doubles + 1 Doubles − 1	(4 + 5, 5 + 6, 6 + 7, 7 + 8, 8 + 9) and the commutative facts
9, 8, 7: Make 10 plus more	(9 + 4, 9 + 5, 9 + 6, 9 + 7, 8 + 4, 8 + 5, 8 + 6, 7 + 4, 7 + 5, 7 + 8) and the commutative facts

Subtraction Strategies	Subtraction Combinations	
Facts with zero Zero rule: "Any number take away zero is the same number."	(0, 1, 2, 3, 4, 5, 6, 7, 8, 9) − 0	
Facts with the same number: "Any number minus the same number is zero."	$n - n = 0$	
Count back: − 1 One less than	(10, 9, 8, 7, 6, 5, 4, 3, 2) − 1	
Count back: − 2 Two less than	(11, 10, 9, 8, 7, 6, 5, 4, 3) − 2	
Count back: − 3 Three less than	(12, 11, 10, 9, 8, 7, 6, 5, 4) − 3	
Count up +1, +2, +3. Start with the smaller number and count up to the bigger number (e.g., 9 − 7, start with 7 and count up to 9, the answer is 2).	(12, 11) − 9	(11, 9) − 8
	(9, 8) − 7	(9, 8, 7) − 6
	(8, 7, 6) − 5	(7, 6, 5) − 4
Double, then "fact family" (4 + 4 = 8; 8 − 4 = 4)	(8 − 4, 10 − 5, 12 − 6, 14 − 7, 16 − 8, 18 − 9)	

(Continued)

TABLE 11.5 (CONTINUED)

9, 8, 7: Up to 10, then add	(17 − 9, 17 − 8, 16 − 9, 15 − 9, 15 − 8, 15 − 7, 14 − 9, 14 − 8, 13 − 9, 13 − 8, 13 − 7, 12 − 9, 12 − 8, 12 − 7, 11 − 9, 11 − 8, 11 − 7)
Down to 10, then add	(16 − 7, 16 − 9, 15 − 7, 15 − 6, 14 − 9, 14 − 6, 14 − 5, 13 − 7, 13 − 6, 13 − 5, 13 − 4, 12 − 7, 12 − 5, 12 − 4, 11 − 7, 11 − 6, 11 − 5, 11 − 4)

Multiplication Strategies	**Multiplication Combinations**
Skip counting: 2's, 5's	(2, 3, 4, 5, 6, 7, 8, 9) × 2; (2, 3, 4, 5, 6, 7, 8, 9) × 5 and the commutative facts
Nifty 9's: Multiply, then check	9 × 2 = 18 (1 + 8 = 9), 9 × 3 = 27 (2 + 7 = 9), 9 × 4 = 36 (3 + 6 = 9), 9 × 5 = 45 (4 + 5 = 9), 9 × 6 = 54 (5 + 4 = 9), 9 × 7 = 63 (6 + 3 = 9), 9 × 8 = 72 (7 + 2 = 9), 9 × 9 = 81 (8 + 1 = 9) and the commutative facts
Zero rule: Any $n \times 0 = 0$	(0, 1, 2, 3, 4, 5, 6, 7, 8, 9) × 0
Identity rule: Any $n \times 1 = n$	(1, 2, 3, 4, 5, 6, 7, 8, 9) × 1
Same n: Count by itself	3 × 3, 4 × 4, 6 × 6, 7 × 7, 8 × 8
	Example: 3 × 3 = 3, 6, 9
Harder facts: Distribute, then add	8 × 7 = 8 × 2 = 16 + 8 × 5 = 40 = 56
	8 × 6 = 8 × 1 = 8 + 8 × 5 = 40 = 48
	8 × 4 = 8 × 2 = 16 + 8 × 2 = 16 = 32

Division Strategies	**Division Combinations**
Any $n \div n = 1$	9 ÷ 9, 8 ÷ 8, 7 ÷ 7, 6 ÷ 6, 5 ÷ 5, 4 ÷ 4, 3 ÷ 3, 2 ÷ 2, 1 ÷ 1
Any $n \div 1 = n$	(9, 8, 7, 6, 5, 4, 3, 2, 1) ÷ 1
Related facts in division	Example: 72 ÷ 8 = 9 and 72 ÷ 9 = 8
Fact families divide/multiply	Example: 72 ÷ 8 = 9, 72 ÷ 9 = 8, 9 × 8 = 72, 8 × 9 = 72

SOURCES: Bley and Thornton (2001); Bryant, Bryant, et al. (2011); Stein, Kinder, Silbert, and Carnine (2006); Van de Walle et al. (2012).

is frequently limited. It often develops conceptual understanding using concrete representations too briefly and moves on to pictorial representations (pictures, tallies) sooner than appropriate for some students.

DIFFICULTIES WITH PLACE VALUE

Students may demonstrate a variety of problems related to their conceptual understanding of place value. Insufficient time spent with concrete representations results in poor understanding of the notion of place and value. According

ADAPT *in action*

MS. HART: ARITHMETIC COMBINATIONS

Ms. Hart is concerned about three students who have not learned addition combinations to 18. Through informal diagnostic teaching, she finds they can recognize and write numerals quickly. They can also solve simple addition combinations, including sums to 10 and "doubles." However, more difficult combinations involving sums to 11 through 18 are challenging for the students. Ms. Hart uses a clinical interview procedure wherein she asks each student to "think aloud" how he or she would solve problems such as $7 + 4$, $8 + 6$, and $9 + 7$. Consistently, the three students read the first number and use their fingers to count on to arrive at the solution. Ms. Hart recalls from her teacher preparation program that "counting on" is a good strategy when students are first learning some facts, particularly when one addend is 1, 2, or 3. But it is not an efficient strategy for solving harder combinations. She decides to teach the three students the "Make Ten Plus More" strategy. Keep in mind that Ms. Hart has other students who have trouble with more difficult addition combinations, so they too may benefit from the adaptations. Also, Ms. Hart can use this lesson for any of her students who are still not proficient with addition combinations. Instructional Strategy 11.1 shows the Make Ten Plus More strategy.

Following the lesson, Ms. Hart reviews the progress-monitoring data for her students. She learns they are missing an important concept of "Ten Plus More" and decides to use the ADAPT framework to make decisions about the next steps for instruction.

(A) **Ask, "What am I requiring the student to do?"** Ms. Hart wants the students to add combinations with sums 11 to 18. She wants them to show the addition strategy using concrete representations (ten-frames and counters).

(D) **Determine the prerequisite skills of the task.** "I know students need to decompose one number to make 10 and to know how much to add to get to 10. Students also need to be able to say the answer to 'Ten plus x is the same as?'"

(A) **Analyze the student's strengths and struggles.** The students did a good job of decomposing one number by using the ten-frames to make 10. But they could not tell how much to add to 10 to make it the same as 13 (equal to). However, quickly saying the answer to "Ten plus a number equals what number?" was problematic. For example, quickly saying $10 + 3 = 13$ or $10 + 6 = 16$ was difficult for the students.

(P) **Propose and implement adaptations from among the four categories.** Ms. Hart decides to adapt the Make Ten Plus More lesson by teaching a lesson just on "Ten Plus More" (instructional content). She will have students use the ten-frames and counters to show $10 +$ more and to tell what number. She will then put these combinations on flash cards and have students say the answers quickly.

(Continued)

BONUS Instructional Strategy
11.1: Make Ten Plus More

(Continued)

Test to determine whether the adaptations helped the student accomplish the task. Ms. Hart will continue to collect progress-monitoring data to determine whether the reduced instructional content helps the students learn the Ten Plus More strategy. Then she will return to Make Ten Plus More and add a "fast facts" component to progress monitoring.

Benchmark. Use the "benchmark" procedure to build fluency. For instance, given a worksheet of facts and working from left to right, designate a fact as the benchmark to reach by the end of the one-minute timing. Students can star or circle the designated fact to identify it.

You can choose the benchmark fact by (a) identifying the number of correct problems answered in a previous one-minute timing, (b) multiplying that number by 25%, and (c) adding the 25% figure to the original figure. This new number becomes the benchmark for the next one-minute marathon. The benchmark strategy is very motivating because it promotes self-competition ("beat yesterday's score"). Distribute rewards to students who reach their benchmark.

Timed drills. You can use periodic timed drills, distributed practice (over several days or across weeks), and data analysis of student performance to monitor automaticity abilities on lower level, cognitive skills. Developing automaticity of such cognitive skills is particularly important at the elementary level because students are learning mathematical skills. At the secondary level, automaticity development must continue in life skills areas (working with money and time). If students were already exposed to a strong proficiency program at the elementary level but are still struggling, however, review their educational goals, transitional needs, and curriculum. For some students with more severe learning problems or severe ID, automaticity in basic facts might be limited. In these cases, calculator instruction is the obvious choice. Examine Instructional Strategy 11.1 for examples of teaching procedures, progress monitoring, and prerequisite abilities and adaptations for procedural strategies.

to Ross (1989), as cited in Van de Walle et al. (2012), there are five levels of place-value difficulties.

1. **Single numeral:** Individual digits in numerals such as 52 are not understood as representing specific values in the number. Rather, 52 is regarded as a single numeral.

2. **Position names:** The student can name the position of the digits (in 52, 5 is in the tens place and 2 is in the ones place), but value is not associated with the position.

3. **Face value:** Each digit is taken at face value. In 52, the student selects 5 blocks to go with 5 and 2 blocks to go with 2. This indicates the value of the position is not understood.

ADAPT *framework:* MS. HART

ASK "What am I requiring the student to do?"	DETERMINE the prerequisite skills of the task.	ANALYZE the student's strengths and struggles.		PROPOSE and implement adaptations from among the four categories.	TEST to determine whether the adaptations helped the student to accomplish the task.
		Strengths	Struggles		
The students will add combinations with sums 11 to 18 showing the addition strategy using concrete representations (ten-frames and counters).	1. Decomposes one number to make 10.	1			
	2. Knows how much to add to get to 10.		2	2. Instructional content: Focus on 10 + 1, 2, 3, 4, 5, 6, 7, 8 in random order. Instructional delivery: Students start on the 10 on the number line and count on to solve the equation for each combination. Instructional material: Number line.	2. Give an equation (e.g., 10 + 6 =) and have students use the number line to solve it.
	3. Says automatically what "Ten Plus More" equals.		3	3. Instructional content: 10 + addends = 11 − 18. Instructional delivery: Provide multiple opportunities to practice. Instructional activity: Play "what number solves this equation?" Show students cards with different equations to solve by retrieving the answers automatically. Instructional material: Ten Plus More Cards.	3. Give students a number and have them make the number using cubes and the five-frame. Record the number of ways they can represent a number; all possibilities should be shown by students.

4. **Transition to place value:** In 52, 2 blocks are selected for the ones place, and the remaining 50 blocks are selected for the 5; no grouping of tens is demonstrated.

5. **Full understanding:** In 52, five groups of 10 are selected for the 5, and 2 remaining blocks are chosen for the 2.

STRATEGIES TO TEACH ARITHMETIC COMBINATIONS

- ### Addition: Count On (+ 1, + 2, + 3)[1, 2]

PROCEDURE

1. Tell students to "start big" by selecting the larger of the two addends and then to count on by the amount of the second number.

2. Emphasize + 1, + 2, or + 3, depending on the number. For example, 9 + 3 = is computed by saying, "Start big"—9 plus three more, 10, 11, 12 to arrive at 12 as the answer.

3. Have students verbalize the process to ensure accuracy in using the "count on" procedure.

PROGRESS MONITORING: Monitor progress by conducting "fast facts"—containing facts with + 1, + 2, and + 3, where students have to say or write the response quickly (within three seconds).

ADAPTATIONS: Instructional materials, instructional delivery, instructional content

REPRESENTATIONS: Concrete and pictorial

Prerequisite Skills	Adaptations
1. Ability to identify larger number to "start big."	1. Provide two numbers, one of which is 1, 2, or 3. Have students state which number is larger. Use the number line or concrete objects to represent each number if necessary. Have students tap + 1, + 2, or + 3 or show a finger for each number counted on.
2. Ability to "count on" a designated amount (e.g., 2, 3) from a designated number (7, 9).	2. Conduct warm-up of rote counting from designated number (e.g., 7) and counting on by 1, 2, or 3. Use number line as pictorial representation if necessary.
3. Ability to write the last number spoken.	3. Provide a number line or number strip with numbers as a referent.

- ### Subtraction: Count Back or Down (− 1, − 2, − 3)[1]

PROCEDURE

1. Tell students to "start big" by selecting the larger of the two numerals.

2. Have students count back by the amount of the second number, − 1, − 2, or − 3, and then write the answer.

3. Have students verbalize the process to ensure accuracy in using the "count back" procedure.

PROGRESS MONITORING: Monitor progress by conducting "fast facts"—containing facts with − 1, − 2, and − 3, where students have to say or write the response quickly (within three seconds).

ADAPTATIONS: Instructional materials, instructional delivery, instructional content

REPRESENTATIONS: Concrete and pictorial

Prerequisite Skills	Adaptations
1. Ability to identify the larger number to "start big."	1. Conduct a warm-up where students start at 12, 11, or 10 and count back. Have them use a number line if necessary.
2. Ability to write the last number spoken.	2. Give students two numbers between 2 and 12 and ask them to say which number is bigger.
	3. Give students a number between 1 and 9 and have them tell the number that is one less than, two less than, or three less than. Have students show a finger for each number counted back.
	4. Have students practice writing numbers presented orally.

- ### Multiplication: Count By

PROCEDURE

1. Tell students to identify a number in the problem they know how to count by.

2. Make tallies or hold up the number of fingers for the other number in the problem.

3. Count by the number from 1 until all of the tallies or fingers are accounted for; the last number named is the answer.

Example: 4 × 8 = ?

1. I know how to count by 4's.

2. I will hold up eight fingers.

3. I count by 4's eight times: 4, 8, 12, 16, 20, 24, 28, 32.

4. 32 is the answer.

PROGRESS MONITORING: Monitor progress by conducting "fast facts," where students have to say or write the response quickly (within three seconds) to a group of facts (e.g., the 3's, 4's, 5's, 6's, 7's, 8's, 9's). Then mix up the facts.

ADAPTATIONS: Instructional materials, instructional delivery, instructional content

REPRESENTATIONS: Concrete and pictorial

Prerequisite Skills	Adaptations
1. Ability to count by 2, 3, 4, 5, 6, 7, 8, 9.	1. Conduct count-by warm-ups. Use a chart to show the count-by number patterns.
2. Ability to keep track of how many counting by.	2. Have students hold up a finger for each number to be counted.

SOURCES: [1]Bley and C. Thornton (2001); [2]Van de Walle et al. (2012).

• **Division: How Many Groups?[2]**

PROCEDURE

1. Tell students to read the division problem 81 ÷ 9 = x and then ask, "How many groups of 9 are in 81?"

2. Have students count by 9's until they reach 81.

3. Tell them that the number of times they count by 9 represents the number of groups of 9 in 81.

PROGRESS MONITORING: Monitor progress by having students say answers for "fast facts."

ADAPTATIONS: Instructional materials, instructional delivery, instructional content

REPRESENTATIONS: Concrete and pictorial

Prerequisite Skills	Adaptations
1. Ability to count by a number.	1. Show students pictorial groups of the number being counted by.
2. Ability to keep track of how many counting by.	2. Focus initially on easier count-by facts, such as count by 2's and count by 5's.
	3. Have students hold up a finger for the number counted by.

Young children, of course, do not fully understand place value, and it should not be surprising that older students who struggle with learning mathematics have not achieved full understanding of the base-10 system. **Diagnostic teaching**—giving problems and asking students questions—can help teachers understand what level of development students have reached in learning about place value.

TEACHING PLACE VALUE

The following techniques can be applied to teaching place-value concepts.

- **Diagnosis:** Using the clinical interview procedure and manipulatives, and having students write numbers to represent place values, assess their level of place-value understanding.

- **Instructional materials:** You can use a variety of manipulatives to teach place value and the concept of whole-number computation with and without regrouping: rods, cubes, base-ten blocks, and bean sticks help teach whole-number computation at the concrete level, as do base-ten mats and place-value charts. Figure 11.1 shows examples of manipulatives and other materials.

- **Vocabulary:** Teach and regularly use the vocabulary of place value. Students should use base-ten language such as 53 represents 5 tens and 3 ones. Other vocabulary should include regrouping to describe how 10 ones are "bundled" to add to the tens place or how a 10 is "unbundled" to add to the ones place during whole-number addition. Similarly, the vocabulary related to hundreds and thousands should be used for larger place-value groupings. Refer to Table 11.4 for examples of terms to teach.

- **Instructional content:** The idea of zero as a placeholder is one of the most challenging concepts for many students, including struggling students. Provide multiple opportunities for students to use manipulatives to represent numbers containing zero as a placeholder to carry out whole-number operations.

- **Concrete, pictorial, and abstract representations:** Pair the use of manipulatives to concretely represent the place and value of numbers with the use of written numerals to demonstrate how to write the numbers (abstract representation). For example, base-ten blocks are used on the place-value mat to represent numbers; students then write the numbers to show how many in each place. Then move to pictorial representations paired with concrete along with abstract. For example, use pictures of blocks depicting numbers, where students build the number using base-ten blocks to check their pictures; they write the numbers as the final step.

- **Progress monitoring:** Assess student understanding of place value by giving them numbers to represent with base-ten blocks, having them tell the numbers in two ways (base-ten number and standard number) and writing the number. Include numbers with zero as a placeholder on a regular basis, because numbers with zero are the most problematic for students to understand.

Teen Numbers

Have students spend time on teen numbers. These numbers represent another area that is very problematic for struggling students to learn. Use two ten-frames to represent quantity for the teen numbers. Provide a number. Have students build the number in the frames, read the number, and write the number. Ask questions such as the following: How many more is 14 than 11? How many

BONUS Instructional Strategy 11.2: Additional
Strategies to Teach Arithmetic Combinations

do I need to add to 12 to get 15? How many is 2 less than 17? How much is 10 plus 8? Teen numbers should also be taught within the context of hundreds. Repeat the activities described here by using hundreds and teen numbers such as 215, 317, and 411. See Figure 11.1 for an example of a ten-frame. The ten-frame provides students with a visual representation of the concept of 10. It is a useful instructional tool that can be used, for example, for counting, counting by 5, and solving simple addition and subtraction problems.

Need to Trade?

Need to trade is a prerequisite activity to renaming in addition. You can introduce this intervention once students have had practice with addition with renaming. Present a variety of addition problems with and without renaming and ask students to identify those in which renaming is required, that is, in which they need to trade 10 ones for 1 ten (Bley & Thornton, 2001). Have students use base-ten blocks to represent numbers initially and then move to visual representation such as tally marks.

Are There Enough?

"Are there enough?" is used for subtraction problems with and without renaming. Give students different subtraction problems and have them decide whether the top number in the ones place is large enough for them to subtract the bottom number from it. Numbers with various places up to thousands can be used, as well as numbers with zeros as placeholders. This activity focuses students' attention on the ones place, number discrimination, and place value (Bley & Thornton, 2001). The application of place value to whole-number computation is discussed next.

WHAT IS WHOLE-NUMBER COMPUTATION AND HOW IS IT TAUGHT?

Solving problems that contain whole numbers requires an understanding of the relationship between numbers and place value, as well as skill in estimating, determining the reasonableness of answers, using a calculator, and using appropriate algorithms. Instruction in place value and whole numbers should occur throughout the curriculum. It is not necessary for students to master addition before being introduced to subtraction or to be proficient in basic arithmetic combinations before being introduced to whole-number problems.

Whole-number operations include addition, subtraction, multiplication, and division without and with regrouping. Students should understand the meanings of the operations and how they are related to one another. They should also be able to compute fluently. Place-value abilities are a fundamental skill for whole-number computations. Estimation and rounding strategies are important companion skills, particularly with advanced multiplication and division computation (Cathcart, Pothier, Vance, & Bezuk, 2000; Hudson & Miller, 2006). Whole-number computation should include the development of conceptual understanding, instruction in procedural strategies, and the application of computation in story problems (Hudson & Miller, 2006).

DIFFICULTIES WITH WHOLE-NUMBER COMPUTATION

Bley and Thornton (2001) identified the process of solving whole-number computation as complex because it relies on symbols, multiple steps, and a level of abstraction that may be problematic for struggling students. Difficulty with arithmetic combinations can interfere with students' ability to attempt whole number computations. Students may view the task as too difficult because they lack fluency with basic facts. The multistep process of computing whole-number problems can be overwhelming to students who have difficulty remembering multiple steps and sequences for solving problems. Difficulties with understanding number relationships and place value can affect the ability to apply important fundamental skills, such as estimating, rounding, recognizing reasonableness of answers, and doing mental computation when solving whole-number computations. Finally, using algorithmic procedures to compute whole-number problems may cause difficulties for students well beyond the elementary school years.

Teaching Whole-Number Computation

The general steps involved in teaching whole-number computation follow. Note that calculators and other technology have an important role to play.

- **Diagnosis:** Provide three problems each of addition, subtraction, multiplication, and division computation, including problems with and without regrouping and division with remainders. Include problems with zero as a value in the ones, tens, and hundreds place. Provide reasonable time for students to complete the problems. Correct the work, noting what types of errors are made. Refer to Table 11.6 for examples of error patterns identified in whole-number computation and remedial strategies to address these error patterns (Ashlock, 2009).

- **Instructional materials:** Use materials from place-value instruction to support conceptual understanding of whole-number operations. Students who struggle to recall answers quickly for arithmetic combinations can use a basic facts table.

- **Technology:** Provide students with calculators to check their answers for whole-number computations.

- **Vocabulary:** Use visuals to demonstrate concepts such as regrouping and remainder.

- **Instructional materials:** Provide a facts table to support students who need help recalling arithmetic combinations. Pair arithmetic combinations instruction with whole-number computations.

TABLE 11.6	ERROR PATTERNS AND REMEDIAL TECHNIQUES	
Operations	**Type of Errors**	**Remedial Techniques**
1. 76 + 49 ——— 1115	No regrouping of the ones in the ones place.	• Use base-ten blocks to model regrouping. • Use grid paper so only one digit can be recorded in each box, "forcing" the need to regroup. Include highlighted grid boxes above the problem to cue the need to write a numeral from regrouping tens or hundreds.
2. 34 729 +694 ——— 1117	Work begins on left rather than right. Regrouping done backward.	• Insert ↓ above the ones place as the place to start. • Explain that in math, we start opposite from where we start with reading.
3. 4 14 5̸7̸4̸ −268 ——— 206	Work begins on left with "borrowing" 1 from 5 to "regroup" to the tens and to the ones to be able to subtract.	• Insert ↓ above the ones place as the place to start. • Use base-ten blocks and a base-ten mat to model the conceptual understanding of regrouping.
4. 4 10 5̸0̸0̸ −2 8 6 ——— 214	Regrouping for the ones place is partially conducted. No regrouping for the tens place.	• Use base-ten blocks to model the conceptual understanding of regrouping. • Use D + PM to teach the procedural steps. • Give examples of subtraction problems with the zero in the minuend and with it in the subtrahend. Have students circle only those problems that can be computed without regrouping.
5. 534 × 24 ——— 1068	Each column is treated as separate multiplication. The left multiplier continues to be used when the multiplicand has more digits than the multiplier.	• Teach the use of the distributive property as an alternative algorithm. • $532 \times 24 = (20 \times 532) + (4 \times 532)$ • Create a cover so that only one digit of the multiplier is revealed at a time. • Have students check their work using a calculator.
6. 95 4)3620 36 ——— 20 20	The zero in the tens place is missing from the quotient. When the student "brings down" and division is not possible, the next digit is "brought down" with no zero used as a placeholder.	• Give students grid paper to help with placement issues.

(Continued)

TABLE 11.6 (CONTINUED)

Operations	Type of Errors	Remedial Techniques
7. $$\frac{1}{4} = \frac{1}{12}$$ $$+\frac{1}{3} = \frac{1}{12}$$ $$\rule{1cm}{0.4pt}\quad\rule{1cm}{0.4pt}$$ $$\frac{2}{12}$$	The student can identify the lowest common multiplier but merely copies the original numerator.	• Explain the purpose of the equal sign—that it means the same fractional part. • Have students use manipulatives to demonstrate that fractional parts on either side of the equal sign are equivalent.
8. $$6\frac{1}{3}$$ $$-2\frac{2}{3}$$ $$\rule{1cm}{0.4pt}$$ $$4\frac{1}{3}$$	The whole numbers are subtracted. There is no regrouping when the subtrahend is larger than the minuend.	• Have students use fractional parts to work through the problem. Use a cue to signal the need to start working with the fractions before the whole numbers. Have students regroup the whole-number unit for an equal set of fractional parts so the subtraction can be performed. • Have students use markings to signal regrouping of a whole into fractional parts. • Provide examples of mixed fractions that require regrouping for subtraction purposes.
9. $$6.8$$ $$+5.5$$ $$\rule{1cm}{0.4pt}$$ $$11.13$$	The decimal point is in the wrong place in the sum. The tenths are not regrouped as units.	• Have students use rods to show a unit for comparison. Have students use rods to show each addend as tenths as compared with the unit. Have students combine the tenths rods and trade for a unit. • Have students use grid paper with the instruction that only one digit can be placed in each box.

SOURCE: Ashlock (2009).

- **Instructional content—task analysis:** Provide similar types of problems when initially teaching whole-number computation at the abstract representation level. Similar types of problems include 2 digit + 2 digit with no regrouping, 3 digit − 3 digit with 0 in the tens place, and 2 digits × 1 digit with regrouping. Then provide mixed-problem worksheets with the same operation, such as 2 digits + 1 digit with regrouping, 2 digits + 2 digits with regrouping, and 3 digits + 3 digits with regrouping. Finally, provide mixed-problem worksheets with mixed operations.

- **Strategies:** Teach students procedural strategies (examples are described later) to solve whole-number computations. Use "invented strategies" for those students who can benefit from representing whole-number computations in nontraditional ways. Refer to Table 11.7 for examples of "invented algorithms." Choose judiciously which strategies to teach;

Teaching Fractions

too many strategies can confuse students. Work with students to determine the strategy that makes sense to them and that they can use independently, efficiently, and effectively.

- **Generalization:** Promote generalization by having students answer problems with mixed signs and in whole-number computational problems.

- **Technology:** Software programs can be used to support the extra instruction that students may require to learn whole-number computation. Some programs offer excellent visualizations of the process using manipulatives, which is often the type of instruction that teachers do not have sufficient time to provide. In the Tech Notes feature below, the Unifix cubes software program is shown, illustrating how the cubes are partitioned for a simple division problem with a remainder.

TECH *notes*

USING SOFTWARE TO SHOW PICTORIAL REPRESENTATIONS OF MATH CONCEPTS

Unifix Software (Didax Educational Resources, 2015) is a program that shows pictorial representations of abstract math concepts. The Unifix are interlocking cubes students can arrange to display patterning, counting, and operations. *Unifix Software* supports switch access, which means that students with motor problems can use the software with switches that control movement in the software.

You can use the following procedures with the Unifix cubes software to pictorially represent and solve the equation $17 \div 5 = x$.

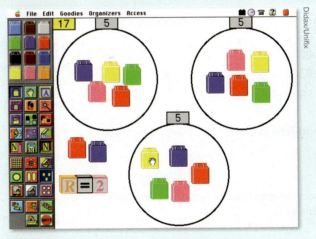

Pictor Unifix Software can be used to provide pictorial experiences with math concepts.

TEACHING PROCEDURE

1. Identify higher and lower performing students who can work together at the computer station.

2. Review the concept of division using the base-ten blocks.

3. Have students work in pairs at the computer with the *Unifix Software*.

4. Monitor progress by having students complete four division problems independently, using paper and pencil.

TABLE 11.7 INVENTED ALGORITHMS

(a) Invented strategies for addition with two-digit numbers

Add Tens, Add Ones, Then Combine	46 + 38 40 and 30 is 70. 6 and 8 is 14. 70 and 14 is 84.	$\begin{array}{r} 46 \\ +38 \\ \hline 70 \\ 14 \\ \hline 84 \end{array}$
Move Some to Make Tens	46 + 38 Take 2 from the 46 and put it with the 38 to make 40. Now you have 44, and 40 more is 84.	46 + 38 76 + 4 → 80 80 + 4 → 84
Add on Tens, Then Add Ones	46 + 38 46 and 30 more is 76. Then I added on the other 8. 76 and 4 is 80, and 4 more is 84.	$\overset{2}{\overbrace{46 + 38}}$ 44 + 40 84
Use a Nice Number and Compensate	46 + 38 46 and 40 is 86. That's 2 extra, so it's 84.	46 + 38 46 + 40 → 86 − 2 → 84

(b) Invented strategies for subtraction by counting up

Add Tens to Get Close, Then Ones	73 − 46 46 and 20 is 66. (30 more is too much.) Then 4 more is 70 and 3 is 73. That's 20 and 7, or 27.	$\begin{array}{l} 46 \\ 66 \\ 70 \\ 73 \end{array} \begin{array}{l} 20 \\ 4 \\ 3 \\ \hline 27 \end{array}$
Add Tens to Overshoot, Then Come Back	73 − 46 46 and 30 is 76. That's 3 too much, so it's 27.	73 − 46 → 46 + 30 → 76 − 3 → 73 30 − 3 = 27
Add Ones to Make a Ten, Then Tens and Ones	73 − 46 46 and 4 is 50. 50 and 20 is 70, and 3 more is 73. The 4 and 3 is 7, and 20 more is 27.	73 − 46 46 + 4 → 50 + 20 → 70 + 3 → 73 27
	Similarly, 46 and 4 is 50. 50 and 23 is 73. 23 and 4 is 27.	46 + 4 → 50 50 + 23 → 73 23 + 4 = 27

(c) Partitioning strategies for multiplication

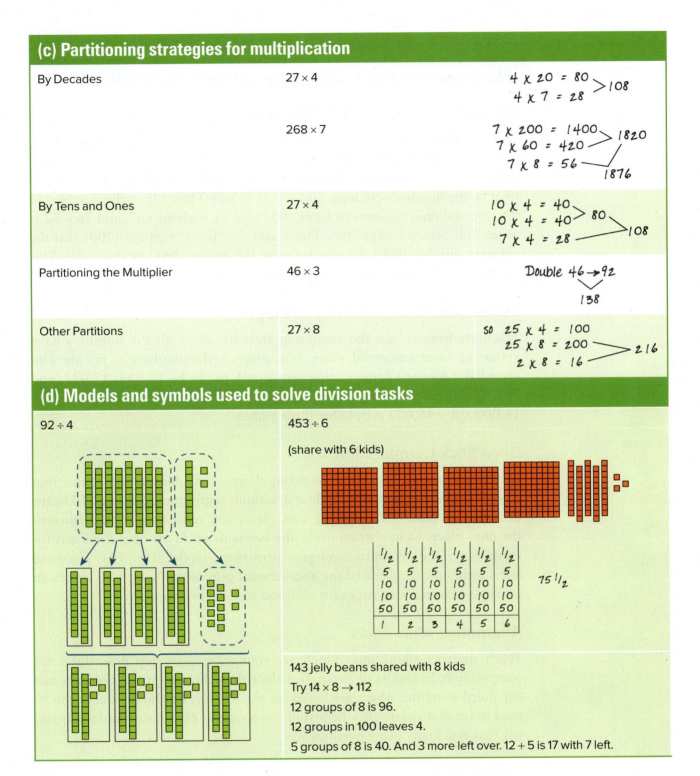

By Decades	27×4	$\begin{array}{l} 4 \times 20 = 80 \\ 4 \times 7 = 28 \end{array} \Big\rangle 108$
	268×7	$\begin{array}{l} 7 \times 200 = 1400 \\ 7 \times 60 = 420 \\ 7 \times 8 = 56 \end{array} \Big\rangle 1820 \quad 1876$
By Tens and Ones	27×4	$\begin{array}{l} 10 \times 4 = 40 \\ 10 \times 4 = 40 \\ 7 \times 4 = 28 \end{array} \Big\rangle 80 \quad 108$
Partitioning the Multiplier	46×3	Double $46 \rightarrow 92$ 138
Other Partitions	27×8	so $\begin{array}{l} 25 \times 4 = 100 \\ 25 \times 8 = 200 \\ 2 \times 8 = 16 \end{array} \Big\rangle 216$

(d) Models and symbols used to solve division tasks

$92 \div 4$

$453 \div 6$

(share with 6 kids)

$1/2$	$1/2$	$1/2$	$1/2$	$1/2$	$1/2$
5	5	5	5	5	5
10	10	10	10	10	10
10	10	10	10	10	10
50	50	50	50	50	50
1	2	3	4	5	6

$75 \, 1/2$

143 jelly beans shared with 8 kids

Try $14 \times 8 \rightarrow 112$

12 groups of 8 is 96.

12 groups in 100 leaves 4.

5 groups of 8 is 40. And 3 more left over. $12 + 5$ is 17 with 7 left.

SOURCE: Van de Walle et al. (2012). Reprinted with permission.

Rounding

Have students round numbers up or down to the nearest 10 or the nearest 100 for whole-number computation, column addition, mental computation, estimation, and determining the reasonableness of an answer. For example, in the division problem 286 divided by 72, it is easy to discover that 4 is a reasonable estimate of how many times 286 can be divided by 72 because $70 \times 4 = 280$.

Estimation: The Front-End Strategy

Teach students the front-end strategy for computing column addition (Reys, 1986). Provide students with a list of numbers to be added, such as $376 + 87 + 432 + 11 =$. Show the students how to first add the numbers in the "front" (that is, the hundreds column: $300 + 400 = 700$). Then adjust the numbers in the tens and ones columns to form 100 ($87 + 11$ is about 100, and $76 + 32$ is about 100, which makes 200). Third, add the "front" number (700) plus the adjusted number (200). Finally, estimate the answer (900 in this case). This strategy can be applied to adding money as well.

Estimation: The Clustering Strategy

Teach students to use the clustering strategy when all the numbers have about the same numerical value. For instance, the numbers of people who attended a football game during one month might be 15,833, 17,021, and 16,682. All the numbers cluster around 16,000, so a reasonable estimate is $16,000 \times 3 = 48,000$ people for three games.

Bean Stick Computation

Have students use bean sticks as manipulatives for addition and subtraction whole-number computation with and without regrouping. Sticks of 10 beans demonstrate place value for the tens place, and remaining beans represent the ones place. Demonstrate using the beans to trade 10 ones for a ten for regrouping. The demonstration plus permanent model (D + PM, discussed later) technique can be used for instructional purposes. Figure 11.2 shows an example of using bean sticks for addition with no regrouping.

Alternative Algorithms

Teach students algorithms, which are routine, step-by-step procedures for computation. Examples of alternative algorithms include partial products and expanded notation, which are based on place value. **Partial products** can be used to teach division; they help students focus on place value and the quantity that is actually being partitioned:

$428 \div 2 = ?$

$400 \div 2 = 200$

$20 \div 2 = 10$

$8 \div 2 = 4$

———

214

FIGURE 11.2 USING BEAN STICKS TO SOLVE COMPUTATIONAL PROBLEMS

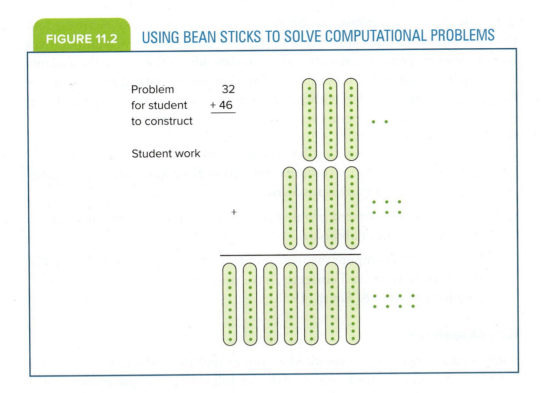

Problem for student to construct

$$\begin{array}{r} 32 \\ + 46 \\ \hline \end{array}$$

Student work

Expanded notation can be used for whole-number subtraction and division. The expanded-notation algorithm helps students show place-value representations of numerals and calculate answers, as illustrated in the following array.

	Subtraction	Division
457	$400+50+7$	$428 \div 2 = ?$
−35	$-30+5$	$(400+20+8) \div 2 =$
	$400+20+2 = 422$	$(200+10+4) = 214$

For both types of alternative algorithms, model and "think aloud" how you solve a division problem. Students imitate and verbalize the steps in applying these algorithms, use manipulatives to represent the process, or work with a partner to solve problems.

Demonstration Plus Permanent Model

Have students use the demonstration plus permanent model (D + PM) intervention, which has proved successful in teaching students explicitly how to solve problems that include addition, subtraction, multiplication, and division of whole-number computation. This intervention takes only a short time to implement, is best applied individually or in small groups, and can greatly facilitate mastery of computation. Teachers using this intervention often report that students catch on very quickly and learn the steps efficiently. The D + PM intervention is at the level of abstract representation but can easily be adapted with visual representations (problems shown using base-ten pictures) and physical representations (problems completed using base-ten manipulatives or bean sticks). Thus, an instructional materials adaptation can help students who require additional conceptual development to understand place value, as well as computing with and without regrouping. The following steps make up the demonstration (D) + permanent model (PM) intervention:

- Demonstrate (D) how to solve a problem by "thinking aloud" the steps in whole-number computation. Stress place-value and regrouping language if regrouping is involved.

- Leave the demonstrated problem as a referent (PM) on the student's worksheet or the chalkboard.

- Have students compute the next problem, saying the steps out loud. If the problem is worked correctly, have students complete the remaining problems (Rivera & Smith, 1988).

Key Questions

Some students become confused when doing multistep whole-number computation (division, multiplication). Ask the following key questions to help students get back on track:

- What is the problem?

- What are the steps?

- What did you just do?

- What do you do next?

Mercer and Mercer (2005) recommended teaching students the following cue or "family strategy" to remember the steps required to solve division problems: **D**addy (divide), **M**other (multiply), **S**ister (subtract), and **B**rother (bring down). Students can be taught to use the "family strategy" or to ask themselves the "key questions" by referring to a chart or cue card, an approach that promotes more self-regulated learning. You can pair these techniques with the D + PM intervention to teach students how to solve division problems.

Sequence of Instruction

Use this approach to promote generalization. Traditionally, teachers present information to students in a task-analyzed, sequenced format, teaching the easiest skill first. Once that skill has been mastered, they present the next one, and so on. Investigations have revealed, however, that students do not have to be taught whole-number computational skills in an easy-to-difficult sequence for learning to occur. Rather, they can be taught the most difficult skill within a group; most will generalize the algorithmic process to the easier problems.

Concrete representations such as bean sticks and base-ten models can promote understanding of place value and renaming.

The following guidelines are suggested:

1. Develop a task analysis of whole-number computation (two digits + one digit, two digits + two digits, three digits + two digits, three digits + three digits—all with no regrouping; two digits + one digit, two digits + two digits, three digits + two digits, three digits + three digits—all with renaming).

2. Test students to identify the skills they have mastered and those that require instruction.

3. Group skills by "no renaming" and "renaming."

4. Select the most difficult skill within a group as the instructional target (say, three digits + three digits with no renaming; three digits + three digits with renaming).

5. Teach this most difficult skill using the demonstration plus permanent model intervention.

6. Present problems representing all the skills within a group for practice (two digits + one digit, two digits + two digits, three digits + two digits, three digits + three digits—all with renaming).

7. Collect student performance data on all the skills on the practice sheet. (Rivera & Smith, 1988)

We now talk about mathematical areas that can be challenging as students progress through the grades.

WHAT ARE RATIONAL NUMBERS AND HOW ARE THEY TAUGHT?

Rational numbers are critical for more advanced mathematics success, especially in algebra (NMAP, 2008). They include the whole numbers and integers; numbers that can be written as the quotient of two integers, a ÷ b, where b is not zero (NCTM, 2000); and fractions, decimals, and percentages. Students should work flexibly with fractions, decimals, and their relationship to percentages, applying these rational numbers to real-life problems related to money, cooking, shopping, and measurement (NCTM, 2000). According to Van de Walle et al. (2012), developing students' understanding of fraction concepts is critical to their success in learning and understanding how to compute with fractions. Students should be taught to view fraction and decimal systems as representing the same concepts. Once they understand this relationship, they should be introduced to percentages and taught the interrelatedness of decimals, fractions, and percentages (Hudson & Miller, 2006).

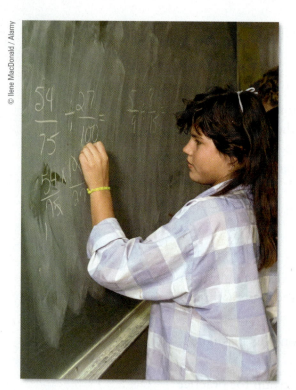

Students encounter a variety of challenges as they engage in work with fractions, decimals, and percentages.

DIFFICULTIES WITH RATIONAL NUMBERS

Students encounter a variety of challenges as they work with fractions, decimals, and percentages. According to Bley and Thornton (2001), those who demonstrate problems with abstract reasoning have difficulties with rational numbers. Research findings from a longitudinal study of 147 students in sixth, seventh, and eighth grade with mathematics learning disabilities (MLD), mathematics difficulties (MD), and typical achievement (TA), found that those with MLD performed poorly on ranking proportions with fractions and decimals (ranking smallest to largest decimals shown as numbers and fractions shown as pictures) compared with the other two groups (Mazzocco & Devlin, 2008). Students with MLD manifested significantly more difficulties in identifying fraction and decimal equivalence ($.50 = \frac{5}{10}$) than did students with MD and students who were TA. Mazzocco and Devlin (2008) suggested poor conceptual understanding of rational numbers (weak number sense) as a possible explanation for low performance in basic tasks, which are associated with earlier grades' content. Students also have difficulties with integers, often due to rules learned in earlier grades that do not apply to the new material (Karp, Bush, & Dougherty, 2014). For example, when we add two negative numbers such as –4 + –6, the sum (–10) is smaller than either of the two addends.

The vocabulary associated with these number systems may be problematic and thus require explicit instruction in the definitions and use of the terms. Number sense regarding the relative sizes of parts, such as thirds, tenths, 0.60, and 25%, and their relationship to a whole unit may be difficult for some students. Problems of this nature will interfere with the ability to judge the reasonableness of answers to questions such as "Is $\frac{3}{4}$ or $\frac{1}{4}$ closer to a whole?" Relating fractions, decimals, and percentages requires a sense of number size and relationship, and without a good sense of number size, even numeral relationships become challenging. Difficulty remembering the meaning of symbols can interfere with interpreting how to solve problems. For example, –1 means negative 1 and not subtract 1. Finally, understanding and recalling the procedural steps necessary in computations is yet another difficult area for students who are struggling.

TEACHING RATIONAL NUMBERS

Our overview of teaching these skills reflects the fact that many students, with and without special needs, need lots of help learning to work with rational numbers and integers.

- **Diagnosis:** Refer to Table 11.6 for examples of error patterns and remedial strategies to address them (Ashlock, 2009).

- **Vocabulary:** Teach terms related to fractions, decimals, percentages, and integers explicitly (Van de Walle et al., 2012).

- **Instructional content:**

  o **Make connections to money:** Talk about and show how decimals such as .25, .10, and .05 are related to money.

  o **Make connections to telling time:** Connect simple fractions ($\frac{1}{2}$, $\frac{1}{4}$) to telling time: half-past the hour, quarter after an hour, or quarter to an hour.

- **Instructional materials:** Use rods, fraction tiles, grid paper, Geoboards, number lines, and pattern blocks to provide activities with quantities in different forms and shapes. Provide multiple exercises for students to represent similar values across the numeration systems using various materials. For example, use a paper strip to show $\frac{1}{4}$ of a region, a Geoboard to show .25 of a region, and grid paper to show 25% of a region. Number lines and integer chips are very useful for teaching integers.

Figure 11.1 shows examples of manipulatives and materials that can be used for instruction in fractions, decimals, and percentages. See the National Library of Virtual Manipulatives (NLVM; http://nlvm.usu.edu/en/nav/vlibrary.html) for multiple manipulative tools for numbers and operations, algebra, geometry, measurement, and data analysis and probability.

- **Strategies:** Use the CSA or D + PM procedure for teaching addition, subtraction, multiplication, and division algorithms.

- **Technology:** Encourage students to check their work using calculators.

- **Progress monitoring:** On a weekly basis, conduct assessments on concepts and skills taught to assess whether students are benefiting from instruction. Error analysis can pinpoint misconceptions you can target for further instruction and review.

Sorting Fractions and Decimals

Given a variety of fractions (or decimals) and the three choices Close to Zero, Close to $\frac{1}{2}$, and Close to 1, have students sort the fractions (or decimals) according to their relationship to the choices. To do this accurately, students must understand the relative sizes of the fractions (or decimals). Have them use manipulatives to demonstrate the accuracy of their choices (Bley & Thornton, 2001).

Fractions and Decimals to Sort

$\frac{1}{9}$	$\frac{4}{5}$	$\frac{1}{20}$	$\frac{5}{8}$	$\frac{6}{7}$	$\frac{2}{3}$
.91	.01	.47	.87	.05	

Close to Zero   Close to $\frac{1}{2}$ Close to 1

Fractions as Equal to or Greater Than 1

Teach students a range of fractional representations when first introducing the concept of a fraction to help develop number sense about relative size. Rather than limiting instruction to 1/2, 1/4, and 1/3, include fractions such as 5/5, 3/1, and 12/4, using fraction strips and shapes such as squares, rectangles, and circles to illustrate physical representations of the fractional concepts. Students then learn from the beginning of fraction instruction that fractions represent relationships, not specific amounts.

Comparisons

Have students make comparisons to see comparative sizes of fractions and the relationship between the sizes. For example, younger children might state that 1/3 is greater than 1/2 because 3 is greater than 2; however, comparisons using manipulatives such as fraction strips or connecting cubes can help them develop an understanding of relative sizes. Note that students must know the identity of the whole (e.g., a cake or a pizza) to discern that 1/2 is indeed greater than 1/3.

Arithmetic Combinations and Fractions

Combine instruction on arithmetic combinations with simple fraction problems. Build fluency in responding to problems, relying on arithmetic combinations, and then present fractions containing the combinations students have been practicing. If the targeted multiplication facts are factors of 8, fraction problems might include the following example:

$$\frac{8}{9} \times \frac{6}{8} = \frac{48}{72} = \frac{2}{3}$$

This technique helps students make the connection between learning multiplication combinations and computing problems with fractions, and it provides additional practice with multiplication combinations.

Money, Decimals, and Percentages

Teach money and decimals together because they have a natural connection. Mastery of money and decimals is a life skill; they may have more relevance for students if taught together. Use number combinations that have been taught and mastered during study of whole-number computation. Use the newspaper or advertising circulars to teach and reinforce money, decimals, percentages, and computational skills. Computing the prices of items, spending a designated amount of money by "shopping the sales," and comparison shopping are all activities that require students to use money, decimals, percentages, and computational skills.

Algebra is an important area that requires careful attention. We take a look at it in the next section.

WHAT IS ALGEBRA AND HOW IS IT TAUGHT?

Algebra uses mathematical statements to describe relationships between things that vary over time. Algebra is about finding the unknown. Algebra is identified as the gateway to college readiness; students must be prepared to be successful with algebraic content (NCTM, 2000; NMAP, 2008). Algebraic reasoning and the development of algebraic concepts require the use of models and algebraic symbols to represent problems and quantitative relationships and strategies to construct and solve simple to complex equations. Algebraic reasoning relies on patterns; variables, equality, and equations; symbolism; and relations, functions, and representations (Allsopp, Kyger, & Lovin, 2007; Van de Walle et al., 2012). For students at risk and students with mathematics disabilities who find mathematics difficult, adaptations are critical to helping them succeed with algebraic content and developing their potential to enter higher education.

DIFFICULTIES WITH ALGEBRA

Difficulties with algebra stem from a variety of problems, including difficulties mastering arithmetic combinations and understanding the vocabulary used in algebraic reasoning. As noted in the problem-solving section later in this chapter, students who demonstrate mathematical difficulties typically exhibit poor performance in solving word problems, which are an important component of algebraic study. Another challenge is understanding patterns and functions. Finally, limited algebraic thinking impedes some students' success. Algebraic thinking is thinking about underlying mathematical structures to analyze, generalize, model, justify, or prove quantitative relationships (Dougherty, Bryant, Bryant, Darrough, & Pfannenstiel, 2015; Kieran, 2004).

TEACHING ALGEBRAIC REASONING

Students who are well on their way to mastering the concepts and skills addressed earlier in this chapter are ready for the exciting challenge of algebraic reasoning.

- **Diagnosis:** Use the think-aloud process with specific problems to assess the level of students' reasoning.

- **Instructional content:** Make connections in activities among patterns, functions, and variables. For example, students can identify and extend a pattern, represent the relationship in a table, identify the functional relationship formula, and predict the next response in a table by using the formula.

- **Instructional content:** Teach the arithmetic properties presented in Table 11.8. These properties are part of algebraic reasoning and are important concepts for students to understand. Even if remembering the name of the property is an issue, students must develop conceptual understanding of how numbers are related and how values are influenced by the properties in this table.

- **Instructional materials:** Use a mathematics balance to help students visualize equalities. Use objects (keys, buttons, blocks, or geometric shapes) that students can categorize according to color, size, and shape.

- **Vocabulary:** Check student understanding of the key vocabulary of algebraic instruction.

TABLE 11.8   MATHEMATICAL PROPERTIES

Property	Formula
Identity Property of Addition: Any number plus zero equals the number; the value does not change.	$n + 0 = n$
Commutative Property of Addition: The order in which numbers are added does not change the answer.	$a + b = b + a$
Associative Property of Addition: When adding, the grouping does not change the answer.	$a + (b + c) = (a + b) + c$
Identity Property of Multiplication: Any number times one equals the number; the value does not change.	$n \times 1 = n$
Commutative Property of Multiplication: The order in which numbers are multiplied does not change the answer.	$a \times b = b \times a$
Associative Property of Multiplication: When multiplying, the grouping does not change the answer.	$a \times (b \times c) = (a \times b) \times c$
Distributive Property of Multiplication: The product can be written as the sum of two products.	$a \times (b + c) = (a \times b) + (a \times c)$

- **Questioning:** Use the examples of the three types of questions in Table 11.9 to generate problems for students to solve.

- **Strategies:** Provide specific strategies and teach using the "think aloud" procedure so students learn how to solve equations and word problems.

- **Technology:** Teach students how to use graphing calculators to plot points and draw curves when graphing patterns (Van de Walle et al., 2012). Refer to the applets on the *e-Standards* published by the NCTM. The applets feature the connection between word problems as real-life situations and graphs and equations. For instance, students can manipulate a situation involving runners and their speed, distance, and time from a starting point. As the students manipulate the variables, the relationship among these variables can be graphed. Finally, review the NLVM to determine how algebraic concepts can be represented using virtual manipulatives.

TABLE 11.9   A FRAMEWORK OF THREE QUESTIONS TO PROMOTE ALGEBRAIC THINKING

Type of Question	Fractions $\frac{1}{2} \times \frac{3}{4}$	Integers $-3 + -8$
1. Reversibility question	What are two fractions whose product is $\frac{3}{8}$?	What are two integers whose sum is -11?
2. Flexibility question	$\frac{1}{2} \times \frac{3}{4}$ $\frac{1}{2} \times \frac{2}{4}$ $\frac{1}{2} \times \frac{1}{4}$ How are these problems alike?	$-3 + (-8)$ $-4 + (-8)$ $-5 + (-8)$ How are these problems alike?
3. Generalization question	If the factors of a multiplication problem are between 0 and 1, what can you predict about the size of the product?	What are two negative integers whose sum is negative? What are a positive integer and a negative integer whose sum is negative? What are two positive integers whose sum is negative? What do you notice about the integers that you found?

SOURCE: Dougherty et al. (2015). Reprinted with permission.

Fact Families

Explain to students that fact families are three numbers that are related, just as the people in a family are related. For example, the numbers 2, 5, and 7 can be used to make two addition problems ($2 + 5 = 7$ and $5 + 2 = 7$) and two subtraction problems ($7 - 5 = 2$ and $7 - 2 = 5$). Demonstrate with the manipulatives the commutative property and that subtraction is the inverse of addition. Provide students with many opportunities to create their own "families." Have them write equations for their problems. Use Figure 11.3 to convey the notion of family and to give students a place to write the number sentences for their fact families.

Solving Algebraic Equations

Teach students a strategy for solving algebraic equations. The following strategy requires students to ask themselves questions to guide their thinking through the steps (Allsopp et al., 2007):

Solve: $5x = 25$

1. Is there a letter?

   "There is a letter that represents a variable. I need to figure out the value of the variable."

2. What is on each side of the equals sign?

   "There is $5x$ and 25, and $5x$ means 5 times x."

3. What is the value for x?

   "I know that 5 times 5 equals 25, so the value of x is 5."

Order of Operations

Teach students the order in which operations are used to solve equations. The correct order follows:

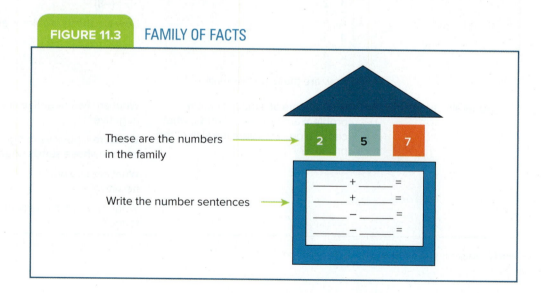

FIGURE 11.3   FAMILY OF FACTS

These are the numbers in the family

Write the number sentences

1. Perform all operations within parentheses and brackets.

2. Evaluate each power (exponent).

3. Do all multiplications and divisions, from left to right.

4. Do all additions and subtractions, from left to right.

Teachers frequently teach students to use the mnemonic "Please Excuse My Dear Aunt Sally" as a way to remember the order of operations. "Please" is a reminder for parentheses, "Excuse" stands for exponents, "My" refers to multiplication, "Dear" means division, "Aunt" is a reminder for addition, and "Sally" means subtraction.

Provide examples of equations for which students have to explain how to solve the problem using the order of operations rules. Create a poster and bookmark with the order information as a cue for those students who may need help remembering it.

Graphic Organizers

Use graphic organizers as a way to help students visualize mathematical relationships, vocabulary, and concepts. Venn diagrams can demonstrate similarities and differences between two concepts; hierarchical diagrams can show subordinate relationships to a superordinate concept; and mapping diagrams (see Figure 11.4) can visually depict how information about concepts can be organized (Maccini & Gagnon, 2005). Figure 11.4 shows the four operations and

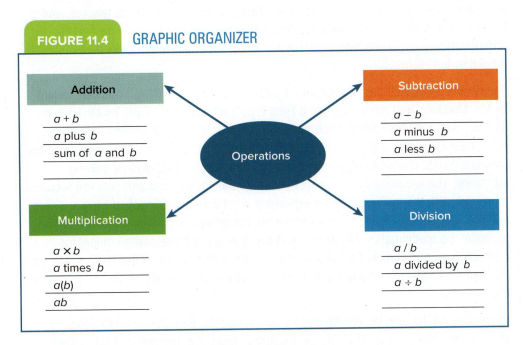

FIGURE 11.4 GRAPHIC ORGANIZER

Operations

Addition
$a + b$
a plus b
sum of a and b

Subtraction
$a - b$
a minus b
a less b

Multiplication
$a \times b$
a times b
$a(b)$
ab

Division
a / b
a divided by b
$a \div b$

SOURCE: Adapted from Maccini and Gagnon (2005). Reprinted with permission.

terms that convey each. Students must understand what operation each term represents as they encounter them in algebraic equations.

Problem solving is one of the most important areas in mathematics. In the next section, we discuss a variety of ways to teach this subject.

The Working Together feature shows how individuals with different expertise collaborate to provide mathematics instruction to all students and intensive interventions to those students who require additional support. You will see how teachers structure algebra instruction, making use of a block model to increasingly intensive instruction for struggling students.

WORKING *together*

COLLABORATING TO SUPPORT STRUGGLING STUDENTS IN ALGEBRA

Parkview High School is located in an urban school district in which a large percentage of students are eligible for free or reduced-price lunch. All students take algebra; those who require more intensive intervention have a double block of algebra each day. Approximately one-third of the ninth graders need this type of model because of low performance and behavioral issues such as low attendance and task completion. The principal and the mathematics department chair worked with the data management team to pull other sources of data to develop profiles of students' mathematics difficulties. Ms. Martinez, the mathematics teacher, and Mr. Wilson, the mathematics interventionist teacher, worked together to provide differentiated and supplemental instruction when progress-monitoring data indicated a need to intervene.

The double block includes regular, Tier 1 intervention in the first part of class, taught by Ms. Martinez, and more intensified Tiers 2 or 3 intervention taught by Mr. Wilson and Ms. Bell, the special education inclusion teacher, during the second part of the block class. Students are grouped into small homogeneous groups, based on progress monitoring data related to algebraic concepts, and taught strategies for solving equations. The vocabulary of each lesson is carefully taught, and students are required to engage with the mathematics by explaining what they are doing, justifying answers, and problem solving. Students use various manipulatives and visual representations to model the mathematics. Mr. Wilson and Ms. Bell use a three-station model for instruction. In one station, Mr. Wilson teaches the mathematics; in the second, Ms. Bell teaches the strategies; and in the third station, students work with a partner to practice the content.

Depending on the day, Mr. Wilson can be reviewing, Ms. Bell can be reteaching, and the independent station might be devoted to progress monitoring. During their planning time, the two teachers review each student's data to choose next steps for the following day, which could include regrouping students and intensifying instruction.

QUESTIONS:

1. Is there another coteaching model Mr. Wilson and Ms. Bell could consider for the double block of algebra intervention? What might this other model offer that is different than the stations model?

2. What activities might Mr. Wilson and Ms. Bell develop together for the stations model where students are working independently so they remain engaged?

3. How can Mr. Wilson and Ms. Bell work together to help students who have struggled for years in mathematics deal with possible motivation issues?

WHAT IS PROBLEM SOLVING AND HOW IS IT TAUGHT?

Problem solving is a basic life skill as well as an essential component of a total mathematics program (NCTM, 2000; NMAP, 2008; Woodward et al., 2012), emphasized in the CCSSM (2010).

You can develop word problems from classroom and daily-life situations that require problem solving. Connect conceptual and skill development to problem solving by integrating whole-number computations, fractions, decimals, percentages, and algebraic equations into word problems students can solve that reflect real-life situations.

Mayer (1998) identified five types of knowledge needed to solve word problems: linguistic (English language and syntax), semantic (understanding of the meaning of words), schematic (knowledge of word problem types and recognition of irrelevant information), strategic (ability to plan and monitor solution strategies), and procedural (ability to perform a sequence of operations). As noted by Montague, Enders, and Dietz (2011), good problem solvers use a variety of cognitive and metacognitive strategies to solve word problems, such as rereading, drawing pictures, identifying important information, and disregarding extraneous information.

iStock/dlewis33

DIFFICULTIES WITH PROBLEM SOLVING

Students with mathematical difficulties struggle to solve word problems for a variety of reasons. They may not

Solving real-world word problems is a basic life skill and is recommended as a major component of the mathematics curriculum.

VIDEO CASE 11.2

Math Problem Solving

1. What is the MSI problem-solving strategy and how does it benefit students who struggle with math? What are the steps in the MSI problem-solving process?

2. How does Lisa Sigafoos guide her students in applying the MSI strategy to a math word problem? What questioning techniques does she use to scaffold her students' success?

understand how to use the five types of knowledge or schema for solving word problems (Jitendra et al., 2007). They may not recognize the types of word problem structures or choose an appropriate solution strategy to solve the problem (Powell, 2011; Shin & Bryant, 2015). They may have problems applying multiple steps within word problems (Shin & Bryant, 2015) or selecting and using the correct algorithms (Hecht, Close, & Santisi, 2003). Moreover, students have been shown to have difficulties paraphrasing what they were being asked to do in the problem and visually representing the process and solution (Krawec, 2014).

TYPES OF WORD PROBLEMS

The word problems typically found in elementary curricula require (a) join, part-part-whole, separate, and compare for addition and subtraction, and (b) equal-groups, multiplicative comparisons, combinations, and product-of-measures problems for multiplication and division (Van de Walle et al., 2012). Mayer (1998) indicated that interest, area, mixture, river current, probability, number, work, navigation, progressions, exponentials, triangles, distance/rate/ time, averages, scale conversion, and ratio problem categories are typically included in secondary-level textbooks.

In some cases, students with limited reading abilities may have difficulty solving story problems simply because they are unable to read the words. Adapting instruction might be the answer to this type of problem. For instance, story problems could be presented on audiotape as well as on paper so that difficult words are read aloud to the students. Another way to address reading level is to have students work in cooperative learning or peer-tutoring arrangements. A student with a more advanced reading level could be the designated reader for the other student or students. A third possibility is to have students work individually or in small groups with the teacher, a family member volunteer, or the paraprofessional. This individualized attention could easily address the reading-level problem and provide additional support in solving story problems. A fourth option could include controlling the reading level of the word problems to more closely match the reading level of the students. By carefully selecting words, teachers can address the reading level more adequately in some cases.

TEACHING PROBLEM SOLVING

The general steps for teaching problem solving follow:

- **Diagnosis:** Use clinical interview procedures to assess the reasons for difficulty solving problems. (These might include language, numbers that are too big, reading problems, extraneous information, or linguistic structure.) Rewrite problems accordingly. In some cases, problems may have to be read to students who have serious reading issues.

- **Instructional delivery:** Include problems with too little or too much information; ask students to tell what is needed or what is extra.

- **Instructional delivery:** Have students write story problems for peers to solve.

- **Instructional delivery:** Have students substitute smaller numbers for larger numbers that may be troublesome. Students can (a) use manipulatives to depict problems, (b) use charts and tables to organize information, (c) solve problems containing more than one right answer, (d) devise their own story problems, (e) solve real problems (situations in the classroom or current events), and (f) focus on the language of the story problem by explaining problems with varying linguistic, symbolic, and extraneous information in their own words.

- **Strategy instruction:** Teach explicit strategies. Refer to Instructional Strategy 11.2 for ways to teach problem solving. Refer to What Works Clearinghouse for an evidence-based practice guide on problem solving (http://ies.ed.gov/ncee/wwc/PracticeGuide.aspx?sid=16).

- **Calculations:** Have students use calculators to check their work.

- **Progress monitoring:** Monitor student performance regularly. Provide several problems for students to solve independently. Ask them to show their work, including the ways they both make a plan and perform their calculations.

FAST DRAW[1]

1. **F** ind what you're solving for.
2. **A** sk yourself, "What are the parts of the problem?"
3. **S** et up the numbers.
4. **T** ie down the sign.

1. **D** iscover the sign.
2. **R** ead the problem.
3. **A** nswer, or draw and check.
4. **W** rite the answer.

(Continued)

(Continued)

Questions and Actions

Step	Questions	Actions
1. Read the problem.	Are there words I don't know? Do I know what each word means? Do I need to reread the problem? Are there number words?	Underline words. Find out definitions. Reread. Underline.
2. Restate the problem.	What information is important? What information isn't needed? What is the question asking?	Underline. Cross out. Put in own words.
3. Develop a plan.	What are the facts? How can they be organized? How many steps are there? What operations will I use?	Make a list. Develop a chart. Use manipulatives. Use smaller numbers. Select an operation.
4. Compute the problem.	Did I get the correct answer?	Estimate. Check with partner. Verify with a calculator.
5. Examine the results.	Have I answered the question? Does my answer seem reasonable? Can I restate the question and answer?	Reread the question. Check the question and answer. Write a number sentence.

Math Scene Investigator[2]

Step	Actions Within Each Step
1. Inspect and Find Clues	Read the problem. Underline the question and the unit. Circle important information. Cross out distractible information.
2. Plan and Solve	Draw a picture to solve. Write the equation.
3. Retrace	Write the inverse fact equation. Recount the picture.

SOURCES:

[1]Adapted from Mercer and Miller (1992); [2]Pfannenstiel, Bryant, Bryant, and Porterfield (2015).

GEOMETRY, MEASUREMENT, PROBLEM SOLVING: BUYING SOD FOR THE BACKYARD

INSTRUCTIONAL OBJECTIVE

The student will use a strategy to solve a multistep problem.

INSTRUCTIONAL CONTENT

Problem solving, number and operation, geometry, measurement, algebra (conceptual understanding)

INSTRUCTIONAL MATERIALS

Graph paper, recording sheet

INSTRUCTIONAL DELIVERY

Grouping: Small group of students

Vocabulary: area, square, foot

Before teaching the lesson, review the vocabulary terms. Have students define the terms in their own words. Use visuals for English language learners.

TEACHING PROCEDURE

1. Provide directions to the whole class for the activity:

In small groups, you are going to work together to generate a solution to the following problem. You are going to lay sod in your backyard. Sod is sold in squares measuring 12 inches by 12 inches. The backyard is 50 feet by 72 feet. Draw on graph paper a diagram of the backyard area you wish to sod. Sod goes for $.85 a square. How much will enough sod to complete the project cost? Solve the problem and record your group's answer and reasoning.

2. Tell students that each one of them should write, on his or her recording sheet, what the problem is asking, strategies for solving the problem, and the calculations.

3. Circulate among groups, asking questions to promote discussion and problem solving.

4. Have a speaker from each small group explain to the whole class how the group solved the problem.

PROGRESS MONITORING (Independent Practice)

After the lesson, give each student four problems to solve independently. Ask students to draw a diagram to represent each problem and to show all calculations.

SOURCE: Bryant, Kim, Hartman, and Bryant (2006).

One of the most useful applications of algebraic reasoning is in using equations to solve word problems. *Fast Draw, Questions and Actions,* and *Math Scene Investigator* are three strategies that have been suggested for analyzing and solving problems. Instructional Strategy 11.2 provides an example of teaching procedures that focuses on geometry instruction.

Think back to the Opening Challenge with Mrs. Reid. ADAPT in Action provides information about how Mrs. Reid approached problem-solving instruction with her students with mathematics difficulties and disabilities.

ADAPT *in action*

MRS. REID: PROBLEM-SOLVING INSTRUCTION

Mrs. Reid has students with identified mathematics disabilities who are having trouble, and other students are struggling as well. She decides to provide a problem-solving lesson that incorporates skills from the different areas of the curriculum. The problem will require the use of geometry, measurement, and algebra. She wants students to develop their strategies for solving the problems and to present their solution strategies to the class as a learning experience.

During group work, Mrs. Reid will look for students' ability to read the problem, paraphrase what the problem is asking, identify relevant information, identify and use a strategy with visuals, and calculate the answer. She will also observe the students' engagement by sitting with each group for 10 minutes to observe who is participating, how frequently, and what is being discussed.

Following the lesson, Mrs. Reid reviews her progress-monitoring data and learns that at least one student in each group makes infrequent or no contributions to the discussion of how to solve the problem. Her struggling students who did not perform well on the progress-monitoring problems need adapted instruction. She decides to use the ADAPT framework to figure out her next steps.

(A) **Ask, "What am I requiring the student to do?"** Mrs. Reid wants the students to solve problems using strategies, including visual representations. She also wants them to compute the calculations correctly.

(D) **Determine the prerequisite skills of the task.** "I know students need to read the problem, figure out what it is asking (including identifying whether there is extraneous information and whether it is a multistep problem), set up a plan using visuals, and calculate the answer."

(A) **Analyze the student's strengths and struggles.** At least five students in each class period had difficulty identifying a plan to solve the problem, did not show the work for each step of a multistep problem, and made calculation errors.

(P) **Propose and implement adaptations from among the four categories.** Mrs. Reid decides to use the *Questions and Actions* strategy shown earlier to help students work through each step of the problem-solving process. This strategy taps both the cognitive (steps) and metacognitive (self-questioning) aspects of problem solving.

(T) **Test to determine whether the adaptations helped the student accomplish the task.** Mrs. Reid will continue to collect progress-monitoring data and group observation information to determine whether students use the steps of the "Questions and Actions" strategy in their small group work and whether their independent performance improves.

ADAPT *framework*: PROBLEM SOLVING

		Strengths	Struggles		
ASK "What am I requiring the student to do?"	**DETERMINE** the prerequisite skills of the task.	**ANALYZE** the student's strengths and struggles.		**PROPOSE** and implement adaptations from among the four categories.	**TEST** to determine whether the adaptations helped the student to accomplish the task.
Solve problems using strategies, including visual representations.	1. Read the problem.	**1**			
	2. Figure out what it is asking.	**2**			
	3. Set up a plan using visuals.		**3**	3. Instructional activity: Use the *Question and Actions* strategy.	3 and 4: Use progress monitoring and observations to determine progress and success.
	4. Calculate the answer.		**4**	4. Instructional material: Use a calculator to self-check.	

UDL *in action*

Universal Design for Learning Lesson

Note: This UDL-based lesson was developed, in part, using the CAST UDL Lesson Builder: http://lessonbuilder.cast.org/create.php?op=new.

The UDL framework (version 2.0) is comprised of three main principles (I. Representation, II. Action and Expression, and III. Engagement).

Each principle has three guidelines and several checkpoints that define them further. In this lesson plan, we delineate how various instructional strategies meet the UDL checkpoints.

Title: Using grids to learn percentages.

(Continued)

(Continued)

Subject: Mathematics: Number and operation-percentage

Grade Level: 6

Duration: 45 minutes

Unit Description: This lesson is part of a group of lessons that focus on the relationship among percentages, fractions, and decimals.

Lesson Description for Day:

Prerequisite skills: Ability to communicate verbally

Unit Goals:

The goal of this unit is to understand the relationship among percentages, fractions, and decimals.

Lesson Goals:

The purpose of this lesson is to introduce the concept of percentage using a 10 × 10 grid.

Methods:
Anticipatory Set:

Tell the students that the purpose of the day's lesson is to help them become familiar with the concept of a percentage to prepare for further lessons about the relationship among percentages, fractions, and decimals. They will need to understand how these concepts are related and ways for representing similar quantities.

Introduce and Model New Knowledge:

1. Introduce the mathematical term *percent* and the symbol that denotes percent. Explain that percent means one part in a hundred. Show pictures from newspaper clippings that use percent and the % symbol to discuss sales (*Checkpoint 2.1—Clarify vocabulary and symbols*). Have students provide real-life examples of items that they and their family buy on sale and what bargains they look for such as 50% off (*Checkpoint 3.1—Activate or supply background knowledge*).

2. Explain that they are going to use the concept of percent for planting a garden. Read the problem to the students:

   - *Ms. Sanchez is going to plant a garden this spring. She has a plot of land that she will partition into parts so that she can plant both flowers and vegetables. Ms. Sanchez knows that she wants more land devoted to flowers and that the remaining land will be for different types of vegetables. She decides to draw a grid to help her visualize what the garden might look like.*

3. Show students models using the virtual manipulative grids of what Ms. Sanchez's garden might look like using NLVM (http://nlvm.usu.edu/en/nav/vlibrary.html) (*Checkpoint 5.2—Use multiple tools for construction and composition*).

4. Show a percentage and ask students what the grid would look like given the percentage so that they can work from a number to shading a grid and from a shaded grid to providing a percentage to help students become comfortable with using the virtual manipulatives (*Checkpoint 3.3—Guide information processing, visualization, and manipulation*).

Provide Guided Practice:

1. Have students work in pairs at computer stations to use the virtual manipulative grid to create pictorial scenarios of what Ms. Sanchez's garden might look like.

2. Have student pairs share with each other their ideas and use the term *percent* as they describe their plot of land's partitions (*Checkpoint 7.1— Optimize individual choice and autonomy*).

Provide Independent Practice:

At the end of the lesson, give students scenarios for the garden and have them show their gardens.

SUMMARY

It is important for teachers to challenge their students to achieve mathematical competence. It is equally important for teachers to provide appropriate instructional adaptations for those students who are most in need of academic assistance. For students with mathematics disabilities, adaptations are important to help them participate in classroom discussions and learn mathematical skills and concepts emphasized in the NCTM standards.

Instructional adaptations are necessary to help students benefit from instruction in the general education setting. This chapter offers ideas about adaptations for early number development; arithmetic combinations; place value; whole-number computation; fractions, decimals, and percentages; algebra; and problem solving. Keep in mind that other areas addressed in the NCTM standards (such as measurement, geometry, and statistics and probability) also require adapted instruction.

REVIEW THE LEARNING OBJECTIVES

Let's review the learning objectives for this chapter. If you are uncertain and cannot talk through the answers provided for any of these questions, reread those sections of the text.

- **What are the attributes of students with mathematics difficulties?**

  Students with mathematics difficulties have different disabilities and may display difficulties with language processing, working memory and executive functioning, and cognitive development. Students exhibit problems with a variety of math skills and concepts, including arithmetic and whole number computation, place value, rational numbers, algebraic thinking, and problem solving.

- **What is early number development and how is it taught?**

  Early number development describes a variety of skills and concepts—which involve number sense—that typically emerge and are taught in

preschool, kindergarten, first grade, and second grade. Teaching early numbers involves number and operation concepts.

- **What are arithmetic combinations and how are they taught?**

  Instruction in arithmetic combinations consists of developing declarative and procedural knowledge and conceptual understanding. In the elementary grades, students are taught different strategies, such as counting on, for learning these arithmetic combinations.

- **What is place value and how is it taught?**

  Place value refers to the base-ten system, which is an important component of mathematics instruction. Teaching place value involves the use of manipulatives and activities to promote the concept of regrouping and the base-ten system.

What is whole-number computation and how is it taught?

Whole-number computation requires an understanding of the relationship between numbers and place value, estimating, determining the reasonableness of answers, and using appropriate algorithms. Teaching whole number computation involves error analysis to determine remedial strategies, the use of manipulatives, and strategies or algorithms for solving problems.

What are rational numbers and how are they taught?

Rational numbers include the whole numbers and integers, numbers that can be written as the quotient of two integers, a ÷ b, where b is not zero, and fractions, decimals, and percentages. Teaching involves the use of manipulatives and opportunities to practice the concepts associated with rational numbers.

What is algebra and how is it taught?

Algebra uses mathematical statements to describe relationships between things that vary over time. Algebraic reasoning and the development of algebraic concepts require the use of models and algebraic symbols to represent problems and quantitative relationships and strategies to construct and solve simple to complex equations.

What is problem solving and how is it taught?

Problem solving is a process that involves understanding word problem structures and how to translate these structures into equations to solve the problem. Problem solving is taught through various strategies and should include real-world problems.

$SAGE edge™ Test your understanding of chapter content. Take the practice quiz. edge.sagepub.com/bryant

REVISIT THE OPENING CHALLENGE

Check your answers to the Reflection Questions from the Opening Challenge and revise them on the basis of what you have learned.

1. What mathematical learning characteristics might be contributing to the students' learning difficulties?

2. How can Ms. Hart and Mrs. Reid use the features of effective mathematics instruction to structure their lessons?

3. What instructional adaptations can be implemented to help students access the mathematics curriculum?

4. What suggestions do you have on ways in which these teachers can monitor student progress?

KEY TERMS

base ten, 476

diagnostic teaching, 489

dyscalculia, 467

executive functioning, 473

long-term memory, 473

number sense, 467

partial products, 498

think aloud, 481

working memory, 473

$SAGE edge™ Review key terms with eFlashcards. edge.sagepub.com/bryant

PROFESSIONAL STANDARDS AND LICENSURE

For a complete description of Professional Standards and Licensure, please see Appendix on page 569.

CEC Initial Preparation Standards

Standard 1: Learner Development and Individual Learning Differences

Standard 3: Curricular Content Knowledge

Standard 4: Assessment

Standard 5: Instructional Planning and Strategies

INTASC Core Principles

Standard 1: Learner Development

Standard 2: Learning Differences

Standard 4: Content Knowledge

Standard 6: Assessment

Standard 7: Planning for Instruction

Standard 8: Instructional Strategies

Standard 9: Professional Learning and Ethical Practice

Praxis II: Education of Exceptional Students: Core Content Knowledge

I. Understanding Exceptionalities: Human development and behavior

III. Delivery of Services to Students: Background knowledge

COMMON CORE STATE STANDARDS

Mathematical Practices

- Make sense of problems and persevere in solving them.
- Reason abstractly and quantitatively.
- Construct viable arguments and critique the reasoning of others.
- Model with mathematics.
- Use appropriate tools strategically.
- Attend to precision.
- Look for and make use of structure.
- Look for and express regularity in repeated reasoning.

Domains

- Counting and Cardinality K.CC
- Operations and Algebraic Thinking K, 1,2,3,4,5.OA
- Number and Operations in

- Base Ten K, 1,2,3,4,5.NBT
- Number and Operations—Fractions 3,4,5.NF
- Ratios and Proportional Relationships 6,7.RP

- The Number System 6,7,8.NS
- Expressions and Equations 6,7,8.EE
- Functions 8,HS.F
- Measurement and Data K,1,2,3,4,5.MD
- Geometry K,1,2,3,4,5,6,7,8,HS.G

- Statistics and Probability 6,7,8,HS.SP
- Number and Quantity HS
- Algebra HS
- Modeling HS

Review ➡ Practice ➡ Improve

Get the tools you need to sharpen your study skills. Access practice quizzes, eFlashcards, video, and multimedia: **edge.sagepub.com/bryant**

12

FACILITATING CONTENT-AREA INSTRUCTION AND STUDY SKILLS

LEARNING OBJECTIVES

After studying this chapter, you will be able to answer the following questions:

- What difficulties do students demonstrate with content-area instruction?

- How can teachers teach content-area vocabulary and concepts?

- How can teachers teach students to monitor their reading comprehension?

- How can students learn from textbook instruction?

- How can teachers promote student participation?

- How can teachers help students with difficulties in study skills?

- What are ways to facilitate memorization and test taking?

ELEMENTARY GRADES Mr. Davis is in his 13th year of teaching fifth grade in a middle-class suburban school district whose demographics reflect a rich cultural diversity. Fewer than 30% of enrolled students are eligible for free or reduced-cost meals. Several of Mr. Davis's 27 students have learning disabilities, and two are being referred for possible ADHD. Reviewing results from the survey he gave the class, Mr. Davis found that few had time management skills or strategies to help them understand content-area expository texts. He reflects, *"Most of my students have good decoding skills and can read fairly fluently. However, clearly I have to help them read their content textbooks successfully. Time management skills showed similarly poor results on the survey. My students did not identify a plan for taking notes or studying for tests, and few spend uninterrupted time studying. Those who have learning disabilities are extremely capable, but they need help to benefit from content-area instruction and to implement effective study skills. Some of my English language learners also need help with vocabulary and comprehension strategies for textbook reading if they are to avoid being at a serious disadvantage when they go into middle school next year."*

SECONDARY GRADES Mrs. Marks is in her ninth year of teaching honors and general history in the 10th, 11th, and 12th grades in an urban school district. Her students span a range of academic abilities, and most are eligible for free or reduced-cost lunch. Several have reading disabilities, one has a mild developmental disability, and several are English language learners. Her classes range in size from 15 to 37 students and encompass many ethnic and linguistic backgrounds. Mrs. Marks recognizes that students need strategies to learn the content and concepts in their history textbooks. She wants to prepare them to handle the demands of a postsecondary education, but many cannot describe what good note-taking and test-preparation practices look like or how to budget their time. She reflects, *"I use the textbooks as a starting point for my teaching and build on the information in them through lectures and hands-on activities. History has to come alive for my students, not just be a recounting of the past. But my students have to be able to grasp the concepts and learn the vocabulary from the text to understand what I am teaching."*

REFLECTION QUESTIONS In your journal, write down your answers to the following questions. After completing the chapter, check your answers and revise them on the basis of what you have learned.

1. What difficulties might students in both teachers' classes exhibit with regard to content-area instruction and study skills?

2. How can the teachers effectively work with their students to help them become efficient learners in content-area instruction and study skills?

3. How can these teachers provide adapted lessons to students who require intensive intervention, while keeping the rest of the class busy with relevant work?

4. How can study skills assessment be used to identify how students, including struggling students, become more efficient learners?

As students progress from the upper elementary grades to middle school and high school, a new pattern evolves in which teachers teach their content-area material and students employ study skills such as taking notes and learning subject matter. Students are now required to read textbooks at their grade level or above; write reports and papers, often using technology such as laptops, desktop computers, or tablets; take notes, often using portable devices such as tablets or smartphones in a library; and participate in discussions and activities. They must also complete homework, take tests, conduct research, and manage their time across multiple subject areas. Because teachers will cover a great deal of instructional content, the pace of instruction may not match the learning needs of struggling students who require a lot of practice to master material. Thus, students with special learning needs may be challenged to keep up with their classmates.

Content-area instruction focuses on teaching students subject knowledge in areas such as mathematics, social studies, science, and literature. Secondary teachers use various instructional approaches for teaching content-area material to students. For example, middle and high school content-area instruction is often teacher directed; that is, teachers present lectures on textbook content, and students read their textbooks to identify important facts and concepts in preparation for weekly tests (Bryant, Bryant, Kim, & Hou, 2015). Content-area instruction may also include student-centered activities, which actively engage students in the learning process to solve problems, discuss issues, and create products. Teachers focus more of their time on facilitating student learning through hands-on activities, questioning, and discussions. Thus, in content-area classes, students must be able to read and understand textbooks and engage in activities such as class discussions and questioning.

To learn from textbooks, teachers' lectures, and class discussions, students must use effective study skills. "Study skills are specific skills employed to acquire, record, remember, and use information efficiently" (Hoover & Patton, 2007, p. 2). Students must also be able to manage their time and concentrate in class and while they are studying. They must be able to listen effectively to lectures and discussions so they can distinguish important from irrelevant information to take notes. They must know how to memorize information and take objective and short-answer tests to pass their classes. Unfortunately, study skills are not often directly taught (Lavenstein, 2015); rather, students may have to acquire these skills by getting tips from helpful teachers, peers, or parents.

We know that secondary teachers who teach in inclusive settings must help all students access and learn the general education curriculum. Because of the problems many students demonstrate with literacy skills, there is increasing emphasis at the state and national levels on the literacy needs of this group of students and on identifying ways to help them learn content-area material. Teachers want strategies to help their students comprehend material in textbooks, including key concepts and terminology, and to engage in classroom activities that lead to successful learning (Bryant et al., 2015; Vaughn & Bos, 2015).

In this chapter, we provide an overview of content-area instruction and study skills, and you will learn about the difficulties faced by students who struggle in these areas. Instructional strategies and adaptations based on the ADAPT framework are provided to help you teach students who need extra instructional support.

WHAT DIFFICULTIES DO STUDENTS DEMONSTRATE WITH CONTENT-AREA INSTRUCTION?

Reading and understanding content in textbooks is one of the major challenges for students with reading difficulties. Many struggling older students read well below grade level and have difficulty learning content (Bryant et al., 2015; Vaughn et al., 2010). They lack strategies for learning vocabulary and concepts, monitoring their reading, and tackling content in textbooks. Activities that demand discussion and small-group participation may also be problematic because students have not learned the content well enough to contribute.

In terms of vocabulary and concept knowledge, all students will not learn meanings at the same rate. Those who have reading disabilities will have poorer vocabularies than better readers, because a great deal of vocabulary learning occurs through reading different types of materials. Thus, the gap between good and poor readers will widen over time (Stone & Urquhart, 2008). Students who lack strategies for learning vocabulary and concepts typically are not familiar with the multiple meanings of words, word origins, or derivational meanings, that is, meanings of words that are formed from other words, sometimes adding prefixes, suffixes, or inflectional endings. Using a dictionary to look up the meanings of words and using context clues in text may not be helpful strategies. Dictionaries may be too difficult to understand, or the context may not provide helpful clues for figuring out word meanings.

Reading comprehension calls on us to think and construct meaning before, during, and after reading by integrating information from the author with our own background knowledge (Clewell, 2015). Self-monitoring reading comprehension requires many skills. Readers must activate their prior knowledge about a topic, question themselves, identify main ideas and supporting details, paraphrase, and summarize information. Good readers monitor their understanding of reading as they read text, and they use strategies to promote comprehension and retention (Honig, Diamond, & Gutlohn, 2008). We know that students who struggle with monitoring their reading comprehension do

VIDEO CASE 12.1

Building Prior Knowledge in the Content Areas

1. In the video, Jan Evans stimulates her students' prior knowledge of food that grows on farms in Texas. What methods does she use to activate and enhance their prior knowledge before she introduces the lesson?

2. How does Ms. Evans incorporate authentic language learning experiences, such as reading, writing, speaking, thinking, and listening, in her content-area instruction? In what ways will these opportunities benefit her students?

not establish a purpose for reading or activate background knowledge. They lack self-questioning abilities to ensure comprehension, and their summarizing strategies are deficient (Schumaker & Deshler, 2006). Any one of these problems can seriously interfere with reading text and learning new concepts. Combined, they impose serious reading challenges on struggling students.

Content-area instruction in science, history, and social studies that focuses primarily on the textbook as a source of information assumes students can read and comprehend **expository text**, which is explanatory/factual in structure and includes multisyllabic, technical words; various expository text structures (such as cause/effect, compare/contrast); and concepts and facts (Schumaker & Deshler, 2006). Research has shown a strong relationship between students' understanding of text structure and reading comprehension (Butler, Urrutia, Buenger, & Hunt, 2010). Students with reading difficulties do not understand text structures and thus have difficulty getting meaning from their content-area reading materials. They do not take advantage of the physical features of the text, such as headings, tables, boldfaced terms, and chapter organizers and summaries.

Finally, in classrooms where teachers include student-centered activities, learners with special needs may be challenged by instruction that requires group interactions, discussions, and product development. For example, students may not possess the basic reading and writing skills to function well in group work. They may not be able to make connections to or remember previously taught material from an earlier chapter or unit that is now integrated into group activities. Difficulty understanding figurative and literal meanings and trouble distinguishing **connotative meanings**—associated meanings that enrich a word's primary meaning—from **denotative meanings**—dictionary definitions—may hamper students' ability to understand readings and engage in discussions. Let's turn now to ways to teach content-area vocabulary and concepts.

HOW CAN TEACHERS TEACH CONTENT-AREA VOCABULARY AND CONCEPTS?

Good readers acquire vocabulary rapidly during their school years (Honig & Gutlohn, 2008). They learn about 3,000 new words each year as they read content-area materials and read independently. By the time they graduate from high school, most will have encountered more than 88,500 word families (consisting of a base word and its derivatives, such as *success* and *successfully*), many during the course of their independent reading (Beck, McKeown, & Kucan, 2013).

Each content area has its own concepts and technical vocabulary, the language students must learn if they are to comprehend specific information. A concept is a general idea or understanding; it is a crucial word or phrase critical for grasping the content. Technical vocabulary includes words that relate specifically to each content area. For example, in history, students must understand the meaning of the

Content Area Inclusion

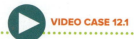

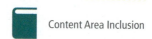

Content Area Inclusion

technical term *transcontinental* as they read about westward migration and railroad expansion in the United States. They also need to understand the relationship between *transcontinental* and migratory patterns and the reasons people migrated west. To learn content-area material, students need strategies to develop an understanding of the meaning of concepts, in this case *migration*, and their relationships to the content and the meaning of vocabulary words (Honig & Gutlohn, 2008). Let's review some ideas for teaching technical vocabulary and concepts.

Teaching the content-area vocabulary is a critical component of promoting reading comprehension. What method is this teacher using to teach vocabulary? What other methods might be helpful?

TEACHING TECHNICAL VOCABULARY AND CONCEPTS

Vacca, Vacca, and Mraz (2014) provided suggestions for helping students learn the meanings of new words and concepts that they encounter in content-area texts. We have blended these suggestions with the adaptation categories from the ADAPT framework:

- **Instructional delivery:** Present new vocabulary in semantically related groups, which are groups of words with meaningful relationships (see the semantic feature analysis grid in Table 12.1; Stahl & Nagy, 2006).

- **Instructional delivery:** Teach students the meaning of the prefixes and the Greek and Latin roots used most frequently in specific content areas. For example, in social studies, teach *trans* (over, across, beyond), *geo* (earth), and *port* (carry); in science, teach *bio* (life), *ex* (from, former), and *meter* (measure).

- **Instructional activity:** Have students link new vocabulary with their background knowledge by describing what they already know about the topic (Beck et al., 2013).

- **Instructional activity:** Have students make up sentences using new vocabulary (Stahl & Nagy, 2006).

- **Instructional materials:** Have students develop word lists or banks.

- **Instructional materials:** Have students use typographic cues such as footnotes, italics, boldface print, and parenthetical definitions to define words.

- **Instructional materials:** Have students use visual displays, including graphic organizers such as **hierarchical charts** (charts with broader concepts listed first, connected to supporting narrower concepts), **Venn**

Teaching Vocabulary and Concepts

diagrams (intersecting shapes that show how concepts are similar and different), **semantic maps** (maps or webs of related words, vocabulary, concepts), and graphs.

- **Instructional delivery:** Help English language learners by teaching academic language.

CONSIDERING *diversity*

TEACHING STUDENTS WHO ARE GIFTED AND TALENTED

Although secondary students who are gifted and/or talented (GT) may take advanced placement (AP) classes, you may find that your class includes students who are GT. Bauer, Benkstein, Pittel, and Koury (n.d.) provided a number of recommendations that can be used to meet these students' unique needs. These suggestions are examples of good teaching and can be used with many students.

- **Compact the curriculum and provide enrichment activities**. Provide environments that are stimulating and address students' cognitive, physical, emotional, and social needs in the curriculum. Let the students move quickly through the required curriculum content and onto more advanced material. Allow for academic rigor.

- **Allow students to pursue independent projects based on their own individual interests.** Assign independent projects based on your students' ability level. Encourage creativity and original thinking among gifted students. Allow them to explore ways of connecting unrelated issues in creative ways.

- **Teach interactively**. Have students work together, teach one another, and actively participate in their own and their classmates' education. Note: This does not advocate gifted children being peer tutors in the classroom; the gifted student should be challenged as well.

SOURCE: Adapted from Bauer et al. (n.d.).

Emphasis should be on working together in the classroom. Cluster gifted children together as a table within your classroom and utilize advanced materials, as well as other suggested resources and modification, to meet their exceptional needs.

- **Explore multiple points of view about contemporary topics and provide students with opportunities to analyze and evaluate material.** Allow open forums and debates in the classroom about controversial issues. Utilize specialized training to ensure your ability to meet the needs of gifted students. Share personal interests with all students, to enrich and expand their world.

- **Do not assign extra work to gifted children who finish assignments early.** This is unfair and frustrating to them. Simply offering more of the same only restricts further learning. Instead, allow those children to work on independent projects or other unfinished work when they finish an assignment early.

- **Consider team teaching, collaboration, and consultation with other teachers.** Use the knowledge, skills, and support of other educators or professionals in the schools. In addition, attend professional development sessions that offer strategies to meet the needs of students who are gifted and/or talented.

SEMANTIC FEATURE ANALYSIS—CIVIL WAR BATTLES

INSTRUCTIONAL OBJECTIVE

The student will create a graphic display to connect a concept to related key vocabulary terms.

INSTRUCTIONAL CONTENT

Vocabulary from lessons

INSTRUCTIONAL MATERIALS

Concept, semantic feature analysis grid, vocabulary

INSTRUCTIONAL DELIVERY

Grouping: Whole class for initial instruction; small groups for practice and sharing

TEACHING PROCEDURES

1. Identify the concept to teach.

2. Model how to complete a semantic feature analysis grid.

3. List the related vocabulary words down the left-hand column, and write the names of the features across the top row.

4. Review the vocabulary words to see whether they contain any of the features listed under characteristics; if so, have the students put a + in the corresponding box. If not, have students put a − in the box.

5. Have students provide a reason why they chose to put + or − in the box.

6. Have students work in small groups to complete a semantic feature analysis grid for a concept to be studied and related vocabulary words.

7. Have students explain their grids to the class.

A completed semantic feature analysis grid for some of the Civil War battles is shown in Table 12.1.

PROGRESS MONITORING

Give students key concepts from a lesson, and have them generate related vocabulary.

See BONUS Instructional Strategy 12.1 for an effective strategy related to the keyword mnemonics.

SOURCE: Vacca et al. (2014).

- **Instructional delivery:** Provide opportunities for gifted and talented students to work together to develop and expand their content vocabularies.

Now we examine specific instructional strategies to promote the understanding of content-area concepts and related vocabulary.

EVIDENCE-BASED INSTRUCTIONAL STRATEGIES

The following evidence-based instructional strategy provides effective ways to help students learn the meanings of technical words and concepts.

The semantic feature analysis grid is implemented as part of instruction. Returning to our Opening Challenge, recall the issues Mrs. Marks faces with her class in terms of reading and vocabulary. The ADAPT in Action feature shows how she adapts instruction to address Samantha's needs.

Now we focus on ways in which students can monitor their own reading comprehension.

··································

BONUS Instructional Strategy
12.1: Keyword Mnemonics

| TABLE 12.1 | SEMANTIC FEATURE ANALYSIS GRID |

Concept: Civil War Battles	Characteristics			
	Fought in South	South Victories	1863	Ulysses S. Grant Involved
Vicksburg	+	–	+	+
Gettysburg	–	–	+	–
First Bull Run	+	+	–	–
Chattanooga (3rd)	+	–	+	+

ADAPT *in action*

SAMANTHA: ORGANIZING TO LEARN

Samantha is a student in Mrs. Marks's class. She was diagnosed as having learning disabilities that affect spoken language (with particular deficits in listening) and reasoning and thinking (executive functioning). This diagnosis explains in part why she gets confused with verbal directions and is extremely disorganized.

Mrs. Marks finds Samantha one of her greatest challenges. "She is so bright but seemingly doesn't care a bit about her schoolwork. I know that's not the case, because she often shares with me her frustration at not being able to get straight A's. She likes to read when she can find her books, but she is constantly missing assignment due dates and misplacing items needed for each assignment. She also loses her completed assignment when she does get something done. Her attention span is short compared with that of the other students, which affects her ability to listen to directions and her peers. Sustaining attention on reading varies; thus, her comprehension abilities vary. Tackling new vocabulary is also hampered by her difficulties focusing and keeping her attention on her reading. The referral for an ADHD evaluation may reveal why she has organization and concentration difficulties, which in turn affect her academics."

Following the lesson, Mrs. Marks reviewed the progress-monitoring data for each student. Given Samantha's difficulties with the reading assignment, Mrs. Marks decides to use the ADAPT framework to make decisions about the next steps in instruction for Samantha. Consider the ADAPT framework, and then identify adaptations that might be useful.

A **Ask, "What am I requiring the student to do?"** Mrs. Davis noted, "Students have to use the visual display, semantic feature analysis, to connect the concept of Civil War battles with related words and ideas in print."

D **Determine the prerequisite skills of the task. Mrs. Marks comments,** "The students need to be able to skim the chapter to find the battles and then read carefully to find out where and when the battles were fought, learn who won them, and determine whether General Ulysses S. Grant was a participant. So, they have to find key vocabulary terms (the names of battles) and comprehend what they read in the sections that describe each battle. Also, they need to have their materials (textbook, notebook, and semantic feature analysis grid) available, take notes, and then decipher what they have written so they can complete their grid. This will take some time, so they must stay on task and keep from being distracted, all the while attending to what they are doing as they work in small groups."

A **Analyze the student's strengths and struggles.** All the students have the requisite skills except Samantha. "She does well working in small groups, but she has trouble understanding the semantic features as we discuss them before moving into small groups. She has no problem reading the text, but she doesn't always have her book or notebook with her. She can take and read her notes. She stays on task for only about 5 to 10 minutes at a time. If she has her book, she should be able to complete part of the grid."

P **Propose and implement adaptations from among the four categories.** Mrs. Marks decides to pair Samantha with another student before the small group work to help her understand the semantic features they will be discussing (instructional delivery). She will have Samantha work on only one battle at a time (instructional content). The day before the lesson, Mrs. Marks will make sure Samantha records in her "schoolwork diary" that she needs to bring her history book to class (instructional material).

T **Test to determine whether the adaptations helped the student accomplish the task.** After the lesson, Mrs. Marks evaluated Samantha's understanding of the lesson. She was satisfied, based on the progress-monitoring data she collected, that Samantha understood semantic features and was able to complete a section of the grid successfully.

Let's take a look at the adaptations Mrs. Marks chose to help Samantha. She decided to continue using them.

ADAPT *framework:* FOR SAMANTHA

ASK "What am I requiring the student to do?"	DETERMINE the prerequisite skills of the task.	ANALYZE the student's strengths and struggles. Strengths	Struggles	PROPOSE and implement adaptations from among the four categories.	TEST to determine whether the adaptations helped the student accomplish the task.
Create a visual display to connect Civil War battles with related words and ideas in print.	1. Be able to skim the chapter to find the battles.	1			
	2. Read carefully about the battles.	2			
	3. Find key vocabulary terms (the battles).		3	3. Instructional delivery: Samantha will be paired with another student before the small group work to help her understand the semantic features they will be discussing and help her stay on task.	3. Check to see if Samantha is understanding the vocabulary and semantic features in text.
	4. Comprehend what is read in the sections that describe each battle.	4			
	5. Have materials available.		5	5. Instructional materials: The day before the work is to be done, Mrs. Marks will make sure Samantha records in her "schoolwork diary" that she needs to bring her history book to class.	5. Check diary for reminder, and monitor her bringing text to class.
	6. Take notes.	6			
	7. Decipher what was written in the notes.	7			
	8. Complete the grid.	8			
	9. Stay on task and keep from being distracted.		9	9. Instructional content: Samantha will work on only one battle at a time.	9. Monitor to ensure that Samantha focuses on one battle at a time.
	10. Work in small groups.	10			

HOW CAN TEACHERS TEACH STUDENTS TO MONITOR THEIR READING COMPREHENSION?

Good readers monitor their understanding of reading as they proceed through the text and use strategies to comprehend and retain the material (Wright, 2010). Students who are able to monitor their comprehension are aware of whether they are understanding and/or remembering what they are reading. Monitoring entails regulating comprehension during reading so students can prevent faulty understanding. It means (a) activating background knowledge, (b) clarifying the purposes for reading, (c) identifying the important information, (d) summarizing information, (e) engaging in self-questioning about the text, (f) using text structure formats to comprehend text, and (g) correcting problems when comprehension is inadequate. Students benefit from instruction on when and how to use different strategies to monitor comprehension so they will be able to fix any comprehension problems. Let's review ways to teach students how to monitor their reading comprehension.

TEACHING STUDENTS TO MONITOR THEIR READING COMPREHENSION

Students should engage in multiple activities before, during, and after reading to ensure that comprehension monitoring is an ongoing process. You can adopt the following suggestions to teach comprehension monitoring. We have blended them with the adaptation categories from the ADAPT framework.

Instructional delivery: Teach students to ask questions before, during, and after reading.

Questions before reading:

- What is my purpose for reading?
- What do I already know about this topic?
- What do I think I will learn about this topic (make predictions)?

Questions during reading:

- Does what I am reading make sense?
- Is this what I expected? Should I revise my predictions or suspend judgment until later?
- How are the important points related to one another? What parts are similar and/or different?
- Should I read on, reread, or stop and use a fix-up strategy? Are there any words I don't understand?

Questions after reading:

- What were the most important points?

VIDEO CASE 12.2

After Reading Strategy

1. How does using the SWBST strategy help Tema Khieu's students to summarize a familiar short story? How can this strategy enhance students' comprehension when they read other texts?

2. What additional methods does Ms. Khieu use to guide her students' reading comprehension? How does she incorporate cooperative learning, mnemonics, and technology into her instruction?

- What is my opinion? How do I feel? Do I agree or disagree?

- What new information did I learn? (Vacca et al., 2014)

Instructional delivery: Help students link background knowledge with topics to be studied before reading. For example,

- Students can make predictions about the reading based on such physical features of the text as pictures, graphs, and headings.

- Students can watch a video that depicts a time era or science concept to be studied.

- Students can make a semantic map (see Figure 12.1) to activate their prior knowledge.

Instructional delivery: Teach students ways to think about the text during reading:

- Students can use the paraphrasing strategy to help monitor their understanding of content in each paragraph (see BONUS Instructional Strategy 12.2 for more information).

FIGURE 12.1 **SEMANTIC MAP FOR SHARKS**

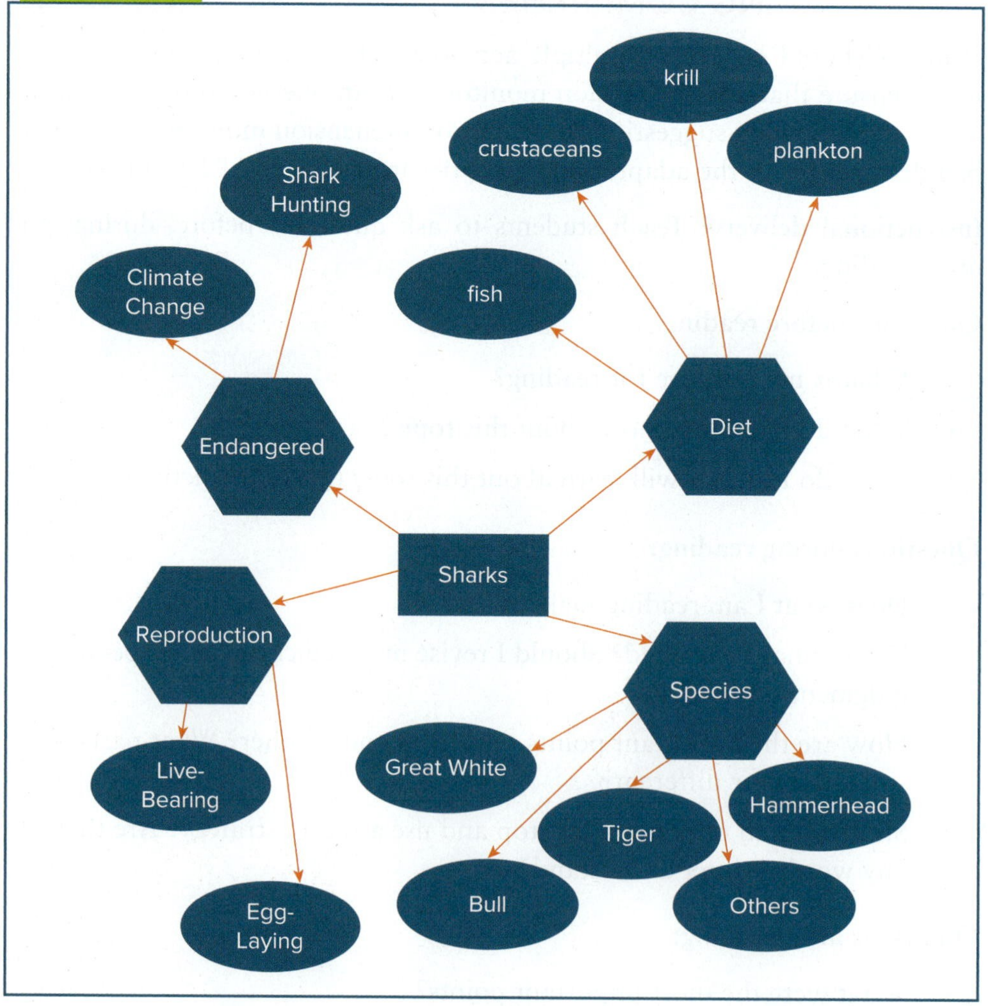

BONUS Instructional Strategy 12.2: Comprehension-Monitoring Activities

- Students can use fix-up strategies to repair faulty comprehension, such as checking their understanding using the questions listed earlier, rereading difficult sentences, and paraphrasing sentences or paragraphs (fix-up strategies were discussed in Chapter 10).

- Students can turn headings into questions and answer the questions after they read sections of the text.

- Students can complete graphic organizers (discussed in the next section) to organize their thoughts about the reading. For instance, Figure 12.2 shows a character map for Stuart Little that was constructed during reading in response to questions about character traits.

Instructional delivery: Help students think about the content after reading. For example,

- Students can summarize text in small chunks, such as chapter sections, and then combine the smaller summaries into a chapter summary.

- Students can write reports to answer questions about the reading.

Now we review specific instructional strategies for comprehension monitoring.

FIGURE 12.2   STUART LITTLE CHARACTER MAP

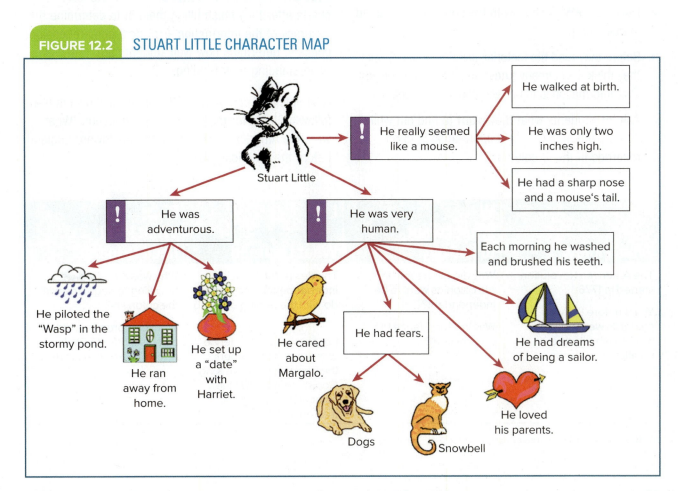

SOURCE: Bryant and Bryant (2011).

KWLS

INSTRUCTIONAL OBJECTIVE: Before, during, and after reading, the students will create a KWLS chart to determine what they know about the topic and what they are learning as they read.

INSTRUCTIONAL CONTENT: Reading comprehension: Activating prior knowledge and acquiring new knowledge

INSTRUCTIONAL MATERIALS: KWLS chart, history text

INSTRUCTIONAL DELIVERY:

Grouping: Whole class group

TEACHING PROCEDURE

1. Determine the core concept.

2. Develop a KWLS chart with the core concept stated in question form.

3. Before they read the material, ask the students what they think they already **know** about the core concept. That information is to be recorded in the K column.

4. Ask the students what they **want** to find out while reading the material. That information is to be recorded in the W column.

5. After reading a portion of the text, return to the KWLS chart and confirm or deny the knowledge in the K (What I know) column.

6. Complete the L (What I learned) column by writing the answers to the questions written in the W (What I want to find out) column and entering other pertinent information that students have **learned** from the reading.

7. Complete the S (What I **still** need to learn) column as they are reading.

8. Repeat steps 5, 6, and 7 until the reading has been completed.

PROGRESS MONITORING: Review students' charts after they finish filling them in to determine the accuracy of the information. Provide a comprehension check to determine how well students are understanding their reading.

A sample of a completed KWLS chart is shown in the following table for the core concept question "What were the American colonists' attitudes toward England before the American Revolution?"

K What I know	W What I want to find out	L What I learned	S What I still need to learn
The American Revolution started in 1776. Years before the war, colonists were unhappy with British rule and taxation.	Why did the people in the colonies want to be independent? Was independence the original goal?	The desire for independence had a lot to do with the feeling of being overtaxed. For some, independence was the goal; for others, the goal was to make King George realize that the colonies needed to be treated fairly.	Why was King George unwilling to negotiate with the colonists? What compromises did the colonists offer to England in return for being less taxed?

SOURCES: KWLS chart adapted from Casareno (2010); D. M. Ogle (1986).

EVIDENCE-BASED INSTRUCTIONAL STRATEGIES

The evidence-based methods in Instructional Strategy 12.2 and BONUS Instructional Strategy 12.2 provide effective ways to help students learn how to monitor their reading comprehension.

Now we return to the Opening Challenge to revisit information about Mr. Davis' class. We will learn how he plans adaptations to the KWLS strategy to help Andre monitor his comprehension of instructional material.

ADAPT *in action*

ANDRE: KWLS

Andre is a student in Mr. Davis's class who knows a great deal about science and how to find the answers to questions. He has great spoken-language skills, both listening and speaking, and can make incredible displays for his class presentations and science fairs. He is a hard worker when it comes to science, but he becomes easily bored with other topics. Andre has a reading disability that makes reading content-area text difficult. He has difficulty with decoding skills and comprehension monitoring, and his reading fluency is slow.

Looking at Instructional Strategy 12.2, think about the challenges Mr. Davis and Andre face in their efforts to meet the instructional objectives associated with completing a KWLS chart. Consider the task associated with the lesson. What is Andre required to do to complete the assigned task and meet the objective? Which of the requisite skills draw on his strengths, and which might be struggles? Examine our sample adaptations, and then think of others that might be ideally suited to Andre and to students with similar characteristics.

Following the lesson, Mr. Davis reviewed the progress-monitoring data for each student and decided to use the ADAPT framework to make decisions about next steps for instruction for Andre.

(A) **Ask, "What am I requiring the student to do?"** Mr. Davis thinks about the task he is having the students complete. "They have to complete each section of the KWLS chart as they read the section on the years leading up to the American Revolution."

(D) **Determine the prerequisite skills of the task.** Mr. Davis comments, "Students have to be able to think about the topic and write down what they know about it. They also need to be able to skim the text and gather clues about the content from headings, key vocabulary terms in boldface print, pictures, and the like, so that they can write down what they need to learn. Then students have to read the text and write down information about what they noted they want to learn. Finally,

(Continued)

(Continued)

all the students have to think about what may still be missing from their readings and write that down on the chart. So what does all that entail? Accessing prior knowledge; skimming; getting clues as they skim and scan; reading individual words; understanding what those words mean, especially key vocabulary terms; comprehending passages; writing legibly; and thinking about what they now know and what they still need to find out."

A **Analyze the student's strengths and struggles.** All the students except Andre have the requisite skills. "Andre has a great memory, so if he already knows something about the topic, he holds his own in a discussion. He can look for bold print and other text features to get a sense of what the passage is about and can identify what he would like to know more about the topic. But when given a textbook to read, he quits before he starts. He lacks important reading skills to do the task. At that point, everything breaks down."

P **Propose and implement adaptations from among the four categories.** Mr. Davis decided to work with Andre alone to help him complete the KWLS chart (instructional delivery). He will have Andre complete the first section by himself. Mr. Davis was at a workshop recently where he heard about a "recordings for the blind and dyslexic" program titled Learning Through Listening that makes CD-ROMs available for students who are blind or who have reading disabilities. Andre qualifies for such a program that can provide electronic books (instructional materials, instructional delivery).

T **Test to determine whether the adaptations helped the student accomplish the task.** Mr. Davis will collect progress-monitoring data to determine whether the adaptations helped Andre access the chapter and complete the KWLS chart.

Before the lesson, Mr. Davis evaluated the activity and determined that Andre's reading disability presented a major challenge to his ability to access print. He decided to make the following adaptations after considering the ADAPT framework.

In the next section, we focus on ways to help students use textbooks effectively.

HOW CAN STUDENTS LEARN FROM TEXTBOOK INSTRUCTION?

Textbooks are an integral part of content-area instruction. They typically consist largely of expository text, although stories (narrative text) are sometimes included to provide a humanistic perspective. For example, in a social studies text, an account of events surrounding the Civil War can be personalized with stories about the effects of the war on individuals and their families.

ADAPT *framework:* FOR ANDRE

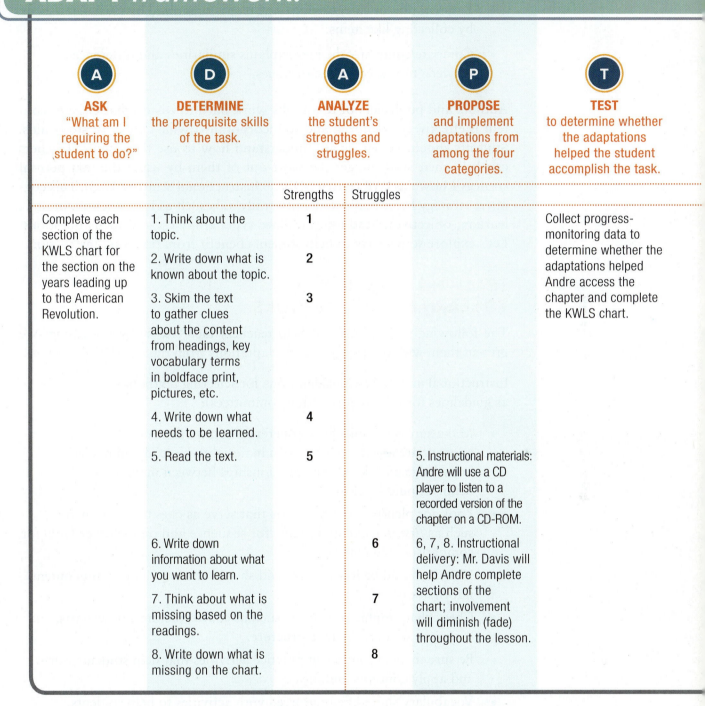

		Strengths	Struggles		
ASK "What am I requiring the student to do?"	**DETERMINE** the prerequisite skills of the task.	**ANALYZE** the student's strengths and struggles.		**PROPOSE** and implement adaptations from among the four categories.	**TEST** to determine whether the adaptations helped the student accomplish the task.
Complete each section of the KWLS chart for the section on the years leading up to the American Revolution.	1. Think about the topic.	1			Collect progress-monitoring data to determine whether the adaptations helped Andre access the chapter and complete the KWLS chart.
	2. Write down what is known about the topic.	2			
	3. Skim the text to gather clues about the content from headings, key vocabulary terms in boldface print, pictures, etc.	3			
	4. Write down what needs to be learned.	4			
	5. Read the text.	5		5. Instructional materials: Andre will use a CD player to listen to a recorded version of the chapter on a CD-ROM.	
	6. Write down information about what you want to learn.		6	6, 7, 8. Instructional delivery: Mr. Davis will help Andre complete sections of the chart; involvement will diminish (fade) throughout the lesson.	
	7. Think about what is missing based on the readings.		7		
	8. Write down what is missing on the chart.		8		

Expository text conveys information in a variety of ways through the use of text structure:

- Problem solution—the text presents a problem and offers possible solutions, usually identifying one solution as most appropriate.
- Description—the text provides details about a topic, person, event, or idea.

- Cause/effect relationships—the text links events (effects) with their causes.

- Enumeration or categorizing—the text is organized by means of lists or by collecting like items.

- Compare/contrast—the text explains similarities and differences between topics, concepts, or issues.

Authors and publishers of textbooks work hard to ensure that chapter content is effectively organized and to incorporate a wide variety of study aids. Students should recognize and understand how to use these tools. Teachers can help their students get the most out of them by using the text perusal strategy known as PARTS (see BONUS Instructional Strategy 12.3). This cognitive strategy helps readers identify study aids such as introduction, outline, learning objectives, headings, boldface type, graphics, and focus questions. Let's explore some ways to help students benefit from textbook instruction.

TEACHING STUDENTS HOW TO LEARN FROM TEXTBOOKS

The following suggestions can help teachers facilitate student learning. We present them with the categories of adaptations from the ADAPT framework.

Instructional materials: Considerations for selecting textbooks (can also serve as guidelines for textbook selection committees):

- Make sure textbooks have coherence (logical flow of ideas) and appropriateness (match between material to be read and reader's knowledge and skills). The relationships between main ideas and details should be clear.

- Look for plenty of **signal words** that serve as cues to text structure, such as *first, second,* and *finally* for sequence and *on the other hand* for comparison and contrast.

- Visuals should be informative and should reinforce important content information.

- Check that graphic organizers such as charts, pictures, flowcharts, and diagrams support the text structure.

- Be sure there are sufficient practice activities that help students learn and apply concepts and ideas.

- Vocabulary should be reinforced with activities to help students develop an understanding of concepts.

Instructional delivery:

- Divide reading assignments into meaningful segments and plan the lesson around these segments.

BONUS Instructional Strategy 12.3:
PARTS Cognitive Strategy

- Introduce the topic by having your students think about what they already know about it (e.g., "What do you know about . . . ? What connections can you make?").

- Have students preview the reading segment by examining the illustrations, headings, and other clues to the content.

- Ask students to make predictions about what they will learn. They may write individual predictions, write with a partner, or contribute to an oral discussion, creating a list of class predictions.

- Have students read the selection and evaluate their predictions. Were their predictions verified? Were they on the wrong track? What evidence supported or contradicted the predictions? Have them discuss their predictions and the content of the reading.

- Close the lesson with a review of the content of the reading and a discussion of the prediction strategies students should use as they read any text.

- Teach words that signal text structures. For example,
  - Sequence—*first, second, next*
  - Cause/Effect—*causes, effects, as a result of*
  - Problem/Solution—*the problem is, the question is, difficulty*
  - Compare/Contrast—*is similar, is different, however, in the same way*
  - Description—*for example, also, another feature*
  - Enumerative—*includes the following*

- Teach text structures using graphic organizers. Model how to use the graphic organizers. Figure 12.3 shows an examples of a graphic organizer that can be used as a study guide and sources of information for test questions.

SOURCE: Instructional strategies that facilitate learning across content areas (n.d.).

Promoting students' participation is an important part of teaching. In the next section, we take a look at ways to engage students in the learning process.

The following list uses the "What's Old" and "What's New" strategy and discusses ways to help students with comprehension monitoring. In the next section, we discuss how teachers can promote student participation in class discussions and activities.

1. Break the class into small groups. Give each group a chapter to review. Instruct students to peruse the topics and special features within their sections.

2. Ask the groups to consider the primary topics covered and list them on a chart under the column headings What's Old and What's New.

FIGURE 12.3   QUESTION EXPLORATION GUIDE FOR THE QUESTION "HOW DO PROBLEMS WITH THE LAYER TEACH US ABOUT HUMAN EFFECTS ON THE ENVIRONMENT?"

Effectiveness of Question Exploration

Text Reference   chapter 7, pages 101-116   **Name:**   Marie David

Course _____

Unit   x _____   **Title** ____ Our Environment _____

Lesson _____   **Critical Question #:** 3 _____   **Date:** 1-25-16

① What is the critical question?

How do problems with the ozone layer teach us about human effect on our environment?

② What are the key terms and explanation?

What is our environment?	All the things surrounding us (air, land, living things)
What is the ozone layer?	Invisible layer of gas that shields us from UV radiation
What is UV?	Ultraviolet radiation, or harmfull rays from the sun
What are CFCs?	Chlorofluorocarbons-chemicals with chlorine

③ What are the supporting questions and answers?

What has happened in the past?	In the past, a protective ozone layer was formed when UV rays hit the oxygen in the air around the earth.
What is a PROBLEM and its CAUSES?	The ozone layer is being destroyed by CFCs we may not even know about in everyday products (cleaning products, foam containers, refrigerator coolants and spray cans).
What are the EFFECTS?	The effects include: 1. physical harm (skin cancer & cataracts) 2. environmental harm (crops and ocean plants) 3. change in weather patterns 4. greenhouse warming of the earth
What are SOLUTIONS?	Solution include: 1. voluntary cutbacks of CFC products 2. use of alternatives to CFCs (HCFCs) 3. world conferences to cut CFCs
What are other concerns?	Some people didn't know or still don't think it's a problem.

④ What is the main idea answer?

People can harm the environment without intending it or even believing it.

⑤ Explore and use the main idea.

How can we explore the facts ourselves?
(Experiments with balloons show that oxygen can be changed to ozone.)

⑥ Extend the main idea to your world.   What can an individual do?
(An individual can decide to do research on which products cause damage to ozone.)

SOURCE: Bulgren, Marquis, Lenz, Schumaker, and Deshler (2009).

To categorize the topics, ask them to consider whether the content has been covered in past classes. There may be some disagreement among group members, so encourage them to develop a consensus.

3. Instruct students upon chart completion to return to the What's Old column and place an asterisk beside topics they have reviewed several times. In the What's New column, ask them to circle items that are so new that they had never heard of them before this exercise.

4. Have each group come forward in turn to display the charts. Allow students to lead their classmates on a chapter walk, pointing out old and new concepts. Encourage them to seek feedback from the class about their lists.

Textbooks are the materials used most often by content-area teachers as the basis for their instruction. What other kinds of materials in this classroom are helping students learn about geography and culture?

SOURCE: Garber-Miller (2006).

HOW CAN TEACHERS PROMOTE STUDENT PARTICIPATION?

Students learn by actively engaging in the learning process through discussions, questioning, and small group activities. Along with textbook instruction, active engagement can help students with learning difficulties understand and interact with the material.

Heather Walport-Glawron wrote an article for the Edutopia.org website in 2012 (updated in 2014) in which she summarized responses from middle-school students to the question "What engages students?" Their answers follow:

1. Let us work with our classmates.

2. Let us work with technology.

3. Connect the real world to the work we do.

4. Love what you do (as a teacher).

5. Get me out of my seat.

6. Bring in visuals.

7. Give us choices.

8. Understand your clients—us!

9. Mix it up!

10. Be human, and have fun (as a teacher).

SOURCE: Adapted from Walport-Glawron (2014).

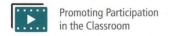

Promoting Participation in the Classroom

Which of these, if any, can you relate to? Do you feel there are important items on this list? What might you add to the list? Think back on your own education. Do you recall any of your teachers (or professors) offering any of these engagement enhancers? Based on what you have learned so far, are there any activities or strategies that you might use in your classroom to promote student engagement?

USING CLASS DISCUSSIONS TO ENGAGE STUDENTS

Teachers can include all students in class discussions through various activities and techniques. Questioning strategies can facilitate discussions by engaging students in asking and answering. Requiring students to write their responses and share their ideas within a small group is good preparation for whole class instruction. Teachers should work among small groups checking for understanding, modeling how to respond to questions, and asking probing questions to stimulate student thinking. The following suggestions can be implemented in all content-area classes. Again, we've incorporated them with the categories of adaptations from the ADAPT framework.

- **Instructional materials/delivery:** Provide a discussion guide with questions students should answer alone, with a partner, or in a small group before class discussions begin. For example, in a small group setting, each group could be responsible for summarizing content for an assigned element of a novel such as setting, characters, problem, and resolution. In social studies or science, students may be assigned a specific part of a chapter to summarize or chapter headings to turn into questions and then answer.

- **Instructional delivery:** Provide a question stem card with stem questions such as "How are _____ and _____ alike and different?" "What explanation can you offer about . . . ?" "Why do you think . . . ?" "How would you describe . . . ?" and a topic, character, event, or issue to go with the stem. Students should prepare an answer to the question before discussion, working with a partner or in a small group.

- **Instructional delivery:** Divide students into small groups and give them one question representing each level of Bloom's taxonomy: knowledge, comprehension, application, analysis, synthesis, and evaluation. Questions can be the same across groups, so when groups share their responses after the activity, the class can identify multiple perspectives about questions that require higher order thinking, such as synthesis and evaluation.

- **Instructional activity:** Have students record their questions about content and put the questions in a box. Draw questions and have students answer the questions.

In the next section, we present information about anchoring instruction as a means for promoting student participation. **Anchored instruction** begins with an event or problem situation (the anchor) presented in a video or movie that provides background and creates a shared experience among students to facilitate learning (Thomas & Rieth, 2011). The anchor can be the main focus or a supplement to facilitate student discussions (Kumar, 2010). Although more research is needed, the technique shows promise for teaching secondary students with academic problems (Bottge et al., 2014). It has been shown to foster students' higher level thinking during class discussions (Thomas & Rieth, 2011). Instructional Strategy 12.3 shows how to use the technique.

Teachers can include all students in class discussions through various activities and techniques. What are some examples of techniques that may be useful in your classroom?

Referring back to the Opening Challenge and issues in Mrs. Marks's class, let us see how she will use the ADAPT framework and anchored instruction using *To Kill a Mockingbird* to ensure Colleen's successful participation in group work.

As noted in Chapter 7, UDL is a powerful means for promoting access to the curriculum for all learners. We have discussed using anchoring instruction as a way to facilitate group participation. Now we present a UDL lesson that focuses on using *To Kill a Mockingbird* and incorporates the UDL principles and checkpoints.

We now turn our attention to study skills, which are critical for successful learning at all grade levels. Students develop study skills in the elementary grades, maintain their use in the middle grades, refine their skills in high school, and generalize the use of study skills in adult contexts (Hoover & Patton, 2007). Students with learning difficulties exhibit problems with study skills. Teachers must be prepared to facilitate the development and use of effective study skills for all students.

HOW CAN TEACHERS HELP STUDENTS WITH DIFFICULTIES IN STUDY SKILLS?

Students with special learning needs must be explicitly taught study skills, because many have not learned how to strategically approach academic tasks in a way that will help them effectively gain and use information taught via text, lecture, and media (IRIS Center, 2015). Managing study and exam preparation time is critically important for success in secondary and postsecondary classes. Those with special needs may demonstrate problems with time management because they organize their time poorly, are easily distracted from tasks or

Creative Study Skills

ANCHORING INSTRUCTION

INSTRUCTIONAL OBJECTIVE: The students will learn content using an anchor and present their knowledge in a group presentation.

INSTRUCTIONAL CONTENT: Expository or narrative text presented through a video

INSTRUCTIONAL METERIALS: Video anchor, computers, writing materials

INSTRUCTIONAL DELIVERY:

Grouping: Whole class or small group

TEACHING PROCEDURES

1. Identify a video that corresponds with the text to be read. In this case, we will use *To Kill a Mockingbird* as the video anchor to teach human relationships, social studies events (post–World War I, World War II, the Great Depression), and themes such as racism, authority, power, and socioeconomic status. Students will be divided into small groups, and each group will work to prepare a multimedia presentation about researched topics that will be presented to the class after the assignments are completed.

2. PHASE 1: Setting the Stage. This phase consists of activities to help students develop interviewing and research skills for their final multimedia project. Students learn how to conduct interviews, ask questions to research a topic, and use their background knowledge to learn more about a topic. As an example, the jigsaw cooperative learning procedure (see Chapter 10) can be used, where members of one jigsaw group conduct research about the author, in this case Harper Lee. Part of the multimedia presentation can include a video where, after students return to their primary groups, one member of the group interviews "Ms. Lee" about her life and how her life experiences may have influenced her writing. Table 12.2 shows the three procedures employed in Phase 1.

TABLE 12.2	ANCHORING INSTRUCTION PROCEDURES FOR PHASE 1

Learning How to Interview

1. Ask students to bring in boxes that contain two to four objects they feel best represent them. Let them brainstorm possible items to include in their boxes.

2. Tell students that today they will work in small groups to learn more about each other by examining the objects each person brought in and by asking questions about the objects. They should ask different types of questions. These might be "why," "how," or "what" questions, or they might come up with other types of questions.

3. Divide students into groups of three. Assign students the following roles: recorder, question asker, responder. These roles will be changed every time.

4. Students begin questioning another student about his or her object box. Allow approximately 10 minutes per person for questioning. Encourage students to ask questions that explore issues such as "Who is this person?" "What do these objects tell me about him or her?"

5. Once the small groups of three have finished questioning, join each group with another group of three. Ask this group of six the following:

   - What types of questions gave you the most information about a person? Why?
   - What types of questions didn't seem to give you much information? Why not?
   - Ask students to share their responses from the small group sessions, and record their responses on paper.

Learning How to Research a Topic

1. Show students a picture depicting a scene from the 1930s.

2. Ask students the following, encouraging them to discuss the photograph:

   - What's going on in this picture?
   - What do you see?
   - Who are the people in this picture?
   - What do you think they are doing? Why?
   - When do you think this took place?
   - Where do you think it took place?
   - How would you describe what is going on in the photograph?

3. Tell students to think of the photograph as similar to an object box. Different elements of the photograph come together to give us a portrait of a particular time and place, just as different objects come together to give us a portrait of a person. Ask the following:

   - What did the photographer want to capture when she took this picture? What is she trying to show us?
   - What message do you think she wanted to convey?
   - What elements of the photograph are essential for our understanding of that message?
   - What information is missing? (What are you wondering about that would help your understanding of the photographer's message?)

4. Record students' questions on the board.

Transitioning to the Anchor

Following student responses, return to the photograph. Ask students the following:

   - Do you think this picture is typical of the 1930s? Why or why not?
   - What have you learned about this time in history?
   - What are you learning about the kinds of questions that get you the most information?
   - What did you learn about people in the 1930s?
   - Who had power? Who had money? How did people get along with one another?

---

3. PHASE 2: Watching the Anchor/Retelling. This phase occurs over several days and introduces students to the themes of the story, for example, power, money, and human relationships in *To Kill a Mockingbird*. After watching the film, students retell the events and identify scenes they think are important to the story. Retelling descriptions are written on sentence strips and ordered according to their place in the story. If students recognize that information is missing, additional strips can be created and added to the descriptions. Students answer questions about the movie related to the themes, setting, characters, and events. Students then engage in a discussion to confirm conclusions and clarify misconceptions.

4. PHASE 3: Segmenting. In this phase, students segment the movie into scenes and label them for use during Phase 5, when they will conduct their research. Strategies used for segmenting include looking for logical breaks between scenes based on plot, scene changes, and character appearances. For instance, if the students choose Mayella Ewell's courtroom scene as a segment, it might be labeled "Mayella's Testimony."

(Continued)

(Continued)

TABLE 12.3	ANCHORING INSTRUCTION, PHASE 4, CHARACTERIZATION

Character Research Procedure

1. Explain to the students that they will use video segments to develop portraits of important characters in *To Kill a Mockingbird*. Ask the class to identify the main characters of the story.

   - What are the most important relationships in *To Kill a Mockingbird*?

2. Model how to create a character web and how to find scenes using film segments.

For example:

   - Choose Mayella Ewell. On the board, create a character web around her name. Ask students to identify Mayella's qualities, her relationships with others, her power in Macon, and her financial situation.
   - Choose the scene from the movie that best illustrates Mayella's character in terms of money, power, and human relationships (Mayella's courtroom testimony).

3. Explain that students will choose a character and, working in groups, will find the most important scenes for that character that reveal money, power, and human relationships.

4. Have groups present their findings on characters to the class.

---

5. **PHASE 4: Characterization.** In this phase, students conduct character analysis. Students work in small groups, and each group chooses one character to portray. The students create an acrostic for their character. For example, for Scout: S—secretive, c—curious, o—outward, u—unpredictable, and t— tomboy. Students identify scenes from the video that depict that character's personality and show how the character relates to the themes of power, money, and human relationships. Characterization activities are shown in Table 12.3.

6. **PHASE 5: Student Research and Presentations.** Students work in small groups to develop a research question on issues that stem from their discussions. Group members conduct research to gather information to answer their questions and create a multimedia presentation. Students must use library and Internet resources. For instance, one question might be, "How did the stock market work?" Students would research this question and relate it to the stock market crash that occurred during the Great Depression in the United States, the period of time depicted in *To Kill a Mockingbird*. The teacher helps students with researching their topic and developing their presentation. A group multimedia presentation is the final event.

SOURCE: H. J. Rieth, D. P. Bryant, C. K. Kinzer, L. K. Colburn, S.-J. Hur, P. Hartman, & H.-S. Choi (2003), An analysis of the impact of anchored instruction on teaching and learning activities in two ninth-grade language arts classes, *Remedial and Special Education, 24*(3), 173–184. PRO-ED. Reprinted with permission.

---

projects, lack "stick-to-it-ness" or persistence, and are unable to organize their ideas into a cohesive plan of action (Bryant et al., 2015). Difficulty in any one of these areas results in trouble completing a task. When students have multiple difficulties, their time management problems are aggravated.

ADAPT *in action*

COLLEEN: CREATING A GROUP PRESENTATION

Colleen, a ninth grader in an urban high school, has a mild developmental disability that manifests itself in numerous ways. She reads at the fourth-grade level, struggles with abstractions, has trouble with fine motor activities, and has some social skills challenges. At the same time, she is eager to please and interacts well with her fellow students. She takes notes when she is assigned a task and has a time management calendar that she uses regularly. She is adept with technology and spends two hours a night on the Internet, researching information for school and chatting with her online friends.

In thinking about Instructional Strategy 12.3, consider the activity's task and requisite skills. Which fall within Colleen's areas of strength, and which might be problematic? Examine our list of sample adaptations, and then think of others that may help Colleen and other students with similar characteristics.

Following the lesson, Mrs. Marks reviewed the progress-monitoring data for each student and decided to use the ADAPT framework to make decisions about next steps for instruction for Colleen.

(A) **Ask, "What am I requiring the student to do?"** Mrs. Marks thinks, "The objective of the lesson is for students to use research and technology skills to create a presentation on a topic related to *To Kill a Mockingbird.* Students have to learn skills to do their part of the project, complete their part of the project, and share new information with their peers."

(D) **Determine the prerequisite skills of the task.** Mrs. Marks notes, "Students have to be able to work in small groups to obtain information and then share that information when they convene in their original groups. They have to be able to access the Internet, read the content presented, extract useful information, determine how to use that information when they return to their jigsaw groups (see Instructional Strategy 12.2), know what to present to their fellow students, and then use their individual skills to fulfill their roles. I want not only to facilitate their success but also to provide explicit instruction and give them practice opportunities."

(A) **Analyze the student's strengths and struggles.** All the students have the prerequisite skills except Colleen, but even she has skills she can utilize. "Colleen works well in small groups, and I have made sure she will be the webmaster, because she is knowledgeable about searching the Internet. She knows PowerPoint also. But I think she'll struggle with accessing online information, because the information found online may be written at a reading level that exceeds her abilities. She will also need help in her presentation to other members of the jigsaw cooperative learning group."

(Continued)

(Continued)

Propose and implement adaptations from among the four categories. Mrs. Marks decides to work with Colleen alone before her group convenes so that they can access websites containing webmaster information. In that way, Colleen will have prior knowledge she can use. Mrs. Marks will also pair Colleen with another member of the group to jointly prepare their presentation to their original groups. And she has asked Colleen's mother to edit Colleen's work and suggest modifications to improve the final project. All these steps are adaptations of instructional delivery. Mrs. Marks sees no reason to adapt the instructional content. She will have Colleen verbally record notes into a tape recorder (instructional materials), rather than writing notes in a notebook. She will instruct Colleen to speak softly into the recorder so as not to disturb others as they take their notes.

Test to determine whether the adaptations helped the student accomplish the task. Mrs. Marks will collect progress-monitoring data to assess whether the adaptations helped Colleen learn the material and share it with her classmates.

After the lesson, Mrs. Marks evaluated the extent to which Colleen met the instructional objective. She was satisfied, on the basis of the progress-monitoring data, that Colleen fulfilled her cooperative learning role of webmaster. In fact, Colleen's group achieved the highest score.

Listening is a skill students use to obtain meaning from spoken language, to promote more efficient study habits, and to foster communication in general. Listening is not synonymous with paying attention, nor is it synonymous with hearing, although both contribute to good listening.

Research studies show that despite the amount of time students spend listening to someone and its importance as a study skill, teachers spend little time on listening instruction (Hoover & Patton, 2007). The ability to listen, to receive and understand information, is a crucial skill for students to be taught explicitly. You can facilitate listening skills in your students.

Students must listen to take notes during lectures or discussions and to follow directions (Hoover & Patton, 2007). Listening requires understanding spoken language, including sentence structure and vocabulary. Students must also be able to grasp the meaning of the message by organizing the content and ignoring irrelevant information. According to Hoover and Patton (2007), students with special learning needs may exhibit the following listening problems:

- Are unable to concentrate during listening activities.
- Frequently lose attention due to visual distractions during listening activities.

BONUS Instructional Strategy
12.4: Conducting Research

ADAPT framework: FOR COLLEEN

A	**D**	**A**		**P**	**T**
ASK "What am I requiring the student to do?"	**DETERMINE** the prerequisite skills of the task.	**ANALYZE** the student's strengths and struggles.		**PROPOSE** and implement adaptations from among the four categories.	**TEST** to determine whether the adaptations helped the student to accomplish the task.
		Strengths	Struggles		
Create a presentation on a topic about *To Kill a Mockingbird*.	1. Assume a role in a cooperative learning group.	1			Collect progress-monitoring data to ensure that the information collected and recorded is correct.
	2. Work in small groups (jigsaw).	2			
	3. Access the Internet.	3			
	4. Read the content presented to obtain information.		4	4. Access screen reader software to obtain information online.	
	5. Take notes.		5	5. Utilize speech-to-text technology.	
	6. Share information with the original group members.	6			
	7. Help create a PowerPoint presentation.	7			

- Frequently lose attention due to auditory distractions during listening activities.
- Are unable to identify primary and secondary points in verbal messages.
- Are unable to follow verbal directions when repeated several times.
- Are unable to state purposes of a listening activity. (p. 67)

As students listen to lectures and discussions, they are expected to take notes to study. Those with special learning needs may have trouble taking notes for several reasons (Boyle, 2011). They may not be able to identify the most important information or write fast enough to keep up with the lecturer. Even

UDL *in action*

Universal Design for Learning Lesson

Note: This UDL-based lesson was developed, in part, using the CAST UDL Lesson Builder (http://lessonbuilder.cast.org/create.php?op=new).

The UDL framework (version 2.0) is comprised of three main principles (I. Representation, II. Action and Expression, and III. Engagement). Each principle has three guidelines and several checkpoints that define them further. In this lesson plan, we delineate how various instructional strategies meet the UDL checkpoints.

Title: English I Lesson: Dramatic Structure

Subject: English I Lesson on Literature

Grade Level: 9

Duration: 45 minutes

Unit Description: This lesson is part of a group of lessons centering on Harper Lee's *To Kill a Mockingbird*.

Lesson Description for Day: Prerequisite skills: Ability to communicate verbally, attend to a short video clip, work collaboratively

Unit Goals: The goal of this unit is to understand the interplay of heroism and courage during the 1930s in the Deep South.

Lesson Goals: The purpose of this lesson is to teach students to complete a project that conveys the phases of plot: exposition, rising action, climax, falling action, and denouement.

Methods: Anticipatory Set: Tell students that the purpose of the day's lesson is to help them understand dramatic structure as it relates to literature. They will be working with print and digital copies of Harper Lee's novel *To Kill a Mockingbird*, as well as the film version that came out in 1962. The movie does a good job of following the events of the book, so the three can be used in conjunction with one another.

Introduce and Model New Knowledge

1. Introduce new vocabulary (exposition, rising action, climax, falling action, denouement) by saying the words, having students repeat the words, writing the words on the board, discussing definitions, and providing strategies for remembering the definitions (e.g., **d**enouement = **d**ecision or **d**one).

2. Read a section of *To Kill a Mockingbird* to the class and diagram the plot on the board using a plot diagram and the new vocabulary words. Provide a print copy of the text for students to follow along.

3. Play a short clip of the movie *To Kill a Mockingbird (Checkpoint 1.3—Offer alternatives for visual information)* that picks up from the material just read. Have students work in small groups to diagram the plot.

4. Provide scaffolds as needed *(Checkpoint 4.2—Optimize access to tools and assistive technologies; Checkpoint 6.3—Facilitate managing information and resources).*

   a. Demonstrate to students how they can change the fonts and backgrounds of digital text by copying and pasting to Microsoft Word; also, for students who are using text-to-speech technology, make sure they understand how to adjust the volume and speed of the audio *(Checkpoint 1.1—Offer ways of customizing the display of information).*

b. Provide graphic organizers (e.g., word maps, semantic maps) to help struggling students better understand key vocabulary terms (*Checkpoint 2.1—Clarify vocabulary and symbols*).

Provide Guided Practice

1. Provide print, digital, and video versions of *To Kill a Mockingbird*.

2. Select a chapter that will be the focus of the activity.

3. Have students work in small groups to diagram the plot of the selected chapter (*Checkpoint 8.3—Foster collaboration and community*). Allow students to choose groupings for learning activities.

4. Allow students to choose what they will produce:

   a. Create a PowerPoint, Animoto, or Prezi presentation.

   b. Create a performance or scenes.

   c. Create a poster or diorama.

   d. Other (as approved by the teacher).

5. Be prepared to model, for example, PowerPoint procedures.

6. Check for understanding and provide corrective feedback as needed.

7. Support self-regulation skills by assisting students in setting and monitoring learning and behavioral goals (*Checkpoint 9.2—Facilitate personal coping skills and strategies*).

Provide Independent Practice

1. At the end of each day, students answer questions related to the new information as they leave the classroom (e.g., What is exposition?).

2. When student projects are completed, they will be evaluated using a scoring rubric designed for the product type.

SOURCE: Johnson-Harris and Mundschenk (2014).

UDL Guidelines are available at http://www.udlcenter.org/aboutudl/udlguidelines/downloads.

when they do record notes, they may have problems making sense of their notes after the lecture if they are illegible or unorganized.

Students with special learning needs demonstrate difficulties with short-term, long-term, and working memory. Short-term memory is a temporary store of information that we tap for immediate endeavors, like remembering two tasks to accomplish today or a short list of items to buy at the supermarket. Long-term memory is a permanent store of information whose permanence is aided by the way information is stored. **Working memory** is the mental function by which we simultaneously process and store information (Swanson, Zheng, & Jerman, 2009). Memorizing information for class work and tests relies on all three types of memory.

Struggling students experience a number of difficulties related to memorizing and test taking. For memorizing, they may lack efficient strategies such as chunking, rehearsing, and creating mnemonics for studying material that will be tested. They may not make associations between new and learned material to help them memorize content. They may lack efficient strategies for approaching a test, such as managing time or tackling multiple-choice questions methodically, and they may not use memory strategies to retrieve information as they take the test. Finally, they may have difficulties reading and understanding test instructions. Given this list, it is not surprising that students struggle taking exams, even if they know the content being tested.

We return to Mr. Davis, who had his students complete a survey to help him learn about their content-area and study skills. The survey is shown in Table 12.4, which you may want to use with your students.

TABLE 12.4 STUDY SKILLS QUESTIONNAIRE

The purpose of this survey is to find out about your own study habits and attitudes. Read each statement and indicate (by writing 1, 2, 3, or 4 in the blank) how well it applies to you.

1 = Sounds not at all like me	2 = Sounds a little like me
3 = Sounds quite a bit like me	4 = Sounds just like me

Reading Textbooks

____ 1. I browse the headings, pictures, chapter questions, and summaries before I start reading a chapter.

____ 2. I make up questions from a chapter before, during, and after reading it.

____ 3. I try to get the meaning of new words as I see them for the first time.

____ 4. I look for familiar concepts as well as ideas that spark my interest as I read.

____ 5. I look for the main ideas as I read.

Taking Notes

____ 6. I take notes as I read my textbooks.

____ 7. I take notes during class lectures.

____ 8. I rewrite or type up my notes after class.

____ 9. I compare my notes with those of a classmate.

____ 10. I try to organize main ideas and details meaningfully.

Studying

____ 11. I study where it is quiet and there are few distractions.

____ 12. I study for a length of time and then take a short break before returning to studying.

____ 13. I have all my supplies handy when I study, such as pens, paper, calculator, etc.

____ 14. I set study goals, such as the number of problems I will do or the pages I will read.

____ 15. I study at least two hours for every hour I am in class each week.

Memorizing		16.	I try to study when my energy is at its peak to increase my concentration level.
	____	17.	I quiz myself over material that could appear on future exams and quizzes to ensure quick recall.
	____	18.	I say and repeat difficult concepts out loud to understand them and recall them better.
	____	19.	I change my notes into my own words, for better understanding.
	____	20.	I try to create associations between new material I am trying to learn and information I already know.
Preparing for Tests	____	21.	I study with a classmate or group.
	____	22.	When I don't understand something, I get help from tutors, classmates, and my instructors.
	____	23.	I do all homework assignments and turn them in on time.
	____	24.	I can easily identify what I have learned and what I have not yet learned before I take a test.
	____	25.	I anticipate the questions that may be asked on tests and make sure I know the answers.
Managing Time	____	26.	I use a calendar to mark upcoming academic and personal deadlines and events.
	____	27.	I use a "to do" list to keep track of academic and personal tasks I must complete.
	____	28.	I start studying for quizzes and tests at least several days before I take them.
	____	29.	I start papers and projects as soon as they are assigned.
	____	30.	I have enough time for school and fun.

SOURCE: Adapted from Red Rocks Community College, Connect to Success, T+ (n.d.).

Next, we talk about ways to help students improve their time management skills.

TEACHING TIME MANAGEMENT SKILLS

Some students with learning problems have difficulties with organizational skills in general; managing and organizing time is one component of the bigger self-management picture. Time management requires students to (a) identify what they must accomplish, (b) understand how long each task will take to complete, and (c) schedule blocks of time to get the job done efficiently. Time management entails making judgments and estimates about the time requirements of various tasks; your students may struggle with time management if they lack good estimation skills and conceptual understanding of time. For example, the student who does not begin a research paper until three days before the due date either has not demonstrated sufficient understanding of the demands of the task or lacks the time management skills to complete the task by the deadline. You can use the following activities to help students with their time management skills (see *Study Guides and Strategies: Time Management:* http://www.studygs.net/timman.htm):

- Block out study time and breaks during the day.
- Dedicate study spaces.

Teaching Organizational Skills

- Conduct weekly reviews.

- Prioritize assignments.

- Achieve "stage one"—get something done!

- Postpone unnecessary activities until the work is done.

- Identify helpful resources.

- Use free time wisely.

- Review notes and readings just before class.

- Review lecture notes just after class.

More than ever before, students are being held to higher standards, as evidenced by the increasing number of states that have adopted the Common Core State Standards. With increased accountability comes an increased workload, and students are required to complete assignments on time for all of their classes. As shown in the Tech Notes feature, technology can provide students like Colleen with time management options.

TEACHING LISTENING AND NOTE-TAKING SKILLS

According to Steimle, Brdiczka, and Mühlhäuser (2009), classroom lectures too often lead to passive listeners, but that does not need to be the case; note taking requires students to be able to listen actively, recognize important points and supporting details, utilize an organizational framework, know some personal shorthand method for abbreviating information, and write quickly. Taking personal notes can help students actively follow the lecture, select relevant information, and restate it in their own words. Given the importance of note taking and its relationship to higher quiz scores, test scores, and grades (Boyle, 2011; Boyle & Rivera, 2012), your students must know how to listen effectively to obtain the information for which you will hold them accountable.

If your students are encountering obstacles to effective listening, their learning may suffer. Here are some barriers that often impede learning from lectures (Hopper 2016, p. 130, cited in Strang, 2016):

- Talking instead of listening.

- Thinking of what you're going to say instead of listening.

- Mentally arguing with the speaker.

- Thinking about something else while the speaker is talking.

- Getting impatient with the speaker.

- Giving in to a poor environment—too noisy, too hot, too hungry.

- Dividing your attention—texting, finishing homework, staring at someone else in the class.

BONUS Instructional Strategy 12.5: Time Management Evaluation

TECH *notes*

ELECTRONIC CALENDARS AS TIME MANAGEMENT TOOLS

For students like Colleen, who habitually turn in assignments late, electronic calendars can be useful tools for time management. Programs such as Google Calendar or one of the many inexpensive smartphone calendar apps help students organize their schedules so that they can complete assignments on time. For example, Colleen has a paper that is due November 15 for her English I class. Noting that date on a calendar is all well and good, but Colleen is better served by breaking the assignment into manageable steps and placing each event into her electronic calendar. For example,

- Begin research on topic on October 1.

- Create an outline based on the research by October 10.

- Annotate the outline by October 20.

- Write first draft by October 30.

- Revise the draft by November 10.

- Edit the revision by November 12.

- Turn in the paper on November 15.

Electronic calendars can send out alerts when a deadline is approaching, often in the form of an e-mail or text message. Of course, students must pay attention to the calendars as deadlines approach, and parents can help by entering important dates on their calendars as well. Numerous products are available for such purposes. To see a listing of the more popular family-based calendars, simply type "family electronic calendars"

into your favorite search engine. Techdialogue (2013) offered these suggestions for using Google Calendar for the classroom, but they apply to any electronic calendar with similar features.

1. Lesson plans and objectives can be added quickly from any computer (and most mobile devices) with internet access.

2. As teachers get more experienced using Google Calendar, they can embed their calendars on their classroom websites.

3. Advanced users can add their Google Calendar to their smart phones and help students and parents subscribe to the classroom calendar so that they can set up reminders on their devices.

4. Educators can use Google Calendars to share schedules with colleagues, from computer lab schedules to athletics practice.

Think about your needs as a student and how electronic calendars can help you develop more efficient study skills. Then project ahead to how you might use this technology in your own classroom to help your students plan schedules and become more efficient learners.

Have students keep a record of how their time was spent for one week. Then you can perform an analysis of their time management with them so you can set up a plan to address any problems the students are having with time. BONUS Instructional Strategies 12.5 and 12.6 offer some concrete ideas for promoting better time management.

- Not listening actively—not taking notes, not asking questions, and so on.

- Not being motivated to listen—thinking the subject is boring.

- Being distracted by the speaker's mannerisms, voice, or appearance.

Fortunately, Hopper (2016, pp. 131–132, cited in Strang, 2016) provided some suggestions your students can use to improve their listening skills:

- Before you even get to class, be prepared—complete all assigned readings and coursework, and bring all needed materials with you.

- Sit as close to the front of the room as you can.

- Get to class on time—if not early.

- Establish and maintain eye contact with the speaker throughout the lecture.

- Listen for verbal cues. (These can be specific words, such as "first," "then," "however," or "my main point is . . . "—or, they can be found in the speaker's tone of voice or level of enthusiasm.)

- Watch the speaker's gestures and other non-verbal behaviors.

- Have your notebook (and pen or pencil), tablet, or laptop ready at all times.

- Respond to and reflect on the lecture as it proceeds. As questions come to mind, jot them down to ask later.

- Eliminate distractions (such as those mentioned above) . . . and steer yourself away from them!

SOURCE: Hopper (2016). Reprinted with permission.

Bragstad and Stumpf (1987) identified note-taking steps with key words and procedures that students can learn to help them recall lecture and textbook material. Model the steps that follow, offer examples of poorly written and well-written notes, and then allow students opportunities to practice with feedback. (Do not use your students' own work as examples of poor notes.) Students can take notes from a lecture or textbook and then work in small groups to discuss what they did for each step. You can use students' notes in the note shrink quiz box (see Step 2) to construct quizzes to test understanding of the lecture or textbook material. The following steps are recommended to improve students' note-taking skills:

STEP 1: *Note-take,* which requires taking notes of important facts during the lecture.

STEP 2: *Note shrink,* wherein students survey their notes, identify important points and "thought chunks," and record chunks in a quiz box.

STEP 3: *Note talk,* in which students put the content into their own words.

These students are writing out notes as they listen. How can you help your students develop better listening and note-taking skills?

STEP 4: *Note think,* which entails linking the new information to existing knowledge and experiences.

STEP 5: *Note review,* which schedules 10 minutes a day for going over the notes.

Finally, Susan Vogel (1997), a leading researcher in postsecondary learning disabilities, offered the following suggestions, which are useful in helping students learn and remember information. You can put these steps in a handout for students to help them remember how to take notes more effectively:

- Color code, enlarge, underline, and highlight your notes to learn the material.

- Copy your notes over if writing helps you memorize.

- Rehearse, either orally or in writing, material to be mastered.

- Write out concepts in full.

- Read your notes, silently or aloud.

- Paraphrase or explain concepts to a friend.

Think about strategies you have used in the past to learn and remember information presented in text or during lectures. How are they similar to what has been presented here? What additional strategies have you used to help retain information that was presented? How might you share the information presented here, along with strategies that you have used successfully, to your students?

WHAT ARE WAYS TO FACILITATE MEMORIZATION AND TEST TAKING?

Students need memorization skills to facilitate the learning of information. For example, they will be asked to memorize a great deal of information in various subject areas and to reproduce that information on tests and in class discussions. Therefore, it is vital for students to possess strategies that help them learn, store, and retrieve information. Research studies have shown that students with learning problems tend to exhibit difficulties with short-term and working memory that result from ineffective information-processing abilities (Johnson, Humphrey, Mellard, Woods, & Swanson, 2010). Their problems stem from a lack of efficient memory strategies (chunking, organizing), a lack of automaticity with basic knowledge (computational facts, sight words), and inefficient self-regulation (meta-memory) strategies.

You can help students improve their memory skills by (a) teaching them how to create mnemonic devices to assist them in memorizing and recalling content, such as lists of information, important people, and steps in a procedure; (b) discussing how they can remember some information by creating mental images—have them provide specific examples of images they create; (c) teaching them to "chunk"

BONUS Instructional Strategy
12.6: Developing and
Implementing a Scheduling Plan

related information for easier memorization and recall—this necessitates discussing the concepts of compare and contrast; and (d) giving them opportunities to recite information through verbal rehearsal—you can do this in student-mediated groups or in a whole group setting. Clearly, if your students with special needs are to learn, retain, and recall content information, they have to know and apply strategies to facilitate these cognitive, or thinking, processes. Now let's look at some ways to help students recall information and take tests successfully.

TEACHING MEMORIZATION AND TEST-TAKING SKILLS

Memorizing information in preparation for tests requires reviewing the material frequently and committing it to memory. Memory strategies that enhance recall, such as listing, categorizing, drawing, visualizing, alphabetizing, devising acronyms, applying mnemonic strategies, and creating associations, are techniques that students with good study skills use.

There are several ways teachers can help their students become better test takers. Hoover and Patton (2007) offered the following suggestions:

- Show students how to take different types of tests.
- Explain different methods of study and types of materials necessary to study for objective and essay tests.
- Review completed tests with students, highlighting test-taking errors.
- Explore test-taking procedures with students, and explain different types of questions.
- Identify and discuss key vocabulary terms found in test instructions, such as *compare, contrast, match,* and *evaluate.*
- Teach students general strategies to use when taking tests: Review the entire test, know the time allotted for test completion, recognize the point values of specific test items, read and reread the directions and test questions, identify key words in questions, and respond to more difficult items after answering the easier items.
- Teach students specific strategies to use when taking multiple-choice tests: Know the number and kind of answers to select, remember the question, narrow down the possible correct answers by eliminating obviously incorrect ones, and record each answer carefully.

Earlier, we mentioned that mnemonic strategies can be helpful when preparing to take tests. One such strategy is called PIRATES, which has been researched extensively and proven to be effective. Table 12.5 illustrates how PIRATES can be taught to help students develop efficient test-taking skills.

We conclude this chapter with an example of how educators can collaborate to meet the needs of a student who has a visual impairment. These students need to be able to access the curriculum, including content-area material, and be prepared in the area of study skills as well. To accomplish both of

TABLE 12.5 THE PIRATES TEST-TAKING STRATEGY

Step 1: Prepare to succeed	
Put "PIRATES" and name on the test.	Say something positive.
Allot time and order to sections.	Start within two minutes.

Step 2: Inspect the instructions	
Read the instructions carefully.	Notice special requirements.
Underline how and where to respond.	

Step 3: Read, remember, and reduce	
Read the whole question.	Reduce choices.
Remember with memory strategies.	

Step 4: Answer or abandon	
Answer the question.	Abandon the question if you're not sure.

Step 5: Turn back	
Turn back to abandoned questions when you get to the end of the test.	Tell yourself to earn more points.

Step 6: Estimate	
Estimate unknown answers using the "ACE" guessing technique.	Choose the longest or most detailed choice.
Avoid absolutes.	Eliminate identical choices.

Step 7: Survey	
Survey to ensure that all questions are answered.	Switch an answer only if you're sure.

SOURCE: Hughes, Schumaker, Deshler, and Mercer (2005). Reprinted with permission.

these objectives, educators must consider the individual needs of each student and the adaptations necessary to promote successful learning. The Working Together feature provides information about technology considerations that need to be planned in sufficient time so that the student is able to start learning along with his or her peers when the school bell rings in the fall.

WORKING *together*

COLLABORATING TO TEACH STUDENTS WITH VISUAL IMPAIRMENTS

Most teachers need assistance when they are working with students who have sensory disabilities. Access to the general education curriculum for these students is of great importance, so consultation about their needs is a critical part of a special educator's and general educator's job. Professionals collaborating in their work with students who are blind or visually impaired should address the following issues. Together, these professionals can make decisions about materials, Braille text, and grading. Susan J. Spungin, an internationally renowned expert on the education and rehabilitation of individuals who are blind or visually impaired, offers suggestions to general education teachers who have students who are blind or visually impaired in their classroom.

- Consider the child as more like other children than different from them. Talk with the child about his or her interests and experiences and expect the child to follow rules that are appropriate to his or her developmental level.

- Always let a visually impaired child know when you are approaching or leaving. Identify yourself by name, especially if the child doesn't know you well. Never make a game of having a child guess who you are. To do so can be confusing, frightening, or frustrating to a child.

- Briefly describe aspects of the environment that might be of importance or interest to the child that he or she cannot see.

- Always ask before providing physical assistance. If the child cannot understand words, offer your hand or arm for assistance. If the child does not know you well, touch him or her only on the hands or forearms, as you might touch another person in a social situation. Reserve hugging and close physical contact for children who know you well, especially if the child is older than preschool age.

- Use words like "blind" or "visually impaired" in normal conversation with the child, but only when they are important to the topic being discussed. Feel free to use words like "look" and "see," just as you would with any other child.

- When walking with a child, encourage him or her to hold your arm near or above the elbow and to use a cane, if he or she has one. A young child might hold your wrist or forefinger. Discourage hand holding as a means of providing travel assistance; help the child understand that it is a way of expressing affection and is different from travel assistance.

SOURCE: Spungin (2013).

QUESTIONS

1. What are some considerations for teaching students who have visual impairments?

2. How should teachers collaborate to ensure students with visual impairments can access the curriculum?

3. Which of the items on this list did you already know? What information is new to you?

4. If you learn that you are to have a student who is blind or visually impaired in your classroom, where would you go for assistance? What questions might you have?

SUMMARY

Content-area instruction is the focus of upper elementary and secondary teaching. Students use textbooks to learn content, listen to teachers lecture on subjects, and engage in activities that help them apply their knowledge. Study skills become increasingly important and are crucial at the secondary level because students must (a) manage their time efficiently to study notes from class and the textbook, (b) memorize material, and (c) take tests that enable them to advance to the next grade level and eventually graduate from high school. Yet we know that students with special needs demonstrate a variety of difficulties in learning and studying content that interfere with their ability to access and master content-area material. For example, reading and understanding textbooks are often major difficulties for students with reading problems. Acquiring information through lectures and learning this information well enough to take tests successfully are challenging for many struggling students. For content-area instruction, we discussed instructional techniques to facilitate student learning in the areas of content-area vocabulary and concepts, self-monitoring of reading comprehension, textbook reading, and student participation. For study skills, techniques were identified for time management, listening and note taking, and memorization and taking tests.

REVIEW THE LEARNING OBJECTIVES

Let's review the learning objectives for this chapter. If you are uncertain and cannot "talk through" the answers provided for any of these questions, reread those sections of the chapter.

- **What difficulties do students demonstrate with content-area instruction?**

  Some students are slow readers orally and silently, have limited sight vocabularies, have trouble decoding words with inflectional endings and multisyllabic words, and/or have difficulty constructing mental images of text descriptions and structures. They have particular difficulty when they attempt to summarize text, generate and answer different types and levels of questions, draw inferences, and monitor their comprehension. They may also struggle to understand derivational, denotative, and connotative meanings and to apply word meanings across content areas.

- **How can teachers teach content-area vocabulary and concepts?**

  When using textbooks, students will benefit from using graphic organizers and comprehension monitoring strategies. They should learn to decode the meaning of unfamiliar words through mapping, associations, and context clues. Teachers can foster student participation with class discussion guides and questioning. Students can also participate in learning by conducting research, using anchors to promote understanding, and using technology to create multimedia projects.

- **How can teachers teach students to monitor their reading comprehension?**

  Teachers can help students master the steps in comprehension monitoring, which are (a) activating background knowledge, (b) clarifying the purposes for reading, (c) identifying the important information, (d) summarizing information, (e) engaging in self-questioning about the text, (f) using text structure formats to comprehend text, and (g) correcting problems when comprehension is inadequate.

- **How can students learn from textbook instruction?**

  Students can benefit from explicit instruction that helps them recognize and use text structures and features that aid comprehension, such as introductions, outlines, objectives, headings, boldface type, graphics, and focus questions. Because textbooks are the materials used most often by content-area teachers as the basis for their instruction, selecting textbooks is an important consideration for teachers and students.

- **How can teachers promote student participation?**

Teachers can include all students in class discussions through questioning strategies that facilitate discussions and by requiring students to write their responses and share their ideas within a small group. Teachers should work among small groups checking for understanding, modeling how to respond to questions, and asking probing questions to stimulate student thinking.

- **How can teachers help students with difficulties in study skills?**

Teachers can help students to audit their time by having them use electronic calendars and other useful devices. Students can also be taught how to learn content by color-coding, enlarging, underlining, highlighting, and rewriting their notes. Finally, teachers can suggest tips for being more astute test takers.

- **What are ways to facilitate memorization and test taking?**

There are numerous ways to help students improve their memory skills, such as (a) teaching students how to create mnemonic devices to assist them in memorizing and recalling content such as lists of information, important people, and steps in a procedure; (b) discussing how some information can be remembered by creating mental images—have students provide specific examples of images they create; and (c) teaching students to "chunk" related information for easier memorization and recall—this necessitates discussing the concepts of compare and contrast, where students must attend to specific categorical features to be able to state how things are similar and how they are different. Strategies such as PIRATES can also be helpful.

$SAGE edge Test your understanding of chapter content. Take the practice quiz. edge.sagepub.com/bryant

REVISIT THE OPENING CHALLENGE

Check your answers to the Reflection Questions from the Opening Challenge and revise them on the basis of what you have learned.

1. What difficulties might students in both teachers' classes exhibit with regard to content-area instruction and study skills?

2. How can the teachers effectively work with their students to help them become efficient learners in content-area instruction and study skills?

3. How can these teachers provide adapted lessons to students who require intensive intervention, while keeping the rest of the class busy with relevant work?

4. How can study skills assessment be used to identify how students, including struggling students, become more efficient learners?

KEY TERMS

anchored instruction, 546

connotative meanings, 528

content-area instruction, 562

denotative meanings, 528

expository text, 528

hierarchical charts, 529

semantic maps, 530

signal words, 542

Venn diagrams, 529

working memory, 555

$SAGE edge Review key terms with eFlashcards. edge.sagepub.com/bryant

PROFESSIONAL STANDARDS AND LICENSURE

For a complete description of Professional Standards and Licensure, please see Appendix on page 569.

CEC Initial Preparation Standards

Standard 1: Learner Development and Individual Learning Differences

Standard 3: Curricular Content Knowledge

Standard 4: Assessment

Standard 5: Instructional Planning and Strategies

INTASC Core Principles

Standard 1: Learner Development

Standard 2: Learning Differences

Standard 4: Content Knowledge

Standard 6: Assessment

Standard 7: Planning for Instruction

Standard 8: Instructional Strategies

Standard 9: Professional Learning and Ethical Practice

Praxis II: Education of Exceptional Students: Core Content Knowledge

I. Understanding Exceptionalities: Human development and behavior

III. Delivery of Services to Students: Background knowledge

COMMON CORE STATE STANDARDS

Reading

- Literacy
- Craft and Structure
- Integration of Knowledge and Ideas
- Range of Reading and Level of Text Complexity

Writing

- Text Types and Purposes
- Production and Distribution of Writing
- Research to Build and Present Knowledge
- Range of Writing

Review ➡ Practice ➡ Improve

Get the tools you need to sharpen your study skills. Access practice quizzes, eFlashcards, video, and multimedia: edge.sagepub.com/bryant

PRACTICE AND APPLY WHAT YOU'VE LEARNED

▶ edge.sagepub.com/bryant

CHECK YOUR COMPREHENSION ON THE STUDY SITE WITH

- Mobile-friendly practice quizzes on the open-access study site that give you opportunities for self-guided assessment and practice!

APPENDIX: PROFESSIONAL STANDARDS AND LICENSURE AND COMMON CORE STATE STANDARDS

CHAPTER 1

CEC STANDARDS

Standard 1: Learner Development and Individual Learning Differences

1.0 Beginning special education professionals understand how exceptionalities may interact with development and learning and use this knowledge to provide meaningful and challenging learning experiences for individuals with exceptionalities.

INTASC

Standard 1: Learner Development

The teacher understands how learners grow and develop, recognizing that patterns of learning and development vary individually within and across the cognitive, linguistic, social, emotional, and physical areas, and designs and implements developmentally appropriate and challenging learning experiences.

Standard 2: Learning Differences

The teacher uses understanding of individual differences and diverse cultures and communities to ensure inclusive learning environments that enable each learner to meet high standards.

PRAXIS II: EDUCATION OF EXCEPTIONAL STUDENTS: CORE CONTENT KNOWLEDGE

I. Understanding Exceptionalities

Basic concepts in special education, including:

- Attention deficit/hyperactivity disorder, as well as the incidence and prevalence of various types of disabilities
- The nature of behaviors, including frequency, duration, intensity, and degrees of severity
- The classification of students with disabilities

II. Legal and Societal Issues

Federal laws and legal issues related to special education, including:

- Public Law 94-142
- Public Law 105-17
- Section 504
- Americans with Disabilities Act (ADA)
- Important legal issues

The school's connections with the families, prospective and actual employers, and communities of students with disabilities—for example:

- Parent partnerships and roles
- Cultural and community influences on public attitudes toward individuals with disabilities

Historical movements/trends affecting the connections between special education and the larger society—for example:

- Inclusion
- Transition
- Advocacy
- Accountability and meeting educational standards

III. Delivery of Services to Students with Disabilities

Background knowledge, including:

- Conceptual approaches underlying service delivery to students with disabilities
- Placement and program issues such as early intervention; least restrictive environment; inclusion; role of individualized education program (IEP) team; due process guidelines; and others

Curriculum and instruction and their implementation across the continuum of education placements, including:

- The individualized family service plan (IFSP)/individualized education program (IEP) process
- Career development and transition issues as related to curriculum design and implementation

CHAPTER 2

CEC

Standard 1: Learner Development and Individual Learning Differences

1.0 Beginning special education professionals understand how exceptionalities may interact with development and learning and use this knowledge to provide meaningful and challenging learning experiences for individuals with exceptionalities.

INTASC

Standard 1: Learner Development

The teacher understands how learners grow and develop, recognizing that patterns of learning and development vary individually within and across the cognitive, linguistic, social, emotional, and physical areas, and designs and implements developmentally appropriate and challenging learning experiences.

Standard 2: Learning Differences

The teacher uses understanding of individual differences and diverse cultures and communities to ensure inclusive learning environments that enable each learner to meet high standards.

PRAXIS II: EDUCATION OF EXCEPTIONAL STUDENTS: CORE CONTENT KNOWLEDGE

I. Understanding Exceptionalities

- Social and emotional development and behavior.
- Language development and behavior.
- Cognition.
- Physical development, including motor and sensory.

Characteristics of students with disabilities, including the influence of:

- Cognitive factors.
- Affective and social-adaptive factors, including cultural, linguistic, gender, and socioeconomic factors.
- Genetic, medical, motor, sensory, and chronological age factors.

Basic concepts in special education, including:

- Attention deficit hyperactivity disorder, as well as the incidence and prevalence of various types of disabilities.
- The causation and prevention of disability.
- The nature of behaviors, including frequency, duration, intensity, and degrees of severity.
- The classification of students with disabilities.

CHAPTER 3

CEC

Standard 1: Learner Development and Individual Learning Differences

1.0 Beginning special education professionals understand how exceptionalities may interact with development and learning and use this knowledge to provide meaningful and challenging learning experiences for individuals with exceptionalities.

INTASC

Standard 1: Learner Development

The teacher understands how learners grow and develop, recognizing that patterns of learning and development vary individually within and across the cognitive, linguistic, social, emotional, and physical areas, and designs and implements developmentally appropriate and challenging learning experiences.

Standard 2: Learning Differences

The teacher uses understanding of individual differences and diverse cultures and communities to ensure inclusive learning environments that enable each learner to meet high standards.

PRAXIS II: EDUCATION OF EXCEPTIONAL STUDENTS: CORE CONTENT KNOWLEDGE

I. Understanding Exceptionalities

Human development and behavior as related to students with disabilities, including:

- Social and emotional development and behavior.
- Language development and behavior.
- Cognition.
- Physical development, including motor and sensory.

Characteristics of students with disabilities, including the influence of:

- Cognitive factors.
- Affective and social-adaptive factors, including cultural, linguistic, gender, and socioeconomic factors.
- Genetic, medical, motor, sensory, and chronological age factors.

Basic concepts in special education, including:

- Attention deficit hyperactivity disorder, as well as the incidence and prevalence of various types of disabilities.
- The causation and prevention of disability.
- The nature of behaviors, including frequency, duration, intensity, and degrees of severity.
- The classification of students with disabilities.

CHAPTER 4

CEC

Standard 1: Learner Development and Individual Learning Differences

1.0 Beginning special education professionals understand how exceptionalities may interact with development and learning and use this knowledge to provide meaningful and challenging learning experiences for individuals with exceptionalities.

INTASC

Standard 1: Learner Development

The teacher understands how learners grow and develop, recognizing that patterns of learning and development vary individually within and across the cognitive, linguistic, social, emotional, and physical areas, and designs and implements developmentally appropriate and challenging learning experiences.

Standard 2: Learning Differences

The teacher uses understanding of individual differences and diverse cultures and communities to ensure inclusive learning environments that enable each learner to meet high standards.

PRAXIS II: EDUCATION OF EXCEPTIONAL STUDENTS: CORE CONTENT KNOWLEDGE

I. Understanding Exceptionalities

Human development and behavior as related to students with disabilities, including:

- Social and emotional development and behavior.
- Language development and behavior.
- Cognition.
- Physical development, including motor and sensory.

Characteristics of students with disabilities, including the influence of:

- Cognitive factors.
- Affective and social-adaptive factors, including cultural, linguistic, gender, and socioeconomic factors.
- Genetic, medical, motor, sensory, and chronological age factors.

Basic concepts in special education, including:

- Definitions of all major categories and specific disabilities including attention deficit/hyperactivity disorder, as well as the incidence and prevalence of various types of disabilities.
- The causation and prevention of disability.
- The nature of behaviors, including frequency, duration, intensity, and degrees of severity.
- The classification of students with disabilities.

II. Legal and Societal Issues

Federal laws and legal issues related to special education, including:

- Section 504.

The school's connections with the families, prospective and actual employers, and communities of students with disabilities, for example:

- Teacher advocacy for students and families, developing student self-advocacy.
- Parent partnerships and roles.

III. Delivery of Services to Students with Disabilities

Background knowledge, including:

- Placement and program issues.

Assessment, including:

- Use of assessment for screening, diagnosis, placement, and the making of instructional decisions.

CHAPTER 5

CEC

Standard 2: Learning Environments

2.0 Beginning special education professionals create safe, inclusive, culturally responsive learning environments so that individuals with exceptionalities become active and effective learners and develop emotional well-being, positive social interactions, and self-determination.

Standard 6: Professional Learning and Ethical Practice

6.0 Beginning special education professionals use foundational knowledge of the field and their professional Ethical Principles and Practice Standards to inform special education practice, to engage in lifelong learning, and to advance the profession.

Standard 7: Collaboration

7.0 Beginning special education professionals collaborate with families, other educators, related service providers, individuals with exceptionalities, and personnel from community agencies in culturally responsive ways to address the needs of individuals with exceptionalities across a range of learning experiences.

INTASC

Standard 3: Learning Environments

The teacher works with others to create environments that support individual and collaborative learning, and that encourage positive social interaction, active engagement in learning, and self-motivation.

Standard 7: Planning for Instruction

The teacher plans instruction that supports every student in meeting rigorous learning goals by drawing upon knowledge of content areas, curriculum, cross-disciplinary skills, and pedagogy, as well as knowledge of learners and the community context.

Standard 9: Professional Learning and Ethical Practice

The teacher engages in ongoing professional learning and uses evidence to continually evaluate his/her practice, particularly the effects of his/her choices and actions on others (learners, families, other professionals, and the community), and adapts practice to meet the needs of each learner.

Standard 10: Leadership and Collaboration

The teacher seeks appropriate leadership roles and opportunities to take responsibility for student learning, to collaborate with learners, families, colleagues, other school professionals, and community members to ensure learner growth, and to advance the profession.

PRAXIS II: EDUCATION OF EXCEPTIONAL STUDENTS: CORE CONTENT KNOWLEDGESPECIAL

II. Legal and Societal Issues

Federal laws and legal issues related to special education, including:

- Public Law 105-17

The school's connections with the families, prospective and actual employers, and communities of students with disabilities, for example:

- Parent partnerships and roles
- Cultural and community influences on public attitudes toward individuals with disabilities

Historical movements/trends affecting the connections between special education and the larger society, for example:

- Inclusion
- Advocacy
- Accountability and meeting educational standards

III. Delivery of Services to Students with Disabilities

Background knowledge, including:

- Conceptual approaches underlying service delivery to students with disabilities
- Placement and program issues such as early intervention; least restrictive environment; inclusion; role of individualized education program (IEP) team; due process guidelines; and others

Curriculum and instruction and their implementation across the continuum of education placements, including:

- The individualized family service plan (IFSP)/individualized education program (IEP) process
- Instructional development and implementation
- Instructional format and components

Structuring and managing the learning environment, including

- Structuring the learning environment Professional roles, including
- Specific roles and responsibilities of teachers
- Communicating with parents, guardians, and appropriate community collaborators

CHAPTER 6

CEC

Standard 1: Learner Development and Individual Learning Differences

1.0 Beginning special education professionals understand how exceptionalities may interact with development and learning and use this knowledge to provide meaningful and challenging learning experiences for individuals with exceptionalities.

Standard 2: Learning Environments

2.0 Beginning special education professionals create safe, inclusive, culturally responsive learning environments so that individuals with exceptionalities become active and effective learners and develop emotional well-being, positive social interactions, and self-determination.

Standard 3: Curricular Content Knowledge

3.0 Beginning special education professionals use knowledge of general and specialized curricula to individualize learning for individuals with exceptionalities.

Standard 4: Assessment

4.0 Beginning special education professionals use multiple methods of assessment and data-sources in making educational decisions.

Standard 6: Professional Learning and Ethical Practice

6.0 Beginning special education professionals use foundational knowledge of the field and their professional Ethical Principles and Practice Standards to inform special education practice, to engage in lifelong learning, and to advance the profession.

Standard 7: Collaboration

7.0 Beginning special education professionals collaborate with families, other educators, related service providers, individuals with exceptionalities, and personnel from community agencies in culturally responsive ways to address the needs of individuals with exceptionalities across a range of learning experiences.

INTASC

Standard 1: Learner Development

The teacher understands how learners grow and develop, recognizing that patterns of learning and development vary individually within and across the cognitive, linguistic, social, emotional, and physical areas, and designs and implements developmentally appropriate and challenging learning experiences.

Standard 2: Learning Differences

The teacher uses understanding of individual differences and diverse cultures and communities to ensure inclusive learning environments that enable each learner to meet high standards.

Standard 3: Learning Environments

The teacher works with others to create environments that support individual and collaborative learning, and that encourage positive social interaction, active engagement in learning, and self-motivation.

Standard 4: Content Knowledge

The teacher understands the central concepts, tools of inquiry, and structures of the discipline(s) he or she teaches and creates learning experiences that make the discipline accessible and meaningful for learners to assure mastery of the content.

Standard 6: Assessment

The teacher understands and uses multiple methods of assessment to engage learners in their own growth, to monitor learner progress, and to guide the teacher's and learner's decision making.

Standard 7: Planning for Instruction

The teacher plans instruction that supports every student in meeting rigorous learning goals by drawing upon knowledge of content areas, curriculum, cross-disciplinary skills, and pedagogy, as well as knowledge of learners and the community context.

Standard 9: Professional Learning and Ethical Practice

The teacher engages in ongoing professional learning and uses evidence to continually evaluate his/her practice, particularly the effects of his/her choices and actions on others (learners, families, other professionals, and the community), and adapts practice to meet the needs of each learner.

Standard 10: Leadership and Collaboration

The teacher seeks appropriate leadership roles and opportunities to take responsibility for student learning, to collaborate with learners, families, colleagues, other school professionals, and community members to ensure learner growth, and to advance the profession.

PRAXIS II: EDUCATION OF EXCEPTIONAL STUDENTS: CORE CONTENT KNOWLEDGE

I. Understanding Exceptionalities

Basic concepts in special education, including:

- The classification of students with disabilities

II. Legal and Societal Issues

Federal laws and legal issues related to special education, including:

- Public Law 94-142
- Public Law 105-17

- Section 504
- Americans with Disabilities Act (ADA)
- Important legal issues

The school's connections with the families, prospective and actual employers, and communities of students with disabilities—for example:

- Parent partnerships and roles
- Cultural and community influences on public attitudes toward individuals with disabilities
- Interagency agreements
- Cooperative nature of the transition-planning process

Historical movements/trends affecting the connections between special education and the larger society—for example:

- Inclusion
- Transition
- Advocacy
- Accountability and meeting educational standards

CHAPTER 7
CEC

Standard 1: Learner Development and Individual Learning Differences

1.0 Beginning special education professionals understand how exceptionalities may interact with development and learning and use this knowledge to provide meaningful and challenging learning experiences for individuals with exceptionalities.

Standard 2: Learning Environments

2.0 Beginning special education professionals create safe, inclusive, culturally responsive learning environments so that individuals with exceptionalities become active and effective learners and develop emotional well-being, positive social interactions, and self-determination.

Standard 3: Curricular Content Knowledge

3.0 Beginning special education professionals use knowledge of general and specialized curricula to individualize learning for individuals with exceptionalities.

Standard 5: Instructional Planning and Strategies

5.0 Beginning special education professionals select, adapt, and use a repertoire of evidence-based instructional strategies to advance learning of individuals with exceptionalities.

Standard 6: Professional Learning and Ethical Practice

6.0 Beginning special education professionals use foundational knowledge of the field and their professional Ethical Principles and Practice Standards to inform special education practice, to engage in lifelong learning, and to advance the profession.

Standard 7: Collaboration

7.0 Beginning special education professionals collaborate with families, other educators, related service providers, individuals with exceptionalities, and personnel from community agencies in culturally responsive ways to address the needs of individuals with exceptionalities across a range of learning experiences.

INTASC

Standard 4: Content Knowledge

The teacher understands the central concepts, tools of inquiry, and structures of the discipline(s) he or she teaches and creates learning experiences that make the discipline accessible and meaningful for learners to assure mastery of the content.

Standard 7: Planning for Instruction

The teacher plans instruction that supports every student in meeting rigorous learning goals by drawing upon knowledge of content areas, curriculum, cross-disciplinary skills, and pedagogy, as well as knowledge of learners and the community context.

Standard 8: Instructional Strategies

The teacher understands and uses a variety of instructional strategies to encourage learners to develop deep understanding of content areas and their connections, and to build skills to apply knowledge in meaningful ways.

PRAXIS II: EDUCATION OF EXCEPTIONAL STUDENTS: CORE CONTENT KNOWLEDGE

II. Legal and Societal Issues

Historical movements/trends affecting the connections between special education and the larger society, for example:

- Inclusion
- Application of technology
- Advocacy
- Accountability and meeting educational standards

III. Delivery of Services to Students with Disabilities

- Background knowledge, including:
- Conceptual approaches underlying service delivery to students with disabilities
- Integrating best practices from multidisciplinary research and professional literature into the educational setting

Curriculum and instruction and their implementation across the continuum of education placements, including:

- Instructional development and implementation
- Teaching strategies and methods
- Instructional format and components
- Technology for teaching and learning in special education settings

Structuring and managing the learning environment, including:

- Structuring the learning environment

CHAPTER 8

CEC

Standard 1: Learner Development and Individual Learning Differences

1.0 Beginning special education professionals understand how exceptionalities may interact with development and learning and use this knowledge to provide meaningful and challenging learning experiences for individuals with exceptionalities.

Standard 3: Curricular Content Knowledge

3.0 Beginning special education professionals use knowledge of general and specialized curricula to individualize learning for individuals with exceptionalities.

Standard 4: Assessment

4.0 Beginning special education professionals use multiple methods of assessment and data-sources in making educational decisions.

INTASC

Standard 1: Content Pedagogy

He or she must understand the central concept and structure of discipline must be created in such a way that students can learn from it effectively.

Standard 3: Diverse Learners

The teacher must know that the students have different capabilities of learning and based on that must train them.

Standard 8: Assessment

The teacher assesses the students formally or informally to evaluate the social, intellectual, and physical development of the students.

PRAXIS II: EDUCATION OF EXCEPTIONAL STUDENTS: CORE CONTENT KNOWLEDGE

III. Delivery of Services to Students with Disabilities

Assessment, including:

- Use of assessment for screening, diagnosis, placement, and the making of instruction decisions.
- Procedures and test materials, both formal and informal, typically used for pre-referral, screening, referral, classification, placement, and ongoing program monitoring.
- How to select, construct, conduct, and modify informal assessments.

CHAPTER 9

CEC

Standard 1: Learner Development and Individual Learning Differences

1.0 Beginning special education professionals understand how exceptionalities may interact with development and learning and use this knowledge to provide meaningful and challenging learning experiences for individuals with exceptionalities.

Standard 2: Learning Environments

2.0 Beginning special education professionals create safe, inclusive, culturally responsive learning environments so that individuals with exceptionalities become active and effective learners and develop emotional well-being, positive social interactions, and self-determination.

Standard 3: Curricular Content Knowledge

3.0 Beginning special education professionals use knowledge of general and specialized curricula to individualize learning for individuals with exceptionalities.

INTASC

Standard 1: Learner Development

The teacher understands how learners grow and develop, recognizing that patterns of learning and development vary individually within and across the cognitive, linguistic, social, emotional, and physical areas, and designs and implements developmentally appropriate and challenging learning experiences.

Standard 2: Learning Differences

The teacher uses understanding of individual differences and diverse cultures and communities to ensure inclusive learning environments that enable each learner to meet high standards

Standard 3: Learning Environments

The teacher works with others to create environments that support individual and collaborative learning, and that encourage positive social interaction, active engagement in learning, and self-motivation.

Standard 4: Content Knowledge

The teacher understands the central concepts, tools of inquiry, and structures of the discipline(s) he or she teaches and creates learning experiences that make the discipline accessible and meaningful for learners to assure mastery of the content.

Standard 6: Assessment

The teacher understands and uses multiple methods of assessment to engage learners in their own growth, to monitor learner progress, and to guide the teacher's and learner's decision making.

Standard 8: Instructional Strategies

The teacher understands and uses a variety of instructional strategies to encourage learners to develop deep understanding of content areas and their connections, and to build skills to apply knowledge in meaningful ways.

Standard 9: Professional Learning and Ethical Practice

The teacher engages in ongoing professional learning and uses evidence to continually evaluate his/her practice, particularly the effects of his/her choices and actions on others (learners, families, other professionals, and the community), and adapts practice to meet the needs of each learner.

PRAXIS II: EDUCATION OF EXCEPTIONAL STUDENTS: CORE CONTENT KNOWLEDGE

I. Understanding Exceptionalities

Human development and behavior as related to students with disabilities, including:

- Social and emotional development and behavior.

III. Delivery of Services to Students

Curriculum and instruction and their implementation across the continuum of educational placements, including:

- Instructional development for implementation.
- Teaching strategies and methods.
- Instructional format and components.

Assessment, including:

- How to select, construct, conduct, and modify informal assessments.

Structuring and managing the learning environment, including:

- Classroom management techniques.
- Ethical considerations inherent in behavior management.

Professional roles, including:

- Influence of teacher attitudes, values, and behaviors on the learning of exceptional students.

Communicating with parents, guardians, and appropriate community collaborators.

CHAPTER 10

CEC

Standard 1: Learner Development and Individual Learning Differences

1.0 Beginning special education professionals understand how exceptionalities may interact with development and learning and use this knowledge to provide meaningful and challenging learning experiences for individuals with exceptionalities.

Standard 3: Curricular Content Knowledge

3.0 Beginning special education professionals use knowledge of general and specialized curricula to individualize learning for individuals with exceptionalities.

Standard 4: Assessment

4.0 Beginning special education professionals use multiple methods of assessment and data-sources in making educational decisions.

Standard 5: Instructional Planning and Strategies

5.0 Beginning special education professionals select, adapt, and use a repertoire of evidence-based instructional strategies to advance learning of individuals with exceptionalities.

INTASC

Standard 1: Learner Development

The teacher understands how learners grow and develop, recognizing that patterns of learning and development vary individually within and across the cognitive, linguistic, social, emotional, and physical areas, and designs and implements developmentally appropriate and challenging learning experiences.

Standard 2: Learning Differences

The teacher uses understanding of individual differences and diverse cultures and communities to ensure inclusive learning environments that enable each learner to meet high standards.

Standard 4: Content Knowledge

The teacher understands the central concepts, tools of inquiry, and structures of the discipline(s) he or she teaches and creates learning experiences that make the discipline accessible and meaningful for learners to assure mastery of the content.

Standard 6: Assessment

The teacher understands and uses multiple methods of assessment to engage learners in their own growth, to monitor learner progress, and to guide the teacher's and learner's decision making.

Standard 7: Planning for Instruction

The teacher plans instruction that supports every student in meeting rigorous learning goals by drawing upon knowledge of content areas, curriculum, cross-disciplinary skills, and pedagogy, as well as knowledge of learners and the community context.

Standard 8: Instructional Strategies

The teacher understands and uses a variety of instructional strategies to encourage learners to develop deep understanding of content areas and their connections, and to build skills to apply knowledge in meaningful ways.

Standard 9: Professional Learning and Ethical Practice

The teacher engages in ongoing professional learning and uses evidence to continually evaluate his/her practice, particularly the effects of his/her choices and actions on others (learners, families, other professionals, and the community), and adapts practice to meet the needs of each learner.

PRAXIS II: EDUCATION OF EXCEPTIONAL STUDENTS: CORE CONTENT KNOWLEDGE

I. Understanding Exceptionalities

Characteristics of students with disabilities, including the influence of:

- Cognitive factors
- Genetic, medical, motor, sensory, and chronological age factors

III. Delivery of Services to Students

Curriculum and instruction and their implementation across the continuum of educational placements, including:

- Instructional development for implementation

- Teaching strategies and methods
- Instructional format and components

Assessment, including:

- How to select, construct, conduct, and modify informal assessments

Structuring and managing the learning environment. Professional roles, including:

- Specific roles and responsibilities of teachers

COMMON CORE STATE STANDARDS

Reading: Key Ideas

Literacy:

CCRA.R.1 Read closely to determine what the text says explicitly and to make logical inferences from it; cite specific textual evidence when writing or speaking to support conclusions drawn from the text.

CCRA.R.2 Determine central ideas or themes of a text and analyze their development; summarize the key supporting details and ideas.

CCRA.R.3 Analyze how and why individuals, events, or ideas develop and interact over the course of a text.

Craft and Structure:

CCRA.R.4 Interpret words and phrases as they are used in a text, including determining technical, connotative, and figurative meanings, and analyze how specific word choices shape meaning or tone.

CCRA.R.5 Analyze the structure of texts, including how specific sentences, paragraphs, and larger portions of the text (e.g., a section, chapter, scene, or stanza) relate to each other and the whole.

CCRA.R.6 Assess how point of view or purpose shapes the content and style of a text.

Integration of Knowledge and Ideas:

CCRA.R.7 Integrate and evaluate content presented in diverse media and formats, including visually and quantitatively, as well as in words.

CCRA.R.8 Delineate and evaluate the argument and specific claims in a text, including the validity of the reasoning as well as the relevance and sufficiency of the evidence.

CCRA.R.9 Analyze how two or more texts address similar themes or topics in order to build knowledge or to compare the approaches the authors take.

Range of Reading and Level of Text Complexity:

CCRA.R.10 Read and comprehend complex literary and informational texts independently and proficiently.

Writing

Text Types and Purposes:

CCRA.W.1 Write arguments to support claims in an analysis of substantive topics or texts using valid reasoning and relevant and sufficient evidence.

CCRA.W.2 Write informative/explanatory texts to examine and convey complex ideas and information clearly and accurately through the effective selection, organization, and analysis of content.

CCRA.W.3 Write narratives to develop real or imagined experiences or events using effective technique, well-chosen details, and well-structured event sequences.

Production and Distribution of Writing:

CCRA.W.4 Produce clear and coherent writing in which the development, organization, and style are appropriate to task, purpose, and audience.

CCRA.W.5 Develop and strengthen writing as needed by planning, revising, editing, rewriting, or trying a new approach.

CCRA.W.6 Use technology, including the Internet, to produce and publish writing and to interact and collaborate with others.

Research to Build and Present Knowledge:

CCRA.W.7 Conduct short as well as more sustained research projects based on focused questions, demonstrating understanding of the subject under investigation.

CCRA.W.8 Gather relevant information from multiple print and digital sources, assess the credibility and accuracy of each source, and integrate the information while avoiding plagiarism.

CCRA.W.9 Draw evidence from literary or informational texts to support analysis, reflection, and research.

Range of Writing:

CCRA.W.10 Write routinely over extended time frames (time for research, reflection, and revision) and shorter time frames (a single sitting or a day or two) for a range of tasks, purposes, and audiences.

CHAPTER 11

CEC

Standard 1: Learner Development and Individual Learning Differences

1.0 Beginning special education professionals understand how exceptionalities may interact with development and learning and use this knowledge to provide meaningful and challenging learning experiences for individuals with exceptionalities.

Standard 3: Curricular Content Knowledge

3.0 Beginning special education professionals use knowledge of general and specialized curricula to individualize learning for individuals with exceptionalities.

Standard 4: Assessment

4.0 Beginning special education professionals use multiple methods of assessment and data-sources in making educational decisions.

Standard 5: Instructional Planning and Strategies

5.0 Beginning special education professionals select, adapt, and use a repertoire of evidence-based instructional strategies to advance learning of individuals with exceptionalities.

INTASC

Standard 1: Learner Development

The teacher understands how learners grow and develop, recognizing that patterns of learning and development vary individually within and across the cognitive, linguistic, social, emotional, and physical areas, and designs and implements developmentally appropriate and challenging learning experiences.

Standard 2: Learning Differences

The teacher uses understanding of individual differences and diverse cultures and communities to ensure inclusive learning environments that enable each learner to meet high standards.

Standard 4: Content Knowledge

The teacher understands the central concepts, tools of inquiry, and structures of the discipline(s) he or she teaches and creates learning experiences that make the discipline accessible and meaningful for learners to assure mastery of the content.

Standard 6: Assessment

The teacher understands and uses multiple methods of assessment to engage learners in their own growth, to monitor learner progress, and to guide the teacher's and learner's decision making.

Standard 7: Planning for Instruction

The teacher plans instruction that supports every student in meeting rigorous learning goals by drawing upon knowledge of content areas, curriculum, cross-disciplinary skills, and pedagogy, as well as knowledge of learners and the community context.

Standard 8: Instructional Strategies

The teacher understands and uses a variety of instructional strategies to encourage learners to develop deep understanding of content areas and their connections, and to build skills to apply knowledge in meaningful ways.

Standard 9: Professional Learning and Ethical Practice

The teacher engages in ongoing professional learning and uses evidence to continually evaluate his/her practice, particularly the effects of his/her choices and actions on others (learners, families, other professionals, and the community), and adapts practice to meet the needs of each learner.

PRAXIS II: EDUCATION OF EXCEPTIONAL STUDENTS: CORE CONTENT KNOWLEDGE

I. Understanding Exceptionalities

Human development and behavior as related to students with disabilities, including:

- Cognition

Characteristics of students with disabilities, including the influence of:

- Cognitive factors

- Affective and social-adaptive factors, including cultural, linguistic, gender, and socioeconomic factors

III. Delivery of Services to Students

Background knowledge, including:

- Integrating best practices from multidisciplinary research and professional literature into the educational setting

Curriculum and instruction and their implementation across the continuum of educational placements, including:

- Instructional development and implementation
- Teaching strategies and methods
- Instructional format and components Assessment, including
- How to select, construct, conduct, and modify informal assessments

COMMON CORE STATE STANDARDS

Mathematical Practices

- Make sense of problems and persevere in solving them.
- Reason abstractly and quantitatively.
- Construct viable arguments and critique the reasoning of others.
- Model with mathematics.
- Use appropriate tools strategically.

- Attend to precision.

- Look for and make use of structure.

- Look for and express regularity in repeated reasoning.

Domains

- Counting and Cardinality K.CC

- Operations and Algebraic Thinking K, 1,2,3,4,5.OA

- Number and Operations in Base Ten K, 1,2,3,4,5.NBT

- Number and Operations—Fractions 3,4,5.NF

- Ratios and Proportional Relationships 6,7.RP

- The Number System 6,7,8.NS

- Expressions and Equations 6,7,8.EE

- Functions 8,HS.F

- Measurement and Data K,1,2,3,4,5.MD

- Geometry K,1,2,3,4,5,6,7,8,HS.G

- Statistics and Probability 6,7,8,HS.SP

- Number and Quantity HS

- Algebra HS

- Modeling HS

CHAPTER 12

CEC

Standard 1: Learner Development and Individual Learning Differences

1.0 Beginning special education professionals understand how exceptionalities may interact with development and learning and use this knowledge to provide meaningful and challenging learning experiences for individuals with exceptionalities.

Standard 3: Curricular Content Knowledge

3.0 Beginning special education professionals use knowledge of general and specialized curricula to individualize learning for individuals with exceptionalities.

Standard 4: Assessment

4.0 Beginning special education professionals use multiple methods of assessment and data-sources in making educational decisions.

Standard 5: Instructional Planning and Strategies

5.0 Beginning special education professionals select, adapt, and use a repertoire of evidence-based instructional strategies to advance learning of individuals with exceptionalities.

INTASC

Standard 1: Learner Development

The teacher understands how learners grow and develop, recognizing that patterns of learning and development vary individually within and across the cognitive, linguistic, social, emotional, and physical areas, and designs and implements developmentally appropriate and challenging learning experiences.

Standard 2: Learning Differences

The teacher uses understanding of individual differences and diverse cultures and communities to ensure inclusive learning environments that enable each learner to meet high standards.

Standard 4: Content Knowledge

The teacher understands the central concepts, tools of inquiry, and structures of the discipline(s) he or she teaches and creates learning experiences that make the discipline accessible and meaningful for learners to assure mastery of the content.

Standard 8: Instructional Strategies

The teacher understands and uses a variety of instructional strategies to encourage learners to develop deep understanding of content areas and their connections, and to build skills to apply knowledge in meaningful ways.

Standard 6: Assessment

The teacher understands and uses multiple methods of assessment to engage learners in their own growth, to monitor learner progress, and to guide the teacher's and learner's decision making.

Standard 7: Planning for Instruction

The teacher plans instruction that supports every student in meeting rigorous learning goals by drawing upon knowledge of content areas, curriculum, cross-disciplinary skills, and pedagogy, as well as knowledge of learners and the community context.

Standard 9: Professional Learning and Ethical Practice

The teacher engages in ongoing professional learning and uses evidence to continually evaluate his/her practice, particularly the effects of his/her choices and actions on others (learners, families, other professionals, and the community), and adapts practice to meet the needs of each learner.

PRAXIS II: EDUCATION OF EXCEPTIONAL STUDENTS: CORE CONTENT KNOWLEDGE

I. Understanding Exceptionalities

Human development and behavior as related to students with disabilities, including:

- Language development and behavior.
- Cognition.
- Physical development.

Characteristics of students with disabilities, including the influence of:

- Cognitive factors.
- Affective and social-adaptive factors.

III. Delivery of Services to Students

Background knowledge, including:

- Integrating best practices from multidisciplinary research and professional literature into the educational setting.

Curriculum and instruction and their implementation across the continuum of educational placements, including:

- Instructional development and implementation.
- Teaching strategies and methods.
- Instructional format and components.
- Technology for teaching and learning in special education settings.

COMMON CORE STATE STANDARDS

Reading: Key Ideas

Literacy:

CCRA.R.1 Read closely to determine what the text says explicitly and to make logical inferences from it; cite specific textual evidence when writing or speaking to support conclusions drawn from the text.

CCRA.R.2 Determine central ideas or themes of a text and analyze their development; summarize the key supporting details and ideas.

CCRA.R.3 Analyze how and why individuals, events, or ideas develop and interact over the course of a text.

Craft and Structure:

CCRA.R.4 Interpret words and phrases as they are used in a text, including determining technical, connotative, and figurative meanings, and analyze how specific word choices shape meaning or tone.

CCRA.R.5 Analyze the structure of texts, including how specific sentences, paragraphs, and larger portions of the text (e.g., a section, chapter, scene, or stanza) relate to each other and the whole.

CCRA.R.6 Assess how point of view or purpose shapes the content and style of a text.

Integration of Knowledge and Ideas:

CCRA.R.7 Integrate and evaluate content presented in diverse media and formats, including visually and quantitatively, as well as in words.

CCRA.R.8 Delineate and evaluate the argument and specific claims in a text, including the validity of the reasoning as well as the relevance and sufficiency of the evidence.

CCRA.R.9 Analyze how two or more texts address similar themes or topics in order to build knowledge or to compare the approaches the authors take.

Range of Reading and Level of Text Complexity:

CCRA.R.10 Read and comprehend complex literary and informational texts independently and proficiently.

Writing

Text Types and Purposes:

CCRA.W.1 Write arguments to support claims in an analysis of substantive topics or texts using valid reasoning and relevant and sufficient evidence.

CCRA.W.2 Write informative/explanatory texts to examine and convey complex ideas and information clearly and accurately through the effective selection, organization, and analysis of content.

CCRA.W.3 Write narratives to develop real or imagined experiences or events using effective technique, well-chosen details, and well-structured event sequences.

Production and Distribution of Writing:

CCRA.W.4 Produce clear and coherent writing in which the development, organization, and style are appropriate to task, purpose, and audience.

CCRA.W.5 Develop and strengthen writing as needed by planning, revising, editing, rewriting, or trying a new approach.

CCRA.W.6 Use technology, including the Internet, to produce and publish writing and to interact and collaborate with others.

Research to Build and Present Knowledge:

CCRA.W.7 Conduct short as well as more sustained research projects based on focused questions, demonstrating understanding of the subject under investigation.

CCRA.W.8 Gather relevant information from multiple print and digital sources, assess the credibility and accuracy of each source, and integrate the information while avoiding plagiarism.

CCRA.W.9 Draw evidence from literary or informational texts to support analysis, reflection, and research.

Range of Writing:

CCRA.W.10 Write routinely over extended time frames (time for research, reflection, and revision) and shorter time frames (a single sitting or a day or two) for a range of tasks, purposes, and audiences.

GLOSSARY

ability grouping A form of acceleration wherein students of comparable abilities work together in courses or activities in which they excel

acceleration An approach that allows gifted and talented students to move through the curriculum at faster rates than their peers who learn in more typical ways

access to the general education curriculum A requirement of IDEA '04; gives students with disabilities the right to receive evidence-based instruction in the general education curriculum, to the greatest extent possible

accommodations Supports to compensate for disabilities; adjustments to assignments or tests

acquisition stage of learning Stage of learning in which learners may not know how to perform a skill, and the aim is for the individual to learn how to perform it

acronym A memory aid that consists of a word made from the first letters of the words that convey the information to be learned

acrostic A memory aid that consists of a sentence wherein the first letters of the words stand for

both the items to be recalled and their proper order

active listening A method of listening that involves ways to listen and respond to communication partners more effectively

active process assessment Flexible interviewing where the student discusses aloud what is being thought during computation

ADAPT framework Steps used to differentiate instruction; provides questions to assist teachers in making instructional and evaluation decisions for individual students

adequate yearly progress The progress of students toward their end-of-year goals, as tracked by the use of assessment data

advance organizer Activities to prepare students for the lesson's content

advanced placement courses Classes that provide more in-depth course content and college credit

affixes Prefixes and suffixes

age equivalents Derived developmental scores reported in years and months

alternative portfolios Schoolwork that becomes

part of the documentation about some students' progress at school; usually replaces high-stakes tests for students with disabilities

Americans with Disabilities Act (ADA) Antidiscrimination legislation guaranteeing basic civil rights to people with disabilities

analytical evaluation scale Scoring that is broken down to consider specific elements; contrast with use of a holistic evaluation scale, wherein student work is considered as a whole

anchored instruction An instructional technique that begins with an event or problem situation (a video or movie can be the anchor). The video is used to provide background information about the event or problem situation and to create a context that contributes to a shared experience among students to facilitate learning

anorexia Intense fear of gaining weight, disturbed body image, and chronic absence or refusal of appetite for food, causing severe weight loss (25% of body weight)

application stage of learning Stage of learning in which the aim is for students to use learning and extend it to new situations

array of services Constellation of special education services, personnel, and educational placements

articulation problems Abnormal production of speech sounds

Asperger's syndrome One of the autism spectrum disorders (ASD) wherein cognition is usually in the average or above-average range

assistive technologist A related services provider who assists with the selection, acquisition, or use of assistive technology

assistive technology (AT) Equipment (devices) or services that help compensate for an individual's disabilities

Assistive Technology Act of 2004 (ATA) Law that facilitates increased accessibility through technology

assistive technology device A unit such as an item, piece of equipment, or product system that helps compensate for an individual's disabilities

assistive technology services A service that assists an individual with a disability regarding AT devices

association-processing level The vocabulary acquisition level wherein words are thought of in terms of synonyms, definitions, or contexts

asthma The most common chronic health condition among children, resulting in difficulty breathing

astigmatism A refractive error, that is, a problem with how the eye focuses light

at risk Students who have experiences, living conditions, or characteristics that have been shown to contribute to school failure

attention deficit/hyperactivity disorder (ADHD) A condition characterized by hyperactivity, impulsivity, and inattention; included in the "other health impairments" category in *DSM-IV-TR*

audience In writing, the person(s) who will read the paper

audience sense In writing, the process for determining the probable reader

audiologist A related services provider who diagnoses hearing losses and auditory problems

augmentative and alternative communication devices (aug com) Methods for communicating, such as communication boards, communication books, sign language, and computerized voices; assistive technology that helps individuals communicate, including devices that actually produce speech

authentic assessments Performance measures that use work generated by the student

authentic text Nonfiction and fictional literature

autism One of the autism spectrum disorders (ASD); ranges from low functioning to high functioning

autistic savant An individual who displays many behaviors associated with autism but also possesses discrete abilities and unusual talents

automaticity Practicing skills until they require less cognitive processing

basal textbook The textbook that is used by the classroom teacher to teach subject-area content

basals Textbooks adopted by school districts to serve as a primary source for subject-area content

base-ten Decimal numeral system that has 10 as its base

base word *See* root word

behavior intervention plan Includes a functional assessment and procedures to prevent behavioral infractions and to intervene if they occur

behavioral strategies Include techniques to increase or decrease targeted behaviors

benchmark In assessment, a predetermined standard for success or failure

bilingual education Instruction that is provided in two languages

Braille A system of reading and writing that uses dot codes embossed on paper; tactile reading. In 1824, Louis Braille created a precursor to the method used today

brainstorm To think of several ideas related to a topic, write notes as one thinks, and use the notes to generate further ideas

bulimia Chronically causing oneself to vomit or otherwise remove food to limit weight gain

checking for understanding During a lesson, periodically determining whether students are learning the content

child find A requirement of IDEA '04 that educators help refer and identify children and youth with disabilities

childhood disintegrative disorder (CDD) One of the autism spectrum disorders (ASD) wherein the individual has typical development until about the age of 5 or 6

chromosomal abnormality A gene disorder

chunking Organizing information by groups or topics

classroom management Purposeful planning, delivery, and evaluation of techniques and procedures that ensure a classroom environment conducive to teaching and learning

clinical interview A procedure to examine a student's knowledge of and thinking about how to solve problems

clinical teaching cycle Sequenced instruction, reteaching if necessary, and informal assessment procedures, including assessment of academic and conversational language proficiency

closed-circuit television (CCTV) An assistive visual input technology that uses a television to increase the size of objects or print

coexisting disability The situation of having more than one disability; comorbidity

cognitive development Understanding and using declarative, procedural, and conceptual knowledge

cognitive disabilities or mental retardation A disability characterized by impaired intellectual functioning, limited adaptive behavior, need for supports, and initial occurrence before age 18; intellectual disabilities

collaboration Professionals working in partnerships to provide educational services

collaborative consultation A partnership between the general education and special education teachers, tapping the expertise of both to provide appropriate services to students with disabilities

community-based instruction (CBI) Teaching functional skills in real-life situations or in environments where they occur

comprehension-processing level The vocabulary acquisition level wherein knowledge of word associations can be used to place words in categories, create sentences, and generate multiple word meanings

computational fluency Knowing and using efficient methods for accurate computing

concepts A general idea or understanding; a crucial word or a few words that are critical for understanding the content

conceptual knowledge Understanding ideas and relationships

conflict A disagreement of interests or ideas

congenital Present at birth or originating during early infancy

connotative meaning An associated meaning added to the primary meaning

construct validity A form of technical adequacy in assessment that reflects whether tests provide results that are associated with the construct being measured

content-area instruction Teaching students subject knowledge in areas such as social studies, science, and literature

content validity A form of technical adequacy in assessment that reflects whether tests contain items that come from a legitimate source and meet basic statistical criteria

contingent observation A behavior management approach in which a disruptive student is removed from an activity but is still able to observe the activity

continuum of services Pattern in which each level of special education services is more restrictive than the one before, and services come in a lock-step sequence

convention skills In writing, the skills associated with spelling, punctuation, and capitalization; mechanics

convergent, lower order questions Questions that usually have one answer and start with *who, what, where,* or *when*

cooperative learning A grouping practice in which small, mixed-ability groups work collaboratively to complete activities

core curriculum Content that is taught to all students in the general education classroom

coteaching Team teaching by general education and special education teachers

criterion-referenced interpretations Interpretations of assessment measures for purposes of comparing performance to standards that signal mastery of the content being tested

criterion-related validity A form of technical adequacy in assessment that has to do with whether tests produce results similar to established tests, either presently (concurrent criterion-related validity) or in the future (predictive criterion-related validity)

criterion-specific rewards A reward system in which students earn privileges only when they reach desirable levels of the target behavior

critical thinking Reasoning to learn new concepts, ideas, or problem solutions

cues Visual or verbal prompts provided to increase the likelihood of correct student responses

cultural characteristics Beliefs, norms, and customs that differ within and between groups

culture Way of perceiving the world and of interacting within it

curriculum-based measurement (CBM) A direct measurement system used to monitor students' progress mastering basic academic skills

data-based decision making Used to identify students who require additional instruction and to determine whether intensive intervention supports are effective

declarative knowledge Understanding of factual information

decodable text Text that contains words made up of the sounds and patterns that students have mastered

decoding Identifying unknown words by using knowledge of letter-sound correspondences

deductive reasoning Reasoning from the general to the specific and problem solving

denotative meaning Literal, dictionary meaning

derived scores Normative scores (such as age equivalents, grade equivalents, ratio IQs, percentiles, and standard scores) into which raw scores are converted

developmental disabilities Severe disabilities that often combine intellectual and physical problems; often used interchangeably with *multiple-severe disabilities*

deviations from print In oral reading, words that are not identified correctly

diagnostic teaching Giving problems and asking students questions to determine their thinking

differentiated curriculum For gifted and talented students, different learning experiences beyond those provided to typical learners through the general education curriculum

differentiated instruction Provision of an individualized array of instructional interventions

differentiating instruction Instruction that is responsive to the diverse needs of all students with a focus on curriculum, instructional adaptations, services, and instruction intensity

direct instruction Teacher-directed instruction that focuses on using explicit, systematic procedures such as modeling, practice opportunities, pacing, error correction, and progress monitoring

disabilities Results of impairments or medical conditions

discrepancy formulas Calculations used to determine the gap between a student's achievement and her or his potential; used to identify students with learning disabilities

discrimination The ability to distinguish one item (such as a letter, number, letter sound, math sign, state, or piece of lab equipment) from another

distributive practice Practice opportunities presented over time on skills that have been taught

divergent, higher order questions Questions that require students to make inferences, to analyze or synthesize information, and to evaluate content

drafting In writing, the stage in which the author attempts to put words on paper using the planning and organization information developed during prewriting

due process hearing Noncourt proceeding before an impartial hearing officer, used when parents and school personnel disagree on a special education issue

duration recording An observational system to measure how long a discrete target behavior occurs

dyscalculia A disorder in learning mathematics skills and concepts

dysgraphia A disorder in writing that involves problems with handwriting, spelling, and composition

dyslexia A language-based reading disability

e-books Electronic versions of textbooks allowing for the application of universal design for learning

ecological assessment An assessment approach that explores the student's relationship to his or her environment, rather than simply focusing on student strengths and deficits

editing In writing, the stage in which writers focus on the mechanical aspects of spelling, capitalization, and punctuation

Education for All Handicapped Children Act *See* Public Law (PL) 94-142

efficacy The power to produce an effect

engaged time The amount of time that students are involved in learning

English language learners (ELLs) or English learners (ELs) Students who are learning English as their second (or third) language

enrichment Addition, to the traditional curriculum, of further topics and skills for the instruction of gifted and talented students

epilepsy or seizure disorders A tendency to experience recurrent seizures resulting in convulsions; caused by abnormal discharges of neurons in the brain

error correction The teacher's provision of immediate feedback to correct error responses

event recording An observational system to measure each occurrence of a discrete behavior (that is, a behavior with an observable beginning and end, such as hand raising)

evidence-based practices Instruction proved effective through rigorous research; also known as validated practices

executive functioning Ability to self-monitor by using working memory, inner speech, attention, and rehearsal

exempt In high-stakes testing, a student who does not have to participate in testing

expanded notation Shows place value representations of numerals

explicit, systematic instruction Teachers model the task and provide extensive feedback as students work through multiple opportunities to practice and respond

externalizing behaviors Behaviors directed toward others (such as aggressive behaviors)

factual knowledge Information that is based on facts and is memorized, retained, and recalled as part of learning

family systems approach An approach in which families' needs and support are defined according to resources, interactions, functions, and the life cycle

fidelity Following the protocol or lesson steps as developed for the instructional practice; ensuring the research measures are valid and reliable

flexible grouping practices Same-ability groups and mixed-ability groups for instructional purposes

form In writing, the type of written product (such as a letter, story, essay, shopping list, or poem)

free appropriate public education (FAPE) Ensures that students with disabilities receive necessary education and services without cost to the family

frustration reading level The level at which the student has less than 90% word recognition and less than 90% comprehension

full inclusion or pull-in programming Special education or related services delivered exclusively in the general education classroom

function words Words such as *on*, *in*, and *from* that are relatively easy for most students to learn because their presence helps students make sense of sentences and because they account for about half of the words seen in text

functional behavioral assessment (FBA) Behavioral evaluations, interviews, observations, and environmental manipulations conducted to determine the exact nature of problem behaviors

functional capability Student strengths related to specific tasks

functional dissonance Conflict between what a student is being asked to do and what the student can do

functional skills Skills used to manage a home, cook, shop, commute, and organize personal living environments with the goal of independent living; also known as life skills

general vocabulary Words that are used on a regular basis during conversation

generalization stage of learning Stage of learning in which the aim is for mastered skills to be employed across all appropriate situations

generation-processing level Vocabulary acquisition level wherein words can be used for discussion purposes or in activities

gifted and talented Students who are identified at the preschool, elementary, or secondary level as possessing demonstrated or potential abilities that give evidence of high performance capability

grade equivalent Derived developmental score reported in years and tenths of years

grade skipping Process in which students advance to a grade ahead of their classmates of the same age

graphic organizers Visual aids to help students organize, understand, see relationships, and remember important information

group homes Community-based living arrangements in which a small number of adults with disabilities live together and receive supports they need for independence

guided practice A teacher's providing students with multiple opportunities to respond and practice

hand over hand Sign language for individuals with deaf-blindness wherein signs are conveyed through touch

handicap A challenge or barrier imposed by others, or by society, because of a condition or disability

heterogeneity A great variety, such as a wide range of strengths and abilities in a group

hierarchical charts Charts on which broader concepts are listed first and then connected to smaller, supporting concepts

high-frequency words The most commonly occurring words in text

high-incidence disabilities Special education categories with the most students

high-stakes assessments State and district-wide assessments to ensure that all students are making satisfactory progress

holistic evaluation scale Evaluation scale in which a single, overall rating is assigned to achievement in learning the curriculum; contrast with the use of an analytical evaluation scale

home-bound instruction Special education services delivered to the student's home, usually as a consequence of the student's fragile health

honors sections An example of ability grouping

hyperactivity Impaired ability to sit or concentrate for long periods of time

I-message A communication technique that involves stating the behavior of concern, the effect of the behavior on the person sending the I-message, and the feelings that the person sending the I-message has as a result

impulsivity Impaired ability to control one's own behavior

inattention Inability to pay attention or focus

inclusive education Educational setting in which students with disabilities have access to the general education curriculum, participate in school activities alongside students without disabilities, and attend their neighborhood school

independent practice Practice that does not require direct teacher supervision or guidance; may occur in the classroom or as homework

independent reading level The reading level at which the student has at least 95% word recognition and at least 95% comprehension

independent study Study of curriculum topics in greater depth or exploration of a topic that is not part of the general education curriculum

individualized education program (IEP) Management tool to identify needed services and to specify and organize them in detail; developed through collaboration among general and special educators, administrators, medical professionals, related services providers, the student's family, and (if appropriate) the student who will receive special education services

individualized family service plan (IFSP) Management tool to identify and organize services and resources for infants and toddlers (birth to age 3) and their families

Individuals with Disabilities Education Act (IDEA) The special education law that protects the rights of students with disabilities to a free appropriate public education; originated with PL 94-142 in 1975

inferential thinking skills Reasoning skills

informal reading inventories (IRI) Unique reading tests that consist of graded word lists and graded passages and for which test scores are reported in terms of grade equivalents

information processing The flow of information that leads to understanding, knowledge, and the ability to act on information

input adaptations How students access test stimuli and questions

inquiry-based approach An approach to teaching

mathematics wherein students interact with their teachers and peers to develop multiple solution strategies for problems

in-school supervision Removing a student from one or more classes and requiring him or her to spend the time in a designated school area

instructional activity A lesson that teaches and reinforces skills and concepts; one of four instructional adaptations included in the ADAPT framework described in this book

instructional content The skills and concepts that are taught; one of four instructional adaptations included in the ADAPT framework described in this book

instructional delivery How an activity is taught, including grouping, instructional steps, presentation, and practice; one of four instructional adaptations included in the ADAPT framework described in this book

instructional materials Instructional aids such as textbooks, kits, hardware, software, and manipulatives; one of four instructional adaptations included in the ADAPT framework described in this book

instructional reading level The reading level at which the reader has either 90% to 94% word recognition and 90% to 100% comprehension *or* 95% word recognition and 90% to 94% comprehension

intellectual and developmental disabilities Significant subaverage general intellectual functioning, existing concurrently with

deficits in adaptive behavior and manifested during the developmental period, that adversely affects a child's educational performance.

intelligence quotient (IQ) Score on a standardized test that is supposed to reflect learning ability

intensity of supports The level of assistance needed for individuals to function as independently as possible; often described as intermittent, limited, extensive, or pervasive

interactional behaviors Ways in which people interact with one another across cultures

interdependent group contingency Arrangement in which individuals earn reinforcement when they achieve a goal established for the group

interim alternative educational setting (IAES) A special education placement to ensure progress toward IEP goals, assigned when a serious behavioral infraction necessitates removal from current placement

internalizing behaviors Behaviors directed inward (e.g., withdrawn, anxious, depressed)

internships A form of enrichment instruction

interval recording A system designed to measure the number of intervals of time in which continuous, highly frequent behavior occurs during the observation period

intraindividual differences In assessment, the strengths and weaknesses a person exhibits across test scores

irregular words Words in which some or all of the letters do not make their common sounds

itinerants Professionals who work in different locations

keyword method A mnemonic device that involves linking information, such as a word, with response information, such as the word's definition. The information is reconstructed either pictorially or verbally

language delays Slowed development of language skills; may or may not result in language impairments

language different Students who are just beginning to learn a second language or are using nonstandard English

language impairment Difficulty in mastering, or inability to master, the various systems of rules in language, which then interferes with communication

least restrictive environment (LRE) Educational placement of students with disabilities that provides as much inclusion in the core curriculum, and as much integration with typical learners, as possible and appropriate

legibility The extent to which what is written can be deciphered or understood

letter combinations Two or more consecutive letters that represent a single sound (/sh/) or multiple sounds (/bl/) in words

letter-sound correspondence Association of a common sound with specific letters or letter combinations in a word

level of concern Amount of student interest in the instruction

long-term memory The permanent storage of information

loudness An aspect of voice, consisting of the intensity of the sound produced while speaking

low-incidence disabilities Special education categories with relatively few students

macroculture The overarching cultural factors exhibited by the society at large

mainstreaming A term formerly used to signify including students with disabilities in school activities alongside students who do not have disabilities

maintenance stage of learning The stage of learning in which the aim is for the mastered skills to remain at the same level of performance as during the proficiency stage

manifestation determination Determination of whether a student's disciplinary problems are due to her or his disability

massed practice Extra practice of a skill to ensure mastery

medically fragile A term used to describe the status of individuals with health disabilities

mental retardation *See* intellectual and developmental disabilities

mentorships Arrangement in which students with special interests pair with adults who have expertise in those areas

microculture A group, within the larger society, whose members share similar language, belief systems, and values

mixed-ability grouping structure Arrangement of students into groups whose members are performing at various levels on the skills targeted for instruction

modeling A demonstration of how to perform the steps involved in solving a problem

modifications Adjustments to assignments or tests that reduce the requirements

morpheme The smallest unit of language that conveys meaning

multicultural education Instruction that provides students with ways to see themselves reflected in the curriculum, as well as to learn about others

multidisciplinary teams Groups of professionals with different areas of expertise, assembled to meet the special needs of individual students

multiple means of action and expression Encouraging students to respond in different ways, in accordance with their strengths

multiple means of engagement Involving students in activities by using a variety of modes of representation and expression to address their interests

multiple means of representation Presenting information in various formats to reduce or avoid sensory and cognitive barriers to learning

multisyllable word recognition Recognition of words that have two or more syllables

multitiered instructional support Tiered levels of increasingly intensive intervention at the primary, secondary, and tertiary levels

National Instructional Materials Standard (NIMAS) A standard in the IDEA '04 regulations requiring states to provide instructional materials in accessible formats to students with disabilities (e.g., electronic versions of textbooks)

No Child Left Behind Act (NCLB) Reauthorization of the Elementary and Secondary Education Act mandating higher standards for both students and teachers, including an accountability system

norm-referenced interpretations Interpretations of assessment measures for purposes of examining performance

normal curve Theoretical construct of the typical distribution of human traits such as intelligence; also known as a bell-shaped curve

normative sample The people who are given a test and whose scores provide a basis with which later test takers' scores are compared

number sense Good intuition about numbers and the relationships among them

observation In assessment, watching students do something, thinking about what they are doing, determining why they are doing it, and identifying what the behavior means to the students and those around them

occupational therapist (OT) A related services provider who directs activities that improve muscular control and develop self-help skills

on-task behavior Behavior focused on the task at hand

orientation and mobility specialist A related services provider who teaches individuals who are blind or have low vision techniques to move safely and independently at school and in the community

orthopedic impairments The term used in IDEA '04 for physical disabilities or physical impairments

other health impairments In *DSM-IV-TR,* a category that consists of health conditions that create special needs and disabilities but are not described specifically in any other category; also known as special heath care needs

outcome assessments Measurements that allow teachers and others to check the results of instruction

overlearn To continue to practice beyond the point of mastery

overrepresentation The assignment, to a special education category, of more students from a diverse group than would be expected on the basis of the proportion of that diverse group in the overall population of students

pacing Providing instruction at an appropriate rate to keep students engaged in learning and to promote understanding

paraeducators *See* paraprofessionals

paraprofessionals Teacher assistants who work in a supportive role under the supervision of licensed professionals

partial products Partitioning quantities to help students focus on place value

pedagogy Instructional practices, teaching

peer conferencing Students discussing each other's written products; considered an effective feedback and editing activity in the writing process

peer or expert consultation Teachers observing their peers providing interventions to learners, such as English language learners, who need supplemental instruction

peer tutoring A grouping practice wherein pairs of students work on their skills, usually for extra practice

percentiles Scores reported on norm-referenced tests that indicate the percentage of scores (determined from a normative sample) that fall below a person's raw score; percentile rank

perinatal During birth

peripheral vision The outer area of a person's visual field

pervasive developmental disorder—not otherwise specified (PDD-NOS) One of the autism spectrum disorders (ASD); the category used when not all three ASD characteristics (problems with communication, social interaction, and repetitive or manneristic behaviors) are present or when they are mild

phonograms Parts of a word to which consonants or blends are added to make a word (examples include *an, ip,* and *un*); also known as rimes

phonological awareness (PA) One's sensitivity to, or explicit awareness of, the phonological structure of words in one's language

physical features of the text Headings, tables, bold-faced terms, chapter organizers and summaries, and the like

physical therapist (PT) A related services provider who treats physical disabilities through many nonmedical means and works to improve motor skills

pitch An aspect of voice; its perceived high or low sound quality

planned ignoring Deliberate, systematic withdrawal of attention by the individual from whom attention is sought

postnatal After birth

prenatal Before birth

prereferral process Steps taken before the actual referral of a child to special education

prevalence Total number of cases at a given time

prewriting The writing stage that involves activities, such as planning and organizing, that are conducted by the writer prior to writing

prior knowledge What a student already knows about a topic

procedural knowledge Understanding of rules and procedures

process assessment Procedures used to determine the manner in which students derive a particular answer when solving a problem

proficiency stage of learning The stage of learning in which the aim is for the learner to perform the skill accurately and quickly

project-based learning A learning approach wherein students investigate relevant problems and discuss their work with other students

prompts *See* cues

Public Law (PL) 94-142 Originally passed in 1975 to guarantee a free appropriate public education to all students with disabilities; also known as the Education for All Handicapped Children Act (EHA)

publishing In writing, the stage in which the author's work is complete and is publicly shared in some format

pullout programs Part-time special services provided outside of the general education classroom, such as in a resource room

purpose In writing, the reason for writing (e.g., to convey a message, to make a request, or to express feelings)

reading comprehension The ability to understand what is read

reading fluency The ability to read text accurately, quickly, and (if reading aloud) with expression

reading vocabulary Word comprehension

recreational therapist A related services provider who assesses leisure function and provides therapeutic recreation and leisure education

recursive In writing, the act of moving back and forth between stages as one writes and polishes one's work

reinforcement The application of an event that increases the likelihood that the behavior it

follows will occur again. Thus reinforcement is functionally related to an increase in frequency of that behavior

related services Special education services from a wide range of disciplines and professions

reliability In assessment, the consistency of measurement results

resistant to treatment A defining characteristic of learning disabilities. Validated methods typically applied in general education settings are not adequate to bring about sufficient learning; the student requires more intensive and sustained explicit instruction

response to intervention (RTI) A multitiered prereferral method of applying increasingly intensive interventions; can be used to identify students with learning disabilities and provide intensive instruction to struggling students

Rett syndrome One of the autism spectrum disorders (ASD) that has a known genetic cause and occurs only in girls

revising In writing, the stage in which authors make changes to the sequencing and structure of the written work to refine the content

rewards Representations of targeted improvement, including tangible items, privileges, free time, or honors

rimes *See* phonograms

root word The primary lexical unit of a word; also known as the base word

rules Procedures that must be followed

same-ability grouping structure Groups in which all students are performing at a similar level

school counselor A related services provider who provides psychological and guidance services

school nurse A related services provider who assists with medical services at school, delivers health services, and designs accommodations for students with special health care needs

scientifically based (or evidence-based) **instruction** Instructional practices employed in schools that are based on findings from research studies that involved systematic, rigorous procedures using experimental or quasiexperimental research designs

screening The use of assessment data to identify quickly and efficiently who is struggling in a particular area

Section 504 of the Rehabilitation Act of 1973 First law to outline the basic civil rights of people with disabilities

self-advocacy Capacity to understand, ask for, and explain one's need for accommodations; expressing one's rights and needs

self-determination Ability to identify and achieve goals for oneself

semantic maps Visual display of a map or web of related words, vocabulary, or concepts

semantically related groups Groups of words with meaningful relationships

service manager A case coordinator who oversees the implementation and evaluation of IFSPs

short-term memory The temporary store of information that is tapped for immediate use

sickle-cell anemia A hereditary blood disorder that inhibits blood flow; African Americans are most at risk for this health impairment

sight word recognition The ability to read a word automatically when encountering it in text or in a list of words

signal words Words that indicate the use of a text structure (for example, *first*, *second*, and *third* for sequence and *on the other hand* for contrast)

signals Visual, auditory, and verbal cues that teachers use to gain student attention

silent reading fluency The number of words read at a certain comprehension level at a certain reading level

sociogram A depiction of peer relationships in graphic form

special education Individualized education and services for students with disabilities and sometimes for students who are gifted and talented

special education categories System used in IDEA '04 to classify disabilities among students

specialized vocabulary Words that have multiple meanings depending on the context

specific praise Complimenting or verbally rewarding others for their accomplishments

speech impairment A disability characterized by abnormal speech that is unintelligible, is unpleasant, or interferes with communication

speech/language pathologist (SLP) A related services provider who diagnoses and treats speech or language impairments

sponge Activities that students can complete independently and are intended to "soak up" time

statement of transition services A component of IEPs for students age 16 or older to help them move to adulthood

stay put provision Prohibits students with disabilities from being expelled because of behavior associated with their disabilities

strategy instruction The use of cognitive strategies to facilitate the learning process

structural analysis Using knowledge of word structure to decode unknown words

student-centered learning Learning in which students are actively engaged in hands-on tasks, discussions, and decision making

stuttering The lack of fluency in an individual's speech pattern, often characterized by hesitations or repetitions of sounds or words; dysfluency; a speech impairment

survey batteries Compilations of tests that assess different areas and provide an overview of achievement

survey tests Tests that survey, or assess, numerous areas

systems of supports Networks of supports that everyone develops to function optimally in life

target behavior A specific behavior, either positive or inappropriate, that the teacher focuses on to increase or decrease that behavior

teacher assistance team process A collaborative approach in which the team discusses a student's problem, identifies possible interventions, and assists the teacher as needed in implementing strategies

teacher-directed instruction At the secondary level, teachers providing lectures on textbook content and students reading their textbooks to identify important facts and concepts in preparation for weekly tests

teacher presence The use of assertive behaviors, teacher proximity, and nonverbal communication to manage student behavior and promote a positive classroom environment in which effective instruction can occur

teacher proximity The teacher positioning himself or herself close to a student to prevent or eliminate problem behavior

technical vocabulary Words that are used in a particular content area

think aloud The teacher saying out loud the steps he or she is taking while solving a problem

time sampling Recording the number of intervals in which a target behavior occurs during the period of observation

timeout-seclusion For severe, out-of-control behavior, placement of the pupil in an isolated room

tone In writing, the "voice" of a written product, which can be lighthearted, serious, optimistic, pessimistic, and so forth

traffic patterns Paths that students frequently follow as they move about the classroom

transition The interval of time occurring prior to, during, or after instruction within the classroom and between locations within the school

typical learners Students and individuals without disabilities

unexpected underachievement A defining characteristic of learning disabilities; poor school performance cannot be explained by other disabilities or limited potential

universal design Barrier-free architectural and building designs that meet the needs of everyone, including people with physical challenges; materials and instructions designed in a way to allow access for all students, including those with sensory, motor, and cognitive disabilities

universal design for learning (UDL) Design that increases access to the curriculum and instruction for all students

universal screening Testing of everyone, particularly newborns, to determine the existence or risk of disability

validated practices Thoroughly researched or evidence-based practices; scientifically validated instruction

validity The extent to which an assessment device measures what it is supposed to measure

Venn diagrams Intersecting shapes that show how concepts are similar and how they are different

vocational rehabilitation counselor A professional who provides training, career counseling, and job placement services

with-it-ness A teacher's awareness of what is going on in his or her classroom at all times

word family A base word and its derivatives

words correct per minute A measure of reading fluency, the number of words a student reads accurately in one minute

working memory The simultaneous processing and storing of information

CHAPTER 1. INCLUSIVE TEACHING AS RESPONSIVE EDUCATION

Allen, M., & Ashbaker, B. Y. (2004). Strengthening schools: Involving paraprofessionals in crisis prevention and intervention. *Intervention in School and Clinic, 39*, 139–146.

American Psychiatric Association (APA). (2013). *Diagnostic and statistical manual of mental disorders* (DSM-5; 5th ed.). Arlington, VA: Author.

Americans with Disabilities Act of 1990. PL No. 101-336, 104 STAT. 327.

Arlington Central School District Board of Education v. Murphy, 548 U.S. 291 (2006).

Artiles, A. J. (2003). Special education's changing identity: Paradoxes and dilemmas in views of culture and space. *Harvard Educational Review, 73*, 164–202.

Assistive Technology Act of 2004. PL No. 108-364.

Ballard, J., Ramirez, B. A., & Weintraub, F. J. (1982). *Special education in America: Its legal and governmental foundations.* Reston, VA: Council for Exceptional Children.

Branson, J., & Miller, D. (2002). *Damned for their difference: The cultural construction of deaf people as disabled.* Washington, DC: Gallaudet University Press.

Browder, D. M., & Cooper-Duffy, K. (2003). Evidence-based practices for students with severe disabilities and the requirement for accountability in "No Child Left Behind." *The Journal of Special Education, 37,* 157–163.

Brown v. Board of Education, 347 U.S. 483 (1954).

Burlington School Committee v. Department of Education, 471 U.S. 359 (1985).

Carey, A. C., Friedman, M., & Bryan, D. N. (2005). Use of electronic technologies by people with intellectual disabilities *Mental Retardation, 43*(5), 322–333. doi:10.1352/0047

Carter v. Florence County School District 4, 950 F. 2d 156 (1993).

Cedar Rapids School District v. Garret F., 106 F.3rd 822 (8th Cir. 1997), cert. gr. 118 S. Ct. 1793 (1998), aff'd, 119 S. Ct. 992 (1999).

Children's Defense Fund (CDF). (2004). *The state of America's children: 2004.* Washington, DC: Author.

Coyne, M. D., Kame'enui, E. J., & Carnine, D. W. (2011). *Effective teaching strategies that accommodate diverse learners* (4th ed.). Boston, MA: Pearson.

Deno, S. (2003). Developments in curriculum-based measurement. *The Journal of Special Education, 37,* 184–192.

Deshler, D. (2001). SIM to the rescue? Maybe . . . maybe not! *Stratenotes, 9,* 1–4.

Doe v. Withers, 20 IDELR 422 (1993).

Dymond, S. K., & Orelove, F. P. (2001). What constitutes effective curricula for students with severe disabilities? *Exceptionality, 9,* 109–122.

Education for All Handicapped Children Act (EHA). PL No. 94-142 (1975).

Education for All Handicapped Children Act (EHA; reauthorized). PL No. 99-457 (1986).

Elementary and Secondary Education Act. PL No. 107-110 (2001).

Finn, C. E.,Jr., Rotherham, A. J., & Hokanson, C. R., Jr. (Eds.). (2001). *Rethinking special education for a new century.* Washington, DC: Thomas B. Fordham Foundation and the Progressive Policy Institute.

Fisher, D., Frey, N., & Thousand, J. (2003). What do special educators need to know and be prepared to do for inclusive schooling to work? *Teacher Education and Special Education, 26,* 42–50.

Florian, L. (2007). Reimagining special education. In L. Florian (Ed.), *The Sage handbook of special education* (pp. 7–20). Thousand Oaks, CA: Sage.

Forest Grove School District v. TA, 129 S. Ct. 987, Supreme Court (2009).

Friend, M. (2000). Myths and misunderstandings about professional collaboration. *Remedial and Special Education, 21,* 130–132, 160.

Fuchs, D., Fuchs, L. S., & Compton, D. L. (2004). Identifying reading disabilities by responsiveness-to-instruction: Specifying measures and criteria. *Learning Disabilities Quarterly, 27,* 216–227.

Fuchs, L., Fuchs, D., & Powell, S. (2004). *Using CBM for progress monitoring*. Washington, DC: American Institutes for Research.

Fuchs, L. S., & Vaughn, S. (2012). Responsiveness-to-intervention: A decade later. *Journal of Learning Disabilities, 45*(3), 195–203.

Futernick, K. (2006). *A possible dream: Retaining California teachers so all students learn*. Sacramento, CA: CSU Center for Teacher Quality.

Garcia, E. E. (2001). *Hispanic education in the United States*. New York, NY: Rowman & Littlefield.

Gartner, A., & Lipsky, D. K. (1987). Beyond special education: Toward a quality system for all students. *Harvard Educational Review, 57,* 367–395.

Grossman, H. (2002). *Ending discrimination in special education* (2nd ed.). Springfield, IL: Charles C Thomas.

Hallahan, D. P., Kauffman, J. M., & Pullen, P. C. (2011). *Exceptional learners*. Boston, MA: Pearson.

Harry, B. (2007). The disproportionate placement of ethnic minorities in special education. In L. Florian (Ed.), *The Sage handbook of special education* (pp. 67–84). Thousand Oaks, CA: Sage.

Hitchcock, C., & Stahl, S. (2003). Assistive technology, universal design, universal design for learning: Improved learning opportunities. *Journal of Special Educational Technology, 18,* 45–52.

Honig v. Doe, 484 U.S. 305, 108 S. Ct. 592 (1988).

Individuals with Disabilities Act of 1988. PL 100-407, 29 USC 2201.

Individuals with Disabilities Education Act. PL No. 101-476. (1990).

Individuals with Disabilities Education Act. PL No. 105-17, 111 STAT. 37 (1997).

Individuals with Disabilities Education Improvement Act of 2004. PL No. 108-446.

Irving Independent School District v. Tatro, 468 U.S. 833 (1984).

Katsiyannis, A., & Yell, M. L. (2000). The Supreme Court and school health services: Cedar Rapids v. Garret F. *Exceptional Children, 66,* 317–326.

Keysor, J. (2006). How does the environment influence disability? Examining the evidence. In M. J. Field, A. M. Jette, & L. Martin (Eds.), *Workshop on disability in America: A new look* (pp. 88–100). Washington, DC: The National Academies Press.

Longmore, P. (2003). *Why I burned my book and other essays on disability*. Philadelphia, PA: Temple University Press.

Lynch, E. W., & Hanson, M. J. (2004). *Developing cross-cultural competence: A guide for working with children and their families* (3rd ed.). Baltimore, MD: Brookes.

MacMillan, D. L., & Siperstein, G. N. (2002). Learning disabilities as operationally defined by schools. In R. Bradley, L. Danielson, & D. P. Hallahan (Eds.), *Identification of learning disabilities: Research to practice* (pp. 287–333). Mahwah, NJ: Lawrence Erlbaum.

McMasters, K., Fuchs, D., Fuchs, L., & Compton, D. (2000). Monitoring the academic progress of children who are unresponsive to generally effective early reading intervention. *Assessment for Effective Intervention, 27,* 23–33.

Mills v. Board of Education of the District of Columbia, 348 F. Supp. 866 (1972).

Moody, S. W., Vaughn, S., Hughes, M. T., & Fischer, M. (2000). Reading instruction in the resource room: Set up for failure. *Exceptional Children, 66,* 305–316.

National Council on Disability (NCD). (2001, June 21). *The accessible future: Transmittal letter*. Washington, DC: Author.

No Child Left Behind Act of 2001. PL 107-110.

Office of Special Education Programs (OSEP). (2006). Students served under IDEA, Part B, by disability category and state: Fall 2005.

Retrieved from http://www.ideadata.org

Office of Special Education Programs (OSEP). (2013). Students served under IDEA, Part B, by disability category and state. Retrieved from http://www.ideadata.org.

Pennsylvania Association for Retarded Children v. Commonwealth of Pennsylvania, 343 F. Supp. 279 (E.D. Pa. 1972).

Rehabilitation Act of 1973. Section 504, 19 U.S.C. section 794.

Riddell, S. (2007). A sociology of special education. In L. Florian (Ed.), *The Sage handbook of special education* (pp. 34–45). Thousand Oaks, CA: Sage.

Roos, P. (1970). Trends and issues in special education for the mentally retarded. *Education and Training of the Mentally Retarded, 5,* 51–61.

Rowley v. Hendrick Hudson School District, 458 U.S. 176 (1982).

Sailor, W. (1991). Special education in the restructured school. *Remedial and Special Education, 12,* 8–22.

Smith v. Robinson, 468 U.S. 992 (1984).

Snell, M. E., & Brown, F. (2006). *Instruction of students with severe disabilities* (6th ed.). Upper Saddle River, NJ: Prentice Hall.

Swanson, H. L., Hoskyn, M., & Lee, C. (1999). *Interventions for students with learning disabilities. A meta-analysis of treatment outcomes*. New York, NY: Guilford Press.

Timothy W. v. Rochester, New Hampshire, School District, 875 F. 2d 945 (1989).

Trautman, M. L. (2004). Preparing and managing paraprofessionals. *Intervention in School and Clinic, 39,* 139–146.

Turnbull, A., Turnbull, H. R., & Wehmeyer, M. L., & Shogren, K. A. (2016). *Exceptional lives: Special education in today's schools* (8th ed.). Boston, MA: Pearson.

U.S. Department of Education. (1995). *Seventeenth annual report to Congress on the implementation of the Individuals with Disabilities Education Act.* Washington, DC: U.S. Government Printing Office.

U.S. Department of Education. (2006). Assistance to states for the Education of Children with Disabilities Program and the Early Intervention Program for Infants and Toddlers with Disabilities; final rule. *Federal Register, 34,* CRF Parts 300 and 301.

U.S. Department of Education, Office of Special Education Programs. (2013). Individuals with Disabilities Education Act (IDEA) database. Retrieved from http://tadnet.public .tadnet.org/pages/712

Utley, C. A., & Obiakor, F. (2001). Multicultural education and special education. In C. A. Utley & F. Obiakor (Eds.), *Special education, multicultural education, and school reform: Components of quality education for learners with mild disabilities* (pp. 1–29). Springfield, IL: Charles C Thomas.

Vaughn, S., Elbaum, B., & Boardman, A. G. (2001). The social function of students with learning disabilities: Implications for inclusion. *Exceptionality, 9,* 47–65.

Villa, R. A., Thousand, J. S., & Nevin, A. I. (2004). *A guide to coteaching.* Thousand Oaks, CA: Corwin.

Wehmeyer, M. L., Lattin, D. L., Lapp-Rincker, G., & Agran, M. (2003). Access to the general education curriculum of middle school students with mental retardation: An observational study. *Remedial and Special Education, 24,* 262–272.

West, J. (1994). *Federal implementation of the Americans with Disabilities Act, 1991–1994.* New York, NY: Milank Memorial Fund.

Winzer, M. A. (2007). Confronting difference: An excursion through the history of special education. In L. Florian (Ed.), *The Sage handbook of special education* (pp. 21–33). Thousand Oaks, CA: Sage.

Zigmond, N. (2003). Where should students with disabilities receive special education services? Is one place better than another? *The Journal of Special Education, 37,* 193–199.

Zobrest v. Catalina Foothills School District, 963 F. 2d 190 (1993).

CHAPTER 2. UNDERSTANDING LEARNERS WITH SPECIAL NEEDS: HIGH-INCIDENCE DISABILITIES OR CONDITIONS

American Association on Mental Retardation (AAMR). (2002). *Mental retardation: Definition, classification, and systems of support* (10th ed.). Washington, DC: Author.

American Psychiatric Association (APA). (2003). *Diagnostic and statistical manual of mental disorders* (4th ed., text rev.). Arlington, VA: Author.

American Psychiatric Association (APA). (2013). *Diagnostic and statistical manual of mental disorders* (DSM-5; 5th ed.). Arlington, VA: Author.

American Speech-Language-Hearing Association Ad Hoc Committee on Service Delivery in the Schools. (1993). Definitions of communication disorders and variations. *ASHA, 35* (Suppl. 10), 40–41.

Arc, The. (2005, May). Causes and prevention of mental retardation. *Frequently asked questions.* Retrieved from http://www.thearc.org

Archwamety, T., & Katsiyannis, A. (2000). Academic remediation, parole violations, and recidivism rates among delinquent youth. *Remedial and Special Education, 21,* 161–170.

Baca, L. M., & Cervantes, H. T. (Eds.). (2004). *The bilingual special education interface* (4th ed.). Columbus, OH: Merrill.

Bakken, J. P., & Whedon, C. K. (2002). Teaching text structure to improve reading comprehension. *Intervention in School and Clinic, 37,* 229–233.

Bender, W. N. (2007). *Learning disabilities: Characteristics, identification, and teaching strategies* (6th ed.) Boston, MA: Pearson.

Bernthal, J. E., & Bankson, N. W. (2004). *Articulation and phonological disorders* (5th ed.). Boston, MA: Pearson.

Bishop, D. V. M. (2006). What causes specific language impairment in children? *Current Directions in Psychological Science, 15*(5), 217–221. doi:10.1111/j.1467-8721.2006.00439.x

Bradley, R., Danielson, L., & Hallahan, D. P. (Eds.). (2002). *Identification of learning disabilities: Research to practice.* Mahwah, NJ: Lawrence Erlbaum.

Bryan, T., Burstein, K., & Ergul, C. (2004). The social-emotional side of learning disabilities: A science-based presentation of the state of the art. *Learning Disability Quarterly, 27,* 45–51.

Bryant, B. R., Bryant, D. P., Porterfield, J., Falcomata, T., Shih, M., Valentine, C., . . . Bell, K. (2014). The effects of a tier 3 intervention for second grade students with serious mathematics difficulties. *Journal of Learning Disabilities.* Advance online publication. doi:10.1177/0022219414538516

Bryant, B. R., Seok, S., Ok, M., & Bryant, D. P. (2012). Individuals with intellectual and/or developmental disabilities use of assistive technology devices in support provision. *Journal of Special Education Technology, 27*(2), 41–57.

Bryant, B.R., Shih, M., Bryant, D. P., & Seok, S. (2010). The role of assistive technology in support needs assessments for children with intellectual disabilities [Special series]. *Exceptionality, 18*(4), 203–213.

Bryant, D. P., Bryant, B. R., Gerten, R., Scammacca, M., & Chavez, M. (in press). Mathematics interventions for first and second grade students with mathematics difficulties: The effects of Tier 2 intervention delivered as booster lesson. *Remedial and Special Education.*

Bryant, D. P., Bryant, B. R., & Hammill, D. D. (2000, March/April). Characteristic behaviors of students with LD who have teacher-identified math weakness. *Journal of Learning Disabilities, 33*, 168–177, 199.

Bryant, D. P., Bryant, B. R., Roberts, G., Vaughn, S., Hughes, K., Porterfield, J., & Gersten, R. (2011). Effects of an early numeracy intervention on the performance of first-grade students with mathematics difficulties. *Exceptional Children, 78*(1), 7–23.

Bullis, M., Walker, H. M., & Sprague, J. R. (2001). A promise unfulfilled: Social skills training with at-risk and antisocial children and youth. *Exceptionality, 9*, 67–90.

Carlson, C. L., Booth, J. E., Shin, M., & Canu, W. H. (2002). Parent, teacher-, and self-rated motivational styles in ADHD subtypes. *Journal of Learning Disabilities, 35*, 103–113.

Centers for Disease Control (CDC). (2004). Fetal alcohol syndrome. *Fast facts.* Retrieved from http://www.cdc.gov

Chadsey, J., & Beyer, S. (2001). Social relationships in the workplace. *Mental Retardation and Developmental Disabilities Research Reviews, 7*, 128–133.

Children and Adults with Attention-Deficit/Hyperactivity Disorder (CHADD). (2004). *Fact sheet.* Retrieved from http://www.chadd.org

Compton, D. L., Fuchs, L. S., Fuchs, D., Lambert, W., & Hamlett, C. L. (2012). The cognitive and academic profiles of reading and mathematics learning disabilities. *Journal of Learning Disabilities, 45*, 79–85. doi:10.1177/0022219410393012

The Consortium for Evidence-Based Early Intervention Practices. (2010). *A response to the Learning Disabilities Association of America (LDA) white paper on specific learning disabilities (SLD) identification.* Retrieved from http://www.isbe.net/spec-ed/pdfs/LDA_SLD_white_paper_response.pdf

Conture, E. G. (2001). *Stuttering: Its nature, diagnosis, and treatment.* Boston, MA: Pearson.

Davis, S., & Davis, L. A. (2003). Fetal alcohol syndrome. *Frequently asked questions.* Retrieved from http://www.thearc.org

Dimitrovsky, L., Spector, H., & Levy-Schiff, R. (2000). Stimulus gender and emotional difficulty level: Their effect on recognition of facial expressions of affect in children with and without LD. *Journal of Learning Disabilities, 33*, 410–416.

Fabiano, G. A., Pelham, W. E., Coles, E. K., Gnagy, E. M., Chronis-Tuscano, A., & O'Connor, B. C. (2009). A meta-analysis of behavioral treatments for attention-deficit/hyperactivity disorder. *Clinical Psychology Review, 29*(2), 129–140. doi:10.1016/j.cpr.2008.11.001

Fisher, D., Frey, N., & Thousand, J. (2003). What do special educators need to know and be prepared to do for inclusive schooling to work? *Teacher Education and Special Education, 26*, 42–50.

Fisher, K. W., & Shogren, K. A. (2012). Integrating augmentative and alternative communication and peer support for students with disabilities: A social-ecological perspective. *Journal of Special Education Technology, 27*(2), 23–39.

Fletcher, J. M., Lyon, G. R., Barnes, M., Stuebing, K. K., Francis, D. J., Olson, R. K., . . . Shaywitz, B. A. (2002). Classifications of learning disabilities: An evidence-based evaluation. In R. Bradley, L. Danielson, & D. P. Hallahan (Eds.), *Identification of learning disabilities: Research to practice* (pp. 185–250). Mahwah, NJ: Lawrence Erlbaum.

Forness, S. R., & Knitzer, J. (1992). A new proposed definition and terminology to replace "serious emotional disturbance" in IDEA. *School Psychology Review, 21*, 13.

Freeman, S. N., & Kasari, C. (2002). Characteristics and qualities of the play dates of children with Down syndrome: Emerging or true friendships? *American Journal on Mental Retardation, 107*, 16–31.

Frey, K. S., Hirschstein, M. K., & Guzzo, B. A. (2000). Second step: Preventing aggression by promoting social competence. *Journal of Emotional and Behavioral Disorders, 8*, 102–112.

Fuchs, D., & Fuchs, L. S. (2006, July). *Curriculum based measurement and response to intervention (RTI).* Kansas City, MO: Progress Monitoring Center, Summer Institute.

Fuchs, D., Fuchs, L. S., Thompson, A., Al Otaiba, S., Yen, L., Yang, N. J., . . . Braun, M. (2002). Exploring the importance of reading programs for kindergarteners with disabilities in mainstream classrooms. *Exceptional Children, 68*, 295–311.

Fuchs, D., Fuchs, L.S., & Vaughn, S.R. (in press). What is intensive instruction and why is it important? *Teaching Exceptional Children.*

Fuchs, L. S., & Fuchs, D. (2001). Principles for the prevention and intervention of mathematics difficulties. *Learning Disabilities Research & Practice, 16*, 85–95.

Fuchs, L. S., Fuchs, D., & Compton, D. L. (2013). Intervention effects for students with comorbid forms of learning disability: Understanding the needs of nonresponders. *Journal of Learning Disabilities, 46*, 534–548. doi:10.1177/0022219412468889

Fuchs, L. S., & Vaughn, S. (2012). Responsiveness-to-intervention: A decade later. *Journal of Learning Disabilities, 45*(3), 195–203. doi:10.1177/0022219412442150

Futernick, K. (2006). *A possible dream: Retaining California teachers so all students learn.* Unpublished manuscript, Center for Teacher Quality at The California State University, Sacramento.

Gargiulo, R. M. (2003). *Special education in a contemporary society: An introduction to exceptionality.* Belmont, CA: Wadsworth-Thomson.

Goldberg, R. J., Higgins, E. L., Raskind, M. H., & Herman, K. L. (2003). Predictors of success in individuals with learning disabilities: A qualitative analysis of a 20-year longitudinal study. *Learning Disabilities Research and Practice, 18*, 222–236.

Gotsch, T. (2002, March 13). Medication issue could emerge in IDEA debate. *Special Education Report, 28,* 1–2.

Graham, S., & Harris, K. R. (2011). Writing and students with disabilities. In J. M. Kauffman & D. P. Hallahn (Eds.), *Handbook of special education.* New York, NY: Routledge.

Gregg, N., & Mather, N. (2002, February). School is fun at recess: Informal analyses of written language for students with learning disabilities. *Journal of Learning Disabilities, 35,* 7–22.

Gresham, F. M., Lane, K. L., & Lambros, K. M. (2000, Summer). Comorbidity of conduct problems and ADHD: Identification of "fledgling psychopaths." *Journal of Emotional and Behavioral Disorders, 8,* 83–93.

Hall, B. J., Oyer, H. J., & Haas, W. H. (2001). *Speech, language, and hearing disorders: A guide for the teacher.* Boston, MA: Pearson.

Hallahan, D. P., Kauffman, J. M., & Pullen, P. C. (2015). *Exceptional children: Introduction to special education* (13th ed.). Boston, MA: Pearson.

Hammill, D. (2004). What we know about correlates of reading. *Exceptional Children, 70,* 453–468.

Harris, K. R., & Graham, S. (1999). Programmatic intervention research: Illustrations from the evolution of self-regulated strategy development. *Learning Disability Quarterly, 22,* 251–262.

Hartung, C. M., & Scambler, D. J. (2006). Dealing with bullying and victimization in schools. *Emotional & Behavioral Disorders in Youth, 6,* 73–96.

Hughes, C., & Carter, E. W. (2006). *Success for all students: Promoting inclusion in secondary schools through peer buddy programs.* Boston, MA: Pearson.

IDEA Practices. (2002). *Youth with disabilities in the juvenile justice system.* Retrieved from http://www.ideapractices.org

The IRIS Center. (2006). *The Response to Intervention (RTI) Module Series.* Nashville, TN: Vanderbilt University. Retrieved from http://www.iris.peabody.vanderbilt.edu

Jenkins, J. R., & O'Connor, R. E. (2002). Early identification and intervention for young children with reading/learning disabilities. In R. Bradley, L. Danielson, & D. P. Hallahan (Eds.), *Identification of learning disabilities: Research to practice* (pp. 99–149). Mahwah, NJ: Lawrence Erlbaum.

Kauffman, J. M. (2005). *Characteristics of behavioral disorders of children and youth* (8th ed.). Columbus, OH: Merrill.

Kennedy, C. H., & Horn, E. (2004). *Including students with severe disabilities.* Boston, MA: Pearson.

Kuhne, M., & Wiener, J. (2000). Stability of social status of children with and without learning disabilities. *Learning Disability Quarterly, 23,* 64–75.

Kukic, S., Tilly, D., & Michelson, L. (2005). *Addressing the needs of students with learning difficulties through the response to intervention (RtI) strategies.* Alexandria, VA: National Association of State Directors of Special Education (NASDSE).

Lane, K. L. (2004). Academic instruction and tutoring interventions for students with emotional/behavioral disorders: 1990 to present. In R. B. Rutherford, M. M. Quinn, & S. R. Mathur (Eds.), *Handbook of research in emotional and behavioral disorders* (pp. 462–486). New York, NY: Guilford.

Lane, K. L., & Wehby, J. (2002). Addressing antisocial behavior in the schools: A call for action. *Academic Exchange Quarterly, 6,* 4–7.

Lerner, J., & Kline, F. (2006). *Learning disabilities and related disorders* (10th ed.). Boston, MA: Houghton Mifflin.

Luckasson, R., Borthwick-Duffy, S., Buntinx, W. H. E., Coulter, D. L., Craig, E. M., Reeve, A., . . . Tassé,

M. J. (2002). *Mental retardation: Definition, classification, and systems of supports* (10th ed.). Washington, DC: American Association on Mental Retardation.

Luckasson, R., & Schalock, R. L. (2013). What's at stake in the lives of people with intellectual disability? Part II: Recommendations for naming, defining, diagnosing, classifying, and planning supports. *Intellectual and Developmental Disabilities, 51*(2), 94–101. doi:10.1352/1934-9556-51.2.094

Maag, J. W. (2000). Managing resistance. *Intervention in School and Clinic, 35,* 131–140.

Manley, R. S., Rickson, H., & Standeven, B. (2000). Children and adolescents with eating disorders: Strategies for teachers and school counselors. *Intervention in School and Clinic, 35,* 228–231.

Mayes, S. D., Calhoun, S. L., & Crowell, E. W. (2000). Learning disabilities and ADHD: Overlapping spectrum disorders. *Journal of Learning Disabilities, 33,* 417–424.

McLaughlin, M. J., & Nolet, V. (2004). *What every principal needs to know about special education.* Thousand Oaks, CA: Corwin.

Mercer, A. (2004). *Students with learning problems* (7th ed.). Columbus, OH: Merrill/Prentice Hall.

Müller, E., & Markowitz, J. (2004). *Disability categories: State terminology, definitions & eligibility criteria.* Alexandria, VA: National Association of State Directors of Special Education (NASDSE), Project Forum.

National Center for Educational Statistics (NCES). (2005). *Quick tables and figures.* http://www.nces.ed.gov/quicktables

National Down Syndrome Society. (2006). *Education and schooling.* Retrieved from http://www.ndss.org

National Institute of Mental Health (NIMH). (2005). *What is attention deficit hyperactivity disorder?* Retrieved from http://www.nimh.nih.gov

National Institutes of Health, National Institute of Neurological Disorders and Stroke (NINDS). (2006). What is learning disabilities? *NINDS Learning Disabilities Information Page.* Retrieved from http://www.ninds.nih.gov

Office of Special Education Programs (OSEP). (2001). Special education in correctional facilities. The twenty-third annual report to Congress on the implementation of IDEA. *U.S. Department of Education.* Washington, DC: U.S. Government Printing Office.

Office of Special Education Programs (OSEP). (2006). *Students served under IDEA, Part B, by disability category and state: Fall 2005.* Retrieved from http://www.ideadata.org

Olmeda, R. E., Thomas, A. R., & Davis, C. P. (2003). An analysis of sociocultural factors in social skills training studies with students with attention deficit/hyperactivity disorder. *Multiple Voices, 6,* 58–72.

Parrish, T., & Esra, P. (2006). The special education expenditure project (SEEP): Synthesis of findings and policy implications. *Forum: Policy Brief Analysis.* Alexandria, VA: Project Forum, The National Association of State Directors of Special Education.

Payne, K. T., & Taylor, O. L. (2006). Multicultural influences on human communication. In N. B. Anderson & G. H. Shames (Eds.), *Human communication disorders: An introduction* (7th ed., pp. 93–125). Boston, MA: Pearson.

Pierangelo, R., & Giuliani, G. (2006). *Learning disabilities: A practical approach to foundations, assessment, diagnosis, and teaching.* Boston, MA: Pearson.

Pierce, K. (2003). Attention-deficit/hyperactivity disorder and comorbidity. *Primary Psychiatry, 10*(4), 69–70, 75.

Ramig, P. R., & Shames, G. H. (2006). Stuttering and other disorders of fluency. In N. B. Anderson &

G. H. Shames (Eds.), *Human communication disorders: An introduction* (7th ed., pp. 183–221). Boston, MA: Pearson.

Reid, R., Riccio, C. A., Kessler, R. H., DuPaul, G. J., Power, T. J., Anastopoulos, A. D., . . . Noll, M. B. (2000). Gender and ethnic differences in ADHD as assessed by behavior ratings. *Journal of Emotional and Behavioral Disorders, 8,* 38–48.

Reschly, D. J. (2002). Minority overrepresentation: The silent contributor to LD prevalence and diagnostic confusion. In R. Bradley, L. Danielson, & D. P. Hallahan (Eds.), *Identification of learning disabilities: Research to practice* (pp. 361–368). Mahwah, NJ: Lawrence Erlbaum.

Roizen, N. J. (2001). Down syndrome: Progress in research. *Mental Retardation and Developmental Disabilities Research Reviews, 7,* 38–44.

Salend, S. J. (2005). *Creating inclusive classrooms: Effective and reflective practices for all students* (5th ed.). Columbus, OH: Merrill/Prentice Hall.

Schalock, R. L., Borthwick-Duffy, S., Bradley, V. J., Buntinx, W. H. E., Coulter, D. L., Craig, E. M., . . . Yeager, M. H. (2010). *Intellectual disability: Definition, classification, and systems of supports* (11th ed.). Washington, DC: American Association on Intellectual and Developmental Disabilities.

Small, L. H. (2005). *Fundamentals of phonetics: A practical guide for students* (2nd ed.) Boston, MA: Pearson.

Spencer, T. J., Bierderman, J., & Wilens, T. W. (2010). Medications used for attention-deficit/hyperactivity disorder. In M. K. Dulcan (Ed.), *Dulcan's textbook of child and adolescent psychiatry.* Retrieved from http://www.psychiatryonline.com/

Sunderland, L. C. (2004). Speech, language, and audiology services in public schools. *Intervention in School and Clinic, 39,* 209–217.

TASH. (2004). *Inclusive quality education.* Retrieved from http://www.tash.org

Taylor, R. L., Richards, S. B., & Brady, M. P. (2005). *Mental retardation: Historical perspectives, current practices, and future directions.* Boston, MA: Pearson.

Thompson, J. R., Wehmeyer, M., Hughes, C., Copeland, S. R., Little, T. D., Obremski, S., . . . Tassé, M. J. (2008). *Supports Intensity Scale for Children.* Washington, DC: American Association for Intellectual and Developmental Disabilities. Manuscript in preparation.

Torgesen, J. K. (2002). Empirical and theoretical support for direct diagnosis of learning disabilities by assessment of intrinsic processing weaknesses. In R. Bradley, L. Danielson, & D. P. Hallahan (Eds.), *Identification of learning disabilities: Research to practice* (pp. 565–652). Mahwah, NJ: Lawrence Erlbaum.

U.S. Department of Education. (2006). Assistance to states for the Education of Children with Disabilities Program and the Early Intervention Program for Infants and Toddlers with Disabilities; final rule. *Federal Register, 34,* CRF Parts 300 and 301.

U.S. Department of Education, National Center for Education Statistics [NCES], Common Core of Data [CCD]. (2012). "State Nonfiscal Survey of Public Elementary/Secondary Education," 1996–97 through 2010–11; Private School Universe Survey (PSS), selected years 1997–98 through 2009–10; and National Elementary and Secondary Enrollment Model, 1972–2010.

U.S. Department of Education, Office of Special Education and Rehabilitative Services, Office of Special Education Programs. (2014). *36th Annual Report to Congress on the Implementation of the Individuals with Disabilities Education Act, 2014.* Washington, DC: U.S. Department of Education.

U.S. Department of Education, Office of Special Education Programs (OSEP). (2013). Individuals with

Disabilities Education Act (IDEA) database. Retrieved from http://tadnet.public.tadnet.org/pages/712

U.S. Senate Appropriations Committee. (2004, September 15). *Senate Appropriations Committee report on the Labor/HHS/Education bill.* Washington, DC: U.S. Senate.

Vaughn, S. (2005, June 8). *Evidence-Based Reading Interventions for the 2%.* Paper presented at the OSEP 15th Annual Technical Assistance and Dissemination Conference, Washington, DC.

Vaughn, S., Elbaum, B., & Boardman, A. G. (2001). The social function of students with learning disabilities: Implications for inclusion. *Exceptionality, 9,* 47–65.

Vaughn, S., & Linan-Thompson, S. (2004). *Research-based methods of reading instruction: Grades K–3.* Alexandria, VA: Association for Supervision and Curriculum Development.

Vaughn, S., Wexler, J., Leroux, A. J., Roberts, G., Denton, C. A., Barth, A. E., & Fletcher, J. M. (2011). Effects of intensive reading intervention for eighth grade students with persistently inadequate response to intervention. *Journal of Learning Disabilities, 45*(6), 515–525. doi:10.1177/0022219411402692

Vaughn, S. R., & Bos, C. S. (2012). Strategies for teaching students with learning and behavior problems (8th ed.). Boston, MA: Pearson.

Walker, H. M., Nishioka, V., Zeller, R., Bullis, M., & Sprague, J. R. (2001). School-based screening, identification, and service delivery issues. *Emotional and Behavioral Disorders in Youth, 1,* 51–52.

Walker, H. M., Ramsey, E., & Gresham, F. M. (2004). *Antisocial behavior in school: Evidence-based practices* (2nd ed.). Belmont, CA: Wadsworth.

Wehmeyer, M. L., Tassé, M. J., Davies, D. D., & Stock, S. (2012). Support needs of adults with intellectual disability across domains: The role of technology. *Journal of Special Education Technology, 27*(2), 11–21.

Wetherby, A. M. (2002). Communication disorders in infants, toddlers, and preschool children. In G. H. Shames & N. B. Anderson (Eds.), *Human communication disorders: An introduction* (6th ed., pp. 186–217). Boston, MA: Pearson.

Yates, J. R., & Ortiz, A. A. (2004). Classification issues in special education for English language learners. In A. M. Sorrells, H. J. Rieth, & P. T. Sindelar (Eds.), *Critical issues in special education* (pp. 38–56). Boston, MA: Pearson.

CHAPTER 3. UNDERSTANDING LEARNERS WITH SPECIAL NEEDS: LOW-INCIDENCE DISABILITIES OR CONDITIONS

American Association of Neurological Surgeons. (2012). *Epilepsy.* Rolling Meadows, IL: Author. Retrieved from http://www.aans.org/Patient%20information/conditions%20and%20treatments/epilepsy.aspx

American Foundation for the Blind. (2014a). *Glossary of eye conditions.* Retrieved from http://www.afb.org/info/living-with-vision-loss/eye-conditions/12

American Foundation for the Blind. (2014b). *Educational interventions for students with low vision.* Retrieved from http://www.afb.org/info/programs-and-services/professional-development/teachers/educational-interventions-for-students-with-low-vision-2646/1235

American Psychiatric Association (APA). (2013). *Diagnostic and statistical manual of mental disorders* (DSM-5; 5th ed.). Washington, DC: Author.

American Society of Neuroradiology. (2012–2013). *Traumatic brain injury (TBI) and concussion.* Oak Brook, IL: Author. Retrieved from http://www.asnr.org/patientinfo/conditions/tbi.shtml#sthash.EkaKMqxF.dpbs

American Speech-Language-Hearing Association (ASHA). (2014). *Facts about pediatric hearing loss.* Retrieved from http://www.asha.org/aud/Facts-about-Pediatric-Hearing-Loss

American Speech-Language-Hearing Association (ASHA). (2015). *Causes of hearing loss in children.* Retrieved from http://www.asha.org/public/hearing/disorders/causes.htm

Asthma and Allergy Foundation of America. (n.d.). *Asthma facts and figures.* Retrieved from https://www.aafa.org/display.cfm?sub=42&id=8

Bryant, B. R., Seok, S., Ok, M., & Bryant, D. P. (2012). Individuals with intellectual and/or developmental disabilities use of assistive technology devices in support provision. *Journal of Special Education Technology, 27*(2), 41–57.

Bryant, D., & Bryant, B. (2011). *Assistive technology for people with disabilities* (2nd ed.). Boston, MA: Pearson.

Center for Head Injury Services. (2014). *Brian injury statistics.* Retrieved from http://www.headinjuryctr-stl.org/statistics.html

Centers for Disease Control and Prevention (CDC). (2005). *Vision impairment.* Atlanta, GA: National Center on Birth Defects and Developmental Disabilities.

Centers for Disease Control and Prevention (CDC). (2010). *A fact sheet for teachers, counselors, and school professionals.* Washington, DC: Author.

Centers for Disease Control and Prevention (CDC). (2014). *Traumatic brain injury in the United States: Fact sheet.* Retrieved from http://www.cdc.gov/traumaticbraininjury/get_the_facts.html

Cerebralpalsy.org. (2014). *Prevalence of cerebral palsy.* Novi, MI: **Stern Law Group.** Retrieved from http://cerebralpalsy.org/about-cerebral-palsy/prevalence-and-incidence/

Child and Adolescent Health Measurement Initiative. (2011).

How many children have health care needs? Retrieved from http://childhealthdata.org/browse/survey/results?q=1792

Cook, A. M., & Polgar, J. M. (2012). *Essentials of assistive technologies.* St. Louis, MO: Mosby.

Ellison, J. (2002). *Miracles happen: One mother, one daughter, one journey.* New York, NY: Hyperion.

Epilepsy Foundation of America (EFA). (2014). *Epilepsy stats and facts.* Retrieved from http://www.epilepsy.com/node/986825

Fisher, K. W., & Shogren, K. A. (2012). Integrating augmentative and alternative communication and peer support for students with disabilities: A social-ecological perspective. *Journal of Special Education Technology, 27*(2), 23–39.

Guiding Eyes for the Blind. (2014). *General information.* Retrieved from https://www.guidingeyes.org/about-us/general-information/#6

Hands and Voices. (2014). *Communications considerations A-Z: Deaf culture and community.* Boulder, CO: Author. Retrieved from http://www.handsandvoices.org/comcon/articles/pdfs/deafculture.pdf

Heward, W. L. (2010). *Characteristics of children with autism spectrum disorders.* Retrieved from http://www.education.com/reference/article/children-autism-spectrum-disorders/

Hill, C., Raymond, G., & Yeung, I. (2013). *Ambient assisted living technology.* Unpublished manuscript.

Hoffmeister, R. J., & Caldwell-Harris, C. L. (2014). Acquiring English as a second language via print: The task for deaf children. *Cognition, 132,* 220–242.

Individuals with Disabilities Education Improvement Act of 2004. PL No. 108–446.

Interagency Autism Coordinating Committee. (2011, January 18). *The 2011 Interagency Autism Coordinating Committee strategic plan for autism spectrum disorder research.* Retrieved from http://iacc.hhs.gov/strategic-plan/2011/index.shtml

Jackson, R. M. (2014). *Curriculum access for students with low-incidence disabilities: The promise of universal design for learning.* Retrieved from http://aem.cast.org/about/publications/2005/ncac-curriculum-access-low-incidence-udl.html#.VduASvn2BD8

Keller, H. (1988). *The story of my life.* Mineola, NY: Dover Thrift Editions.

Kohnle, D. (2014, May 8). Health tip: Dealing with an autism spectrum disorder. *U.S. News & World Report.* Retrieved from http://health.usnews.com/health-news/articles/2014/05/08/health-tip-dealing-with-an-autism-spectrum-disorder

Macular Degeneration Foundation. (2012). *Low vision aids & technology: A guide.* Sydney, Australia: Author. Retrieved from http://www.mdfoundation.com.au/resources/1/MDF_LowVisionAids.pdf

Marin County Office of Education. (2010). *Emergency plan for students with special needs for Marin County School District.* Retrieved from http://www.marinschools.org/SafeSchools/Documents/EmergencyServices/MCOE2013EmerPlan.pdf

Miles, B. (2008). *Overview on deaf-blindness.* Retrieved from http://www.nationaldb.org/documents/products/Overview.pdf

National Center for Education Statistics. (2013). *Fast facts: Students with disabilities.* Retrieved from http://nces.ed.gov/fastfacts/display.asp?id=64

National Dissemination Center for Children with Disabilities (NICHCY). (2012). *Traumatic brain injury. Fact sheet 18.* Washington, DC: National Dissemination Center for Children with Disabilities.

National Human Genome Research Institute. (2014). *Learning about sickle cell disease.* Retrieved from http://www.genome.gov/10001219

National Infant & Toddler Child Care Initiative. (2010). *Infant/toddler development, screening, and assessment.* Washington, DC: Author. http://www.zerotothree.org/public-policy/state-community-policy/nitcci/multidisciplinary-consultant-module-2.pdf

National Institute of Environmental Health Sciences (NIEHS). (2012). *Asthma and its environmental triggers.* Retrieved from http://www.niehs.nih.gov

National Institute of Mental Health (NIMH). (2014). *What is autism spectrum disorder?* Retrieved from http://www.nimh.nih.gov/health/topics/autism-spectrum-disorders-asd/index.shtml

National Institute on Deafness and Other Communication Disorders. (2014). *Cochlear implants.* Retrieved from http://www.nidcd.nih.gov/health/hearing/pages/coch.aspx

New Mexico Public Education Department Special Education Bureau. (2011). *Disabilities—Exceptionalities, in policies and procedures for the provision of special education services for students with disabilities and gifted students.* Albuquerque, NM: Author.

Office of Special Education Programs (OSEP). (2006). *Students served under IDEA, Part B, by disability category and state: Fall 2005.* Retrieved from http://www2.ed.gov/about/reports/annual/osep/2006/index.html

Park, A. (2009, September 9). Autism symptoms disappeared with behavioral therapy in babies. *Time.* Retrieved from http://time.com/3305027/autism-symptoms-disappeared-with-behavioral-therapy-in-babies/

Smith, D. D., & Tyler, N. C. (2010). *Introduction to special education: Making a difference* (7th ed.). Columbus, OH: Merrill/Pearson.

Snell, M. E., & Brown, F. (2010). *Instruction of students with severe disabilities* (7th ed.). Upper Saddle River, NJ: Merrill/Prentice Hall.

Stern Law Group. (2015). Definition of cerebral palsy. Retrieved from http://cerebralpalsy.org/about-cerebral-palsy/definition/

Szymanski, C., Lutz, L., Shahan, C., & Gala, N. (2013). *Critical needs of students who are deaf or hard of hearing: A public input summary*. Washington, DC: Laurent Clerc National Deaf Education Center, Gallaudet University.

U.S. Department of Education. (1996). *Nineteenth annual report to Congress on the implementation of the Individuals with Disabilities Education Act*. Washington, DC: U.S. Government Printing Office.

U.S. Department of Education, National Center for Education Statistics. (2013). *Digest of education statistics, 2012* (NCES 2014-015, Chapter 2). Retrieved from http://nces.ed.gov/fastfacts/display.asp?id=59

U.S. Department of Education, Office of Special Education and Rehabilitative Services, Office of Special Education Programs. (2014). *35th Annual Report to Congress on the Implementation of the Individuals with Disabilities Education Act, 2013*. Washington, DC: Author.

U. S. Department of Health and Human Services. (2010). *Child health USA 2010*. Retrieved from http://www.mchb.hrsa.gov/chusa10/index.html

U.S. Department of State, Bureau of International Information Programs. (2013, August 28). *Overcoming barriers to equal education*. Washington, DC: Author. Retrieved from http://iipdigital.usembassy.gov/st/english/pamphlet/2013/08/20130823281583.html#axzz3G8MTbniJ

U.S. Government Accountability Office (GAO). (2011, May). *Deaf and hard of hearing children* (GAO-11-257). Retrieved from http://www.gao.gov/assets/320/318711.html

World Health Organization. (2014). *Visual impairment and blindness*. Retrieved from http://www.who.int/mediacentre/factsheets/fs282/en/

CHAPTER 4. OTHER STUDENTS WITH SPECIAL LEARNING NEEDS

American Association of University Women. (1992). *How schools shortchange girls*. Washington, DC: Author.

Au, K. H. (1980). Participation structures in a reading lesson with Hawaiian children: Analysis of a culturally appropriate instructional event. *Anthropology & Education Quarterly, 11*(2), 91–115. doi:10.1525/aeq.1980.11.2.05x1874b

Bardack, S. (2010), *Common ELL terms and definitions*. Washington, DC: English Language Learner Center, American Institutes for Research.

Boulder Valley School District Office of Advanced Academic Services. (2010). Identifying talented and gifted students from culturally, linguistically, and ethnically diverse (CLED) populations. Retrieved from http://bvsd.org/tag/Documents/CLED%20Identification.pdf

Brown, J. E., & Ortiz, S. O. (2014). Intervention for English learners with learning disabilities. In J. T. Mascolo, V. C. Alfonso, & D. O. Flanagan (Eds.), *Essentials of planning, selecting, and tailoring interventions for unique learners* (pp. 274–275). Hoboken, NJ: John Wiley & Sons.

Bryant, B. R., Bryant, D. P., Porterfield, J., Falcomata, T., Shih, M., Valentine, C., . . . Bell, K. (2014). The effects of a tier 3 intervention for second grade students with serious mathematics difficulties. *Journal of Learning Disabilities*. Advance online publication. doi:10.1177/0022219414538516

Children's Defense Fund. (2014). *The state of America's children*. Washington, DC: Authors. Retrieved from http://www.childrensdefense.org/library/state-of-americas-children/

Council on Social Work Education. (2010).

DeNavas-Walt, C., Proctor, B. D., & Smith, J. C. (2012). *Income, poverty, and health insurance coverage in the United States: 2011*. Washington, DC: U.S. Department of the Census.

Fletcherm, J. L., & Speirs Neumeister, K. L. (2012). Research on perfectionism and achievement motivation: Implications for gifted students. *Psychology in the Schools, 49*(7), 668–677.

Friend, M. (2008). *Special education: Contemporary perspectives for school professionals* (2nd ed.). Boston, MA: Pearson.

Gardner, H. (1983). *Frames of mind*. New York, NY: Basic Books.

Gardner, H. (1993). *Multiple intelligences: The theory in practice*. New York, NY: Basic Books.

Goldenberg, C. (2008). Teaching English language learners: What the research does—and does not—say. *American Educator, 32*(2) 8–23, 42–44.

Gollnick, D. M., & Chinn, P. C. (2012). *Multicultural education in a pluralistic society* (9th ed.). Columbus, OH: Merrill.

Gregory, G. H., & Chapman, C. (2013). *Differentiated instructional strategies: One size doesn't fit all* (3rd ed.). Thousand Oaks, CA: Corwin.

Hammer, P. C. (2012). *Effects of disability labels on students with exceptionalities: A brief review of the literature*. Charleston: West Virginia Department of Education. Retrieved from http://wvde.state.wv.us/research/reports2012/LitReview_EffectsofDisabilityLabelsonStudentswithExceptionalities2012.pdf

Heath, S. B. (1983). *Ways with words: Language, life, and work in communities and classrooms*. New York, NY: Cambridge University Press.

Hernández, D., & Napierala, J. S. (2012). Children in immigrant families: Essential to America's future. *Child and Youth Well-Being Index Policy Brief*. New York, NY: Foundation for Child Development.

Hill, C., Corbett, C., & St. Rose, A. (2010). *Why so few? Women in science, technology, engineering, and mathematics.* Washington, DC: American Association of University Women. Retrieved from http://www.aauw.org/resource/why-so-few-women-in-science-technology-engineering-mathematics/

Housing Assistance Council. (2011). Poverty in rural America. Retrieved from http://www.ruralhome.org/storage/documents/info_sheets/povertyamerica.pdf

Individuals with Disabilities Education Improvement Act of 2004. PL No. 108-446.

Jacob K. Javits Gifted and Talented Students Education Act of 1988.

Kauffman, J. M. (1999). Commentary: Today's special education and its message for tomorrow. *Journal of Special Education, 32*(4), 244–254.

Klingner, J. (2014). *Distinguishing language acquisition from learning disabilities.* New York, NY: Division of Specialized Instruction and Student Support Office of English Language Learners.

Klingner, J. K., Boelé, A. L., Linan-Thompson, S., & Rodriguez, D. (2014). Essential components of special education for ELLs with LD: Position statement of the Division for Learning Disabilities of the Council for Exceptional Children. *Learning Disabilities Research & Practice, 29*(3), 93–96.

Klingner, J. K., Vaughn, S., Boardman, A., & Swanson, E. (2012). *Now we get it! Boosting comprehension with collaborative strategic reading.* San Francisco, CA: Jossey-Bass.

Kutz, M., Dyer, S., & Campbell, B. (2013). Multiple intelligence profiles of athletic training students. *The Internet Journal of Allied Health Sciences and Practice, 11*(1), 2. Retrieved from http://ijahsp.nova.edu/articles/Vol11Num1/pdf/Kutz.pdf

Montgomery County Public Schools. (n.d.). *Twice exceptional students: A guidebook for supporting the achievement of gifted students with special needs.* Retrieved from http://www.montgomeryschoolsmd.org/uploadedFiles/curriculum/enriched/programs/gtld/2010%20Twice%20Exceptional%20Students-At%20A%20Glance.pdf

Naidoo, J. C. (2014). *The importance of diversity in library programs and material collections for children.* Chicago, IL: Association for Library Service to Children.

National Assessment of Education Progress (NAEP). (2013). *Scores by student group.* Washington, DC: U.S. Department of Education. Retrieved form http://www.nationsreportcard.gov/reading_2013/vocabulary/#student-groups

National Association for Gifted Children (NAGC). (n.d.). *NAGC position statements & white papers.* Retrieved from http://www.nagc.org/about-nagc/who-we-are/nagc-position-statements-white-papers

National Center for Education Statistics (NCES). (2014). *Nation's report card.* Washington, DC: U.S. Department of Education. Retrieved from https://nces.ed.gov/nationsreportcard/

National Center for Homeless Education (NCHE). (2007). *Supporting homeless students with disabilities: Implementing IDEA.* Retrieved from http://center.serve.org/nche/downloads/briefs/idea_qa.pdf

National Center for Homeless Education (NCHE). (2014). *Identifying children and youth in homeless situations.* Retrieved from http://center.serve.org/nche/downloads/briefs/identification.pdf

National Council of Teachers of English. (2008). *English language learners: A policy research brief produced by the National Council of Teachers of English.* Retrieved from http://www.ncte.org/library/NCTEFiles/Resources/PolicyResearch/ELLResearchBrief.pdf

Neuliep, J. W. (2015). *Intercultural communication: A contextual approach* (6th ed.). Thousand Oaks, CA: Sage.

Nieto, S., & Bode, P. (2008). *Affirming diversity: The sociopolitical context of multicultural education* (5th ed.). Boston, MA: Pearson.

No Child Left Behind Act of 2001, 20 U.S.C. § 6319 (2008).

Orosco, M. J., & Klingner, J. K. (2010). Bilingual first grade instruction. In D. Haager, J. K. Klingner, & T. Jiménez, *How to teach English language learners: Effective strategies from outstanding educators, grades K–6* (pp. 53–79). San Francisco, CA: Jossey-Bass.

Purcell, C. (1978). *Gifted and talented children's education act of 1978, Congressional Record.* Washington, DC: U.S. Government Printing Office.

Rehabilitation Act of 1973. Section 504, 19 U.S.C. section 794.

Ryan, C. (2013). *Language use in the United States: 2011.* Washington, DC: U.S. Department of Commerce.

Shealey, M. W., McHatton, P. A., & Wilson, V. (2011). Moving beyond disproportionality: The role of culturally responsive teaching in special education. *Teaching Education, 22*(4), 377–396.

Smith, D. D., & Tyler, N. C. (2010). *Introduction to special education: Making a difference* (7th ed.). Columbus, OH: Pearson/Merrill.

Starkes, T. (2013). The *other* dropout problem in urban schools. *American Thinker.* Retrieved from http://www.americanthinker.com/articles/2013/09/the_other_dropout_problem_in_urban_schools.html

Sullivan, A. L., & Bal, A. (2013). Disproportionality in special education: Effects of individual and school variables on disability risk. *Exceptionality, 79*(4), 475–494.

Tannenbaum, A. J., & Baldwin, L. J. (1983). Giftedness and learning disability: A paradoxical combination. In L. Fox, L. Brody, & D. Tobin (Eds.), *Learning disabled/gifted children: Identification and programming* (pp. 11–36). Baltimore, MD: University Park Press.

Trail, B. (2011). *Twice exceptional gifted children*. Austin, TX: Prufrock Press.

U.S. Census Bureau. (2010). *Census 2000 redistricting* (PL 94-171, summary file, tables PL1 and PL2). Washington, DC: U.S. Department of Commerce.

U.S. Census Bureau. (2011, April 2). *U.S. Census Bureau, population division*. Retrieved from http://www.census.gov/population/www/cen2000/phc-t1.html

U.S. Census Bureau. (2012). *The 2012 statistical abstract*. Washington, DC: Author.

U.S. Department of Commerce. (2013). *U.S. Department of Commerce, Census Bureau, American Community Survey (ACS), 2008 and 2013*. Washington, DC: Author.

U.S. Department of Education, National Center for Education Statistics [NCES], Common Core of Data [CCD]. (2012). "State Nonfiscal Survey of Public Elementary/Secondary Education," 1996–97 through 2010–11; Private School Universe Survey (PSS), selected years 1997–98 through 2009–10; and National Elementary and Secondary Enrollment Model, 1972–2010.

U.S. Department of Education, Office for Civil Rights. (2014). *Civil rights data collection data snapshot: College and career readiness*. Washington, DC: Author. Retrieved from http://www2.ed.gov/about/offices/list/ocr/docs/crdc-college-and-career-readiness-snapshot.pdf

U.S. Department of Education, Office of Special Education and Rehabilitative Services, Office of Special Education Programs [USDE]. (2014). *36th annual report to Congress on the implementation of the individuals with disabilities education improvement act*. Washington, DC: Author.

U.S. Department of Housing and Urban Development. (2013). *The 2013 annual homeless assessment report (AHAR) to Congress*. Washington, DC: Author.

Vaughn, S., Cirino, P. T., Linan-Thompson, S., Mathes, P. G., Carlson, C. D., Hagan, E. C., . . . Francis, D. J. (2006). Effectiveness of a Spanish intervention and an English intervention for English-language learners at risk for reading problems. *American Educational Research Journal, 43*, 449–487.

Vaughn, S., Mathes, P. G., Linan-Thompson, S., & Francis, D. J. (2005). Teaching English language learners at risk for reading disabilities to read: Putting research into practice. *Learning Disabilities Research & Practice, 20*, 58–67.

Vermont Department of Education. (2010). *Section 504—A manual for parents, families, and schools* (4th ed.). Montpelier, VT: Author.

Webb, J. T., Gore, J. L., Amend, E. R., & DeVries, A. R. (2007). *A parent's guide to gifted children*. Scottsdale, AZ: Great Potential Press.

Wrightslaw. (2015). *Inclusion: Answers to frequently asked questions from the NEA*. Retrieved from http://www.wrightslaw.com/info/lre.faqs.inclusion.htm

Yell, M. L. (2012). *The law and special education* (3rd ed.). Boston, MA: Pearson.

CHAPTER 5. DEVELOPING COLLABORATIVE PARTNERSHIPS IN SCHOOLS AND WITH FAMILIES

Bernal, C., & Aragon, L. (2004). Critical factors affecting the success of paraprofessionals in the first two years of career ladder projects in Colorado. *Remedial and Special Education, 25*(4), 205–213.

Chalfant, J., & Van Dusen Pysh, M. (1989). Teacher assistance teams: A descriptive study of 96 teams. *Remedial and Special Education, 10*, 49–58.

Chopra, R. V., Sandoval-Lucero, E., Aragon, L., Bernal, C., De Balderas, H. B., & Carroll, D. (2004). The paraprofessional role of connector. *Remedial and Special Education, 25*(4), 219–231.

Cloud, N. (2002). Culturally and linguistically responsive instructional planning. In A. J. Artiles & A. A. Ortiz (Eds.), *English language learners with special education needs* (pp. 107–133). Washington, DC: Center for Applied Linguistics and McHenry, IL: Delta Systems.

Downing, J., Ryndak, D., & Clark, D. (2000). Paraeducators in inclusive classrooms. *Remedial and Special Education, 21*, 171–181.

Figueroa, R. (2002). Toward a new model of assessment. In A. J. Artiles & A. A. Ortiz (Eds.), *English language learners with special education needs* (pp. 51–63). Washington, DC: Center for Applied Linguistics and McHenry, IL: Delta Systems.

French, N. K. (2004). Connecting schools and communities: The vital role of paraeducators. *Remedial and Special Education, 25*(4), 203–204.

Friend, M. (2006). *Special education: Contemporary perspectives for school professionals*. Boston, MA: Pearson.

Friend, M., & Cook, L. (2010). *Interactions: Collaboration skills for school professionals* (6th ed.). Columbus, OH: Merrill.

Friend, M., Cook, L., Hurley-Chamberlain, D., & Shamberger, C. (2010). Co-teaching: An illustration of the complexity of collaboration in special education. *Journal of Educational and Psychological Consultation, 20*(1), 9–27. doi:10.1080/10474410903535380

Garcia, S. B. (2002). Parent-professional collaboration in culturally sensitive assessment. In A. J. Artiles & A. A. Ortiz (Eds.), *English language learners with special education needs* (pp. 87–103). Washington, DC: Center for Applied Linguistics and McHenry, IL: Delta Systems.

Garcia, S. B. (2014, March). *The intercultural dimensions of schooling in dual language schools*. Paper presented at the Massachusetts Association for Bilingual Education

Annual Conference for Dual Language Programs: Cross-Cultural Connections, New Haven, CT.

Giangreco, M. F., & Doyle, M. B. (2007). Teacher assistants in inclusive schools. In L. Florian (Ed.), *The Sage handbook of special education* (pp. 429–439). Thousand Oaks, CA: Sage.

Gordon, T. (1980). *Leadership effectiveness training.* New York, NY: Wyden.

Heron, T. E., & Harris, K. C. (2000). *The educational consultant: Helping professionals, parents, and students in inclusive classrooms* (4th ed.). Austin, TX: PRO-ED.

Hoover, J., Eppolito, A., Klingner, J. K., & Baca L. (2012). Collaborative decision making in multicultural contexts. In B. Billingsley, J. Crockett, & M. L. Boscardin (Eds.), *Handbook on special education leadership* (pp. 191–208). New York, NY: Routledge.

Idol, L., Nevin, A., & Paolucci-Whitcomb, P. (2000). *Collaborative consultation* (2nd ed.). Austin, TX: PRO-ED.

Individuals with Disabilities Education Act, 20 U.S.C. § 1400 (2004).

Individuals with Disabilities Education Improvement Act of 2004. PL No. 108-446.

Klingner, J. K., Edwards, P., & Dunsmore, K. (2010). Assessing students with special needs. In D. Lapp & D. Fisher (Eds.), *Handbook of research on teaching the English language arts* (pp. 336–342). New York, NY: Routledge.

Lavoie, R. (2008). *The teacher's role in home/school communication: Everybody wins.* Retrieved from http://www.ldonline.org/article/28021#top

Minondo, S., Meyer, L., & Xin, J. (2001). The roles and responsibilities of teaching assistants in inclusive education: What's appropriate? *Journal of the Association for Persons With Severe Handicaps, 24*(4), 253–256.

Murawski, W. W., & Swanson, H. L. (2001). A meta-analysis of coteaching research: Where are the data? *Remedial and Special Education, 22*(5), 258–267.

Murray, C. (2004). Clarifying collaborative roles in urban high schools. *Teaching Exceptional Children, 36*(5), 44–51.

No Child Left Behind Act of 2001. PL No. 107-110.

Ortiz, A. (2002). Prevention of school failure and early intervention for English language learners. In A. J. Artiles & A. A. Ortiz (Eds.), *English language learners with special education needs* (pp. 31–50). Washington, DC: Center for Applied Linguistics and McHenry, IL: Delta Systems.

Ortiz, A. A., & Yates, J. R. (2001). A framework for serving English language learners with disabilities. *Journal of Special Education Leadership, 14*(2), 72–80.

Pickett, A. L., & Gerlach, K. (2003). *Supervising paraeducators in school settings* (2nd ed.). Austin, TX: PRO-ED.

Pugach, M. C., & Johnson, L. J. (1995). *Collaborative practitioners, collaborative schools.* Denver, CO: Love.

Riggs, C. G. (2005). To teachers: What paraeducators want you to know. *Teaching Exceptional Children, 36*(5), 8–12.

Rivera, D. P., & Smith, D. D. (1997). *Teaching students with learning and behavior problems* (3rd ed.). Boston, MA: Pearson.

Salend, S. J., Gordon, J., & Lopez-Vona, K. (2002). Evaluating cooperative teaching teams. *Teaching Exceptional Children, 37*(4), 195–200.

Scruggs, T. E., Mastropieri, M. A., & McDuffie, K. A. (2007). Co-teaching in inclusive classrooms: A metasynthesis of qualitative research. *Exceptional Children, 73,* 392–416.

Turnbull, A., Turnbull, H. R., & Wehmeyer, M. L., & Shogren, K. A. (2016). *Exceptional lives: Special education in today's schools* (8th ed.). Boston, MA: Pearson.

U.S. Department of Education, National Center for Education Statistics [NCES], Common Core of Data [CCD]. (2012). "State Nonfiscal Survey of Public Elementary/Secondary Education," 1996–97 through 2010–11; Private School Universe Survey (PSS), selected years 1997–98 through 2009–10; and National Elementary and Secondary Enrollment Model, 1972–2010.

Vaughn, S., Bos, C. S., & Schumm, J. S. (2013). *Teaching exceptional, diverse, and at-risk students in the general education classroom* (6th ed.). Boston, MA: Pearson.

Villa, R. A., Thousand, J. S., & Nevin, A. (2008). *A guide to co-teaching: Practical tips for facilitating student learning.* Thousand Oaks, CA: Corwin.

Walther-Thomas, C. (1997). Co-teaching experiences: The benefits and problems that teachers report. *Journal of Learning Disabilities, 30*(4), 395–407.

Walther-Thomas, C., Korinek, L., McLaughlin, V. L., & Williams, B. T. (2000). *Collaboration for inclusive education: Developing successful programs.* Boston, MA: Pearson.

Weiss, M. P., & Lloyd, J. W. (2002). Congruence between roles and actions of secondary special educators in co-taught and special education settings. *The Journal of Special Education, 36*(2), 58–68.

Werts, M. G., Harris, S., Tillery, C. Y., & Roark, R. (2004). What parents tell us about paraeducators. *Remedial and Special Education, 25*(4), 232–239.

White, R. (2004). The recruitment of paraeducators into the special education profession: A review of progress, select evaluation outcomes, and new initiatives. *Remedial and Special Education, 25*(4), 214–218.

Yates, J. R., & Ortiz, A. A. (2004). Classification issues in special education for English language learners. In A. M. Sorrells, H. J. Rieth, & P. T. Sindelar (Eds.), *Critical issues in special education* (pp. 38–56). Boston, MA: Pearson.

CHAPTER 6. DELIVERY OF APPROPRIATE SERVICES TO STUDENTS WITH SPECIAL NEEDS

Barnett, D. W., Daly, E. J., Jones, K. M., & Lentz, F. E., Jr. (2004). Response to intervention: Empirically based special service decisions from single-case designs of increasing and decreasing intensity. *Journal of Special Education, 38,* 66–79.

Barnhill, G. P. (2005). Functional behavior assessment in schools. *Intervention in School and Clinic, 40,* 131–143.

Bigby, L. M. (2004). Medical and health related services: More than treating boo-boos and ouchies. *Intervention in School and Clinic, 39,* 233–235.

Borthwick-Duffy, S. A., Palmer, D. S., & Lane, K. L. (1996). One size doesn't fit all: Full inclusion and individual differences. *Journal of Behavioral Education, 6,* 311–329.

Bradley, R., Danielson, L., & Hallahan, D. P. (Eds.). (2002). *Identification of learning disabilities: Research to practice.* Mahwah, NJ: Lawrence Erlbaum.

Brown, M. R., Paulsen, K., & Higgins, K. (2003). Remove environmental barriers to student learning. *Intervention in School and Clinic, 39,* 109–112.

Bryant, D. P., & Bryant, B. R. (2003). *Assistive technology for people with disabilities.* Boston, MA: Pearson.

Bryant, D. P., Bryant, B. R., Roberts, G., Vaughn, S., Hughes, K., Porterfield, J., & Gersten, R. (2011). Effects of an early numeracy intervention on the performance of first-grade students with mathematics difficulties. *Exceptional Children, 78*(1), 7–23.

Bryant, D. P., Pfannenstiel, K., & Bryant, B. R. (2014, April). *Project AIM: Algebra-readiness intervention modules for at-risk middle school students.* Paper presented at the CEC Conference, Philadelphia, PA.

Buehler, V. (2004, July/August). Easy as 1-2-3 IEPs. *Volta Voices, 11,* 20–23.

Cartledge, G., Kea, C. D., & Ida, D. J. (2000). Anticipating differences, celebrating strengths: Providing culturally competent services for students with serious emotional disturbance. *Teaching Exceptional Children, 32,* 30–37.

Chambers, A. C. (1997). *Has technology been considered? A guide for IEP teams.* Reston, VA: Council of Administrators of Special Education and Media Division of the Council for Exceptional Children.

Cook, B. G. (2001). A comparison of teachers' attitudes toward their included students with mild and severe disabilities. *Journal of Special Education, 34,* 203–213.

Cook, B. G., Tankersley, M., Cook, L., & Landrum, T. J. (2000). Teachers' attitudes toward their included students with disabilities. *Exceptional Children, 67,* 115–135.

Dabkowski, D. M. (2004). Encouraging active parent participation in IEP team meetings. *Teaching Exceptional Children, 36,* 34–39.

Darling-Hammond, L. (2005, April). *Correlation between teachers and student achievement.* Paper presented at the annual conference of the American Educational Research Association (AERA), Montreal, Canada.

Darling-Hammond, L. (2006a). Constructing 21st-century teacher education. *Journal of Teacher Education, 57,* 300–314.

Darling-Hammond, L. (2006b, November). *Developing a profession of teaching.* Paper presented to the 2006 CalTEACH Annual Faculty Professional Conference, San Jose, CA.

de Fur, S. H. (2003). IEP transition planning—from compliance to quality. *Exceptionality, 11,* 115–128.

Denton, C. A. (2012). Response to intervention for reading difficulties in the primary grades: Some answers and lingering questions. *Journal of Learning Disabilities, 45,* 232–243.

Downing, J. A. (2004). Related services for students with disabilities: Introduction to the special issue. *Intervention in School and Clinic, 39,* 195–208.

Dworetzky, B. (2004). Effective practices for involving families of children with disabilities in schools. *Newsline: The Federation of Children With Special Needs, 24,* 1, 12.

Earles-Vollrath, T. L. (2004). Mitchell Yell: IDEA 1997 and related services. *Intervention in School and Clinic, 39,* 236–239.

Etzel-Wise, D., & Mears, B. (2004). Adapted physical education and therapeutic recreation in schools. *Intervention in School and Clinic, 39,* 223–232.

Fisher, D., Frey, N., & Thousand, J. (2003). What do special educators need to know and be prepared to do for inclusive schooling to work? *Teacher Education and Special Education, 26,* 42–50.

Fuchs, L., Fuchs, D., & Powell, S. (2004). *Using CBM for progress monitoring.* Washington, DC: American Institutes for Research.

Fuchs, L. S., Fuchs, D., & Compton, D. L. (2012). The early prevention of mathematics difficulties: It's power and limitations. *Journal of Learning Disabilities, 45,* 257–269.

Fuchs, L. S., Fuchs, D., Hosp, M., & Jenkins, J. R. (2001). Oral reading fluency as an indicator of reading competence: A theoretical, empirical, and historical analysis. *Scientific Studies of Reading, 5,* 239–256.

Fuchs, L. S., & Vaughn, S. (2012). Responsive-to-intervention: A decade later. *Journal of Learning Disabilities, 45,* 195–203.

Futernick, K. (2006). *A possible dream: Retaining California teachers so all students learn.* Sacramento, CA: CSU Center for Teacher Quality.

Haager, D., & Klingner, J. K. (2005). *Differentiating instruction in inclusive classrooms: The special educator's guide*. Boston, MA: Pearson.

Hanley, G. P., Iwata, B. A., & McCord, B. E. (2003). Functional analysis of problem behavior: A review. *Journal of Applied Behavior Analysis, 36*, 147–185.

Hoover, J. J., & Patton, J. R. (2004). Differentiating standards-based education for students with diverse needs. *Remedial and Special Education, 25*, 74–78.

Hughes, M. T., Valle-Riestra, D. M., & Arguelles, M. E. (2002). Experiences of Latino families with their child's special education program. *Multicultural Perspectives, 4*, 11–17.

Individuals with Disabilities Education Improvement Act of 2004. PL No. 108-446. 118 STAT. 2647.

Kern, L., Delaney, B., Clarke, S., Dunlap, G., & Childs, K. (2001). Improving the classroom behavior of students with emotional and behavioral disorders using individualized curricular modifications. *Journal of Emotional and Behavioral Disorders, 9*, 239–247.

Kravetz, J. (2005, January 7). Under new IDEA, districts no longer required to provide, maintain implants. *The Special Educator, 20*, 1, 6.

Layton, C. A., & Lock, R. H. (2007). Use authentic assessment techniques to fulfill the promise of No Child Left Behind. *Interventions, 27*, 169–173.

Madaus, J. W., & Shaw, S. F. (2006). The impact of the IDEA 2004 on transition to college for students with learning disabilities. *Learning Disabilities Practice, 21*, 273–281.

Magiera, K., Smith, C., Zigmond, N., & Gebauer, K. (2005). Benefits of co-teaching in secondary mathematics classes. *Teaching Exceptional Children, 37*, 20–24.

Mastropieri, M. A., & Scruggs, T. E. (2014). *The inclusive classroom: Strategies for effective differentiated instruction*. Boston, MA: Pearson.

McMaster, K. L., Fuchs, D., Fuchs, L. S., & Compton, D. L. (2005). Responding to nonresponders: An experimental field trial of identification and intervention methods. *Exceptional Children, 71*, 445–463.

McNamara, K., & Hollinger, C. (2003). Intervention-based assessment: Evaluation rates and eligibility findings. *Exceptional Children, 69*, 181–193.

National Association of School Nurses (NASN). (2004). Impact of Cedar Rapids Community School District vs. Garret F. on school nursing services. School Health Nursing Services' role in health care: Issue brief. Retrieved from http://www.nasn.org

National Center for Education Statistics (NCES). (2006). *Fast facts: Dropout rates of high school students*. Retrieved from http://www.nces.ed.gov

National Center on Secondary Education and Transition (NCSET). (2005). Key provisions on transition: IDEA 1997 compared to H.R. 1350 (IDEA 2004). Minneapolis: University of Minnesota. Retrieved from http://www.ncset.org

Neal, J., Bigby, L. M., & Nicholson, R. (2004). Occupational therapy, physical therapy, and orientation and mobility services in public schools. *Intervention in School and Clinic, 39*, 218–222.

Neubert, D. A. (2003). The role of assessment in the transition to adult life process for students with disabilities. *Exceptionality, 11*, 63–75.

Obiakor, F. W., & Ford, B. A. (2002). Educational reform and accountability: Implications for African Americans with exceptionalities. *Multiple Voices, 5*, 83–93.

Office of Special Education Programs (OSEP). (2006a). Building the legacy of IDEA 2004. Topical brief: Individualized education program (IEP), team meetings, and changes to the IEP. Retrieved from http://idea.ed.gov

Office of Special Education Programs (OSEP). (2006b). *Building the legacy: IDEA 2004*. Model Forms: IEP. Available from http://idea.ed.gov

Office of Special Education Programs (OSEP). (2006c). *Students served under IDEA, Part B, by disability category and state: Fall 2005*. Retrieved on December 30, 2006, from www.ideadata.org

Rodríguez, M. A., Gentilucci, J., & Sims, P. G. (2005, November 11). *Preparing principals to support special educators: Interactive modules that enhance course content*. Paper presented at the annual meeting of the University Council for Educational Administration, Nashville, TN.

Ryan, A. L., Halsey, H. N., & Matthews, W. J. (2003). Using functional assessment to promote desirable student behavior in schools. *Teaching Exceptional Children, 35*, 8–15.

Salend, S. (2010). *Creating inclusive classrooms: Effective and reflective practices* (7th ed.). Boston, MA: Pearson.

Sanford, C., Newman, L., Wagner, M., Cameto, R., Knokey, A.-M., & Shaver, D. (2011). *The post-high school outcomes of young adults with disabilities up to 6 years after high school. Key findings from the National Longitudinal Transition Study-2 (NLTS2)* (NCSER 2011–3004). Menlo Park, CA: SRI International.

Shippen, M. E., Simpson, R. G., & Crites, S. A. (2003). A practical guide to functional behavioral assessment. *Teaching Exceptional Children, 35*, 36–44.

Shriner, J. G., & Destefano, L. (2003). Participation and accommodation in state assessment: The role of individualized education programs. *Exceptional Children, 69*, 147–161.

Smith, D. D. (2007). *Introduction to special education: Making a difference*. Boston, MA: Pearson.

Sopko, K. M. (2003). *The IEP: A synthesis of current literature since 1997*. Washington, DC: National Association of State Directors of Special Education (NASDSE), Project Forum.

Sugai, G., Horner, R. H., Fixen, D., & Blase, K. (2010). Developing systems-level capacity for RTI implementation: Current efforts and future directions. In T. A. Glover & S. Vaughn (Eds.), *The promise of response to intervention: Evaluating science and practice* (pp. 286–309). New York, NY: Guilford.

Test, D. W., Mason, C., Hughes, C., Konrad, M., Neale, M., & Wood, W. M. (2004). Student involvement in individualized education program meetings. *Exceptional Children, 70*, 391–412.

Thompson, S., Lazarus, S., Clapper, A., & Thurlow, M. (2004). *Essential knowledge and skills needed by teachers to support the achievement of students with disabilities: EPRRI issue brief five*. College Park, MD: The Institute for the Study of Exceptional Children and Youth, Educational Policy Reform Research Institute.

Tomlinson, C. A., & Moon, T. R. (2013). *Assessment and student success in a differentiated classroom*. Alexandria, VA: Association for Supervision and Curriculum Development.

Tornatzky, L. G., Pachon, H. P., & Torres, C. (2003). *Closing achievement gaps: Improving educational outcomes for Hispanic children*. Los Angeles: The Center for Latino Educational Excellence, The Tomás Rivera Policy Institute, University of Southern California.

U.S. Department of Education. (2006). Assistance to states for the Education of Children with Disabilities Program and the Early Intervention Program for Infants and Toddlers with Disabilities; final rule.

Federal Register, 34, CRF Parts 300 and 301.

Vaughn, S., Cirino, P. T., Wanzek, J., Wexler, J., Fletcher, J. M., Denton, C. A. . . . Francis, D. J. (2010). Response to intervention for middle school students with reading difficulties: Effects of a primary and secondary intervention. *School Psychology, 39*, 3–21.

Vaughn, S., & Fletcher, J. M. (2012). Response to intervention with secondary school students with reading difficulties. *Journal of Learning Disabilities, 45*, 244–256.

Vaughn, S., & Fuchs, L. S. (2003). Redefining learning disabilities as inadequate response to instruction: The promise and potential problems. *Learning Disabilities Research and Practice, 18*, 137–146.

Vaughn, S., Wanzek, J., Murray, C. S., Scammacca, N., Linan-Thompson, S., & Woodruff, A. L. (2009). Response to early reading interventions: Examining higher responders and lower responders. *Exceptional Children, 75*, 165–183.

Wagner, M., Newman, L., Cameto, R., Levine, P., & Garza, N. (2006). *An overview of findings from wave 2 of the National Longitudinal Transition Study-2 (NLTS2)*. (NCSER 20063004). Menlo Park, CA: SRI International.

Wood, W. M., Karvonen, M., Test, D. W., Browder, D., & Algozzine, B. (2004). Promoting student self-determination skills in IEP planning. *Teaching Exceptional Children, 36*, 8–16.

Yates, J. R., & Ortiz, A. A. (2004). Classification issues in special education for English language learners. In A. M. Sorrells, H. J. Rieth, & P. T. Sindelar, *Critical issues in special education* (pp. 38–56). Boston, MA: Pearson.

Ziegler, D. (2002). *Reauthorization of the elementary and secondary education act: No Child Left Behind Act of 2001*. Arlington, VA: The Council for Exceptional Children, Public Policy Unit.

CHAPTER 7. PROMOTING ACCESS TO THE CURRICULUM

Anderson, L. W., Krathwohl, D. R., Airasian, P. W., Cruikshank, K. A., Mayer, R. E., Pintrich, P. R., . . . Wittrock, M. C. (2001). *A taxonomy for learning, teaching, and assessing: A revision of Bloom's taxonomy of educational objectives*. New York: Longman.

Ayllon, T., & Azrin, N. H. (1965). Reinforcement and instructions with mental patients. *Journal of Experimental Analysis of Behavior, 7*(4), 327-331. doi: 10.1901/jeab.1964.7-327.

Bloom, B. S., Engelhart, M. D., Furst, E. J., Hill, W. H., & Krathwohl, D. R. (1956). *Taxonomy of educational objectives: The classification of educational goals. Handbook I: Cognitive domain*. New York, NY: David McKay.

Bryant, B. R. (2015). *Application evaluation form*. Austin, TX: Psycho-Educational Services.

Bryant, B. R., Bryant, D. P., Porterfield, J., Falcomata, T., Shih, M., Valentine, C., . . . Bell, K. (2014). The effects of a tier 3 intervention for second grade students with serious mathematics difficulties. *Journal of Learning Disabilities*. Advance online publication. doi:10.1177/0022219414538516

Bryant, D. P., & Bryant, B. R. (2003). *Assistive technology for people with disabilities*. Boston, MA: Pearson.

CAST. (2011). *Universal Design for Learning Guidelines version 2.0*. Wakefield, MA: Author.

Coyne, M. D., Kame'enui, E. J., & Carnine, D. W. (2011). *Effective teaching strategies that accommodate diverse learners* (4th ed.). Boston, MA: Pearson.

Delquadri, J., Greenwood, C. R., Whorton, D., Carta, J. J., & Hall, R. V. (1986). Classwide peer tutoring. *Exceptional Children, 52*, 535–542.

Edyburn, D. (2010). Would you recognize universal design for learning if you saw it? Ten propositions for new directions for the second decade of UDL. *Learning Disability Quarterly, 33,* 33–41.

Fuchs, D., Fuchs, L. S., Mathes, P. G., & Simmons, D. C. (1997). Peer-Assisted learning strategies: Making classrooms more responsive to diversity. *American Educational Research Journal, 34*(1), 174–206.

Gersten, R., Beckmann, S., Clarke, B., Foegen, A., Marsh, L., Star, J. R., & Witzel, B. (2009). *Assisting students struggling with mathematics: Response to Intervention (RtI) for elementary and middle schools* (NCEE 2009-4060). Washington, DC: National Center for Education Evaluation and Regional Assistance, Institute of Education Sciences, U.S. Department of Education. Retrieved from http://ies.ed.gov/ncee/wwc/publications/practiceguides/

Gersten, R., Carnine, D., & Woodward, J. (1987). Direct instruction research: The third decade. *Remedial & Special Education, 8*(6), 48–56.

Hall, T. E., Cohen, N., Vue, G., & Ganley, P. (2014). *Learning Disability Quarterly.* Advance online publication. doi:10.1177/0731948714544375

Heron, T. E., Villareal, D. M., Yao, M., Christianson, R. J., & Heron, K. (2006). Peer tutoring systems: Applications in classroom and specialized environments. *Reading & Writing Quarterly, 22,* 27–45.

Higher Education Opportunity Act of 2008 (HEOA). PL No. 110-315.

Hopkins, B. I. (1968). Effects of candy and social reinforcement, instructions, and reinforcement schedule learning on the modification and maintenance of smiling. *Journal of Applied Behavior Analysis, 1,* 121–129.

Johnson, D. W., Johnson, R. T., & Holubec, E. J. (1994). *Cooperative learning in the classroom* (6th ed.). Alexandria, VA: Association for Supervision & Curriculum Development.

Kagan, S. (1990). *Cooperative learning resources for teachers.* San Juan Capistrano, CA: Resources for Teachers.

Kennedy, M. J., Thomas, C. N., Meyer, P., Alves, K. D., & Lloyd, J.

W. (2014). Using evidence-based multimedia to improve vocabulary performance of adolescents with LD: A UDL approach. *Learning Disability Quarterly, 37*(2), 71–86. doi:10.1177/0731948713507262

King-Sears, M. (2009). Universal design for learning: Technology and pedagogy. *Learning Disability Quarterly, 32,* 199–201.

King-Sears, M. E., Johnson, T. M., Berkeley, S., Weiss, M. P., Peters-Burton, E. E., Evmenova, A. S., . . . Hursh, J. C. (2014). An exploratory study of universal design for teaching chemistry to students with and without disabilities. *Learning Disability Quarterly.* Advance online publication. doi:10.1177/0731948714564575

Lemons, C. J. (2000). *Comparison of parent and teacher knowledge and opinions related to augmentative and alternative communication* (Unpublished master's thesis). The University of Texas at Austin.

Lenz, B. K., & Deshler, D. D. (2004). Adolescents with learning disabilities: Revisiting the educators' enigma. In B. Wong (Ed.), *Learning about learning disabilities* (3rd ed., pp. 535–564). Atlanta, GA: Academic Press/Elsevier.

Mastropieri, M. A., & Scruggs, T. E. (2014). *The inclusive classroom: Strategies for effective differentiated instruction.* Boston, MA: Pearson.

McMaster, K. L., Fuchs, D., & Fuchs, L. S. (2006). Research on peer-assisted learning strategies: The promise and limitations of peer-mediated instruction. *Reading & Writing Quarterly, 22*(1), 5–25.

National Center on Intensive Instruction (NCII). (2014). *Academic intervention technical review.* Washington, DC: American Institutes for Research.

National Governors Association Center for Best Practices, Council of Chief State School Officers. (2010). *Common Core State Standards.* Washington, DC: National Governors Association Center for Best Practices, Council of Chief State School Officers.

Pintrich, P. R. (2002). The role of metacognitive knowledge in learning, teaching, and assessing. *Theory Into Practice, 41*(4). doi:10.1207/s15430421tip4104_3

Price, K. M., & Nelson, K. L. (2003). *Daily planning for today's classroom* (2nd ed.). Belmont, CA: Wadsworth-Thomson.

Rao, K., Ok, M. W., & Bryant, B. R. (2014). A review of research on universal design educational models. *Remedial and Special Education, 35*(3), 153–166.

Raskind, M., & Bryant, B. R. (2002). *Functional evaluation for assistive technology.* Austin, TX: Psycho-Educational Services.

Rose, D. H., Harbour, W. S., Johnston, C. S., Daley, S. G., & Abarbanell, L. (2006). Universal design for learning in postsecondary education: Reflections on principles and their application. *Journal of Postsecondary Education and Disability, 19,* 135–151.

Schumaker, J. B., & Deshler, D. D. (2006). Teaching adolescents to be strategic learners. In D. D. Deshler & J. B. Schumaker (Eds.), *Teaching adolescents with disabilities: Accessing the general education curriculum* (pp. 121–156). Thousand Oaks, CA: Corwin.

Schumm, J. S., Moody, S. M., & Vaughn, S. (2000). Grouping for reading instruction: Does one size fit all? *Journal of Learning Disabilities, 33*(5), 477–488.

Scruggs, T. E., & Mastropieri, M. A. (1992). Classroom applications of mnemonic instruction: Acquisition, maintenance, and generalization. *Exceptional Children, 58,* 219–229.

Slavin, R. E. (1991). Synthesis of research on cooperative learning. *Educational Leadership, 48*(5), 71–82.

Smith, D. D., & Lovitt, T. C. (1976). The differential effects of reinforcement contingencies on arithmetic performance. *Journal of Learning Disabilities, 9,* 11–29.

Stokes, T. F., & Baer, D. M. (1977). An implicit technology of generalization. *Journal of Applied Behavior Analysis, 10,* 349–367.

Stowitschek, J. J., Stowitschek, C. E., Hendrickson, J. M., & Day, R. M. (1984). *Direct teaching tactics for exceptional children*. Rockville, MD: Aspen.

Swanson, H. L., Cooney, J. B., & O'Shaughnessy, T. E. (1998). Learning disabilities and memory. In B. Wong (Ed.), *Learning about learning disabilities* (2nd ed., pp. 107–162). San Diego, CA: Academic Press.

Swanson, H. L., & Deshler, D. (2003). Instructing adolescents with learning disabilities: Converting a meta-analysis to practice. *Journal of Learning Disabilities, 36*, 124–135.

Swanson, H. L., Hoskyn, M., & Lee, C. (1999). *Interventions for students with learning disabilities. A meta-analysis of treatment outcomes*. New York, NY: Guilford Press.

Technology and Media. (n.d.). *The AT quick wheel*. Arlington, VA: Council for Exceptional Children.

Tieso, C. (2005). The effects of grouping practices and curricular adjustments on achievement. *Journal for the Education of the Gifted, 29*(1), 60–89.

Vaughn, S., & Bos, C. (2011). *Strategies for teaching students with learning and behavior problems* (8th ed.). Boston, MA: Pearson.

Vaughn, S., Hughes, M. T., Moody, S. W., & Elbaum, B. (2001). Instructional grouping for reading for students with learning disabilities: Implications for practice. *Intervention in School and Clinic, 35*, 131–137.

Wong, B. Y. (1993). Pursuing an elusive goal: Molding strategic teachers and learners. *Journal of Learning Disabilities, 26*(6), 354–357.

CHAPTER 8. ASSESSMENT AND DATA-BASED DECISION MAKING

Bryant, B. R., Kim, M. K., Ok, M. W., Kang, E. Y., Bryant, D. P., Lang, R., & Son, S. H. (in press). A comparison of the effects of reading interventions on engagement and performance for 4th grade students with learning disabilities. *Behavior Modification.*

BVSD Office of Advanced Academic Services. (2010). *Identifying talented and gifted students from culturally, linguistically, and ethnically diverse (CLED) populations*. Retrieved from http://bvsd.org/tag/Documents/CLED%20Identification.pdf

CAST. (2011). *Universal Design for Learning Guidelines version 2.0*. Wakefield, MA: Author.

Conners, C. K. (2008). *Conner-III*. San Antonio, TX: The Psychological Corporation/Pearson.

Cuillos, S., SoRelle, D., Kim, S. A., Seo, Y. J., & Bryant, B. R. (2011). Monitoring student response to mathematics intervention: Using data to inform tier 3 intervention. *Intervention in School and Clinic, 47*, 121.

Dumont Willis. (n.d.). Score conversion tables for commonly used tests. Retrieved from http://alpha.fdu.edu/psychology/score_conversion_tables.htm

Flower, A., McKenna, J., Muething, C., Bryant, D. P., & Bryant, B. R. (2013). Effects of the Good Behavior Game on classwide off-task behavior in a high school basic algebra resource classroom. *Behavior Modification, 38*, 45–68. doi:10.1177/0145445513507574

Hammill, D., Brown, L., & Bryant, B. R. (1992). *A consumer's guide to tests in print* (2nd ed.). Austin, TX: PRO-ED.

McLoughlin, J. A., & Lewis, R. B. (2008). *Assessing students with special needs* (7th ed.). Upper Saddle River, NJ: Pearson.

Miller, M. N., Linn, R. L., & Gronlund, N. E. (2013). *Measurement and assessment in teaching* (11th ed.). Upper Saddle River, NJ: Pearson.

National Center on Educational Outcomes (NCEO). (2013). *Alternate assessments for students with disabilities: Overview*. Retrieved from http://www.cehd.umn.edu/nceo/topicareas/alternateassessments/altassesstopic.htm

National Governors Association Center for Best Practices & Council of Chief State School Officers. (2010). *Common Core State Standards*. Washington, DC: Authors.

Overton, T. (2011). *Assessing learners with special needs: An applied approach* (7th ed.). Upper Saddle River, NJ: Pearson.

Partnership for Assessment of Readiness for College and Careers (PARCC). (2013). *Expanding access: Accessibility features and accommodations for students with disabilities in PARCC assessments—A parent's guide*. Retrieved from http://www.parcconline.org/resources/parent-resources

Rashotte, C., Torgesen, J. K., & Wagner, R. W. (2012). *Test of Word Reading Efficiency*. Austin, TX: PRO-ED.

Reynolds, C. R., Livingston, R. B., & Willson, V. (2009). *Measurement and assessment in education* (2nd ed.). Boston, MA: Pearson.

Salvia, J., Ysseldyke, J., & Bolt, S. (2010) *Assessment: In special and inclusive education* (12th ed.). Boston, MA: Houghton Mifflin.

Schrank, F. A., McGrew, K. W., Mather, N., & Woodcock, R. (2014). *Woodcock-Johnson IV*. Itasca, IL: Riverside.

Smith, D. D., & Tyler, N. C. (2010). *Introduction to special education: Making a difference* (7th ed.). Columbus, OH: Pearson/Merrill.

Statewide Vision Resource Centre. (2012). *Teaching the use of magnifiers for reading*. Retrieved from http://www.svrc.vic.edu.au/CUmagnifiers.shtml

Taylor, R. L. (2008). *Assessment of exceptional students* (8th ed.). Boston, MA: Pearson.

Thompson, S. J., Johnstone, C. J., & Thurlow, M. L. (2002). *Universal design applied to large scale assessments*. Minneapolis, MN: National Center on Educational Outcomes.

Torgesen, J., & Bryant, B. R. (2005). *Test of Phonological Awareness* (2nd ed.; TOPA-2+). Austin, TX: PRO-ED.

Wagner, R. W., Torgesen, J. K., Rashotte, C., & Pearson, N. (2013). *Comprehensive Test of Phonological*

Processes (CTOPP-2). Austin, TX: PRO-ED.

Wiederholt, J. L., & Bryant, B. R. (2012). *Gray Oral Reading Test* (5th ed.). Austin, TX: Pro-Ed.

Woodcock, R. (2011). *Woodcock Reading Mastery Test* (3rd ed.). San Antonio, TX: The Psychological Corporation/Pearson.

CHAPTER 9. PROMOTING POSITIVE BEHAVIOR AND FACILITATING SOCIAL SKILLS

Alberto, P. A., & Troutman, A. C. (2012). *Applied behavior analysis for teachers* (9th ed.). Englewood Cliffs, NJ: Merrill.

Allen, K. E., Hart, B. M., Buell, J. S., Harris, F. R., & Wolf, M. M. (1964). Effects of social reinforcement on isolate behavior of a nursery school child. *Child Development, 35,* 511–518.

American Psychological Association. (2013). Preventing violence against teachers. *Monitor on Psychology, 44*(10), 58. Retrieved from http://www.apa.org/monitor/2013/11/ce-corner.aspx

American Psychological Association. (2014). *Classroom management.* Retrieved from http://www.apa.org/education/k12/classroom-mgmt.aspx

Barrish, H. H., Saunders, M., & Wolf, M. M. (1969). Good behavior game: Effects of individual contingencies for group consequences on disruptive behavior in a classroom. *Journal of Applied Behavior Analysis, 2,* 119–124.

Belgrave, F. Z., & Brevade, J. (2014). *African American boys: Identity, culture, and development.* New York, NY: Springer.

Canter, L. (2010). *Assertive discipline: Positive behavior management for today's classroom* (3rd ed.). Bloomington, IN: Solution Tree Press.

Cohen, M. R. (2011). *Social literacy.* Baltimore, MD: Brookes.

Corrol, E., Tynan, D., & Lines, M. M. (2009). Planned ignoring. *Nemours Foundation.* Retrieved from https://www.nemours.org/content/dam/nemours/wwwv2/filebox/service/health/parenting/tips/13plannedignoring.pdf

Council for Children with Behavior Disorders. (2009). *CCBD's position summary on the use of seclusion in school settings.* Retrieved from http://www.casecec.org/pdf/seclusion/Accepted,%20CCBD%20on%20Use%20of%20Seclusion,%207-8-09.pdf

Do2Learn. (2013). *Paying attention & listening to others.* Retrieved from http://do2learn.com/organizationtools/SocialSkillsToolbox/PayingAttention.htm

Dreikurs, R. (1968). *Psychology in the classroom: A manual for teachers* (2nd ed.). New York, NY: Harper & Row.

Dreikurs, R., & Cassel, P. (1972). *Discipline without tears.* New York, NY: Hawthorn Books.

Education Portal. (2015). *Applying the Premack principle in the classroom.* Retrieved from http://education-portal.com/academy/lesson/applying-the-premack-principle-in-the-classroom.html#lesson

Emmer, E. T., & Evertson, C. M. (2008). *Classroom management for middle and high school teachers* (8th ed.). Boston, MA: Pearson.

Espelage, D., Anderson, E. M., Brown, V. E., Jones, A., Lane, K. L., McMahin, S. D., . . . Reynolds, C. R. (2013). Understanding and preventing violence directed against teachers. *American Psychologist, 68*(2), 75–87. Retrieved from https://www.apa.org/pubs/journals/releases/amp-68-2-75.pdf

Evertson, C. M., & Emmer, E. T. (2012). *Classroom management for elementary teachers* (9th ed.). Boston, MA: Pearson.

Flower, A., McKenna, J., Muething, C., Bryant, D. P., & Bryant, B. R. (2013). Effects of the Good Behavior Game on classwide

off-task behavior in a high school basic algebra resource classroom. *Behavior Modification, 38,* 45–68. doi:10.1177/0145445513507574

Glasser, W. (1969). *Schools without failure.* New York, NY: Harper & Row.

Gordon, T. (2003). *Teacher effectiveness training.* New York, NY: Three Rivers Press.

Haydon, T., & Musti-Rao, S. (2011). Effective use of behavior-specific praise: A middle school case. *Beyond Behavior, 20*(2), 31–39.

Hernandez, H. (2001). *Multicultural education: A teacher's guide to linking context, process, and content.* Upper Saddle River, NJ: Prentice Hall.

Intervention Central. (n.d.). *Jackpot! Ideas for classroom reward.* Retrieved from http://www.interventioncentral.org/behavioral-interventions/rewards/jackpot-ideas-classroom-rewards

Klingner, J. K., Boelé, A. L., Linan-Thompson, S., & Rodriguez, D. (2014). Essential components of special education for ELLs with LD: Position Statement of the Division for Learning Disabilities of the Council for Exceptional Children. *Learning Disabilities Research & Practice, 29*(3), 93–96.

Lane, K. L. (2007). Identifying and supporting students at risk for emotional and behavioral disorders within multi-level models: Data driven approaches to conducting secondary interventions with an academic emphasis. *Education & Treatment of Children, 30*(4), 135–164. doi:10.1353/etc.2007.0026 Retrieved from http://www.pbis.org/common/pbisresources/presentations/PBIS_ImplementationLeadership_oct29_2012.pdf

Lewandowski, J. A. (1989). Using peer forums to motivate students. *Teaching Exceptional Children, 21*(3), 14–15.

Licciardello, C. C., Harchik, A. E., & Luiselli, J. K. (2008). Social skills intervention for children with autism during interactive play at a public elementary school. *Education and Treatment of Children, 31*(1), 27–37.

The National Professional Development Center on Autism Spectrum Disorders. (n.d.). *Evidence-based practice: Functional behavior assessment.* Retrieved from http://autismpdc.fpg.unc.edu/sites/autismpdc.fpg.unc.edu/files/imce/documents/Functional-Behavior-Assessment-Complete10-2010.pdf

Neo, M., Neo, K. T.-L., & Tan, H. Y.-J. (2012). Applying authentic learning strategies in a multimedia and web learning environment (MWLE): Malaysian students' perspective. *The Turkish Online Journal of Educational Technology, 11*(3), 50–60. Retrieved from http://www.tojet.net/articles/v11i3/1135.pdf

Powel, M. (2013). *5 ways to make your classroom student-centered.* Retrieved from http://www.edweek.org/tm/articles/2013/12/24/ctq_powell_strengths.html

Pressman, B. (2011, October 14). *Withitness in the classroom.* Retrieved from http://www.education.com/reference/article/using-xray-vision-substitute-teacher/

Raskaukas, J., & Scott, M. (2011). Modifying anti-bullying programs to include students with disabilities. *Teaching Exceptional Children, 44*(1), 60–67.

Rose, C. A., Swearer, S. M., & Espelage, D. L. (2012). Bullying and students with disabilities: The untold narrative. *Focus on Exceptional Children, 45*(2), 1–10.

Ryan, J. B., Pierce, C. D., & Mooney, P. (2008). Evidence-based teaching strategies for students with EBD. *Beyond Behavior, 17*(3), 22–29.

Saylor, C. F., & Leach, J. B. (2009). Perceived bullying and social support in students accessing special inclusion programming. *Journal of Developmental and Physical Disabilities, 21,* 69–80. doi:10 1007/s 10882-008-9126-4

Smith, D. D., & Tyler, N.C. (2010). *Introduction to special education: Making a difference* (7th ed.). Boston, MA: Pearson.

Sugai, G., & Horner, R. H. (2009). Defining and describing schoolwide positive behavior support. In W. Sailor, D. Dunlao, G. Segai, & R. Horner (Eds.), *Handbook of positive behavior support* (pp. 307–326). New York, NY: Springer.

Sullivan, A. L., & Bal, A. (2013). Disproportionality in special education: Effects of individual and school variables on disability risk. *Exceptionality, 79*(4), 475–494.

University of Nebraska–Lincoln, Office of Graduate Studies. (n.d.). *Twenty tips on motivating students.* Retrieved from http://www.unl.edu/gradstudies/current/teaching/motivating

U.S. Census Bureau. (2010). *Statistical abstract of the United States.* Washington, DC: Author.

U.S. Department of Education. (2004). *Twenty-sixth annual report to Congress on the implementation of the Individuals with Disabilities Education Act.* Washington, DC: U.S. Government Printing Office.

White, N. A., & & Loeber, R. (2008). Bullying and special education as predictors of serious delinquency. *Journal of Research in Crime and Delinquency, 45*(4), 380–397. doi:10.1177/0022427808322612

Wolfgang, C. H. (2008). *Solving discipline problems* (4th ed.). Boston, MA: Pearson.

Zakrzewski, V. (2012, September 18). Four ways teachers can show they care. Retrieved from http://greatergood.berkeley.edu/article/item/caring_teacher_student_relationship

CHAPTER 10. TEACHING LITERACY

Atwell, N. (2010). *Writing in the middle—reading in the middle: DVD bundle.* Portsmouth, NH: Heinemann.

Bos, C. S., & Vaughn, S. (2006). *Teaching strategies for students with mild to moderate disabilities* (6th ed.). Boston, MA: Pearson.

Bryant, B. R., Bryant, D. P., Hammill, D. D., & Sorrells, A. M. (2004). Characteristic reading behaviors of poor readers who have learning disabilities. *Assessment for Effective Intervention, 19,* 39–46.

Bryant, B. R., Wiederholt, J. L., & Bryant, D. P. (2012). *Gray Diagnostic Reading Test* (2nd ed.). Austin, TX: PRO-ED.

Bryant, D. P., & Bryant, B. R. (2011). *Assistive technology for people with disabilities* (2nd ed.). Boston, MA: Allyn & Bacon/Prentice Hall.

Bryant, D. P., Bryant, B. R., Langley, J., Flower, A., Hou, V., McKenna, J., . . . Tausiani, J. (2011). Secondary special education observation and intervention study: Technical report. Meadows Center for Preventing Educational Risk, College of Education, University of Texas at Austin and Texas Education Agency.

Butler, S., Urrutia, K., Buenger, A., Gonzalez, N., Hunt, M., & Eisenhart, C. (2010). *A review of the current research on vocabulary instruction.* Portsmouth, NH: National Reading Technical Assistance Center.

Cunningham, P. M. (2013). *Phonics they use: Words for reading and writing* (6th ed.). Upper Saddle River, NJ: Pearson.

Englert, C. S., Zhao, Y., Dunsmore, K., Collings, N. Y., & Wolbers, K. (2007). Scaffolding the writing of students with disabilities through procedural facilitation: Using an Internet-based technology to improve performance. *Learning Disability Quarterly, 30*(1), 9–29.

Graham, S. (2009–2010). Want to improve their writing? Don't neglect their handwriting. *American Educator, 33*(4), 20–40.

Graham, S., & Harris, K. R. (2005). *Writing better: Teaching writing processes and self-regulation to students with learning problems.* Baltimore, MD: Brookes.

Graham, S., & Harris, K. R. (2011). Writing and students with disabilities. In J. M. Kaufmann & D. P. Hallahan (Eds.), *Handbook of special education* (pp. 422–433). New York, NY: Routledge.

Graham, S., Harris, K. R., & Larson, L. (2001). Prevention and intervention of writing difficulties with students with learning disabilities. *Learning Disabilities Research & Practice, 16,* 74–84.

Graham, S., & Perin, D. (2007). *Writing next: Effective strategies to improve writing of adolescents in middle and high schools—A report to Carnegie Corporation of New York.* Washington, DC: Alliance for Excellent Education.

Haager, D., & Klingner, J. K. (2005). *Differentiating instruction in inclusive classrooms.* Boston, MA: Pearson.

Hammill, D. D., & Bryant, B. R. (1998). *Learning Disabilities Diagnostic Inventory.* Austin, TX: PRO-ED.

Harris, K. R., & Graham, S. (2013). "An adjective is a word hanging down from a noun": Learning to write and students with learning disabilities. *Annals of Dyslexia, 63*(1), 65–79. doi:10.1007/s11881-011-0057-x

Harris, K. R., Lane, K. L., Graham, S., Driscoll, S., Sandmel, K., Brindle, M., & Schatschneider, C. (2012). Practice-based professional development for self-regulated strategies development in writing: A randomized controlled study. *Journal of Teacher Education, 63*(2), 103–119.

Hasbrouck, J., & Tindall, G. (2005). Oral reading fluency: 90 years of measurement. Retrieved from http://files.eric.ed.gov/fulltext/ED531458.pdf

Honig, B., Diamond, L., & Gutlohn, L. (2008). *Teaching reading sourcebook* (2nd ed.). Novato, CA: Arena Press.

Johnson, A. P. (2008). *Teaching reading and writing.* Lanham, MD: Rowman & Littlefield Education.

Kim, M.-K. Bryant, D. P., & Bryant, B. R. (2015). Synthesis of interventions for improving oral reading fluency of elementary students with learning disabilities. Manuscript submitted for publication (copy on file with author).

Lane, K. L., Harris, K., Graham, S., Driscoll, S., Sandmel, K., Morphy, P., . . . Schatschneider, C. (2011). Self-regulated strategy development at tier 2 for second-grade students with writing and behavioral difficulties: A randomized controlled trial. *Journal of Research on Educational Effectiveness, 4*(4), 322–353. doi:10.1080/19345747.2011.558987

Mercer, C. D., & Pullen, P. C. (2004). *Students with learning disabilities* (7th ed.). Upper Saddle River, NJ: Prentice Hall.

Moats, L. C. (2005/2006). How spelling supports reading. *American Educator, 29,* 12–43.

National Assessment of Educational Progress. (2013). *The nation's report card.* Washington, DC: National Center for Educational Statistics.

National Reading Panel. (2000). *Teaching children to read: An evidence-based assessment of the scientific research literature on reading and its implications for reading instruction.* Bethesda, MD: National Institutes of Health, National Institute of Child Health and Human Development.

Santangelo, T., & Graham S. (2014). Selecting and tailoring interventions for students with written expression difficulties. In J. T. Mascolo, V. C. Alfonso, & D. P. Flanagan (Eds.), *Essentials of planning, selecting, and tailoring interventions for unique learners* (pp. 204–230). Hoboken, NJ: Wiley.

U.S. Department of Education. (2002). *Guidance for the Reading First program.* Washington, DC: Author. Retrieved from http://www.ed.gov/programs/readingfirst/guidance.doc

Wanzek, J., & Roberts, G. (2012). Reading interventions with varying instructional emphases for fourth graders with reading difficulties. *Learning Disability Quarterly, 35*(2), 90–101. doi:10.1177/0731948711434047

CHAPTER 11. TEACHING MATHEMATICS

Allsopp, D. H., Kyger, M. H., & Lovin, L. H. (2007). *Teaching mathematics meaningfully: Solutions for reaching struggling learners.* Baltimore, MD: Brookes.

Ashlock, R. B. (2009). *Error patterns in computation* (10th ed.). Boston, MA: Pearson.

Berch, D. B. (2005). Making sense of number sense: Implications for children with mathematical disabilities. *Journal of Learning Disabilities, 38,* 333–339. doi:10.1177/00222194050380040901

Blair, C., & Razza, R.P. (2007). Relating effortful control, executive function, and false-belief understanding to emerging math and literacy ability in kindergarten. *Child Development, 78,* 647–663.

Bley, N., & Thornton, C. (2001). *Teaching mathematics to students with learning disabilities* (4th ed.). Austin, TX: PRO-ED.

Browder, D. M., Spooner, F., Ahlgrim-Delzell, L., Harris, A., & Wakeman, S. (2008). A meta-analysis on teaching students with severe cognitive disabilities. *Exceptional Children, 74,* 407–432.

Bryant, B. R., Bryant, D. P., Kethley, C., Kim, S., Pool, C., & Seo, Y. (2008). Preventing mathematics difficulties in the primary grades: The critical features of instruction in textbooks as part of the equation. Special series, *Learning Disability Quarterly, 31*(1), 21–35.

Bryant, D. P., Bryant, B. R., Gersten, R., Scammacca, N., & Chavez, M. (2008). Mathematics intervention for first- and second-grade students with mathematics difficulties: The effects of tier 2 intervention delivered as booster lessons. *Remedial and Special Education, 29*(1), 20–32.

Bryant, D. P., Bryant, B., & Hammill, D. D. (2000). Characteristic behaviors of students with LD who have teacher-identified math weaknesses. *Journal of Learning Disabilities, 33*(2), 168–177.

Bryant, D. P., Bryant, B. R., Roberts, G., Vaughn, S., Hughes, K., Porterfield, J., & Gersten, R. (2011). Effects of an early numeracy intervention on the performance of first-grade students with mathematics difficulties. *Exceptional Children, 78*(1), 7–23.

Bryant, D. P., Kim, S. A., Hartman, P., & Bryant, B. R. (2006). Standards-based mathematics instruction and teaching middle school students with mathematical disabilities. In M. Montague & A. Jitendra (Eds.), *Teaching mathematics to middle school students with learning difficulties* (pp. 7–28). New York, NY: Guilford.

Bryant, D. P., Roberts, G., Bryant, B. R., & DiAndreth-Elkins, L. (2011). Tier 2 early numeracy number sense interventions for kindergarten and first-grade students with mathematics difficulties. In R. Gersten & B. Newman-Gonchar (Eds.), *RtI mathematics* (pp. 65–83). Baltimore, MD: Brookes.

Butler, F. M., Miller, S. P., Crehan, K., Babbitt, B., & Pierce, T. (2003). Fraction instruction for students with mathematics disabilities: Comparing two teaching sequences. *Learning Disabilities Research & Practice, 18,* 99–111.

Cathcart, W. G., Pothier, Y. M., Vance, J. H., & Bezuk, N. S. (2000). *Learning mathematics in elementary and middle schools.* Upper Saddle River, NJ: Merrill/Prentice Hall.

Chard, D. J., Baker, S., Clarke, B., Jungjohann, K., Davis, K., & Smolkowski, K. (2008). Preventing early mathematics difficulties: The feasibility of a rigorous kindergarten mathematics curriculum. *Learning Disability Quarterly, 31,* 11–20.

Council of Chief State School Officers & National Governors' Association. (2010, June). *Common Core Sate Standards for Mathematics. Common Core State Standards Initiative.* Retrieved from http://www.corestandards.org/assets/CCSSI_Math%20Standards.pdf

Coyne, M. D., Kame'enui, E. J., & Carnine, D. W. (2011). *Effective teaching strategies that accommodate diverse learners* (4th ed.). Boston, MA: Pearson.

Doabler, C. T., & Fien, H. (2013). Explicit mathematics instruction: What teachers can do for teaching students with mathematics difficulties. *Intervention in School and Clinic, 48,* 276–285.

Dougherty, B., Bryant, D. P., Bryant, B. R., Darrough, R. L., & Pfannenstiel, K. H. (2015). Developing concepts and generalizations to build algebraic thinking: The reversibility, flexibility, and generalization approach. *Intervention in School and Clinic, 50,* 273–281. doi:10.1177/1053451214560892

Fuchs, L. S., Geary, D. C., Compton, D. L., Fuchs, D., Hamlett, C. L., & Bryant, J. D. (2010). The contributions of numerosity and domain general abilities to school readiness. *Child Development, 81,* 1520–1533. doi:10.1111/j.1467-8624.2010.01489.x

Fuson, K. C. (1982). An analysis of the counting-on solution procedure in addition. In T. P. Carpenter, J. M. Moser, & T. A. Romberg (Eds.), *Addition and subtraction: A cognitive perspective* (pp. 67–81). Hillsdale, NJ: Lawrence Erlbaum.

Geary, D. C. (2004). Mathematics and learning disabilities. *Journal of Learning Disabilities, 37,* 4–15. doi:10.1177/00222194040370010201

Geary, D. C. (2011). Consequences, characteristics, and causes of mathematical learning disabilities and persistent low achievement in mathematics. *Journal of Developmental & Behavioral Pediatrics, 33*(30), 250–263. doi:10.1097/DBP.0b013e318209edef

Gelman, R., & Gallistel, C. R. (1978). *The child's understanding of number.* Cambridge, MA: Harvard University Press.

Gersten, R., Beckmann, S., Clarke, B., Foegen, A., Marsh, L., Star, J. R., & Witzel, B. (2009). *Assisting students struggling with mathematics: Response to intervention (RtI) for elementary and middle schools* (NCEE 2009-4060). Washington, DC: National Center for Education Evaluation and Regional Assistance, Institute of Education Sciences, U.S. Department of Education. Retrieved

from http://ies.ed.gov/ncee/wwc/publications/practiceguides/

Gersten, R., Jordan, N. C., & Flojo, J. R. (2005). Early identification and intervention for students with mathematics difficulties. *Journal of Learning Disabilities, 38*(4), 293–304.

Gevarter, C., Bryant, D. P., Bryant, B. R., Zamora, C., Sammarco, N., & Watkins, L. (2015). *Mathematics interventions for individuals with autism spectrum disorder: A systematic review.* Manuscript submitted for publication.

Groen, G. J., & Parkman, J. M. (1972). A chronometric analysis of simple addition. *Psychology Review, 79,* 329–343.

Hecht, S., Close, L., & Santisi, M. (2003). Sources of individual differences in fraction skills. *Journal of Experimental Child Psychology, 86*(4), 277–302.

Hudson, P., & Miller, S. P. (2006). *Designing and implementing mathematics instruction for students with diverse learning needs.* Boston, MA: Pearson.

Individuals with Disabilities Education Improvement Act of 2004. PL No. 108-446.

Jitendra, A. K., Griffin, C., Haria, P., Leh, J., Adams, A., & Kaduvetoor, A. (2007). A comparison of single and multiple strategy instruction on third grade students' mathematical problem solving. *Journal of Educational Psychology, 99,* 115–127. doi:10.1037/0022-0663.99.1.115

Jordan, N. C., Glutting, J., & Ramineni, C. (2009). The importance of number sense to mathematics achievement in first and third grades. *Learning and Individual Differences.* Advance online publication. doi:10.1016/j.lindif.2009.07004

Jordan, N. C., Hanich, L. B., & Kaplan, D. (2003). Arithmetic fact mastery in young children: A longitudinal investigation. *Journal of Experimental Child Psychology, 85,* 103–119.

Jordan, N. C., Kaplan, D., Ramineni, C., & Locuniak, M. N. (2009). Early math matters: Kindergarten number competence and later mathematics outcomes. *Developmental*

Psychology, 45, 850–867. doi:10.1037/a0014939

Karp, K., Bush, S., & Dougherty, B. J. (2014). Avoiding rules that expire. *Teaching Children Mathematics, 21*(1), 18–25.

Kieran, C. (2004). Algebra thinking in the early grades: What is it? *Mathematics Educator, 8,* 139–151.

Krawec, J. L. (2014). Problem representation and mathematical problem solving of students of varying math ability. *Journal of Learning Disabilities, 47*(2), 103–115. doi:10.1177/0022219412436976

Maccini, P., & Gagnon, J. C. (2005). *Math graphic organizers for students with disabilities.* Washington, DC: The Access Center: Improving Outcomes for All Students K–8. Retrieved from http://www.k8accesscenter.org/ training_resources/documents/ MathGraphicOrg.pdf

Mayer, R. E. (1998). Cognitive, metacognitive, and motivational aspects of problem solving. *Instructional Science, 26,* 49–63.

Mazzocco, M. M. M., & Devlin, K. T. (2008). Parts and "holes": Gaps in rational number sense among children with vs. without mathematical learning disabilities. *Developmental Science, 11*(5), 681–691.

McLoughlin, J. A., & Lewis, R. B. (2008). *Assessing students with special needs* (7th ed.). Upper Saddle River, NJ: Pearson.

Mercer, C. D., & Mercer, A. R. (2005). *Teaching students with learning problems* (7th ed.). New York, NY: Macmillan.

Mercer, C. D., & Miller, S. P. (1992). Teaching students with learning problems in math to acquire, understand, and apply basic math facts. *Remedial and Special Education, 13*(3), 19–35, 61.

Miller, S. P., & Mercer, C. D. (1993). Mnemonics: Enhancing the math performance of students with learning difficulties. *Intervention in School and Clinic, 29,* 78–82.

Miller, S. P., Mercer, C. D., & Dillon, A. (1992). CSA: Acquiring and retaining math skills. *Intervention in School and Clinic, 28,* 105–110.

Montague, M. M., Enders, C., & Dietz, S. (2011). Effects of cognitive strategy instruction on math problem solving of middle school students with learning disabilities. *Learning Disability Quarterly, 34*(4), 262–272. doi:10.1177/0731948711421762

Murphy, M. M., Mazzocco, M. M. M., Hanich, L. B., & Early, M. C. (2007). Cognitive characteristics of children with mathematics learning disability (MLD) vary as a function of the cutoff criterion used to define MLD. *Journal of Learning Disabilities, 40,* 458–478. doi:10.1177/00222194070 400050901

National Council of Teachers of Mathematics (NCTM). (2000). *Principles and standards for school mathematics.* Reston, VA: Author.

National Mathematics Advisory Panel (NMAP). (2008). *Foundations for success: The final report of the National Mathematics Advisory Panel.* Washington, DC: U.S. Department of Education.

National Research Council. (2009). *Mathematic learning in early childhood: Paths toward excellence and equity.* Washington, DC: Author.

Peterson, S. K., Mercer, C. D., & O'Shea, L. (1988). Teaching learning disabled students place value using the concrete to abstract sequence. *Learning Disabilities Research, 4*(1), 52–56.

Pfannenstiel, K. H., Bryant, D. P., Bryant, B. R., & Porterfield, J. A. (2015). Cognitive strategy instruction for teaching word problems to primary-level struggling students. *Intervention in School and Clinic, 50,* 291–296. doi:10.1177/1053451214560890

Powell, S. (2011). Solving word problems using schemas: A review of the literature. *Learning Disabilities Research & Practice, 26*(2), 94–108.

Powell, S. (2014). The influence of symbols and equations on understanding mathematical equivalence. *Intervention in School and Clinic, 50,* 266–272. doi:1053451214560889

Powell, S. R., & Fuchs, L. S. (2010). Contribution of equal-sign instruction beyond word problem tutoring for third-grade students with mathematics difficulty. *Journal of Educational Psychology, 102,* 381–394. doi:10.1037/a0018447

Rispoli, M., O'Reilly, M., Lang, R., Machalicek, W., Davis, T., Lancioni, G., & Sigafoos, J. (2011). Effects of motivating operations on problem and academic behavior in classrooms. *Journal of Applied Behavioral Analysis, 44*(1), 187–192. doi:10.1901/jaba.2011.44-187

Rivera, D., & Smith, D. D. (1988). Using a demonstration strategy to teach midschool students with learning disabilities how to compute long division. *Journal of Learning Disabilities, 21,* 77–81.

Ross, S. H. (1989). Parts, wholes, and place value: A developmental view. *Arithmetic Teacher, 36*(6), 47–51.

Shin, M., & Bryant, D. P. (2015). A synthesis of mathematical and cognitive performances of students with mathematics learning disabilities. *Journal of Learning Disabilities, 45,* 96–112. doi: 10.1177/0022219413508324

Siegler, R., Carpenter, T., Fennell, F., Geary, D., Lewis, J., Okamoto, Y., . . . Wray, J. (2010). *Developing effective fractions instruction for kindergarten through 8th grade: A practice guide* (NCEE No. 2010-4039). Washington, DC: National Center for Education Evaluation and Regional Assistance, Institute of Education Sciences, U.S. Department of Education. Retrieved from http:// www.whatworks.ed.gov/publications/ practiceguides

Siegler, R. S., & Shrager, J. (1984). Strategy choice in addition and subtraction: How do children know what to do? In C. Sophian (Ed.), *Origins of cognitive skills* (pp. 229–293). Hillsdale, NJ: Lawrence Erlbaum.

Sorto, A. (2012). *Mathematics instructional strategies for English language learners.* Austin: Meadows

Center for Preventing Educational Risk, University of Texas.

Stasolla, F., Perilli, V., & Damiani, R. (2014). Self monitoring to promote on-task behavior by two high functioning boys with autism spectrum disorders and symptoms of ADHD. *Research in Autism Spectrum Disorders, 8,* 472–479.

Stein, M., Kinder, D., Silbert, J., & Carnine, D. W. (2006). *Designing effective mathematics instruction.* Upper Saddle River, NJ: Prentice Hall.

Strickland, T. K., & Maccini, P. (2013). The effects of the concrete-representational-abstract-integration strategy on the ability of students with learning disabilities to multiply linear expressions within area problems. *Remedial and Special Education, 34*(3), 142–153.

Swanson, H. L., & Jerman, O. (2006). Math disabilities: A selective meta-analysis of the literature. *Review of Educational Research, 76*(2), 249–274.

Van de Garderen, D., & Scheuermann, A. M. (2014). Diagramming word problems: A strategic approach for instruction. *Intervention in School and Clinic.* Advance online publication. doi:10.1177/1053451214560889

Van de Walle, J. A., Karp, K. S., & Bay-Williams, J. M. (2012). *Elementary and middle school mathematics: Teaching developmentally* (8th ed.). Boston, MA: Pearson.

Wei, X., Christiano, E. R., Yu, J. W., Wagner, M., & Spiker, D. (2015). Reading and math achievement profiles and longitudinal growth trajectories of children with an autism spectrum disorder. *Autism, 19*(2), 200–210. doi:10.1177/1362361313516549

Wiig, E. H., & Semel, E. M. (1984). *Language assessment and intervention for the learning disabled* (2nd ed.). New York, NY: Macmillan.

Williams, D. L., Goldstein, G., Kojkowski, N., & Minshew, N. J.

(2008). Do individuals with high functioning autism have the IQ profile associated with nonverbal learning disability? *Research in Autism Spectrum Disorders, 2,* 353–361.

Wong, C., Odom, S. L., Hume, K., Cox, A. W., Fettig, A., Kucharczyk, S., . . . Schultz, T. R. (2013). *Evidence-based practices for children, youth, and young adults with autism spectrum disorder.* Chapel Hill: The University of North Carolina, Frank Porter Graham Child Development Institute, Autism Evidence-Based Practice Review Group.

Woodward, J., Beckmann, S., Driscoll, M., Franke, M., Herzig, P., Jitendra, A., . . . Ogbuehi, P. (2012). *Improving mathematical problem solving in Grades 4 through 8: A practice guide* (NCEE 2012-4055). Washington, DC: National Center for Education Evaluation and Regional Assistance, Institute of Education Sciences, U.S. Department of Education. Retrieved from http://ies.ed.gov/ncee/wwc/publications_reviews.aspx#pubsearch/

CHAPTER 12. FACILITATING CONTENT-AREA INSTRUCTION AND STUDY SKILLS

Bauer, S., Benkstein, P., Pittel, A., & Koury, G. (n.d.). *Gifted students: Recommendations for teachers.* Retrieved from http://www.education.udel.edu/wp-content/uploads/2013/01/GiftedStudents.pdf

Beck, I. L., McKeown, M. G., & Kucan, L. (2013). *Bringing words to life: Robust vocabulary instruction* (2nd ed.). New York, NY: Guilford.

Bottge, B. A., Toland, M. D., Gassaway, L., Butler, M., Choo, S., Griffen, A. K., & Ma, X. (2014). Impact of enhanced anchored instruction in inclusive math classrooms. *Exceptional Children, 81*(2), 158–175.

Boyle, J. R. (2011). Thinking strategically to record notes in content classes. *American Secondary Education, 40*(1), 51–66.

Boyle, J. R., & Rivera, T. Z. (2012). Note-taking techniques for students with disabilities: A systematic review of the research. *Learning Disability Quarterly, 35*(3), 131–143. doi:10.1177/0731948711435794

Bragstad, B. J., & Stumpf, S. M. (1987). *A guidebook for teaching study skills and motivation* (2nd ed.). Boston, MA: Allyn & Bacon.

Bryant, B. R., Bryant, D. P., Kim, M.-K., & Hou, F. (2015, April). *High school English I support for students with learning disabilities.* Paper presented at the Council for Exceptional Children Annual Conference, San Diego, CA.

Bryant, D. P., & Bryant, B. R. (2011). *Assistive technology for people with disabilities* (2nd ed.). Boston, MA: Pearson.

Bulgren, J. A., Marquis, J. G., Lenz, B. K., Schumaker, J. B., & Deshler, D. D. (2009). Effectiveness of question exploration to enhance students' written expression of content knowledge and comprehension. *Reading & Writing Quarterly, 25,* 271–289. doi:10.1080/10573560903120813

Butler, S., Urrutia, K., Buenger, A., & Hunt, M. (2010). *A review of the current research on comprehension instruction.* Portsmouth, NH: RMC Research Corporation.

Casareno, A. B. (2010). When reading in college is a problem. In S. C. Brown & M. A. Fallon (Eds.), *Teaching inclusively in higher education* (p. 48). Charlotte, NC: Information Age Publishing.

Clewell, S. (2015). Strategies for helping readers: Activating prior knowledge. *Thinkport.* Retrieved from http://www.thinkport.org/career/strategies/reading/activate.tp

Garber-Miller, K. (2006). Playful test previews: Letting go of familiar mustache monologues. *Journal of Adolescent & Adult Literacy, 50*(4), 284–288. doi:10/1598/LAAL.50.4.4

Honig, D. L., & Gutlohn, L. (2008). *Teaching reading sourcebook* (2nd ed.). Oakland, CA: Consortium on Reading Excellence.

Hoover, J. J., & Patton, J. R. (2007). *Teaching students with learning problems to use study skills* (2nd ed.). Austin, TX: PRO-ED.

Hopper, C. H. (2016). *Practicing college learning strategies* (7th ed.). Boston, MA: Cengage Learning.

Hughes, C. A., Schumaker, J. B., Deshler, D. D., & Mercer, C. D. (2005). *Learning strategies curriculum: The test-taking strategy: PIRATES*. Lawrence, KS: Edge Enterprises.

Instructional strategies that facilitate learning across content areas. (n.d.). Retrieved from http://www.sde .ct.gov/sde/lib/sde/pdf/curriculum/ section7.pdf

IRIS Center. (2015). *Study skills strategies (Part 1): Foundations for effectively teaching study skills*. Retrieved from http://iris.peabody. vanderbilt.edu/module/ss1/

Johnson, E., Humphrey, M., Mellard, D., Woods, K., & Swanson, H. L. (2010). Cognitive processing deficits and students with specific learning disabilities: A selective meta-analysis of the literature. *Learning Disability Quarterly, 33*, 3–18.

Johnson-Harris, K. M., & Mundschenk, N. A. (2014). Working effectively with students with BD in a general education classroom: The case for universal design for learning. *The Clearing House: A Journal of Educational Strategies, Issues and Ideas, 87*(4), 168–174. doi:10.1080/0 0098655.2014.897927

Kumar, D. D. (2010). Approaches to interactive video anchors in problem-based science learning. *Journal of Science Education and Technology, 19*, 13–19. doi:10.1007/s10956-009-9154-6

Lavenstein, H. (2015). Not happy with your teenager's midterm grades? Start now with these steps toward better grades. *Rhode Island Tutorial & Educational Services*. Retrieved from http://www.ritutorial.org/tag/ high-school-study-skills/

Ogle, D. M. (1986). A teaching model that develops active reading of expository text. *The Reading Teacher, 39*, 564–570.

Red Rocks Community College, Connect to Success, T+. (n.d.). Retrieved from http://www.rrcc .edu/sites/default/files/instructional-services-step_5.pdf

Rieth, H. J., Bryant, D. P., Kinzer, C. K., Colburn, L. K., Hur, S.-J., Hartman, P., & Choi, H.-S. (2003). An analysis of the impact of anchored instruction on teaching and learning activities in two ninth-grade language arts classes. *Remedial and Special Education, 24*(3), 173–184.

Schumaker, J. B., & Deshler, D. D. (2006). Teaching adolescents to be strategic learners. In D. D. Deshler & J. B. Schumaker (Eds.), *Teaching adolescents with disabilities: Accessing the general education curriculum* (pp. 121–156). Thousand Oaks, CA: Corwin.

Spungin, S. J. (2013, August 15). *For teachers: Basic tips for when you have a visually impaired student in your class*. Retrieved from http:// www.afb.org/BLOG/AFB-BLOG/ FOR-TEACHERS-BASIC-TIPS-FOR-WHEN-YOU-HAVE-A-VISUALLY-IMPAIRED-STUDENT-IN-YOUR-CLASS/12

Stahl, S. A., & Nagy, W. E. (2006). *Teaching word meanings* (Literacy teaching series). Mahwah, NJ: Erlbaum.

Steimle, J., Brdiczka, O., & Mühlhäuser, M. (2009). Collaborative paper-based annotation of lecture slides. *Educational Technology & Society, 12*(4), 125–137.

Strang, T. (2016). *Tips for students: Become a better listener*. Retrieved from http://blog.cengage.com/TIPS-STUDENTS-BECOME-BETTER-LISTENER/

Swanson, H. L., Zheng, X., & Jerman, O. (2009). Working memory, short-term memory, and reading disabilities: A selective meta-analysis of the literature. *Journal of Learning Disabilities, 42*, 260–287.

Stone, B., & Urquhart, V. (2008). *Remove limits to learning with systematic vocabulary instruction*. Denver, CO: McREL.

Techdialogue. (2013, January 3). *An intro to using google calendar for the classroom*. Retrieved from https:// techdialogue.wordpress.com/ 2013/01/03/an-intro-to-using-google-calendar-for-the-classroom/

Thomas, C. N., & Rieth, H. J. (2011). A research synthesis of the literature on multimedia anchored instruction in preservice teacher education. *Journal of Special Education Technology, 26*(2), 1–22.

Vacca, R. T., Vacca, J. L., & Mraz, M. E. (2014). *Content area reading: Literacy and learning across the curriculum* (11th ed.). Boston, MA: Pearson.

Vaughn, S., & Bos, C. S. (2015). *Strategies for teaching students with learning and behavior problems* (9th ed.). Boston, MA: Pearson.

Vaughn, S., Cirino, P. T., Wanzek, J., Wexler, J., Fletcher, J. M., Denton, C. A. . . . Francis, D. J. (2010). Response to intervention for middle school students with reading difficulties: Effects of a primary and secondary intervention. *School Psychology, 39*, 3–21.

Vogel, S. (1997). *College students with learning disabilities: A handbook*. Pittsburgh, PA: Learning Disabilities Association of America.

Walport-Glawron, H. (2014). *Kids speak out on student engagement*. Retrieved from http://www.edutopia .org/blog/student-engagement-stories-heather-wolpert-gawron

Wright, J. (2010). *How to: Improve reading comprehension with a cognitive strategy: Ask-read-tell*. Retrieved from http://www .interventioncentral.org/sites/ default/files/pdfs/pdfs_blog/ cognitive_strategy_reading_ comprehension_ART.pdf

INDEX